DESIGNING: AN INTRODUCTION

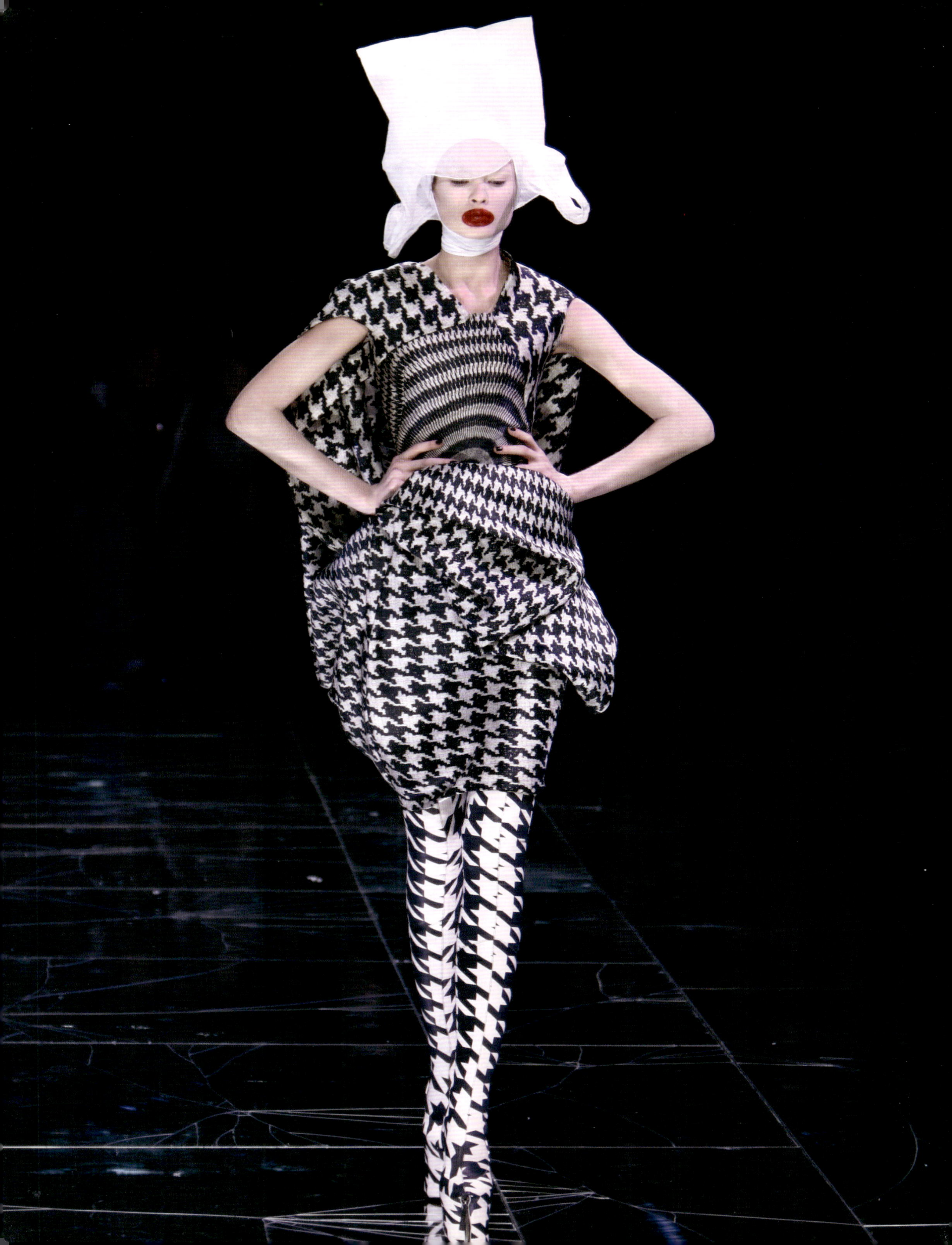

DESIGNING: AN INTRODUCTION

KARL ASPELUND
UNIVERSITY OF RHODE ISLAND

FAIRCHILD BOOKS
An Imprint
of Bloomsbury
Publishing Inc.

Fairchild Books
An imprint of Bloomsbury Publishing Inc.

1385 Broadway
New York
NY 10018
USA

50 Bedford Square
London
WC1B 3DP
UK

www.bloomsbury.com

First published in 2015

Library of Congress Cataloging-in-Publication Data
2013048839

ISBN: PB: 978-1-60901-496-4

Typeset by Precision Graphics
Cover Design by Eleanor Rose
Text Design by Cara David Design
Printed and bound in China

FOR

Julia, Karl, Colin, and Brenda.

CONTENTS

EXTENDED CONTENTS

PREFACE

D*esigning in the early 21st century* inhabits a vast terrain. We live in a world of design, by design: interiors, fashionable apparel, accessories, architecture, computers, Web-based applications, and on and on. This book is an introduction to the concepts, history, methods, and practices required for a working knowledge of the profession of design. It allows the student and teacher to explore and examine the basic structures involved before branching out into designing or working with designers in any of the numerous fields available. The discussion is wide-ranging, touching on large and small, industrial and artisanal, high-tech, virtual, luxe, and mundane. Functionality and problem solving are highlighted, as well as showing design in an artistic light. All the chapters reflect a view of design and designing as seen in the present day of global markets and instant communications. As a result *four-dimensional design* and experience as a design element are added to the discussion and highlighted. Observing the practice as a whole is also emphasized, as is creating an awareness of designed objects in the students' everyday environment.

ORGANIZATION OF THE TEXT

The content of this book is modular, with well-contained chapters and sections. This should allow for efficient course planning for instructors as well as nonlinear use of sections for reference by students in workshops and seminars. By addressing both functional and aesthetic needs over a broad range of applications, the books encourages the student's perception of design to develop in both two and three dimensions. The first section introduces the profession of design, its nature and history, and the elements and principles of design. The second tackles the problems of planning and presentation. The third section then considers the different approach and stance in designing for two, three, and four dimensions by considering user interface, environments, and experiences over time.

PART 1: THE NATURE, ELEMENTS, AND PRINCIPLES OF DESIGN

The first section introduces the current profession of design as it evolved in the industrialized world. Designing is defined as a practice, its history presented, and the elements and principles of design introduced. Chapter 1 provides a description of the nature of the designer and of designing: What does it mean to *design* something, and what are the basic steps of the process? After demonstrating the nature of design and designing, by showing it in various guises, the chapter ends with a step-by-step description of what a designer *does,* in practice, during the span of one project. Then the chapter closes with a discussion and demonstration of how constraints and needs define a design solution.

Chapter 2 anchors the present day in history, by examining the most impactful design movements of the 19th and early 20th centuries. Their theories, methods, influence, and ultimate fading are discussed, leading to practical discussions and definitions of the Modernist movement and designing in the Postmodern condition of the late 20th century.

Chapter 3 is a heavily illustrated demonstration and discussion of the basic elements of design. They are defined as the classic group of line, shape, color, texture and pattern, and space, but time is also presented as an element in order to involve the user experience at the beginning stage of conceptual thinking.

A demonstration and discussion, also heavily illustrated, of the basic principles of design follows in Chapter 4. As with the elements of design, these are defined by the classic headings. Following the inclusion of time as an element, *usability* is included as a principle to further discuss the user experience and bring home the concerns of present-day markets and technology.

PART 2: INFORMING DESIGN

The second section presents the practical aspects of conceptualizing, researching, planning, and presenting designs. With many illustrations, the two chapters are intended as a guide and reference for novice designers that show the very practical and multifaceted nature of the designer's profession. Chapter 5 focuses on how an idea may become a fleshed-out and clearly defined concept. The chapter takes a very practical slant, showing the designer's concerns from finding and identifying the idea to expanding it, relating it to the world around, and considering the constraints of time and production. Chapter 6, on the other hand, considers the techniques, modes, and methods of creating and presenting designs to an audience of either collaborators or clients. Different media is discussed, as well as different situations, and the chapter wraps up by considering the designer's dual role as a performer and salesperson when presenting.

PART 3: THINKING DESIGN

The third section is devoted to the methods and practices of professional designers. The four chapters it contains identify and discuss the modes of thinking involved for two-, three-, and four-dimensional design, as well as designing for onscreen applications. This is approached in each case from the practical considerations involved in materials, ergonomics and user experience.

Chapter 7 is a discussion of the nature of graphic design and its relationship to fine art composition. The mechanics, elements, and inherent meaning of graphic design elements are also discussed from a very practical standpoint. In Chapter 8 the nature of three dimensions as a design challenge is discussed, followed by a presentation of the application of three dimensions in design and the need to understand 3D as a physical sensory experience. Time and experience arrive in Chapter 9, where design as an element of culture is considered through such issues as human perception and memory, among other things. The chapter also introduces experience over time as a design problem, by contemplating practical aspects of time and perception relating to usability and user satisfaction. Concluding the section, graphic design, three-dimensionality, and four-dimensional design then come together in Chapter 10, which considers designing for on-screen applications.

TEXT FEATURES

Designing: An Introduction is heavily illustrated with more than 250 images providing constant visual inspiration to the reader. Numerous sidebars and end-of-chapter review questions, exercises, and assignments should prompt in-class discussion and allow the forming of research projects, both in and in-between classes.

DISCUSSION AND REVIEW QUESTIONS AND EXERCISES AND ASSIGNMENTS

The chapters conclude with discussion and review questions and activities and exercises, which reinforce the instructional material and key concepts. The discussion questions encourage engaging with design problems and prompt discussion.

SIDEBARS

Each chapter includes several sidebars. A quotation or two from a designer has been chosen to illuminate the matter under discussion in each chapter. Considering these should prompt thought and discussion and can be the basis for a home assignment or *thought experiment.* Networking sidebars provide information on websites to peruse for further information on the chapter material. The websites were chosen for a high likelihood of permanence, but relevant keywords are also provided to use in search engines. Ergonomics sidebars use that term in the widest sense by relating the design issues of each chapter to human constraints and needs. This can prompt thoughts and discussions on the user experience and four-dimensional design in each case. Timeline sidebars highlight historical moments relevant to the discussion of the chapter to encourage thinking about continuity and connectivity with culture and history. Finally, Sustainability sidebars highlight an example or case study related to the chapter material and a related quotation from literature or periodicals.

ACKNOWLEDGMENTS

This book is, despite the solo-author name on the cover, a group effort. It would never have happened without the students, colleagues, clients, collaborators, and family that assisted, inspired, and provided for the material herein over many past years. I am indebted to them all, named and unnamed, near and far, in space and time.

My Department Heads and Deans of the Textiles, Fashion Merchandising and Design Department at URI's College of Human Science and Services deserve many thanks for their willingness to hand me the reins and develop courses and curricula from which this book grew. Thanks to Dr. Linda Welters, Dr. Martin Bide, Dean Lori E. Ciccomascolo and her predecessor, Dean Lynn McKinney. Thanks to the hundreds of students whom I have enjoyed meeting in TMD327 and TMD126 for their patience and willingness to experiment and contribute. I am also grateful for the constructive criticism of proposal and manuscript and reviewers: Rose Casterline, Valencia College; Dawn Sealy, Art Institute of Jacksonville and Daytona Beach Community College; Cecilia Mandrile, University of New Haven; Jeff Boshart, Eastern Illinois University; Michael Kroeger, College of Mount St. Joseph; Barbara Arlen, the Fashion Institute of Technology; Barry Underhill, Art Institute of Austin; Linda Johnson, Florida Atlantic University; Diane Sparks, Colorado State University; Christine David, The Art Institute of Fort Lauderdale; Beverly Kissinger, University of Alabama; Richard Withem, The Art Institute of Charlotte; Joey Manson, Clemson University; Diane Zatz, The Art Institute of Philadelphia; Norton Young, The Art Institute of Portland; Linda W. Wood, The Art Institute of Atlanta; Tamara Peterson, Columbus College of Art and Design; Andrew Furman, Ryerson University; Joseph Cory, Judson University; James Housefield, UC Davis; and, Janet Hethorn, University of Delaware.

This would have been a far rougher journey without my wonderful editor, Julie Vitale, whose cheer, patience and guidance have sustained the project through both rocky terrain and smooth sailing (and an actual hurricane or two.) This is mirrored in the entire team at Fairchild/Bloomsbury, who have been as fun to work with and as magnificent as ever, they include Priscilla McGeehon, publisher; Olga Kontzias, former executive editor; Joe Miranda, development manager; Edie Weinberg, art editor; Avital Aronowitz-Krasilovsky, photo researcher; Rebecca Reid Marshall, composition project manager; and Eric Bramer, compositor.

Finally, my wife Brenda and my children Júlía, Karl, and Colin Thor. Without their joy, interest, and forbearance nothing is really ever worth doing. They deserve thanks that cannot ever be large enough.

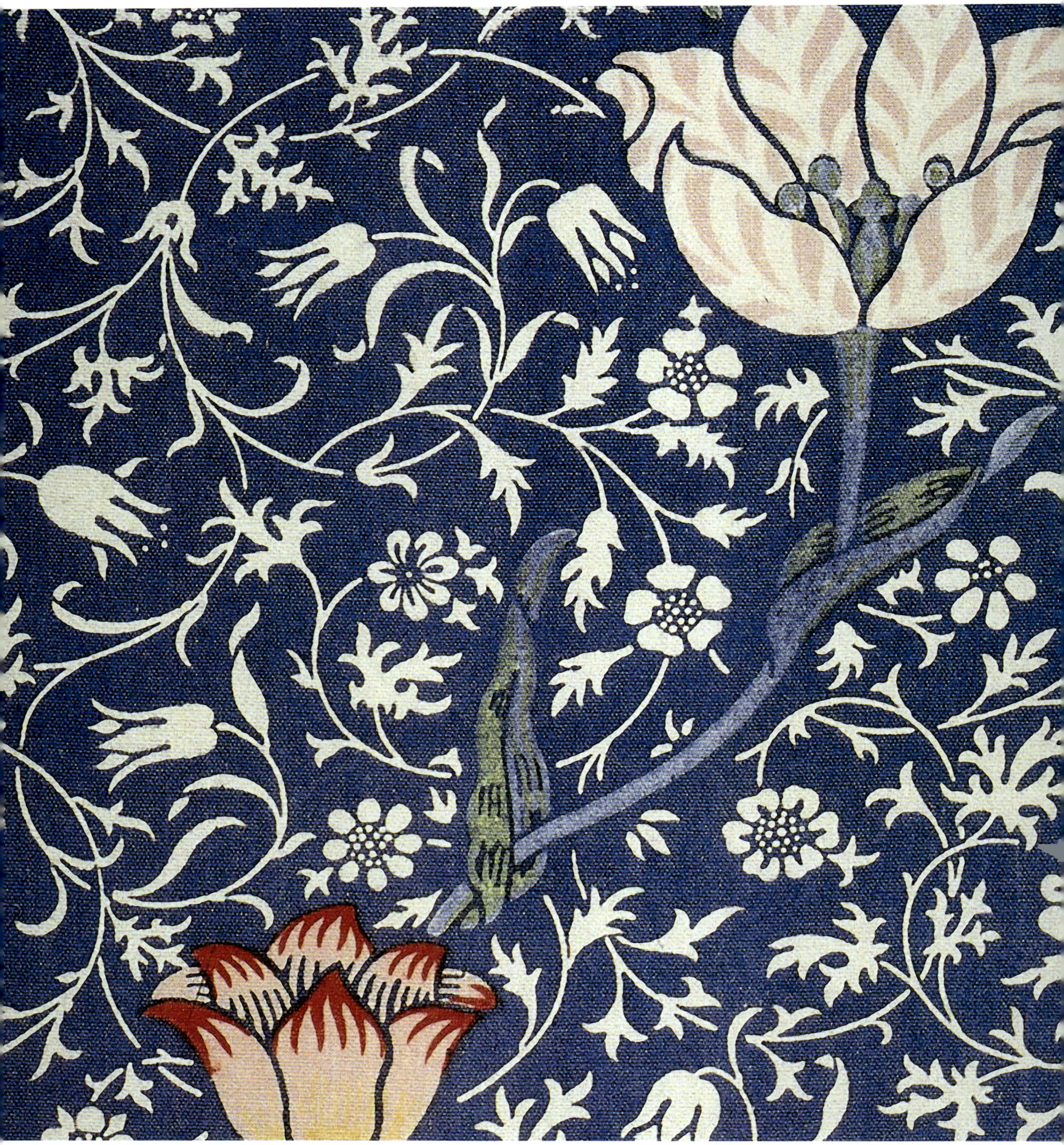

PART I

THE NATURE, ELEMENTS, AND PRINCIPLES OF DESIGN

Part I introduces the profession of design as it evolved in the industrialized world. Designing is defined as a practice, its history presented, and the elements and principles of design introduced. Chapter 1 considers the nature of design in modern industrialized society, what it is, what the process is, and how to approach it. Chapter 2 gives a brief historical overview of the modern movements that led to our current condition in design. Chapter 3 takes a look at the basic elements of design and explains their use and how they connect, adding *time* to the traditional list. Chapter 4 subsequently explains the principles within which these elements are applied and further develops the addition of time by considering the user experience.

OPPOSITE
Wallpaper design from 1885 by William Morris. The debt owed by Mucha and others to the romantic nostalgia of the Arts and Crafts Movement is clear: The floral swirls and asymmetries, contrasting colors and vivid patterns all continue.

CHAPTER 1

WHAT IS DESIGNING?

DESIGNERS SPEAK

"People think it's this veneer—that the designers are handed this box and told, 'Make it look good!' That's not what we think design is. It's not just what it looks like and feels like. Design is how it works."

—STEVE JOBS, quoted in Rob Walker, "The Guts of a New Machine," *New York Times Magazine,* November 30, 2003.

"It's important not to overstate the benefits of ideas. Quite frankly, I know it's kind of a romantic notion that you're just going to have this one brilliant idea and then everything is going to be great. But the fact is that coming up with an idea is the least important part of creating something great. It has to be the right idea and have good taste, but the execution and delivery are what's key."

—SERGEY BRIN, quoted in Jemima Kiss, "Secrets of a Nimble Giant," *The Guardian,* June 17, 2009.

OBJECTIVES

Identify the place of designing in human society.

Recognize the significance of designing as a basic human activity.

Identify the stages of the process that designers work within.

Understand the distinct demands of each stage of the design process.

Detect the importance of defining the constraints and needs involved in a design project.

Designing is a basic component of human experience and culture through history that has become a globalized profession dedicated to the needs defined by modern, urban, industrialized society. It has a process involving several stages, and bringing an idea from the world of imagination to the world of objects requires touching on each of these stages with an awareness of the needs and constraints involved and a well-defined goal in sight. The designer's job is to guide the project throughout the entire journey, creating a new product or system that fulfills all the apparent needs within the given constraints.

THE DESIGNED WORLD: WHERE IS DESIGN?

Humans are a designing species. If the basic definition of **human culture** may be said to be the things we do and the things we do them with over time, then practice of designing lies at the core of our nature and has been essential to human culture from its very beginnings. We have designed ourselves and our societies into various shapes and cultures by continually reshaping ourselves by the careful construction of apparel, tools, environments, habitats, and systems. The creating of an object with form that is more elaborate or beyond the needs of the basic function (e.g., carefully shaping a stone axe, beyond just making it sharp) is often considered a criterion of the "modern human." The ability to combine symbolic thinking with the utilitarian has been interpreted as a criterion of distinctly human "culture."[1]

We may not be the only species that creates habitats and uses tools, but we may be the only one that decorates them. The tradition of decorating caves with symbols and images, for example, extends back at least 40,000 years, with the clear use of stencils to create "cave art" arriving on the scene at least 37,000 years ago (Fig. 1.1).[2] However, the creation of tools and even "jewelry" of some kind, with imposed (and therefore designed) forms appears even earlier, at least on the cusp of Neanderthal and Homo sapiens cultures 50,000 to 60,000 years ago. This inclination may well have also been a trait of Neanderthal and other early-hominid species predating the biologically "modern" human, *Homo sapiens,* by tens of thousands of years. The ability to design a better way of getting by would likely have been a deeply rooted and early addition to the traits that eventually became common human behavior. Whether carried out of Africa and adopted by Neanderthals or developing independently in several places and species at once, something sparked this "designing" mode 50,000 to 60,000 years ago. Therefore, at some particular point in the evolution of the species, a shift occurred and the species was headed for organized culture. We, as a species, have since deliberately, repeatedly, and systematically modified our surroundings and equipment to shape our own behavior.

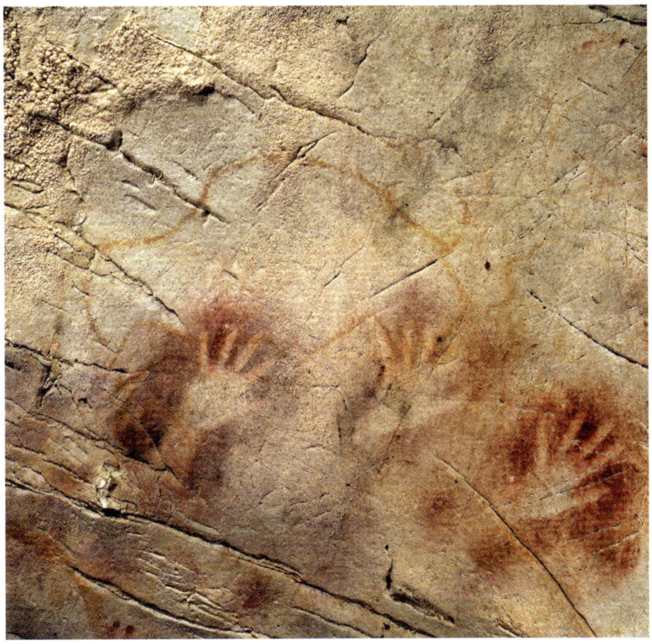

1.1 The oldest cave art yet dated is estimated to be around 40,000 years old. Located in the El Castillo cave in northern Spain, it places art and design at the very beginnings of human culture (if not even earlier). The act of deliberately decorating or symbolically marking the environment shows a culture operating by design.

Source: Pedro Saura/dapd

By the Late Stone Age (50,000 years ago), the pace of innovation and the general skill level had both increased. The level of craft knowledge had also improved dramatically, and different groups of early humans formed their own cultural identity and developed their distinct ways of making things. The designing of better and better tools, over thousands of years, allowed for the development of human environments and more efficient habits. Habitats became villages and towns that then grew into cities, and these increasingly needed planning. The structures these imposed, in turn, led to societies that demanded services and industries and required distinction among groups and classes.

Eventually, **mass production,** the standardization of the production goods in large quantities, replaced handcraft practices, and the design of more efficient technology both led and followed in a wave of **industrialization** among the colonial powers, when machine technology

BOX 1.1

SPEAKING OF DESIGNING . . .

HOW TO SPEAK OF "DESIGNING"? The objective of this book is to provide a broad introduction to it, and this first chapter begins appropriately by addressing the question, "what *is* designing?" The beginning of the answer lies in the wording of the question itself. The choice of the word "designing" as opposed to "design" is deliberate and significant. We will be looking at what a designer *does*, at the actions and events involved, rather than the resulting products. "A design" is a *result,* and "the design of . . . " is the style, feel, or system arrived at by the "designing" involved.

To clarify, designing is about working with ideas: finding, examining, planning, defining, and explaining ideas. These are ideas about the creation of things, environments, systems, or even events. Designing is solving problems that we perceive in our environments and existence—problems of comfort, practicality, and aesthetics; problems of individual and collective behavior—as well as the definitions and methods involved in the solving of these problems. The world is not as we would have it, and so we will fix it. We have a vision to fulfill, or we need a solution to a particular problem, or a need must be fulfilled.

Designing is the actions within a *process* that produces a formalized system. The system thus created is the solution to a problem. The design that fulfills the need. The system can be any combination of materials, techniques, and orderings of operations that creates a solution. In this sense, a shirt is a system, and so is a car, a chair, a neighborhood development, the "look" of a rock concert, a book cover, and a travel mug.

Referring in this way to "designing" (the doing) rather than "design" (that which has been done, or the style, form, or mode resulting) reminds us that we are looking at a thoroughly integrated human *action* that, in being constantly active, transcends human eras, artistic movements and political philosophies. Introducing designing involves the analysis of *processes* of thought and action, as well as the *elements* and *principles* involved in those thoughts and actions. Understanding the *historical and cultural structures* that have prompted—and been created by—this systematic manipulation of human experiences and existence is also necessary, as it shows *how* designing is a constant feature of human society and possibly even *why*. With the *how* and the *why* clarified, an understanding of *what* should follow close behind.

expanded the production capabilities in a number of industries and economic sectors. Better looms, for example, led to large-scale textile production, factories increased output of all goods, better roads led to faster transportation, and better vehicles accelerated the movement of goods, people, and ideas. All this led to increased commerce at every step along the way (Fig. 1.2). The oversight and planning required gradually resulted in a profusion of designers in an enormous variety of fields. Their work subsequently became a social and political force in modern society. Design became a function of civic life in high-fashion and social events as well as in the myriad objects required for the new standards of living among the moneyed classes in the growing

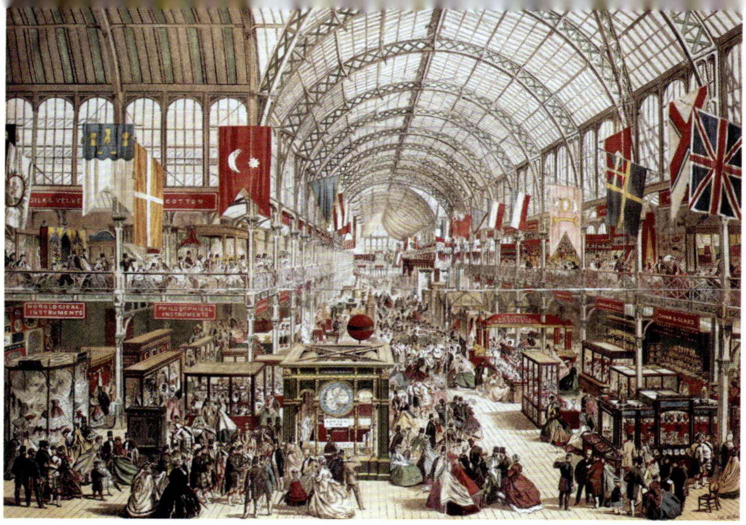

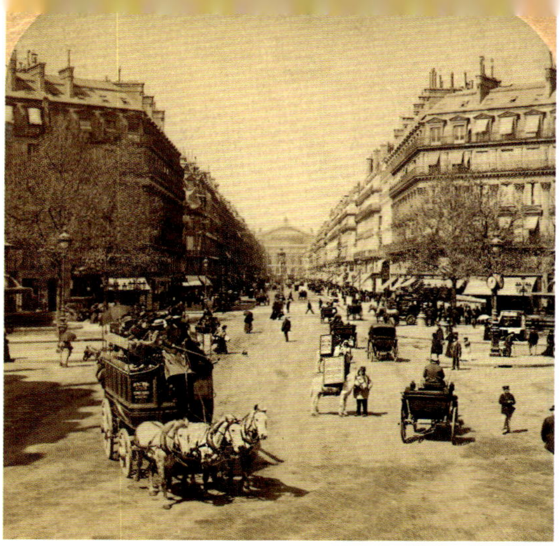

ABOVE LEFT

1.2 From The Great Exhibition of 1851 in London. As the commercial industrialized society became the reigning system and political expediency began to revolve around imports, exports, production, and consumption, the problems facing manufacturing became greater and greater. The *designer* as a profession was established in service to the marketplace. New products needed to be brought to market in order to produce demand and keep the wheels of commerce going (literally keeping the factories in motion).

Source: The Granger Collection, NYC-

ABOVE RIGHT

1.3 The Avenue de l'Opera in Paris, France, 1900. In the mid-1800s during the height of the reign of Napoleon III, Baron Haussmann redesigned the center of Paris, creating large, wide boulevards and uniform streetscapes. These reflected the needs of the new modern society, but also the political necessities of a regime that needed to display its power and maintain control over its cities. City planning and design began to reflect the desire for order and regimentation of industrial society.

Source: Courtesy of Claudio De Grano collection

cities. Furniture and flatware, carpets and wall hangings, clothing and accessories, gardens and carriages—all needed to be produced in styles demanded by status and fashionable display. (See Box 1.1.)

From its contribution to official architecture and city planning, design was also very soon a force in the service of prevailing powers and dominant groups. The idea that a society could be designed into a shape desired by the ruling class is seen in the application of design to the shape and size of city streets, government buildings, places of worship, and communal housing (Fig. 1.3). It also has been effectively applied in the field of fashionable apparel, especially in the creation of codes of socially acceptable and non-acceptable fashions (Fig. 1.4). The message "this is who we are" is encoded in the environment, showing ourselves how *we* live. The code embedded in the buildings, furniture, clothing and goods is there to be read to determine who belongs within and who is outside the circle of society. This allows the ruling classes to include and exclude members by simply switching the rules at will. The development of design as a profession in Europe in the 19th century has its roots in empire building and colonial

BELOW

1.4 From *The Ladies Gazette of Fashion* 1860. The mid-1800s saw an explosion in the capabilities for production of fashionable apparel. Social acceptance and the signaling of social position began to require the wearing of the "correct" and acceptable designs. The designing of high fashions therefore both reflected and directed the social order.

Source: New York Public Library Picture Collection/Digital Gallery

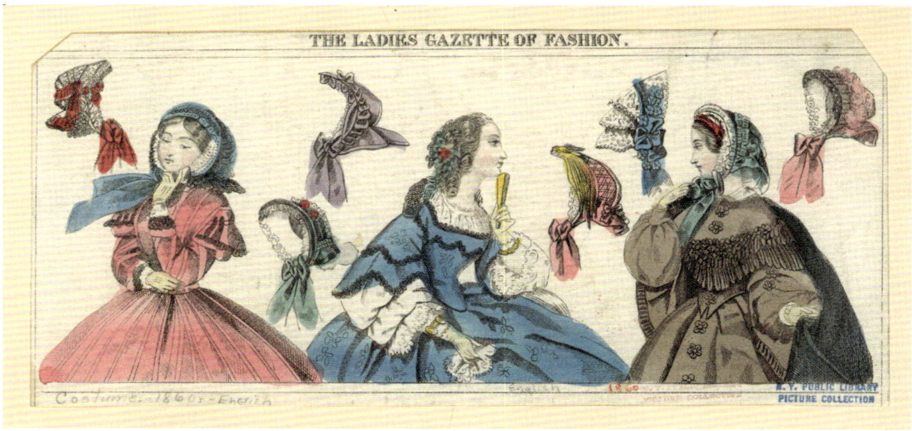

TIMELINE

Each chapter contains a sidebar labeled "Timeline" addressing matters relevant to the chapter's material from a historical perspective. It may be an actual timeline with dates and events, or it may contain a historical discussion. Despite the forward-looking and often fashion-oriented aspects of the designer's profession, a connection to—and awareness of—history and tradition is an absolutely vital part of a designer's toolkit.

They may address a trend or fashion-oriented concern, or they may explore a question of tradition, methods, and knowledge of paths taken in the past. Knowing how one connects to the world and the past can be a very powerful inspiration and a motivation to move forward with one's own work.

Use these timelines as prompts to investigate the history and traditions involved in your interests in design, whatever they may be. As you will see in Chapter 2, the story of design is deep and multilayered.

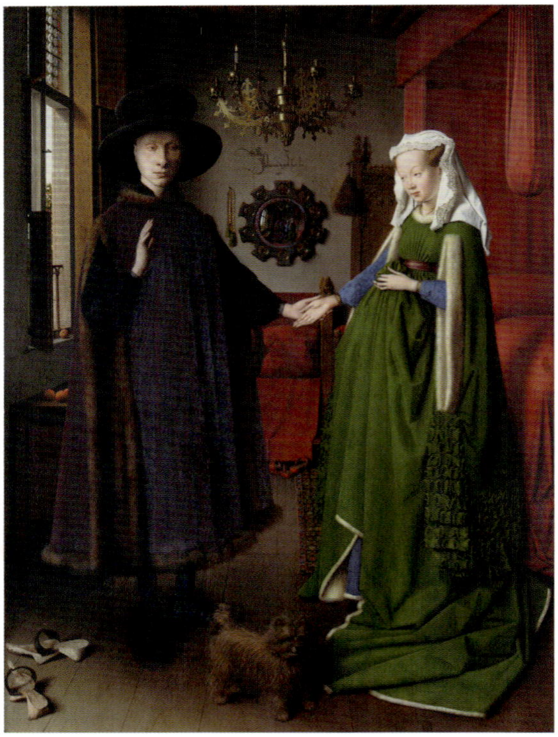

1.5 *The Arnolfini Portrait*, 1434, by Jan van Eyck. We define and present ourselves as individuals, societies, and cultures by the objects and surroundings we design, own, and inhabit. Even in the earliest portraits of the new urban upper class, such as this one, we see the display of material goods as a way of defining status and identity. All the items surrounding the couple—their clothes, bedding, and even the dog and pieces of fruit—are items of value that show them to be people of significant means.

Source: Jan van Eyck: *The Arnolfini Portrait* (1434)

domination. The representation of power and display of wealth was fueled by conquest, and the wealth and valuable materials taken from the conquered colonies flooded the economic systems of Europe with ostentatious materials and designed goods. In a society of spectacle, where appearance is everything, the class with the money and means of production can encode its message in buildings, clothing, and goods, and then manipulate, edit, and tailor the result as long as it remains in control of the way the designs are created.

Designing is, however, about much more than creating products on shelves—it is also the forming of the shelves themselves, the building the shelves are in, the lighting in the building, the building's layout and surroundings, the layout of the streets and neighborhoods, and the theories and practices involved in city planning. Design can encompass the systems of factories that create the products, the transportation methods of getting the products to the shelves, and the advertisements and the layout of the pages the ads are on. It also encompasses the machines in factories; cars, highways, and bridges; ships; aircraft; satellites and navigation systems; and on and on. Human culture is defined not only by the things around us, but how those things are used over time and to what end. In fact, the act and art of designing is so completely entwined with human experience it is fair to say that if we are defined by what we do and how we do it, for a large part of humanity the sum of our designing *is* the world in which we live (Fig. 1.5).

THE PROCESS: WHAT DOES A DESIGNER DO?

Designers are as different as their jobs are many, and there is no standard environment in which they may be found. A designer has a command of the technical as well as the sensual and emotional. A designer knows enough about materials and techniques to recognize what is needed and how to head toward the correct solution. A designer has enough knowledge of the history and tradition of the field to know how to follow rules—and how to break them. Finally, a designer has an unending interest in the field but also develops trains of thought that allow the field to expand and be altered.

In general, the job description of a designer is pretty straightforward: Create a concept, specifications, and plan of production for a new product, within a budget, before a deadline. But depending on the product involved, once the day-to-day operations begin, one designer's job may be wildly different from another. A designer of clothing, for example, and a designer of cars are dealing with extremely different sets of materials, methods, engineering, and client needs. Designers must be trained in the various technical abilities specific to their discipline. A good designer of clothing may not necessarily be a good designer of furniture or cars; the knowledge of techniques, needs, and constraints of the product is too variable. Yet the basic principles and elements are the same, the traditional tools of sketching and illustration are the same, they may use some of the same software, and their vocabulary and sources of inspiration can overlap. For example, many of the concerns of design have to deal with size, shape, and tolerances of the human body, but how designers can and must incorporate these into their designs is very different (Fig. 1.6). Designers can be working on technical aspects of a project, considering structures or diagrammatic solutions, or they can be working on entirely conceptual or decorative aspects. Each of these aspects is a function of the design problem involved: Fulfill the needs of the project as defined by the prospective client (or whoever has requested the design). The project then has to be completed inside the time frame allotted, within the given budget, and in accordance with the manufacturing parameters.

With so much variation in scope and style, one would think a definition of the designer's role would be tricky, but in fact it is fairly easy to frame: The designer's main

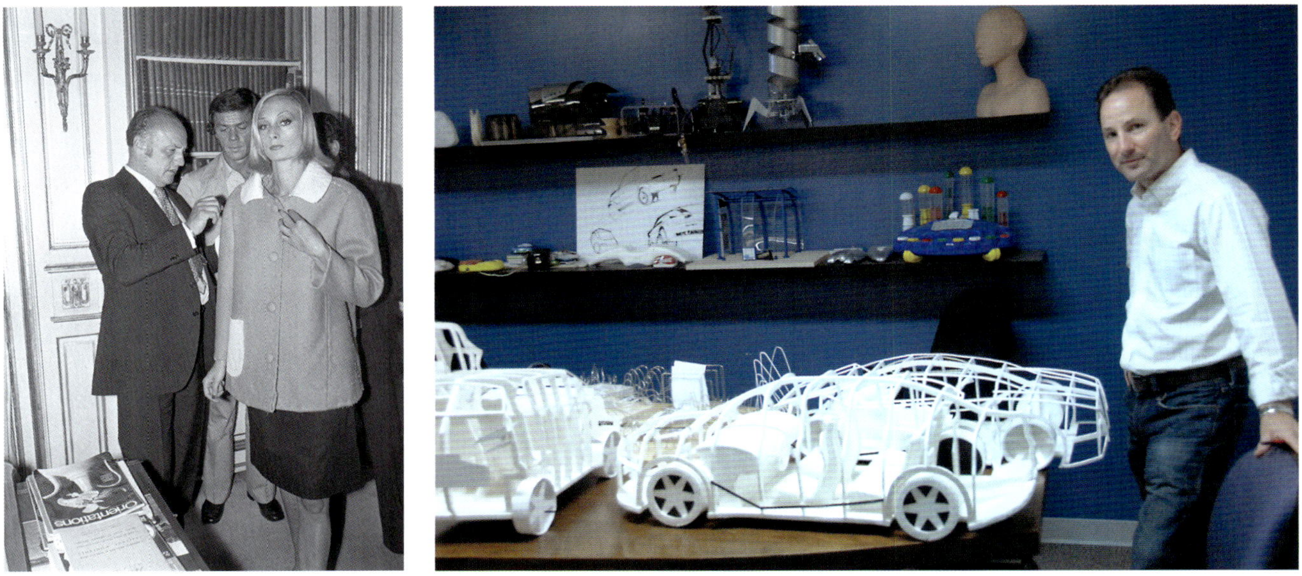

1.6 A designer of high-fashion dresses and a designer of cars may, for example, be dealing with many of the same elements and principles, but the techniques, needs, and constraints of different disciplines of design also vary wildly. Both designers consider shape, volume, materials, colors, and so on, but the construction methods, industry standards, and collaborative methods are vastly different, to name but a few.

Sources: L: Courtesy of WWD; R: Photo by Clover Sterling; ©2010 Humber ITAL

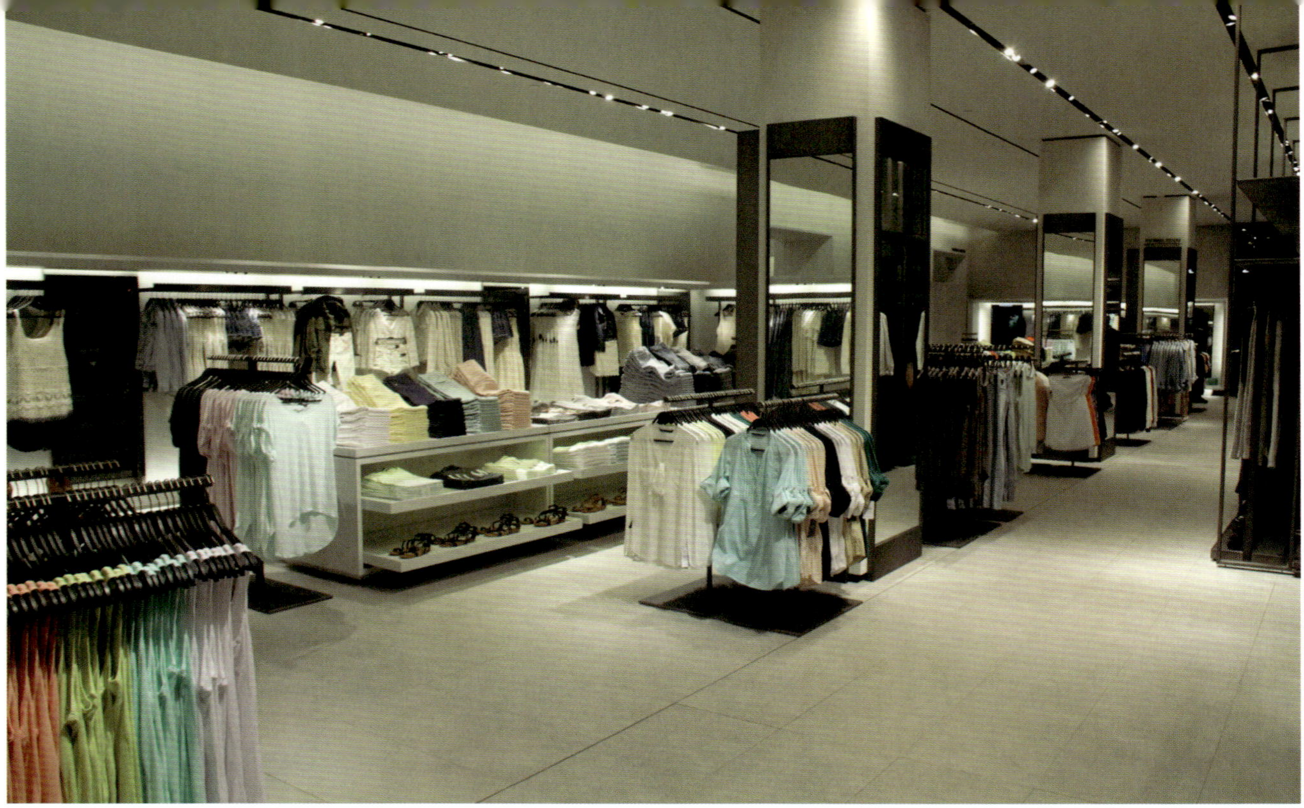

1.7 Designing is about improving a current situation or developing something new and useful, sometimes focusing on beauty, sometimes on function, sometimes both. Sometimes function is beauty, and sometimes the beauty is the function. The room, the furnishings, the products, the lighting are all designed for a need.

Source: Courtesy of Kyle Ericksen/WWD

objective is to make sure everyone involved in the production of the design has the practical, aesthetic, and technical information they need. The designer places this information in context and solves any problems that may appear to stand in the way of a solution to the design problem. The designer is also an *intermediary* between the client and the production side, and then between both of these and the marketing group. Finally, the designer also can be seen as the most familiar avatar of the profession—an *illustrator* that provides information by creating images of the final design.

The process of designing can vary depending on the intention of the design. Sometimes design is concerned with developing something new and useful—sometimes focusing on beauty, sometimes on function, and sometimes on both (Fig. 1.7). At times function *is* beauty, and at other times the beauty is the function. In addition, design often involves rethinking the nature of our interaction with everyday objects and environments.

So, what are the basic steps of the process? If designing is what is done "by design," what *is* that precisely? An introduction to the nature of design and designing must show it in its various guises, along with a step-by-step description of what a designer actually *does* in practice. This requires a discussion and demonstration of how constraints and needs define a design solution, as most of the time a designer is making choices and decisions based on predefined parameters of a specific problem. In such cases, designing quickly encompasses more than the basic elements of the product involved; it comprises knowledge, technology, aesthetics, methods, budgets, time, and capabilities applied in a process containing a series of stages: inspiration, identification, conceptualization, exploration, definition, communication, and production.

INSPIRATION

The first stage, **inspiration,** the infusion of creative energy, might be the most difficult to pin down, but understanding its importance is vital to the successful completion of a project. The first step in any creative project should be the inspiration of the

SUSTAINABILITY

The problems of sustaining human culture and "life as we know it" are bound up with the problems of sustaining our methods of production, manufacturing, commerce, and use of goods. It is fairly clear to most people that current practices are headed toward a crisis in the near future as the number of humans on the planet demanding resources for a industrialized middle-class lifestyle increases exponentially. Each chapter in this book also contains a sidebar, highlighting (all too briefly) issues relating to sustainable practices that can be considered in parallel with one or more of the chapter's topics. This reflects the view that designers in today's globalized economy hold a great deal of power over the environmental impact of the life cycle of the goods we use. Designers can influence the choice and amount of materials, production methods, style, durability, and recyclability of the product. Designers are also the link in the production chain that probably has a dialogue with most other links—suppliers, manufacturers, retailers, and clients, to name a few. Consider this your responsibility if you are involved with design: You can make a difference to the health and well-being of future generations by basing choices on the environmental impact of your work.

participants. Inspiration is the fuel that keeps the designers and collaborators engaged and willing to work on the project, even when the going is rough. It is what drives the creative person to take on a project even when the next steps are completely hidden from view.

The designer's initial task is to consider what might inspire engagement with the project. Is there an aesthetic excitement? A personal goal? The thrill of achieving something no one has before? The satisfaction of creating something that meets a need in a way that is wholly new? Perhaps the inspiration is simply the thought of creating a moneymaker for the company, or perhaps it is the lift to the morale of the team by including them in a project's success. The project might have gains that are their own end, in that they lead toward a larger goal, and solving one objective might bring the next one closer.

So, what can inspire a designer? Answering the question by saying "anything at all" is actually accurate but ultimately unhelpful. We must look closer. Inspiration for a design project can come from a creative side; it can be technical, emotional, or situational. Technical inspiration might, for example, be stirred by the designer being intrigued by a material or a method and how it will be used to solve a design problem. For example, creating a pattern for a fabric might be inspired simply by the mechanics of making a certain rhythm work within a set of shapes and colors. A solution to a technical problem of how to build something more efficiently may contain its own reward, and the inspiration comes from the satisfaction of a puzzle solved.

But inspiration may be a purely emotional drive involving the desire to see something come to fruition—that is, having an initial vision of how things should be in the design of an environment or in the appearance of an object and then making that a reality. Nostalgia and the emotionality of revisiting familiar ground and reliving the past through one's own creativity might play a part. All of this is part of the human experience. Emotions *do* count and are not trivial or indulgent.

The modernist technical view of design and architecture that defined the profession in the late 19th and early 20th centuries tended to sideline the emotional side of creativity. After the emotionality of the romantic movement of the early 19th century, the

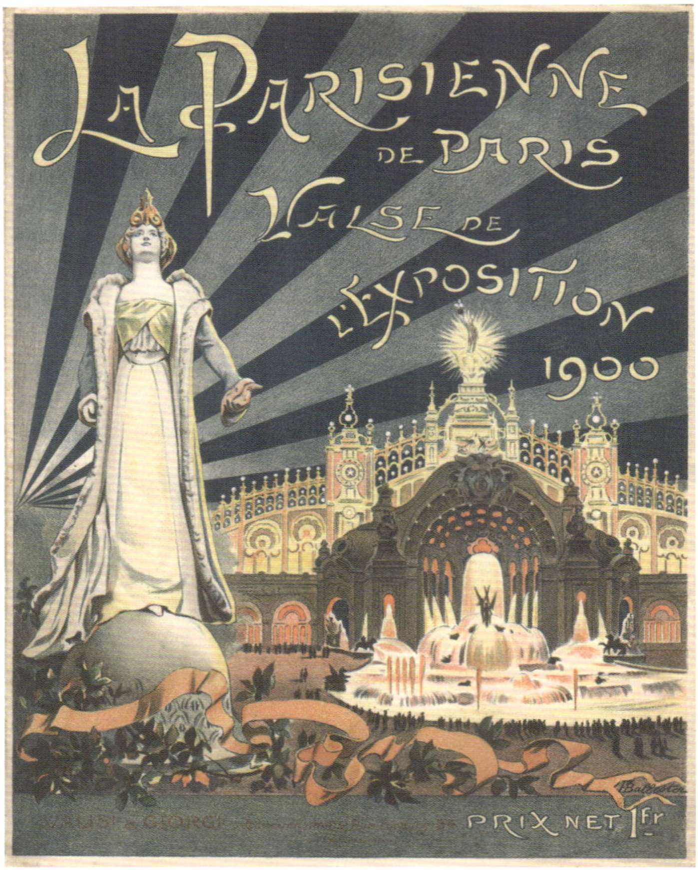

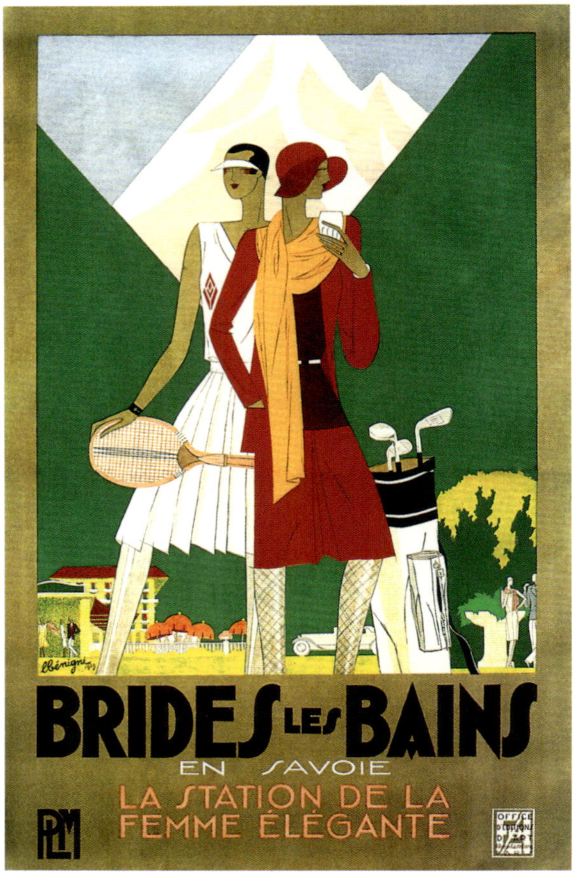

1.8 As the 20th century arrived, modern style rid itself of the romanticism of the 19th century, as seen in these two posters, both typical of their time. The soft curvature of Art Nouveau style on the left has become the high modernist angularity on the right. (The flowing style of Art Nouveau would return in the 1960s when "flower power" tempered the edges of modernism.) (Posters left to right: 1900—Sheet music cover, La Parisienne De Paris [Valse De L'exposition 1900]; 1922: Chrysler ad, part of a European series.

Sources: L: Courtesy of http://exposition-universelle-paris-1900.com; and R: © Lordprice Collection/Alamy

technical masculine-oriented society that was developing turned toward an enforced seriousness and allowed little space for frivolity. Emotion was relegated to "the feminine" and considered at best evidence of overwrought "artistic" sensibilities and at worst weakness. In design, emotion was largely expressed in a romantic emotionality in the 19th century, but this was answered by a shift toward a more controlled emotionless style as the 20th century demanded a modern technical approach. This pendulum would swing back and forth several times during the 20th century. (Fig. 1.8).

However, whatever emotion is required is that which grows from *care*. If the designer cannot display care for the project, it is unlikely that anyone else will feel inspired to do so. Without caring, there is no anger or humor; there is also little joy at the successfully completed project. Without care, the idea that finishing the project somehow solves a problem, overcomes a constraint, or fulfills a need becomes a technical question rather than an emotional investment.

IDENTIFICATION

The first practical step in a design project, beyond a sense of inspiration, is to identify the problems involved. What exactly (to the extent that precision is possible at the beginning of a project) is being asked of the designer or design team? What are the needs that the design must fulfill? What are the constraints that bind the project to a certain range of possible solutions? Budgets will play a part, but so will the nature and

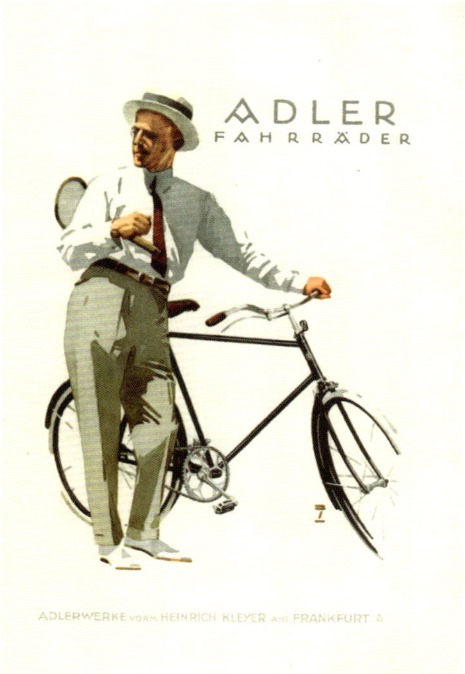

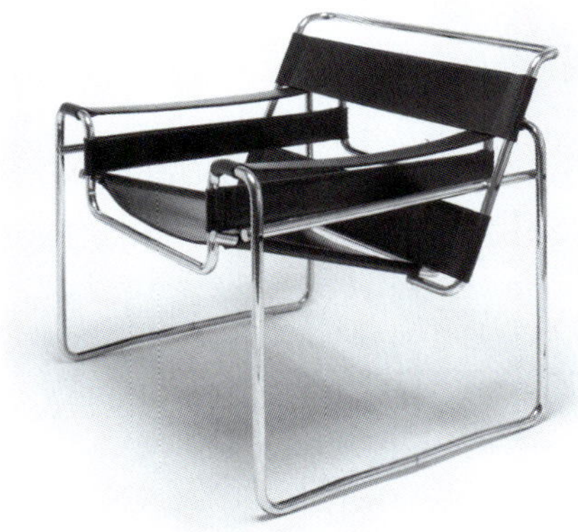

1.9 How designers approach one problem may solve another: The revolutionary design of the 1926 "Wassily" Chair (bottom) by Marcel Breuer was said to have been inspired by the hollow metal tubing Breuer used when designing the "Adler" bicycle (top).

Sources: Top: Mary Evans/Retrograph Collection; Bottom: © G. Jackson/Arcaid/Corbis

personality of the clients, the geographical situation of the project, its projected longevity, and any number of other factors.

Identification often takes place through research and investigation of the needs and constraints of the client and the situations involved, but it also comprises brainstorming and imagining, as the actual situation may leave plenty of room for the creative spirit to inject ideas. Identifying a design project properly is key to its success, and doing so creates a safe place where objectives can be delineated, parameters established, and risks determined beforehand.

A designer in the identifying stage may be seen as a connector who identifies how concepts can be brought together in a new way. This is the core of innovation: the ability to connect two or more known ideas in a new way to bring something into the world that has not been seen or done before or that performs better than anything so far. Creating connections between ideas also may involve creating connections among disciplines where the way something is approached in one place may be the solution of how it is done elsewhere. For example, lightweight frames developed for bicycles were found to be excellent for furniture in the 1920s, and methods from the space program have supported thinking about design for a number of more earth-bound products (Fig. 1.9).

Making connections requires that a designer be versed in more than one area, and these skills are vital not just in training but in maintaining abilities. A constant curiosity and willingness to step outside the comfort zone of one's own discipline will always serve a designer well. It is not only helpful but necessary.

Finally, being a connector also may be about connecting people, where skills as a people manager must come into play in recognizing how members of a design team will work together and who will benefit from working with whom.

CONCEPTUALIZATION

The image that often emerges is the designer as problem solver. Every design project is a problem requiring a solution. The solution encompasses methods, uses, approaches, materials, costs, weights, contexts, moods, and emotions, but in the end, a solution—that is, a *concept*—begins to emerge of the direction that must be followed. The concept can be entirely mundane, such as how to improve a simple kitchen gadget. Or it can be large and profound, such as a vision for the future of an entire city or a life-changing, culture-evolving device that changes everyone's method of engagement in daily life.

In dealing with **conceptualization** as well as the application of technical solutions and precise definitions, the designer's mind overlaps with the scientist's mind, the artists mind, and the philosopher's mind: Here is a problem of existence . . . here is a problem of interaction with people and things . . . here is a problem of day-to-day living . . . here is a problem of societal existence and operation . . . a specific need . . . a strict constraint . . . a need for materials . . . a precise measurement—all of these may

1.10 Designer's mind, artist's mind, scientist's mind, philosopher's mind. . . . Here we see the British fashion designer Vivienne Westwood in Africa working with the United Nations Ethical Fashion Initiative, focusing her designer´s mind on problems of social and ethical significance.

Source: Courtesy of Chloe Mukai, The Ethical Fashion Initiative, International Trade Centre

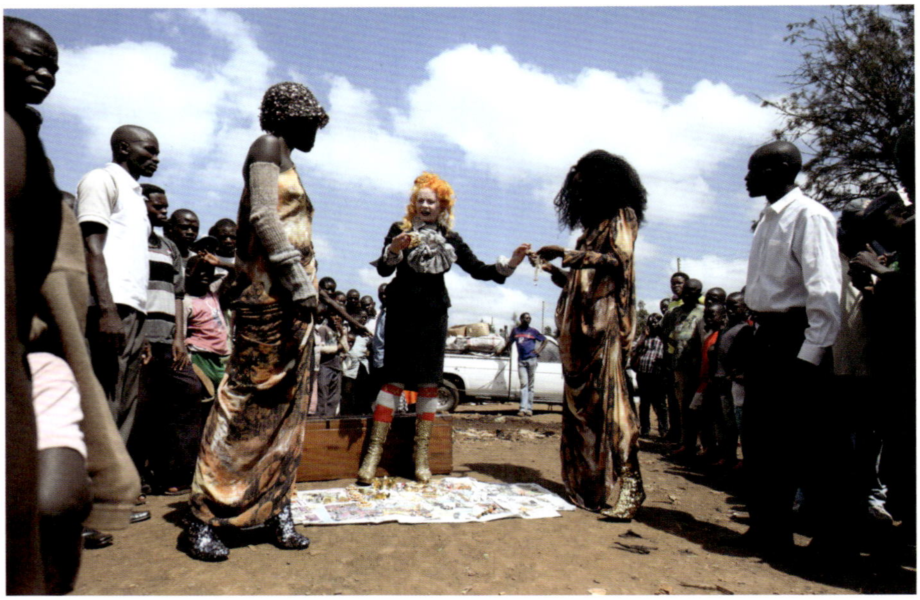

require a solution by design, and the designer brings in and presents the information, the connection, the context, and the technical know-how to solve this particular problem. The designer may bring in visuals, diagrams, writing, artwork, and any number of references to previous solutions. How this approach evolves over time also is a way of looking at the development of civilization itself and the human experience, as will be discussed in Chapter 2. (Fig. 1.10.)

EXPLORATION

Eventually the conceptual phase must lead to exploration of the practical matters at hand and a "kicking around" of the concept to see what it actually contains. Here **exploration** begins. The idea as fleshed out in brainstorming is conceptualized and outlined. What is its nature? Where does it fit into a previously existing scheme? Where does it break out and create new areas for the end users to experience? The idea is explored for hidden possibilities and new perspectives. Various techniques and exercises have been developed, such as the very powerful SCAMPER method developed by engineers at NASA to move a project out of a corner (see Box 1.2).

The turning of raw material into an object requires precise definitions and technical specifications. Technical diagrams, prototypes, mock-ups, testing, and planning are either performed or directed by the designer to test functionality and to try out new materials. Connecting is one thing. Putting it in context is another. A good designer must find where things fit. How does a material belong? How does a shape "speak of" a concept? What is the space in which a designed object will fit in the life of a person, a city, a society, a culture? Thinking in terms of context requires much more than knowledge of materials and techniques. It also requires knowledge of cultures and people, beliefs and behaviors, ways, structures, and methods of people's lives. The designer must be able to place him- or herself within a situation. What is (or will be) the context of the design? How does it fit into the life, into the system, into the prevailing trend of

ERGONOMICS

In each chapter there is a sidebar concerned with *ergonomics* as it relates to the chapter's material. From the Greek *ergon* (work) and *nomos* (laws), ergonomics is literally the "science of work." Following is the definition of ergonomics as approved by the Council of the International Ergonomics Association (www.iea.cc) in 2000:

> Ergonomics (or human factors) is the scientific discipline concerned with the understanding of the interactions among humans and other elements of a system, and the profession that applies theoretical principles, data, and methods to design in order to optimize human well-being and overall system performance.
>
> Practitioners of ergonomics, ergonomists, contribute to the planning, design, and evaluation of tasks, jobs, products, organizations, environments, and systems in order to make them compatible with the needs, abilities, and limitations of people.

As a discipline, ergonomics applies to all activity: physical, cognitive, social, environmental, and organizational. It is therefore extremely important that designers understand and apply its methods. *Physical ergonomics* is the primary of these in traditional design, as it is concerned with human anatomy and physical activity. This might involve considering posture, materials, repetitive movements, work-related musculoskeletal disorders (such as carpal tunnel syndrome and muscle strains), workplace layout, and safety and health in general. *Cognitive ergonomics*, on the other hand, is concerned with mental processes that relate to people's interactions as well as people as elements of a system. This may involve considering issues of perception, memory, reasoning, and motor response. In human system design, there may be issues of mental workload, decision making, skilled performance, human–computer interaction, human reliability, work stress, and training. Finally, *organizational ergonomics* is concerned with the optimizing of systems in terms of their organizational structures, policies, and processes. It may involve designers in the application of technical aspects of systems or the effects of physical layout on a system or process.

how things are done? The structures and habits of people—the schemes within which they operate—must be brought into focus.

DEFINITION

Designers have to adhere to deadlines. Like it or not, the time arrives when the SCAMPER-ing must end and the decision must be made to go with one or another of the possible solutions. Now designing becomes about precise choices and confirmation of these choices: this color and not that, these textures, that equipment, this finish, and on and on until the concept is delivered as closely as possible to the desired form. In the **definition** stage, the thinking tends toward the technical as the elements of design have to move from overall concepts and abstract notions of color schemes, line, and space to definite measurements, color codes, and tolerances. It is here that the production team may show up to weigh in on the best solutions for constructing the designed object.

COMMUNICATION

Although the **communication** skills of the designer factor heavily toward the end of a project when the design is taken to production, the need for communication is vital throughout the process. The designer must provide material for inspiration, identify the design problem to the team, explore the concepts and consider all possibilities, and determine technical solutions and specifications, communicating as much as possible with everyone during the process.

BOX 1.2

SCAMPER: A BRAIN-STORMING TECHNIQUE

IN THE EARLY STAGES OF A PROJECT, designing is about exploring ideas in order to find out what they contain and what constrains them. The best way to evaluate the constraints in all directions is to isolate the idea's components and deliberately change things around to find the limits of the total concept. Push and prod the intended design to see what it's capable of and whether there are other directions in which it might go. Once it's gone too far, there's your limit.

Brainstorming usually refers to a group getting together to examine a situation with the express purpose of solving a problem. This is not limited to designing but is found in any structured planning or systematic creativity where a solution must be found by generating new ideas. In a brainstorming session, everyone's voice must be heard and no ideas are to be dismissed or criticized during the discussion. Critical analysis takes place after a predetermined period of when a certain number of ideas have been generated.

A number of good brainstorming techniques have been developed to assist in a creative process dialogue. The SCAMPER technique is an excellent example of how designing can be systematically approached. It is a very good way of exploring the possibilities of idea, as it can easily be applied to any kind of creative venture and is easily done as either a solo activity or as a prompt for group brainstorming. The technique was formally defined by Robert F. Eberle, an educational administrator who wrote on creativity for both children and teachers. SCAMPER is an acronym for:

<u>**S**</u>ubstitute

<u>**C**</u>ombine

<u>**A**</u>dapt

<u>**M**</u>odify (**m**inimize *or* **m**agnify)

<u>**P**</u>ut to other use(s)

<u>**E**</u>liminate or **e**laborate

<u>**R**</u>everse or **r**earrange

Taking an initial idea and running it down the list allows a team or individual designer to examine the project from various angles, considering various elements and aspects, without getting hung up on any one particular element of the design or even on the nature of the design itself. SCAMPER-ing simply provides a way to rearrange the existing concept and attack it from various levels to get as much out of it as possible. By not binding the discussion to any individual aspect, it allows the idea as a system—to be taken outside habitual frames of reference and possibly be improved in unexpected ways.

Take an idea and do as many of the following as you can. The results may overlap; some may be silly. This is normal and means that you have found a boundary to examine. Consider individual parts of your design, but also think of it as a *system* (you might even be designing an actual system):

SUBSTITUTE

Take something out; put something else in its place. For example, swap colors or components. Substitute a technique or a method of construction. If there's a process, isolate a step. Then consider doing something else at that point. Where does this lead?

COMBINE

Take two or more components of your idea and combine them. For example, make two pieces into one piece, or several steps into one operation. Combine your entire concept with another idea. Combine styles. Now what?

ADAPT

How can your design be adapted to another situation, or for another purpose? For example, a design for a specific climate is adapted to another, or a system directed at one situation is modified to work for another. Note that adapting involves change, as opposed to *putting to other uses* (below) where the unchanged idea is directed to another purpose.

MODIFY (MINIMIZE OR MAGNIFY)

This step is probably the most open-ended, as *modification* can have a variety of meanings. In any case, begin, without adding new elements, by changing the *quality* of one or more elements of the design. Make something bigger or smaller, lengthen or shorten a process, make something angular curvy, and so on. Then consider modifying the *functionality* of your design; make it do something differently. Finally, consider modifying the overall design by adding a component to the object or a step to the process.

PUT TO OTHER USE(S)

How could your idea be applied to another problem? How could your design be used elsewhere? What would happen if it were used by someone entirely different than the end user you imagined?

ELIMINATE OR ELABORATE

Is everything necessary? All the components? Every step in the process? What if you randomly remove an element or function? ("Can't have color," or "mustn't move.") How much can you remove before your idea is no longer what you intended? Conversely, did you leave any thought half-finished? What can be increased or made more complex? What can be taken further? At what point is there "too much"? (When is "too much" "just right"?)

REVERSE OR REARRANGE

Reverse in whole or in part: put the back in the front, the end at the beginning, the left on the right, and so on. What does "inside-out" mean in the context of your idea? Is there an order to things that can be rearranged or broken up? Is there an assumption or belief about the order of things that can be challenged out of existence?

The art of communication lies largely in clarity and trust. All the information must be completely clear, and even when it is not, the unknowns must be delineated ("This we know. This we *don't* know. This we have to find out."). The ability to evaluate the talents and knowledge of a production team and to speak of problems without embarrassment and hesitation is often the difference between a successful production and one that winds up being an awkward compromise.

Communication is on more than one level. The communication of strictly practical information is one thing. The other is inspiring communication of the care and aesthetic sense involved. Lining up specifications clearly and thoroughly is perhaps the easier of the two. The key to inspiring a crew is to be inspired yourself. After all, an uninspired person cannot inspire anyone else.

Finally, in terms of communication, there is the image of the designer that seems to hold the most sway in popular imagination: that of someone sketching away on a pad with a marker or pencil, quickly drawing the shape of whatever the object is with a few lines on a page. The designer as "illustrator" has come to us through such popular mythmaking as that which took place around fine art in the early 20th century, where the sense of immediate inspiration being placed onto a canvas or sketchpad with no preparation or investigation beforehand was the mark of a "true" artist.

This was affirmed during the renaissance of high-fashion design in the 1950s, when authoritative designers, such as Dior or Saint Laurent, were frequently shown with sketches in hand next to the finished models of their designs (Fig. 1.11). It is still seen today in the frequent stories of iconic buildings and new concepts being designed on a napkin.[3] It happens all the time: a design has to begin somewhere—every journey begins with a first step. The sketch on the napkin, however, is probably itself a result of work that has already taken place. A designer may have researched the client's needs, thought about materials, and looked at tradition and history before picking up that napkin (Fig. 1.12).

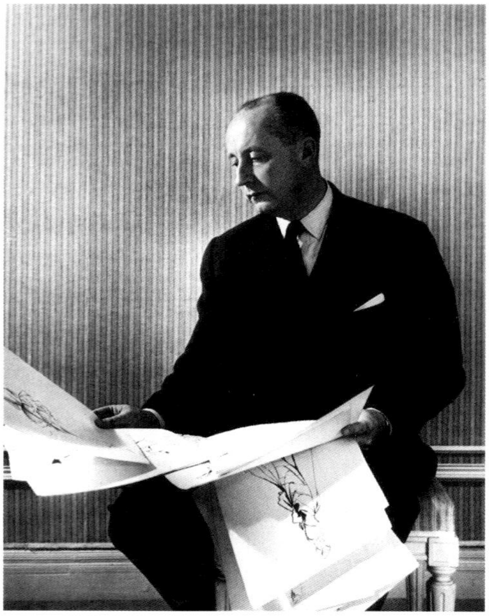

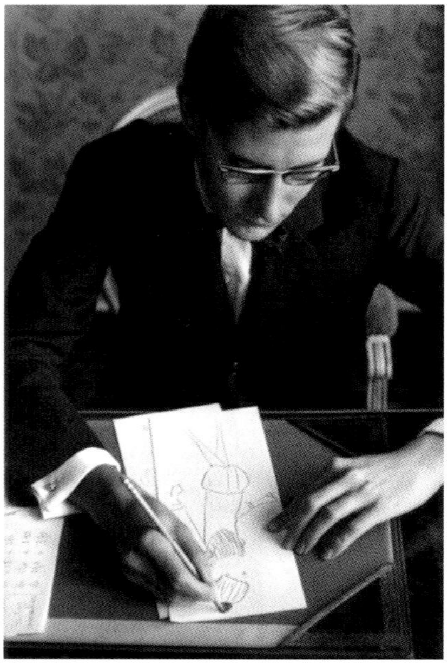

1.11 The designer as illustrator: With so much of the designer's job being intangible, cerebral, and piecemeal, the popular image of the designer as sketch artist was solidified through staged photographs such as these in the heyday of high fashion. Christian Dior in 1948 (left); Yves Saint Laurent in 1957 (right), shortly after being named as Dior's successor.

Sources: L: © Everett Collection Historical/Alamy; R: © Photos 12/Alamy

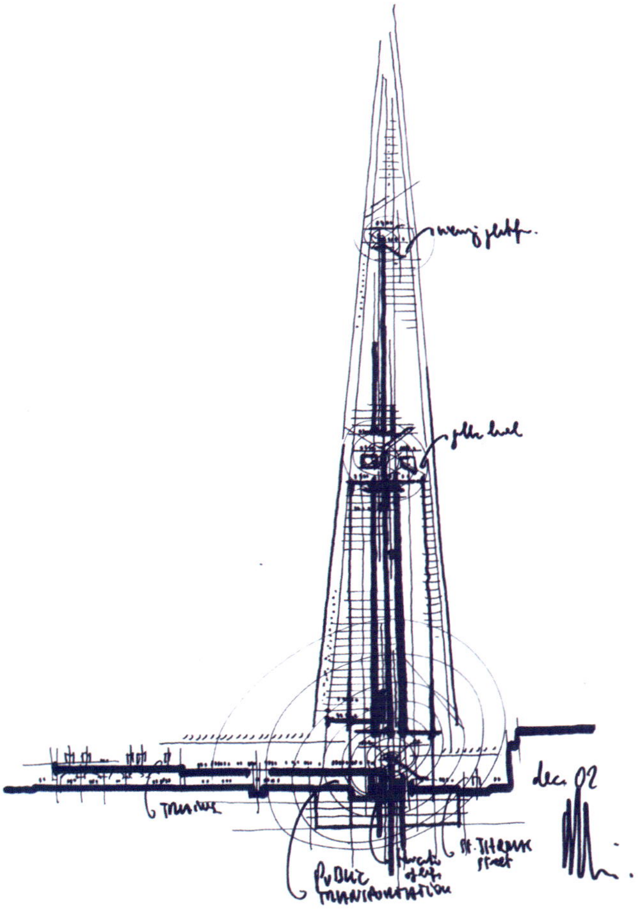

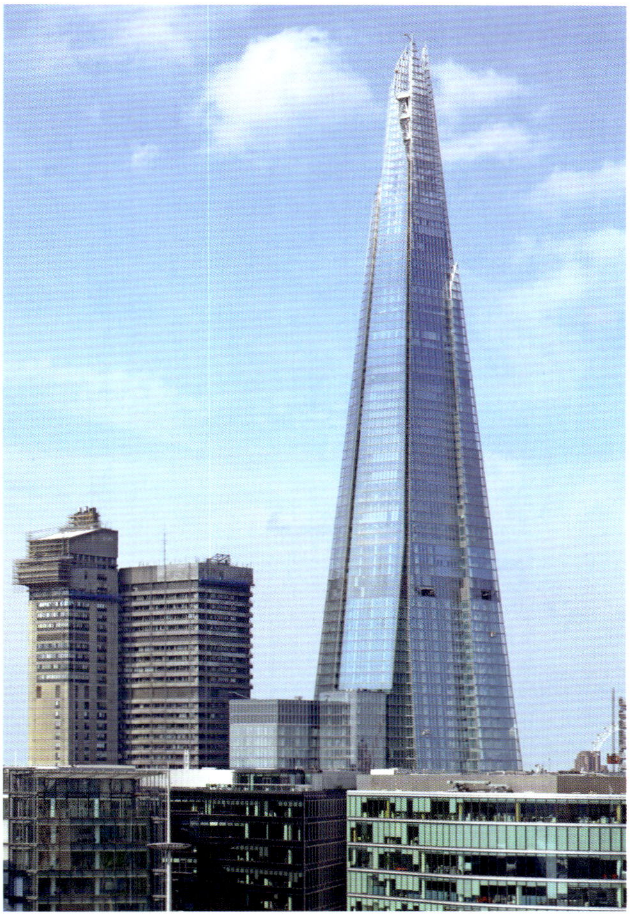

1.12 The architect Renzo Piano's "The Shard" in London. It is said to have begun as a sketch on the back of a napkin in a Berlin restaurant in 2000. True or not, this kind of myth reveals the instinctive and impulsive beginnings of design ideas. Sketch from 2002 (left); "The Shard" (right), nearing completion 10 years later.

Sources: L: The London Bridge Tower, Renzo Piano Building Workshop Architects; R: © Justin Kase z12z/Alamy

The sketching-image makes the designer's craft into an artistic image and thus continues to romanticize it. This, however, does not (and must not) take away from the fact that a large part of a designer's craft revolves around creating visuals of the concept and the idea in its various stages.

PRODUCTION

In the **production** phase, the biggest challenge to the designer may be to actually let go of the project and let the production process take over. Possibly this may be as easy as seeing the project sent off to being manufactured in a far country. However, production also may involve hands-on supervision throughout a long process, such as watching a building go up or an interior being assembled.

The difficulty lies in having to compromise the design vision with the reality of physical objects and tactile, organic materials that are by their very nature flawed and imperfect. A surface is never quite as flawless as it is imagined, a color perhaps not quite as intense as it looks on a computer screen or marker sketch, and the fit of a garment not quite as perfect on the model in motion as it seemed to be on a static mannequin. But these are all overcome by experience, and a designer learns when to push for "perfection" and when to give in to the imperfections of the world.

NETWORKING

To obtain an idea of what design is in human society, visiting a design museum might be a good start, before heading out into the streets, stores, and public spaces.

Here are twelve major design museums:

DESIGN MUSEUM DANMARK (COPENHAGEN)
designmuseum.dk

VICTORIA AND ALBERT MUSEUM (LONDON)
www.vam.ac.uk

DESIGN MUSEUM (LONDON)
designmuseum.org

THE RISD (RHODE ISLAND SCHOOL OF DESIGN) MUSEUM
risdmuseum.org

DESIGN MUSEUM BOSTON
designmuseumboston.org

SMITHSONIAN COOPER-HEWITT, NATIONAL DESIGN MUSEUM IN NEW YORK
www.cooperhewitt.org

VITRA DESIGN MUSEUM (GERMANY)
www.design-museum.de

MUSEUM OF MODERN ART (NEW YORK)
www.moma.org

DESIGN MUSEUM GENT (BELGIUM)
www.designmuseumgent.be

DESIGN EXCHANGE (CANADA'S DESIGN MUSEUM)
www.dx.org

RED DOT DESIGN MUSEUM (SINGAPORE)
museum.red-dot.sg

MUSEUM OF AFRICAN DESIGN (SOUTH AFRICA)
www.moadjhb.com

DESIGNING: A HUMAN EXPERIENCE

We are surrounded by products that have all been thought through in a design process (i.e., to varying degrees of artistic and aesthetic sensibilities). The building, the interiors, the furniture, the objects, and clothing, the handheld gadgets and computers that have become ubiquitous—themselves containing virtual environments that are heavily designed.

Has this always been so? Perhaps not in the mass-manufactured way that we now live our lives, but human society in general is very far away from a non-designed state (and as implied earlier, any human society by its very nature is always designed). It is an inherent part of human condition to alter, adapt, and improve upon nature—even though the nature of the improvement often is hotly debated, especially in recent years, as the destructive impact of human technology and systems on the natural world is becoming ever clearer.

The Canadian social theorist Marshall McLuhan is well known for his statement **"the medium is the message."** This statement finds a meaning in the study of designing. Our communication and distribution technologies have developed to the point where to a large portion of human beings' connectivity to each other and the world is instantaneous and without pause. The content of these communications are beside the point, as McLuhan pointed out. It is not what is *on* the screen (McLuhan was writing about television, before the advent of the Internet), but the fact that we get the majority of our information about the world *from* a screen in a constant stream of broken-up imagery and information. We are increasingly reliant on the design of systems and the design of gadgets that steer our understanding of the world into bytes and bits of information that we cannot access without electronic devices (Fig. 1.13).

Therefore, the design of the gadgets we use matters. The size of the screen, the interactivity of the hardware and software, the websites or program involved—all

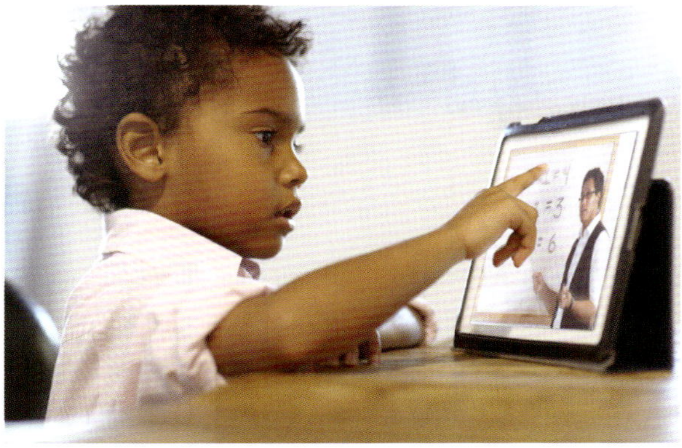

ABOVE
1.13 We increasingly get our information about the world from a screen. The design of the delivery system changes how we interact with the world. Children growing up with new communication technology incorporate it very quickly and develop a worldview based on the information flow it affords them.

Source: © Ron Royals/Corbis

influence our worldview. More than ever, social interaction is restricted to the communication of isolated thoughts, packaged into small messages—short notices, tweets, statuses, and headline-style phrases or images. The disembodied state of online communication and presence may make us forget that environments are more than just the physical manifestation of things. In worrying about the effects of all this messaging and virtual interaction, we may have forgotten that all human interaction requires environments and we will create them if they are not there already. We are never without a world to be in, be it imagined on a cave wall, built as a city of gleaming skyscrapers, inhabited by people wearing designer labels, or a collection of bursts of information and images on a small handheld screen.

The constant flow of information through multiple channels creates a fragmented worldview of multiple streams of text, images and sound, that had already begun with the increase in information delivered by accelerating publication, radio, television, and film. Design as a whole has therefore less of a total feel than was the case in the early decades of the 20th century. This may be a self-perpetuating culture, as the consumers who are the audience for the incessant stream of online material are habituated to the fragmentation, variation, and appeal of the constant new thing. The online reposting and blogging creates a totality of its own, reinforcing the image of a world of assorted combinations (Fig. 1.14).

The structures of early 21st century design are those defined by media that is global, non-localized, largely geared toward a consumer identity that is not bound to place or specific national culture, and the offspring of late 20th-century corporate culture and marketing. As the speed of ideas compounded by the sheer mass of information available to consumers makes trends far harder to spot, much less predict or create, designers are followers more often than leaders. Style cultures tend to feed on

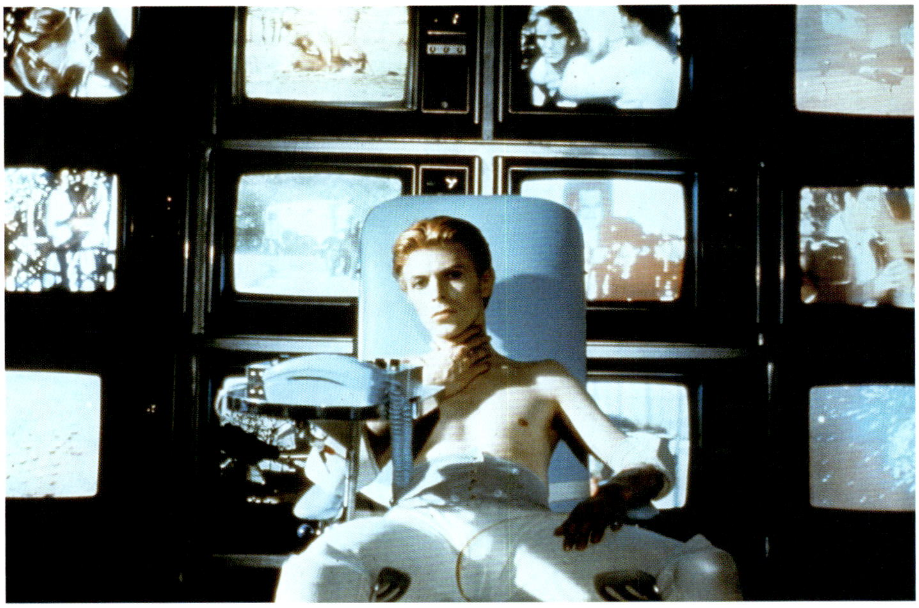

BELOW
1.14 The audience for an incessant stream of digital material becomes habituated to the fragmentation, variation, and appeal of the constant new thing. As the number of options increase, instead of becoming overloaded, the audience alters its way of viewing. Attention spans altered and multitasking with multiple streams of information began to be observed as television channels multiplied. Now blogging and texting have become the reigning mode, and a room of multiple TVs (as seen here behind David Bowie in *The Man Who Fell to Earth* in 1976) seems almost a quaint image.

Source: STUDIOCANAL Films Ltd.

themselves in a loop: A culture creates its own structures and is in turn perpetuated by its own structures, such as in the dress codes of a subculture, or the rules of high-society etiquette. Communications technologies, such as print, radio, film, television, and the World Wide Web, simply speed up the process by facilitating the delivery and the reach of the information needed by the participants in order that they may adhere to the correct behavior.

It is very important to remember the context in which these issues are being discussed and from what vantage point a book, such as this, is written. The placing of design as a subject of study and analysis in a classroom is part of a modern tradition that is a product of—and embedded in—a culture that can be traced back for centuries and spans a large portion of the globe. But it is not the *entire* culture of the globe, nor does it encompass *all* of human history and experience. Despite the fact that humans are the designing species, the idea of design as a formal and important element of society is not everywhere, and there are certainly a number of places on the globe where designer creations are of minimal importance. Design is approached differently in different places, just as it was approached differently in different historical eras and cultures all around the world. Even in a globalized market and corporate world, people's needs and constraints on the ground are still extremely different from one part of the world to the next.

CONSTRAINTS AND NEEDS

To Igor Stravinsky, composing music was a process of solving musical problems, problems that he insisted on precisely defining before he started to work. "The more constraints one imposes, the more one frees one's self," he said. "And the arbitrariness of the constraint serves only to obtain precision of execution." Before beginning to write a ballet, for example, he wrote to ask for the exact dimensions of the hall in which it would be performed, the number of seats, and the direction in which the orchestra would be facing.[4]

Just as in Stravinsky's musical creativity, constraints place limits on the designer's mobility. To have to navigate around an obstacle requires a solution, and restrictions on a creative process create in this way a basis for interaction and dialogue. Placing arbitrary obstacles may well spark thoughts that would not appear otherwise. Courting constraints in a systematic way is therefore a way to move through a design project, by solving one problem at a time, or to find a way out of a dead end, by forcing the idea to go in another direction.

A design will have both **inherent** and **imposed constraints**. On one hand, the *inherent* qualities that make the object into the very thing that it is: What are the specific qualities and elements that make a table a table and a chair a chair? When is a shirt a shirt and not something else? What needs to happen to something for it to be called a "jacket"? These particular qualities and elements that are necessary for the thing to be what it is meant to be are the inherent constraints involved. What it *must* be (Fig. 1.15).

On the other hand, there are the constraints of the designing itself: the qualities and elements that can be *imposed* to make it the thing we would like it to be—this type of chair, table, shirt, or jacket, defined by its materials, colors, desired textures or patterns, and other elements that the designer has control over and can choose rather than be forced into. The initial work of a designer is often in the choosing of these

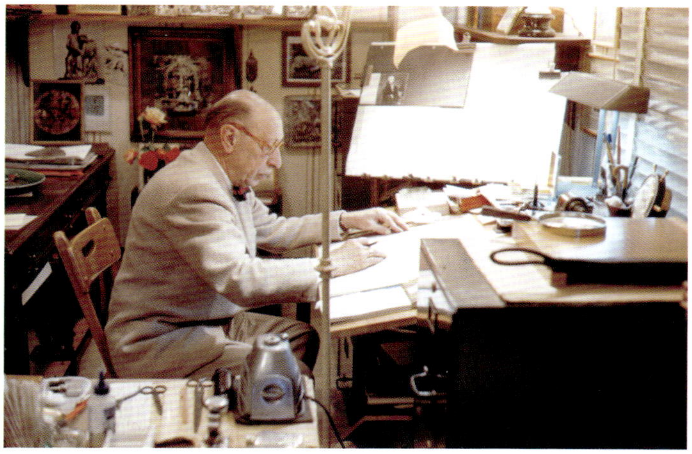

1.15 "The more constraints one imposes, the more one frees oneself of the chains that shackle the spirit" said the composer Igor Stravinsky, seen here at his desk. "The arbitrariness of the constraint only serves to obtain precision of execution." By framing the problem precisely, the design problem becomes a clearly defined puzzle with a set of clearly indicated areas that need solving. The freedom arrives from knowing exactly how far one can move and where to at each point.

Source: © Marvin Koner/Corbis

imposed constraints ("I will only use recycled materials"). In some cases, navigating the imposed constraints defines most of the work on a design project.

The inherent constraints tend to be given. The constraints that arrive from the client or end user are more often of the imposed kind. The end user requires a chair. But what kind? For what purpose? Made of what materials? To what tolerances? What colors? What kind of decoration (if any)? Is there a price point? And so on. The fact that the end user needs or wants a chair (and the wanting can itself be a "need") is not so much in question.

However, there is a side to designing where the inherent nature of the proposed project needs to be the first thing questioned. The client wishes for a chair. But is it really the chair that is needed? Perhaps what the client really needs is a couch? Or not precisely this kind of chair but another one altogether (the client wants a chaise, but what she really *needs* is a rocking chair). It becomes the designer's mission to investigate the need itself, to determine if the inherent constraints are the correct constraints involving the end user's need. Once that is established, the imposed needs can be considered.

Once the design is in hand, there are further hurdles of constraints to consider. There may be constraints that arrive from the manufacturing process itself. The producers may not be able to handle the materials, may not have the technical expertise to produce the required solution, or may not be able to perform the required operation on time or within the given budget.

The constraints inherent in manufacturing are equally as weighty as any other, but in any innovative project, they will sneak up on the process. The best way to tackle this is to involve the manufacturers in the process as it is underway or at least consult with knowledgeable manufacturers regarding any unsolved or vague elements. Often if the solutions are new or untried methods are involved, prototyping must take place, and it is there that previously unknown or at least unexpected constraints will present themselves.

THE HIERARCHY OF DESIGN NEEDS

The constraints of a design project will tend to become stricter as the design is pushed further up the **hierarchy of design needs**, which is defined by the levels a design must reach to satisfy—and then eventually transcend needs.[5]

These needs include (in rising levels of fulfillment):

- *Functionality.* The design must function as intended.
- *Reliability.* It must do so reliably.
- *Usability.* It must be easy to use, or at least once one has learned how, one must not need to learn again.
- *Proficiency.* The design allows us to do things better than before.
- *Creativity.* The design changes the approach to a problem to the degree that the norms change even to the degree that there is a cultural shift.

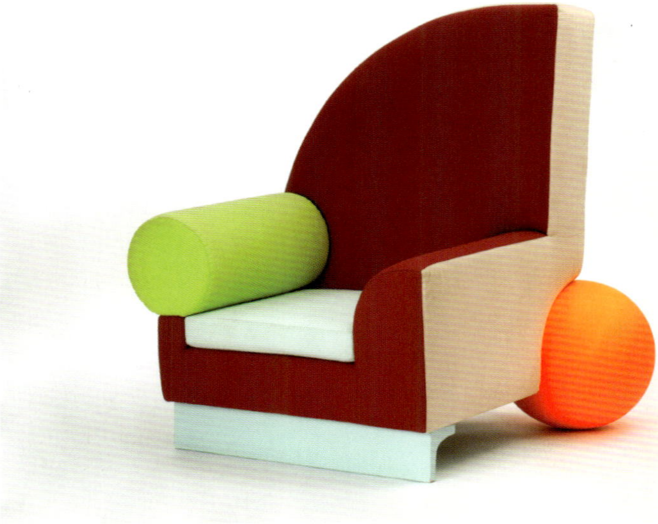

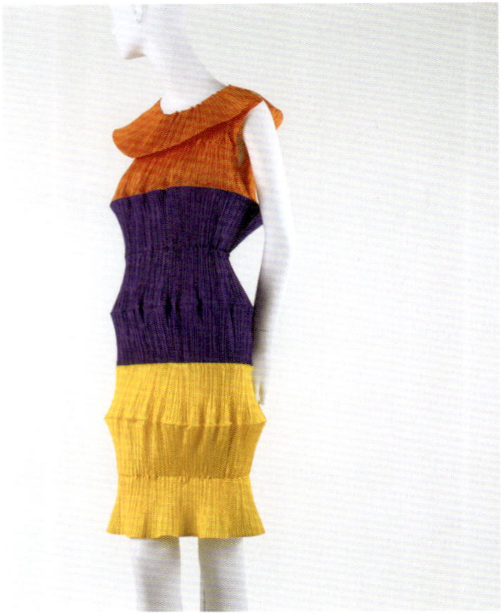

1.16 Considering functionality: What does the design do? What are the technical specifications? Is visual appeal a function? How much of the function of these designs lies in their fulfilling of practical needs, such as support (chair) and shelter (dress), and how much in the sense of visual stimulation and satisfaction?

Sources: L: Bel Air arm chair designed by Peter Shire (1982), V&A Images, London/Art Resource, NY. R: Dress by Issey Miyake (Spring/Summer 1994), Image copyright © The Metropolitan Museum of Art. Image source: Art Resource, NY

The designer's role in ensuring the positioning of the design's solution in the hierarchy's levels becomes more involved and complex as it moves on up the hierarchy. To ensure the *functionality* of the object in question, a certain basic knowledge of the designed object's history and methods and mechanics is necessary and a technical know-how is required in order to make it do what it is supposed to do (Fig. 1.16). The *reliability* also comes from technical know-how and perhaps collaboration with manufacturers on choosing the right components or methods. The designer's challenge when confronted with the desire for *usability* or user-friendliness becomes more involved. Now the designer must become aware of the practices and habits of the end user as they relate to designs of this sort and if none exist (perhaps it is a totally new kind of design), then to imagine and perhaps prototype this knowledge into existence. The designer must be able to consider various scenarios of interaction between the end user and the design and respond to each of them with a good solution, so that in each case the end user is well served.

Much discussion of user-friendliness arose out of the changes that interactive designs created with the advent of computer interfaces, desktop technologies, and eventually handheld devices, touch screens, and so on. The mantra for good program design became usability: The user needed to be able to *intuit* the use of the product without wading through instructions. Clearly this cannot always be the case. But the idea is that once the user achieves a certain level of knowledge, the operations proceed smoothly and with minimal effort.

Proficiency in a design takes us out of the realm of the usual and brings us a design that allows us to do things in a way that is better, is more efficient, is more productive, or in general has a better outcome than any design of this kind has done before. New technologies have a way of allowing such proficiencies on a generational basis. The idea that we can constantly be better at something drives productivity and the marketplace of a consumer society. Each successive design must be perceived to be better than the one before in order to capture our attention (Fig. 1.17).

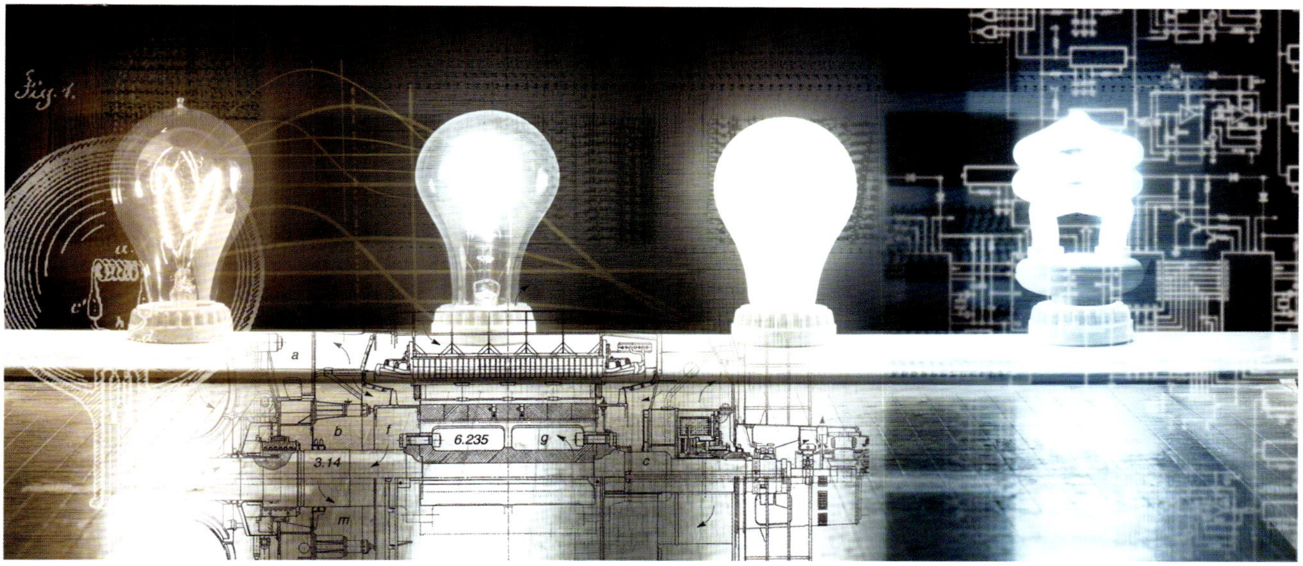

1.17 Proficiency: Each successive design must perform better—that is, allow us to have a better experience than before. Successive technical modifications to the simple lightbulb have not only changed the design, but altered our experience of lit spaces and our relationship with our surroundings. Ecological benefits result from more efficiency and our experience of a well-lit space is enhanced.

Source: © Alamy

The truth of the matter may be different, and it is perhaps less often so than the marketers would have us believe. But that aside, a design that does allow us to be better at things is a delight. To accomplish this, a designer also must be an innovator of the kind that pushes the boundaries of the possible. This requires knowledge of materials, technology, manufacturing processes, user interaction, and methods. This also means that the designer must recognize the limitations that are to be overcome. This can only be done by thorough investigation and an intimate knowledge of the problem, needs, and constraints involved and turning them to the design's advantage.

There is finally the point of *creativity*, where a design is created that changes the way things are done. Not only do we do things better, we also do them differently. Examples of this abound in computing and communications technologies in recent years, but more hands-on and physical moments of creativity in design were equally numerous in, say, the early 20th century as technologies allowed all manner of new products to be designed and improve day-to-day living. Examples abound in relation to electric motors and switches: Power tools, kitchen appliances, medical devices, and office machinery, to name a few.

Recent times have been less optimistic about the continued success of such evolutionary design. The early 20th century optimistic vision of constant improvement through technology was seen to be flawed. The two World Wars and subsequent arms race showed, for example, that modern technology and systems design could lead to massive death and destruction. It also became apparent that much of the modern designs and systems were massively harmful to the environment. However, there is much to be done and learned still. Designers who wish to go to the truly creative route must understand the human behavior and interaction that guide the nature of the product. They must know how people will respond to a new way of behaving with technology, new materials, and new ways of doing.

A designer must therefore be a student of human nature. How do people behave? How do they interact with the design and with each other? It is in the doing of things

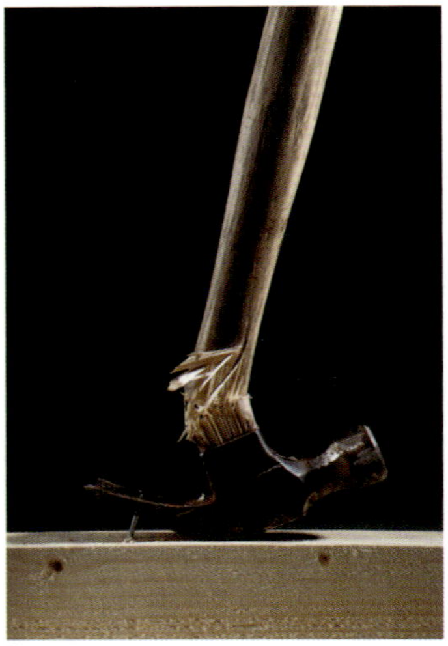

1.18 We hammer away without thinking of the hammer; the tool is transparent to us. If it breaks or ceases to function, it becomes apparent to us again. The awareness of a designed object and its importance is highlighted this way, when it is repurposed, put into a new context, or otherwise improved. You see it again and in a new way. You and the object are reoriented in the world. You *know* it now.

Source: © Caspar Benson/fstop/Corbis

that we prove our humanity. The impact of our actions on our fellow human beings is a yardstick by which we may measure the meaning of our existence. To design for changed action by enabling our fellow humans to have better lives and perhaps improve in turn that of those around them, is to change human society in a subtle but perhaps permanent way. A truly creative designer therefore aims to understand human behavior and the structures within which it develops and evolves in order to understand the relationship of human beings, their designs, their environment, and their basic ways of being. With this understanding a designer can become truly influential.

TRANSPARENT AND APPARENT OBJECTS

To understand how humans encounter a new design, let us consider how we actually approach using things in our day-to-day existence and how things, environments, and objects shape us, even as we use them. The philosopher Martin Heidegger used an example of a carpenter and his hammer. While all goes well with the work and the hammer, a proficient carpenter does not actually think about the hammer. Only when there is a problem with the hammer itself—say it is not the right type of tool or it has some defect, or it breaks—that attention is called to it. The hammer becomes prominent in the carpenter's conscious thought. Suddenly the hammer is *obvious*: It ceases to be (as Heidegger puts it) *transparent*. Otherwise, the carpenter simply continues hammering away at whatever needs hammering (Fig. 1.18).

The things of our daily existence are in this way generally transparent. A new design, if it reaches the level of creativity in the hierarchy, must become obvious for a while, until we incorporate it into our normal way of doing things and it disappears again and normalizes. Then the next design must move in to the space that is left for the new and apparent. What this means it that the designer must recognize where these limits are, in order to force the nontransparency of the design by advancing the concept up the final two steps on the hierarchy of designs into proficiency and creativity.

This also can be done by pulling the design into a new context by repurposing it, recontextualizing individual elements, or making us look at it in a way that we have never seen before. As an old friend with a new look, the design is now a new thing, perhaps even more exciting, but it still remains within the identity of the old concept.

Changes in technology can also force the issue, making it inevitable that the design will become new. For example, in laptop computers, new materials, new manufacturing methods, and miniaturization of components all make for a new experience, even though the *object* itself essentially is the same.

Cultural shifts can do the same: A new way of looking at the design—or something that was not acceptable—becomes acceptable in society. This changes our underlying perception of the design and our behavior around it. Styles and manners that seemed inconceivable are suddenly the norm. For example, tattoos and piercings used to belong to a very specific set of society throughout most of the 20th century, but at the end of the century, they became commonplace in one generation.

CONCLUSION

Finally, each cultural experience builds on—or reacts to—all that have come before, and the gradual layering of knowledge and experience makes even the most radical changes themselves eventually seem routine. We become inoculated to change itself, and a constant state of change becomes normal. We begin to feel we have seen it all before, and to accept the impermanence of styles, ideas, and cultural norms. This expectation of change has, for example, become the norm in the world of designer fashion. This place of constant flux, as we will see in the next chapter, is where the modern history of designing has brought us.

KEY TERMS

Human culture
Mass production
Industrialization
Urban living
Consumerism
Capitalism
Modernity
Stages of design project: inspiration, identification, conceptualization, exploration, definition, communication, and production
Constraints and needs
Inherent and imposed constraints
Hierarchy of design needs
Transparency in experience

DISCUSSION AND REVIEW QUESTIONS

1. Consider how your daily existence is structured by your own design. How do you order things around you? How do you decorate your surroundings? How do you choose your clothing and accessories? What does the designing of your daily existence have in common with early humans from 40,000 years ago? What is different?

2. Consider how the design of your environment influences your behavior. Consider rooms, buildings, streets, shops, restaurants, and public spaces. How does your behavior change from one to the other? How much of this do you suppose is "by design?"

3. Look around the room you are in. How much of what you see is normally *transparent* to you? Why do you suppose this is? What would it take, design-wise, to change this?

EXERCISES AND ASSIGNMENTS

1. Pick an object that you consider to be a good design (for any reason at all).
    a. What would inspire such designing?
    b. How would you communicate what is especially important about the design to someone who had to make it?
    c. How would you describe it to a prospective end user who has never seen it before?
    d. Make a list of the inherent and imposed constraints, and consider how they influenced the outcome.

2. Choose three objects in your immediate surroundings: an item of clothing, a kitchen utensil, and a piece of furniture.

   a. Where does each stand in the "hierarchy of design"?

   b. If it is not at the highest level, what keeps it from going higher?

   c. If you feel it is at the highest level, what makes it so?

   d. How do the three compare? If one achieves a higher level than the others, how could its qualities be translated to the others?

3. For the one of these three that you consider the best design, list the inherent and imposed constraints that a designer would have considered in its designing.

   a. Find three objects you on that are normally transparent to you.

   b. What change in their design would cause them to not be transparent for a while?

   c. Why would these changes work?

   d. Do these changes improve the design or not?

REFERENCES

1. C. S. Henshilwood and C. W. Marean, "The Origin of Modern Human Behavior: Critique of the Models and Their Test Implications," *Current Anthropology* 44, no. 5 (December 2003): 627–651.

2. A. W. G. Pike et al., "U-Series Dating of Paleolithic Art in 11 Caves in Spain," *Science* 336, no. 6087 (June 15, 2012): 1409–1413.

3. BBC World Service, 23:05, June 12th, http://www.BBC.co.uk/radio/player/P00TJZ3X.

4. Donal Henehan, "Obituary: Igor Stravinsky, the Composer, Dead at 88," *New York Times*, April 7, 1971, p. 26.

5. Concept adapted from Will Lidwell, Jill Butler, and Kritina Holden, *Universal Principles of Design* (Gloucester, MA: Rockport Publishers, Inc., 2003), 106.

CHAPTER 2

A BRIEF OVERVIEW OF MODERN DESIGNING

DESIGNERS SPEAK

"All in all, the creative act is not performed by the artist alone; the spectator brings the work into contact with the external world by deciphering and interpreting its inner qualifications and thus adds his contribution to the creative act."

—MARCEL DUCHAMP, *The Writings of Marcel Duchamp (Marchand du Sel)*, edited by Michel Sanouillet and Elmer Peterson (New York: Oxford University Press, 1973), 139–140.

"Space and light and order. Those are the things that men need just as much as they need bread or a place to sleep."

—LE CORBUSIER (Charles-Edouard Jeanneret-Gris), quoted in Ada Louise Huxtable, "Architectural Giant: Le Corbusier's Plans Shaped Cities and He Was Always Ahead of Field," *New York Times*, August 28, 1965.

OBJECTIVES

Recognize the continuous narrative of design in modern culture.

Identify the main periods and movements of design in the modern world.

Understand the dialogue of designing and culture creation.

Be familiar with major trends in design in the modern period.

Recognize the political nature of designing.

An examination of the world of modern design must begin with a detailed look at the most impactful design movements in the industrialized world. In this chapter, their theories, methods, influence, and ultimate fading are discussed, leading to practical discussions and definitions of the Modernist movement and designing in the postmodern condition of the late 20th century. The shift from a Western-dominated to a global market and the implications of multiple cultural perspectives are presented, and design as culture-creation and the influence of culture on design are examined.

DESIGNING OUR WAY TO THE GLOBAL PRESENT

At this writing, design continues to be influenced by globalized industrial-based consumer culture and capitalism. This means that globally people are living in similar houses and apartments, furnished with similar appliances and goods. People shop for the same clothes from the same brands, eat the same kinds of food from their local franchises, see the same movies, and listen to the same music on the same gadgets. All over the world they are doing the same kind of jobs, often for the same companies, to which they drive the same cars and fly the same airlines. This continuing homogenization of design, tastes, and trends has been the hallmark of design in this century.

The political dominance of the Western colonial program has faded since World War II, and with that came a fading of central authorities of culture and their large-scale narratives. The turn toward the cultural past became a tangible force in emerging societies, but the tug-of-war of tradition and novelty is played out more than ever in the field of design. Almost counterintuitively, given the multicultural emphasis, an international style of no particular place is now represented in nearly every urban environment on the globe (Fig. 2.1).

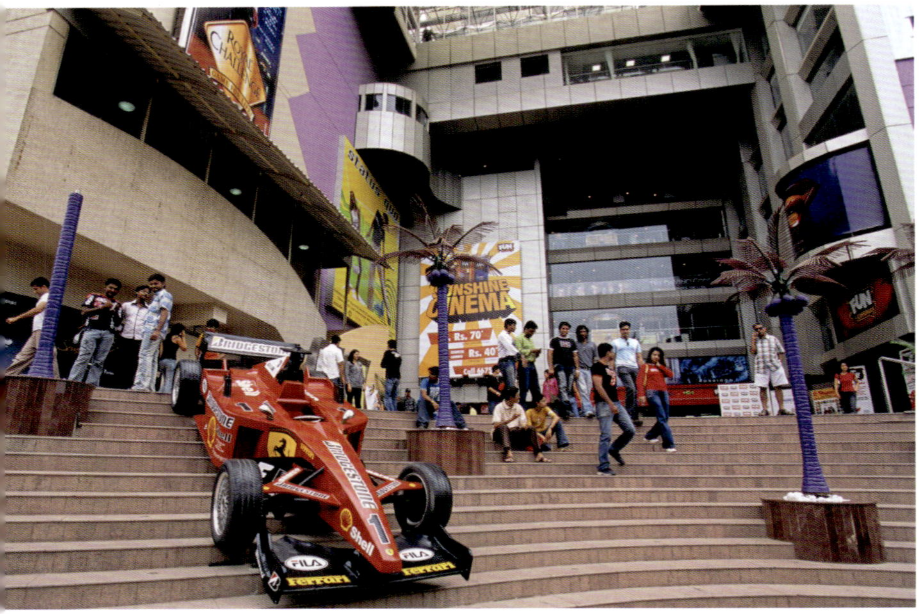

2.1 Global style and design, in an age of media saturation and international brands, has produced a common style that is of nowhere in particular. This mall entrance, the car, even the clothing on the people could be from anywhere and everywhere.

Source: Photograph © Frederic Soltan/Sygma/Corbis

In 1979 French philosopher Jean-François Lyotard articulated the proposition that the status of knowledge was altered in societies that had entered the postindustrial (computerized) age. They were no longer modern cultures—worlds of continuing scientific progress ordered by grand theories of culture and history. Rather, the **postmodern condition** is one where grand narratives—overarching theories or philosophies of the World—are not adequate to represent and contain the world.[1] The focus in this chapter is therefore on designing as both a contributing element as well as a creation of what came to be the modern condition, which has now realigned into the post- or late-modern version of itself.

In modern society, science and technology, mass communication, and transportation reshaped all perception of the world and people's place in it to foster a dominating faith in analysis and systems. This is a world by design. Modernity also saw the rise of urban living and the appearance of the public as a force. We see in this a shift that has taken place culturally across the world since the 1960s. Even as the world order of colonialism and Western dominance gradually began to give way after World War II, computerized and electronic media decentralized communication culture. A questioning of the dominance of the Western (Euro-centric) worldview and the ideas of the ownership of culture began to take place. The rules of society that were held with much conviction are not natural laws. Structures defining gender relationships, hierarchies of cultures, and notions of race and nation were increasingly seen to be artificial, even in non-Western cultures. Even concepts of civilized and primitive, so carefully defined in the colonial period, dissolved along with understandings of high and low culture.

THE HISTORICAL STREAM

Design certainly exists outside the context of modern capitalism. There are cultural approaches to the creation of clothing and habitats that bring their traditions to bear and are localized to the use and practices of a specific people. But in this text the discussion will be focused on the relatively narrow field of how we arrived at the current global marketplace-oriented profession of internationalized style.

The practices and theories that drive today's world of design in a globalized market and increasingly blurred cultural lines developed from lines of thought that can be traced back for centuries to many cultural spheres. The discussion here will stay within a stream of formal knowledge and philosophies (rather than innate or *traditional* practices) that came out of the cultures of the Mediterranean, North Africa, and Arabia, dispersed east to Baghdad and west to Spain, and then headed north over the Alps and the Pyrenees. Exchanging influences all the while, this culture met its counterparts in Asia even as it headed west across the Atlantic, before fragmenting in a flash of technology to become a globalized multicultural practice of no particular place. The history of design as a concept in human society shows us a tension between **classicism** and **modernism,** conservatism and radical thinking, revolution and stasis. A characteristic of designing in the modern age is a tendency to react to globalization by reverting to the local and traditional. The tradition of classicism—exported to cities all over the world by Western empires with degrees of colonial dominance—denied the experience of the local and the present by grounding all culture in the past with classical "ancients" that belonged to no one (Fig. 2.2).

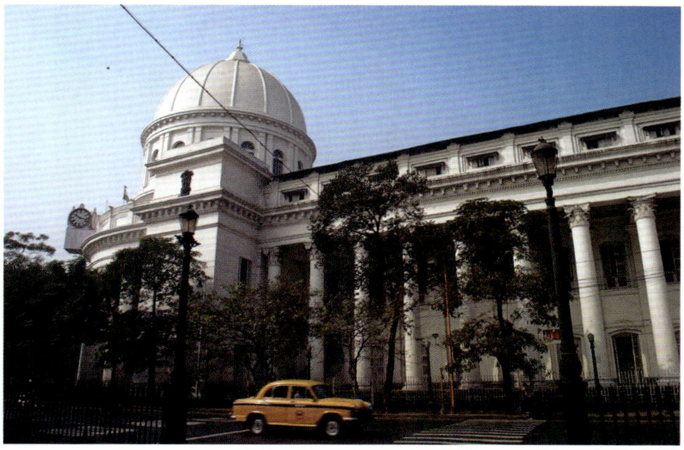

ABOVE
2.2 The General Post office in Kolkata, India, was designed in 1864 and completed in 1868. It is in the classicist style based on the mode of the colonizing power, Great Britain, and not that of the colonized.

Source: Photograph courtesy of Schwiki

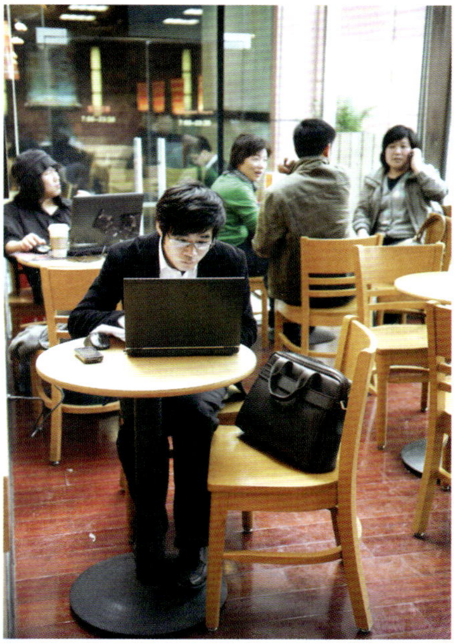

RIGHT
2.3 Global culture in the industrialized (and industrializing) world has become electronic, interactive, and non-localized. Our cultural space now includes whatever sections of the Internet we choose to dwell in.

Source: Photograph ©Justin Guariglia/Corbis

Manuscript culture gave way to print culture in the 15th to 16th centuries. This is where we come in at the beginning of the modern age. Print allows full repeatability at a distance from the source. The visual element of culture becomes fully dominant over the aural/oral and all knowledge becomes linear and systematic; *learning* is *reading*—an individualized and internal experience, rather than a shared, communal, multi-bodied happening. Finally, in our time we see a transition to an electronic age, where the linear, private experience of print culture gradually gives way to the global, non-localized, and interactive culture of electronic media (Fig. 2.3).

But as the information has become more diverse and fragmented, the possibility of precision has greatly increased. We are able to experience more and more of the world in increasingly varied states with better precision and swifter immediacy. This is what modernity has become in its post stage: The systematizing of culture that began with the manuscripts and the transition to the written word of defined, centralized knowledge and book learning. Culture as we know it comes to us designed and packaged in framed discrete units, rather than as lived experience. Or rather, our lived experience *is of* the packaged and framed. Culture became something to be experienced in a linear and logical fashion—analytically, and at a distance, such as in viewing art on walls and theater on stage, rather than creating it ourselves or participating directly.

2.4 A spread from Vitruvius' book on architecture. The fact that the groundwork of design in the Western world was laid with classicism has led to it becoming a baseline for all other designing.

Source: De Architectura by Vitruvius. Detail/Photograph ©Tarker /The Bridgeman Art Library

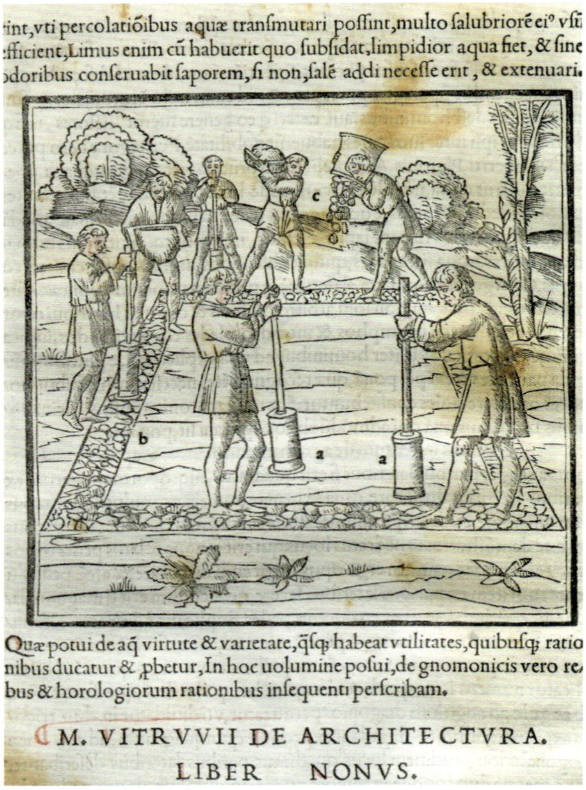
int,vti percolatiōibus aquæ tranſmutari poſſint,multo ſalubriorē ei⁹ vſū
efficient,Limus enim cū habuerit quo ſubſidat,limpidior aqua fiet, & ſine
odoribus conſeruabit ſaporem, ſi non,ſalē addi neceſſe erit , & extenuari.

Quæ potui de aq̄ virtute & varietate,q̄ſq; habeat vtilitates,quibuſq; ratio
nibus ducatur & ꝓbetur, In hoc uolumine poſui,de gnomonicis vero re
bus & horologiorum rationibus inſequenti perſcribam.

M. VITRVVII DE ARCHITECTVRA.
LIBER NONVS.

In the 15th century the recovery of literature from the height of the Roman civilization brought the attention of intellectuals and artists in Europe to ideas that had been part of the culture of the continent before the Roman Empire split and collapsed. The discovery of two manuscripts by the book hunter Poggio Bracciolini in the early 1400s were hugely influential in a rebirth of intellectual and artistic life in Europe. One is directly related to designing, and the other was influential in sparking the trends of thought that led to the development of modern secular society, with its emphasis on the individual.

De Architectura by the Roman Vitruvius was a treatise on architecture, and as it began to be copied and spread over the continent in the two centuries that followed, it became the primary text for the revival of classical methods in architecture with reference to Roman and Greek architecture. The modern age exhibits a story of tension between a culture of classicism and a breaking away from the Greco-Roman ideals and their subsequent interpretations in the Renaissance and Neoclassical revival. Even to this day, the dialogue continues, as can be seen in debates over the choices made in designs for monuments and museums in the late 20th century and the tension between local tradition and globalized style (Fig. 2.4).

The second book to shake the world of medieval Europe was *De Rerum Natura,* in which the Roman poet Lucretius, explaining the philosophy of the Greek Epicurus, emphasizes a very modern view that human beings are central to their own experience, there is no divine providence, and nature is equally cruel and destructive as well as beautiful and creative.[2]

When the Roman Empire degenerated into a religiously dogmatic and static culture, the maintenance of arts and sciences had shifted to the Arabic-speaking world. There they developed extensively from the 8th to the 13th centuries, during what is now known as the Islamic Golden Age. Classical works of Rome and Greece were translated into Persian and Arabic and then combined with influences and knowledge from China and India to be later translated into Turkish, Hebrew, and back into

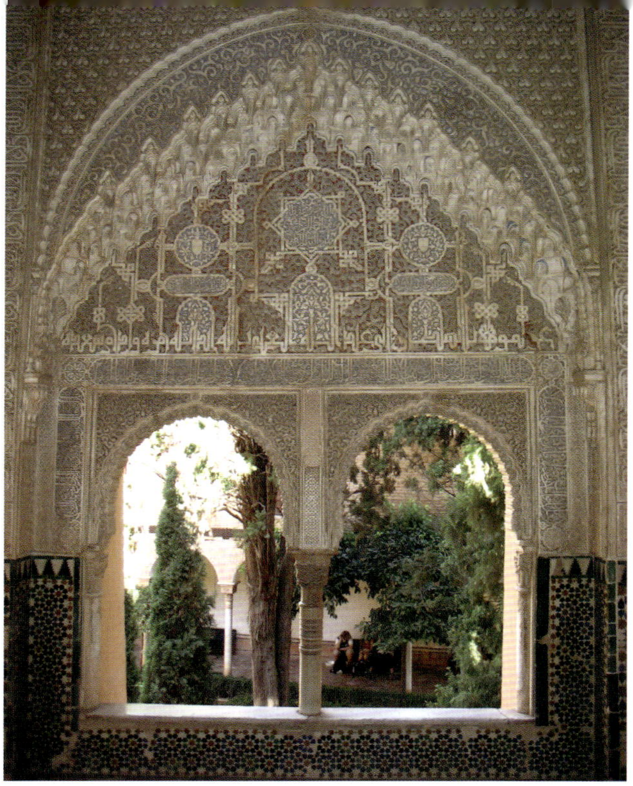

Latin. Architecture and design flourished in the scientific and mathematically innovative Caliphate, with fine detail and patterns with multiple symmetries being developed in decorative arts (Fig. 2.5).

However, the Caliphate also entered a period of scientific denial and went into decline as religious authority began to dominate and suppress innovation in science, art, and design. Then the pendulum swung back and a period of investigation and research began in Europe, with universities founded in Bologna (1150), Paris (1200), and Oxford (1220). The scientific volumes that had been translated into Latin began to produce new scholarship. This in turn prompted a search for books that had been transcribed and kept in monasteries. Although the interaction of the Islamic and European scientific communities continued with successive waves of new translations into the 17th century, it is in the early 1400s that the rising investigative knowledge coupled with improving economies of Europe began to produce the recognizably modern world, where conservative and religiously oriented philosophies had their own tensions building with the worlds of art and science.

ABOVE
2.5 The Alhambra Palace in Spain (detail). Islamic designs show rich patterns and multiple symmetries, which required precision of design and execution and bear witness to the state of knowledge and science involved.

Source: Photo courtesy of Javier Carro

RENAISSANCE

Inspired by the ancients, builders and architects followed the examples set by Vitruvius and created styles that eventually became characteristic of the Renaissance. The cities of Europe were growing by leaps and bounds with ever more artisans and craftspeople fulfilling the needs of the urban high classes for furniture, textiles, housewares, and accessories. Costume and furnishings among the burghers and aristocracy echoed the heaviness of the architecture with a heavy use of materials and layering of fabrics and decoration (Fig. 2.6).

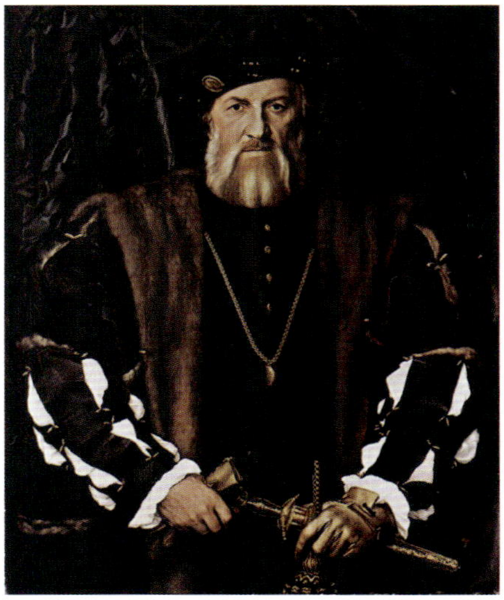

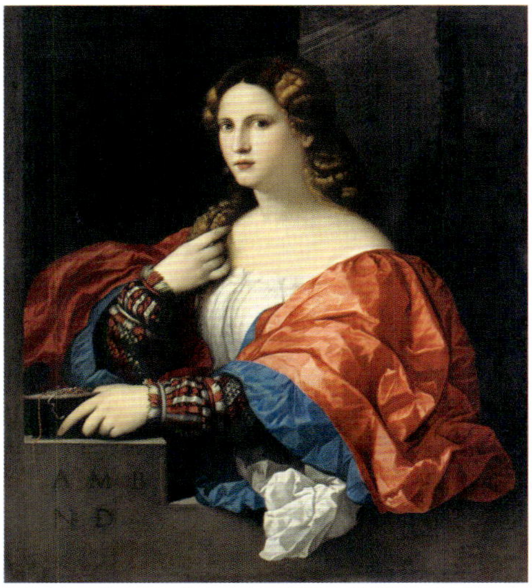

RIGHT
2.6 L: *Portrait of Charles de Solier, Lord of Morette* (1534–1535), by Hans Holbein the Younger (1497–1543), oil on oak, 36.4 x 29.6 inches, Gemäldegalerie, Dresden. R: Portrait of a Woman ("La Bella"), by Palma il Vecchio (Jacopo d'Antonio Negretti, Italian, ca. 1479–1528), oil on canvas, 37.4 x 31.5 inches, ca. 1525. Renaissance fashions were heavy-looking and layered. Climate had the least to do with these choices. Here was a class of people showing off their riches by exhibiting a wealth of fabric on their own bodies.

Source: R: Museo Thyssen-Bornemisza/Scala/Art Resource, NY

TIMELINE: A FEW SIGNIFICANT MOMENTS IN MODERN DESIGN

1860s

- Arts and Crafts Movement—influenced by John Ruskin and William Morris in the United Kingdom and Gustav Stickley in the United States—considers machine production degrading to both workers and consumers. To fight the deadening hand of industry on design, they advocate, and put into practice, an aesthetic based on traditional methods of craftsmanship.

1868

- Charles Worth founds the Chambre Syndicale, which will later become the Fédération Française de la Couture, devoted to maintaining the exclusivity and authenticity of French haute couture. High-fashion design becomes a self-perpetuating system.

1871

- *Hints on Household Taste* is published in the United States. Published three years previously in England, it preaches *simplicity, humility,* and *economy* in design to replace the extravagance of the popular revival styles of the time. The American edition states: "We take our architectural forms from England, our fashions from Paris, the patterns of our manufactures from all parts of the world, and make nothing really original but trotting wagons and wooden clocks."

1883

- Thomas Edison invents the light bulb, which eventually changes the concept of the workday, alters architecture, and becomes a significant aid to communication. Electric light affords the use of brighter colors and more detail and changes the expectation of how interior design can—and should—perform its function.

1885

- The Home Insurance Building, in Chicago, is completed. It is the first building to incorporate the principles of the modern skyscraper, with a steel skeleton above the sixth floor, and curtain walls. The building was designed by William Le Baron Jenney, in whose offices Louis Sullivan completed his apprenticeship. Sullivan would later formulate the maxim of "form follows function" in answer to the question of how to design these new tall office buildings.

1889

- George Eastman places Kodak camera on sale for first time. The habituation of the public to the ability to create images and visual cues for themselves would profoundly change the approach to experience and memory in modern culture. Eventually, monochromatic photos become visual signals of the past and the visual language of nostalgia acquires the patina of old photos as a design cue.
- The Universal Exposition opens in Paris with the Eiffel Tower completed. The high-fashion designer Paul Poiret is thoroughly charmed by the electrically lit fountain, influencing him in his use of color for his entire career.

1893

- The Columbian Exposition in Chicago is a triumph for Beaux-Arts style.

1895

- Siegfried Bing opens a shop in Paris and names it *L'Art Nouveau* (The New Art). Bing sold exceptional works by many of the best-known designers, and the name of his shop became attached to their style. The style, also known as Style Mucha in Spain, Jugendstil in Germany, and Stile Liberty in Italy, achieved a *total* style effect that was available at every level and scale of commodity, from furnishings to clothing to jewelry and graphic design.

1896

- Architect Louis Sullivan proclaims that "form ever follows function" in considering the design of tall office buildings. This will become a mantra for modernist designers.

1900

- The *Exposition Universelle* in Paris highlights the Art Nouveau style, presenting it as the style of the new century.

1901

- Frank Lloyd Wright gives a speech titled "The Art and Craft of the Machine" in which he lays out basic principles of modern industrial design, as he sees them. He praises the Arts and Crafts Movement, but states that Morris's and Ruskin's time is over: " . . . that the machine is capable of carrying to fruition high ideals in art—higher than the world has yet seen!"

1903

- Wiener Werkstätte (German for Vienna Workshop) is established in Vienna in 1903 as an association of artists and craftspeople working together to manufacture fashionable household goods. They aimed to bring good design and art into every part of people's lives, and establish a new art for the new century. Simplified shapes, geometric patterns, and minimal decoration characterized Wiener Werkstätte products. The Werkstätte exerted an enormous influence on artists and Art Deco designers throughout the first part of the 20th century.

1907

- The first commercially successful method for color photography is patented by Auguste and Louis Lumière in Paris.

1913

- Gabrielle "Coco" Chanel opens boutique in Deauville, France; revolutionizes and democratizes women's fashion with tailored suits, chain-belted jerseys, quilted handbags; the most copied fashion designer in history.

1914–1918

- World War I—the last war fought with 19th-century expectations by the major colonial powers—accelerates the development and designs of all manner of technologies, many of which spin off into peacetime usefulness. However, due to the success of those systems and designs that are devoted to quickly killing as many people as possible, the ideals of the modern technological age are found to be very suspect by intellectuals and artists in Europe. Cracks begin to form in the vision of a bright scientific future. Designing, as a result, begins to temper high modernism and futurism with a nostalgic backwards look, especially in apparel, resulting in large swings in trends.

1919

- The Bauhaus School is founded in Germany. The theories and practices incubated and hatched there became models for design that remained in place for the rest of the 20th century, despite challenges of postmodern theory.

1923

- The architect Le Corbusier (Charles-Edouard Jeanneret) publishes *Vers une architecture* ("Toward an Architecture" translated as *Towards a New Architecture*). It is a collection of essays exploring and outlining a theory of architecture for the modern *machine age* and has enormous influence on 20th century architecture and design. Le Corbusier defined houses as "machines for living in," while furniture was "domestic equipment."

1925

- *Exposition des Arts Décoratifs et Industriels Modernes* is held in Paris and gives its name to the style now commonly known as Art Deco. One of the strongest and most influential reactions against the Art Deco movement came from the Swiss architect Le Corbusier. His *Pavilion de l'Esprit Nouveau* at the 1925 Exposition was a forceful rejection of the use of expensive, exotic materials in the extravagant, one-of-a-kind objects that typified Art Deco.

1929

- Raymond Loewy opens his industrial design office in New York. Later it becomes nearly impossible to go through a day in the United States without encountering one of his streamlined designs, such as the Frigidaire refrigerator or the Zippo lighter.

1932

- The Museum of Modern Art in New York (opened 1929) establishes the world's first curatorial department devoted to architecture and design. The merging of art and design in the modern world is thereby acknowledged.

1939–1945

- The needs and constraints of the total warfare of World War II again accelerate the development of materials and designs. It is now clear that technology and science is not necessarily benign in all aspects, as the experience of World War I had already shown. Again, the modernist ideal of better living through technology is scarred by wartime logistics and systems for quickly killing large numbers of people; this time by the ravages of air raids, death camps, and atomic weapons. The Atomic Age quickly becomes one of dread rather than hopeful optimism.

1954

- Coco Chanel, after a 15-year hiatus, returns to the world of apparel design. Over the next five years, she lays the foundation of the "Chanel Look," which was to become a classic staple, copied and revived the world over for the remainder of the 20th century.

1959

- New York sociologist C. Wright Mills refers to a "postmodern period" in which conformity and consumerism have begun to replace the Modern age of liberal ideals.

1962

- Marshall McLuhan publishes *The Gutenberg Galaxy,* where he argues that the communications technology of the electronic age will re-tribalize humankind. He coins the term *global village* to describe this situation.
- *Silent Spring,* by Rachel Carson, is published. The book, a sharp critique of the use of pesticides, is credited with launching the environmental movement.

(continued on next page)

TIMELINE: A FEW SIGNIFICANT MOMENTS IN MODERN DESIGN

1964

- Marshall McLuhan's *Understanding Media: The Extensions of Man* proposes that "the medium is the message"—that the effect of a mode of communication far outweighs the effect of the content being communicated. Television would, for example, have the same effect on society no matter what kind of programming took place. McLuhan's thinking later fell out of favor but has taken on new significance in the Internet age.

1966

- Yves St. Laurent opens his groundbreaking Rive Gauche boutiques in Paris, the first ready-to-wear collections associated with a couture house. High fashion begins a process of fragmentation that results in the breaking down of the old-world fashion system in the late 20th century.
- The architect Robert Venturi begins his influential critique of the modernist ideal, publishing *Complexity and Contradiction in Architecture.* He declares "Less is a Bore" in opposition to the "Less is More" ethic of the modernists.

1967

- The theorist Guy Debord publishes *The Society of the Spectacle,* a critique of modern culture in which consumerism has taken over and "all being has become about having."

1972

- The Pruitt-Igoe housing development in St. Louis, Missouri, is demolished. Charles Jencks asserted that its destruction signaled the end of the modern style of architecture.

1976

- The Sex Pistols release their first single in the United Kingdom. They play their gigs in outfits designed by Vivienne Westwood and become the face of punk rock.

1979

- Francois Lyotard publishes his lecture on "The Postmodern Condition," where he outlines the dissolution of the grand narratives of the colonial system and the decentralization of knowledge in the late 20th century.

1980

- Ettore Sottsass founds the Memphis Group of designers, which then went on to create a sensation at the Milan Furniture Fair in 1981. The goal of the Memphis Group was to direct design away from the European functionalism of the late 1970s by transferring "into the world of the western home the culture of rock music, travel and a certain excess." The group, always intended to be temporary, disbanded in 1988.

1990

- The World Wide Web originates at CERN in Europe. Tim Berners-Lee writes the program. The Internet age will radically alter the state of human knowledge and how people access information on a daily basis.
- Adobe ships Photoshop 1.0. Photos can now be digitally manipulated on a home computer.

1997

- The Guggenheim Museum Bilbao is completed. The architect Frank Gehry brings his style of curved, clashing, freeform surfaces to fruition.

1998

- Google Inc. opens for business. Its search engine will change how information is accessed and how the access is considered.
- Megapixel digital cameras become available at the consumer level. This will quickly alter how people approach photography and images in daily life.
- "Always on, always connected, and always visual" becomes the prevailing mode of the turn of the century.

2004–

- The iPod becomes the "must have" gadget. It is soon followed by iPhones (2007), iPads (2010), and a host of tablets and handheld devices that rearrange the culture of communication and computing. The sleek minimalism of Apple's design program becomes the definitive style of this new family of devices.

The Renaissance style acted at first as a counterpoint to the previous reigning High-Gothic style with its tall spires and thin columns. Buildings built in the Renaissance style were initially solid and wide with a strong visual connection to the ground achieved by layering the textures and scale of the building materials (Fig. 2.7). Very quickly, though, artisan craftspeople achieved greater finesse, creating increasingly finer textures and constructs from basic materials. Craft knowledge developed faster

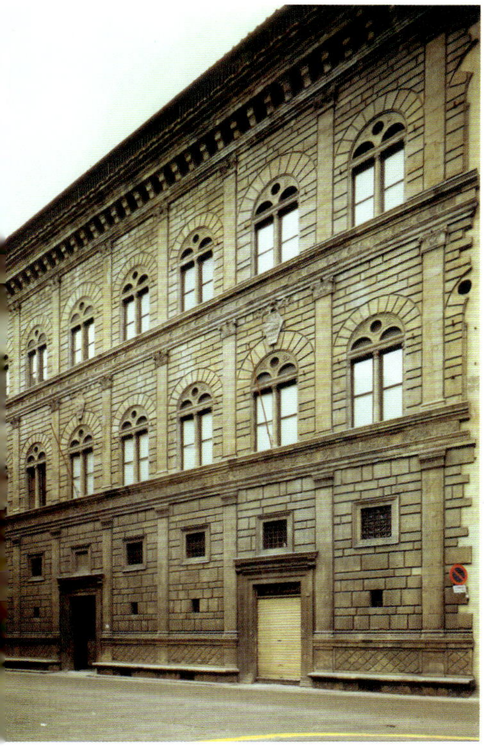

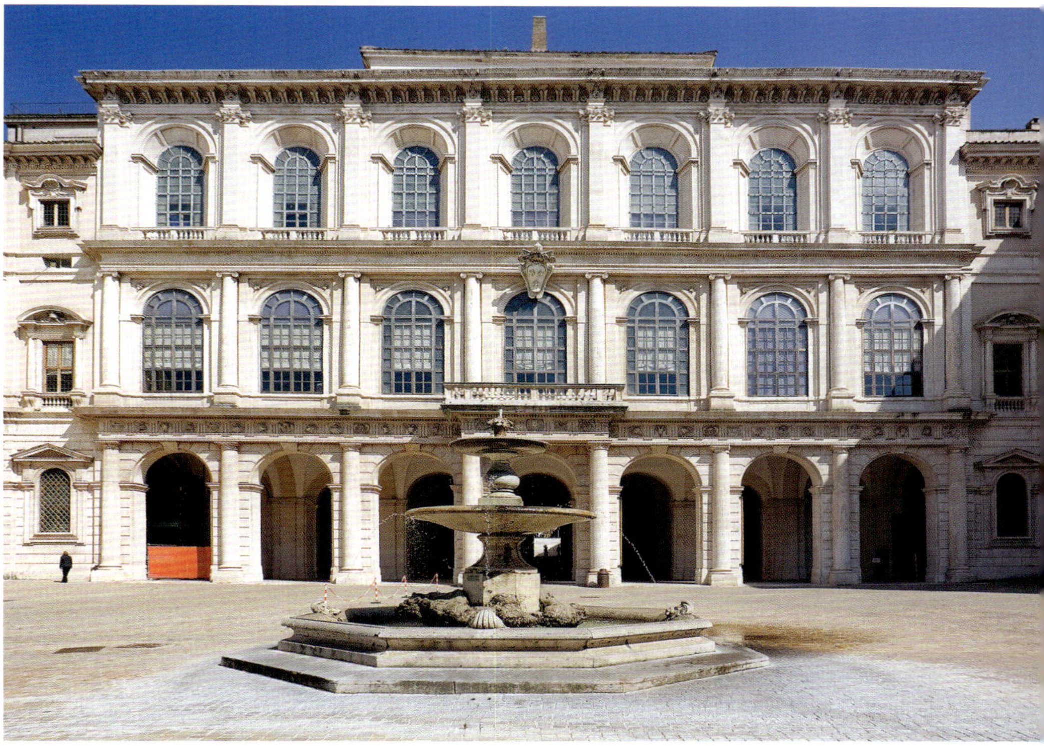

ABOVE LEFT

2.7 The initial building design of Renaissance style reflected the use of materials and construction methods of the time, but the form was nearly straight out of Vitruvius.

Source: R: Museo Thyssen-Bornemisza/Scala/Art Resource, NY

ABOVE RIGHT

2.8 With greater knowledge and developing talent, craftspeople could get more out of their materials. Better craftsmanship and an understanding of load bearing allowed the lightening of walls. The parallel improvements in the art of glassmaking also helped the trend toward more light and larger openings. Palazzo Barberini, Rome. 1627–1633. Maderno, Borromini, Bernini.

Source: Copyright © SIME/eStock Photo—All rights reserved

than styles could migrate, and the styles therefore developed at different paces in different areas. Overall, building became visually lighter by virtue of the ability to create load-bearing walls that could contain larger windows, and glass-making skills and techniques also improved (Fig. 2.8). In addition, garments became finer as mass production of cloth could handle finer spinning and weaving.

The power struggles between secular and papal authority developed into a struggle between the northern Protestant states and the southern Catholic regimes and the papacy. Patronage of artists, craftspeople, and artisans became a required feature of ecclesiastical as well as secular courts, with the crossover of papal palaces and the commissioning of churches by the aristocracy, creating an explosion of construction, decoration, furnishing, and painting.

BAROQUE

Craftmanship improved alongside the incredible increase in wealth and resources that flooded into Europe in the wake of the colonial program. Local resources all over the world were pillaged and shipped back to the capitals of the colonial powers of Portugal, Spain, Italy, France, and England. The Renaissance styles, which had been getting lighter, more open, and more decorated now evolved into openwork styles in which walls seemed to disappear altogether. There was a renewed emphasis on height in buildings and interiors. Furniture echoed this lightness, with curvature heightening the sense of airiness and fluidity of form as the late Renaissance *mannerism* became what is now known as Baroque (Fig. 2.9).

The lower aristocracy and higher urban classes echoed the styles of the ruling classes, creating demand that in turn could be fulfilled by increasing numbers of specialized

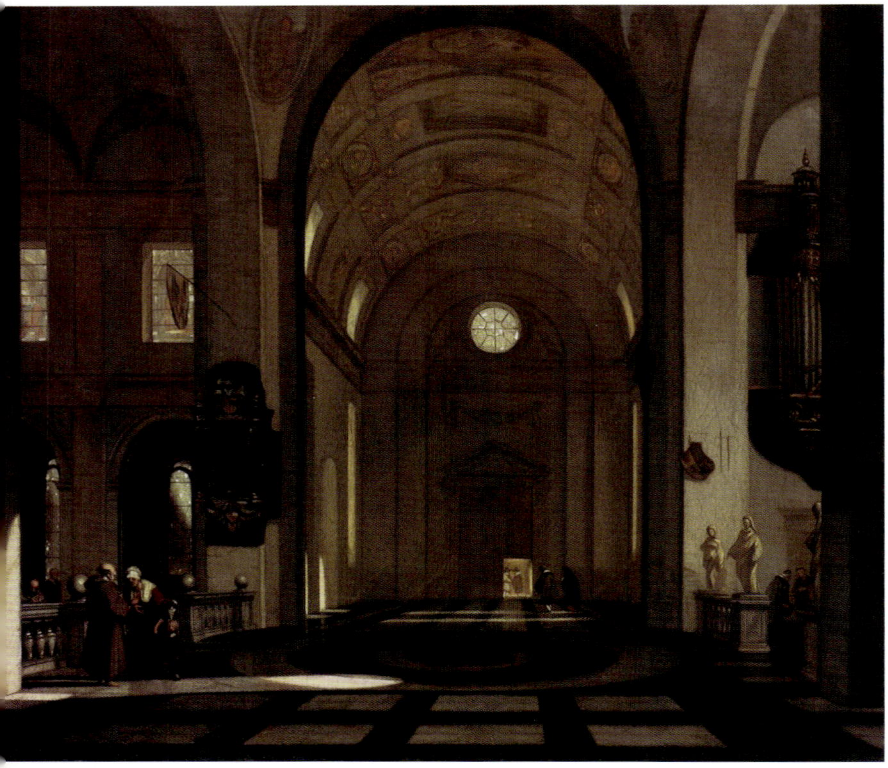

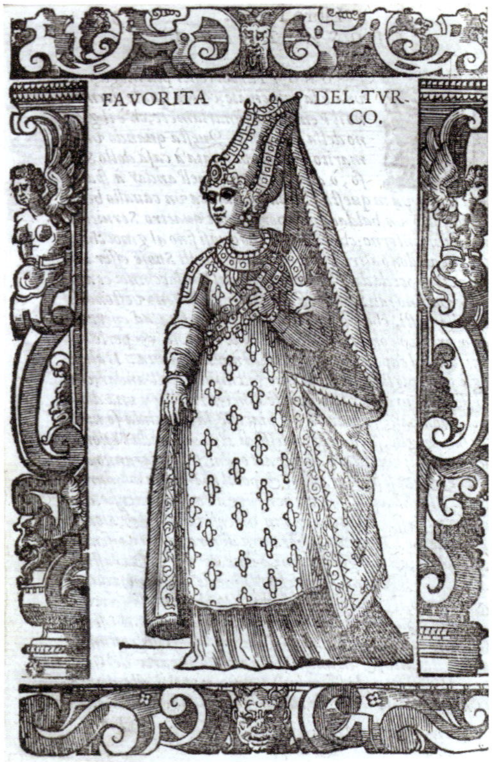

ABOVE LEFT

2.9 The Baroque style, although developing at a different pace in different parts of the globe, is tall rather than broad and light rather than heavy. It embues a sense of motion, where earlier styles were more static.

Source: Emanuel de Witte [Public domain], via Wikimedia Commons

ABOVE RIGHT

2.10 A plate from *De gli Habiti Antichi e Modérni di Diversi Parti di Mondo*, ("Of ancient and modern dress in different parts of the world") showing different styles available to a lady. Now it was possible to pick and choose fashionable designs rather than wait for them to arrive in good time.

Source: Image copyright © The Metropolitan Museum of Art. Image source: Art Resource, NY

craftspeople with ever-increasing standardization of production methods and instruction. Pattern books and templates with designs began to appear to both assist in the creation of these goods and to inform the new aristos and help sort for them a bewildering world of new options. Examples include *Corona delle Nobili et Virtuose Donne* ("Crown of Noble and Virtuous Ladies"), which was a pattern book of Venetian lace, and *De gli Habiti Antichi e Modérni di Diversi Parti di Mondo* ("Of Ancient and Modern Dress in Different Parts of the World"), a book of fashion plates. See Fig. 2.10.

Aristocratic clothing also took on a more flowing, airy, and layered look, with the overload of fabric also being amplified by an overload of décor and ribbon. Men's clothing began to separate from women's, however, in a way that would continue to define the gender difference until the 20th century, with the silhouettes of men and women developing in very different directions. The increase of structure and decoration on the women's side was not echoed in the male costume, and gradually menswear began to emphasize cut and tailoring in the north, where the aristocracy was more rural, while menswear among the southern aristocracy, massed at court in France and Spain, continued the trend of layered finery for a while. The use of accessories went unchanged, with high wigs and powder along with very detailed craftsmanship, just as in housewares and home accessories.

The Baroque period saw an explosion in ecclesiastical music and painting as well, where a heightened sensuality was displayed in a disguise of mythical and religious themes. Intense scenes of physical power and entwined bodies echo the movement and tension found in every aspect of design of the period under the veneer of elegant balance and symmetry of its architecture and music (Fig. 2.11).

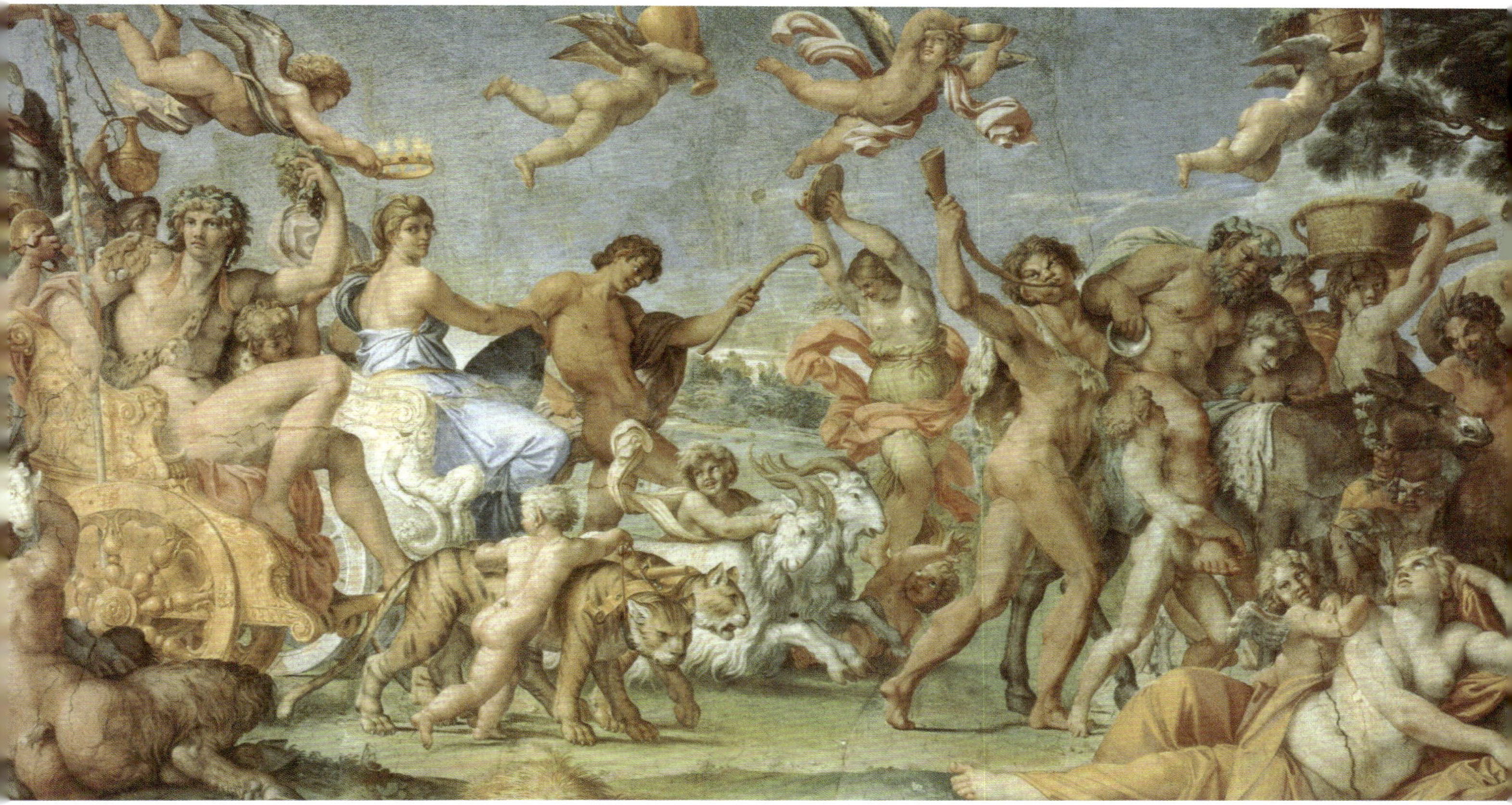

ROCOCO

ABOVE

2.11 Baroque carried with it a pervasive sensuality often disguised as mythological allegories.

Source: Fresco in Rome, Palazzo Farnese. *Triumph of Bacchus and Ariadne*. Artist: Annibale Carracci [Public domain], via Wikimedia Commons

RIGHT

2.12 Portrait of Marie Antoinette in "country garb." Attributed to Louise Élisabeth Vigée Le Brun, 1783. This outfit scandalized the ladies of France who felt it was far too "relaxed" for the Queen to be seen in it. And who could blame them? Compared with previous styles at European courts, this one was practically a state of undress.

Source: Louise Élisabeth Vigée Le Brun (Public domain), via Wikimedia Commons

As secular wealth overtook the place of church riches and the authority of aristocracy and monarch outstripped the clergy, design went toward a more worldly emphasis, and as would become a standard pendulum swing, the wealthy clientele pushed their pursuit of luxury to the furthest possible point. *Rococo* style (essentially late-Baroque) amplified all the characteristics of Baroque, adding layers upon layers of decoration (with the characteristic shell motif, or *rocaille*—a combined form of the French words for shell and for stone—probably giving the style its name). Rococo furniture, art, and apparel all indicate a heightened sensuality. It is here that the physical and emotional distance from country life and direct contact with nature allowed the urbanized upper classes, inspired by the philosopher Rousseau, to romanticize the wild outdoors. Idealizing and over-dramatizing nature became a design feature, with the high formalizing of gardens and landscaping of the Baroque giving way to the introduction of "random" elements and "wild" growth. This is also reflected in a studied "dishabille" in dress along with a romanticizing of peasant and country garb (again Rousseau inspired), which appeared in the studied casualness of French ladies and country gentlemen in the late 18th century (Fig. 2.12).

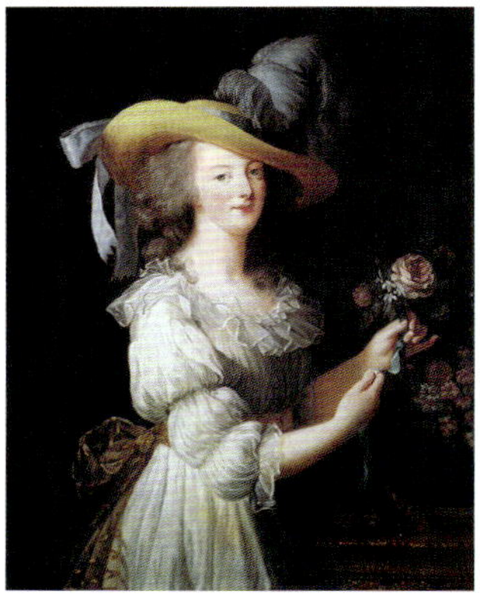

NEOCLASSICISM CA. 1760 TO 1860 TO . . . ?

As the new society of urban commercial wealth gradually displaced the power structures of royalty and church, a couple of vectors combined to bring back classicism in a "pure" form, placing Greco-Roman architecture and references directly into the current designing of buildings and luxury furnishings. In part, **neoclassicism**, the turn toward classicism was a reaction to the perceived decadence of the Rococo style and its attendant culture of sensuality. In part, it was a way of turning away from the influence of the southern European culture of royalist Catholicism, stripping down to a "modern," democratic Protestantism of Western capitalism (Fig. 2.13). Another influence was the discovery of the ruins of ancient Rome found at Herculaneum in 1738 and Pompeii ten years later. The visible evidence of a previous grand civilization was picked up, romanticized, and used as a claim to glory, not just by the descendants of Rome but by any culture that laid claim to political and philosophical ties back to Rome and Athens (Fig. 2.14).

Finally, and no less significant, was the establishment of art history itself as a discipline. The German scholar Johann Joachim Winckelmann established the modern methods of art history in the late 1700s and grounded the idea of the ancient Greek high culture as being "perfection." This moment in history defined the visual language

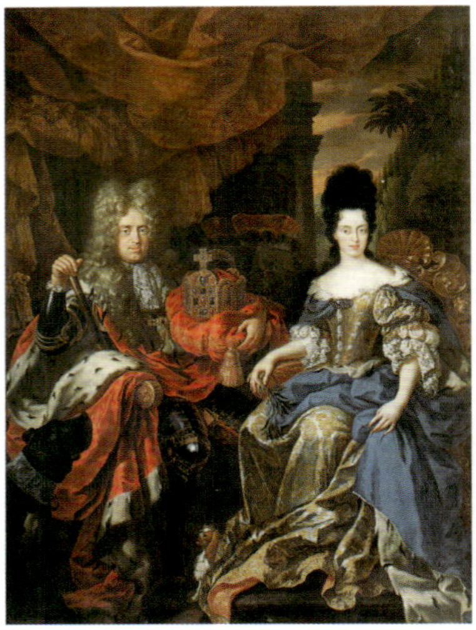

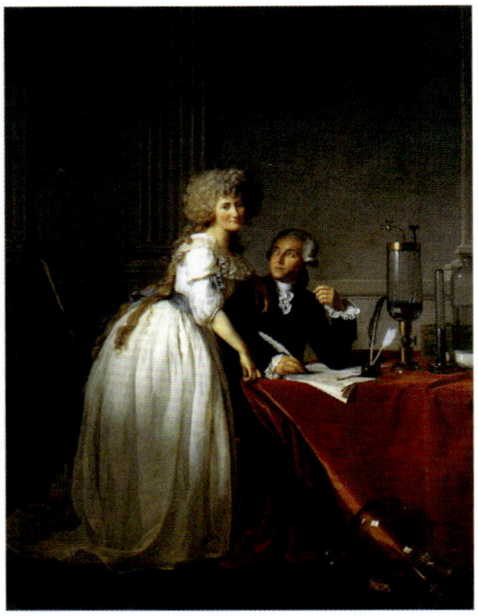

ABOVE

2.13 Left: Portrait of Johann Wilhelm von der Pfalz and Anna Maria Luisa de' Medici (before 1708), by Jan Frans van Douven. Right: Portrait of Antoine-Laurent and Marie-Anne Lavoisier, 1788 by Jacques-Louis David. The new democracies simplified the designs of their garments as well as their furnishings. This was meant to convey a sense of seriousness and purpose after a time of decadence and sensual excess.

Source: L: Jan Frans van Douven [Public domain], via Wikimedia Commons. R: Jacques-Louis David [Public domain], via Wikimedia Commons

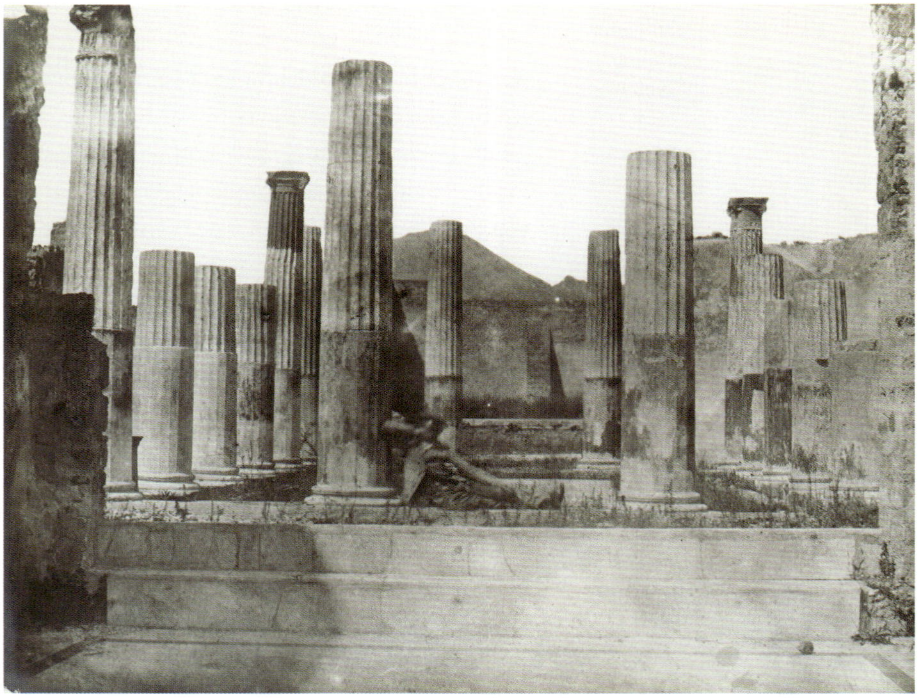

RIGHT

2.14 The ruins of Pompeii. Echoing the romanticizing of nature: The romanticizing of history after the rediscovery of Herculaneum (1738) and Pompeii (1748) further cemented classicism into the culture but also led to an examination of antiquity as a source for art and design.

Photograph copyright © Edinburgh University Library Special Collections Division

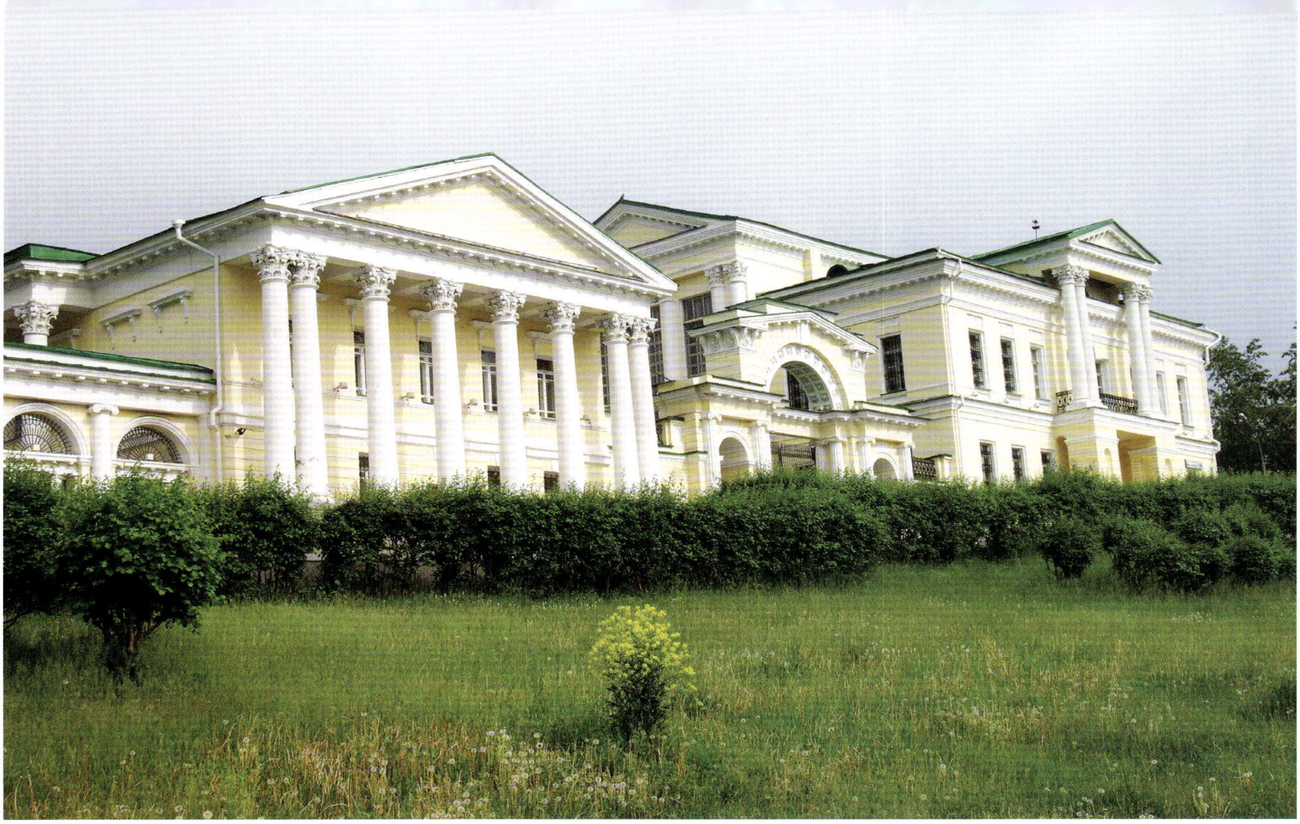

ABOVE

2.15 The classicist model became the visual language of power even in places where the Roman empire had not reached. The code was set in white marble and pillars. Rastorguev-Kharitonov mansion, built in the early 19th century, Yekaterinburg Russia.

Source: ©Shutterstock

RIGHT

2.16 Even when nations tried to design their way into a local identity the baseline always seemed to be the classical world of antiquity. Top: A statue of a Roman vestal virgin 3 AD. Bottom: A paining of the personification of the German nation: Germania, by Philip Veit, 1848.

Source: Top, Corbis. ©Araldo de Luca/Corbis. R: Germania, by Philipp Veit. Bottom, wall fresco, St. Paul's Church, Frankfurt am Main, designed to cover the organ during the Frankfurt Assembly/Parliament, 1848–1849

of Western culture for 250 years and is still part of the vocabulary of modern architecture and design well outside of Europe, due to the exporting of governmental identities in the colonial system. The visual elements of neoclassical architecture and courtly dress of the 19th century became the design language of both governmental and upper-class social power (Fig. 2.15).

The search for national identity by various ethnic groups in Europe created a dialogue that was precisely in opposition to the internationalizing of the style of colonial powers. This led to the designing of romanticized identities based on the group's mythical-historical past, as their present often had little or no specific visual identity to offer. But tracing the group's origins to the ancients meant that the classical culture of the colonial powers and empires became that which had to be measured against for grandeur and heroics. Looking back, the design language therefore often looks very much the same (Fig. 2.16).

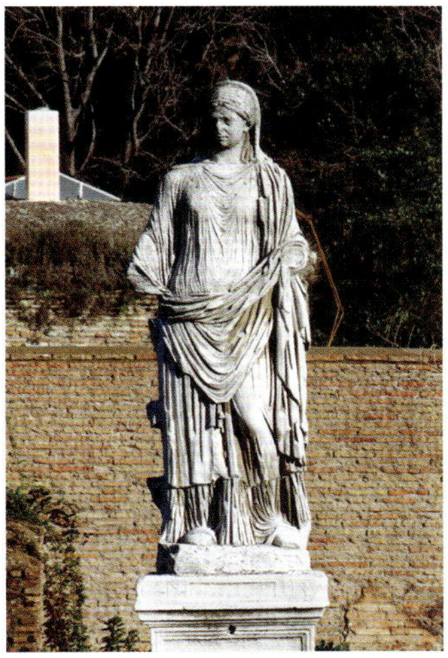

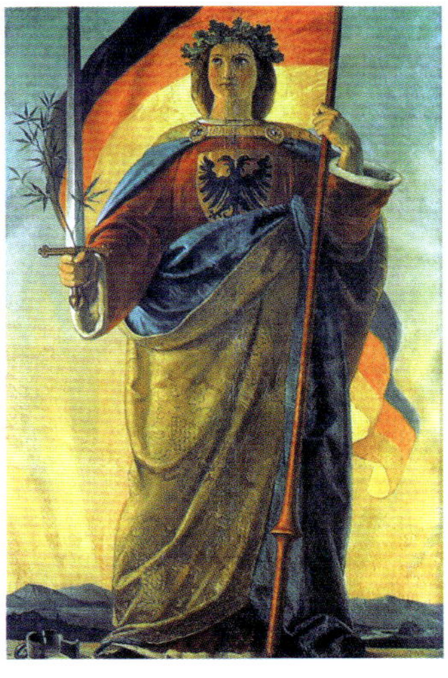

"MUSEUMIFICATION" OF CULTURE—DESIGNING NATIONS

The establishment of museums in the capital cities of Europe brought the elements of the ancient culture where they could be displayed, directly observed, and studied. Colonial powers removed artifacts from dominated nations and set them up for display along with sanctioned artwork derived from the high culture model. Museums became temples of culture and what constituted culture was formulated, introduced, and solidified by these institutions. But the museums also attended to local identities, assisting in the invention of the *national heritage* by placing traditional artifacts behind glass. The exoticizing of the distant "other" went hand in hand with the romanticizing of the local past.

Consequently a three-sided tension appeared between innovative designing, designing in a classical mode, and the design inspiration to be had from the vernacular or traditional crafts. In any given period, one or the other was the fashionable norm for the higher class, depending on the prevailing degree of conservatism or radicalness. Conservative forces, if in power, seem to have tended toward classicism but toward traditional values (often couched in *folk* identity) if in opposition or on war footing. The reigning powers set a style by their own appearance and habitats.

Artists became designers for regimes as easily as they would design for theatrical productions, as public occasions became spectacular in scale and intended impact. Jacques-Louis David designed events and costumes for the French Revolutionary government and then, after its downfall, also for the successors at the court of Napoleon I. David's use of classical motifs in design for propagandist fashion made him the model for similar artists engaged in nationalist imagery all over Europe and cemented the visual relationship of design and politics for more than a century. Classicism thus became the design language of democracy, even as it was the design language of conservatism and counterrevolution (Fig. 2.17).

2.17 Classicism: the code for democracy. Left: The White House in Washington, D.C. Top right: The Château de Rastignac, France. Bottom right: Leinster House, Dublin Ireland.

Source: L: White House Museum. R: © Monuments historiques, 1992. Bottom R: © Geray Sweeney/CORBIS

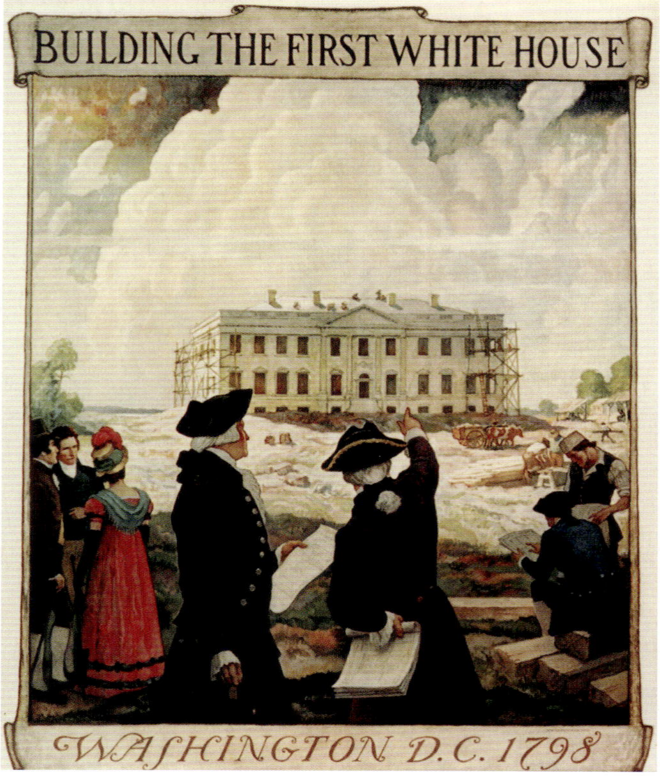

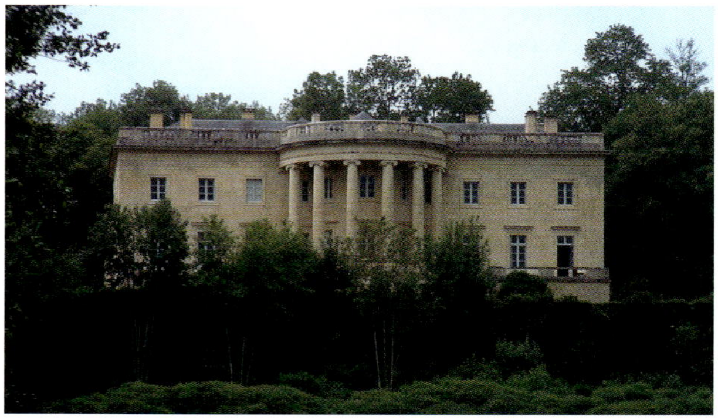

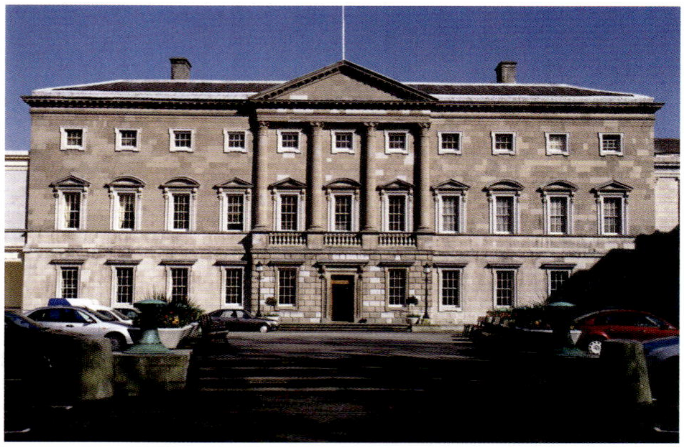

BELOW LEFT

2.18 A scene from the Paris Opera house at the height of the Second Empire in 1860. The Second Empire which lasted from 1852–1870 under Napoleon III and Empress Eugenie saw the invention of a number of upper-class traditions in fashion and social behavior. Along with the developments in Queen Victoria's even longer reign in Great Britain, these set the stage for how style was approached for a century at least. Lithograph by an unknown artist of the Paris Opera (Opéra Le Peletier), 1860—The Grande Salle in 1854.

Source: Lithograph by unknown of the Paris Opera via Wikimedia Commons

BELOW RIGHT

2.19 Ruskin felt that the craftsperson should have enough leeway in the work to allow the individual hand to show through. The craftsperson and artist were one in the same, each had a contribution from him- or herself that went into the work.

Source: Jeter L, from Duke University Archives

DESIGNING SOCIETY

Ritual is at the heart of human society. To navigate human relationships and the interaction of people in society, ritualistic rules serve as structures within which people can safely operate in times of dramatic change. Times of transition require supporting structures. The new societies added modes of civility along with dress codes and rules of "proper" behavior to provide order and a sense of security. Those in power needed to signal their identity to society so the status and class system could be maintained. Strict rules of decorum were set up, and dress codes were equally complex, strict, and in most cases extremely expensive to maintain class boundaries. In this vein, in Paris, where industry, politics, and commerce were aligned in the 1860s, the combined efforts of Charles Worth and the Empress Eugenie under the political guidance of Princess Pauline Metternich set up the high-fashion system for the next 100 years (Fig. 2.18).

But design theories in a middle-class society of commerce and finely turned class distinction had to be about more than government architecture and official high fashions. The developing design thinking was crystallized by John Ruskin, an English art critic and professor who in 1849 wrote a deeply conservative volume titled *The Seven Lamps of Architecture*. There he laid out a strict agenda for the designing of buildings in the modern age. Although Ruskin himself in later years felt it was too strict, his outline revealed the shape to come of the directions and tensions in modern design. For example, the second of Ruskin's "lamps" is *truth*. Here he advocated the use of materials in a *true* fashion, anticipating a key element of the Modernist vision. Stone should be worked as stone, wood should be made to do what wood does, and so on.

On the other hand, his notion of *beauty* was that it should be drawn from nature, and to bolster this, there should be *life* in the construction. That is to say, things should be *visibly* made by hand and not too uniform: The handcraft should be made evident by giving craftspeople freedom of execution so that their individual hand would leave a mark (Fig. 2.19).

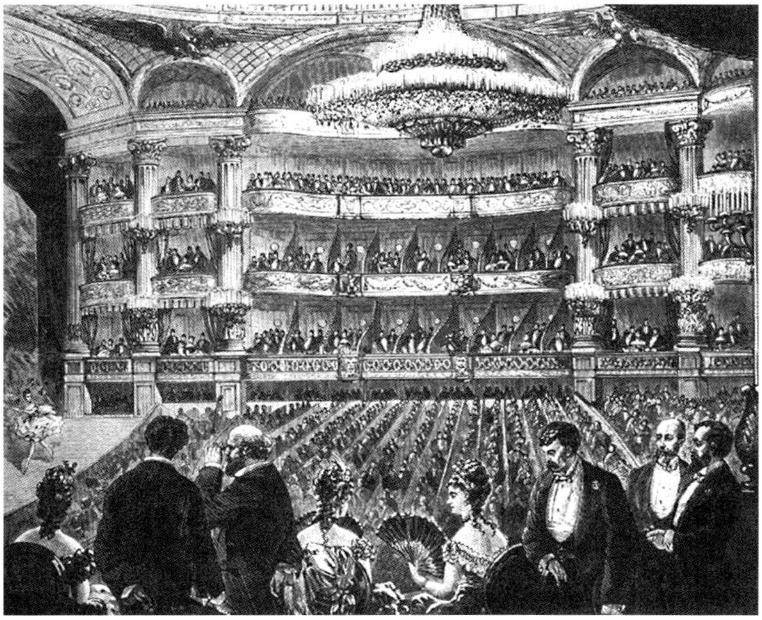

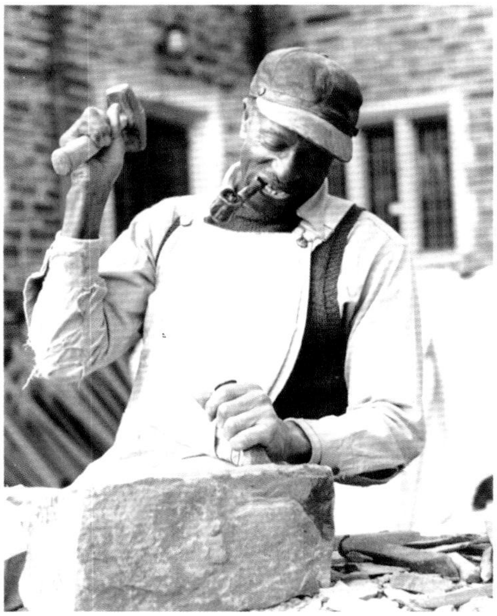

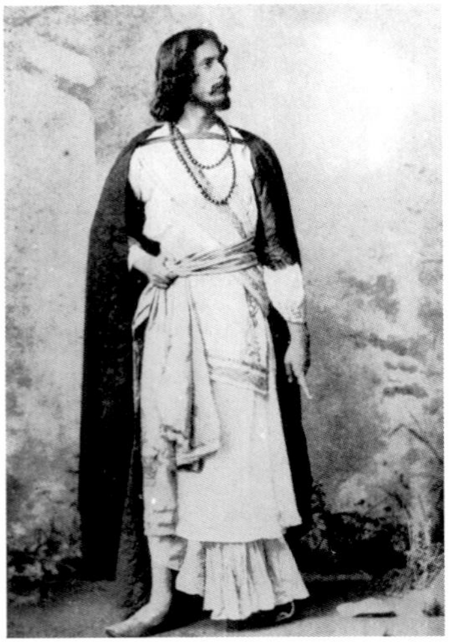

2.20 Rabindranath Tagore (1861–1941) delivered one of his first-published poems at the age of 14 to the Hindu Mela in 1975. He would become the first Asian author to be awarded a Nobel Prize for literature.

Image source: Rabindranath Tagore, c.1880–1890 (b/w photo), Indian photographer, (19th century) /Private Collection /Archives Charmet /The Bridgeman Art Library

Finally, Ruskin felt there should be no originality for its own sake. The designer should show *obedience* to tradition and established methods. Ruskin, although a conservationist, was also dead set against the renovation of buildings, considering it part of their beauty to age and decay.

However, Ruskin was not an advocate of the Greco-Roman style. In two lectures in 1853, he stated that "the Greek style in which much of Edinburgh was built should be replaced by the Gothic."[3] This attempt to disengage with the Greco-Roman classicism was widely echoed in nationalist movements that advocated turning to a local past. For example, in Denmark the priest, philosopher, and educator Nicolaj Grundtvig advocated a "turn to the North" in all things toward a local traditional culture. This gave rise to an admiration of Viking culture and a Scandinavianism that attempted to resist French fashions and Roman influences in art and design. This period is now known as the Golden Age of Danish art. Similarly in Kolakata, India, a decade or so later, the writer Nabagopal Mitra organized the *Hindu Mela,* an association that aimed to inspire nationalist feelings through the creative arts. Mitra hoped to inspire educated youth to revive the Hindu past and to interpret Western education and culture in terms of the local Bengali civilization.[4] Although primarily successful in the nonvisual arts of literature, poetry, and music, the *Mela,* as similar movements elsewhere, prompted an examination of local tradition and handcraft (Fig. 2.20).

ROMANTICS AND ORIENTALISM

Mirroring the nationalist dreams on the empires' edges, Romanticism developed in the late 18th century in a time of upheaval and a realignment of society characterized by the French Revolution. It had roots in literature and a cult of fashionable emotionality or *sensibilité,* in part inspired by writings such as the novel *The Sorrows of Young Werther* (*Die Leiden des Jungen Werthers*), where the German poet and philosopher Goethe highlighted the stifling of personality in modern society.[5] Although chiefly exhibited in literature and fine arts, the Romantics fostered a world view that influenced views of design well beyond their time by prompting criticism of the modern world. This world view attempted to counteract the alienation of the industrial world, with its dislocation of people and traditional life by focusing on emotion: intuition, imagination, impulsiveness, spirituality, and feeling—all advocated by Ruskin in his writing on the Gothic and all of which has circled back into design periodically ever since.

But Romanticism went further by opening up to the uncontrolled forces of nature. Nature became an artistic concept as a representation of a place outside the framework of society and the stifling restrictions of living constantly among "the madding crowd." As such, the Romantics were a rebuke to the modern, while also signaling the full arrival of the most modern concept: the individual (Fig. 2.21).

As the 19th century progressed, the idea of the *talented individual* came into focus. In part, this was a result of the changing practices of industry and art in an urban setting, where on one hand there was mass production of goods and on the other individual acts of creation. The Romantic outlook in art and design emphasized the individual and individual creativity, just as when Ruskin had advocated the free hand of craftspeople. These individual acts had to be properly accredited in order to

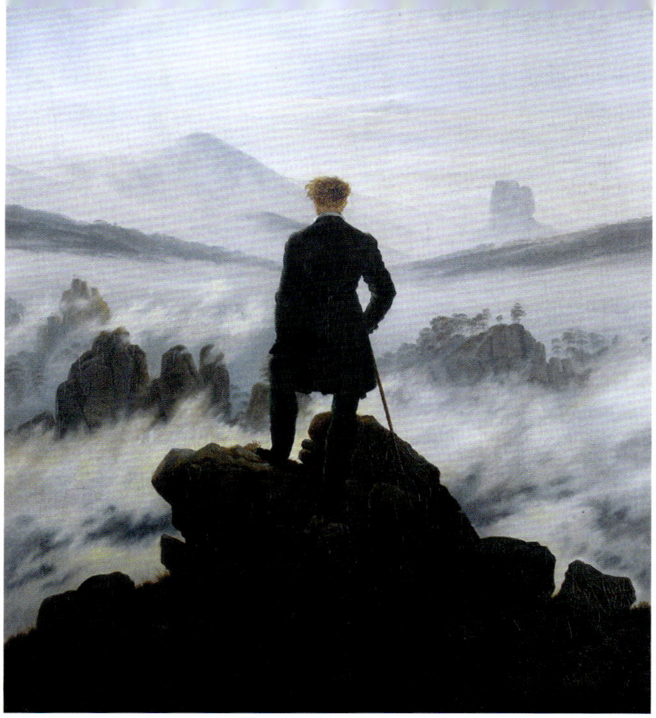

2.21 *The Wanderer above the Sea of Fog* (1818) by Caspar David Friedrich (1774–1840). Friedrich explored the person's inner life as reflected in the observation of nature. He felt that the individual should be looking within as well as around. The solitary romantic figures, immersed in forces beyond their control, became the modern image of the creative life.

Source: Artist: Caspar David Friedrich (1774–1840). The photographic reproduction was done by Cybershot800i

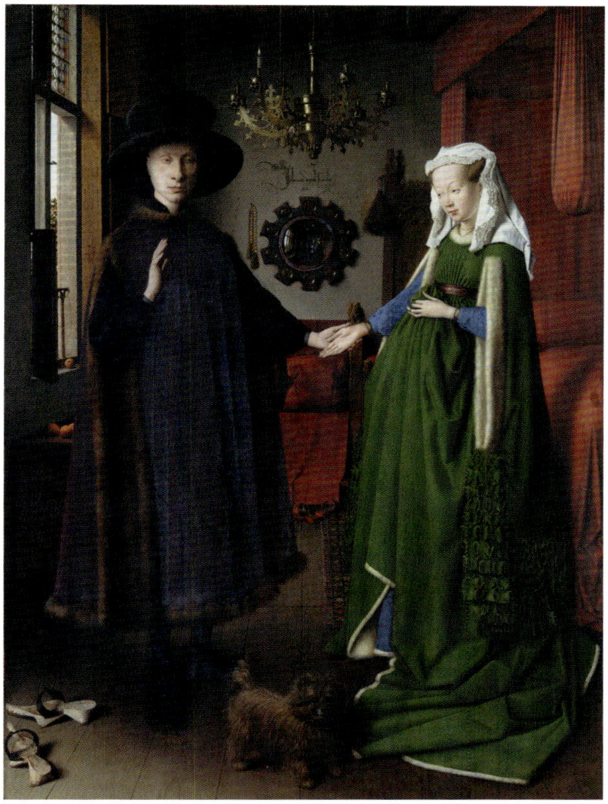

TOP RIGHT

2.22 Jan van Eyck. *The Arnolfini Wedding* ("The Arnolfini Portrait") is thought to be of the Italian merchant Giovanni di Nicolao Arnolfini and his wife, in their home in the Flemish city of Bruges. The couple (whose "wedding picture" this may or may not be) have arrayed around them a host of status markers, goods that they have bought for their home. The painting, whatever other purpose it may have served, is a testament to their social standing. It is an documentation of their consumption.

Source: Jan van Eyck. "The Arnolfini Wedding" ("The Arnolfini Portrait")

distinguish them in the marketplace from the mass of goods produced for conspicuous consumption in the new status-driven society. The idea of originality and artistic vision was thus added to the creative process as an essential component. And so, for example, a gown made by the same designer as the empress became a symbol of status, no less (and possibly more) than the actual created object itself. A much earlier example of this would be a portrait prominently signed by an artist. The 15th-century painting by Jan van Eyck generally known as *The Arnolfini Wedding* shows a couple posing among status symbols with the artist's signature prominently placed as part of the entire status display (Fig. 2.22).

This romanticizing of the past and a desire to be represented by a tradition that could be seen as noble led to the invention of various traditions among ethnic groups all over the world in connection with the development of nationalist movements. The collection of folk materials in art, literature, music, and poetry became a tool for this creation. Local intellectuals began to collect and create origin myths and local styles using myths and structures based on folk and the ancients. The Middle Age Romanticism was heavily connected to the nationalist cultural movements all over Europe that worked toward creating national identities tied to local histories and "Golden Ages" of the past. Meanwhile, the colonial powers were importing goods and influences from their colonies in Asia and Africa and travelers also brought back impressions that were also romanticized and amplified into a mythical and mysterious "Orient" (Fig. 2.23).

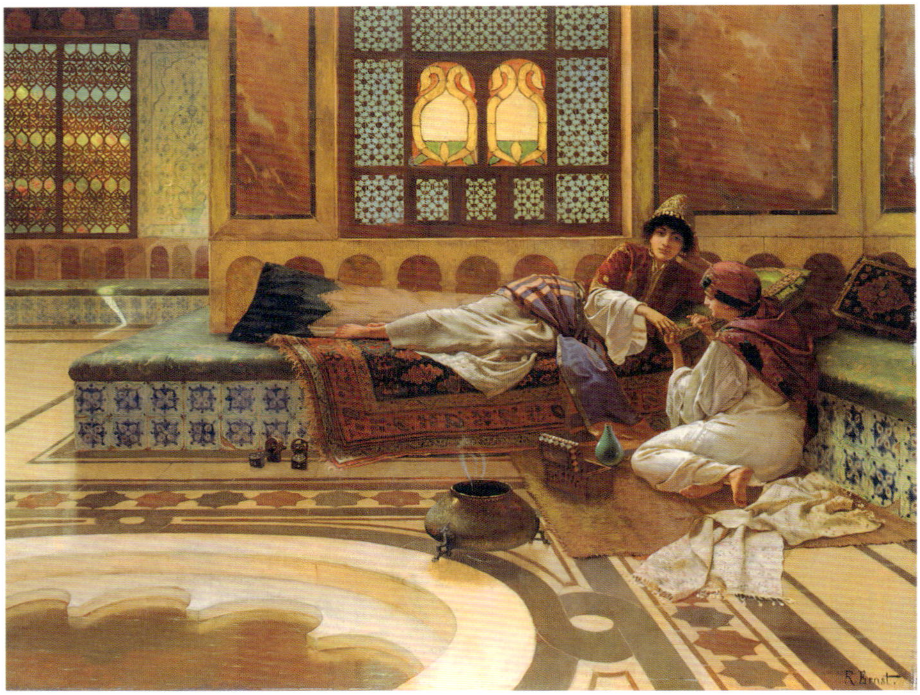

2.23 *The Manicure,* by Rudolph Ernst (Austrian, 1854–1932). The mysterious "Orient" was created in the minds of Westerners with paintings like this which often were made in studios in London, Berlin, Paris or other European cities. The "Orientals" became a mysterious group of *others* against which cultures could be compared and onto which dreams of color and freedom from the rigidity of modern western society could be projected. This escapism demanded the creation of goods for western homes so the colors textures and *feel* could be experienced.

Source: The Manicure (oil on panel), Ernst, Rudolphe (1854–1932) /Private Collection/Photo © Christie's Images/ The Bridgeman Art Library

BELOW
2.24 Turkish carpets, Northern African patterns, Japanese prints medievalist structures and Chinese wallpaper all in a mix, contrasted with the grayness and drabness of the modern urban environment and the monochrome garb of its male upper class. Henry Treffry Dunn (1838–1899). Rossetti and Dunton at 16 Cheyne Walk.

Source: Henry Treffry Dunn (1838–1899) Dante Gabriel Rossetti reading proofs of Sonnets and Ballads to Theodore Watts Dunton in the drawing room at 16 Cheyne Walk, London

THE INVENTION OF "THE ORIENT"

A fascination with mysterious and exotic lands of the East had been building since European ships allowed exploration of the globe, which soon turned to military ventures and trade. As the world view normalized in the 18th century, it became a rite of passage for young aristocrats to travel to foreign climes, and by the early decades of the 19th century, there was a steady stream of young intellectuals, artists, budding scientists, and adventurers heading off for points south and east. Heading east, the mystical Orient began in Turkey at the Bosporus and encompassed roughly the lands that now make up the Middle East and Asia. These travelers brought back journals and artifacts and romanticized and exoticized the Eastern lands and their cultures, creating a mythical image of the people and places. All things "Oriental" became fashionable: Turkish carpets, Northern African patterns, Japanese prints, medievalist structures, and Chinese wallpaper contrasted with the grayness and drabness of the modern urban environment and the monochrome garb of its male upper class (Fig. 2.24).

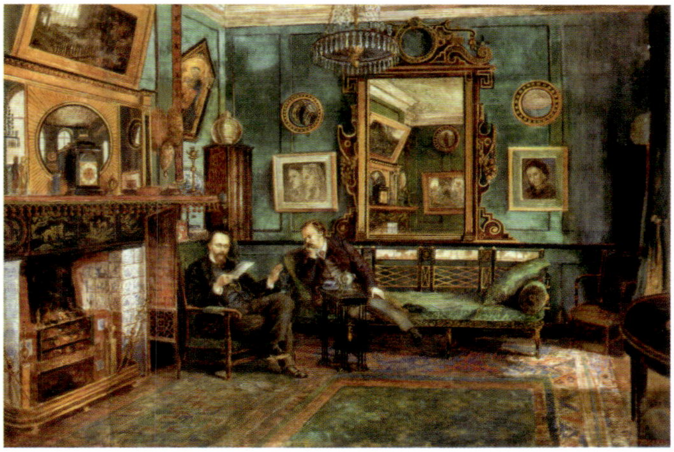

This fascination with the Orient was amplified in the 1870s, especially in Paris, after the Paris Exhibition of 1867 had included a Chinese and a Japanese Pavilion (Fig. 2.25). Capitalizing on this, Siegfried Bing (1838–1905), an enterprising art dealer, imported and promoted Japanese and East Asian art in his shop in Montmartre in Paris (Fig. 2.26). The Japanese woodblock prints known as *ukiyo-e* were especially influential, inspiring graphic designers and artists to rethink their use of surface and color. Among those heavily

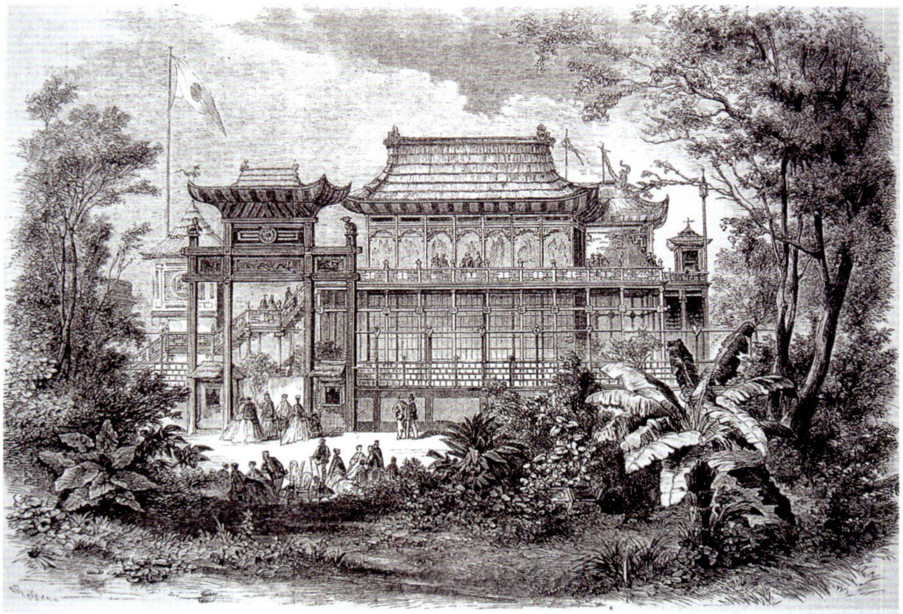

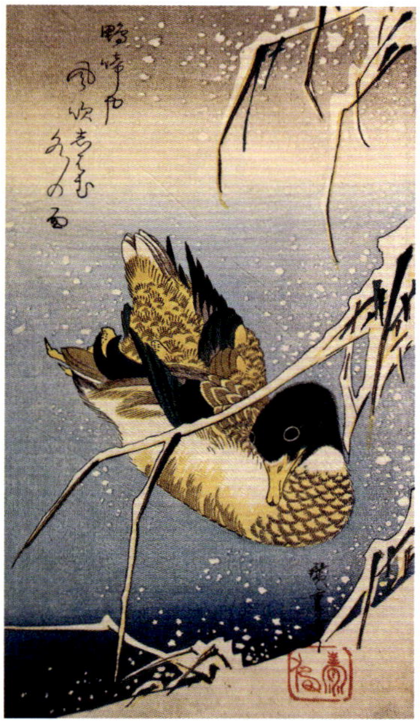

TOP LEFT
2.25 The Japanese pavilion at the Paris Exhibition of 1867. The "Orient" had arrived.

Source: *Le Monde Illustre* 1867. Reproduction in "Soie et Lumieres," Christian Polak

TOP RIGHT
2.26 Siegfried Bing in Paris fuelled the craze by importing and selling Japanese goods and artworks. Cover from *La Japon* artisique.

Source: © Peter Horree/Alamy

influenced were the painters Vincent Van Gogh and Toulouse-Lautrec, who both frequented Bing's shop in the 1880s (Fig. 2.27).

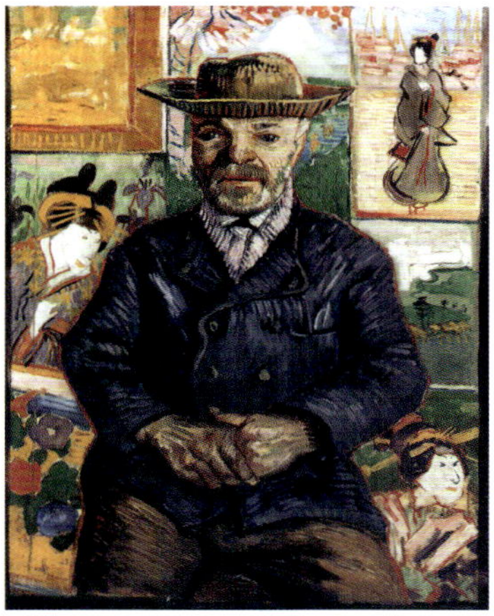

BOTTOM RIGHT
2.27 *Portrait of Pere Tanguy,* by Vincent Van Gogh. Orientalism wasn't all just straight copying and buying of things. Vincent van Gogh was a frequent visitor to Sigfried Bing's shop in Paris. Van Gogh was inspired by the use of color and space in the Japanese *ukiyo-e* and injected it into his own unique style. Here he has painted a portrait with a similar two-dimensionality and used actual *ukiyo-e* as the background.

Source: Artist: Vincent van Gogh, *Portrait of Père Tanguy*

DESIGNS FOR MARKET: DESIGNING AS A PROFESSION

As the commercial industrialized society became the reigning system and political expediency began to revolve around imports, exports, production, and consumption, the central role of mass manufacturing became greater. The designer as a profession was established in service to the marketplace. New products needed to be brought to market in order to produce demand and keep the factories in motion.

Just as artisans of the Middle Ages needed to become more specialized and educated to run efficient operations in the face of the increased demand for their goods, designers in the late 19th century had to increasingly specialize in a field and market and find a niche. But now, in addition, the demand for a "signature style" was added—most obviously in the high-fashion apparel field where the "designer label" began to eclipse the importance of the garment itself.

The *designer* became a vital link in the production chain of the manufactured goods, producing concepts and designs, diagrams and drawings, and overseeing production so that the workers could create goods according to specification. Specialization became the name of the game, and workshops sprouted as precursors to modern-day factories, with a division of labor and specialization driving output by the hundreds and thousands. The numbers involved required a formal separation of the artisan-handcraft from the conceptualizing and technical specification (Fig. 2.28).

2.28 In this photograph from c. 1890, employees use sewing machines to produce garments at the Waist and Dress Factory of the Rosenthal Brothers.

Source: © Schenectady Museum; Hall of Electrical History Foundation/ CORBIS

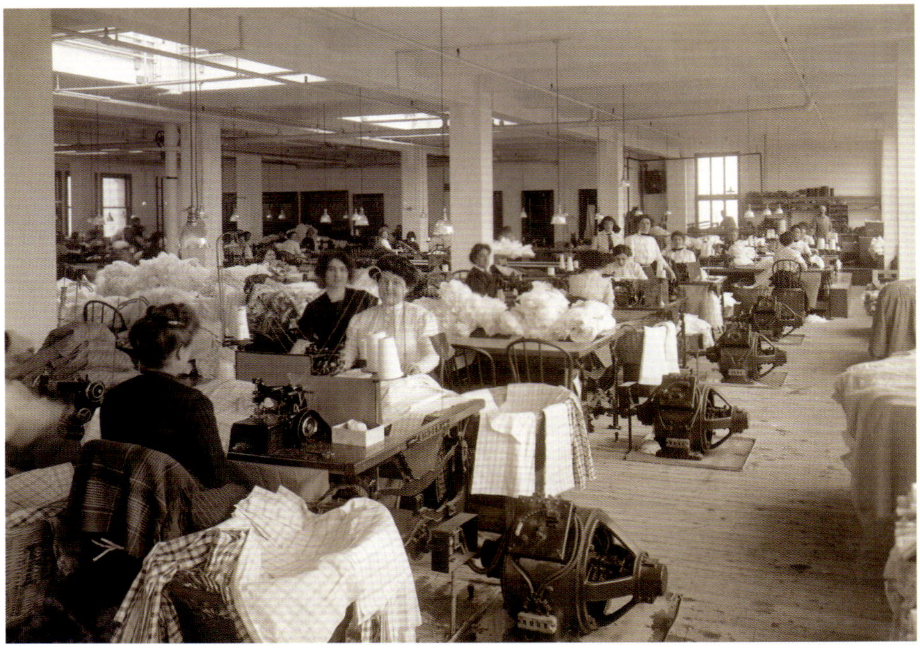

The system of conspicuous consumption that had grown up with the middle class resulted in the culture of planned obsolescence and throwaway, as became evident in the apparel industry early on. Right at the beginning, being about seasons and the latest fashions, it kept the textile mills working and the commercial interests happy. As the consumer society model spread and the marketing of everything became a profession, marketing and design went hand in hand.

ART NOUVEAU: TOTAL DESIGN

Inevitably style itself became a commodity, as mass-produced designs became more affordable and social pressure to conform to commodity culture increased. The style that most commonly came to be known as Art Nouveau was the first of the modern *total designs.* It was "total" in that the style was used on the entire environment: in building details, furniture, graphic design, flatware, carpets, cutlery, clothing, jewelry, and on and on. In a sense, the same could have been said about earlier styles, but although fashionable in many regards, they were not *in themselves* a commodity. The selling of the style as a *declared style produced by an individual* in mass manufactured form is the defining element that sets it apart: This is the beginning of the designer environment.

Art Nouveau was distinguished by dynamic curves creating a flowing line. Designs were often asymmetric, and forms had an organic feel. The use of color was dramatic and intense, owing to the possibility of new synthetic dyes and pigments. The *Exposition International* in Paris in 1900 served to popularize the style, and it became the defining optimistic style of the new modern century. It seems to have appeared in several places at once. In France the style was promoted by Siegfried Bing, who in 1895 changed his gallery devoted to the *Art Japonais* into a total design gallery called *L'Art Nouveau.* In rooms designed with this new curvy style, he exhibited all the wares and

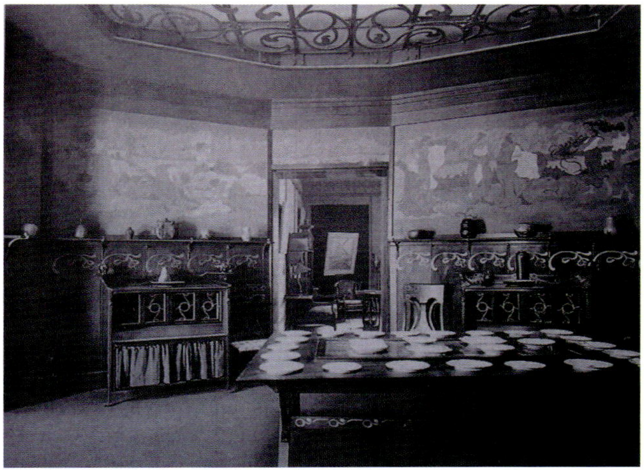

ABOVE
2.29 Interior of Siegfried Bing's store in Paris. Bing re-created his store and called it L'Art Noveau (The New Art), in which he presented all the goods there in an example of total design.

Source: Henri Van de Velde es Paul Elie Ranson: Siegried Bing ebedloje, 1895

BELOW
2.30 Left: Cover of the magazine *Jugend* ("Youth") from 1896. Right: Champagne Advertisement Poster by Alphonse Mucha (1860-1939) from 1898.

Source: R: The front cover of the magazine Jugend of 30 May 1896 PD-Old; L: Snark / Art Resource, NY

artwork to fit in a designed environment for the customers to walk through and experience (Fig. 2.29). In the German-speaking world, the style took its name from the arts journal *Jugend* ("Youth"), and in Spain from the Czech illustrator Alphonse Mucha, who popularized the style in the posters and ads he produced in Paris after 1887. The English, however, became most familiar with the style from seeing it in the store Liberty's in London, where the Liberty print became its most well-known example (Fig. 2.30).

WILLIAM MORRIS AND THE ARTS AND CRAFTS MOVEMENT

At the end of the century designs under a certain style, such as Art Nouveau, could be manufactured en masse and be seen everywhere in versions both expensive and well made as well as cheap knockoffs that could be bought by the less well-off citizenry. Design had in this sense become democratized. However, what some saw as an unfortunate side effect was that the quality of the goods themselves and the aesthetics of the design were of a gradually lessening standard. This was perhaps inevitable given the numbers involved, but it also prompted a backlash. Voices began

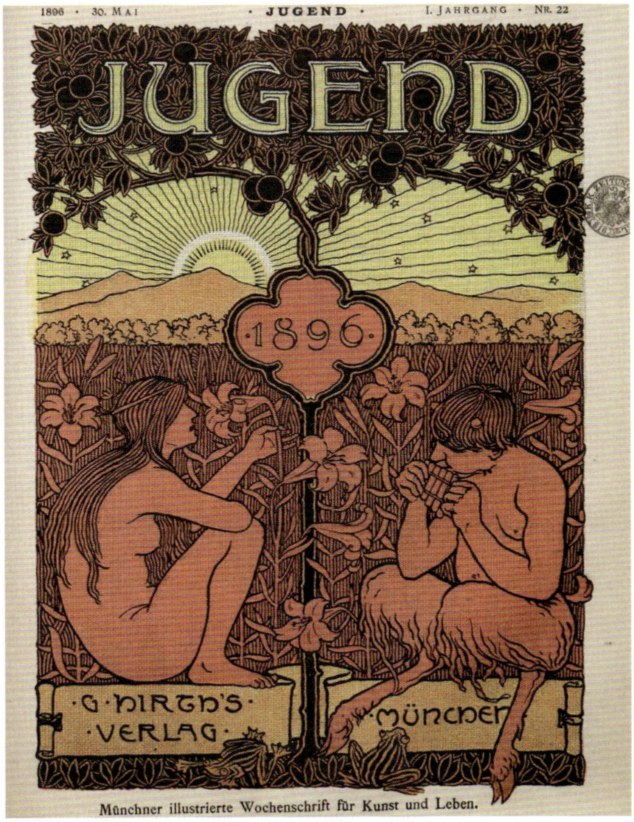

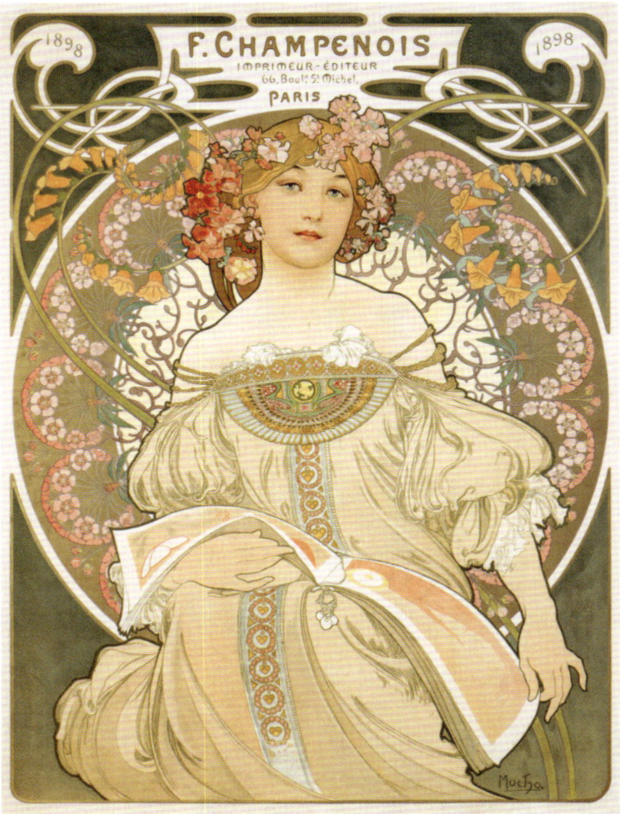

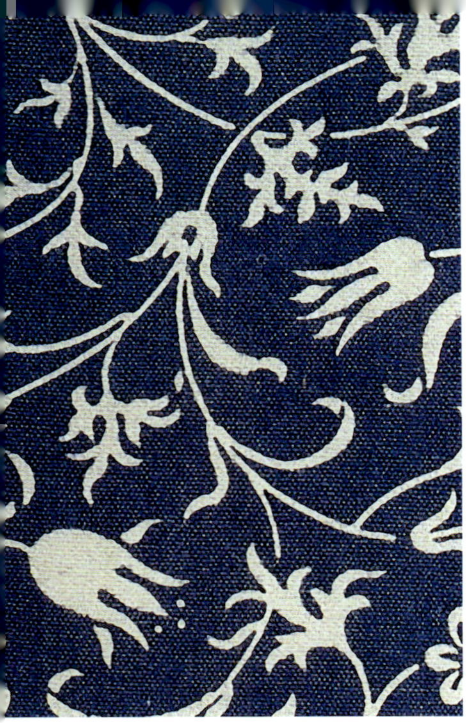

ABOVE

2.31 Wallpaper design from 1885 by William Morris. The debt owed by Mucha and others to the romantic nostalgia of the Arts and Crafts Movement is clear: The floral swirls and asymmetries, contrasting colors and vivid patterns all continue.

Image source: Medway printed cotton and linen designed by William Morris. Planet Art CD of royalty-free PD images William Morris: Selected Works

RIGHT

2.32 Detail from a season ticket for The Arts & Crafts Exhibition Society, by Walter Crane, England, 1890.

Source: Detail from a season ticket for The Arts & Crafts Exhibition Society, by Walter Crane, England, UK, 1890. V&A Images, London/Art Resource, NY

to be heard that protested this cheapening of aesthetics and started to advocate the heightening of artistic sensibilities in all areas of life.

One such voice was that of William Morris in England (1834–1896), who associated with the Pre-Raphaelites, a group of Romantic artists supported and inspired by John Ruskin. The Pre-Raphaelites wished to return to the intense colors and detail of 15th-century painting. Morris, who had studied both architecture and painting, turned to designing and founded a design firm with several artists associated with the Pre-Raphaelites. Morris, Marshall, Faulkner & Co, later renamed Morris & Co., specialized in stained glass at first, but Morris later expanded into tapestries, wallpaper, and graphic design as his interests, and by the 1890s, Morris was publishing manuscripts with typefaces of his own design inspired by 15th-century typography (Fig. 2.31).

Morris became an active spokesman for social reform, and his socialism found an expression in the effort to provide well-designed furnishings for everyone. This ideal spread and became what by 1887 was called the Arts and Crafts movement, after the Arts and Crafts Exhibition Society was formed in London (Fig. 2.32). Its first president, William Crane, (succeeded by Morris in 1881) said early on that they "must turn our artists into craftsmen, and our craftsmen into artists."[6]

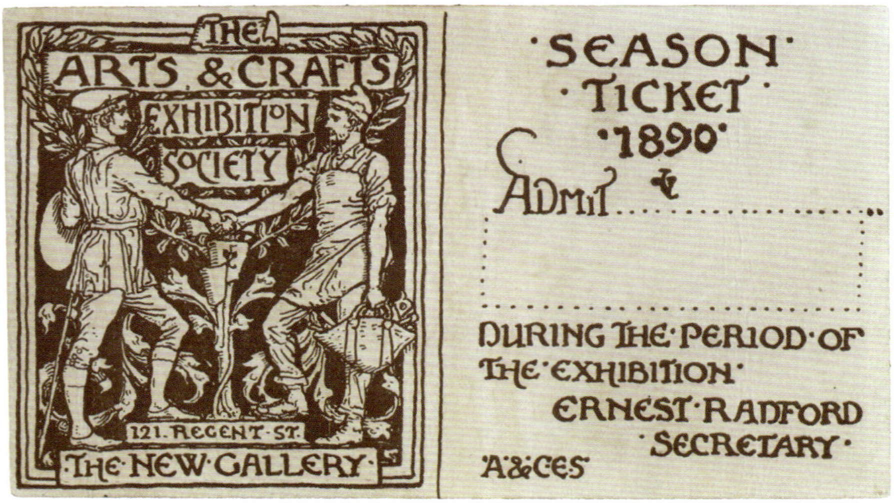

By educating craftspeople and designers together in artistic principles, those involved in the movement hoped to counteract what was perceived as a tendency toward the repetitive unoriginality, cheapness of materials, and lack of care in design and creation of factory-made products. By resurrecting the craftsperson, they attempted to resurrect the ideals of good craftsmanship. But Crane himself, writing in 1905, admitted that they were going against the tide:

> Certainly we cannot hope that the world, just yet, will beat its swords into ploughshares, or its spears into pruning-hooks, still less that it will return to local industry and handicraft for all the wants of life, or look solely to the independent artist and craftsman to make its house beautiful. The organized factory and the great machine industries will continue to work for the million, as well as for the millionaire, under the present system of production; but, at any rate,

they can be influenced by ideas of design, and it must be said that some manufacturers have shown themselves fully alive to the value of the co-operation of artists in this direction.[7]

BIG CITIES, OFFICE BUILDINGS, AND FUNCTIONALITY

The new cities posed a number of design questions, most notably how to approach the design of the tall buildings? With the advent of elevators and electric light, there seemed to be no limit to the design of office buildings and the idea to design upward rather than out, creating vertical communities to maximize the productivity and use of limited space. The answer, it seemed, lay in having their design be guided by functionality. Considering this problem, the architect Louis Sullivan laid down a law that became one of the touchstones of the modernist movement:

> Whether it be the sweeping eagle in his flight or the open apple blossom, the toiling work horse, the blithe swan, the branching oak, the winding stream at its base, the drifting clouds, over all the coursing sun, form ever follows function, and this is the law.[8]

There is, however, a problem with Sullivan's statement in that nature does in fact not *do* anything. Nature simply *appears* as a result of its inherent processes that are themselves a result of numerous factors coming together. To say that the function of an eagle demands it to be shaped a certain way falls into this trap of assuming a *purpose* in the natural formation of anything. A bird does not have wings because it *needs* to fly; it flies because it *can*, and then because it can, it forms an existence that is based on the ability.

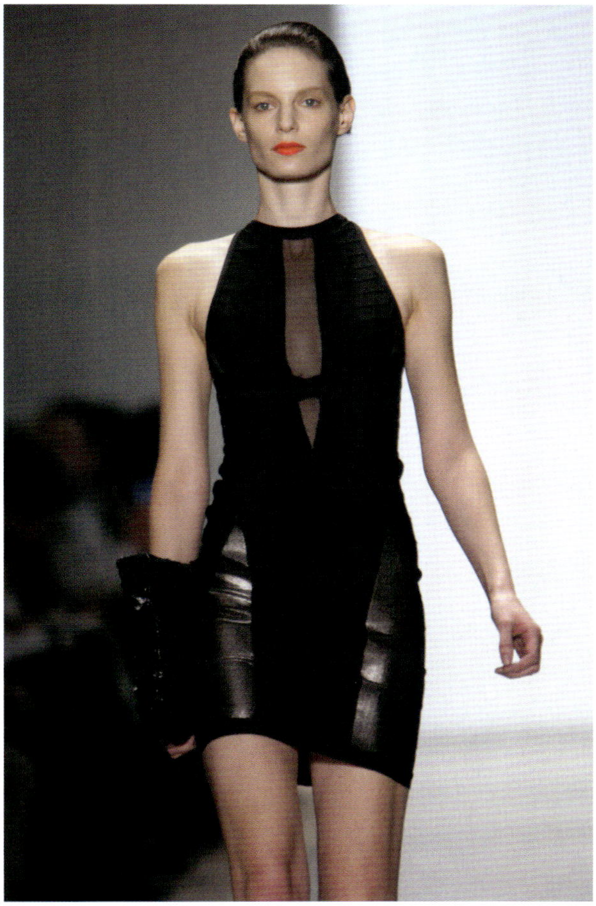

2.33 Decoding the relationship of the form and function of a design becomes less straightforward once emotional and aesthetic impact are considered as functions. The function of a little black dress is far more than just shelter, and its form reflects that. But it is not the same kind of function as the function of an office building.

Source: Thomas Iannaccone/WWD

However, to suggest that "form follows function" is not invalid; it is simply an incorrect framing of the natural relationship. In nature, form and function are a dialogue. One could just as easily say that "function follows form." In design, therefore, if design is to base its approach to problems on a *natural ordering* of things, form and functionality must be considered together.

But a larger problem that Sullivan's directive does not address—and subsequent discussions of Modernist ideals tended to sidestep—is that if it is to apply outside of the architecture of office buildings, it defines function too narrowly. How to understand the function when modern life revolves around so much more than strict physical functionality. What *is* the function of a designed object? Does functional equal practical in every case? Humans in society, with all their rituals, small and large, derive meaning from their constructed environments and possessions. Clothing and architecture are shelter, but also signs of identity. What, for example, do we do with a design that has the function of being decorative or has the only purpose of having a strong visual impact (Fig. 2.33)?

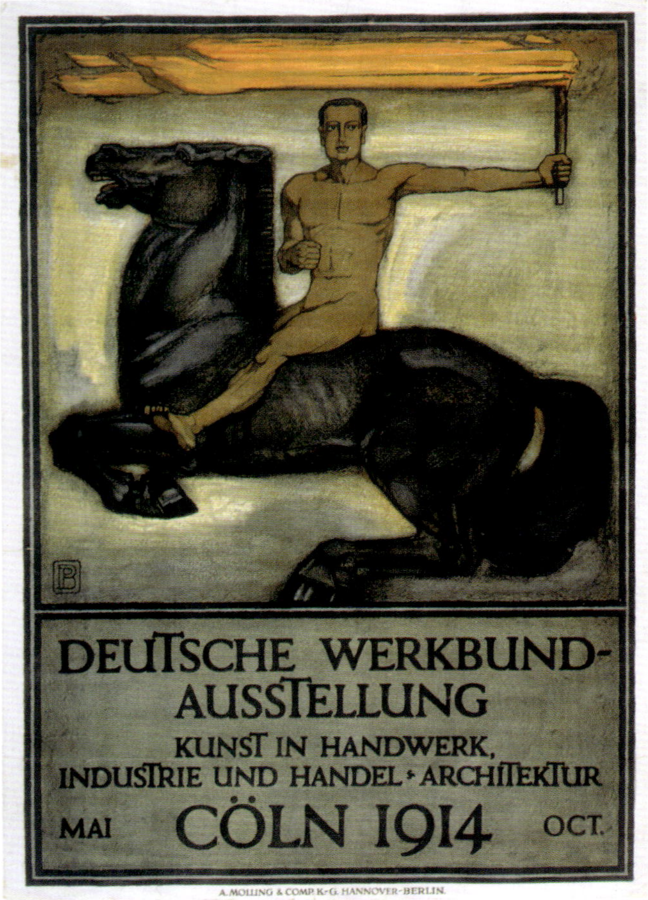

2.34 Poster for the first exhibition by the Deutsche Werkbund in Cologne that was interrupted by the outbreak of World War I in August of 1914. The exhibit's theme is "Art in Craft, Industry, and Commercial Architecture." The poster's style seems much more connected to the 19th century's Romantics and Classicists.

Source: V&A Images, London/Art Resource, NY

THE DEUTSCHER WERKBUND

The rearrangement of political life, the adaptation of society to urban living, and the problems of industrialized society with its disruption of long-unchanged rhythms of life all called for new solutions to the questions of how people were to operate in community. Societies for the advancement of all manner of causes, political groups, literary societies, collaboratives, and artists' salons debated and demanded voting rights, women's rights, education, clean air, better water, and any number of causes. Advocates blended with the increasing crowds, creating the new environment in which we still live in many ways.

Groups devoted to improving the aesthetics and functionality of mass-produced design grew beyond the utopianism of William Morris, as artists and designers banded together to create groups such as the Deutscher Werkbund. Along similar lines, these groups advocated for a synthesis of art and craft but were more open to new production technologies and were not as myopic in their admiration of rural or medieval life (Fig. 2.34).

When it was founded in 1907, the Werkbund still retained much of the spirit of the Arts and Crafts movement. However, instead of fighting against what Morris and his colleagues saw as the evils of the capitalist marketplace, the Werkbund founders declared that industrial production had to be accepted as the reigning method and that their aims would be to bridge the gap between the innovators and production. As the political atmosphere in Germany became more nationalistic and fractured in the years leading up to World War I, the Werkbund split into factions where the more conservative architects and the progressive advocates of craft and individual design disputed the extent to which they should emphasize industrial work or creativity.

FUTURISTS

Meanwhile, in Italy, a group formed that celebrated the modern functional technological age. This loosely organized cohort, led by the Italian F. T. Marinetti, became known as the Futurists. Their extreme stand was an intimation of things to come. In a dramatic swing, the Futurists advocated a rethinking of culture and design. They were the anti-Romantics: Anything and everything old-fashioned was to be eliminated. Science and technical knowledge was to be the source of inspiration instead of history. The Futurists took a ruthless view of design. The new world was to be inspired by the speed of new machines and the intense violence of modern warfare.

Their program was total and even took on the mainstay of male conservatism, the basic suit. Menswear was already becoming a design problem in that the approaching

SUSTAINABILITY

Human society's impact on nature had already begun to cause concern in the late 19th century, as the industrialization of the world progressed by leaps and bounds and improvements in technology and medical sciences afforded a rapid population increase. However, the modernist program and the faith in scientific and technological progress allowed these concerns to be set aside, if not ignored altogether. It wasn't until after World War II that the impact of the accelerating industrial capabilities and factory farming focused the efforts of an environmental movement. Rachel Carson's book *Silent Spring* (1962), aimed at the harm of pesticides, sparked a popular swell of environmentalism, and throughout the 1960s and 1970s more and more scientists were pointing out the finite nature of oil and other resources. In 1987, after almost three years of preparation, the United Nation's World Commission on Environment and Development, headed by Gro Harlem Brundtland, issued the report *Our Common Future.* The committee advocated sustainable development, which it defined as "development that meets the needs of the present without compromising the ability of future generations to meet their own needs." The Brundtland Report, as it came to be known, places particular emphasis on long-term thinking and on improving the lot of the world's poor.

Following on the Brundtland Commission's work, Agenda 21, a plan of action, was presented at the UN Conference on Environment and Development (the "Earth Summit") in Rio de Janeiro in 1992, again after three years of preparation. Progress has, however, not been at the hoped-for level globally, with the agenda becoming heavily politicized, and subsequent Rio conferences such as "Rio+20" in 2012 are perceived as having compromised the goals and agenda.

However, ecologically sustainable design standards are being slowly incorporated into various industries, most notably the LEED standard (Leadership in Energy and Environmental Design) upheld by the U.S. Green Building Council since the late 1990s (see new.usbg.org). The standard "provides building owners and operators with a framework for identifying and implementing practical and measureable green building design, construction, operations, and maintenance solutions" and is both raising awareness of ecological practices as well as significantly contributing to reducing the use of energy.

modernity seemed to be at odds with the dark, stiff formalism of male attire. Giacomo Balla, one of the group, designed a series of suits according to Futurist principles and wrote in his manifesto on "Futurist Men's Clothing," "Let us finish with the humiliating and hypocritical custom of wearing mourning. Our crowded streets, our theatres and cafés are all imbued with a depressingly funereal tonality, because clothes are made only to reflect the gloomy and dismal moods of today's *passéists*."[9] The futurist clothes ("hap-hap-hap-hap-happy clothes" according to Balla) were to have "brilliant," "forceful," and "muscular" colors with lines that were "dynamic" and "asymmetrical." Balla's manifesto continues, "The consequent merry dazzle produced by our clothes in the noisy streets, which we shall have transformed with our Futurist architecture, will mean that everything will begin to sparkle like the glorious prism of a jeweler's." According to another of their manifestos, the "noisy streets" of the Futurist city were to have buildings "like a gigantic machine" and "like an immense and tumultuous shipyard, agile, mobile and dynamic in every detail; the Futurist house must be" with no stairwells, but elevators that "scale the lengths of the façades like serpents of steel and glass." A building was not to be "pretty and pleasing," and superimposed decoration was "absurd." It was to be "glass and steel, stripped of paintings and sculpture, rich only in the innate beauty of its lines and relief, extraordinarily "ugly" in its mechanical simplicity, higher and wider according to need rather than the specifications of municipal laws" (Fig. 2.35).

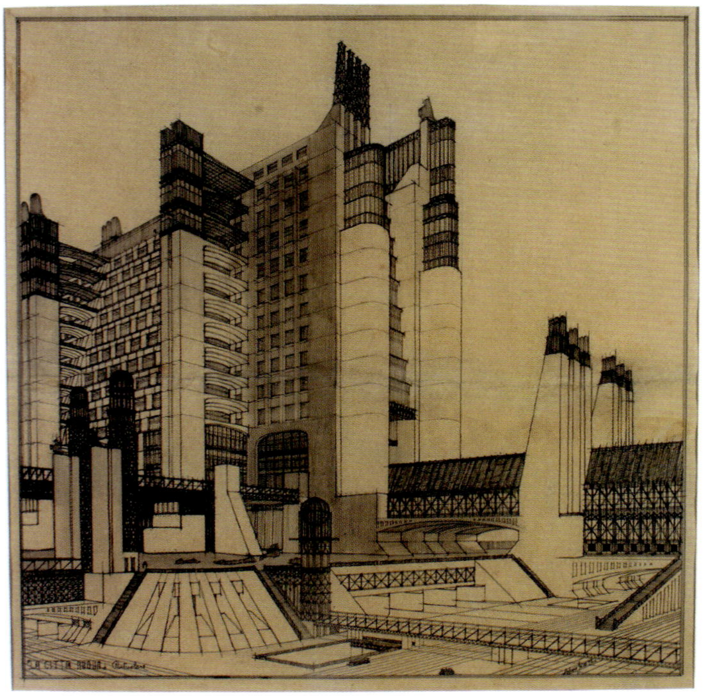

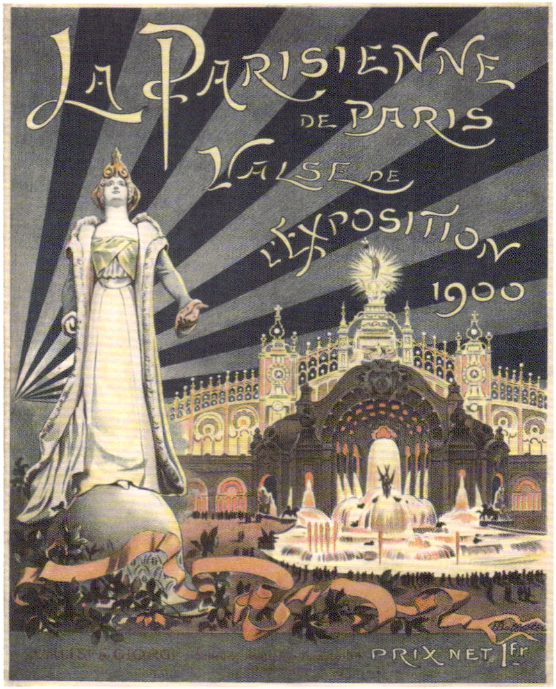

TOP LEFT

2.35 Futurist building design for "The New City" (1912), by Antonio Sant'Elia (1888–1916), who like Giacomo Balla, was a key figure in the Futurist movement.

Source: Antonio Sant'Elia (1888–1916). Part of the series La Città Nuova, 1914. Housing with external lifts and connection systems to different street levels *Utopie metropolitane, la mostra* (in Italian). Style & Design. *L' Espresso* (2013-03-28).

TOP RIGHT

2.36 Poster for the Exposition Universelle of 1900 in Paris. The optimism and excitement about the future and its technological and scientific marvels is very evident.

Source: Courtesy of http://exposition-universelle-paris-1900.com/

And interestingly enough, the Futurists did not intend to design for the future: "The fundamental characteristics of Futurist architecture will be its impermanence and transience. Things will endure less than us. Every generation must build its own city."[10]

Difficult as the Futurist's posturing may be, their positions crystalize many of the modernist philosophies toward design and society. The modernism of the early 20th century was an approach toward culture and design that involved a continuing overthrowing of the present, driven by a sincere belief in technology and progress, systems, and science. In the philosophy of modernists function should define design and beauty was meant to arise from the functional approach. Decoration and playfulness in architecture was generally frowned upon, as it was not considered to be useful. (And Balla's "happy clothes" never took hold.)

As with so much of what modern history brings, the counterpoint was already present at the high point of the movement. Right after the middle of the 20th century, the counterarguments were coming forward. However, at the beginning of the 20th century, the optimism and ideological fervor was strong and the notion that the world and history were thought to have a purpose and narrative allowed the formulation of theories of art and design that placed creativity and innovation in the service of this forward-moving "progress" (Fig. 2.36).

BAUHAUS

The intense, militant **futurism** of the Italians had its more tempered counterpart in the work being produced by designers involved in the Deutscher Werkbund. For example, the architect Walter Gropius designed the radically modern Fagus shoe factory in Germany that was built from 1911 to 1914. The brick-and-glass–walled building's design

ERGONOMICS IN HISTORY

The history of ergonomics as a practice goes back as far as humanity has used tools. Stone axes and bone tools were clearly formed and carved to be a good fit. However, the studied and systematic approach we associate with the science today begins to develop with the machines of the Industrial Revolution. Doctors in the 17th century had begun to notice work-related ailments, but the repetitive motion and monotony of tasks in the factories created a whole new set of problems. With those problems came scientific investigation into their solutions. In 1857 Wojciech Jastrzebowski, in Poland, introduced the term *ergonomics* from the Greek words: *ergos* (work) and *nomos* (laws). Shortly thereafter, Frederick Taylor, in the United States, pioneered what came to be known as scientific management to increase efficiency and productivity among industrial workers. It was during World War II, however, that *human factors engineering* became critical in the assembly of rapidly made complex weaponry (notably aircraft). Ensuring productivity and safety went hand in hand, and psychologists began to work with designers and engineers to optimize the movements of workers and the spaces and lighting of their workplaces. Eventually these investigations expanded to a wide range of disciplines to design systems and spaces that fit.

With the ever-increasing workforce at desk jobs and the new repetitive motion of people working at computer terminals, the science of ergonomics has also become that of small-scale operations and individual comfort. Today's *user-friendliness* is therefore an inheritor of a long line of design concerns of humans, machines, tools, environments, motion, attitude, and fit.

was based on a set of specifications that included, for example, how the building was to be experienced by those going by on nearby train tracks. But Gropius's main source of inspiration during this period was industrial architecture in America. He was fascinated by the very functional American industrial buildings, the grain elevators, daylight factories, and open-plan warehouses with their concrete structures, glass-curtain walls, and flexibility of purpose. These, in his view, were the buildings of the future "exemplars for a better modern industrial architecture" (Fig. 2.37).

In 1919, with an aim to continue the aim of the Werkbund and bring the arts and craftsmanship together in an industrial design frame, Gropius gathered a group of men and women, designers in various disciplines—architecture, graphic design, furniture textiles, and metalwork—and set up the *Bauhaus*, a school that was essentially a research institution creating prototypes for industrial production in the modern age.[11]

Gropius, like William Morris, felt that well-designed furnishings and houses were everyone's right. He saw a world of component-based architecture that would improve both the experience of the construction and the habitation of dwellings for

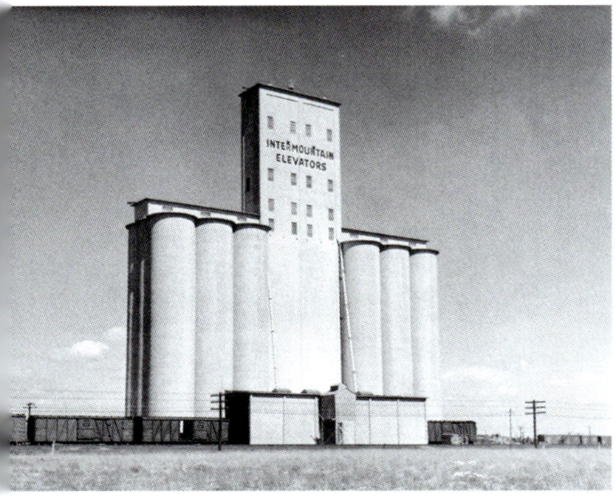

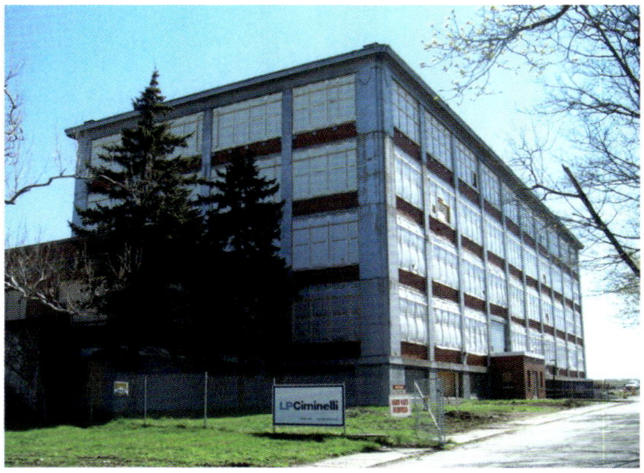

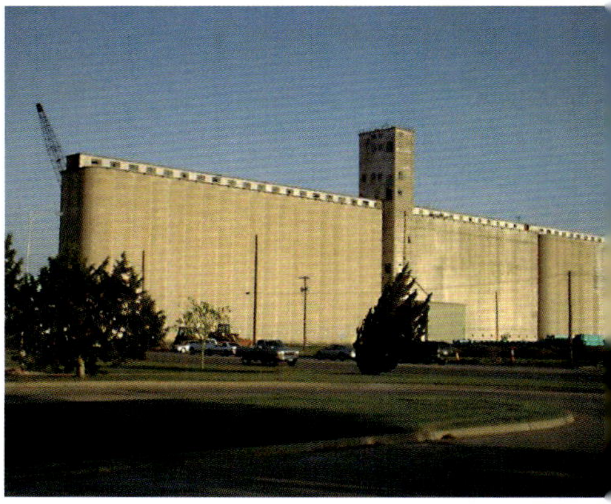

2.37 The needs of industry began to determine the look of buildings in the beginning of the 20th century. Engineers and architects began to arrive at the same conclusions. Left, a grain elevator in the American Mid-West from 1928; Middle, the Buffalo Meter Co. building in NY from 1915; and Right, a warehouse under construction in America in 1904.

Source: ©Horace Bristol/CORBIS

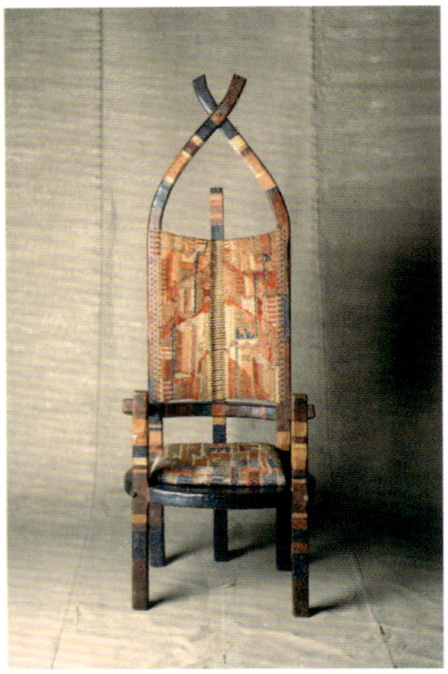

ABOVE

2.38 African or Romantic Chair, 1921. Textile by Gunta Stölzl (1897–1983) on a chair by Marcel Breuer (1902–1981).

Source: Bauhaus-Archiv Berlin, Foto: Hartwig Klappert. Bauhaus-Archiv Berlin/Acquired with funds provided by Ernst von Siemens Kunststiftung

all. Working within the parameters of industrial production, the Bauhaus became the defining institution for design in the 20th century, advancing the culture of design masters in modern society by creating an enormous number of influential designs. Chairs, lamps, hardware, textiles, and interiors—it is revealing that much of what we still perceive as modern in the early decades of the 21st century was actually created nearly 100 years ago.

The textile designer Gunta Stölzl (1897–1983), a student who became a teacher and then one of the very few female masters at Bauhaus, described it so: "We wanted to create living things with contemporary relevance, suitable for a new style of life. Huge potential for experimentation lay before us. It was essential to define our imaginary world, to shape our experiences through material, rhythm, proportion, color and form"[12] (Fig. 2.38).

In keeping with the male-oriented atmosphere of the culture at large and modernist techno-worship in particular, female designers like Stölzl were few and far between, but their influence has been increasingly acknowledged in later years. Lilly Reich, for example, was the first woman elected to the governing board of the Deutscher Werkbund and later another of the female teachers at the Bauhaus. Reich met the architect Ludwig Mies van der Rohe when both were involved with Werkbund projects and was his (romantic and professional) partner for 13 years, collaborating on exhibitions as well as designing furniture. Their most dramatic and famous collaborations perhaps being the Barcelona Pavilion of 1929 and its derivative the Tugendhat House in Brno, with their corresponding chair designs: the Barcelona chair and Brno chair (Fig. 2.39).

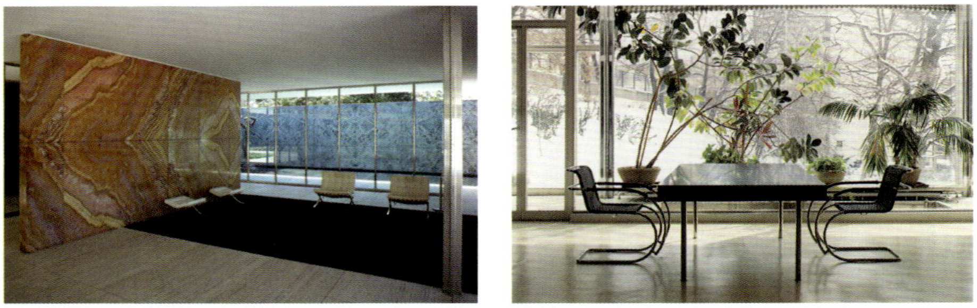

RIGHT

2.39 Barcelona chairs (left) and Brno (right) chairs in their respective surrounding designs by Lily Reich and Mies van der Rohe.

Source: L: © EMILIO FERRER / Alamy. R: © Miroslav Ambroz/Artifice Images.

As time went on, the Bauhaus was considered too radical for the increasingly conservative and intolerant politics of Germany. As the Nazi Party's influence strengthened with Hitler's rise to power in the early 1930s, the Bauhaus was increasingly harassed by Nazis, who saw their work as degenerate and "un-German" in its cosmopolitan style. The Bauhaus was closed shortly after 1933 after a series of compromises, and many of the designers fled, some to America.

CONSTRUCTIVISTS AND DADA

Even as modernism was establishing itself as the revolutionary direction of the 20th century, its fragmentation was already appearing. For example, the move away from a strict functionalism and into the deconstructed mode more familiar to the end of the 20th century appeared among the Constructivists of the new society that was

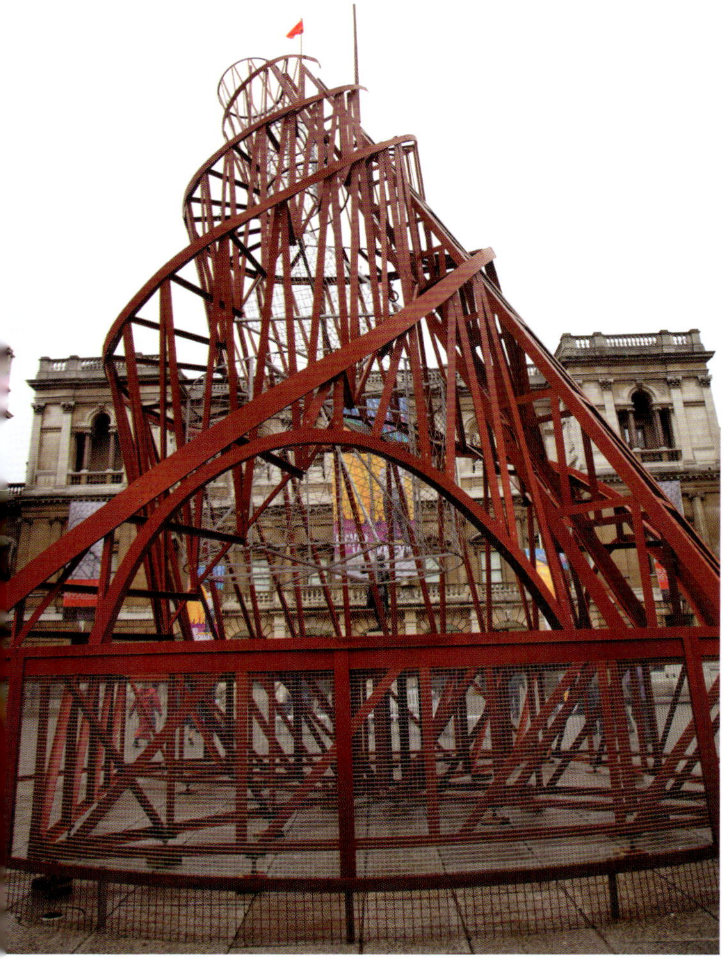

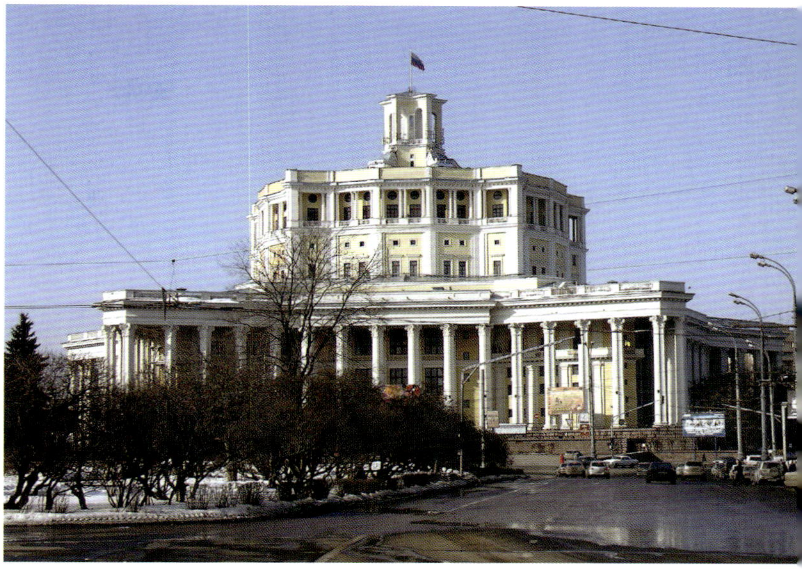

ABOVE LEFT

2.40 The Monument for the Third International by the Constructivist Tatlin was considered too radical a design.

Source: © M.Sobreira/Alamy

ABOVE RIGHT

2.41 The Red Army Theater in Moscow (1940) displays the near-Baroque classicism of the Soviet style.

Source: By NVO (Own work (own photo)) [CC-BY-SA-2.5 (http://creativecommons.org/licenses/by-sa/2.5)], via Wikimedia Commons

being built in the newly formed Soviet Union (Fig. 2.40). The **Constructivists** were the most forward-looking of the Soviet world of art and design and envisaged their work as representing the modern age of science, progress, and human equality. Their vision was thoroughly modernist but equally grandiose as those that came before. To them, in keeping with the revolutionary philosophies of the time, it was vital to develop new concepts of art and beauty. They would get rid of the imagery of the old world and aristocratic elites that had been overthrown and work within a vision of a new world of industry, science, and technology.

To this end, their design language became geometric, angular, and functional, exposing the interiors and constructions of the objects. The denial of classicism was overriding—a symbolic rejection of the imperial classicism of the old world—but the visual language they chose instead became too revolutionary for the comfort of the new totalitarian government, itself a new power elite. Having taken power, the revolutionary elite could not abide further expansion of radical thinking. Power must be consolidated. Art and design had to be brought under control and exhibit the might of the state. After a period of active modernist innovation, a reversion to classicism set in, with even a hint of the Baroque, which became the Soviet style for official buildings and monuments (Fig. 2.41).

DADA

In the years surrounding World War I, a New York–Paris axis appeared in modern art and design, with French artists such as Francis Picabia and Marcel Duchamp living in New York City and Americans—the writers Ernest Hemingway an Ezra Pound among them—forming a group in Paris around the writer and art collector Gertrude Stein. American jazz culture spread to Paris, while Parisian art and design came to New York.

Duchamp and Picabia became friends and collaborators with the American artist Man Ray, who later moved to Paris. All three supported the anti-art movement known as Dada, which had begun in Switzerland and spread to Germany and France. **Dada** was radically antiestablishment and antiwar, and their art, often performance-based and absurd, used a sense of the ridiculous to make statements about the dark side of modern industrial-capitalist society.

One of the originators of Dada in Switzerland was the Romanian-French writer Tristan Tzara, who formed the Cabaret Voltaire in Zurich in 1916 along with the writers and poets Hugo Ball, Emmy Hemmings, Jean Arp, and others. The Cabaret Voltaire was a venue for these socialist and anarchist poets and artists to perform their radical political works.

Their beginnings were inspired by the Italian Futurists, and there was even collaboration between the two groups. But Tzara and the Dadaists eventually aimed to go beyond Futurism, and in 1918 Tzara wrote a new manifesto:

> I write a manifesto and I want nothing, yet I say certain things, and in principle I am against manifestoes, as I am also against principles. . . . And so Dada was born of a need for independence, of a distrust toward unity. Those who are with us preserve their freedom. We recognize no theory. We have enough cubist and futurist academies: laboratories of formal ideas. Is the aim of art to make money and cajole the nice nice bourgeois?[13]

Tzara's Dada aimed to be Futurism's nemesis, and its spirit, with its wild energy and antiestablishment slant, became the cutting edge of modern art and design. Tzara's Manifesto of 1918 ends with the Futurist annihilating rage inverted and anticipates the remainder of the 20th century: "Freedom: Dada Dada Dada, a roaring of tense colors, and interlacing of opposites and of all contradictions, grotesques, inconsistencies: LIFE."

In Germany, as the 1920s wore on, right-wing nationalists, in the guise of the Nazi Party, had a similar reaction to the art being developed in the modern age as the Stalinists in Russia. They emphasized tradition and folkish style, cultivated an extreme intolerance of difference, and were incompatible with the internationalist and experimental program of modernism (Fig. 2.42). In 1937 once their hold on power was complete, the Nazis held an exhibition of "Degenerate Art" that meant to mock the modernists who were now branded enemies of the state and of German culture. Much of the exhibit was especially set up to mock the very influential First International Dada Fair that was held in Berlin in 1920.

But it is in Dada and the outliers of the modernist movement in the 1920s where we see the beginnings of what would follow in the next generations. We need only note the revived interest in Dada in arts in the late 1950s and early 1960s and the Dada-like happenings performed by the radical side of the antiwar hippie movement in the United States of America. Concepts became methods of protest, and the look of protest became the look of the hippies and beatniks. Many progressive movements in the 1960s adopted a nostalgic, romantic stance and presented an antimodernist vision of a multiethnic and preindustrialized society and adopted a premodernist graphic design style echoing Art Nouveau (Fig. 2.43).

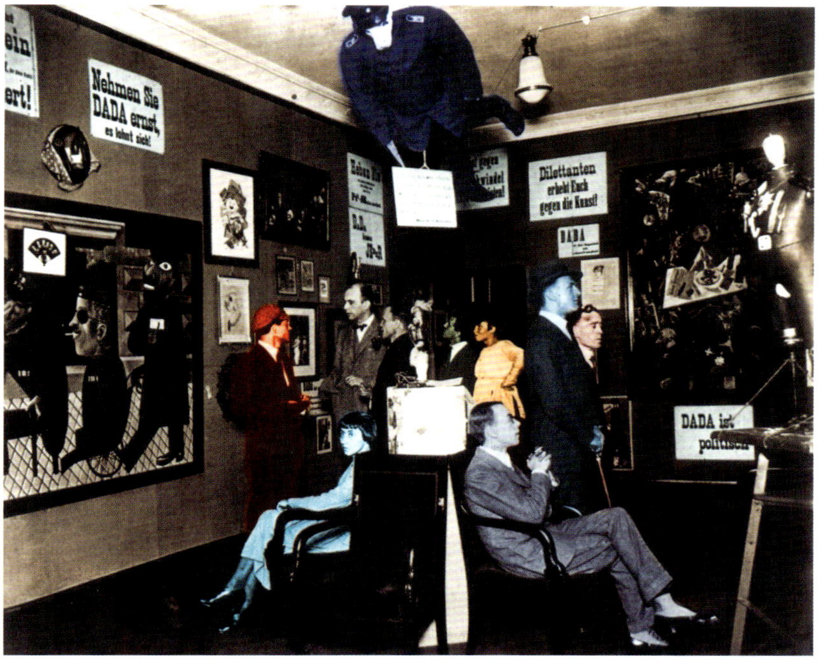

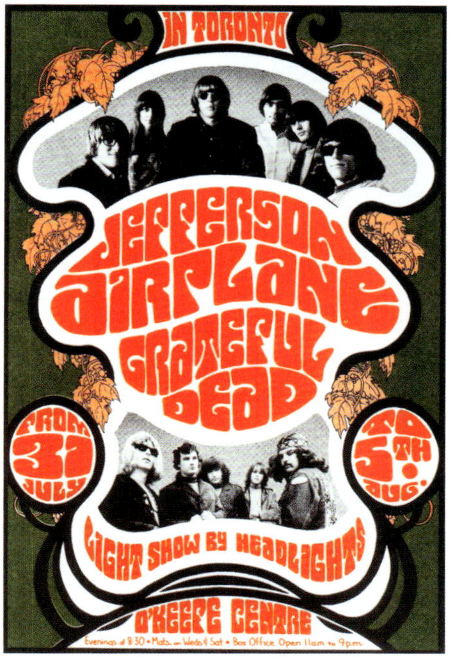

ABOVE LEFT

2.42 A room at the first Dada Fair in Berlin in 1920. Notice the text on the wall to the upper left: Nehmen Sie DADA ernst, es lahnt sig! ("Take DADA seriously, it's worth it!").

Source: © Prisma Bildagentur AG/Alamy

ABOVE RIGHT

2.43 Styles of the 1960s counterculture echoed and resurrected Art Nouveau. Psycheldelic poster from 1967.

Source: © JHPhoto/Alamy

NAUM GABO: THE FUTURE WE LEAVE TO THE FORTUNE-TELLERS

Meanwhile, back in the 1920s the Russian constructivist movement was also edging ahead, and like the Dadaists found themselves putting in stakes beyond the *moderns* in the 1920 *Realist Manifesto* by Naum Gabo (Naum Neemia Pevsner, 1890–1977) and his brother Anton Pevsner. Gabo and Pevsner, like Tzara, begin with a swipe at the Futurists, implying they were overly impressed country bumpkins:

> The pompous slogan of "Speed" was played from the hands of the Futurists as a great trump. We concede the sonority of that slogan and we quite see how it can sweep the strongest of the provincials off their feet.[14]

They then deny the need for romanticizing of the past as well as the quasi-religious worship of the future, both being equally delirious:

> Space and time are re-born to us today. . . . We do not look for justification, neither in the past nor in the future. . . . We assert that the shouts about the future are for us the same as the tears about the past: a renovated day-dream of the romantics. . . . A monkish delirium of the heavenly kingdom of the old attired in contemporary clothes.[15]

Summing up, they write that they will reconsider the use of lines, color, volume, and mass as building blocks of art. Form and line do not matter as principles; color is only decorative, not inherent; and most importantly recognizing time and experience as a way of realizing art. All art is experience, says Gabo. The actual *being with* art is as important as seeing it or studying it. Therefore, says Gabo, coming full circle to Morris and joining with Gropius, it should be a part of life: "at the workbench, at the office, at work, at rest, and at leisure; work days and holidays, at home and on the road, so that the flame of life does not go out in man." Finally, in the experience, where space and time are to be considered together, what matters is the *now*:

> The past we are leaving behind as carrion.
>
> The future we leave to the fortune-tellers.
>
> We take the present day.

ART DECO

L'Exposition des Arts Decoratifs et Industrials Modernes in 1925 gave its name to *Art Deco*, the first truly 20th-century total design movement, involving clothing, vehicles, flatware, and architecture murals, textiles, and wallpaper. In graphic design it outlived perhaps all its other applications (Fig. 2.44). Art Deco represented the Constructivists' ideal and the Futurists' vision without the warfare, characterized by the turning away from European classicism and the introduction of a new language of form and color, by geometric forms, stepped structures, sunbursts, and the Cubist language of broken forms and multiple perspectives. In addition, a streamlining of forms appeared, inspired by the new design paradigm of technology, trains, cars, and airplanes. Art Deco was well suited to represent the new world of speed and engines, and although European by name, birth, and ancestry, it became the first American style by being the first identifiable style of Hollywood films in what is now seen by many as one of the Golden Ages of filmmaking.

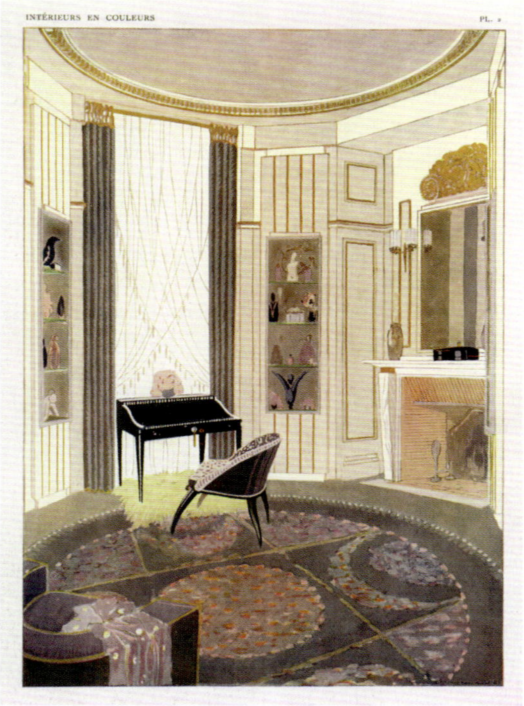

2.44 A design for an interior for the 1925 Paris International Exhibition Arts Decoratifs. Despite the modern tendency of Art Deco, the classicisms of the 19th century are still included. Note the classicist elements, such as the pillars and capitals and even the desk.

Interior with furniture designed by Ruhlmann, from a collection of prints published in 4 volumes by Albert Levy, c.1924–1926 (pochoir print), Ruhlmann, Jacques-Emile (1869–1933)/ Private Collection /The Stapleton Collection/The Bridgeman Art Library.

A side effect of design for filmmaking is that because films take months to create, the fashions and style going in must anticipate the styles of the time following the film's release. To this end, Hollywood filmmaking became an exhibition for high fashion. Grand scenes of the 1920s were set in a glamorous—if imaginary—world of high-modern Art Deco.

The Art Deco exhibition in 1925 was also a nexus of apparel design. It was here that Coco Chanel exhibited what became her signature design: the Chanel Suit. With its machine knit jersey, lack of decoration, and clean lines, it was right in the frame with the most modernist of architecture. Using modern industrial fabrics, basic colors, and delicate but significant accents and above all designed for comfort, it may have been the most significant design to appear in apparel until youth fashions took to the streets in the 1960s.

Significantly, the 1925 exhibition was also where the designer Paul Poiret, coming off the height of his career in female apparel, had his final moment in the sun. Poiret and Chanel had sneered at each other's designs for years (Fig. 2.45). Poiret's designs, whose colorful and Oriental-themed looks had seemed so modern only a generation earlier, now seemed to belong to the 19th century, overworked and fussy. The architect-designer known as Le Corbusier (Charles-Édouard Jeanneret, 1887–1965), whose designs for buildings and cities tended toward the most functional and mechanical of modernist

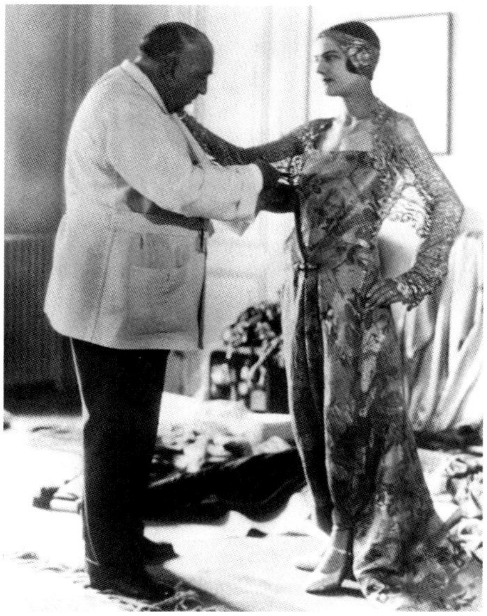

ABOVE

2.45 Paul Poiret with his opulent Orientalism. The visible ostentation of the 19th century was replaced with more subtle signals when Chanel's minimalism took over as the modern style.

Source: ©UNDERWOOD & UNDERWOOD/CORBIS.

visions, realized the significance of this shift: "Woman has got there before us," he exclaimed. "She has brought about the reform of her dress. . . . The courage, the enterprise, inventive spirit with which woman has revolutionized her dress are a miracle of modern times. Thank you!" Like the Futurist Balla, Le Corbusier saw how out-of-synch men's fashions had become with their vision of the future. "What about us men?" he continued. "A dismal state of affairs! In our clothes, we look like generals of the Grand Army and we wear starched collars! We are uncomfortable."[16]

The years of World War I and the 1920s saw the first successful developments of designing in favor of large-scale marketing campaigns. The propaganda efforts for getting the citizens of the United States to back the entry into the war were based on the relatively new theories of psychology, and after the war, the experts involved brought their talents to the private sector. Graphic design and advertising developed a minimalism well suited to print, and meanwhile a graphic visual style was developing in the black-and-white films.

Art Deco continued to dominate through the 1930s, especially in architecture and film, while apparel headed toward an ostentation of form and fabric. With a new world war on the horizon, the competing styles of the 20th century can all be seen in the entrance to yet another World Expo, The Exhibition International in Paris. The ideological battles of the modern age were being fought with classicist iconography (Fig. 2.46). In 1937, the German and Soviet pavilions faced each other. Although showing Art Deco influences, their modernisms are classically tempered by their imperial pretensions, with the Germans edging out the Soviets in classical references but the Soviets going full-bore realist in their socialist hero worship. Between the two stands, the symbolic tower from the exhibition of 1889: The Eiffel Tower, timeless in comparison, but definitely more modern than either of the others.

RIGHT

2.46 The Exhibition Internationale in Paris 1937. The Nazis (on left) and the Soviets (on right) face off in neo-classicist realism, with the Eiffel Tower between them. (Postcard, The Exhibition Internationale in Paris 1937.)

Source: ©DIZ Muenchen GmbH, Sueddeutsche Zeitung Photo/Alamy

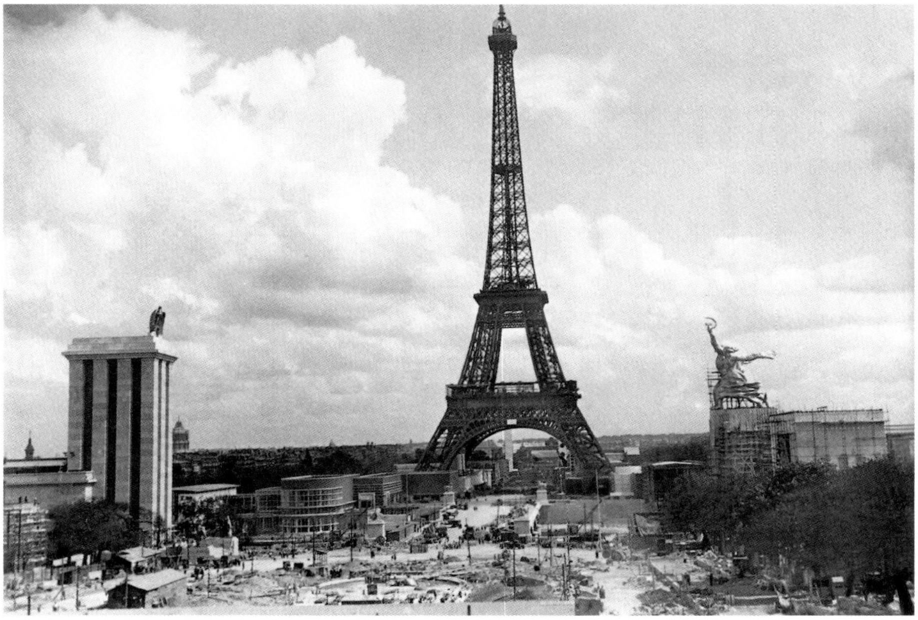

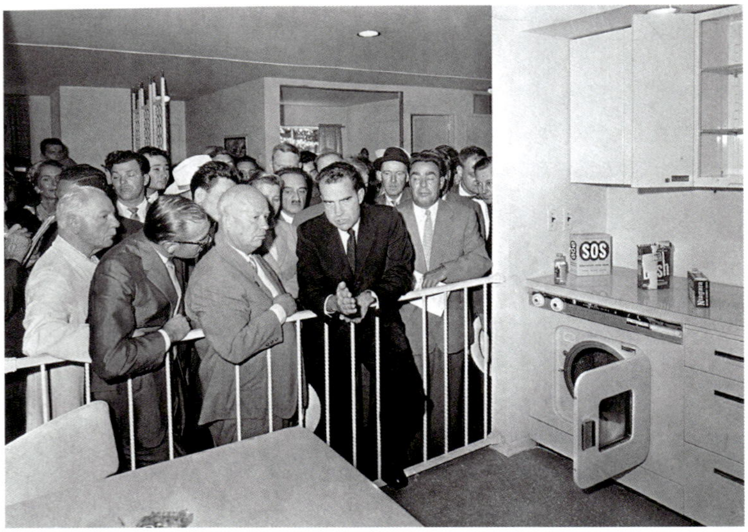

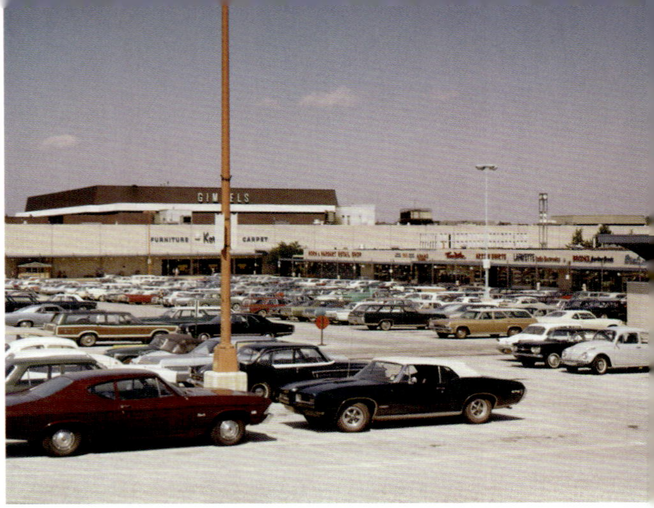

TOP LEFT

2.47 At the Moscow Exhibition in 1959, a "Kitchen Debate" took place on the relative merits of capitalist and communist societies. Capitalism aimed to win with consumer goods and weapons, the Soviets didn't take the hint and set their designers to only one side of the equation. "Nixon eventually steered the topic of competition to weapons. 'Would it not be better to compete in the relative merit of washing machines than in the strength of rockets?' 'Yes, but your generals say we must compete in rockets,' responded [Khrushchev] the Soviet leader. 'We are strong and we can beat you.'" (William Safire. 2009. "The Cold War's Hot Kitchen." *New York Times*, July 24, 2009).

Source: William Safire, 2009, *The New York Times*

TOP RIGHT

2.48 The middle class began to form its identity on consumer goods in the middle of the 19th century. One hundred years later, there seemed little alternative to most as a designed conformism framed all experience.

Source: ©ClassicStock/Alamy

FRAGMENTATION

Two major opposing powers emerged from World War II: The United States of America and the Soviet Union, the former with its infrastructure and economy not only undamaged but revived and revved up. To be able to outperform the enemy economically became the strategy, when a major war could not be fought. If *they* built one, *we* had to build a bigger one. Design related to weaponry and space travel (itself an offshoot of weapons design race) kept pace on either side of the capitalist-communist divide, but the consumer economy needed an ever-faster rotation of products and styles, while the planned economies of the Eastern Bloc had no incentive to innovate. While the Soviets looked at such pursuits as a sign of capitalism's degeneracy that would lead it to an early end, the United States government actively promoted the concept of consumer culture as a measure of freedom, sending, for example, a replica of an entire "average American home" to an exhibition in Moscow in 1959 (Fig. 2.47).

Designers in the United States certainly had their work cut out for them. The new postwar economy was booming, with a number of new households of small families changing the landscape. Like the Arnolfinis of the 15th century, they needed all the new goods to fill these homes with status markers (Fig. 2.48). Designers like Raymond Loewy created an iconic look for the mid-century in the process of creating products for the postwar American Age. From soda bottles and new car models to logos, magazines, and movies posters, there was no end to products and pop culture that needed a look, marketing, packaging, and advertising. With the help of Hollywood, a strong dollar, and a major export market to exploit in the postwar era, the center of modern cultural impact shifted to the United States and with centers of gravity of pop and youth culture in New York and California. Automobiles became the American design icon, and Hollywood films went into a new Golden Age of stardom and fame, even as voices and authors began to be heard in design, music, literature, and filmmaking that appealed to a counterculture that professed an anti-American anti-consumerism (Fig. 2.49).

New inventions flooded into the market. From plastics, man-made clothing fibers such as nylon, miniaturized electronics, and more efficient motors was assembled a Technicolor playground of consumer goods that seemed very exciting after the gray and militarized 1940s. Paris and New York became the dual suns of fashion after the offices

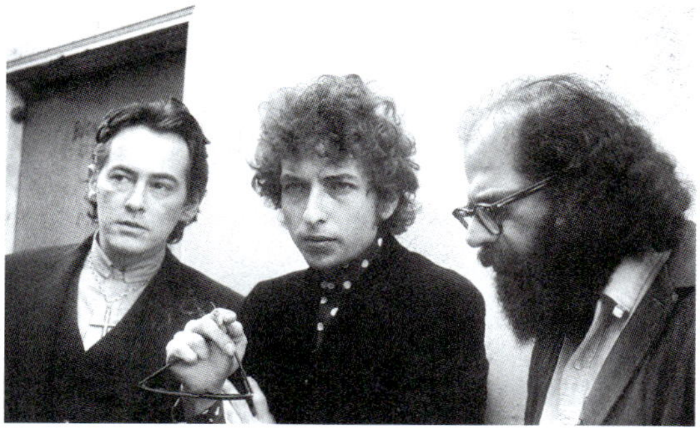

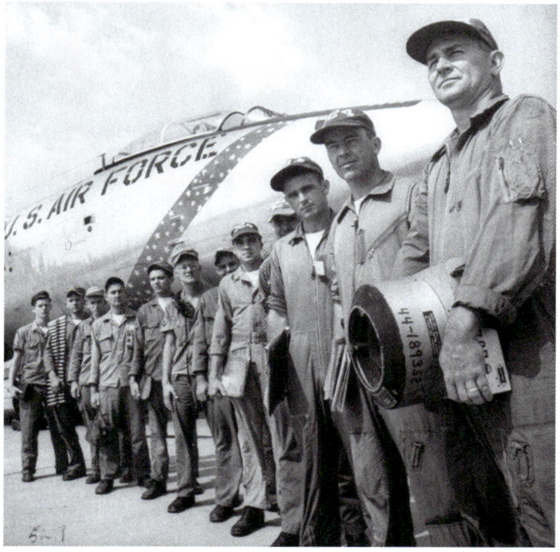

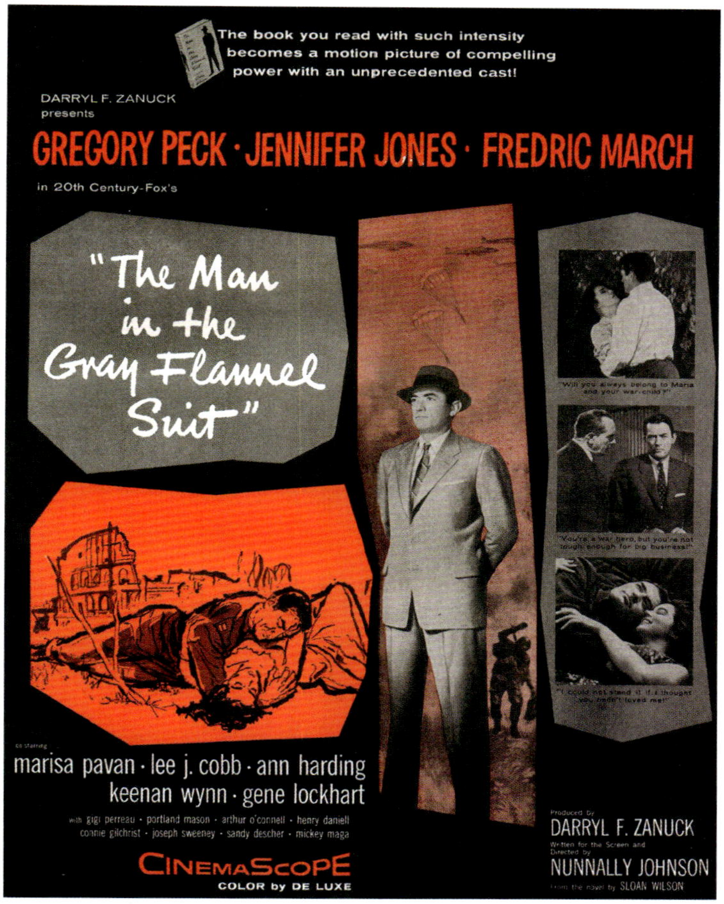

TOP LEFT

2.49 Left to right, Michael McClure, Bob Dylan, and Alan Ginsberg. By the early 1960s, even as the model of the consumer society seemed to be completely solid, counterculture figures, such as these, were voicing doubts about modern industrial society and its approach to nature, wealth, and other human beings.

Source: © 1965, 2013 Dale Smith, all rights reserved

BOTTOM LEFT AND RIGHT

2.50 The counterculture response was driven in large part by the militarization of society and the conformism of civilian life. *The Man in the Gray Flannel Suit* addressed the disillusionment of a Madison Avenue executive and his struggle for individuality.

Source: ©TopFoto/The Image Works. Photo by Peter Stackpole, Time Life Pictures/Getty Images

of *Vogue* moved to New York and the center of women's fashion stayed in Paris with the success of the designs of Christian Dior, hyped to no end by the New York editors.

Meanwhile the first stirrings of a youth revolution were underway, with disaffected youth reacting to the increased conformity and remilitarization of their society. Young artists, poets, and designers began to "drop out" of the "conformist" society they felt was forming in the post-WWII years, with the growth of suburbs and Madison Avenue marketing of consumer goods in a spreading media environment taking on a culturally conservative stance in opposition to the new perceived enemies in the Communist Bloc. The cultural identity of suburbia and Madison Avenue "gray-flannel" business was tied to owning branded consumer goods and conforming to predetermined social norms distributed by centralized media outlets (Fig. 2.50).

THE SOCIETY OF THE SPECTACLE

With the full distancing of consumer from production that was being achieved, the value of the goods packaging, surface, and label increased as fewer consumers (which is what all citizens became) knew what actually went into the making of anything. In a culture where everything has a monetary value, everything becomes a commodity and the potential value of a *name* or a brand becomes its actual value. Designing therefore became a way to add value to an otherwise relatively standard object. With appearance now all, designing was key (Fig. 2.51). This situation was brought into sharp relief by

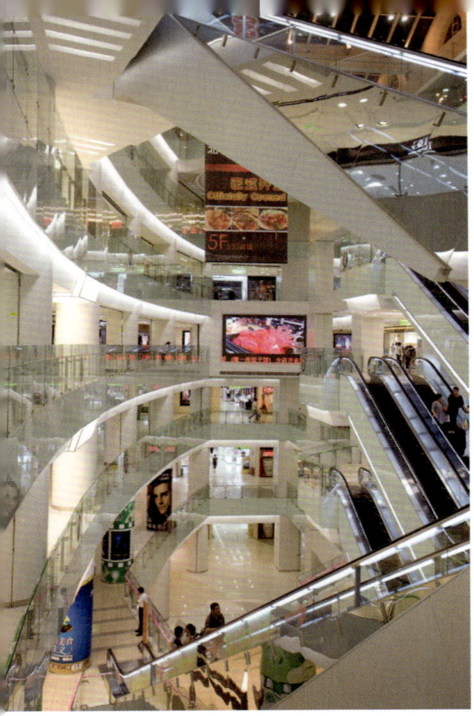

ABOVE

2.51 Thousand of goods are presented and sold, but how many are more than a re-branding of a basic product? The minor differences from one label to the next are designed to make the product the desired object. The design element and the label together make the difference.

Source: © MARKA/Alamy

the French social critic Guy Debord in the late 1960s. Debord wrote in *The Society of the Spectacle* (1968) that "all being has become having and all having derives its prestige from appearances."

He saw in the sixties that the designed society that had been going strong for almost a century had now achieved a reality of its own. There was no reference point beyond it. All our identities are projected, seen, and interpreted by the goods we own, drive, wear, and have around us. But each of these items carries only part of its potential social value if it is not *seen* to be what it is: The prestige comes from the visible affirmation that it is "this kind of thing" or "that label." Logos and branding become the order of the day. A designer label on anything at all became the way for the populace to not only signal its members' status and place in society but also to assure themselves of their own worth and special place within this imaginary world of bought identity.

But it is here that the idea of couture, in apparel for example, yields to the branded label of ready-to-wear. A couture garment is well made, lasts, and is unique. It is also expensive as a result. In the consumer culture the look quickly became more important than the quality and craftsmanship. The importance of all these factors became so lessened toward the end of the 1960s that the designer Balenciaga gave up and closed. "No one left to dress," he was said to have given as the reason. One after the other the couture labels either closed, switched to ready-to-wear, or became loss leaders (items sold at a loss to attract customers for higher priced goods) for the sale of accessories and perfumes. This is often referred to as the "Death of Fashion," but it was not fashion that was dying. On the contrary, fashion was in vigorous health as the marketplace expanded into the affluent suburbs and youth market. It was the 19th century that was fading—at long last letting go of culture. With it went both the aristocratic tendencies of Old Europe and the early modernist ideals of design in service of large social and political theories (Fig. 2.52).

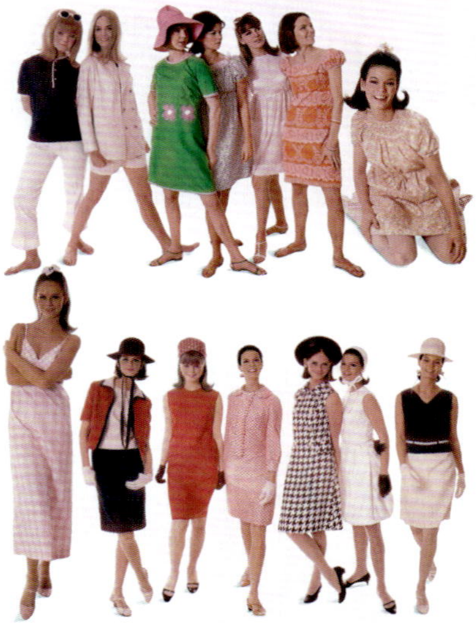

RIGHT

2.52 In the 1960s, designer fashions went mainstream and were no longer the exclusive territory of upper classes. Designers began to focus on the youth market.

Source: Courtesy of WWD

MODERNISM'S END

The organizational aspect of modern design was wearing thin by the mid-20th century. As the high-fashion world fragmented into multiple inspirations and engagements, architects also broke free of the hierarchies of modernism.

An often-cited example is how the complexity of life brought down a housing complex in St. Louis. The Pruitt-Igoe complex was designed in 1951 according to Le Corbusier's principles, by the architect Minoru Yamasaki (who would later design the Twin Towers in New York City). Meant to replace crowded slums and solve housing problems in St. Louis, the 11-story, 33-building complex containing 2,870 apartments was heralded as "Manhattan on the Mississippi." However, cost cutting during the

NETWORKING

The following list contains influential texts and sites on the Modern age of design.

THE BAUHAUS DESSAU

The site of the iconic and influential German design school.
www.bauhaus-dessau.de

THE VKHUTEMAS SCHOOL (HIGHER ART AND TECHNICAL STUDIOS, RUSSIA)

Lesser known than the Bauhaus, but equally interesting and influential.
monoskop.org/VKhUTEMAS

F. T. MARINETTI (1909): "THE FUTURIST MANIFESTO"

vserver1.cscs.lsa.umich.edu/~crshalizi/T4PM/futurist-manifesto.html

NAUM GABO AND ANTOINE PEVSNER (1920): "THE REALISTIC MANIFESTO"

davidrifkind.org/fiu/libraryfiles/gabo.the-realistic-manifesto.lib-iss.pdf

CLEMENT GREENBERG (1961): "MODERNIST PAINTING"

An essay on Modernism in Art by the influential art critic Clement Greenberg.
www.sharecom.ca/greenberg/modernism.html

WALTER BENJAMIN (1936): "THE WORK OF ART IN THE AGE OF MECHANICAL REPRODUCTION"

An essay that can be seen to presage the position and relationship of art and design in the years since.
marxists.org/reference/subject/philosophy/works/ge/benjamin.htm

STANFORD ENCYCLOPEDIA OF PHILOSOPHY: ENTRY ON MULTICULTURALISM

plato.stanford.edu/entries/multiculturalism/

STANFORD ENCYCLOPEDIA OF PHILOSOPHY: ENTRY ON POSTMODERNISM

plato.stanford.edu/entries/postmodernism/

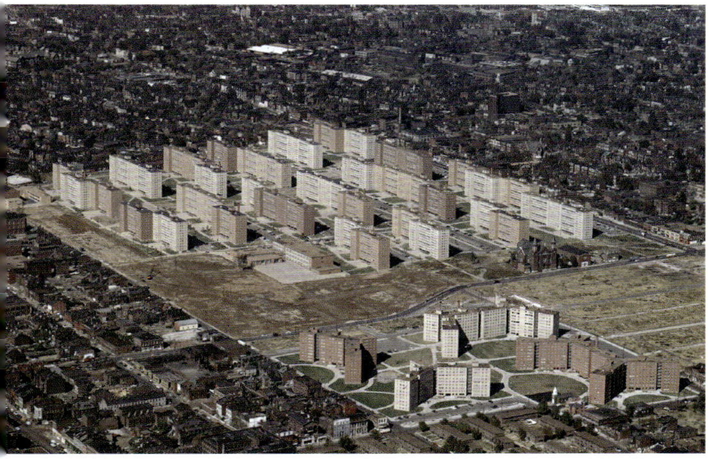

2.53 The Pruitt-Igoe housing complex in St. Louis. Thirty-three 11-story buildings envisaged as "Manhattan on the Mississippi." The reality quickly appeared very different as the community that was envisaged seemed not to be able to form in the environment as designed.

Source: Courtesy of United States Geological Survey.

construction phase led to a lower-quality environment than had been originally envisaged. After completion in 1956, it quickly fell into disrepair. The design of the complex has been blamed for the lack of social cohesion that allowed the area to deteriorate into visual and social decay. A sense of community never developed among the inhabitants, and the complex succumbed to social alienation and urban blight with rising rates of vandalism and crime[17] (Fig. 2.53). By 1968 inhabitants were being encouraged to leave. Starting on July 15, 1972, the entire complex was demolished over the following four years.

Charles Jencks, an architectural theorist, later declared July 15, 1972, the day that "modern architecture died." Blaming architecture for a failure of a number of public policies and the pressures of economic, racial, and industrial politics of a declining city in the 1960s may be an overdramatization.[18] However, it certainly signaled the death of the tech-and-systems worship of the Futurist wing of modern design and highlights the inability of High Modernism to anticipate the irrational messiness of human existence and the importance of the symbolic in a human environment (Fig. 2.54).

The architect Robert Venturi had already begun questioning the laws governing modernist design when writing for the Museum of Modern Art in 1966. He suggested that the simplification process of the modernists' functionality ideal too often led to bland designs that were lacking in excitement. To the Modernist dictum of "less is more," Venturi responded "less is a bore." In opposition to the vision of mechanical organization and high-rise new cities, Venturi maintained that the random

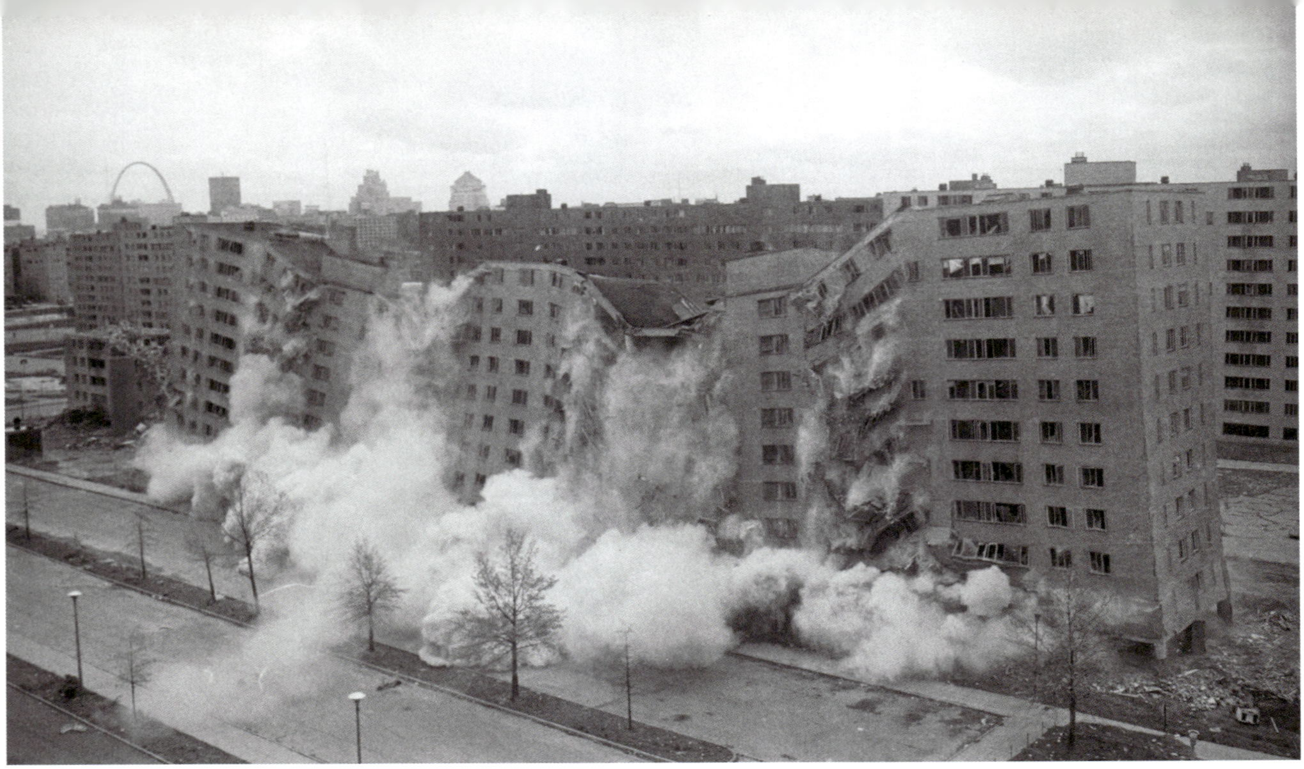

ABOVE
2.54 The failure of Pruitt-Igoe has become a symbol of the failure of the Modernist design program. What failed was much more than what can be laid only at the door of the architects. The grand design itself was flawed from the start, in that the large-scale design of human communities failed –or was unable to– take into account the messiness, randomness and haphazardness of human behavior.

Source: ©Bettmann/CORBIS

complexities of modern environments resulted in cityscapes with an inherent style resulting *from* the "honky tonk" messiness, rather than in spite of it.[19]

Around the time Pruitt-Igoe was being prepared for demolition, Venturi, two other faculty members of the Yale School of Architecture (Denise Scott Brown, and Steven Izenour), and a dozen students went to Las Vegas and studied the urban sprawl, visual intensity, and unfettered development of commercial strips. In their 1972 study—a research project conducted at Yale—one of the observations made on the streetscape of Route 66 jumps out when considering the development of modern design: "The sign is more important than the architecture. . . . The sign at the front is a vulgar extravaganza, the building at back a modest necessity. . . . If you take the signs away, there is no place" (Fig. 2.55).[20]

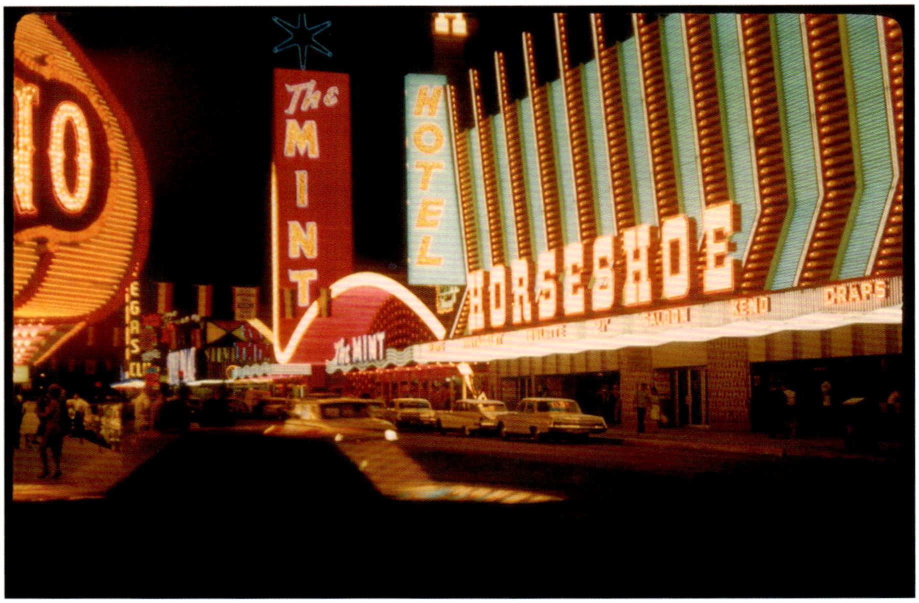

RIGHT
2.55 "If you take the signs away, there is no place," wrote Robert Venturi. The Las Vegas strip of the 1960s is all symbols, but also a realization of Dada-esque freedom, as in the Dada manifesto: ". . . a roaring of tense colors, and interlacing of opposites and of all contradictions, grotesques, inconsistencies: LIFE."

Source: ©Archive Image/Alamy

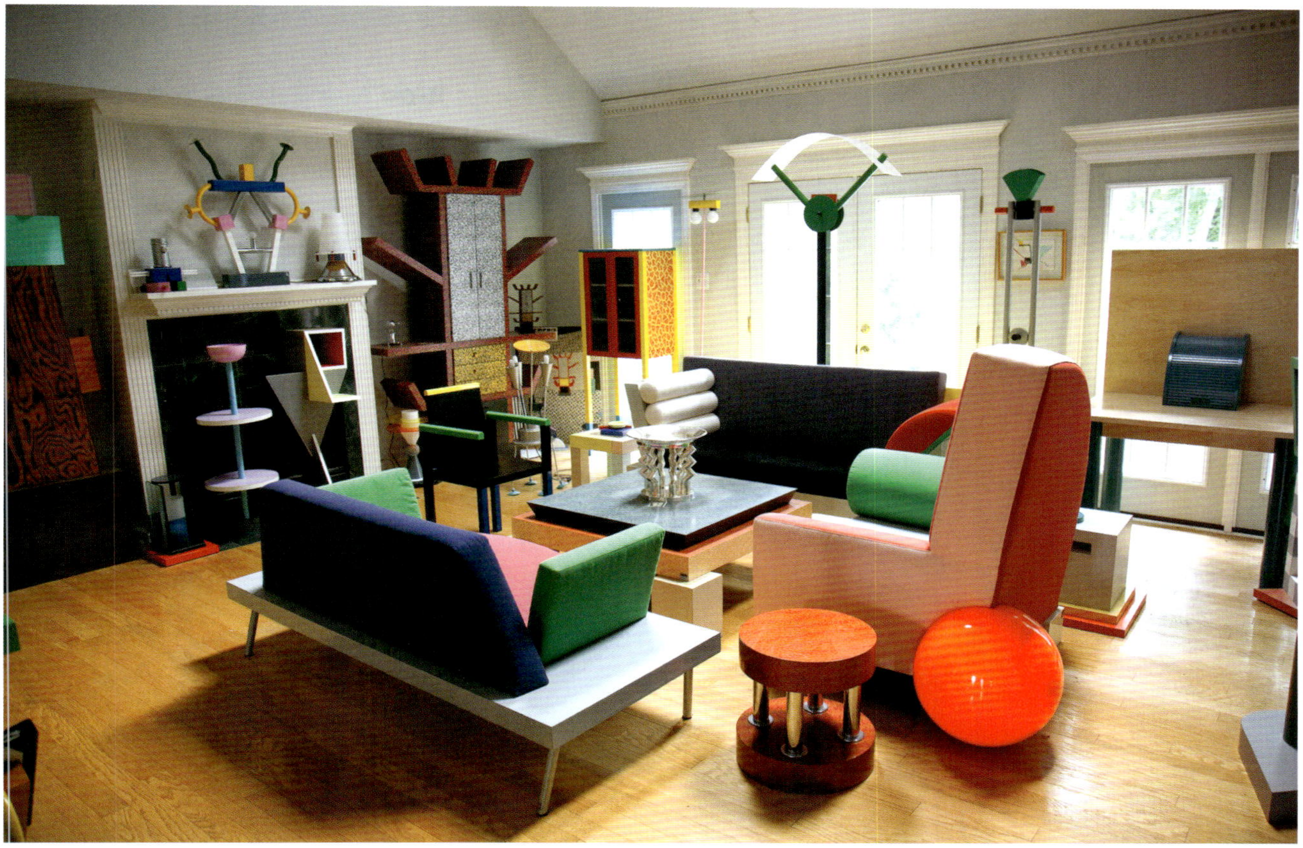

2.56 The Memphis Group's "Milano" design collection. Although perhaps dated a generation later, the Memphis design retains a playfulness with hints of anarchy.

Source: Courtesy of Zanone Studio www.memphis-milano.org

The massed clamor of visual input, the extravaganza brings to mind Tristan Tzara's Dadaist demand for "Freedom: Dada Dada Dada, a roaring of tense colors, and interlacing of opposites and of all contradictions, grotesques, inconsistencies: LIFE." The life that Modernist planners seemed to neglect sprouted of its own accord from underneath the theorized designed surface a few years later when Punk and New Wave fashions led the way out. In the late 1970s and in the early 1980s, an attempt to break away from the reigning direction of sleek black boxes and beige technology was successfully made by a group of architects and designers in Milan under the leadership of Ettore Sottsass. The *Memphis Group* created a sensation when they first exhibited at the 1981 Milan Furniture Fair, by adopting styles as jumbled and colorful as the extravaganza of Las Vegas. They threw out the rules and took on a role of playful experimentation with color, shape, and materials. Memphis became the Dadaist Punk gate-crashing the cool suave *haute-design* of the early 1980s New York–Paris axis (Fig. 2.56).

CONCLUSION

Toward the end of the century, the headquarters of international design shifted from Europe to a rapidly globalizing United States of America. The Americanization of global style that ensued led to a lack of adherence to culture, while a dismissal of tradition allowed the experimentation of styles to multiply, each in its own non-localized world. History in the postmodern condition is not linear: *Retro* is just another style. Even the idea of the designer in the present day is transformed. What used to be a very elite group with all its political leanings and manifestos has now been altered into a working idea of the professional with all the requisite training in any of an enormous number of programs in an equally large number of schools all over the world. Designing has gone fully mainstream and is incorporating all the technologies available.

Designers are less and less instructed in the actual handcraft involved in the area of their ever-narrowing expertise except to develop a familiarity and vocabulary as the relationship of the artisan craftsperson and the designer, separated in the 19th century, has grown more and more distant. A student entering design programs in the second decade of the 21st century may expect not only to be taught the classical elements, principles, methods, and histories from the Renaissance onward but also to be instructed in CAD (computer-aided design), the creation and use of websites and nonphysical methods of modeling, presentation skills, and business practices. The increasing use of digital communication and online social media seems, however, to be resulting in increasing desire to return to the tactile, and likely artisan manufacturing and the trend toward locally versus globally constructed products will continue to rise as the economies change.

KEY TERMS

Classicism	Modernism	Constructivism
Neoclassicism	Futurism	Postmodern condition

DISCUSSION AND REVIEW QUESTIONS

1. Consider your environment. Look at clothing, furniture, buildings, vehicles, objects, and tools. How many design influences from the past 500 years can you identify? Is there a prevalence of one style over another in a particular area of design? Which period styles are not to be seen? Why might this be?

2. Pick one common item in everyday life, such as a gadget, a piece of furniture, or a common item of clothing, and consider its design history. Can you remember significant changes? What did it replace and when? How do you think it might change in the future? Why?

3. How does your cultural identification rely on design? What designed products do you use or wear that make you feel as if you belong to a specific group, nation, or subculture? What are the significant elements that allow this identification?

4. Identify *political designing* in your environment. Consider the streets, buildings, and clothing styles surrounding you. Is there a discernible message about society evident in the designs? ("Conservative?" "Liberal?" "Traditional?" "Avant-garde?") Is there a conflicting message? Why?

EXERCISES AND ASSIGNMENTS

1. Choose a room in your home, school, or workplace where you can spend some time looking around.
   a. List all the different period styles or influences from period styles you can find. Use any resources you can to help you.
   b. Is there a clear difference in where these appear? (For example, all furniture is one style but the architecture of the room is another.) How does this manifest and why do you think this is so?
2. Now consider whether you can observe influences from different cultural spheres.
   a. List any ethnic influences you can find.
   b. List any classical styles.
   c. List any items that seem to be influenced by pop culture.
   d. Why, in each case, do you suppose each style is found in this environment?
3. Consider the three most recent furnishings and/or items of clothing you bought.
   a. Explain whether you chose them for visual appeal, functional ability, or both.
   b. What was the visual appeal? Describe it as best you can. What makes it work visually for you?
   c. What is the function of these items? Do they work? If not, what could be improved by design?
   d. How do you think your design sensibilities are different from those of the previous generations (your parents, teachers, etc.)? What do you value in design that they did not? What about the other way around?

REFERENCES

1. Jean-François Lyotard, *The Postmodern Condition: A Report on Knowledge* (Minneapolis: University of Minnesota Press, 1984).
2. Monica R. Gale, *Myth and Poetry in Lucretius* (Cambridge: Cambridge University Press, 1994) 223.
3. John Ruskin, "The Nature of Gothic," in *The Stones of Venice*, vol. II, 1885 (Project Gutenberg, 2009), http://www.gutenberg.org/files/30755/30755-h/30755-h.htm.
4. Partha Mitte, *Art and Nationalism in Colonial India, 1850–1922: Occidental Orientations* (Cambridge: Cambridge University Press, 1994), 221–223.
5. Georg Lukacs, *Goethe and His Age*, trans. Robert Anchor (London: Grosset & Dunlap, 1969).
6. Walter Crane, *Ideals in Art: Papers Theoretical Practical Critical* (London: George Bell & Son, 1905), http://chestofbooks.com/arts/essays/Theoretical-Practical-Critical-Ideals/index.html.

7. Crane.

8. John Sullivan. *The Tall Office Building Artistically Considered.* (Philadelphia: Lippincott, 1896), https://archive.org/details/tallofficebuildi00sull.

9. Giacomo Balla. "Futurist Men's Clothing: A Manifesto," in *Futurism: An Anthology,* edited by Christine Poggi and Laura Wittman (New Haven, CT: Yale University Press, 2009), 194 ff.

10. Antonio Sant'Elia. "Manifesto of Futurist Architecture," in *Rethinking Architectural Technology,* edited by William W. Braham and Jonathan A. Hale (London: Routledge, 2013), 15 ff.

11. Lucius Burkhardt, *The Werkbund: History and Ideology* (Hauppauge, NY: Barron's, 1980), 13.

12. Ulrike Muller, *Bauhaus Women* (Paris: Flammarion, 2009).

13. Günter Berghaus. "Futurism, Dada, and Surrealism: Some Cross-Fertilization Among the Historical Avant-gardes," in *International Futurism in Arts and Literature* (New York: de Gruyter, 2000), 289–290.

14. Naum Gabo, Antoine Pevsner. "The Realistic Manifesto." (Moscow: Second State Printing House, 1920), http://davidrifkind.org/fiu/library_files/gabo.the-realistic-manifesto.lib-iss.pdf

15. Gabo.

16. Le Corbusier, *Précisions* (Paris: Les Éditions G. *Crès* & Cie, 1930). Quoted in Mary McLeod, "Undressing Architecture: Fashion Gender and Modernity," in *Back from Utopia,* edited by Hubert-Jan Henket and Hilde Heynen (Rotterdam: Uitgeverij 010 Publishers, 2002), 321.

17. Alexander von Hoffman, "Why They Built the Pruitt-Igoe Project," Joint Center for Housing Studies, Harvard University, http://www.soc.iastate.edu/sapp/PruittIgoe.html.

18. See also Katharine G. Bristol, "The Pruitt-Igoe Myth," *Journal of Architectural Education* 44, no. 3 (May 1991), 163–171.

19. Robert Venturi, *Complexity and Contradiction in Architecture,* 2nd ed. (New York: Museum of Modern Art, 1977).

20. Robert Venturi, Denise Scott Brown, Steven Izenour, *Learning from Las Vegas: The Forgotten Symbolism of Architectural Form,* rev. ed. (Cambridge, MA: MIT Press, 1977), 17–18.

CHAPTER 3

THE ELEMENTS OF DESIGN

DESIGNERS SPEAK

"In designing hardware to be used every day, it was important to keep both the human aspects and the machine in mind. What looks good also often feels good."

—MICHAEL GRAVES

"I am also very fascinated by the way one can transform cloth and make it do things that it doesn't always do. Architecture is how the person places herself in the space. Fashion is about how you place the object on the person. That's why for a long time I liked some of the early Japanese work by Issey Miyake and Yohji Yamamoto—they were so structured that it was like wearing a different material. With shoes it's all about sculpture—how to design a column. They have to land somewhere."

—ZAHA HADID, quoted in Louise McCready, "Form in Motion: Architect Zaha Hadid on Her Exhibit at the Philadelphia Museum of Art," *Vogue,* September 23, 2011. www.vogue.com/culture/article/form-in-motion-architect-zaha-hadid-on-her-exhibit-at-the-philadelphia-museum-of-art.

OBJECTIVES

Distinguish the basic elements of design.

Characterize the distinct nature of each element.

Identify ways in which these elements are used to further designing.

Recognize the importance of adding *time* to the traditional list of elements.

To understand the nature of the world and the things in it, we break things down: we investigate the elements. We wonder: "What are the basic ingredients and how do they work?" We may therefore ask: "What are the components of a designer's creativity? What do designers use to appeal to our senses and emotions?" To understand the art and craft of designing, an easy familiarity with the basic elements must be developed. A student of design must investigate the basic elements, just as a craftsperson explores the tools and materials for creating an object. Using a very limited set of sensual elements, designers work according to an equally limited set of aesthetic principles to create an endless array of designs of varying degrees of practicality for an enormous range of clients and audiences. The basic elements of design are considered to be line, shape, color, texture and pattern, and space. Now, however, we will break with tradition and add the consideration of time as an element of design, to incorporate the user experience into the framework.

AN INCREASING DIMENSIONALITY

Just like elements in nature or the basic raw materials of industry, a surprising thing about the elements of design is how few they really are: **color, line, texture** and **pattern, shape,** and **space** have traditionally been listed as the five *elements* of design. It is, however, clear that a sixth element, **time,** must be added to the art of design, just as it was added to our understood framework of dimensions a century ago, when the three dimensions of space were no longer sufficient to describe the nature of the world.

With this in mind, the order in which we will consider the elements of design follows a pattern of increasing dimensionality (Fig. 3.1). We begin with the nondimensional experience of *color*, then look at the single dimension of an implied or mathematical *line*, and then examine the two-dimensionality of *patterns*. Patterns dovetail with *texture* where the third dimension shows up. *Shape*, on the other hand, requires a discussion that lies between (or bridges) two- and three-dimensionality, as shape begins to imply motion. *Space* and *motion* can be implied in two dimensions; however, *actual motion* requires *actual space* to move within as well as *time* for there to be any motion at all. Thus, we have not only the full three dimensions but also a fourth. An *experience* of space requires *time*, but perceiving space is not the only—or even the most obvious—way in which humans perceive the world through time. *Time*, by ordering our perception into *before, during*, and *after*, is present in all our experience of the world and all things in it. It also plays a part in defining our relationship to things by how we engage with the world over time and by an understanding of time passed, through learning, memory, and nostalgia. This means that a designer must be aware of the relationship formed with the designed object over time and know how to incorporate and allow for the lived experience in the design of an object, space, or event.

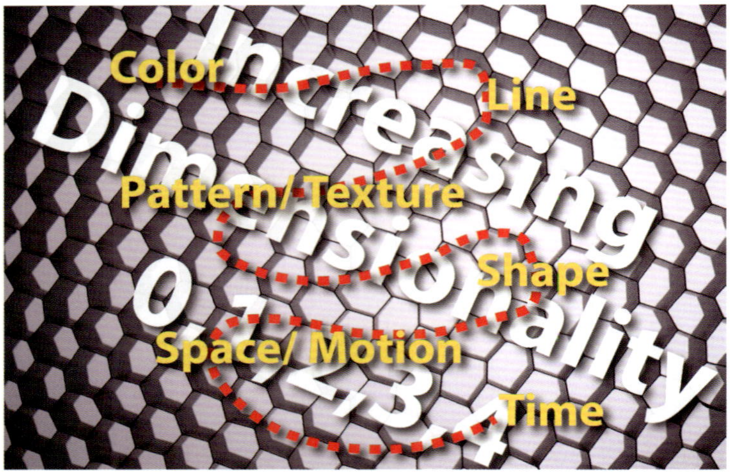

3.1 The elements of design can be considered in a pattern of increasing dimensionality: Color in itself has no dimension, line has one, pattern two and then also three, and so does shape. Then we go on into three-dimensionality with textures. Three dimensions give us space, volume, and ultimately motion (in space) that requires time to be realized.

Source: Illustration by Karl Aspelund

A recent development in human history makes this all the more important a consideration. More and more of our immediate experiences and relationships now take place via electronic screens, changing the lived human experience of the world as it relates directly to design, space, and time. On these screens, time and space are distorted and illusionary; our experience is broken up into separate and irregular units through cuts, hits, links, and various shifts that take place either as a result of our actions or as a part of the structure of the experience (narratives take place in sound bites and scenes; information is fragmented into hyperlinked screens, status updates, and short bursts of text). For this reason, time must be included in this discussion as an element of design: It is underlying our experience of the world and is increasingly significant as our interaction with the world becomes more fragmented, layered, and *in the moment* through electronic media.

COLOR

Color is a topic for lifelong study. Apart from the emotional and psychological directions, it can be approached from many points of departure within industrial applications, art, science, and all different disciplines of design. To begin understanding color in design, we must first construct a framework of terms and concepts as well as take a brief look at the theoretical basis of color study and the appearance and effect of color in the world. First, we will look at color using four basic dimensions: hue, value, intensity, and temperature.

HUE

The *hue* of a color is the name that identifies the pure color as represented on a color wheel, as located in an area on a simple spectrum of primary and secondary colors: red, violet, blue, green, yellow, and orange (Fig. 3.2). This, however, is usually not enough information to work with. Looking around, one might very rapidly spot a dozen different items of any given hue. For example, one might find several colors on different things that all could be said to be the color blue. However, each of these blues may actually be different. Some of them may even be marginally blue, appearing on the edge of green or violet. Some may be darker, some lighter, some pale, some intense, and so on.

Partly, this is a function of language and culture. Some languages have more finely defined names of color than others. Icelandic, for example, does not contain specific words to identify the colors that the English language points to as orange or violet. Rather, it uses composite words to point in a circular fashion to objects of those colors: The words are literally translated as "yellow of [the fruit] orange" (*appelsínugulur)* and "blue of [the flower] violet" (*fjólublár*).

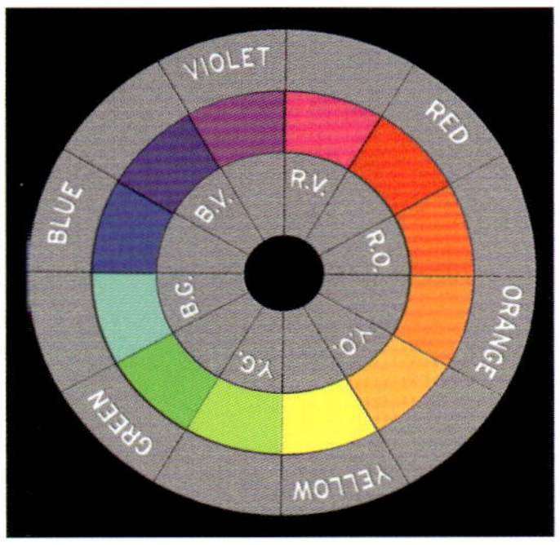

ABOVE
3.2 The *hue* of a color is the name that identifies the pure color as represented on a color wheel, locating it in an area on a simple spectrum of primary and secondary colors: red, violet, blue, green, yellow, and orange.

Source: Illustration by Karl Aspelund

VALUE

The *value* is determined by placing the color in a continuum of light to darkness—that is, white to black (Fig. 3.3). This is the brightness (or darkness) scale, not to be confused with the *intensity* of the color.

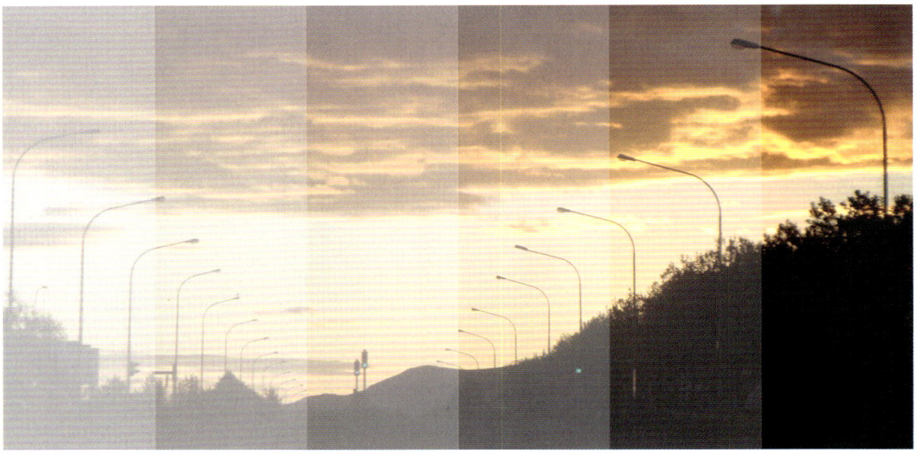

RIGHT
3.3 The *value* is a placing of color in a continuum of light to darkness.

Source: Illustration by Karl Aspelund

INTENSITY

Intensity refers to the saturation of a color on a surface or in solution. It is the *amount* of color, as opposed to the lightness or darkness indicated by *value*. In paint, this would be considered the amount of pigment in the solution. The intensity of a design's color scheme creates an emotional response where a level of excitement tends to increase with higher color saturation (Fig. 3.4).

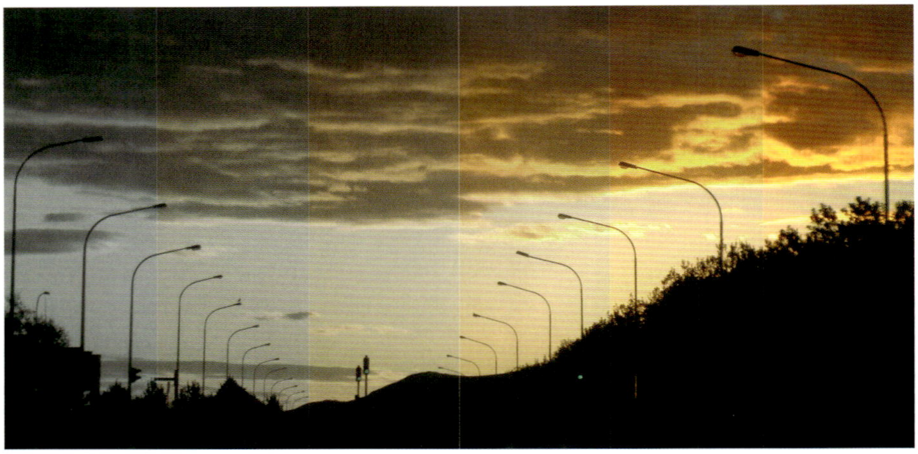

RIGHT
3.4 *Intensity*, also called *chroma*, refers to the saturation of color—the amount of pigment in paint, for example.

Source: Illustration by Karl Aspelund

TEMPERATURE

The *temperature* of a color can be brought into discussion in both a technical and a psychological sense. The latter is of more immediate interest and impact. With color being the design element that most directly appeals to human sensibilities in a very wide range of intensity, the sense of temperature has the most direct physical connection. A sense of *warm* is connected to the yellow-orange-red scale, while the green-blue side is *cool*. This allows a direct path to the viewer's nervous system, by appealing to a nearly innate sense of temperature. Lighting, paint, and dyes can produce a sense of comfort and calm, or urgency and precision, by utilizing color schemes based on a warm or cool scheme (Fig. 3.5). Levels of interest can be created by juxtaposing warm and cool colors to produce focal points and contrast (Fig. 3.6).

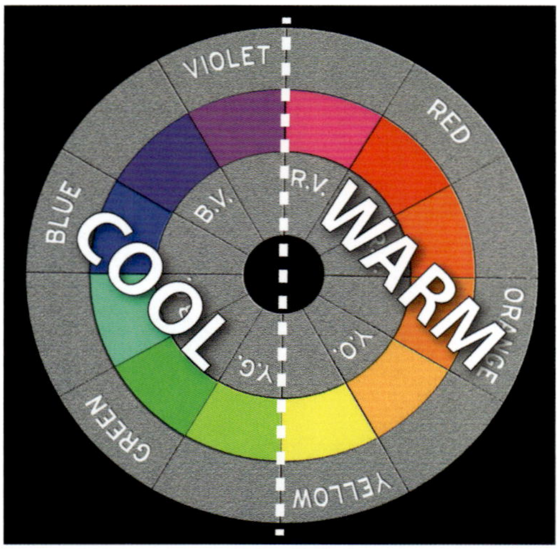

BELOW LEFT
3.5 A sense of *warm* is connected to the yellow-orange-red scale, while the green-blue side is *cool*.

Source: Illustration by Karl Aspelund

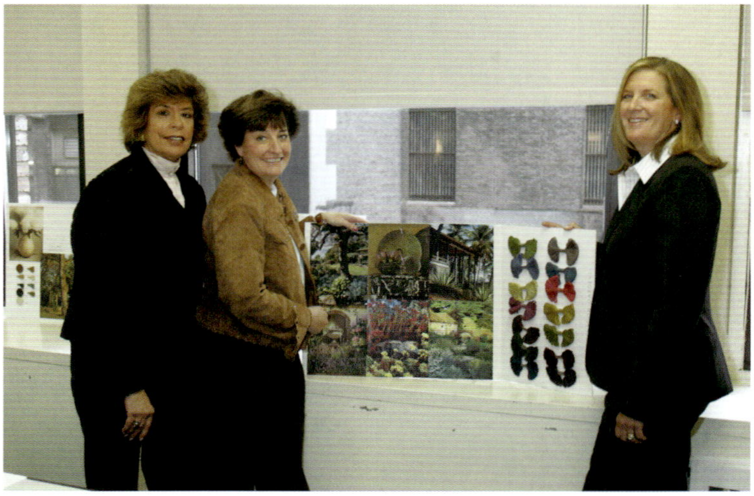

BELOW RIGHT
3.6 Designers use warm and cool schemes directly to create coherence and interest. The schematic colors tie the collection together and create a totality that becomes more interesting to a viewer by being a large, connected whole. The totality of the collection bound together in a color scheme is more impactful than just a collection of disparate parts.

Source: Photographs by Robert Mitra/WWD

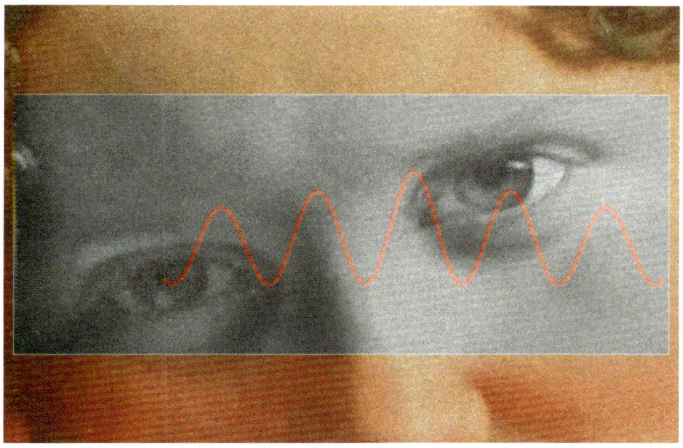

ABOVE

3.7 Color is the result of our nervous system interpreting the energy input of varying wavelengths of light on the nerve endings in our eyes. The height of the wave determines the energy delivered, which we interpret as degrees of brightness.

Source: Illustration by Karl Aspelund.

BELOW

3.8 A rendering of black-body radiation at temperatures ranging from 550 K to 6,500 K (kelvin units) and the color scale above.

Source: Image courtesy of Tim C. Schröder.

COLOR THEORIES

The more technical understanding of color temperature brings us to a discussion of color theories. Color is the result of our nervous system interpreting the energy input of varying wavelengths of light on the nerve endings in our eyes. On one end of the visible spectrum, we have violet and blue, and at the other end, at not quite twice the wavelength, we find red. The height of the wave determines the energy delivered, which we interpret as degrees of brightness (Fig. 3.7). In terms of light, colors are classified technically—scientifically—as cool to warm according to the light an otherwise featureless object (a *black body*) will emit at a certain temperature. This is used to calibrate computer screens and digital photography among a myriad of scientific applications and is important in coordinating digitally produced designs to physical color samples (Fig. 3.8).

But while *scientific* color is about wavelengths of light and *artistic* color is (still) mainly about pigment, the division in design is not that clear-cut. Color for onscreen design also involves light and will therefore continue to increase in relative importance in designs and presentations as communication switches more and more to live-screen events. However, the emphasis in design in still for the most part on physical representations of color in dyes, pigments, paint, and ink.

COLOR SYSTEMS

Color can be either understood as a *subtractive* system of pigments or an *additive* system of light. The *RGB* color model refers to the Red, Green, and Blue light in an *additive* system that creates color on electronic screens. It is referred to as additive because it begins with black (no light) and then light is added until the desired color

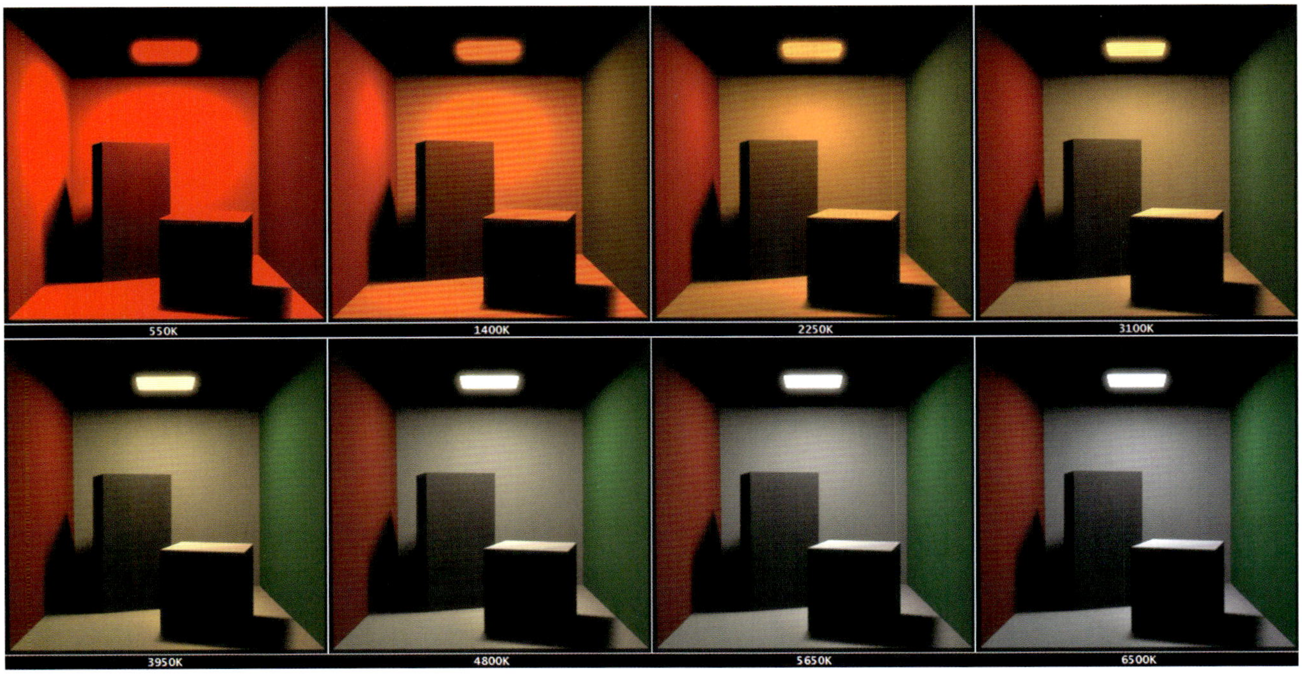

TIMELINE: DESIGN ELEMENTS IN HISTORY

The evolution of human culture and identity is woven through with the development and innovative use of design elements. It is punctuated with innovation related to the approach to them and the technologies involved in their use and creation. Quickly going down the list of elements and observing their historical presence in the design of modern urban culture reveals a continuous flow and experimentation.

The use of *line* has fluctuated between an emphasis on curvature and an emphasis on straight-line geometry since the rise of cities. In modern (*Western*) urban culture, the first shift in line is, however, clearly visible in the transition from vertical to horizontal as the medieval Gothic gave way to the Greco-Roman classic revival of the Renaissance. The disintegration of line was rapid over the course of the 18th century as late-Baroque evolved into Rococo. This was then answered by a return to the structured mathematical geometries of neoclassicism in the 19th century that set the pattern for modern cities. Baron Haussmann's urban planning of Paris, resulting in the long, straight boulevards of Paris, and the grid-plan layout of New York City that was proposed in 1807 and put into effect a few years later, became the templates on which cities all over the world have been planned and renovated.

PATTERNS AND TEXTURE

Using *pattern and texture* has been a part of human culture since its very beginning; it may, in fact, be seen as one of the signals of humanity's arrival. Decorative patterns on accessories and in weaving are an early signal of human culture all over the globe, and evidence is visible from the transition from pre-human to Neanderthal culture. As capabilities and technologies progressed, patterns became more and more complex, with multiple colors and symmetries rising to levels of enormous complexity in the architecture of Islamic culture. Technologies of dyes and synthetic textiles in the 19th and 20th centuries have allowed the mass manufacturing of patterned and textured apparel and interior textiles to the point where there absence is nearly unimaginable in urban society.

SHAPE AND VOLUME

Shape and *volume* has been stretched, expanded, and experimented with, but the tolerances of natural materials kept structures in check until the Industrial Age. Clothes, rooms, and buildings tended toward roughly human proportions, even in grand structures. Entering the 20th century a rethinking of shape and volume began in the constructivist experimentation in the Soviet Union and the men and women of the Bauhaus School in Germany. Meanwhile, Cubists in France were inspired to reevaluate the representation of shape and volume by African art. Classical notions have been very strongly held to, however, but deconstructivist architecture in the late 20th century has pointed to new approaches. Human shape and ergonomics inevitably remain a framework for human design.

SPACE AND MOTION

For thousands of years of human history, *space* and *motion* went unchallenged, as humans were bound to the speeds and ranges defined by gravity and human or animal locomotion. Then trains, telegraph, radio, motorcars, airplanes, and spaceflight redefined the human relationship with space and motion in rapid succession over a century. In the last half-century, the changes in perception of distance and connection have been just as dramatic, with the quick adoption and spread of television and Internet connectivity. Despite this, it is still human space and human motion that is being translated by technology, and the capabilities of humans "on the ground" are inevitably the yardstick. Developments in progress in Internet-connected work at a distance, drones, robotics, and exoskeletal structures may cause a further shift in the experience of human space in coming years.

TIME AND EXPERIENCE

Just as space and motion area altered by technology, *time* and *experience* have been reordered and opened up in the more recent centuries of human culture. The invention of accurate timepieces for navigation and communication brought mechanical order to human culture and the invention of electric light and telegraph changed the approach to how time and information were ordered and planned in business and war. Einstein's work on the relativity of space and time brought a new philosophy of time and experience to the world, while time was reordered much in the same way as space by the advent of radio, television, and the Internet. All the human-experienced dimensions of space and time have indeed been altered in their perception by technology and design.

COLOR

Finally, *color* theories and developments have been enormously affected by scientific and technological developments in the modern age. A brief description of this history is best served as a timeline:

- **1704:** Sir Isaac Newton publishes *Optiks* in which—among other things—he explains the nature of light and how it may be separated into component colors. He also showed how color is produced from the interaction of light with materials, through absorption, reflection, and transmission.
- **1810:** Johan Wolfgang von Goethe publishes his *Theory of Colours.*

- **1839:** *The Law of Simultaneous Color Contrast (De la loi du contraste simultané des couleurs et de l'assortiment des objets colorés.)* by the French industrial chemist Michel Eugène Chevreul.
- **1855:** The three-color method, which is the foundation of virtually all practical color processes whether chemical or electronic, was first suggested in an 1855 paper on color vision by Scottish physicist James Clerk Maxwell.
- **1856:** William Henry Perkin, at the age of 18, discovers a method of creating synthetic dye, inventing the aniline dye mauveine, a strong purple color.
- **1868:** Louis Ducos du Hauron patents the production of photographic three-color prints on paper.
- **1873:** German chemist Hermann Wilhelm Vogel discovers that the addition of small amounts of certain aniline dyes to a photographic emulsion can add sensitivity to colors which the dyes absorbed.
- **1879:** *Modern Chromatics* published by the American physicist Ogden Rood.
- **1905:** Albert H. Munsell publishes *A Color Notation,* in which he begins to develop a system based on how people perceive colors rather than by mathematical definition.
- **1915:** The Textile Color Card Association of the United States (TCCA) is formed to better predict and set upcoming color and style trends.
- **1919–1922:** Johannes Itten teaches at the Bauhaus, developing the innovative "preliminary course," which was to teach students the basics of material characteristics, composition, and color.
- **1932:** Technicolor introduced. It is a new color process—"Process 4," with one negative for each primary color and a *matrix* to improve contrast. This becomes the standard for major Hollywood studio filmmaking.
- **1935:** American Kodak introduces Kodachrome, the first modern integral color film.
- **1955:** The TCCA (1915) becomes the Color Association of the United States (CAUS).
- **1963:** Pantone Company introduces its initial Pantone Matching System Printers' Edition. The Pantone name is known worldwide as the standard language for color communication from designer to manufacturer to retailer to customer.
- **1966:** The first all-color primetime season on television begins in the fall.
- **1981:** IBM's first color graphics card is produced along with the first color computer display standard for the IBM PC.

is achieved (Fig. 3.9a). On electronic screens the light is not mixed as such, but rather, minute dots, *pixels,* are made up of three tiny light sources that switch on as red, green, or blue, which are then blended in our perception into the resulting hue, with their added intensities producing the final color (Fig. 3.9b).

The *CMYK* process, on the other hand, is the *subtractive* printing process method of printing color by using four inks—Cyan, Magenta, Yellow, and black (Key). Nearly all printed material is currently produced under the CMYK process. The colors are referred to as *spot colors,* and by layering color onto (usually) white paper, the ink *subtracts* from the reflected light to produce the hue. Usually a black under-layer controls the intensity of the color, by tempering the amount of light—again by *subtraction* (Fig. 3.9c).

The two most common color theories in use today, those of Goethe and Munsell, have largely been in use for a century (Fig. 3.10). Goethe's system is the most commonly known and uses three primary colors—red, yellow, and blue—to create the entire spectrum. Munsell's system, however, uses green and violet as well, acknowledging that a satisfactory violet or green cannot be produced from pigments by the other three.

Professor Alfred Munsell, of Boston, Massachusetts, developed his color system around the beginning of the 20th century, with the aim to accurately describe colors using numerical references. Each color is represented by three numbers denoting the *hue, value,* and *chroma* (intensity). Munsell arranged colors into a cylindrical shape where the hues go around horizontally, intensities (chroma) are arranged from the central axis outward, and the values are arranged from top (white) to bottom (black).

With manufacturing of designs often taking place at a distance from the designer, in any number of different areas of the world, precise information is crucial. The Pantone company produces a color system that has become close to being a worldwide standard by providing a standardization of colors

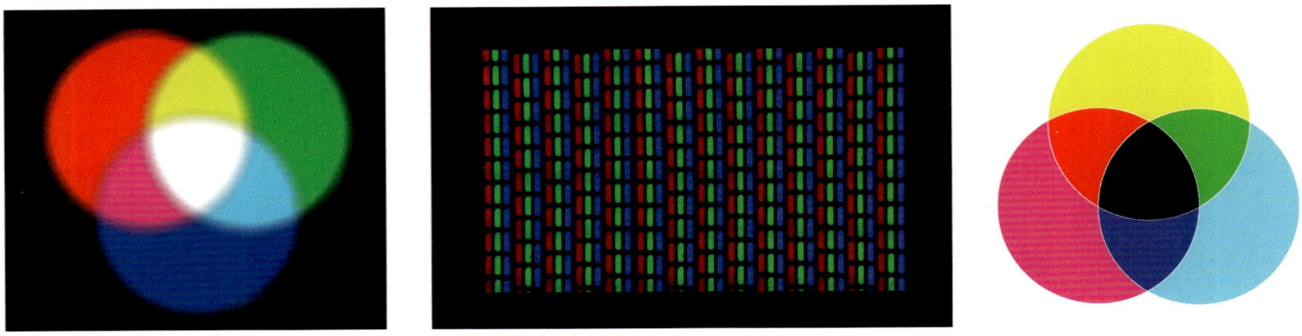

A B C

3.9 (A) The RGB color model refers to the red, green, and blue light in an additive system. It is referred to as additive because it begins with black (no light), and then light is added until the desired color is achieved. (B) On electronic screens, pixels are made up of three tiny light sources that switch on as red, green, or blue, which blend into the requisite hue. Their brightness directs the intensity. (C) Nearly all printed material is currently produced under the CMYK process. The colors are referred to as spot colors, and by layering color onto (usually) white paper, the ink subtracts from the reflected light to produce the hue.

Source: Illustration by Karl Aspelund

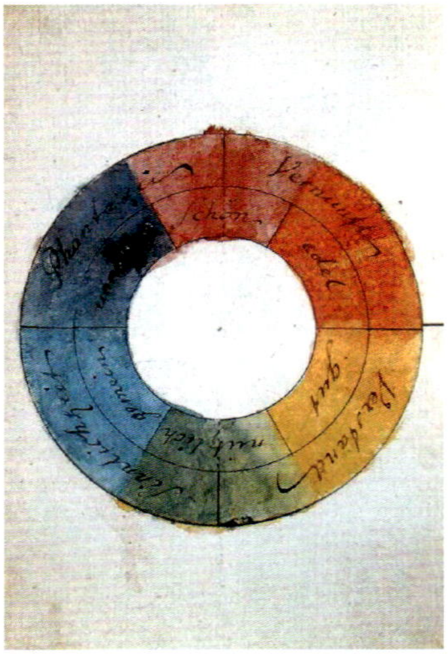

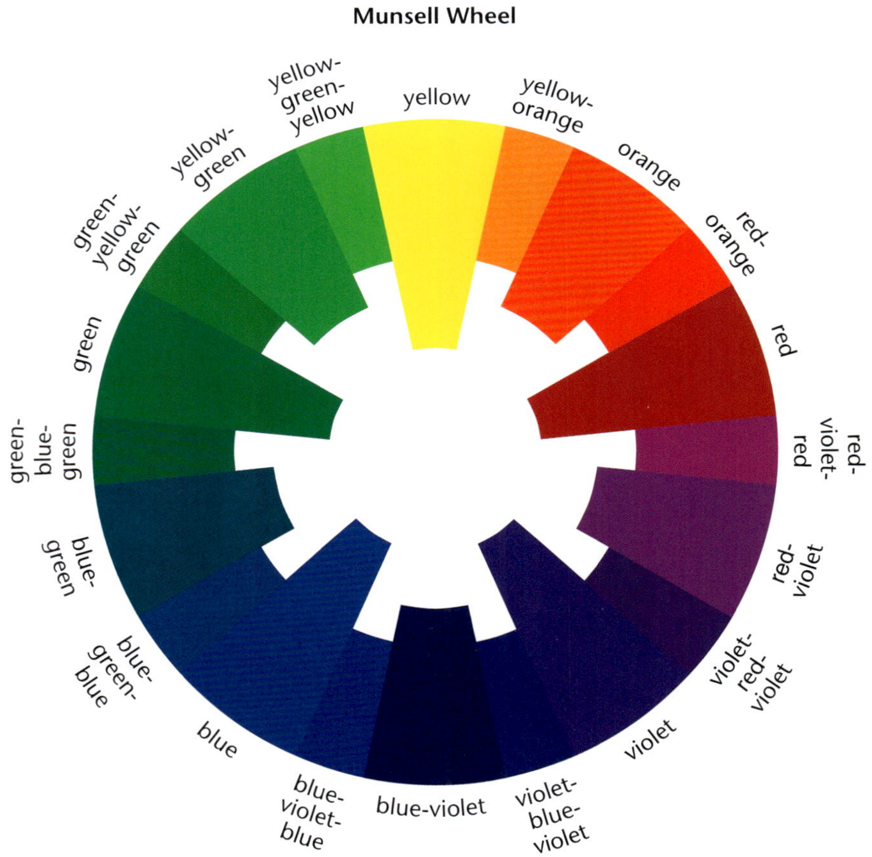

3.10 Left: Goethe's sketch of his symmetric color wheel, consisting of three primary colors of red, yellow, and blue. Right: This twenty-step partitive color wheel from the Munsell color system consists of five primaries, five secondaries, and ten tertiaries.

Source: L: Johann Wolfgang von Goethe by Luestling at de.wikipedia [Public domain], from Wikimedia Commons

with its Pantone Guides. Using these, designers can specify a color to a manufacturer on the other side of the world by indicating the Pantone (PMS, for Pantone Matching System) number. Pantone produces subsets of colors that can be reproduced using four-color, ink-based CMYK and screen-based RGB, as well as a host of other colors produced using 13 base pigments plus black and white (Fig. 3.11).

COLOR SCHEMES

As the designer is setting up a design concept, a *color scheme* usually comes into play very early in the process, and the sourcing of materials will often depend on it. A few basic frameworks, based on the four basic dimensions of color—hue, value, intensity, and temperature—can be used as starting points.

A *monochromatic* color scheme that utilizes only different intensities of a single hue has very different effects depending on the dimensionality and application of the design. Using only grays is the most basic of these. In graphic design a monochromatic scale of gray, brown, or blue tends to imply a historical reference, often tinged with nostalgia, by referring to pre-color-printing eras or tintype, daguerreotype, or black-and-white photography. In clothing a grayscale in a classic outfit will also evoke a classic feel and even a historical sense by evoking a subdued 19th-century sensibility. However, in interiors a grayscale will invariably create a cool, modernist vision, regardless of the historical forms in use, as the modernist vision of controlled use of hues and values overrides the forms and in elements (Fig. 3.12). The effect of using a grayscale is very bound to the width of the scale used. Going for a wider scale of more contrast creates a more dramatic effect, whereas a narrower scale evokes a sense of calm (Fig. 3.13). The same effect appears with a monochrome scale of any hue, but the overall effect takes on the quality

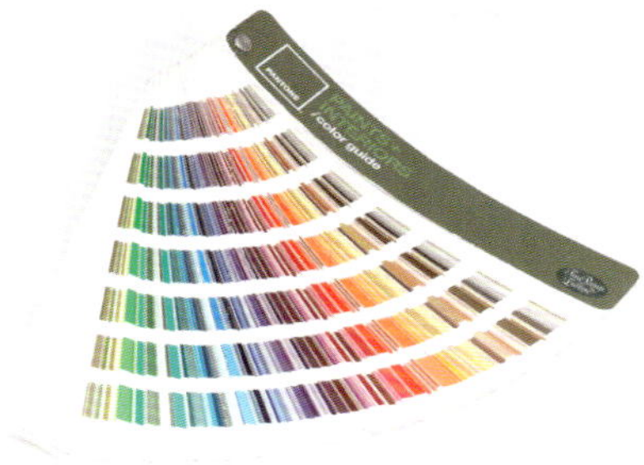

ABOVE

3.11 Pantone, Inc. produces a color system that has become close to being a worldwide standard.

Source: Image courtesy of Grant Cornett/WWD

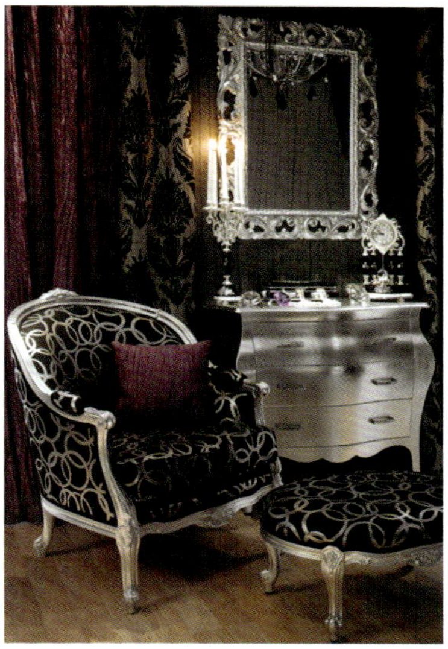

RIGHT

3.12 Putting a grayscale color scheme and metallic textures onto a classic design gives it a "cool" modernist feel. Louis XVI medallion dining chair by Jepara 50 Furniture.

Source: © Zoonar GmbH/Alamy

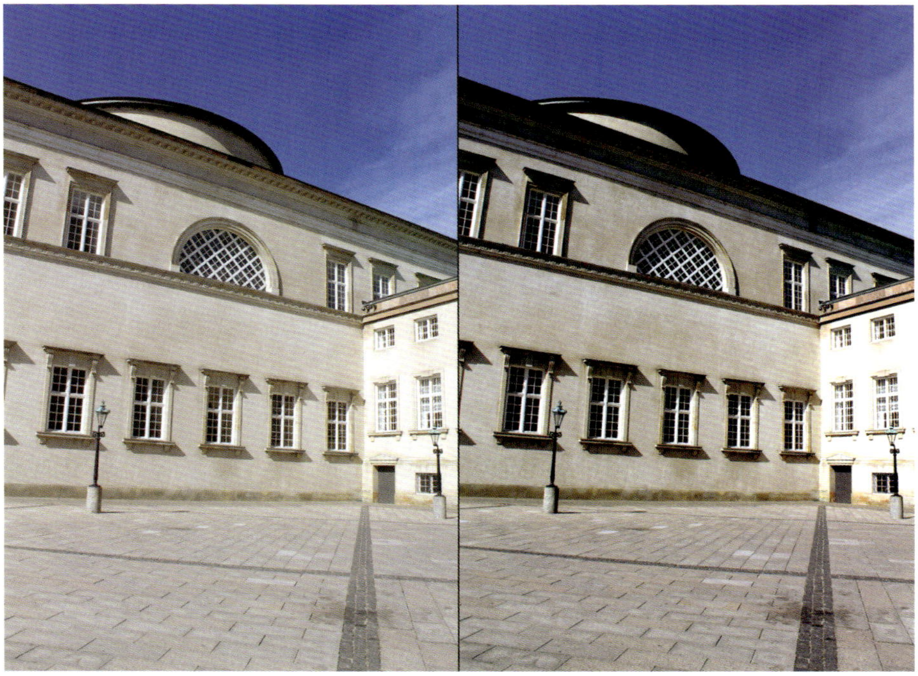

BELOW

3.13 The wider gray scale, from nearly full black to nearly full white, on the right subtly creates a more dramatic effect, while the narrower scale of varying grays on the left produces a calmer feel by not agitating our visual sense quite as much.

Source: Illustration by Karl Aspelund

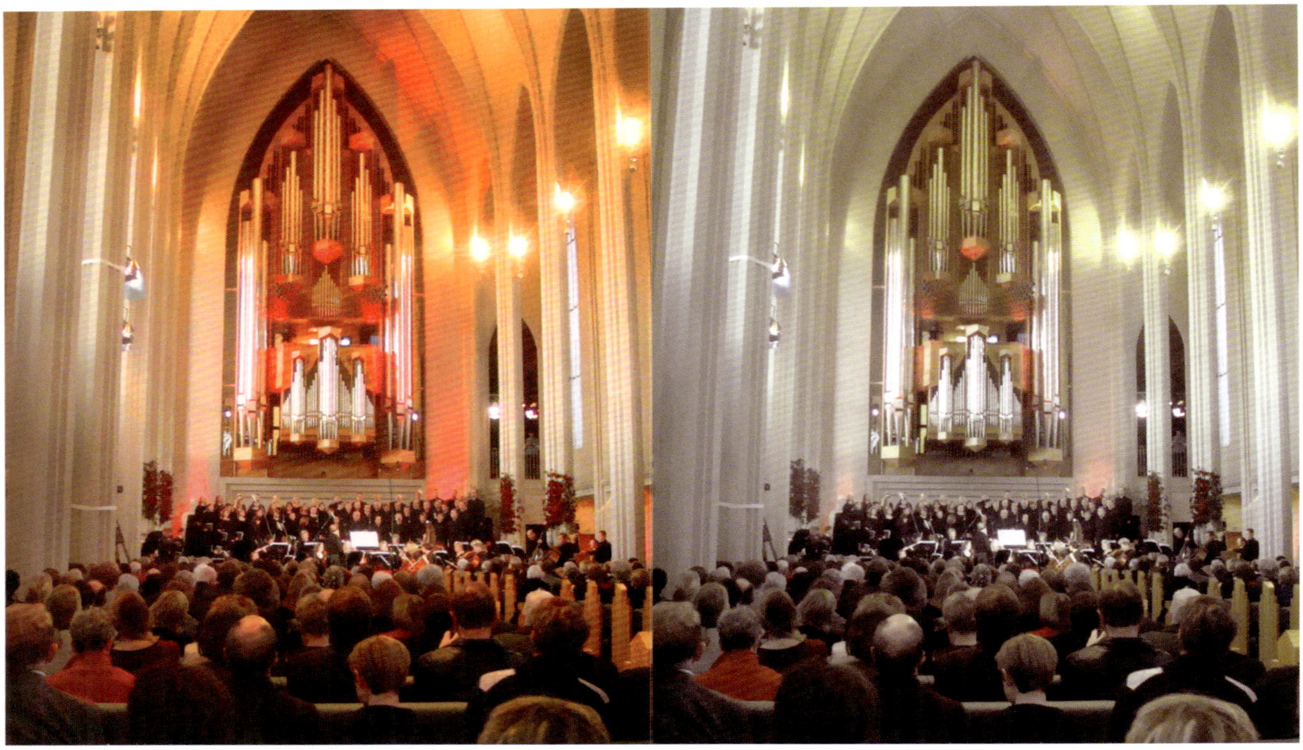

ABOVE

3.14 The intensity of colors, regardless of their placement, has a direct effect on the viewer's perception. A higher-value color scheme (left) provides more stimulus and produces a more intense mood, while a lower overall value (right) produces a calm mood.

Source: Illustration by Karl Aspelund

RIGHT

3.15 The association of colors to temperature is experienced on a physical level. The images have a different emotional feel resulting from the use of cooler (right) and warmer (left) color schemes, even when those schemes are relatively mild. The warmer colors evoke the same feeling in the viewer as if the room were actually warmer.

Source: Illustration by Karl Aspelund

of the base color. Varying intensities of a blue will, for example, produce a very different overall feel than a varied range of a yellow.

Color schemes based on choices of *high* or *low value* in color create environments that feel moody or calm. High-value schemes can produce a visual sense of weight—the darker, the heavier—and also a sense of substance; the lower the value, the more light and therefore a sense of less substance and weight (Fig. 3.14). *High* or *low intensity* of color can also create schemes based on high and low contrast, which can then be further expanded into a dimension of warm and cool color schemes. The cool spectrum of greens through blue violets creates a harder look when dark or a cooler look when the intensity is low. Warm color schemes utilize the yellow-red/red-violet section of the spectrum and, depending on the intensity of the colors, can either create a dramatic impact or a warm feeling (Fig. 3.15).

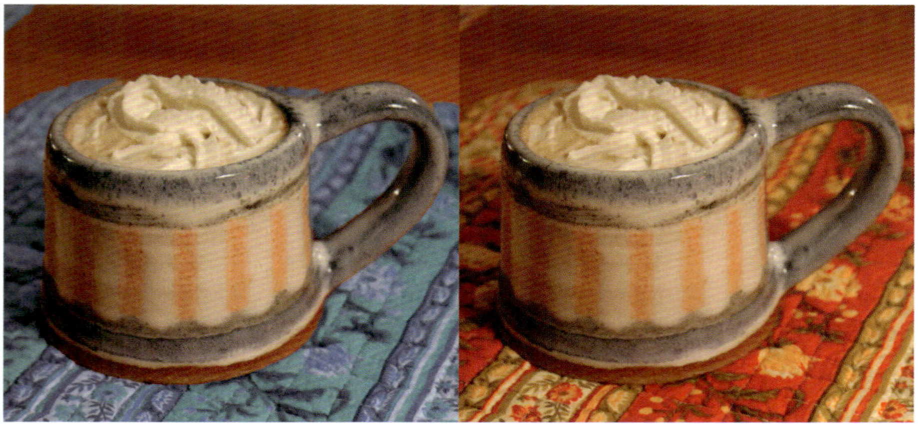

SUSTAINABILITY AND ELEMENTS

Line, shape, color, texture and pattern, space, and *time* all affect the environmental impact of a design. The totality of the design, the "whole of it," greater than the sum of its parts, must be broken down into the constituent elements to properly assess the impact of the design on the environment. Primarily, the issues involved would be how the application of design elements demands resources in materials or energy for production or use and how the elements can be re-used, repaired, or recycled. The *line* and the *shape* of a design may require materials or structures of a certain kind and may put demands on resources, materials, maintenance, or use by being overlarge or needing extra support, for example. A *color* or the creation of *textures* and *patterns* may require the use of harmful pigments, chemicals, or processes. The use of *space* is likewise critical to the sustainability questions as, for example, the extravagant use of space could mean a large difference in energy use. The key for a designer is to consider at each juncture what the choices made will involve over *time.* How much energy use is invovled in the life cycle of a product and the durability of its materials must be assesed over *time.* The distribution and breakdown of harmful materials takes place over *time* and so on and on. Every element has its own way of impacting the question of sustainability, and you as a designer have significant control over how the elements are applied.

COLOR IN ACTION (EXPERIENCING COLOR)

Color in design allows for very dynamic effects. Color gives a sense of action and movement, stillness and quiet, heat and cold. It also has a way of evoking emotions through cultural or nature-based associations—for instance, soothing, exciting, or joyous. Color can be used for emphasis—loud and soft—through contrast, placement, and isolation. It adds variety to patterns that would otherwise be monotonous and can unify a design by creating a tie between otherwise unrelated elements in a design (Fig. 3.16).

Care must be taken when you are looking at color, especially from the point of view of color theory, in that symbolism is *culture-specific* and cultural references and languages may contain more differences than similarities. With color so bound to

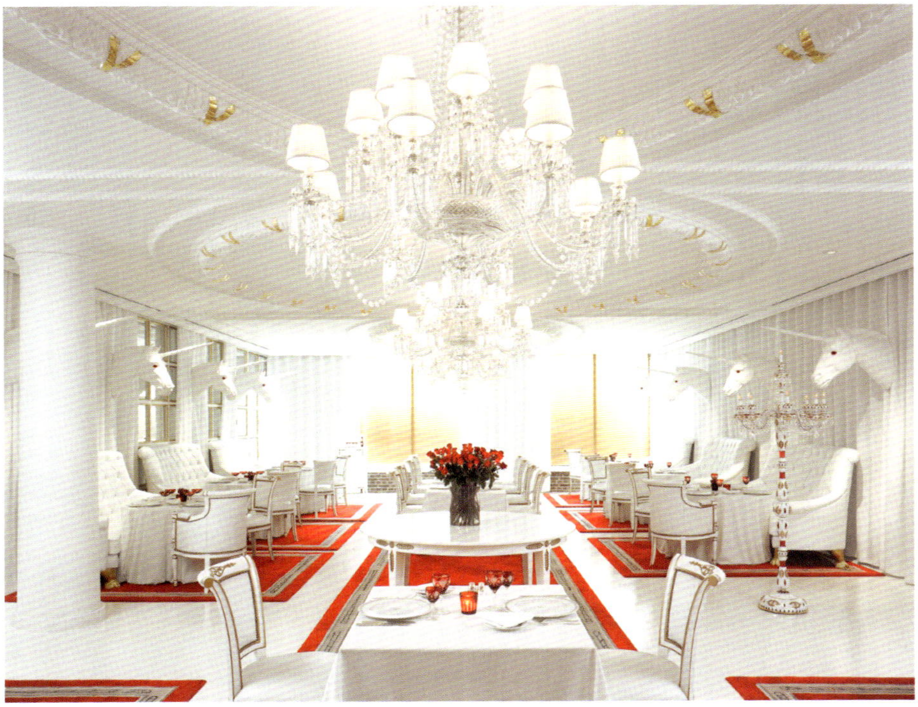

3.16 The room is tied together with red. When the flowers have been placed in the center, the entire room coalesces into the middle. El Bistro Sur del Mundo at Faena Hotel in Buenos Aires.

Source: Image courtesy of Faena Group

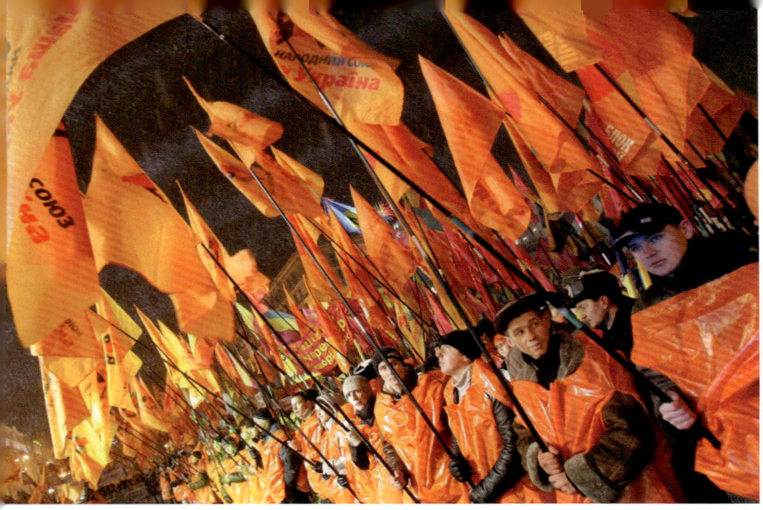

LEFT

3.17 The *meaning* of a color can change from one generation to the next if a suitably strong reference appears in a culture—for example, the connecting of a color to a political party or a revolution. The Orange Revolution in the Ukraine (2004–2005) made the color orange into a coded signal for antigovernment protest in Eastern Europe and elsewhere. Seven years later, supporters of Russia's government were identifying themselves as "anti-Orange."

Source: ©GLEB GARANICH/Reuters/Corbis

cultural interpretation, it is no surprise that the understanding and interpretation of color changes over historical time. The meaning of a color can change from one generation to the next if a suitably strong reference appears in a culture, such as an iconic design in fashion, or if an event is tied to the use of a color, for example, the connecting of a color to a political party or a revolution. This is more often connected to a local context but can spread to other localities (Fig. 3.17).

LINE

The first of our formative elements is *line*. This can either be a *drawn* line marked on a surface, a *formed* line constructed into a design, or an *implied* line where two or more points are connected by association. The implied line is therefore the most elementary kind of *pattern* (which will be considered below). A designed line is thus more than just an element in an illustration on a page, a fact that becomes even more obvious when we considers the lines in our surroundings that are either formed or implied (Fig. 3.18).

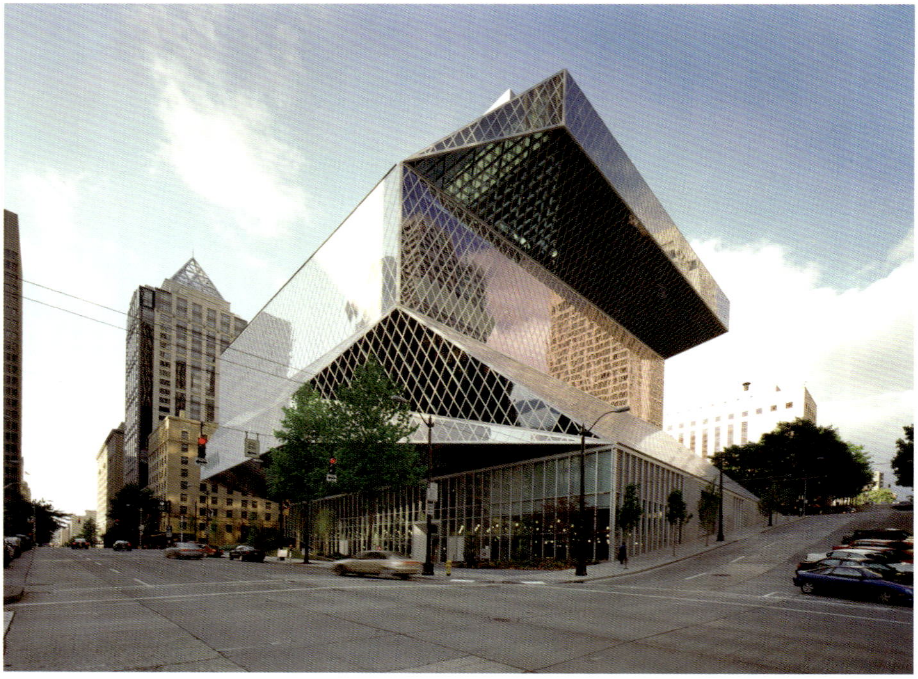

3.18 The first of our formative elements is *line*. Here, in the Seattle Public Library building, designed by Rem Koolhaas, line is used in a number of ways: Criss-crossing lines create the surfaces of the exterior, and vertical and horizontal lines bind the structure visually to the street and surrounding buildings (and may well evoke the older building it replaced.) The lines of the edges going this way and that, then create a sense of motion as if the building were struggling to escape its foundations. The Seattle Public Library.

Source: Photograph: © Arcaid/Corbis

ERGONOMICS AND ELEMENTS

Considering the ergonomics of a designed object from the point of its elements seems obvious, until one notices that it is all too easy to overlook a good portion of what might be important. If the idea is to create objects, systems, and environments that are user-friendly, safe, and comfortable, it is important to consider all the points of contact, impact, and significance to the human user. All the elements may play into the interaction of the human with the design in any combination: line, shape, color, texture and pattern, space, and time—all may have a bearing on the user physically or mentally, in one way or another.

The *line* of a room or machine may create a sense of comfort, or dangerously obscure sight-lines. The *shape* of a tool handle may make a job easier or be uncomfortable or injurious. A *color* may be calming or distracting, or it may send a wrong message. *Textures* and *patterns* may do all of this, and the use of *space* is critical in any ergonomic investigation. The human mind and body react, move, and are impacted by all the elements of a design, not just the obvious or visible. Which brings us to *time*, over which it all takes place. Observing a design in a still moment has little significance ergonomically. It is the experience over time that counts.

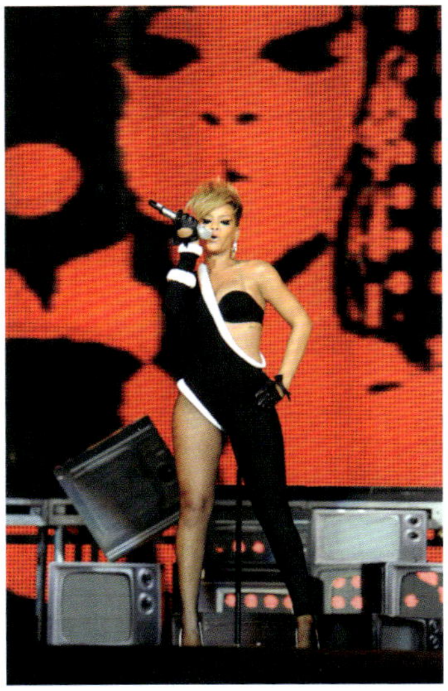

RIGHT

3.19 Outfits with diagonal asymmetry, such as this costume, have an especially dramatic effect as they disrupt the natural left-right symmetry of the human body. Rihanna performs live in concert as part of the Pepsi Super Bowl Fan Jam Concert.

Source: Photograph: © Chris Gordon/Corbis

DIRECTION

A *line*, whether implied or physical, indicates one of three directions: horizontal, vertical, or diagonal. Humans by the nature of the orientation of our bodies and symmetries are inclined toward horizontal and vertical constructs, with diagonals acting to disrupt space and create a sense of movement or even imbalance (Fig. 3.19).

CLARITY

The *line* of a design can have varying degrees of clarity—it can be vague, well defined, or anywhere in between (Fig. 3.20). The feel of a design often is directly related to the clarity of the line. A crisp, clear definition can give a space or an outfit a feel of effortlessness or efficiency, while an elaborate or overlapping line produces a depth and sense of looseness and motion. Contrasting degrees of clarity can produce interesting effects

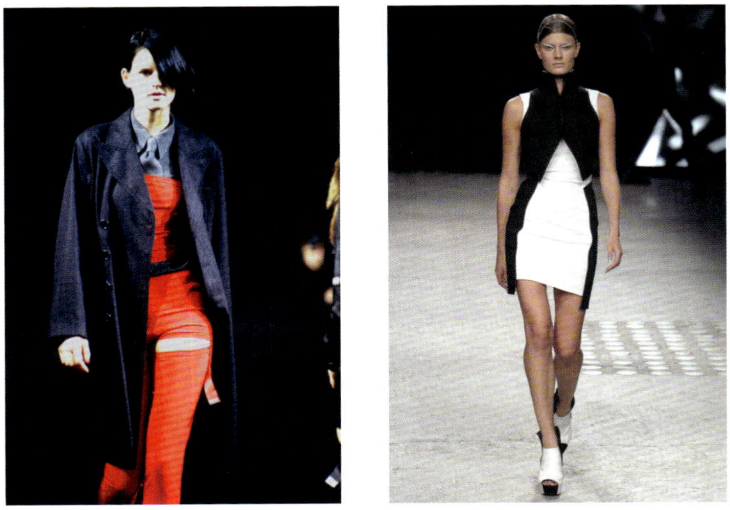

LEFT

3.20 These two outfits vary greatly in the clarity of the *line* involved. Observe how the layering and looseness of the outfit on the left obscures the line both within the design and the overall shape. Left: Bikkembergs A/W 1995, photograph by Niall McInerney, Bloomsbury Fashion Photography Archive. Right: Gareth Pugh. Fall 2013 ready-to-wear collection.

Source: Photograph: Giovanni Giannoni/WWD

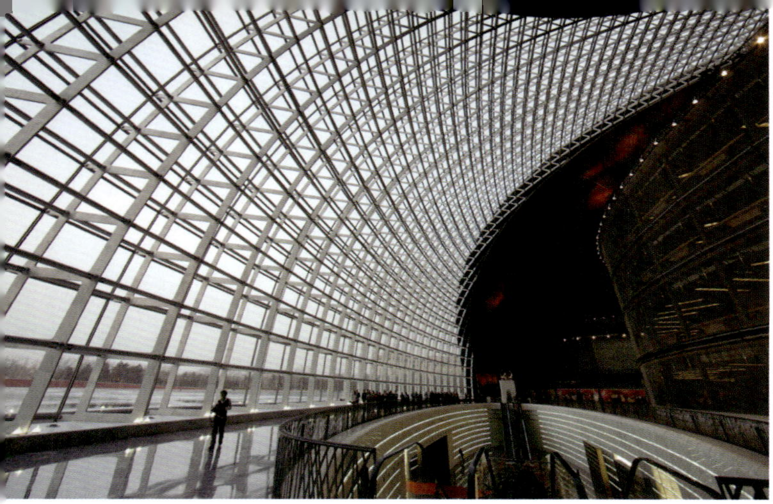

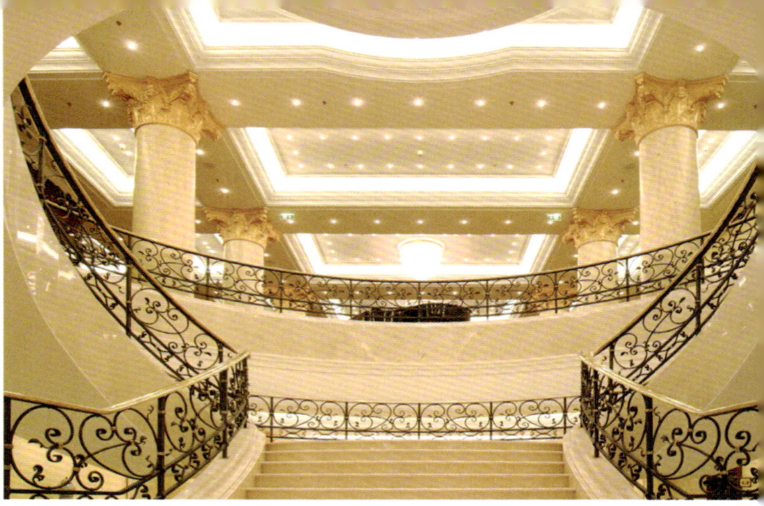

ABOVE

3.21 These different shapes of line convey a sense of movement and space. Curved lines in relation to straight structures in architecture create a feeling of expansiveness and space as well as movement. Left: National Centre for the Performing Arts Beijing. Right: Lobby of the Berlin Ritz-Carlton.

Source: L: The hall inside of the National Grand Theater © Astock/A Stock/Corbis; R: © travelstock44/Alamy

BELOW

3.22 The contrasting curved lines and straight sections in the body shape of this 1935 Mercedes-Benz 540K heightens a sense of speed by creating illusions of motion and fluidity.

Source: Photograph courtesy of Mercedes-Benz Classic Archives.

and focal points, while an overemphasis on either side, clarity or vagueness, may be overwhelming.

SHAPE

A line can be shaped in three different ways: convex, concave, or straight (Fig. 3.21). These different shapes convey a sense of movement and space, determined by what they are in relation to and where the viewer is positioned. For example, in clothing, the shape of the line is usually considered in relation to the underlying body and its movement or by its position relative to a strong determining feature in a garment. A similar sense is conveyed in interiors or structures and when used in the body shape of a vehicle heightens a sense of motion and fluidity (Fig. 3.22).

LENGTH AND WIDTH

The length of a line as a design element is not about measurements (although this does become important in the construction of the designed object) but rather the *relative* lengths of line. Varying lengths of line can produce a sense of structure, a pattern, and a sense of motion Again, the designer's awareness must be focused on the length in relation to the human body or surrounding structures. The same applies to width of line, where the relative width of line can be the entire concept in a design (Fig. 3.23).

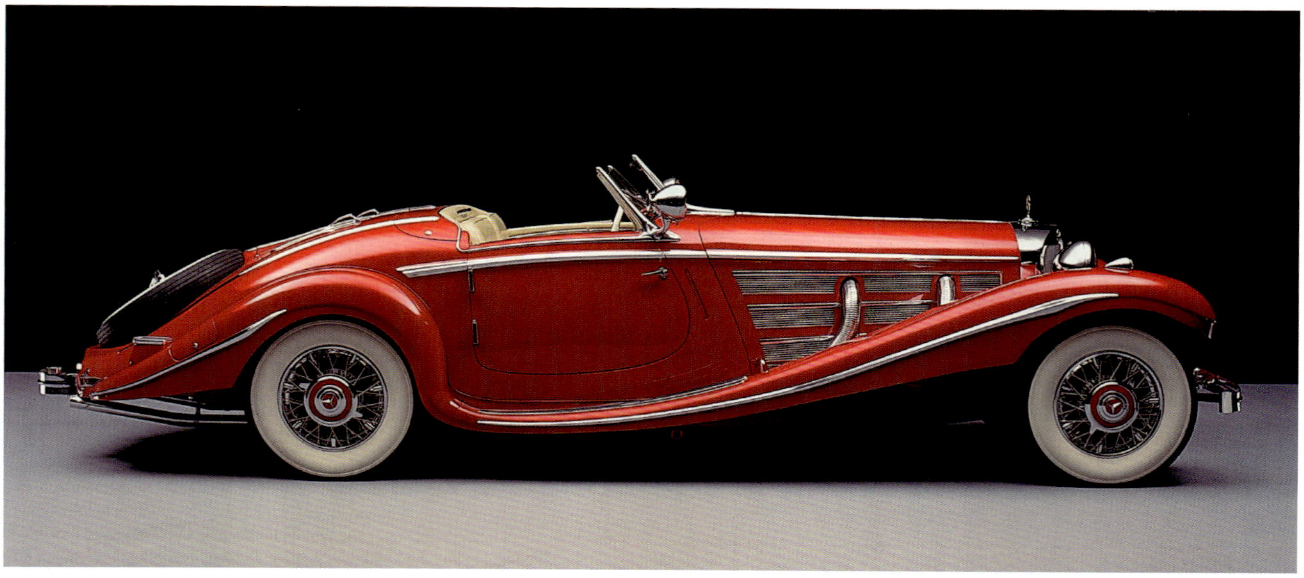

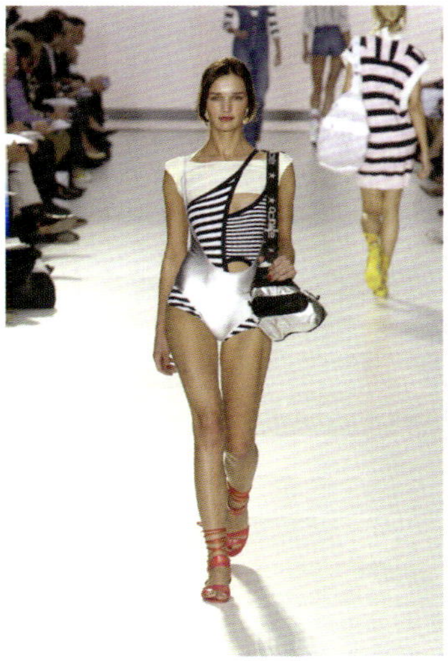

ABOVE LEFT

3.23 The relative width of a line can be a large element of or even the entire design statement as in this outfit. The top, bathing suit, bag, and shoes all play with different widths of line. Chloe Spring/Summer 2004, ready-to-wear.

Source: Photograph courtesy of firstVIEW.com

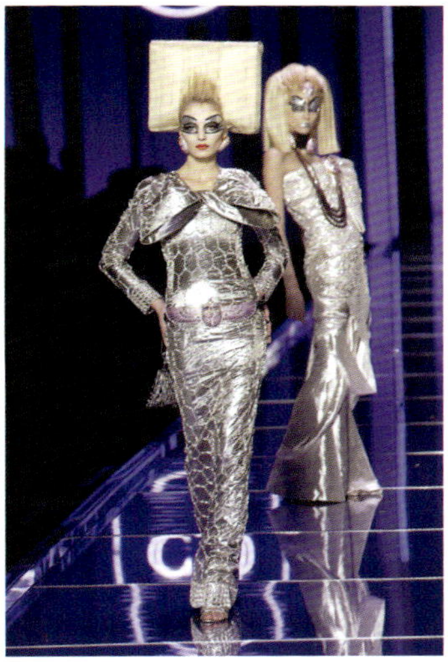

ABOVE RIGHT

3.24 Textures and patterns provide an impact within a spectrum that contains both visual interest and tactile sense. The sense of the dress above is felt through both your eyes and your fingertips (even if you don't touch it). Christian Dior Spring/Summer 2004 couture.

Source: Photograph courtesy of firstVIEW.com

TEXTURE/PATTERN

Texture and pattern must be considered together, as their sensory impact is related and their use in a design can often be thought of as two approaches toward the same goal. Textures and patterns provide an impact within a spectrum that contains both *visual interest* and *tactile sense*. Our sense of the world is from the very beginning of our lives molded by the sensory input from our skin and in textures we are engaging with our whole body. Touching things and other living beings begins even before we engage with the world through sight. Very young babies use their mouths to examine objects, as the sense of touch is most active there. They do this well before they begin to move through the world physically and before their eyes can focus properly. In doing so, they set up correspondences between touch and sight that lasts for a lifetime (Fig. 3.24).

VISUAL INTEREST AND TACTILE SENSE

It is important for a designer to be aware that sensory perception is not exclusive to individual senses. The engaging of more than one of our senses by a single sensory input is known as *synesthesia*. True synesthesia is a relatively rare condition where, for example, people quite literally *see* sounds or *taste* colors. However, it is clear that in most people there is much overlap between the senses, and we understand, on an instinctive level, ideas such as "it tastes green" or "a round kind of sound."

The relationship of patterns and textures is a very good example of this kind of mild synesthesia. *Texture* is experienced and understood both visually and through touch. A tactile sensation can be understood through sight, just as the texture can be conveyed through tactile description. For example, consider whether rough fabric looks or feels rough? How about smooth concrete (Fig. 3.25)?

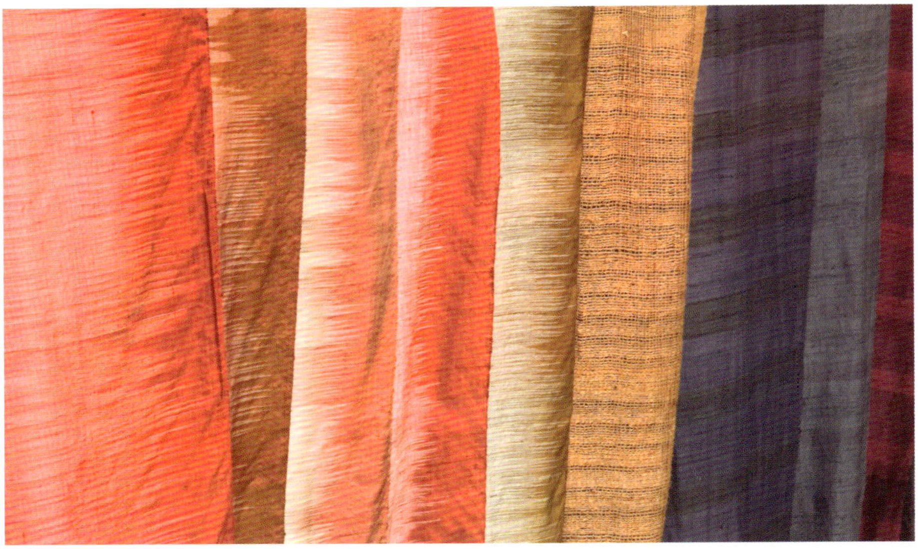

RIGHT

3.25 Texture is experienced both visually and through touch. The terms used are extremely relative. Consider whether raw silk, a rough fabric, looks or feels rough? How about smooth concrete?

Source: L, © Bill Brennan/Design Pics/Corbis; R, © Dieter Heinemann/Westend61/Corbis

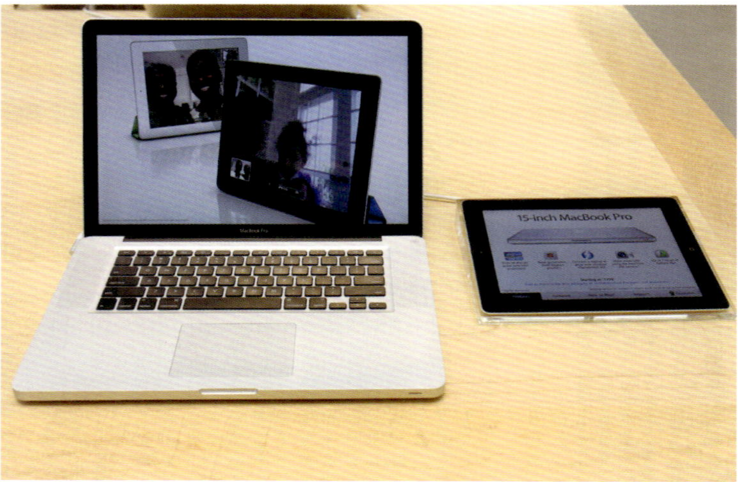

ABOVE
3.26 We increasingly interact with the world through devices that are ever-present in our hands. Counterintuitively, these are creating a new demand for sensations in the texture of cases, keyboard, button surfaces, and tactile screen responses.

Source: Photograph courtesy of Robert Mitra/WWD

On the other hand, a texture may simply be implied by illustrative means or by setting up a pattern on a two-dimensional surface. We have learned to connect visuals with a sense in our fingertips or skin, and the visual appeal of a surface can be an appeal to a much more intimate sense of touch. A surface pattern may be made to project a sense of what might be felt on our skin by referring to a familiar texture. This is becoming increasingly important with the mounting number of virtual environments we navigate in the course of our day-to-day existence. These have greatly increased the amount of visual rather than tactile interaction we have with the world. At the same time, the nature of our interaction with these virtual worlds is impermanent and *in the moment,* while the devices we interact through are increasingly present in our hands, creating a new demand for sensations in the texture of cases, keyboard and button surfaces, and tactile screen responses (Fig. 3.26).

PATTERN

Rhythm is one of the principles of design discussed in the following chapter, but for now, we should understand that the use of pattern generates rhythms. Patterns, whether 2D or 3D—either built in or added on—set up rhythms that can bring both order and variety to a surface or structure. Patterns are instinctively thought of as two-dimensional constructs, as they are most often seen as surface elements. However, three-dimensional patterns have been used in interiors and architecture throughout human culture (Fig. 3.27).

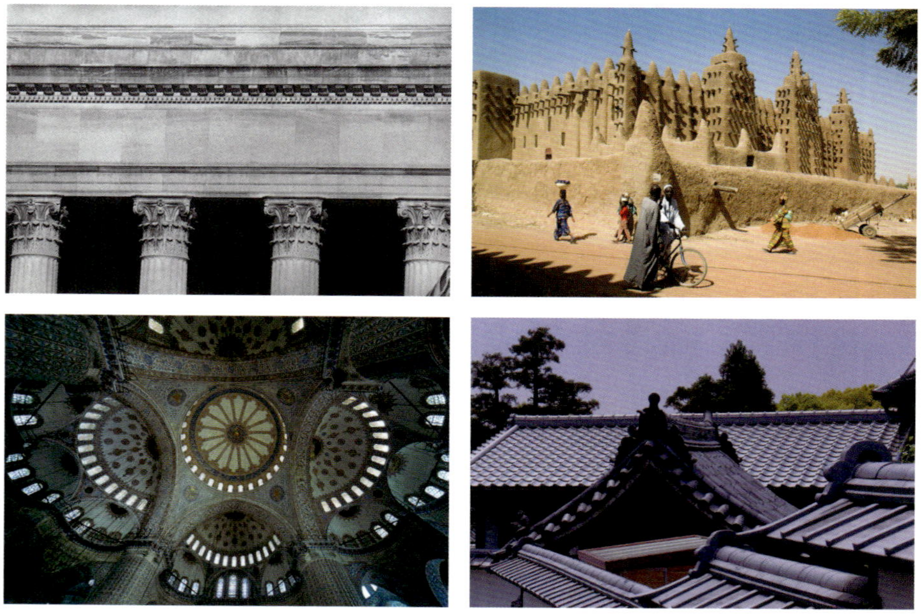

RIGHT
3.27 Three-dimensional patterns are common in interiors and architecture throughout human culture.

Source: Upper L: © David H. Wells/Corbis; Upper R: © Nigel Pavitt/JAI/Corbis; Lower L: © Image Source/Corbis; Lower R: © Dec/lamy

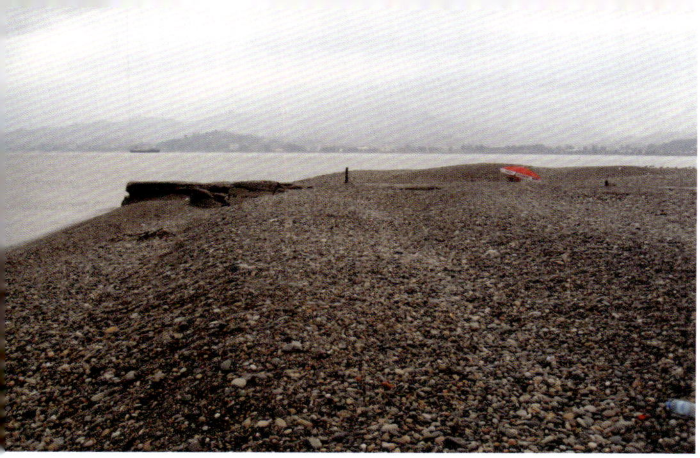

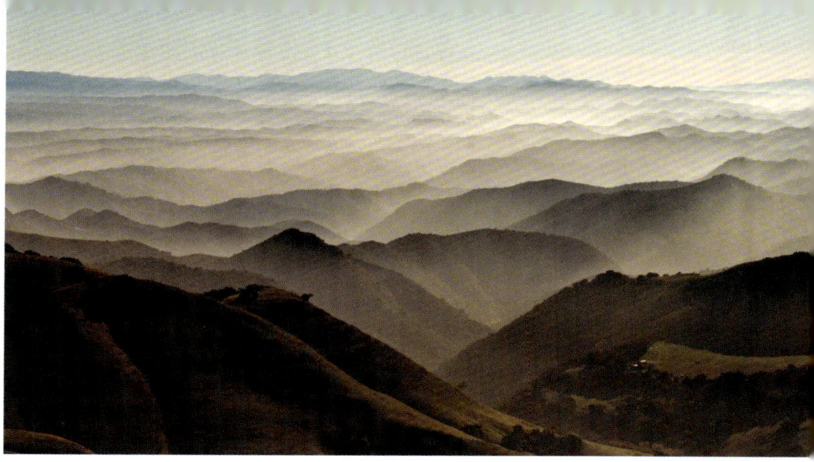

PATTERN AND THE GESTALT

Humans are hard-wired for pattern recognition in order to make sense of the bombardment of sensory stimuli that we are subjected to at every living moment. Our instinctive and unconscious placement of sensory stimuli into patterns not only places order on the universe but also allows much learning and adaptation, as we are able to fill in gaps in information, whether it is visual, aural, or even informational and conceptual (Fig. 3.28). The strength of our abilities is such that even in the absence of a pattern, we will create one that corresponds to the closest known structure we have. We will therefore inevitably see faces in smoke and trees and the unlikeliest of places. But we also will nearly automatically connect unrelated objects or events into perceived sequences. Lights will appear to pulse in time to music, features in landscapes will seem rhythmic, and birdsong or insects will seem to create patterns of sound (Fig. 3.29). The sensory information is grouped into "totalities" (also known as a gestalt, see Box 3.1) where we understand the collected information as something larger than simply the sum of parts. For example, a collection of musical notes played in succession will be understood as a tune and a simple set of lines may be understood as a design for an object of considerable complexity (Fig. 3.30).

ABOVE LEFT

3.28 The human brain processes the observed environment and discerns patterns if at all possible. On this beach, a subtle pattern has developed from how the stones are distributed by the tide. What is initially seen as a random textural surface is soon perceived as a pattern undulating softly along the shore. Batumi Beach, Republic of Georgia.

Source: Photograph © Ephraim Stillberg

ABOVE RIGHT

3.29 Designing for rhythmic effect can rely on the fact that we automatically connect unrelated objects or events into perceived sequences. Natural formations in landscapes may seem rhythmic by dint of the forces that molded them. Coastal California Hills in hazy mist near San Luis Obispo.

Source: Photograph © Proehl Studios/Corbis

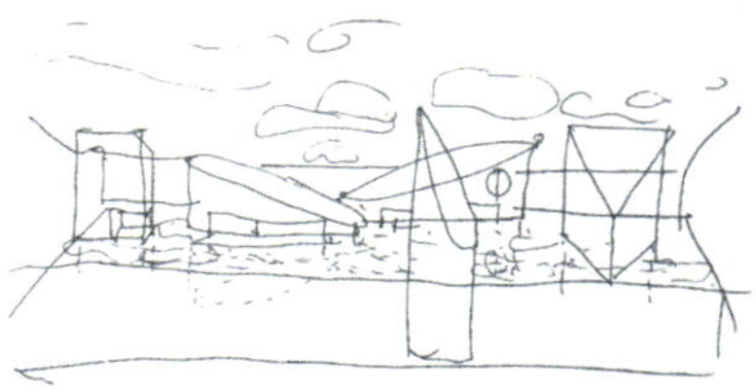

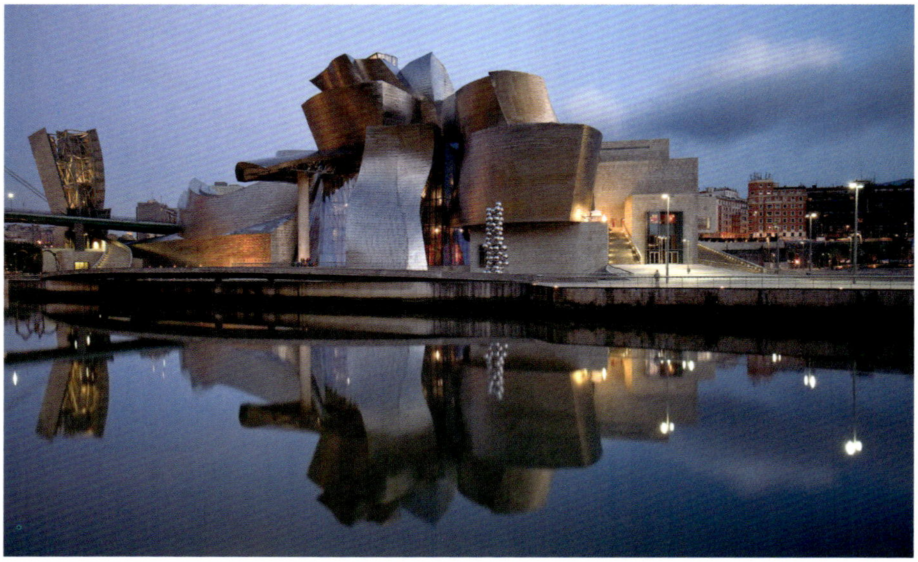

RIGHT

3.30 We understand the collected information—the gestalt—as something larger than simply the sum of parts. A simple set of lines may be understood as a design for an object of considerable complexity. Frank Gehry's sketch of the Bilbao Guggenheim and the building itself.

Source: Sketch, courtesy of the Visual Resources Collection, School of Architecture, The University of Texas at Austin; Photo © Ben Pipe/Robert Harding World Imagery/Corbis

BOX 3.1

THE GESTALT AND ELEMENTS OF DESIGN

IN THE CONTEXT OF PRESENTING A DESIGN TO AN AUDIENCE, it is worth noting that each design element can be seen as a statement adding to the totality of the design, but at the same time each acquires its meaning from the whole. The whole—the gestalt—has its own identity that is larger than the sum of the individual elements. It is good to see this in the frame of writing: The elements of a design contribute to the gestalt in the way words make up a poem. The final *meaning* of the individual words, however, also comes from the context of the poem. The final meaning of the elements in a design will be a product of their own nature and their position in the design itself. Discussing the elements in a design, one should therefore be very careful about keeping the context clear. Be very mindful of the dialogue between the individual elements and the whole. When presenting the elements, keep referring back to the whole design and the overall impact as you discuss their presence and contribution in order that your audience understands their contribution and context within the whole.

Marshall McLuhan's famous maxim "the medium is the message" (see also chapters 1 and 10) points to the idea that the content being broadcast through media is less important for the understanding of culture than the effect of the media technology itself. Television's big effect, for example, was in the possibility of instantly disseminated information passively received, regardless of the content being broadcast. McLuhan gave a clearer example by pointing out that a light bulb is a medium that does not have content at all, but it does have an effect on society by changing how people operate in relation to daylight and darkness.[1]

Taking this thought a little further still, we can understand that the elements of design convey a message on two levels in a version of the gestalt discussion: On one hand, the element itself has an identity; on the other hand, it depends on its meaning from its context in the whole design. The whole design's impact—its *message*—then arrives from the combined effect of the elements on the viewers and users of the designs. But this takes place in the context of the design itself, and the elements acquire their meaning by being placed there.

For example, the color red, as a concept, can have a meaning in itself. This may be personal, cultural, or part of a systemic code. But it isn't until it is placed in the context of a design that it fully speaks to us. The red of an evening dress, for example, has a different message than the same red used on a carpet, or a fire engine, or the cover of a book. At the same time a red fire engine has a different impact than a gray one (if there is such a thing). Red in itself does not have content; it only is content when placed in context. Color is a fairly obvious example, but the same can easily be said about line, pattern, shape, motion, and texture. By transferring these over to other designs, other meanings are created. This is more than semantics. This is about experience. Even time becomes interpreted by the very nature of the actions performed within it, and a design experienced over time may therefore influence our understanding of the meaning or message of that particular slice of time.

BELOW LEFT

3.31 Patterns can be used to create areas of emphasis or focus by placing elements rhythmically, by adding color, or simply by using structure on unadorned fields, such as in the columns and brickwork of this terracotta mosque in Porto Novo, Benin.

Source: © Anthony Asael/Art in All of Us/Corbis

BELOW RIGHT

3.32 The flowers and leaf shapes in William Morris' design clearly maintain the identity of the represented plants. However, they are perfected and presented in an idealized form. Chrysanthemum wallpaper, William Morris, 1877—Victoria and Albert Museum, London.

Source: V&A Images, London /Art Resource, NY

TEXTURE AND PATTERN AS CONTRAST AND EMPHASIS

A simple pattern will easily appear out of any minimally organized sets of lines, colors, or forms, and an effective pattern can be created with a very simple set of elements in either two or three dimensions. A number of classic patterns have been developed over the centuries. By contrasting colors within any regular structure such as a weave, tiling, or brickwork, the craftsperson or designer can set up a visually engaging pattern. Patterns also can be used to create areas of emphasis or focus by the designer placing them on unadorned fields. Simply breaking the pattern will create a strong focal point (Fig. 3.31).

SHAPE

Considering shapes in design, one might think that the endless possibilities would resist classification. However, an immediate difference presents itself to the designer when dealing with how things are represented: Are they natural or ideal? In a *naturalistic* approach, a designer seeks to copy the world, attempting to present an honest visual appearance of shapes in the world around us. Under *idealism*, on the other hand, the designer interprets and presents the world with a vision of how it should be. Perceived imperfections and flaws are corrected and desired characteristics are enhanced (Fig. 3.32).

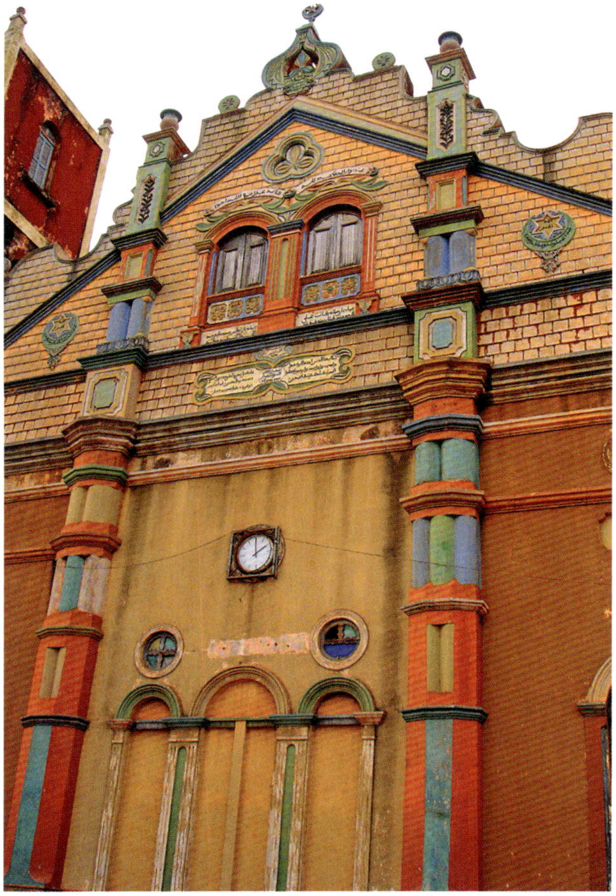

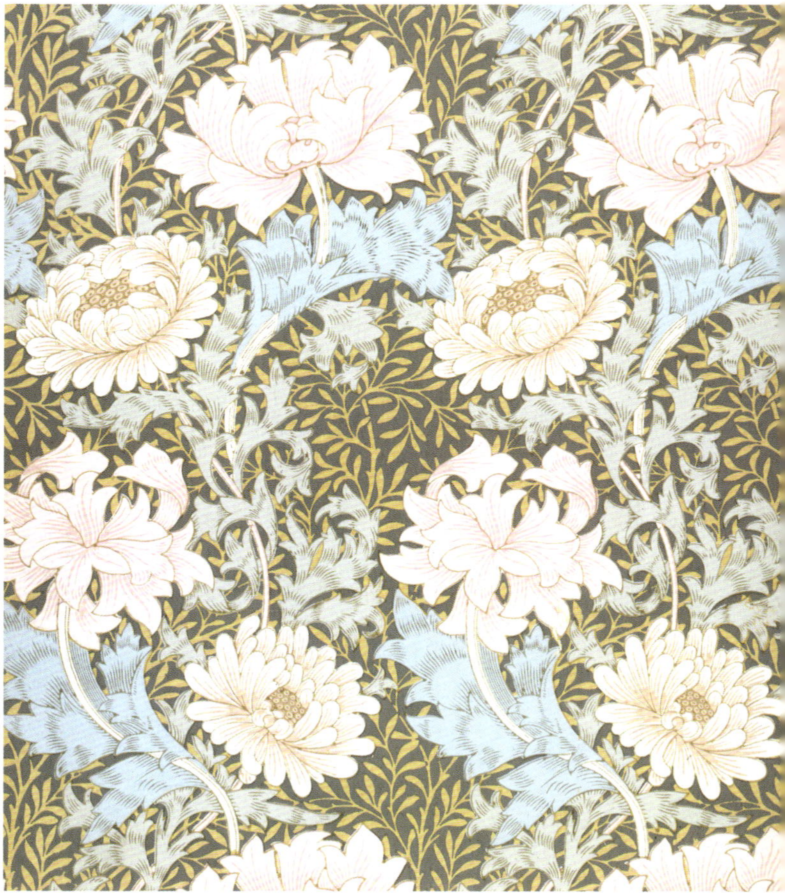

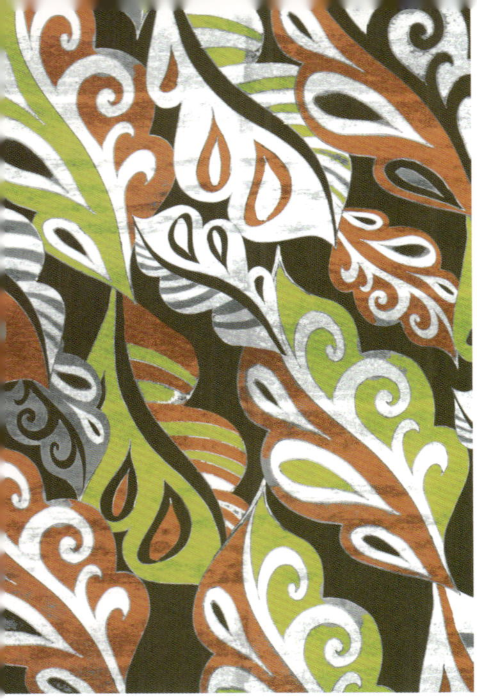

ABSTRACTION AND NONOBJECTIVE FORMS

An *abstraction* shows us the essence of a shape rather than a detailed description. A shape is reduced to an outline or silhouette, simplified to its basic character. Abstractions have dominated the scene, both culturally and historically, as decorative elements of design for as long as humans have engaged in such activities. The stripped down nature of abstractions makes them easily incorporated into patterns, and they are also well suited for execution in mass production (Fig. 3.33).

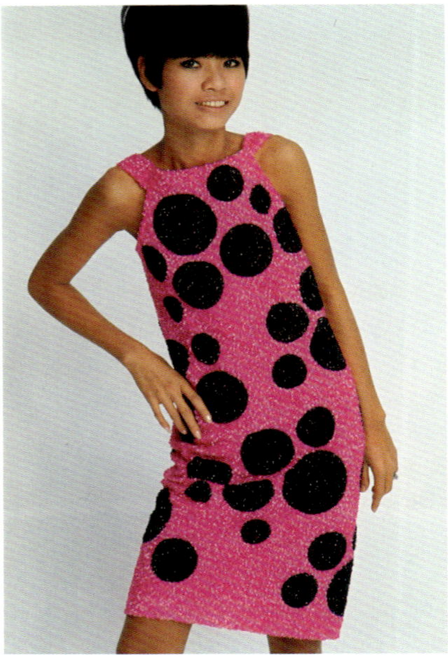

There is, of course, no need for designed shapes to refer to actual entities. Designers can work with *nonobjective shapes*, working with form in a way that uses the qualities of shapes for their own sake. These can be of a varying degree of purity, with the *pure forms* of basic geometry, circles, rectangles, triangles, and ellipses playing a large role (Fig. 3.34).

ABOVE LEFT

3.33 An abstraction shows us the essence of a shape rather than an accurate description. This makes them easily incorporated into woven patterns and well suited for printing in mass production, as in this textile pattern of abstracted tropical leaves.

Source: © Garreau Designs/Corbis

ABOVE RIGHT

3.34 Designed shapes do not need to refer to actual entities. Designers can work with *nonobjective shapes*, working with form for its own sake. Model Nom Srey Neang in a pink beaded dress with black circles by Pierre Cardin, 1965.

Source: © Condé Nast Archive/Corbis

CURVILINEAR AND RECTILINEAR

Whatever the shape in question, it breaks down into two very simple categories when we look at the edges and angles. Shapes can be *curvilinear*, rounded and curving forms that may imply movement or softness, or *rectilinear*, composed of straight lines that will often feel more still, hard, and permanent (Fig. 3.35).

BELOW

3.35 Art Nouveu style (left) emphasized the *curvilinear* shapes, while high modernist design (right) tends with its systematic bent toward the *rectilinear*. Left: Round bar at the Philharmonic Dining Rooms, Liverpool, England. Right: Contemporary bar.

Source: L: Photograph ©Newton; Greg/Arcaid/Corbis. R: Photograph ©Studio Ton Kinsbergen/Beateworks/Corbis

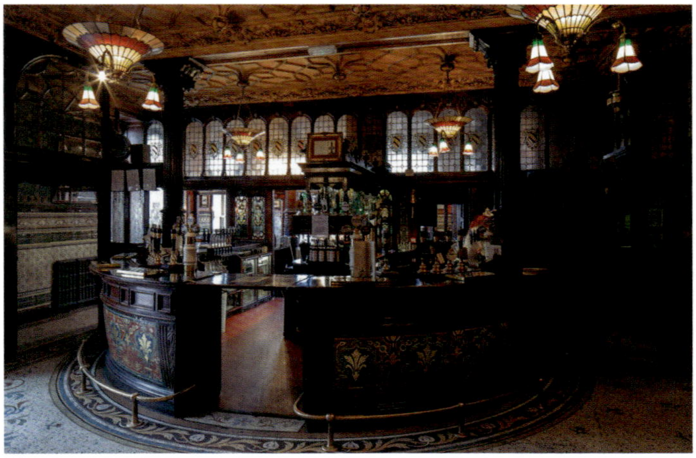

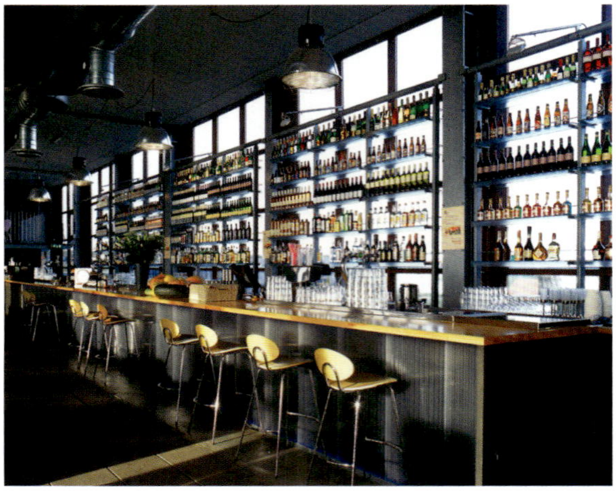

RIGHT

3.36 In the interior of the 2006 Wiesmann-Roadster, the positive shapes of the dashboard, steering wheel, floors, doors, and console envelope the negative spaces (negative shapes) within which the bodies of the driver and passenger fit and operate. The sculptural dialogue of shapes and spaces creates an environment that is both open and enveloping.

Source: Courtesy of www.wiesmann.com

BELOW

3.37 Our understanding of three-dimensional space is closely tied to our understanding of a code displayed in two dimensions. *Above* and *below* become *near* and *far; in front* and *behind* read in two dimensions as distance. So much of our perception of the world is on two-dimensional pages and screens that this is completely transparent to us. Battle of Panipat, British Library.

Source: © British Library Board/Robana/Art Resource, NY

POSITIVE/NEGATIVE SHAPES

But in both two- and three-dimensional design, we must also consider that the crucial shape we are creating may not be the thing itself but what the thing encompasses. We may be working with the *positive shape*—the thing that is there—or we may be interested in the *negative shape*—the shape created around or within any shape or object. It is not always clear which is which, as foreground and background, shape, and absence may not always be well defined, but the presence of a dialogue between the shapes is always apparent (Fig. 3.36).

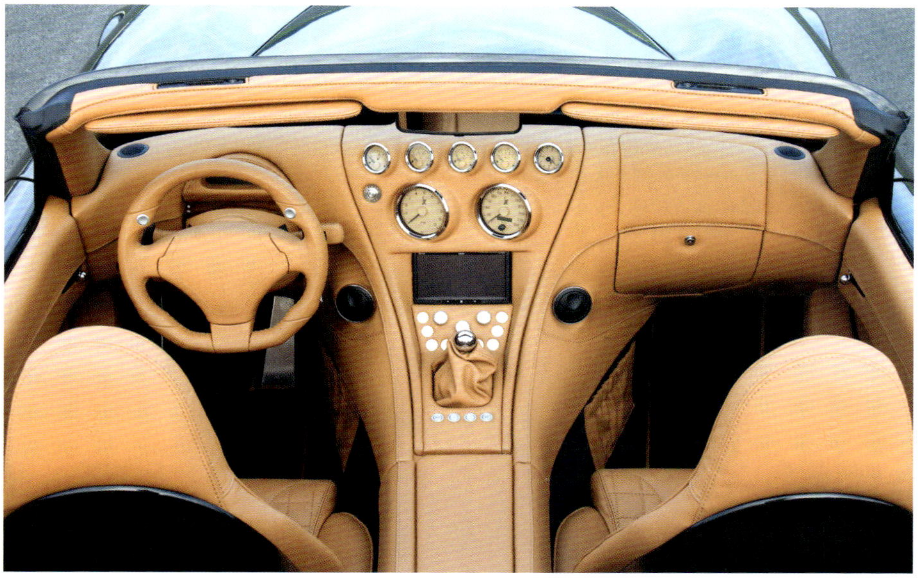

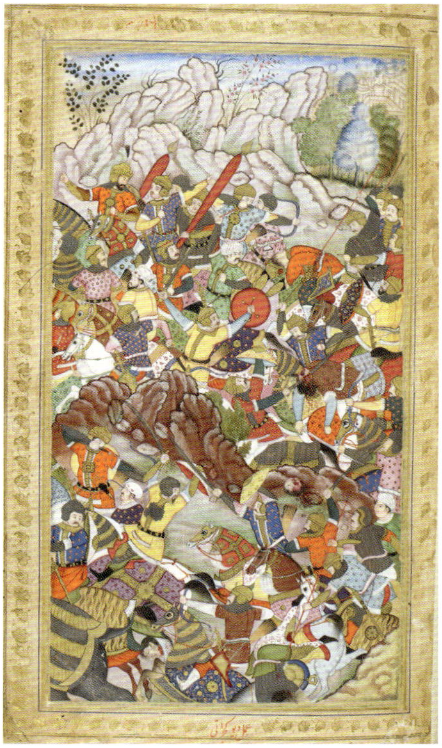

SPACE (AND MOTION)

2D AND 3D SPACE

Although designing can be easily classified into two- and three-dimensional design and the difference is usually obvious, the difference in our spatial perception within them is not (Fig. 3.37). Our understanding of space in two dimensions is a direct result of our learned experience of space in three dimensions. Our experience of the world gradually begins to include learned interpretations of things that signal *space* through a variety of visual cues that allow us to understand three-dimensional space, even in a strictly two-dimensional representation.

Three-dimensional designing will often begin with two-dimensional work on a screen or sketchpad and end with a two-dimensional illustration representation in a photograph or printout, or in ad copy. So much of the back and forth with the idea takes place in a reduced version of the *real* experience, even when the three dimensions are simulated on a screen. A designer must know how to project the design into the extra dimensions required to fully sense, anticipate, and provide for the user experience of the designed object in space and time. It becomes necessary to understand logically how we interpret our surroundings as dimensions, how we understand the visual cues, and what these cues actually are.

ILLUSIONS OF SPACE AND MOTION

Graphic design will depict in two dimensions the illusion of three-dimensional space and motion. This can be done with a number of methods, usually several at once (Fig. 3.38). Although mostly used in two-dimensional art or design, these techniques are also used in set design for theater and can be used to create an illusion of space in interiors. All utilize the way in which we interpret space visually, using the visual cues with which we understand space to deliver an understanding of three dimensions on a two-dimensional plane.

Size is a very good way to create this illusion, as we understand two objects as being at different distances from us if they look to be the same in every way except size. We can use their surroundings to develop a sense of scale. *Overlapping* one thing over another gives us a sense of in front and behind, which immediately conjures up three-dimensions.

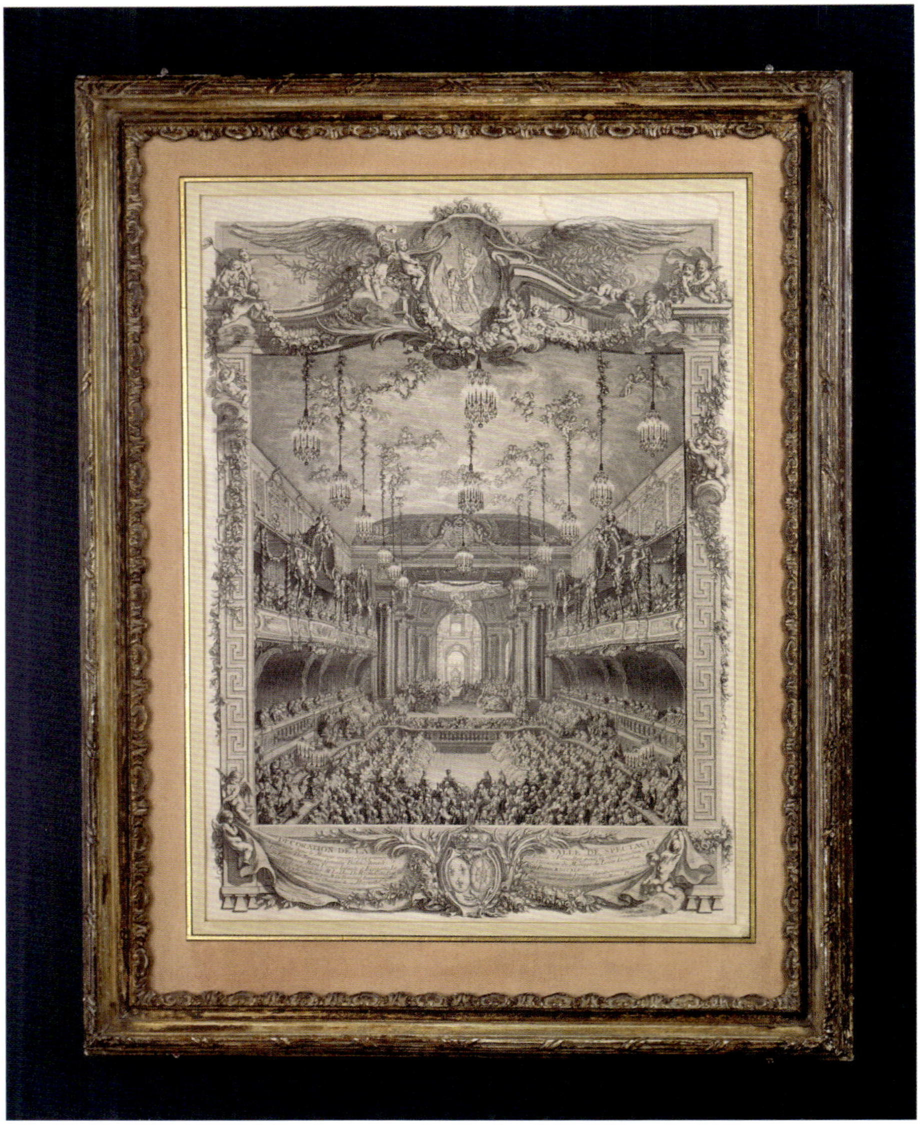

3.38 Two-dimensional artwork easily creates the illusion of three-dimensional space and motion using many different tricks of perception. Ball given at Versailles in 1745 for the marriage of Louis XV of France to Marie-Therese of Spain, by Charles Nicolas Cochin II (1715–1790).

Source: V&A Images, London/Art Resource, NY

Vertical location will also place two-dimensional objects into a three-dimensional relationship, especially if there are other visual cues available. Our sense of *perspective* is trained to interpret the higher object as further away if it is below our horizon line, but closer if above it. *Transparency* will also imply three-dimensionality by showing an in-front/behind relationship.

The rules of perspective, developed during the Renaissance, allow us to systematically create an illusion of depth and distance by altering shapes accordingly. The skewing of forms corresponds to a vanishing point, mimicking our perception of space and thereby implying three dimensions in the field. We recognize also the difference between a larger object and a smaller one of the same kind representing distance, but usually we need a reference to inform us of the scaling—something binding them together or implying the space in which they sit.

We learn to recognize that atmospheric conditions will reduce both the intensity and value of colors as distance increases, allowing color gradation to effectively indicate space. We can read also three dimensions from how shadows are placed, especially if they do so consistently and with corresponding highlights. It is obvious to us that a shadow falls onto an object according to the relationship of the objects to the light source. If we recognize the position of the light source, we can interpret the placement of the objects depending on the shadows they cast and the light they reflect.

IMPLIED SPACE AND MOTION VERSUS ESSENTIAL SPACE AND MOTION

Even when we interpret three-dimensionality from a learned standpoint, our main understanding is instinctual. For example, directionality creates an illusion of motion; we understand *potential* motion by the recognition of what effect gravity will have or the direction implied by the front-back structures of vehicles and animals. We simply *feel* that that the front will move forward and that gravity will pull, even when we are looking at a 2D environment where neither of these factors is actually in operation (Fig. 3.39).

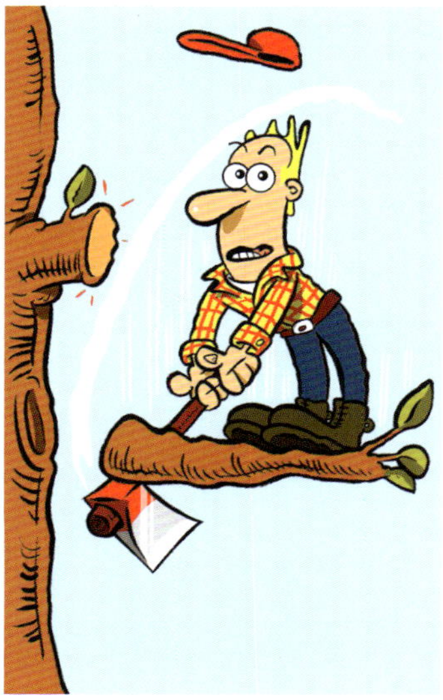

3.39 Directionality creates an illusion of motion, we understand *potential* motion by the recognition of gravity or the front-back structures of vehicles and animals. We *feel* that the *front* will move *forward* and that gravity will pull *downward*.

Source: © Brian Aldred/Alamy

The implied space of two-dimensional design must translate into the physical reality of humans: a world of lived space and motion. Meanwhile, two-dimensional design also is a function of our three- (or four-) dimensional experience and must be read accordingly. The resulting stance the designer must adopt is that all design operates in three or four dimensions but can be codified and examined in two. In other words, graphic space *is* volume, and shape and space are practically interchangeable.

THE LANGUAGE OF MOTION

We have an instinctive understanding of shapes that imply motion and we may think that these are *natural,* but they are not. They are very much acquired and cultural. For example, during the early 20th century a visual language of the *form of speed* developed as cars, trains, airplanes, and rockets took on streamlined forms that became symbols of speed (Fig. 3.40).

This modernist side effect of *form following function* is an understanding based on learning—we have incorporated the visual language of speed and streamlining into our cultural collection of symbols.

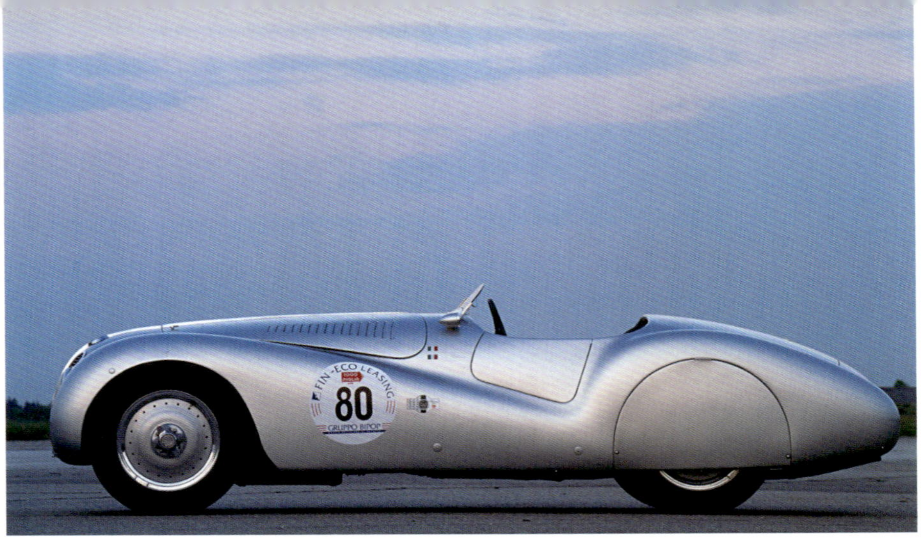

3.40 We have an instinctive understanding of shapes that imply motion that are very much acquired and cultural. During the early 20th century a visual language of the *form of speed* developed as streamlined forms and became symbols of speed. BMW 328 *Mille Miglia,* 1930.

Source: Courtesy of BMW Group Archive

Our sense of space and motion in design is thus always based on our own lived experience that provides us with points of reference to cultural structures. We then project our emotional connections onto these experiences. In this way the *dialogue* of design with its audience evolves from generation to generation.

BOUNDARIES AND EDGES

In our day-to-day lives we constantly negotiate boundaries. Some are actual and physical, some are implied, and some are emotional and psychological. The spaces we inhabit and the clothes we wear surround us, defining areas of personal and communal space. People's spaces collide and intertwine depending on need and social structures involving appropriateness, politeness, gender relations, and tradition, in a complex dance of everyday movement.

Our sense of space and the boundaries we live and move within arrives directly from our physical shape and being. We operate within planes and right angles; we have a sense of *forward* and *back* and *side* based on the geometry of our own left-right symmetry, front-back asymmetry, and the *up* and *down* asymmetrical orientation of our bodies. But with all that, we still navigate our bodies through space with a sensory orientation that is nearly 360 degrees. We have a sense of space and the possibility of movement backward and above our heads.

Therefore, even in our modern state, often so removed from what we consider nature, our spaces—the cityscapes, buildings, interiors, furniture, and clothing—are all a function of human body planes and structures, just as plainly as any animal-created habitat is a function of its shape and mobility. This is who, and what, and also *how* we are.

We build spaces for their *insides* and *outsides. Our positive spaces* are carved out in negative for our habitats, defining space that we live and interact in. We thrive on closeness and the comfort of intimate space, but also luxuriate in open space and large-scale interpretations of our personal environments. And human spaces create human relationships: Architecture has for all known history been used to create spaces that convey power by altering the relationship of the person to the space and the space to itself.

VIRTUAL SPACE

Over the course of the 20th century, human experience began to shift from physical interaction with a world of things to a world of signals perceived electronically, through a series of devices. Although telegraph and radio had foreshadowed this

NETWORKING

The following list contains prominent websites for further exploration:

BROWN UNIVERSITY'S COMPUTER SCIENCE DEPARTMENT

Apps for Color Theory

cs.brown.edu/exploratories/freeSoftware/catalogs/color_theory.html

INTERNATIONAL COLOR CONSORTIUM

Promoting the standardization of color-management systems

www.color.org

KENT STATE UNIVERSITY, EDUCATION IN VISUAL LITERACY: LINE

www.educ.kent.edu/community/vlo/design/elements/line/index.html

STANFORD ENCYCLOPEDIA OF PHILOSOPHY: ENTRY ON THE EXPERIENCE AND PERCEPTION OF TIME

plato.stanford.edu/entries/time-experience/

WOLFRAM MATHWORLD ON PENROSE TILING

Creating aperiodic tilings and non-repeating patterns

http://mathworld.wolfram.com/PenroseTiles.html

SHODOR.COM: INTERESTING PATTERN GENERATOR USING TESSELATIONS

http://www.shodor.org/interactivate/activities/Tessellate/

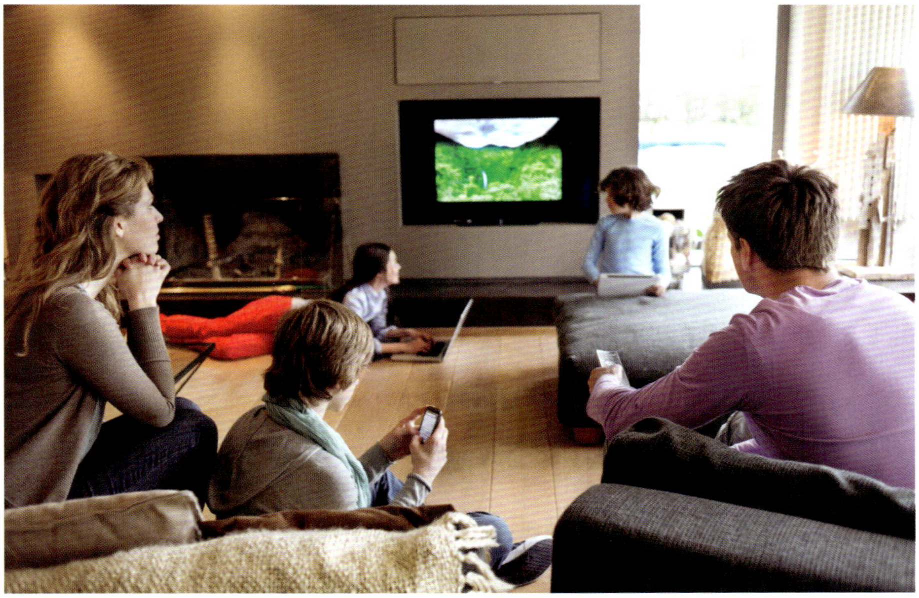

3.41 Over the course of the 20th century, human experience began to shift from physical interaction with a world of things to a world of signals perceived electronically through a series of devices.

Source: © Eric Audras/Onoky/Corbis

development, the real shift came through television, starting in the 1950s, and then the Internet, mobile phones, and other handheld devices in the decades around the beginning of this century (Fig. 3.41). An enormous portion of people's daily lives in the industrialized world now takes place in the virtual space of digital signals.

TIME (AND EXPERIENCE) AS ELEMENTS OF DESIGN

The extension of human experience by electronic means also carries with it an extension of our sense of immediate time, and indeed our changing perception of historical time, with all things present and accessible online at all times.

THE USER EXPERIENCE

Definitions of good design abound and are often couched in such a way as to describe good design as producing something both useful and beautiful. Definitions of this kind don't stand up by themselves for very long, as defining *beauty* immediately becomes a problem and *usefulness* is a very loose term. For example, is a designer dress useful? How beautiful is a well-designed tractor (Fig. 3.42)? And this has several permutations, depending on the viewpoint of the wearer of the dress, the driver of the tractor, or an outside observer.

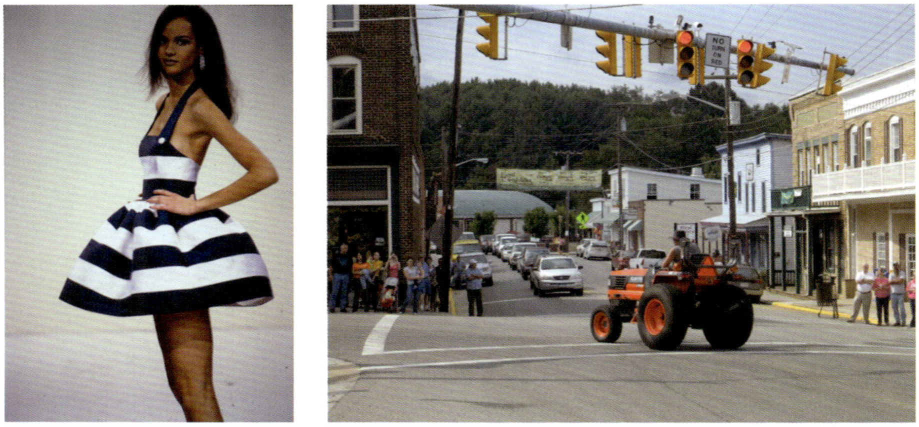

RIGHT

3.42 Is a designer dress more *useful* or *beautiful*? What if we don't think it's beautiful? How beautiful is a well-designed dress or a tractor? The user's concept of beauty matters. A farmer my not appreciate the beauty of a cocktail dress any more than a young socialite would consider a tractor.

Source: L: Photo © Colleen Redman. R: Ellis, Photograph by Niall McInerney, Bloomsbury Fashion Photography Archive

The modernist philosophy of functionality above all runs into difficulties once functionality becomes entwined with emotional needs and responses. Including the element of time allows a more flexible approach than the modernist notion of functionality had room for. Essentially the user experience breaks down into two interrelated sides: the practical and the emotional—on one hand the problem of *usability,* on the other that of *satisfaction.*

DESIGNING FOR LIVED EXPERIENCE

Designing for user satisfaction requires an acknowledgment of the lived experience as an element in design. Designing is in the end not only a dialogue but a series of dialogues. First, there is the dialogue between the designer and the end user in terms of addressing the constraints and needs of the design in relation to the client; then, the dialogue between the end user and the designed object or environment; and finally, between the end user and the internalized experience or memory of the design/environment (Fig. 3.43).

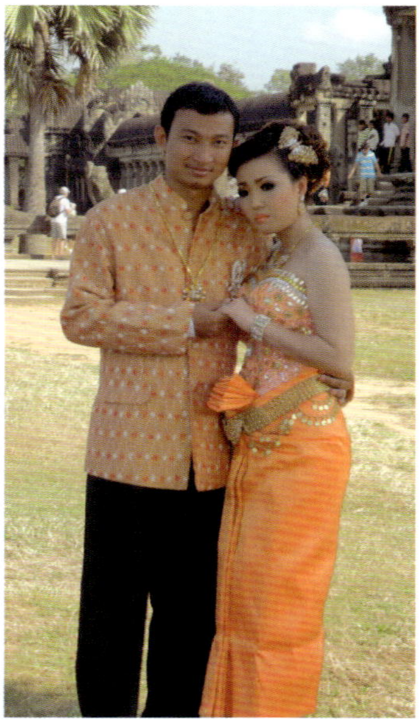

BELOW

3.43 Designing is a series of dialogues. First between the designer and the end user. Then between the end user and the designed object. and finally, between the end user and the internalized experience or memory of the design. This internalization may eventually lead to designs becoming a part of local tradition.

Source: Photo courtesy of Matthew Laird Acred

The first dialogues create references linking the designer's concepts, the client's previous experience, and the design's elements and nature. These references create levels of interest by pointing to new or unusual connections. They can also evoke emotions by appealing to nostalgia or memory or a more abstract sensory experience, such as textures or colors that resonate with the audience. These become attractive, and with time, a relationship with the design's elements forms where the end user is satisfied with the design's performance on both a functional and an emotional level. The design becomes "the way it should be" by fulfilling both.

TIME IN DESIGN

A good design achieves importance over lived historical time. Rhythm and pattern, for example, cannot be considered unless the temporal experience is factored in (What is first? What next?). Space cannot be experienced unless it is traversed (first here, then there). But time is also the dimension that allows us to have memories and a sense of continuous life (what was, what is, what will be).

When considering *time* as an element of design, we must understand a concept of time that is more related to lived experience (sensory time) than measurement (scientific time). Scientific time deals with measurements, schedules, calendars, chronologies, and timelines and is therefore pertinent to the design process itself, but as an element of design, we must consider sensory time—the lived experience. Among the dimensions we live in is the temporal dimension in which we conceive of time as passing and of things being ordered in time, allowing us a sense of now, future, and past. This includes the experience of clock time, a scientific and mechanical development that allows us to perceive time in measured units and use it to measure intervals between occurrences.

Time in design also plays a part in the dialogue that is memory and experience. Over time we create a narrative of our own lives and our relationships with the people and things around us. The designed objects in our environment help create this narrative by becoming collective points of reference and affirmations of the myths and beliefs of our personal and shared existence. There is nothing mysterious about this. We are the animal that designs environments and habitats and our creations are statements of our modes of existence—they become affirmations over time of what we are and how we belong. As individuals, the interpreted experiences of our designed environments and equipment contribute over time to our self-image. For groups, they become *culture* (Fig. 3.44).

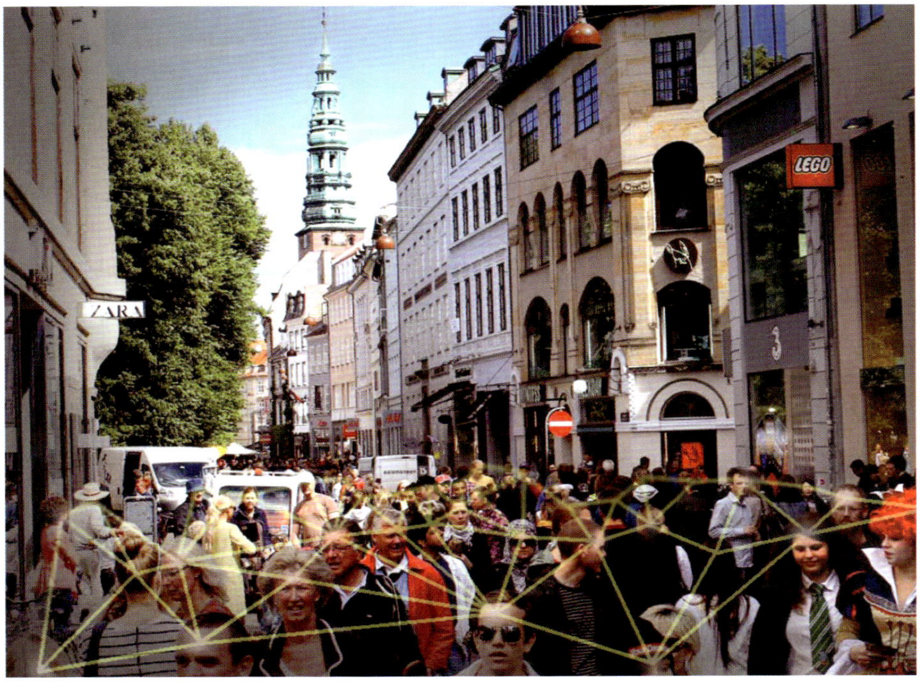

3.44 As individuals in society, the interpreted experiences of our designed environments and equipment contribute over time to our self-image; as groups, they become *culture* over time.

Source: Photograph and illustration by Karl Aspelund

EXPERIENCE IN TIME

The experience we have of our surroundings and designed objects has four stages that bring us into a growing relationship (Fig. 3.45). A designer must be aware of the trajectory of this evolution in order to work for the different levels of engagement it entails.

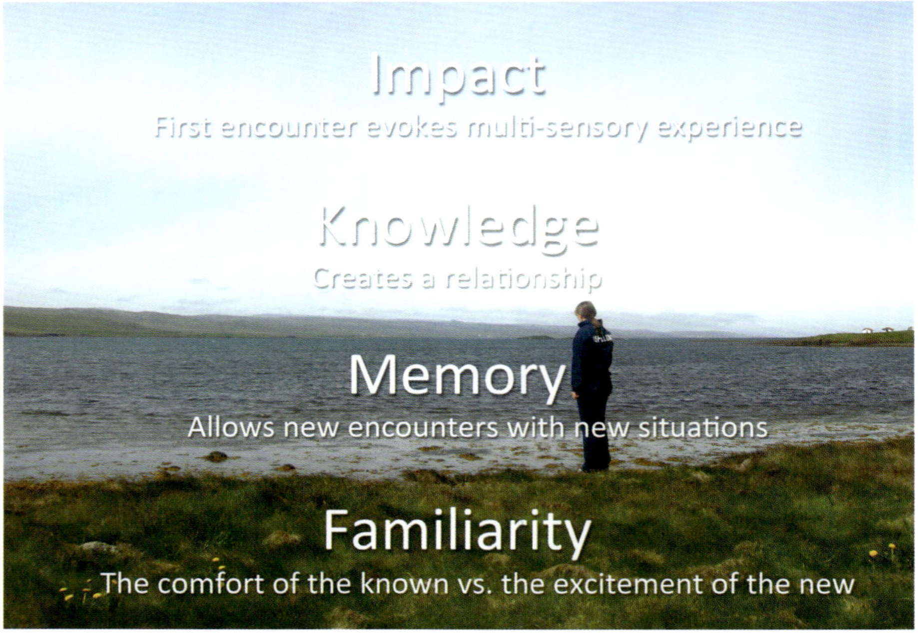

3.45 The experience we have of our surroundings and designed objects has four stages that bring us into a growing relationship and dialogue with a design objects and spaces.

Source: Photograph and illustration by Karl Aspelund

The first time we enter a room, try on a garment, walk through a building, or pick up an object, we are impacted consciously and unconsciously by sight, touch, sound, smell, emotion, and memory creating an impression and comfort level. Our first encounter with a design, like any first impression, is often the key to any future relationship we have with it. We experience *in the moment*—in the now—a series of impressions that become the framework within which the dialogue with the design will take place.

Over time, with repeated encounters, we form a relationship—we know the object, space, or situation, and we form a level of comfort. Previous experience may bring information from memory, but otherwise we form knowledge into memory that begins to inform future encounters with other designs. We learn through the layering of repetition to identify our responses to spaces, equipment, and products and make choices accordingly. Finally, our familiarity allows us to make choices, choosing either of the very human needs for the comfort of the known or the excitement of the new.

CONSIDER: DIFFERENT TIME DEMANDS

A designed object can be initially absorbed whole—almost instantly—through sight and touch. Contrast this with the contents of a book or film, the experience of a website or game, and so on, which require a commitment of time to absorb. However, any object that is in use will be revisited, reread, re-experienced, and the familiarity of the design begins to produce a sense of belonging. For example, texts and music were

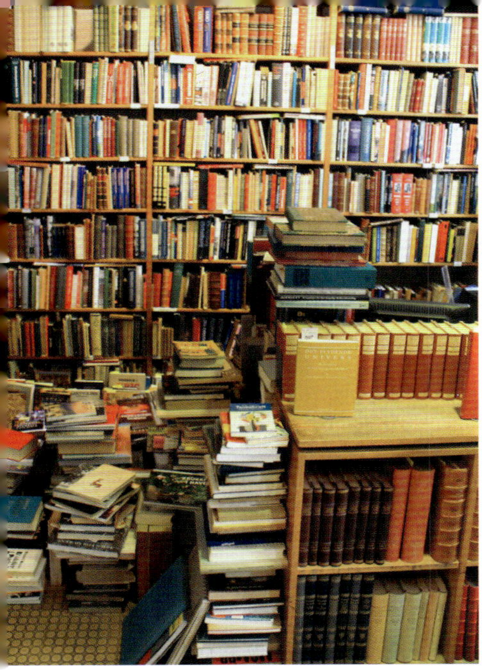

3.46 The design and feel of a book—its pages, its binding—makes a difference in the perception of the book's content before the reader even begins to read. Its physical presence is a factor. E-books are, on the other hand, pure content.

Photograph by Karl Aspelund

primarily sold as objects, that is, bound books and albums. Now they appear more as digital content without physical form. Previously, the design of a book, a book jacket, or an album cover would make a significant difference in the perception of that content. The weight and texture of the cover, the paper and print quality, cover illustrations, typefaces, and colors would inform the audience of the content, before they even began to read or listen (Fig. 3.46).

With downloaded content, that visual/tactile dialogue is no longer part of the experience and a relationship is not necessarily formed in the same way. We can, for example, change fonts, sizes, backgrounds, and formatting on texts in e-readers, so the text itself does not have a recognizable character as we revisit it. We also do not download albums but rather tracks, which may or may not be identified by any static visual at all. The design of a downloaded text or piece of music therefore has no longer any memory component—it has no interaction with the audience over time—altering the experience of reading or listening to music. The multisensory experience has lost an element.

NOSTALGIA, FAMILIARITY, AND NOVELTY

The near-synesthetic nature of experiencing a design through multiple senses must not be overlooked in the design process. Human beings *feel,* they *experience,* and every element counts over time. The excitement of the new becomes a familiarity that can then later bloom as nostalgia for the things that used to be and how they used to be. Nostalgia as a design inspiration grew ever stronger in the late 20th century, and it became ever more popular to present clear *retro* references in all manner of designs.

Human desire for experience eventually tends toward a *home base,* and we become anxious when the unfamiliar surrounds us without end. In the end we must *belong*. It is quite possible that the need for novelty on one hand and familiarity on the other is constantly in tension over time, and as more and more of our experience of the world is on-screen, the need for retro familiarity in the things we touch becomes stronger.

HISTORY, MEMORY, AND NOSTALGIA

The experience we have of our objects and surroundings allows an attachment to develop over time. As we, the things, and the environment age—and show signs of this aging—a sense of belonging emerges. The wear and tear, scars, and patinas brought by use and existence over time create identities and signs of individuality and experience. The sense of having lived with—or been lived in—allows us to consider the design from a point of view where the object or place is connected to times past. It has a life, replete with memory and the mystery of buried knowledge.

But nostalgia, longing, and romantic visions require a view of history in relation to the present. The designer must be able to identify with the audience's lived experience of the designed object or environment over time. As the 20th century wore on, the concept of pre-worn patina became part of the aesthetic of the modern world. A predesigned past began to be built into manufactured goods and clothing. Rather than being fresh and undamaged, a new status arose around being worn and faded—lived and full of lived experience.

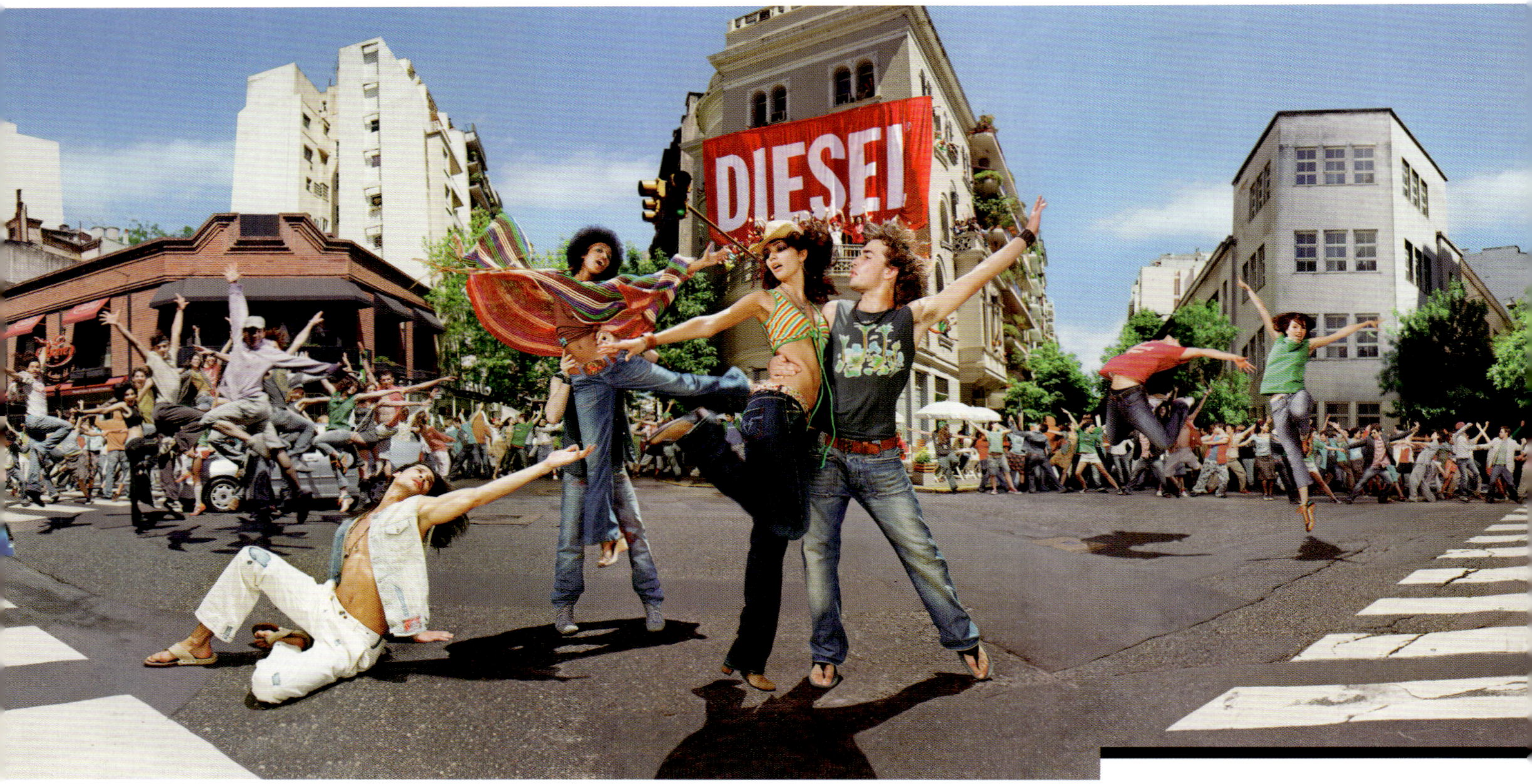

3.47 Our culture has increasingly become a search for the future by continually referencing the past, with styles, periods, and references overlapping into a self-fulfilling vision. This ad uses fashion references to past decades (mainly a polished look at the late 1960s and 1970s) to create a humorous ironic statement that contrasts the overt nostalgia with a slogan of "the future—a musical to believe in." Diesel brand ad campaign poster by KK Los Angeles.

Source: Courtesy of Kessels Kramer and Photography by Elaine Constantine ©2005

LIVED EXPERIENCE OVER TIME

It is here that design begins to be about a dialogue with local culture. A designer must understand the interaction of the local population with the styles and methods that were in place, those that are in the process of being adopted, and those that are emerging. With culture being a collected store of the things we do and the things we do them with over time, we see that an understanding of a culture is also an understanding of a historical narrative.

With a historical narrative being both factual and fanciful at once, knowledge of history in an official sense or in basic textbooks is not necessarily helpful. Rather, history in design must be understood as *lived* history, and this requires a knowledge of the culture of the lived objects and environments within which the designer is working. But with markets and environments ever more global, designers need to be more vigilant about overlapping and varied cultural influences finding their way into the simplest designs through local references and the use of the basic elements of design (Fig. 3.47).

CONCLUSION

The elements of design are both few and apparently simple, but the basic list conceals a world of complex opportunity. The application of *color, line, texture and pattern, shape,* and *space* with the addition of *time* allows for an endless journey of creativity. The addition of time is, however, a factor that must be considered carefully, as its inclusion literally adds a dimension. Considering time as an element allows us much more insight into the role of design as the creation of *experience.* Good knowledge of each set of elements, and the inherent possibilities and their limitations, allows the designer to analyze a design problem and create a solution with confidence and insight. Thinking of design as experience brings us closer to the user involved and can only result in better designing.

KEY TERMS

Line	Texture	Space
Shape	Pattern	Time
Color		

DISCUSSION AND REVIEW QUESTIONS

1. Choose a designed object or environment that you can observe, touch, and move around. Observe how the different elements are experienced by a viewer or user of the design. What is the relationship of sight, touch, and movement for each element?

2. Compare two similar designed objects that use design elements in a very different way (e.g., two chairs, two bicycles, two shirts). How do the elements create the distinct design?

3. Consider each of the design elements in turn and consider how their effect takes place over time: What is the impact in *the moment?* What is the effect over a long period? How might the full experience of the element in question require time?

EXERCISES AND ASSIGNMENTS

1. Consider a designed object and describe it in terms of its elements of design.
   a. Color: What colors are used? How? Is there a color scheme involved?
   b. Line: Formed/implied? Curved/straight? Convex/concave? Clear/ Unclear? Length? Width?
   c. Texture/Pattern: Visual or tactile or both? Both at once or both present?
   d. Shape: Rectilinear/curvilinear?
   e. Space: How does the design use positive and/or negative space?
   f. Time and Experience: What do you think would be the experience of the object over time? Will the object change over time? If so, how will those changes affect the experience? Do you think the changes are desirable or not?

2. Consider changing the each of the elements of the design.

   a. Which elements can be changed without the object losing its specific identity? (When does a chair become *another kind of* chair? When is a shirt no longer *this kind of* shirt) ?

   b. How much can you change before it becomes another object altogether? (When does a chair stop being a chair and become, say, a couch or a chaise? When is a shirt no longer a shirt but a jacket or a blouse)?

   c. How are the elements of this design independent of—or dependent on—each other? (Can the colors change without altering patterns, can line change without altering shape, and so on? How does changing the physical elements (color, texture, etc.) change the experience of the object?

REFERENCES

1. Marshall McLuhan. *Understanding Media*, McGraw-Hill, 1964, pp. 8–9.

CHAPTER 4

THE PRINCIPLES OF DESIGN

DESIGNERS SPEAK

"I design places to be in and, even if existence is not definable, I know a few recurrent motifs: for instance, to look out of the window, to see the sun going through it or filtered by a veranda, to live in high or low rooms, wide or narrow doors, corners to shelter in without having to look outside, to possess a terrace to grow plants on, to go long or short distances—places that don't tell you what they are or places where you just look. I try to design them so that the people living in them can be aware of these different moments."

—Ettore Sottsass, quoted in Barbara Radice, *Ettore Sottsass: A Critical Biography* (New York: Random House, 1993).

"Humanism is probably the thing that connects all of our projects. Whether planning a city, designing a building, designing a piece of furniture, or designing a toaster, first and foremost I think about how people will interact with the design. I embraced this philosophy while studying in Rome, and it is the most important filter that I include in all of our projects, and it is the greatest thing I have instilled in our office. The terms have become almost cliché, but function drives form in good design at every scale."

—Michael Graves, "Interview with Michael Graves," *Design Elements*, http://design-elements-blog.com/2012/04/30/interview-with-michael-graves/

OBJECTIVES

Identify the principles of design.

Comprehend why each principle may be necessary in the creation of a design.

Distinguish the aesthetic effect of each principle's application.

Be familiar with the concept of gestalt perception and its principles.

Recognize the importance of considering usability or user experience when designing.

Now that the elements of design—the fundamental building blocks of a design project—have been introduced, the focus now turns to the principles of design. These are guiding concepts that direct how to work with the elements to produce visually engaging and effective designs. The principles of design grew out of early considerations of art and architecture and appear in similar framings over the course of centuries. Mostly, due to their origins in discourse on fine arts and high architecture, they deal with aesthetic considerations rather than functionality or practicality. For this reason, it is necessary to widen the discussion and add the more recently formulated concept of "usability" to the mix, in the same (and not unrelated) way in which "time" was added to the elements of design in the previous chapter. The six principles of design are therefore presented here as:

- Unity, variety, and harmony
- Proportion and scale
- Balance
- Rhythm
- Emphasis and focus
- Usability (experience)

WHY "PRINCIPLES"?

The principles of design serve as guides to structure a designer's choices and as frames within which the design concept can be questioned and developed. They are not *laws* or *rules* to be followed, but rather effects to be produced by the use of design elements. For example, a choice may be made between a unity or a disarray of elements; a rhythmic solution or an arrhythmic arrangement of forms may be found. Although they are not rules themselves, each of the principles has prompted the formulation of various rules and methods over the centuries. These have had the goal of finding the best way to achieve a desired result or have even detailed specifically what that result should entail. Certain ratios and proportions were considered more pleasing than others in the classical Greek culture, for example, and the Euro-American culture valued regular rhythms and symmetry well into the 20th century (Fig. 4.1). Underlying these are culturally and socially dependent ideas of good aesthetics and the purpose of design in the world. Ideals evolve, are challenged and change, cultural influences realign modes, and the approach to the principles changes right alongside. The principles remain there to be acknowledged, either by adherence or opposition.

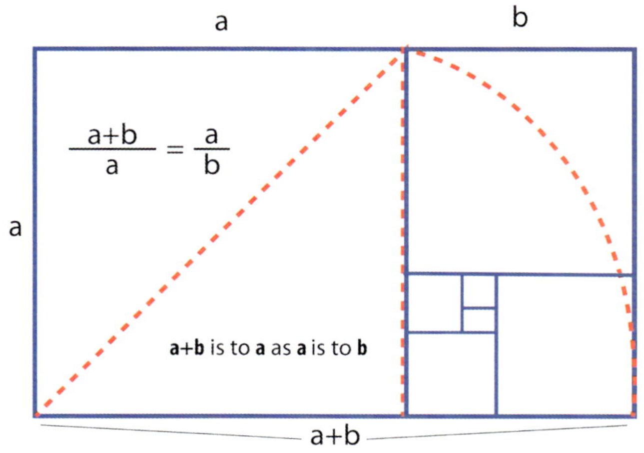

4.1 Certain ratios and proportions are considered more "pleasing" than others and admired for their mathematical properties. The *golden ratio* or *golden section* (approximately 1:1.618) appears frequently in natural formations as well as geometry and was considered a major discovery and evidence of an underlying principle of natural beauty. It appears, for example, in both the overall proportions as well as the details of the Temple of Zeus at Olympia in Athens. The opinion that this is somehow a perfect ratio was reinforced in Western culture when all things Greek and Roman began to be venerated in the Renaissance and Neoclassical periods.

Source: Illustration by Karl Aspelund

TIMELINE: TREATMENT OF PRINCIPLES

Attempting to create a brief timeline of design principles is an odd and ultimately futile undertaking, particularly in light of the historical overview of Chapter 2. Trying to encompass the variations and different approaches through history—at least in a quick overview—would necessitate describing the entire history of design as well as its variations within and among cultures. We would need to consider how design principles have changed and the experimental nature of humanity's approach, from the very beginning of the human endeavor, to molding our surroundings by design. Proceeding through history and around the globe, one observes the shifts in emphasis from one period to the next and one culture to another. The principles of design are formally indicated in different ways in Ancient Egypt, Greece, China, Middle America, and Africa. Harmony is played with, focus is clear and then dispersed, rhythms are emphasized, then broken, balance through symmetry comes and goes, and proportions and scale are blown up and brought down. One could compare Classical Japan with the Western Modernists, African polyrhythms with postmodern playfulness, observe the Greco-Roman classical symmetries in colonial architecture worldwide, and ponder the strange simplicity of thousands of years of pyramids and pyramid-like structures in Egypt, Middle America, and Asia.

Understanding the principles of design historically and across cultures should not be done in a linear fashion or by looking at individual items and "works" museum-style, but by considering design as a dialogue of people and their environment over time. The principles are there as frames to be worked in, around, and through—sometimes inside, sometimes out. Although we as humans have an innate need to categorize and recognize in order to understand, when you are considering the history of these design principles, think of them as a conversation of people and things (at least once you've categorized and recognized).

Each of the elements of design has a unique way of contributing to the work being performed under each of the principles. Working with balance in color, for example, is a very different operation than balancing shapes and balancing textures or patterns. Different disciplines also approach the principles differently, with different priorities. Apparel designers may be less concerned with rhythm than architects, for example, and although both design around constraints of human movement and size, the attention to proportion and scale is quite different.

Technological developments have influenced how the principles are approached from generation to generation. New materials, production methods, and media change what is possible. To incorporate these new capabilities, new trends in design will subsequently arise that in turn challenge or broaden the reigning approach to the principles. Soon, self-images are altered; balances, scale, harmonies, and rhythms shift; new design ideals are embedded in the culture; and a new round of exploration can begin.

UNITY, HARMONY, VARIETY

A designer's approach will involve balancing elements to create a degree of totality in a design impact on our senses and emotions. The relationship between the various elements to the overall design becomes that of *belonging* or *not belonging,* each contributing to the overall effect by strengthening or counterbalancing each other. The contribution of each element is determined by both the overall relationship of the parts *to the whole* as well as the individual effect of each element *within the whole.* An understanding of how we perceive elements, ideas, events, and things to be in union allows designers to create and manipulate such unions in design. It is therefore helpful to begin the discussion of design principles with the concepts of **unity, harmony,** and **variety.** This examination gets to the core of how we perceive designs (or anything) as totalities, even when the individual elements that make them up are an incomplete set. However, an understanding of the perception of totalities requires that we first look at the concepts of gestalt perception.

GESTALT PERCEPTION

Gestalt is the type of word that is adopted into the English language unchanged because the meaning is subtle and difficult to translate perfectly. It is a German word that means something akin to *a totality,* as in "the whole of it," but it also conveys a perception or experience where the "whole of it" is more than a sum of its parts. Gestalt represents a totality where the assembly of elements creates a new experience with qualities that are not represented by the collected elements (e.g., a meal is more than a pile of ingredients). See Fig. 4.2.

The ability of humans to recognize patterns relies on an ability to perceive a gestalt from incoming information. We are generally very good at this. Even the most disjointed, broken-up stimuli can be assembled into meaningful information so well that we frequently will overlay meaning on completely random signals, such as when we see human figures in natural formations and faces in smoke, or when we hear voices in hisses of white noise (Fig. 4.3).

This is fundamentally how we learn and how we structure information over time, by connecting new information with prior knowledge by association. Soon the whole of a perceived concept, experience, or object is greater than the sum of its parts and we have new knowledge to work with. To construct a new idea for an audience—a new concept by design—we may play directly to this innate strength to achieve a new impactful unity from different situations of things or information.

ACHIEVING UNITY

It is important to realize that we process sensual information in this gestalt-creating way, regardless of which combination of our five senses is delivering the information to our brain. We recognize the relationship of elements as unified by the following

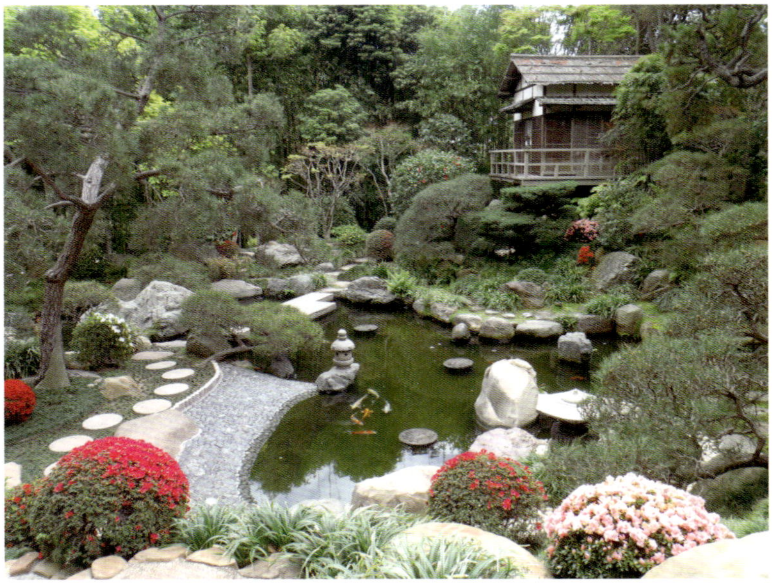

BELOW LEFT

4.2 A gestalt is a totality where the assembly of elements creates a new experience with qualities that are not represented by the elements individually. This garden vista, for example, is more than a collection of rocks, plants, and structures by a pond. Each element works to create the overall design of the place and space. There is "the whole of it"—the way in which the similar shapes, textures, and colors of the rocks, plants, and built structures work together to create the unique gestalt (totality) that is this area.

Source: Courtesy of hannahcarterjapanesegarden.com

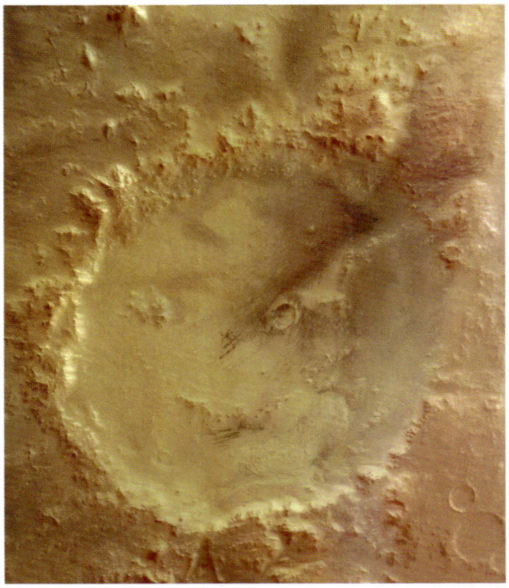

BELOW RIGHT

4.3 Humans process information into knowable structures, frequently overlaying meaning on random visual signals or sounds (a phenomenon known as pareidolia). We see human figures in natural formations and faces in smoke, or hear voices in hisses of white noise, such as the happy face in the Galle Crater on Mars.

Source: Credit: ESA/DLR/FU Berlin (G. Neukum)

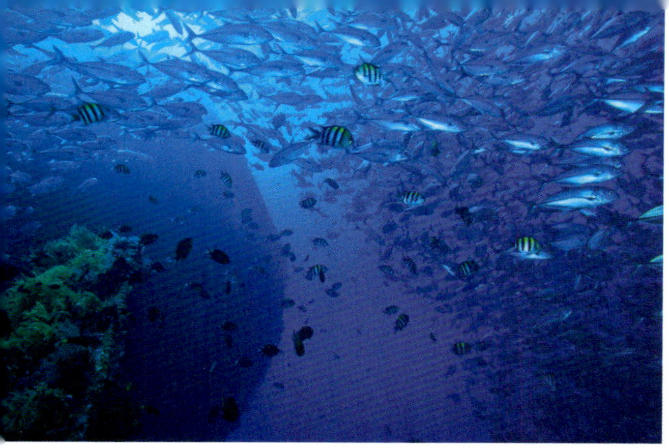

4.4 Similarity: We recognize things that are similar and instinctively group them into categories of belonging and not belonging. If there is any hint of structure or pattern it will very likely emerge and define our understanding of the relationship of the events or things. In this image, we recognize how the fish belong together by noting the several different types. We see quickly that the striped fish are not part of the larger school involved and do not belong with the others.

Source: © Stuart Westmorland/Corbis

subset of the principles of gestalt perception: similarity, proximity, repetition, continuation, and closure (see Box 3.1 in Chapter 3):

Similarity. We recognize things that are similar and instinctively group them into categories of belonging and not belonging. If there is any hint of structure or pattern, it will very likely emerge and define our understanding of the relationship of the events or things (Fig. 4.4).

Proximity. Events or things close together are understood as related, or at least more closely connected, than events or things that are spaced further apart (Fig. 4.5).

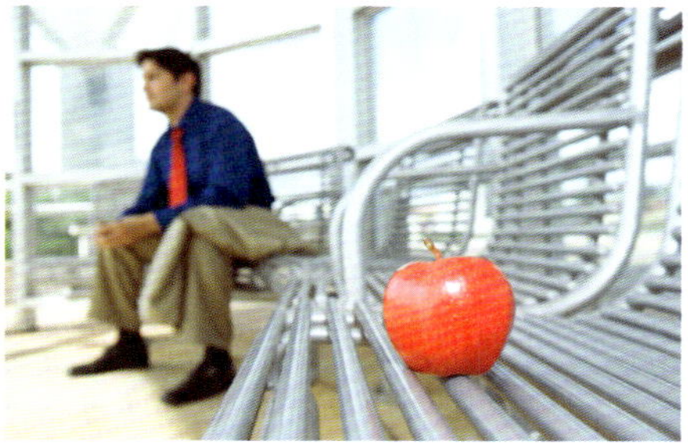

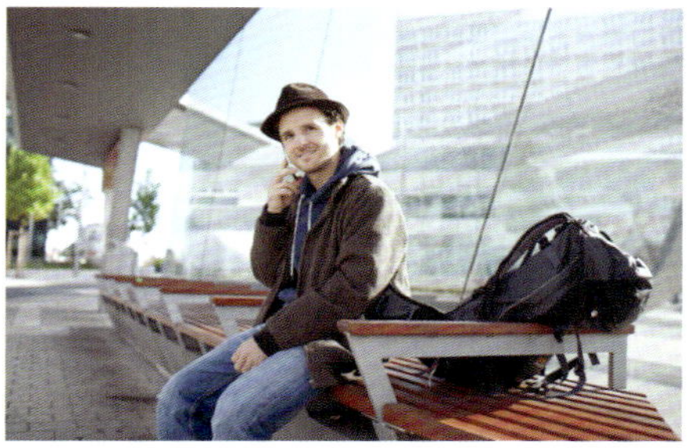

4.5 Proximity: Events or things close together are understood as more closely connected, than events or things that are spaced further apart. In the picture on the left, the distance makes it unclear whether the apple belongs to the man in the blue shirt. It may or may not. In the picture on the right, it seems very likely that the backpack, being so close, belongs to the man with the hat.

Source: L: © Steve Hix/Somos Images/Corbis; R: © Matthias Ritzmann/Corbis

Repetition. Elements that appear or occur repeatedly are grouped and considered to be in unity (Fig. 4.6).

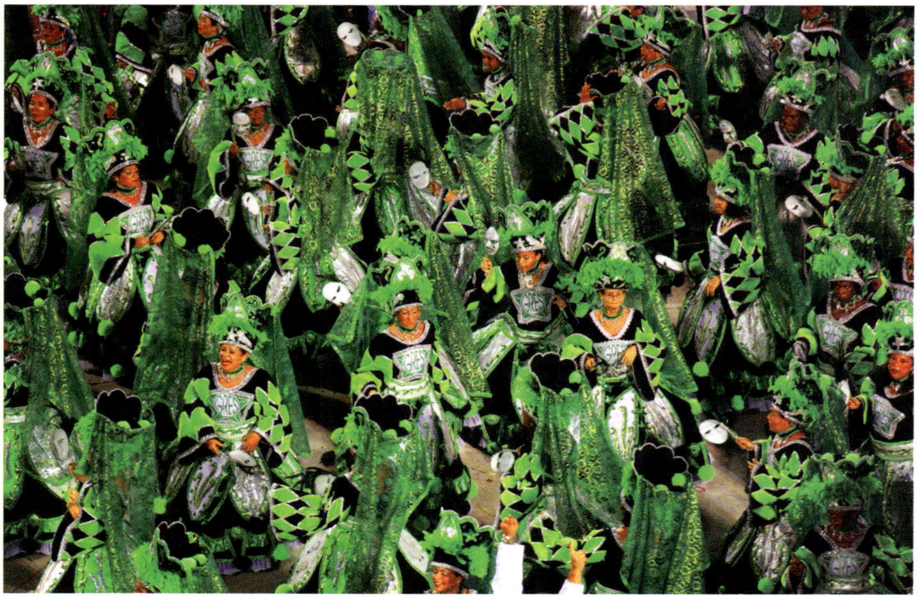

4.6 Repetition: Elements that appear or occur repeatedly are grouped and considered to be in unity. It is an easy assumption that the people in this picture have a unified purpose of some kind, once we have registered their costumes and the closeness of their placement. They all *belong* to each other and the situation they are in. They are *grouped* by their costumes. We do not, for example, guess that they all arrived individually and just happened to stand in the same spot. Carnival in Rio.

© ROBIN UTRECHT FOTOGRAFIE/HillCreek Pictures/Corbis

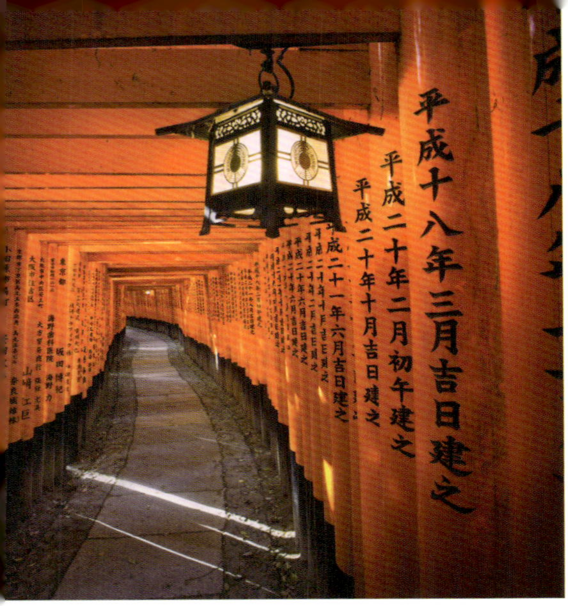

ABOVE

4.7 Continuation: Looking at this section of the arcade of *torii* (shrine gates) in the Fushimi Inari-taisha Shrine in Kyoto, Japan, we would expect the gates to continue around the bed in orange and not suddenly be blue or made of glass.

Source: © Jon Hicks/Corbis

Continuation. Elements that are separate but imply a continuous line or a continuity of development will be understood to be connected. This also applies to a continuous pattern or repetitive form that will be understood to continue beyond what is immediately perceived (Fig. 4.7).

Closure. Where a pattern or form (i.e., either things or events) is incomplete, we fill in the pattern and provide the continuation. This creates a *closed* or *complete gestalt.* The totality is completed (Fig. 4.8).

EMPHASIZING UNITY

The five principles of gestalt perception above are keys to understanding the way unity—or the lack thereof—is communicated in design. By working them backward, a designer can take advantage of people's innate responses to sensory stimuli. Perhaps more importantly, designers can understand their own impulses. By observing their impulsive decisions in hindsight, they may understand the unity they have created or disrupted with their choices.

The human psyche craves unity made interesting by injections of variety. In the largest sense, harmony is achieved when the arrangement of a variety of elements forms a gestalt that is considered pleasing. This is often used very loosely with regard to the compatibility of elements in a design, or good arrangements; the harmony of furniture in interiors, for example, or the harmony of spatial arrangements. Formally, however, sounds are most commonly referred to in this way; for example, when a number of voices sing different notes, which together produce a richer sound than would be possible by any one voice. Colors also are spoken of as harmonizing when a color scheme is constructed in such a way as to include, for example, complementary or analogous colors or color triads (Fig. 4.9).

BELOW

4.8 Gestalt Closure: When a pattern, form, thing, or event is incomplete, we fill in the pattern and provide the continuation. This creates a *closed* or *complete gestalt*. The totality is completed.

Source: © Peter M. Fisher/Corbis

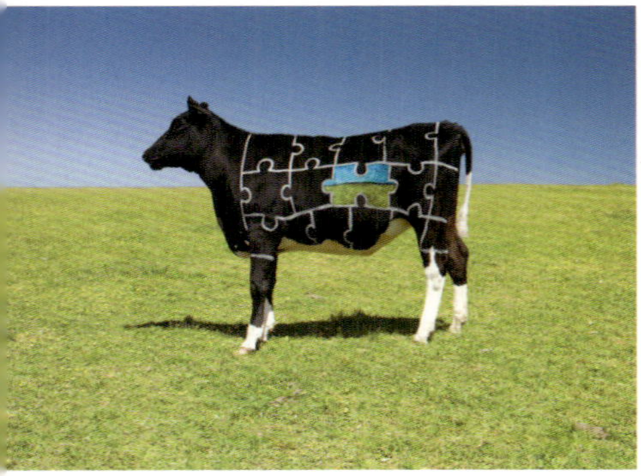

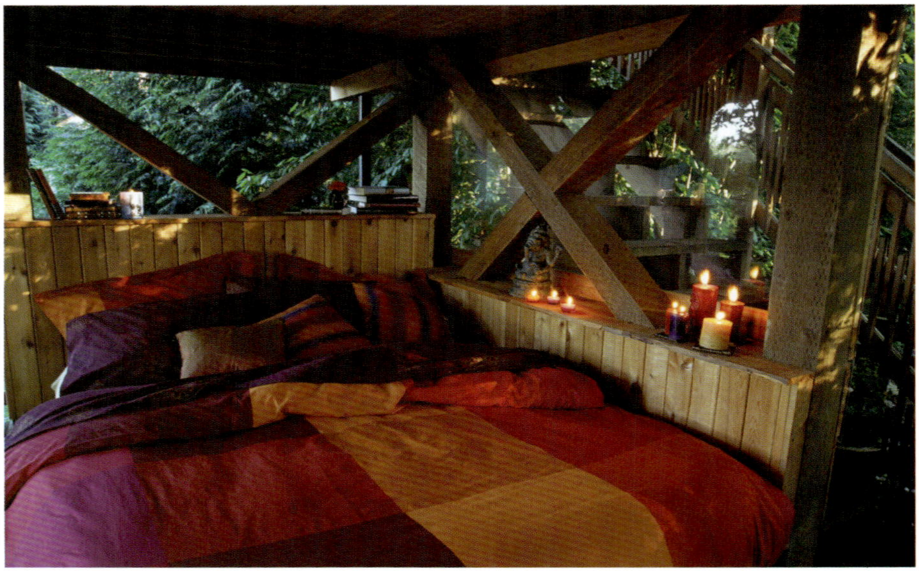

4.9 Colors are spoken of as harmonizing when a color scheme is constructed in such a way as to include, for example, complimentary or analogous colors or color triads, all of which can be seen here if the greenery is included in the scheme.

Source: © Clive Nichols/Arcaid/Corbis

RIGHT

4.10 Even that which is deconstructed often has as much a sense of being a gestalt as any design. This bookshelf, an exercise in the reuse of salvaged construction materials has as totality of its own.

Source: By Lewis Wadsworth, a designer and artist in Boston, Massachusetts (http://lewiswadsworth.net/lw4/contact/)

BELOW LEFT

4.11 Uniformity is used in grand displays and large-scale spectacles to create a sensation of depersonalized grandeur in displays of power. The picture shows the Republic Day celebrations in India.

Source: © National Geographic Image Collection/Alamy

BELOW RIGHT

4.12 Harmony results from a balance of variety and unity on a point residing somewhere on a continuum between the two extremes. In the end it is a value assessment in the moment, rather than the application of rules that allows the achievement of such a balance. Here we have variety in unity producing a visual harmony: The general shapes and textures are very similar, producing unity, but the colors vary largely. They, however, are within a unified frame themselves and the shapes, colors and textures produce a pleasing visual harmony.

Source: © Joe Petersburger/Corbis

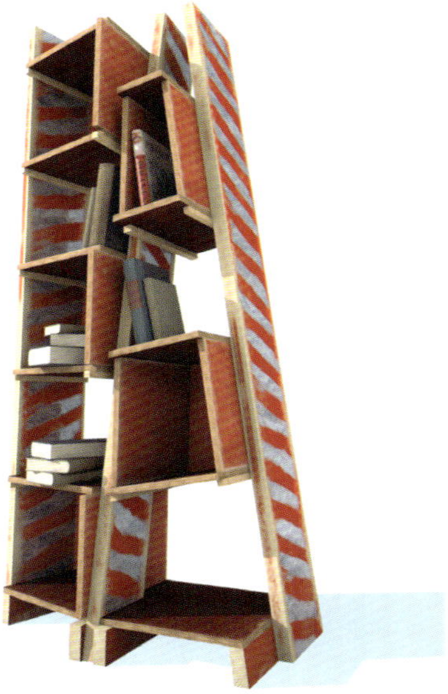

In any case, the essential issue is that in viewing designs, we perceive the gestalt that results from the combination of elements. In perceiving this unity, we develop additional stimulation, or *visual interest,* from any variety we observe within the unity. If the variety is not somehow *disruptive* to our senses (and this, as mentioned above, can be culturally, historically, and socially dependent), we consider the effect successful (i.e., satisfying or pleasing).

The deconstruction of unities only has very recently, in the history of human creativity, come to the forefront of creativity and design, but even with the late-modern/postmodern trend toward deconstruction, design tends toward creating unified totalities. Even that which is *deconstructed* often has as much a sense of being a gestalt as any design from previous centuries (Fig. 4.10). True disunity is extremely hard to find, much less create, just as it is very hard to be deliberately random; there seems to always be method found in any madness.

Designs that tend toward too much unity have, on the other hand, an effect that is blunted by repetition. Such uniformity can have impact when used for emphasis and is often used as such to the maximum possible extent. Strong statements may be created by avoiding variety altogether. By working with only one element or a repetition of a small set of elements, an effect may be produced that is very impactful and overwhelming. Uniformity often is used in grand displays and large-scale spectacles to create a sensation of depersonalized grandeur, and it is hardly surprising that this functions often in displays of power (Fig. 4.11). Conversely, overwhelming variety can create a chaotic effect, giving rise to the feelings of exhilaration that result from being (nearly) out of control and the joy of surprise. In the end, the harmony resulting from a balance of variety and unity must be understood as being found on a point residing on a continuum between the two extremes and not a fixed result determined by universal rules (Fig. 4.12).

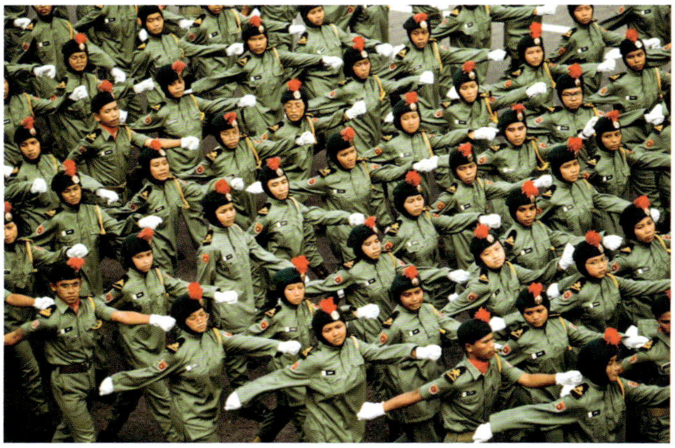

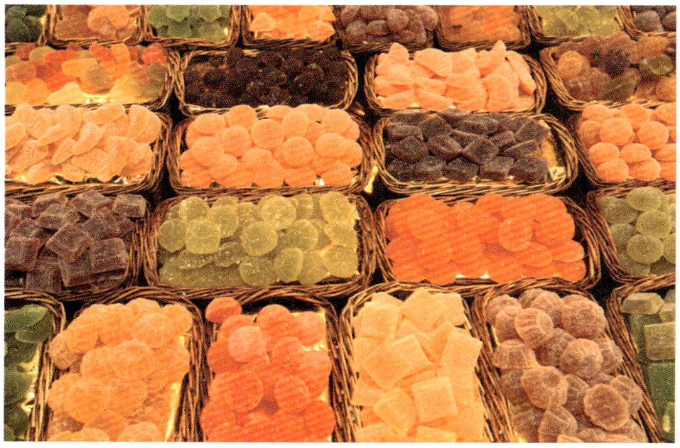

PROPORTION AND SCALE

Proportion refers to the **scale,** or relative size, of elements in a design and is manipulated constantly in all manner of designing. Certain ideals of proportion are held very strongly—and differently—in different cultures, with geometric ideals being expressed as laws. In the Euro-American cultural sphere, for example, Greco-Roman classical ideals of proportion were revitalized in the early 15th century, held sway for nearly 400 years, and are still lingering. These are expressed by concepts, such as the golden ratio, that are meant to be especially pleasing (Fig. 4.13) and the classical *eight-part division* of the human body (Fig. 4.14). However, these have been eroding along with other classical ideals of design over the past 100 years, with modernist experimentation and multicultural references trending in different directions.

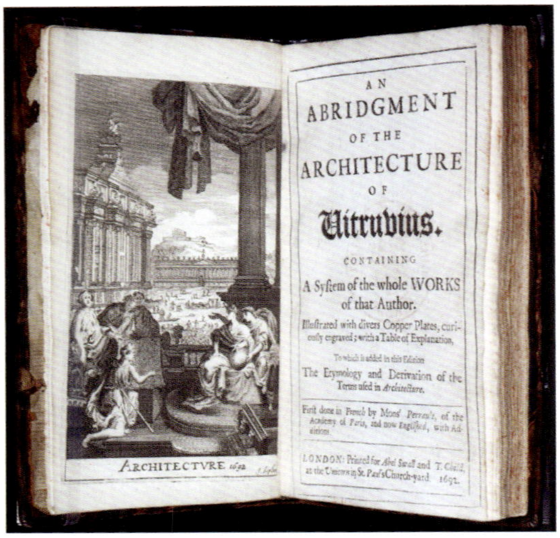

ABOVE

4.13 In the Euro-American cultural sphere, for example, Greco-Roman classical ideals of design were revitalized through architecture in the early 15th century and held sway for nearly 400 years. In many ways they still linger. Frontispiece and title page of the English translation of *An Abridgment of the Architecture of Vitruvius*. (London, 1692).

Source: Copyright: RIBA Library Photographs Collection

EXTERNAL AND INTERNAL SCALE

With regard to proportion, one may be positioned in one of two main frames of reference: the *external*, where one considers the relation of elements to surroundings and interactions, or the *internal*, where the relative scale of elements within the design is considered. The primary point of scale reference in all human design is (perhaps too obviously) the human body. Different as cultures, politics, and historical references may be, the overall scale of humans is a universal reference throughout the world and has been for thousands of years, because humans became the species that designs its environment. In that, the distinction of internal and external takes on a universal dimension of how the design relates to the human body.

First, there is a question of *direct physical contact* determining the scale. The design is literally *on* the body, conforming to its proportions. Apparel, jewelry, accessories, prosthetics, and equipment designed to sit on the body may be discreet or

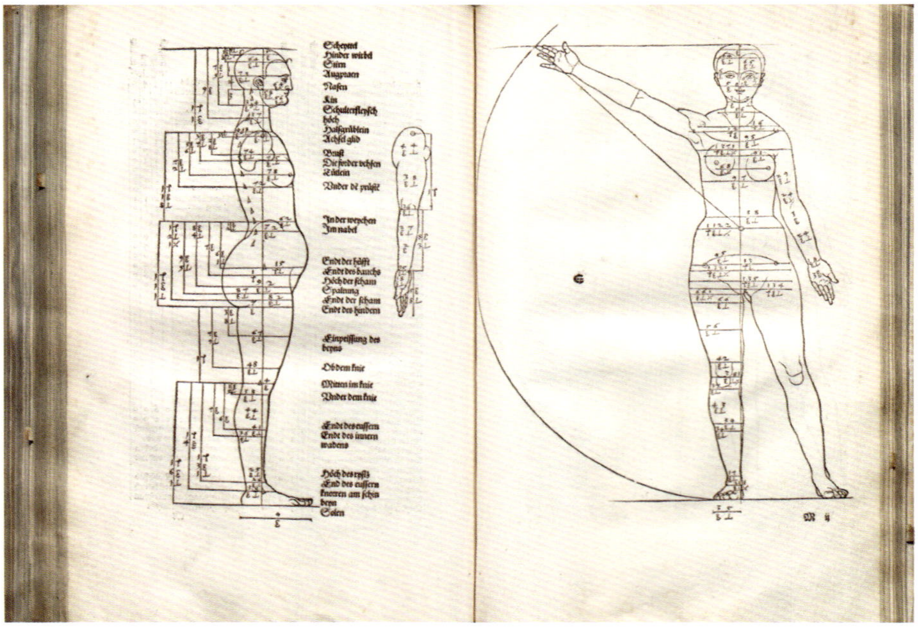

RIGHT

4.14 An analysis of the proportions of the female body as illustrated by the artist Albrecht Dürer, in his De Symmetria Partium in Rectics Formis Humanorum Corporum, a part of his larger work Four Books on Human Proportions.

Source: National Gallery of Art Library (Gift of Robert F Erburu)

SUSTAINABILITY: A PRINCIPLE FOR THE FUTURE

Just as with the elements of design, the principles of design must each be considered when sustainability comes into question. As usability is to be taken into account, this also provides a new point to consider. However, taking each in turn serves little purpose, as the principles are *applied* or *adhered to*, rather than being directly tangible. The point to make, regarding sustainability, is that the six principles of design—unity/variety/harmony, proportion and scale, balance, rhythm, emphasis/focus, and usability (experience)—affect the construction and use of a design and can therefore each make demands on materials and production. The designer considers each in turn, assessing the impact of the design in terms of its use of resources, and whether the aesthetic considerations that the principles apply are putting an undue strain anywhere. For example, the requirement of the placement of a particular element to influence a sense of balance may require more materials, time, energy, and so on. Perhaps a different design decision would retain the aesthetic impact but be less demanding. Play with this kind of thinking on designs around you. Be aware that each design decision has consequences and that aesthetics are in the end the easiest to manipulate.

overwhelming, but they are always so in relation to the body and are understood as such by the viewer by reference to an internalized, instinctive knowledge of what the body is and does. We not only see, we *feel* the interaction on our own skin, bones, and muscles, sensing how our own bodies would relate and interact (Fig. 4.15).

Second are designs that are intended to be *handled and manipulated*. The key here is the *hand* in handled (echoing the latin *manis* in manipulated), although we may be considering designs that are operated by any body part—that is, tools, utensils, or equipment of any kind that are held, moved, powered, or reacted to via physical contact. Such items must be proportioned to allow this interaction comfortably and efficiently. Keys on keyboards must be big enough to accommodate fingertips, pedals must fit feet, cup handles allow fingers, kitchen utensils sit comfortably in hands, and so forth (Fig. 4.16).

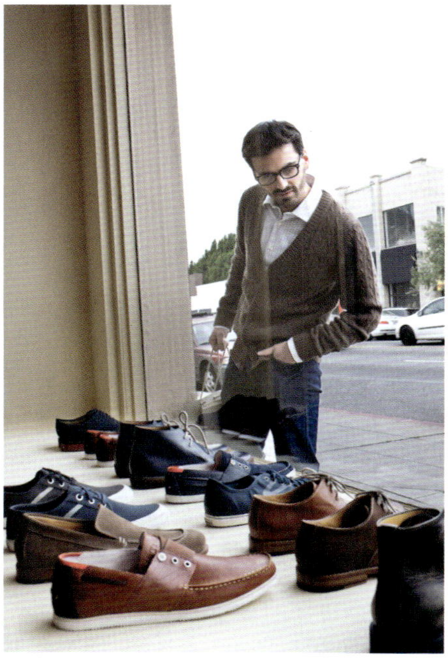

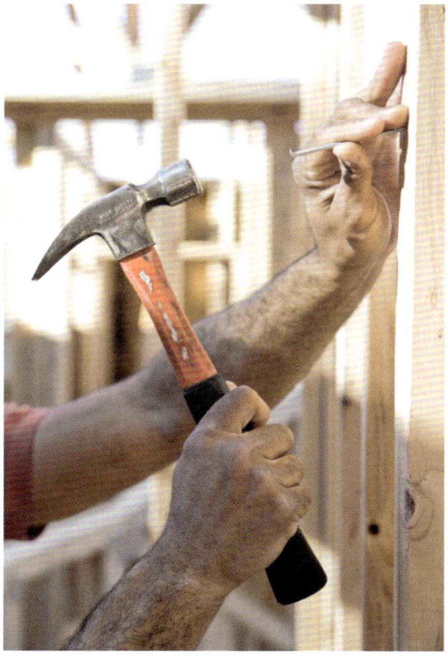

BOTTOM LEFT

4.15 We sense the world with more than one sense at a time. Our memories of experiences are awakened by any of our senses. When looking at a design with which we will interact, we also feel it on our own skin, bones, and muscles, through memories of similar experiences, sensing how our own bodies would relate to it. Looking at a garment or pair of shoes evokes in us the memory of having worn similar items. We know how it would feel if we wore it.

Source: © Helen King/Corbis

BOTTOM RIGHT

4.16 Human activity defines human equipment. The comfortable balance of a tool in the hand is a good example of the importance of proportion, structure, and texture in allowing comfortable and efficient interaction with our designs.

Source: © Colorblind Images/Blend Images/Corbis

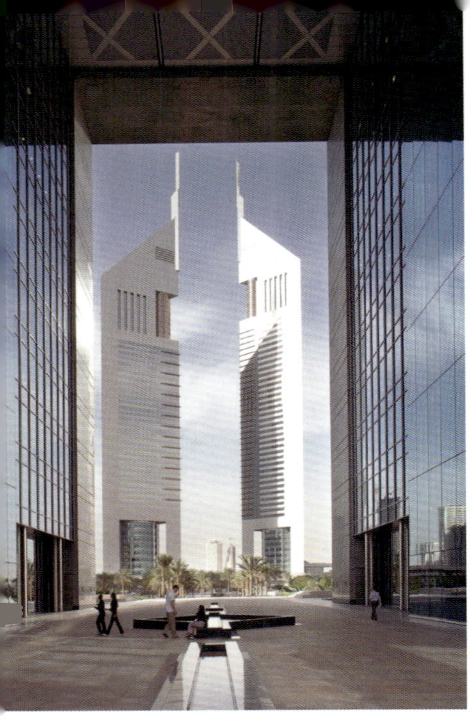

ABOVE

4.17 Through the centuries, architecture and city planning has resulted in designs that specifically and purposefully overwhelm the human body in order to exhibit power or display the status of the ruling classes of the city. Making the viewer seem small by comparison to the buildings is literally a way to make the viewer *feel* small. The Gate, View Through Arch to Surrounding Skyscrapers, Gensler, Dubai, United Arab Emirates.

Source: © Hufton + Crow/VIEW/Corbis

The third category includes designs that *surround or accommodate the body*, such as clothing, furniture, or vehicles, where the entire body must sit or fit comfortably. For this, industries have developed certain standards that accommodate most people, with the apparel industry developing systems of sizing, as it needs to be more precise in its adaptation to the variety of body types and shapes.

Finally, there are designs that specifically and purposefully overpower the human body, by going outside human scale and re-referencing the basic elements. This has habitually been done in architecture and city planning, but also can be seen in fashionable apparel through the centuries (Fig. 4.17).

Then, despite all of the above, there are designs that are not body-dependent. These designs consist of equipment and constructs where the primary function of the design does not involve any direct human interaction. These are usually of a very technical or functional nature, such as satellites, miniaturized scientific equipment, drones, robots, or weapons that once deployed do not require human interaction. They do, however, still require the human hand in their creation and handling, so there is a sense of human scale in their background. (Individual components are generally within the scale of current human perception and manipulation.) Large-scale engineering works, such as dams, rail bridges, or earthworks, also may be considered non-human in scale, but that may be a matter of definition, as they also are created to allow for human construction methods and usually incorporate the human scale in components (e.g., walkways, stairs, doors, lighting). True non-human design as a distinct conceptual area remains a future prospect, but with the increased use of virtual environments and nanotechnology on the horizon, this is not a very distant future (Fig. 4.18).

MANIPULATING SCALE AND PROPORTIONS

References matter when you are working with scale and internal proportions. Designers must therefore understand the human body as a basic reference point. But designers must also be aware of the internal references within the designed object where

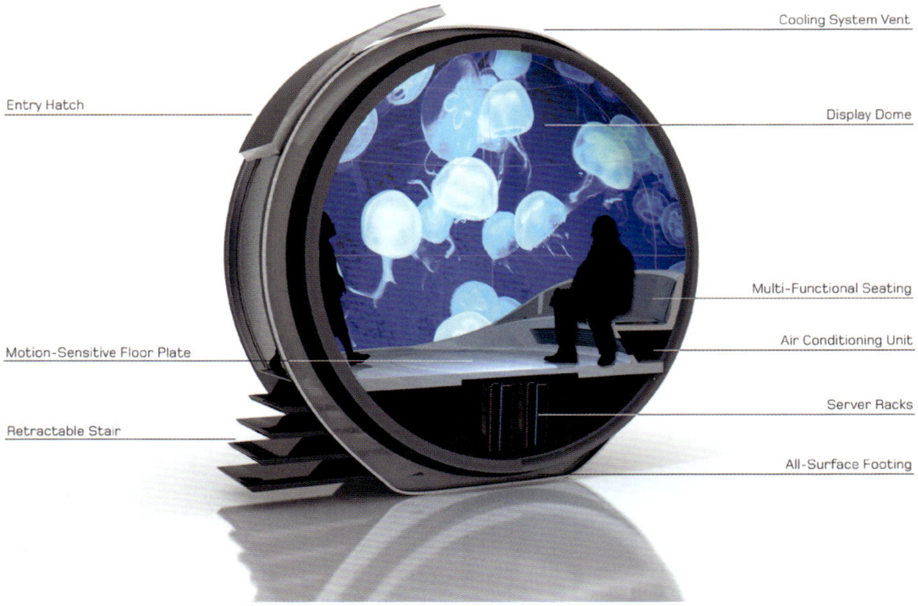

RIGHT

4.18 True non-human design as a distinct conceptual area remains a future prospect. Virtual environments are by their very nature without scale, so once the technology allows us to fully immerse ourselves into the virtual space, they might provide interesting opportunities and experiences, as such environments are not generally experienced by humans.

Source: Tino Schaedler and Michael Brown for NAU

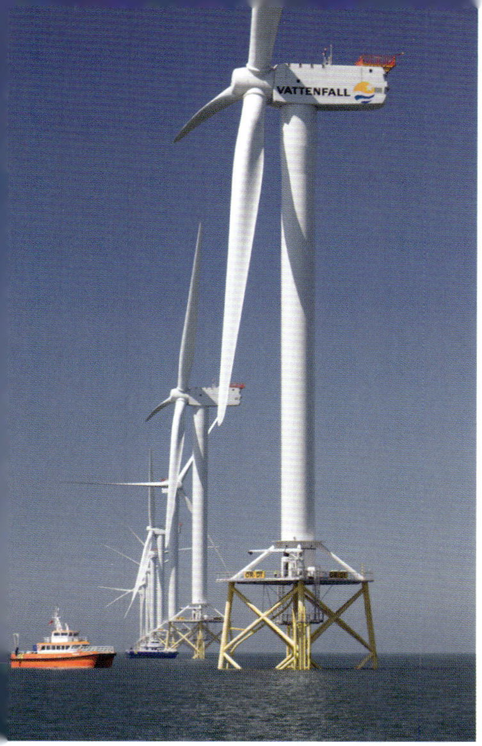

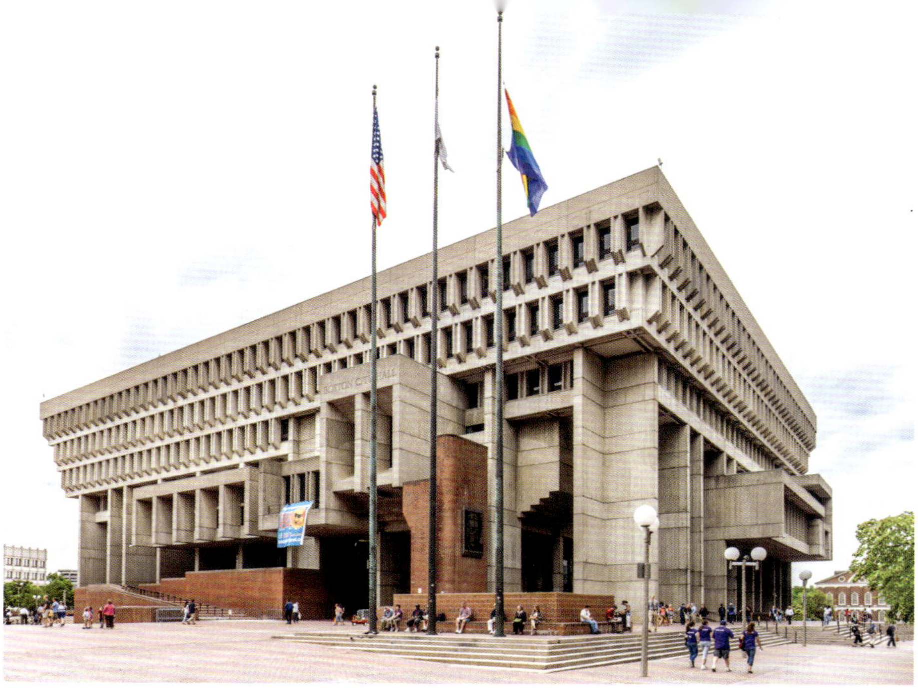

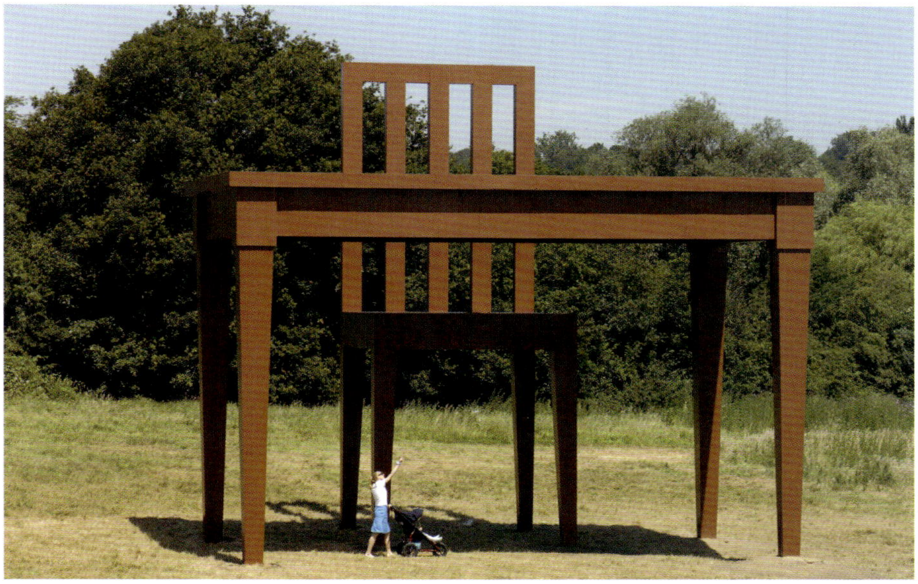

ABOVE
4.19 In the absence of a human figure, we will look for anything that is known to be habitually human scale. Here, the boats, and specifically the windows on the boats, provide a clue to the scale of these wind turbines.

© Anthony West/Corbis

ABOVE RIGHT
4.20 Boston City Hall is seemingly designed to avoid any visible clues to its scale (until you have people around it).

Source: © Nikreates/Alamy

BELOW RIGHT
4.21 Functionality disappears at some stage in over- or under-scaling. At that point the design is serving some other purpose. This over-scale chair with glass mosaic tiles, by the designer and architect Alessandro Mendini, has lost its purpose as a thing to sit on and has become a work of art, a thing to observe and consider. Its purpose is now to engage the viewer in thought over its form, colors, and context.

Source: © Geraint Lewis/Alamy

the known and unknown meet. We only understand the scale of anything in reference to the known, and the first order of perception is therefore to orient ourselves in the scale of the known. A human figure will always provide the quickest way in, but in the absence of the human, we will look for anything that is known to be habitually human scale. Garments, steps, doors, equipment, and furniture provide a second order of clues to scale (Fig. 4.19).

The inclusion of a known scaled object or element serves more purposes than simply orientation. The orientation itself can be a design feature. The contrast in scale may be a part of the design statement, allowing engagement with visual interest over different distances (Fig. 4.20). Over-scaling or under-scaling can even be the design statement in total. But there seem to be no limits to how far scale manipulation can go for visual appeal, especially if one challenges classical notions of beauty. Functionality, however, will be lost at some stage in over- or under-scaling, and there the design comes to a critical point (Fig. 4.21). This again brings us to a

ERGONOMICS: PRINCIPLES IN ACTION

The principles of design are at their core ergonomic concerns, with *usability* encapsulating the concept of ergonomics in itself. Or even the other way around: Ergonomics facilitate usability. The other, classical principles—unity/ variety/ harmony, proportion and scale, balance, rhythm, and emphasis/focus—all affect the physical and mental experience of the user directly and can each be explored in terms of its contribution to comfort, efficiency, safety, and so on. The designer must allow the decisions made in working with the principles of design to produce the desired effect within the given framework: How does the design relate to the human body and experience? What is the effect of balance, rhythm, scale, and so on, on the user—in the moment and over time? How to balance the demands of ergonomic ideals, usability, and aesthetics? Strict functionality may apply at times; aesthetics over comfort may be desirable at others. These are always open questions and the only real mistake is to ignore them.

consideration of the limits of human scale and a realization that the proportions and scale of a design are in the end determined by human interaction at all levels of touch, perception, and motion.

BALANCE

Balance in design comes from an awareness of the distribution of *visual weight.* This involves an awareness of symmetries, focal points, emphasis, and patterns. Just as the basic reference of scale and proportion is the human body, our sense of visual balance results from the physical experience of living in a body in the world. Our world is, in a certain sense, *created* by our perspective of it. That perspective involves a human body that is oriented a certain way with certain symmetries and methods of movement. In this section, we also will explore how the various elements may contribute to balance in a design, often in dialogue with each other.

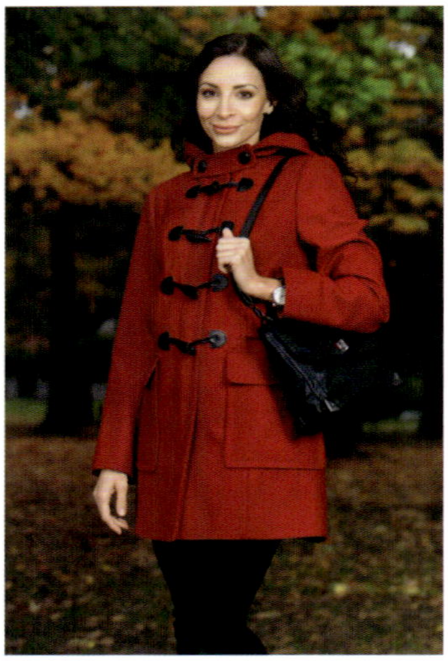

4.22 The rows of buttons create visual interest in the large expanse of unadorned cloth. The large bag provides a bit of balance to the photograph by adding *visual weight* against the focus of the buttons, head, hair, and cap.

Source: © Oleksiy Maksymenko/All Canada Photos/Corbis

DISTRIBUTION OF "VISUAL WEIGHT"

The distribution of visual weight relies mainly on three things: the *proportion* of individual elements, the *placement* of elements, and the visual *effect* of details within the total design. For example, there may be a large expanse of unadorned cloth making up the front of a jacket. This may then be broken up by a row of buttons (Fig. 4.22). The buttons running up the middle create an equal distribution of visual weight on the front of the person wearing the jacket. However, a designer may decide to place an insignia that is colorful and eye-catching on the coat. The visual weight has now shifted up and over, and the *balance* of visual weight in the design has now been thrown off. This could be the desired effect for the coat, but in a photo shoot for a fashion magazine, an art director may choose to place a handbag with the same colors in the hand of the model to regain a visual balance for the photograph and, in doing so, also provide more visual interest.

The designer could then elaborate on the jacket with multiple points of interest in the form of pocket flaps, ribbons, or any number of decorative elements, creating a balance between them. The visual weight of the design is gradually overtaken by the added details as the basic fabric of the jacket front becomes a background for this display.

SYMMETRY

A balance (such as in the coat in Figure 4.22) is bilaterally symmetrical; it has a left/right symmetry. This is a very common way to design anything in the human realm, as that is the inherent symmetry of the human body. Humans have three basic planes of symmetry. We are symmetrical left to right, but we are asymmetrical front to back and top to bottom. These symmetries are echoed in all human design, creating a sense of balance, but symmetries can be of other kinds: diagonal, radial, or with multiple axes. Islamic art, for example, has a strong strain of odd-numbered symmetries running through it.

4.23 Breaking a pattern is one of the more effective ways of creating imbalance in a design.
Source: ©Bettmann/CORBIS

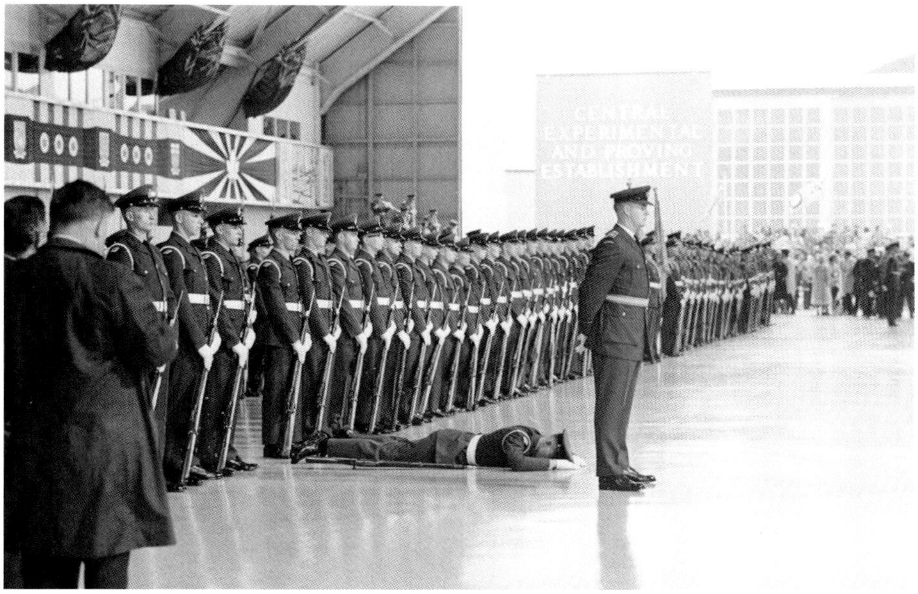

The relationship of balance to pattern emerges when one considers how patterns are set up. An element or series of elements is introduced and then repeated according to a set of rules. For a pattern to emerge, the elements must form a rhythmic repetition over time or distance. A pattern can have its own internal focal points, and it can be broken up by the injection of new elements. This perhaps throws the balance of the patterning off, so it can be rebalanced, just as the coat mentioned above and its pockets. Patterns in design are in this way very influential on our sense of balance in a structure. Our perception returns to the repetitive array of elements that becomes the framework developing a sense of balance. Breaking a pattern is therefore one of the more effective ways of creating imbalance in a design (Fig. 4.23).

"NATURAL" BALANCE

There is in human beings a natural sense of balance. Our body has its symmetries, and the mechanisms in our inner ear are attuned to our position relative to the ground and the direction of gravitational pull. We are fed information about our relative stance toward the world and the stance of things relative to us in a constant feedback loop of sensory information from eyes, ears, and limbs.

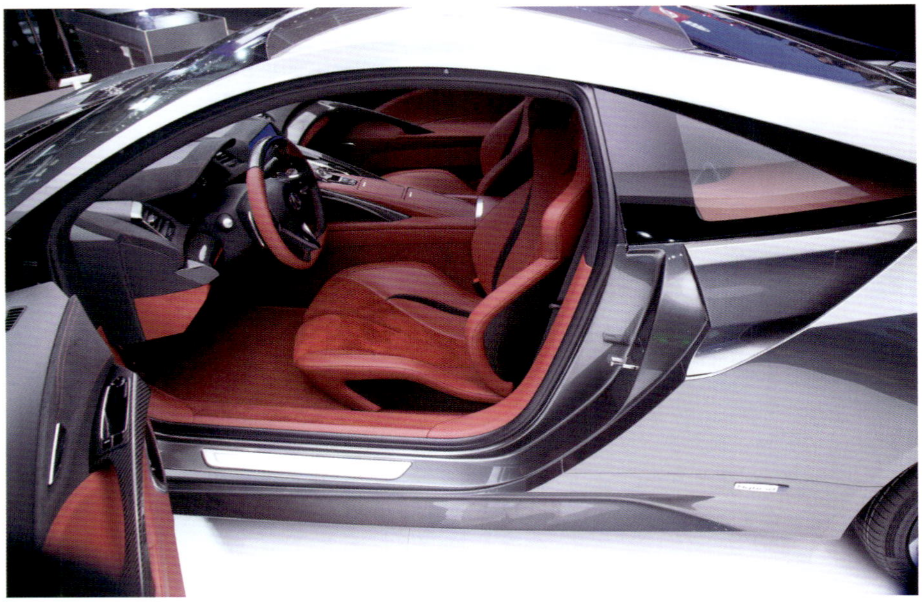

RIGHT

4.24 There is a certain natural order to the idea of balance and symmetry in the design and creation of human environments and equipment that derive from the shape and scale of the human body—how things face, how they fit, where we fit into the negative space and around the positive space of the structure.

Source: © Car Culture/Car Culture/Corbis

BELOW

4.25 The textured surface adds a disproportionate weight in the totality of this design, but position, contrast, and emphasis matter as well. The positive/negative of the fabric versus skin, the lines (actual and implied), and the contrast of textures all have a say in the gestalt of this gown.

Source: Giovanni Giannoni/WWD

This is perhaps so obvious a situation that it takes a step outside our being to grasp it. It is by the three planes of our body that we interpret the world, splitting space, motion, and objects into *front and back, left and right,* and *up and down.* Imagine you were a being with 360-degree locomotion and vision. The sense of *front* and *back* would not be relevant at all. If we flew like birds or floated like fish, our sense of *up* and *down* would be very different. In contrast to the other principles under discussion here, there is a certain natural order to the idea of balance and symmetry in the design and creation of human environments and equipment (Fig. 4.24).

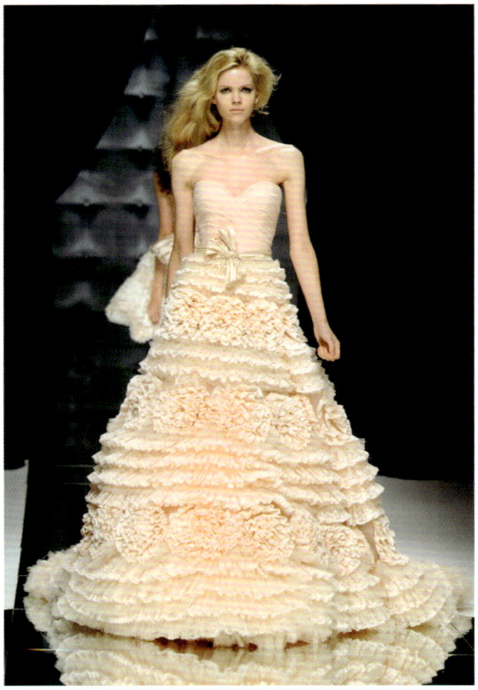

ELEMENTS IN SYMMETRY AND BALANCE

Designers can use each of the elements to create a balance either by referring to other elements of the same type or by working with others in a combination of *position, contrast,* and *emphasis.* Color, for example, has a fairly complex number of ways in which it can balance within a design. Different hues, intensities, and values have different visual weight and can therefore create balance in different-sized areas. Lines and shapes can balance in both two and three dimensions in an interplay of positive and negative, but also in play with color and/or texture, whether the texture is actual or implied in graphic design or built in. Textures can work in similar ways, where a more textured surface can have a disproportionate weight in the totality of the design (Fig. 4.25).

Imbalance and Implication of Motion

Imbalance in design can be achieved by the same means and can be used to imply motion and change. The simple imbalance of a text can, for example, create emphasis on a headline and a picture placed off-center in a layout will draw attention to itself. The pattern recognition that humans are so adept at serves here in the opposite: We very quickly spot

RIGHT

4.26 A picture placed off-center in a layout will draw attention to itself. The pattern recognition that humans are so adept at, serves here in the opposite: We very quickly spot the out-of-place—there is a sense of unease—and are very alert to the danger of something *falling* off the established structure.

Source: Illustration by Karl Aspelund

BELOW

4.27 The measure of balance in clothing perceived from the outside as well as from within is the planes of the human body, and our sense of balance comes from a perceived relation to these. When designers work against this, as Rei Kawakubo did here in 1997, distorting shape and using unfamiliar textures, it produces a sense of unease: The design is not recognizable to us. It is unfamiliar and uncanny.

Source: firstVIEW.com

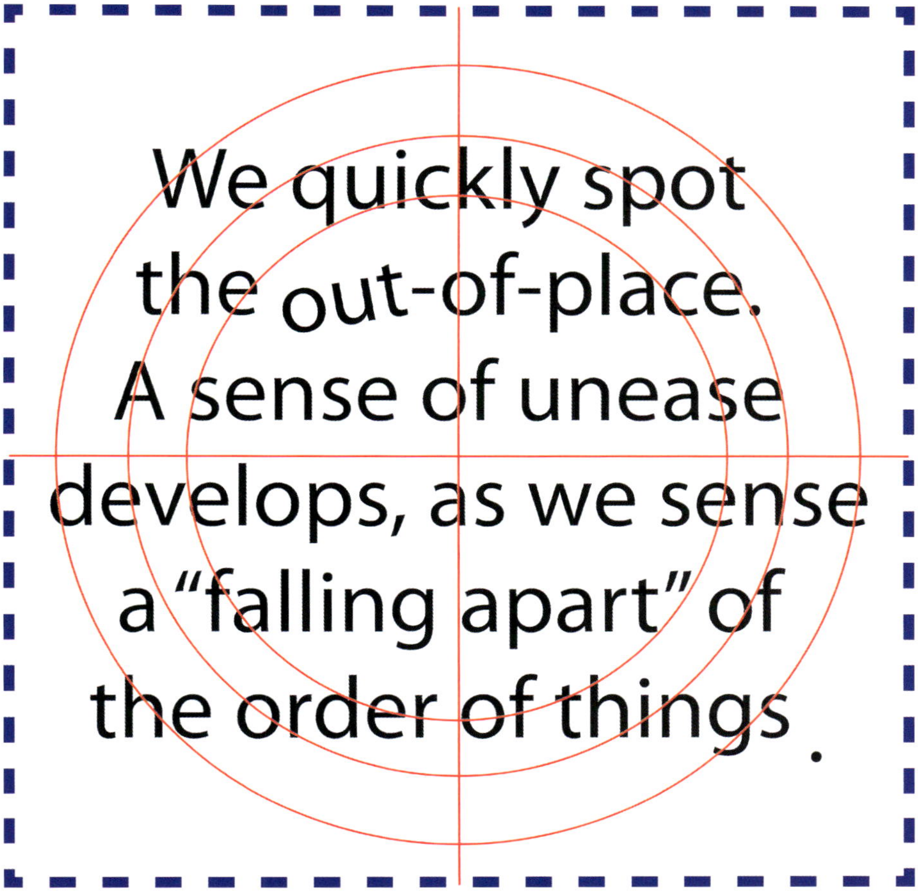

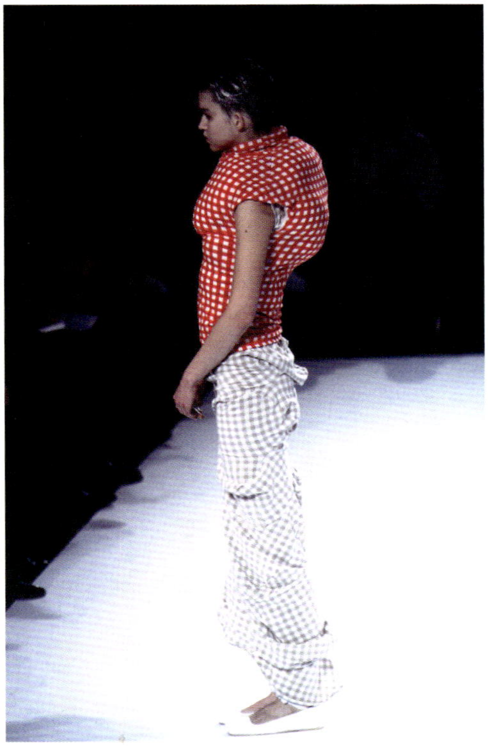

the out-of-place—there is a sense of unease—and are very alert to the danger of something *falling* off the established structure (Fig. 4.26).

A structure—a grounding horizon line of sorts—is always implied in a printed page by virtue of the format, and architecture brings with it at least the flat floor if not a ceiling and orthogonal walls. With clothing, however, the measure of balance, perceived from the outside as well as from within, must always be the planes of the human body and our sense of balance comes from a perceived relation to these (Fig. 4.27).

BALANCE AND POWER SIGNALS

Just as overemphasized unity is frequently used to overwhelm an audience or signal the presence of power, so are symmetries and the resulting balance used in architecture. Classicism had a strong symmetrical tendency with its facades and rotundas. And when the nations of the Euro-American culture were forming identities, neoclassicism became the prevailing style. Well into the 20th century, the strong symmetries of power are evident in architectural structures, with the apparent stability of the buildings signaling the enduring nature of the state. Imposing order became a sign of modern culture. Societies also showed their mastery of nature in well-ordered gardens, while the power of government

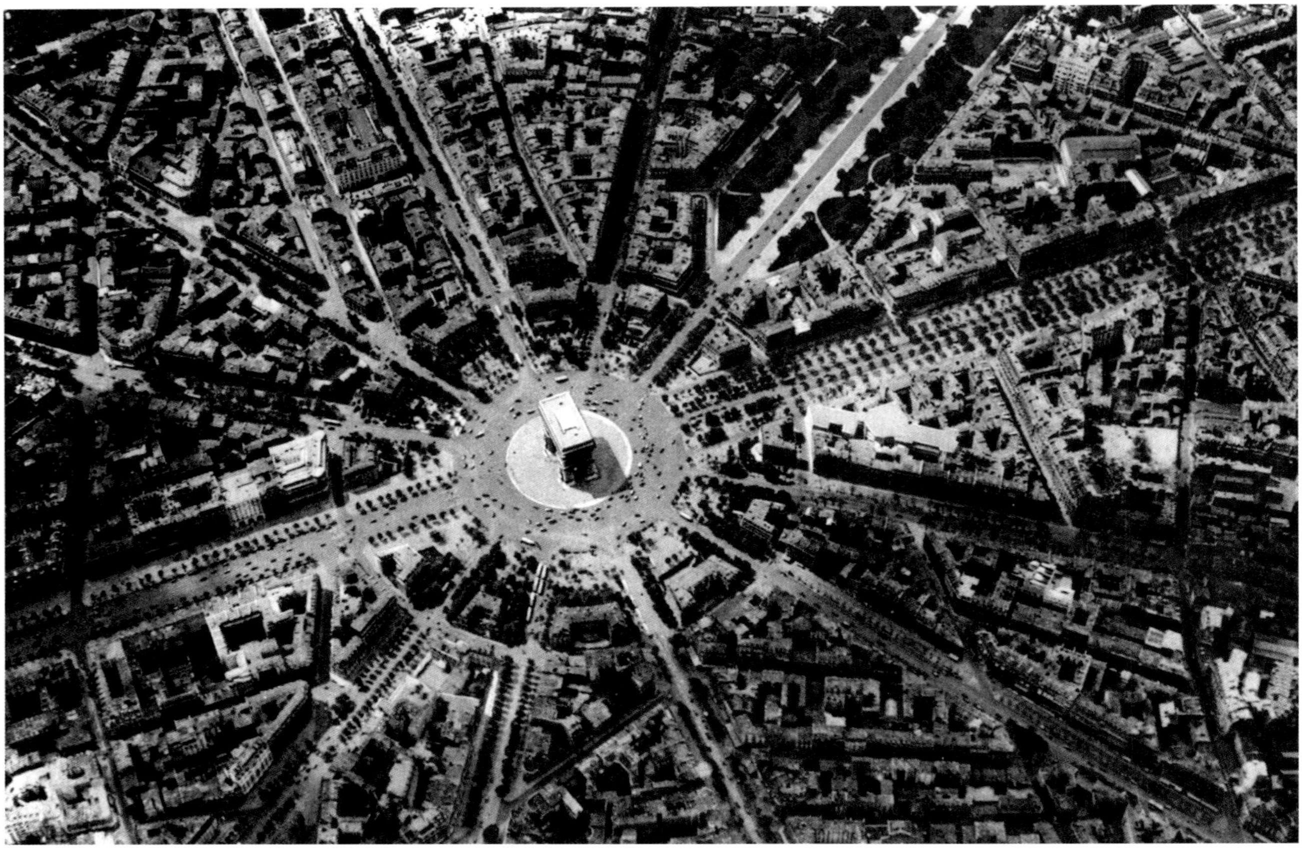

was made evident in the clearing away of old neighborhoods with winding streets and layers of historical periods. Paris became a model for this kind of exercise in the early 19th century through the designs of Baron Haussmann, and the trend was picked up by governments and city planners all over the world (Fig. 4.28).

RHYTHM

Rhythm, generally understood as the repeated pattern of sound or movement, can also be evoked by a repeated element in a design. Whether decorative or structural, it will be perceived on more than one sensory level. The visual input also triggers a response in a physical sense of being able to *feel* the rhythmic quality of the visual. Somewhere between the seen rhythm and the knowledge that allows the visual input to be translated into thoughts of sound and motion an interpretation of the visual input is felt in the body (Fig. 4.29).

Synesthesia, mentioned earlier, is the linking of senses (from the Greek: *syn* = together + *aisthesis* = sensation) when sensory input of one kind triggers (involuntary) responses from another sensory area, such as when sounds or words may invoke the perception of colors. True synesthesia is thought to be a relatively rare and involuntary neurological condition, but many people have some version of experiences like this. Even in daily life the idea of more than one sense being engaged in an experience is so common as to be firmly embedded in language: Food tastes *sharp,* and sounds may also be *sharp;* colors may be *hot* or *cool;* smells can have color. The upshot is that visual rhythm must be considered a multisensory experience and can be approached accordingly in designs.

TOP
4.28 Paris became a model for imposing structural organization to cities in the early 19th century through the designs of Baron Haussmann, and the trend was adopted by governments and city planners all over the world.

Source: © The Print Collector/Alamy

4.29 Sight and prior knowledge allows visual input to be translated into thoughts of sound and motion; an interpretation of the visual input becomes a rhythm that is felt in the body.

Source: © Steve Hix/Somos Images/Corbis

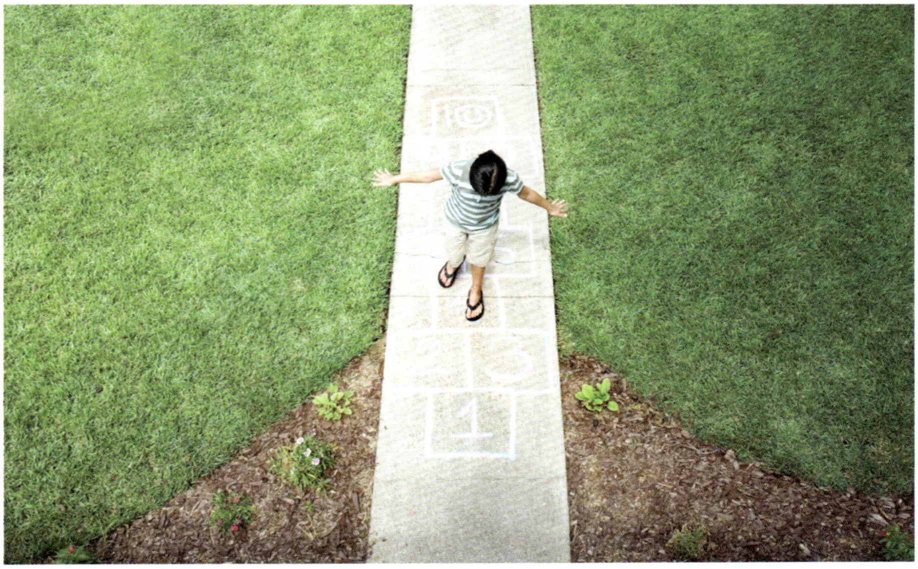

Rhythm in design has obvious relations with pattern. However, there is more to consider, as rhythm in design engages more than one of our senses at a time. A sense of rhythm may be prompted by a visual pattern, but the visual pattern also could produce a physical and sensory experience of movement or touch by direct resonance with body movement, where rhythms are experienced though sense memory rather than seen or felt. Related to this is the idea of *kinesthetic empathy*, where, when watching dancers, for example, a person responds by feeling the movement in his or her own body and unconsciously mimicking them. Rhythms set in motion a sympathetic response and the body responds by moving in synch with the input. Rhythm sensed visually implies movement and may be viewed through motion (as when a rhythm is set up in a structure by walking past it) and so can be prompted by patterns that allow the body to directly experience a sense of motion from an immobile structure (Fig. 4.30).

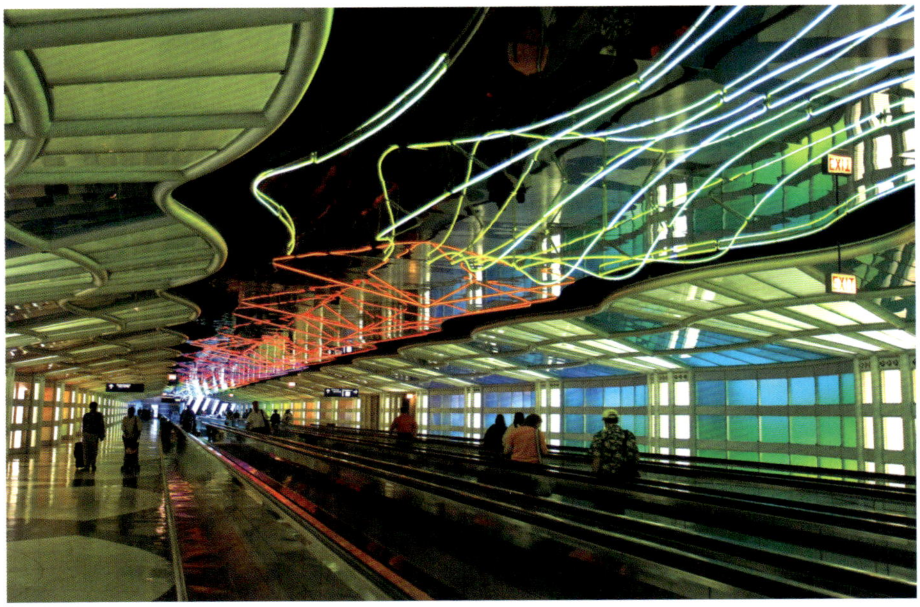

4.30 Rhythm sensed visually implies motion and patterns allow the body to directly experience a sense of motion, even when the motion is the body's and not the observed design's. A rhythmic structure become dynamic when viewed in motion, as when moving down the hall at Chicago International Airport and encountering *Sky's the Limit* by Michael Heyden.

Source: Copyright © Claudia Uripos/eStock Photo—All rights reserved

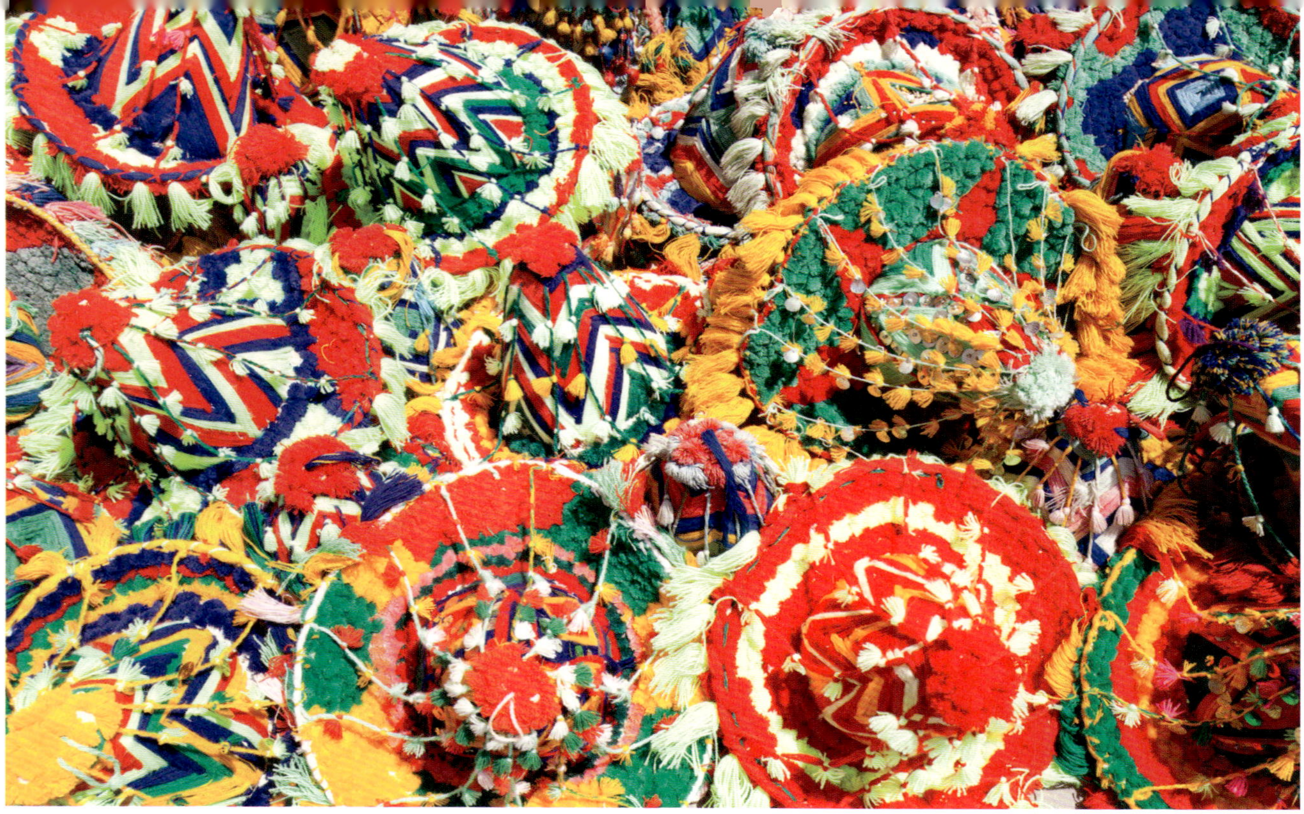

ABOVE

4.31 It is extraordinarily difficult to achieve true "randomness" in a pattern, as the orderliness of the underlying structure immediately begins to imply or even enforce patterns. The pattern elements in these hats, for sale in a street market in Marrakech, are very varied, and yet the totality has a sense of patterned order.

Source: © Ashley Cooper/Corbis

Between our pattern-seeking abilities that seek out rhythms and create totalities out of varied stimuli and our physical multisensory response to patterned structures, we sense rhythms in our environment without any major effort. Tiling and weaving are both especially powerful examples of this. It is extraordinarily difficult to achieve true randomness in a tiled or woven pattern, as the orderliness of the underlying structure begins to imply patterns even when the tiles or yarns are assembled by chance (Fig. 4.31).

VISUAL RHYTHM

Visual rhythm can be set up in three basic ways: The first is a simple tiling, where an element is repeated over an area or through space. A repeat of an element in one row would be the simplest example of this—a one-dimensional rhythm. Adding another row adds a level of geometric complexity through the ability to create overlapping structures. The rhythm can be placed in a different sequence or stepped. The rhythm can be made to be progressive, when more and more layers are added. A new element can be added or one taken away to allow the rhythmic pattern to evolve as the structure develops and the eye travels over it (Fig. 4.32). Again, we are dealing with time, where the designer must consider the order of presentation, the motion of the observer (is the design coming at you or going away?), and the order in which the design will be observed (left to right, top to bottom?). The immediate level of complexity grows very quickly.

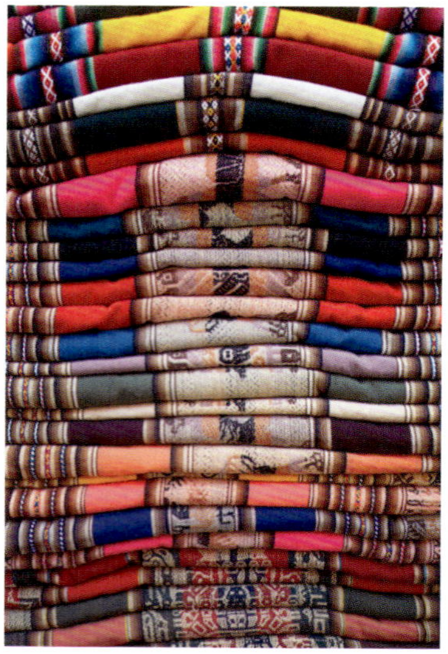

BELOW RIGHT

4.32 The rhythm is progressive, once more and more layers are added. A new element can be added or one taken away to allow the rhythmic pattern to evolve as the structure develops and the eye travels over it. This stack of blankets at Witches' Market in La Paz developed a pattern of its own as each blanket was added.

Source: © Ian Trower/JAI/Corbis

Polyrhythmic Structures

Rhythm involves all manner of surface treatments but also three-dimensional constructs, and rhythm can be more than simple alternating elements. In *polyrhythmic structures,* a number of rhythms come together to create a totality that is larger and more meaningful than the individual patterns involved.

This next step in the development of patterns comes from injecting yet another level of interaction within the pattern. A polyrhythmic pattern or structure is created when differently sequenced patterns meet or are layered. This is easily understood in music when different time signals are used for different instruments or voices (as in the polyrhythmic music of sub-Saharan Africa or that of the composer Philip Glass). If one considers the tilings of a colored pattern to be analogous to musical notes and tempo, then the creation of a polyrhythmic visual pattern is easily understood (Fig. 4.33).

This kind of emergent pattern is sometimes hard to predict if the sequences are large and the cycle is long, but natural patterns emerge this way through the interaction of forces on a cellular level. This could be brought to bear on modern virtual structures once computers had the ability to generate patterns with enormous complexity and mimic natural cellular patterns on seashells and plants (Fig. 4.34).

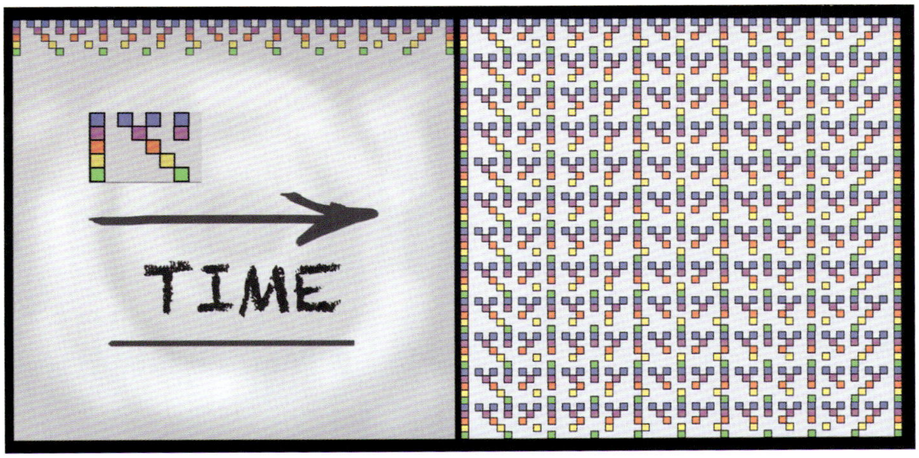

TOP RIGHT

4.33 The tilings of a colored pattern can be understood to be analogous to musical notes and tempo. Here the notes create a polyrhythmic pattern. The different *time structures* are layered one after another until the cycle is achieved. Overall, a whole new structure emerges as each colored tile sequence is added. Smaller internal structures also become evident.

Source: Illustration by Karl Aspelund

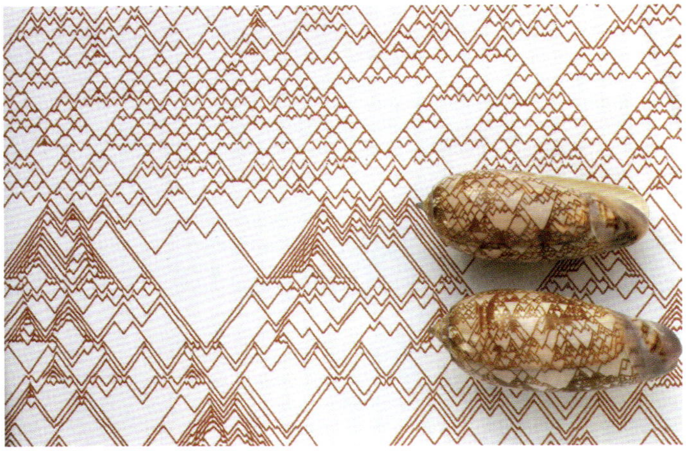

BOTTOM RIGHT

4.34 Natural patterns emerge through the interaction of forces on a cellular level. This was brought to bear on modern virtual structures once computers had the ability to generate patterns with enormous complexity and mimic natural cellular patterns on seashells and plants. The picture shows a pattern generated by a relatively simple computer program developed at the Max Planck Institute in Germany along with two mollusk shells of the type Oliva Porphyria.

Source: Meinhardt, H. and Klingler, M. (1987). A model for pattern formation on the shells of mollusks. *J. theor. Biol* 126, 63–69. [PDF]. Meinhardt, H. (2009). The Algorithmic Beauty of Sea Shells (4th edition). Heidelberg/New York: Springer

EMPHASIS AND FOCUS

By placing focal points or emphasizing certain elements over others, a designer can lead the eye of the viewer and create a narrative of sorts within the design itself. **Emphasis,** the singling out of a specific element within a design, can be created by placing elements in a specific relation to other elements and to the total design. In doing so the emphasized element becomes a point of **focus,** the place toward which our attention is directed to the exclusion of others. Focus points can be singular or multiple, depending on the desired effect, and can help or hinder a sense of balance and symmetry, as we have seen above. But as is true of all the principles of design, the abandonment of the principle or the use of opposition can be equally effective.

The lack of a focal point or absence of emphasis can be a way to make a design statement, and this kind of dissolution is very common. The important thing to realize is that once again we are dealing with the body itself and its responses. We have to understand physically as well as emotionally and logically how audiences view designs and how the eye travels across an object.

FOCAL POINT: LEADING THE EYE

Most human beings view objects in their environment by scanning them from side to side, mostly from left to right. This simple physiological fact is crucial to understanding how emphasis and focal points operate on a fundamental level. When the eye travels over a surface, it continues until it encounters an obstacle. As the scan is side to side, a vertical line is the most impactful obstacle, but any edge will be examined in more detail before the eye continues its journey. We identify the world in this way, by examining its edges: Where does something change into something else (Fig. 4.35)? Armed with this knowledge, a designer can place objects, patterns, colors, and details into the visual field in such a way as to either trip up the eye on its journey or allow it to skid on, or to lead it (by way of a diagonal, perhaps) to another area.

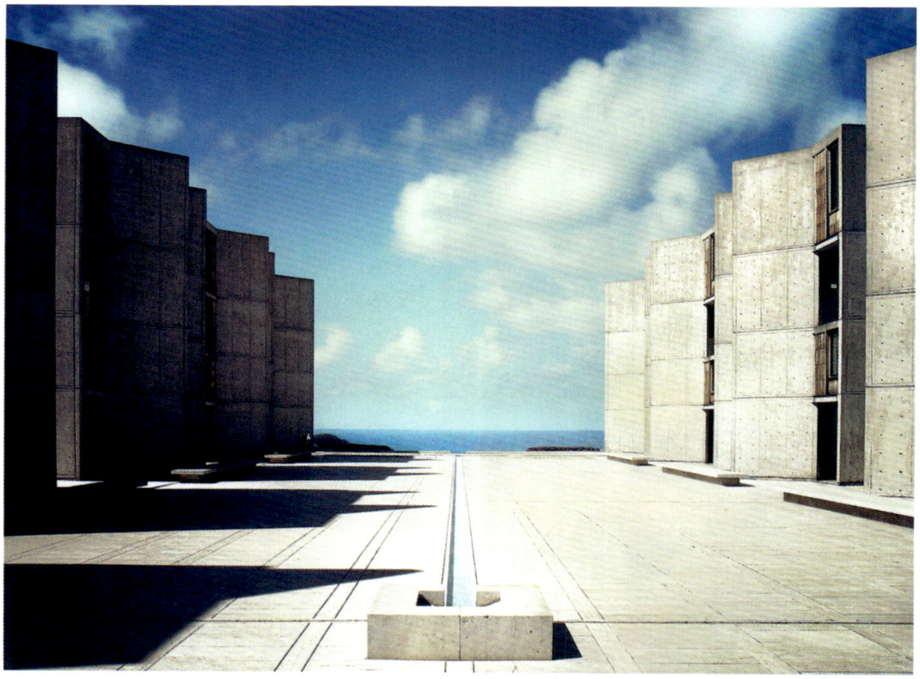

4.35 A vertical line is the most impactful obstacle, but any edge will be scanned and examined before the eye continues its journey. We identify the world by examining its edges and boundaries, finding where something becomes something else or where one area ends and another begins.

Source: The Salk Institute for Biological Studies (http://choupina.wix.com/choupin)

The human body has its own built-in areas of interest, where the most impactful are the face and any erotic zones that may (or may not) be seen. We seem to learn at a very early age to recognize the most elementary face-like shapes and our eyes will immediately go to them and pick them out of an environment. This can be used to great effect in designs where a face becomes a part of the design, as a draw for the attention of the viewer.

EMPHASIS BY CONTRAST OF ELEMENTS

Elements in carefully placed contrast will immediately draw the eye, creating a point of emphasis. Colors in contrast will interact strongly, lines that curve in different directions or interact dynamically create places the eye will be drawn to by virtue of the mimicking of shape or space, and diagonals will draw the eye into contrasting directions (Fig. 4.36). A broken rhythm, a shape out of place, the "wrong" element appearing in a line of items—all of these become focal points and can be used as such in designs. Textures can create emphasis by appearing embedded in a field of an opposing tactile/visual surface: smooth in rough, fuzzy in smooth, patterned in featureless, and so on (Fig. 4.37). In a collection of shapes, the odd one out will immediately become the focal point and sequences that are interrupted will become a point of interest both visually and in terms of experience. Even in the presentation of designs, an effective trick is to present a design out of sequence or in contrast to a series (a long line of black dresses interrupted by a red one, for example, places emphasis both on the red dress and the blackness of the others).

EMPHASIS BY PLACEMENT

Isolation can also serve as a way of emphasizing an object or event; allowing the object to stand alone against a relatively empty background or space brings it into focus immediately. The isolation creates a space where the viewer's eye travels quickly to find the point of interest.

BOTTOM RIGHT

4.36 Elements in carefully placed contrast will immediately create a point of emphasis or focus, drawing the eye in. The color and texture contrasts, between the starry sky and the clouds, along with the direction provided by the vertical center and symmetry, create a powerful focal point in this design for Act I of Mozart's opera *The Magic Flute*.

Source: © The Metropolitan Museum of Art. Image source: Art Resource, NY

BOTTOM LEFT

4.37 Textures can create emphasis by appearing embedded in a field of an opposing tactile/visual surface. The dialogue between the wood and the smooth white porcelain texture reaches a peak between the glass surfaces and the living trees. Photographer: Richard Powers Location: UK.

Source: © Richard Powers/Arcaid/Corbis; License Type: Rights Managed (RM)

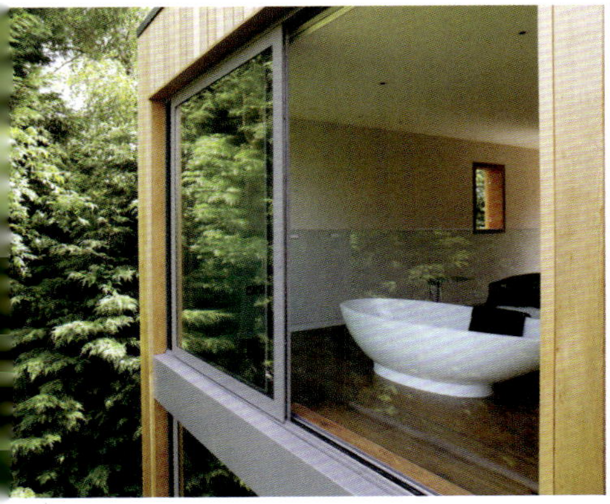

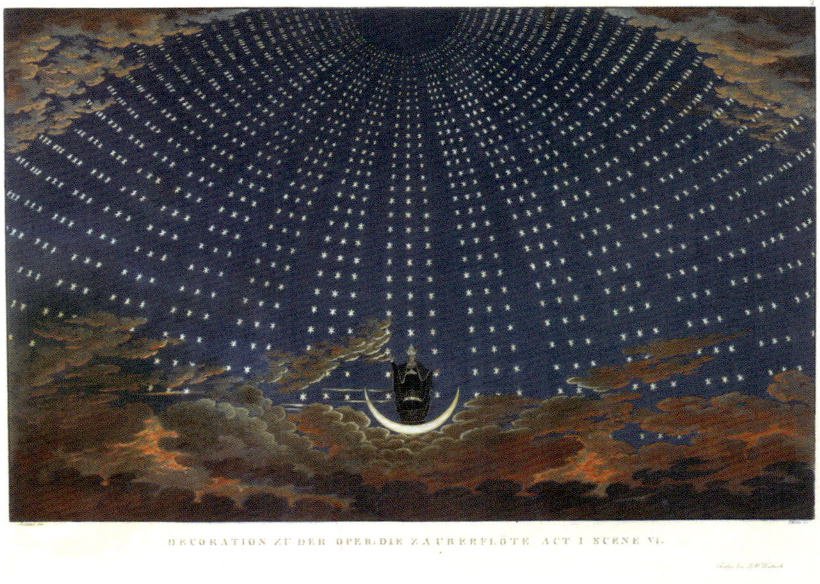

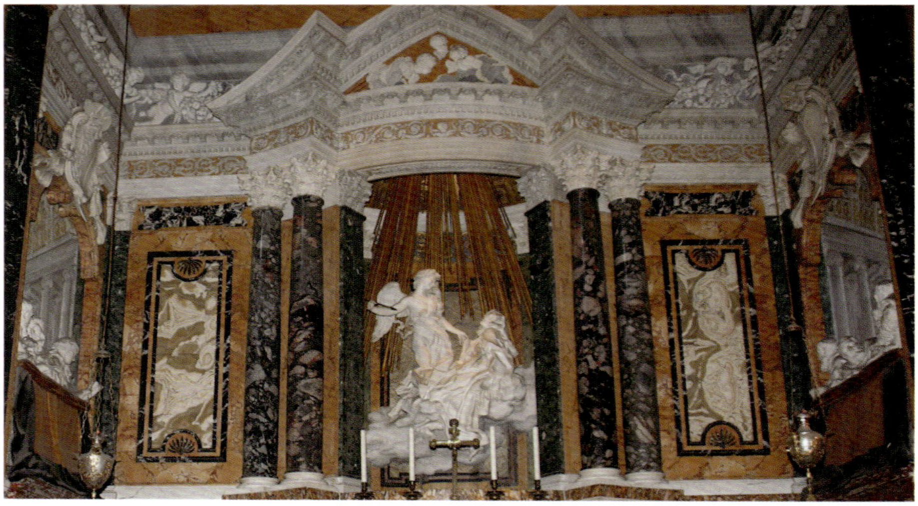

RIGHT

4.38 The sculpture in Giovanni Bernini's design in the Cornaro Chapel in Rome creates a strong point of visual emphasis through texture and color. The contrast between the strong symmetry of the architectural details and the asymmetrical arrangement of the figures emphasizes the sense of movement and creates a stronger focal point.

Source: Photo © Nina Aldin Thune

BELOW

4.39 The button, being a strong focus point, has the extra significance of a textured design, giving it some aesthetic weight, making it worth the central position it holds. Balmain blazer.

Source: Franck Mura/WWD

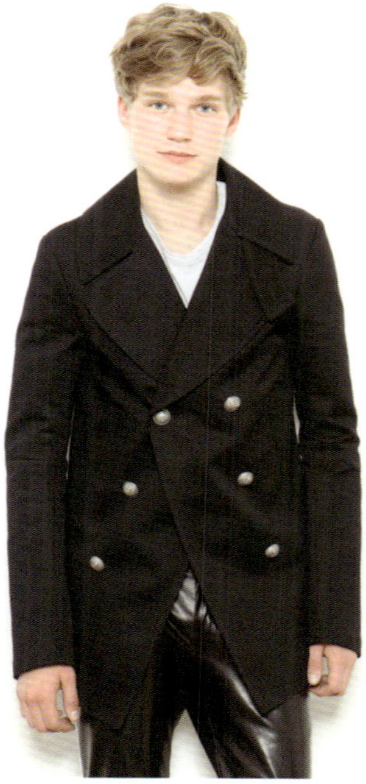

Symmetry and asymmetry also can serve in this respect. As mentioned, we are creatures that seem to desire a certain level of order spiced with variety, and the placing of an element off-center or out of balance immediately draws our interest. In clothing and architecture, this often will involve diagonals or asymmetrical structures that also serve to lead the eye to a destination or across a space. Putting an object dead center in a space is one way of underscoring its importance, but placing it slightly off-center creates a sense of visual interest through the unease this lack of balance evokes in the viewer (Fig. 4.38).

SINGLE FOCUS

Choosing a point of single focus or multiple focus points is a determining decision in the effect of a design, regardless of whether the design is large or small. A singular point of focus has a very different feel and gives immense importance to the element in question. It becomes the message of the design, and in becoming so central, the message acquires meaning. Creating a space for a single focus on a design and then not fulfilling the promise of having that focus be worth something lets the audience down and makes the entire design seem weak. The element in question, a doorway, a piece of furniture, or a button on a jacket, must have some significance, some weight of aesthetics or meaning to make it "worth it" (Fig. 4.39).

There is, however, always the counterpoint, where the singular focus point would be negative space. The creation of a void is however not a disappointment; a void as a single focus becomes mysterious or attractive, unless there is no basis for the emptiness. Sometimes the attraction is literal as the void invites the viewer to come closer and even to enter.

MULTIPLE FOCI

Multiple focus points, on the other hand, provide a very different experience by prompting the eye to wander back and forth over a surface or throughout a space. Multiple focus points in this way create a sense of action and movement: a space becomes dynamic and an outfit has a sense of motion about it (Fig. 4.40).

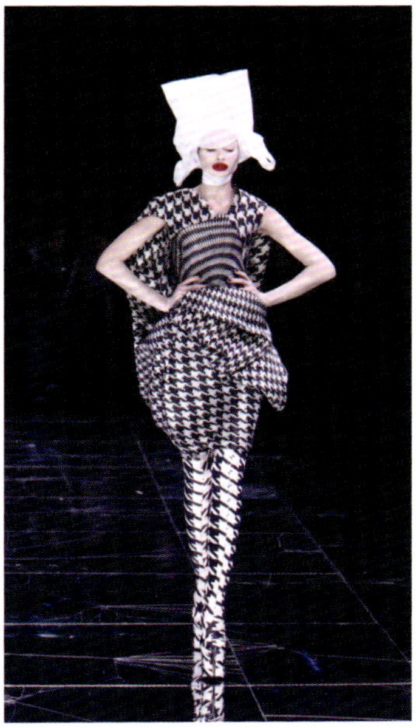

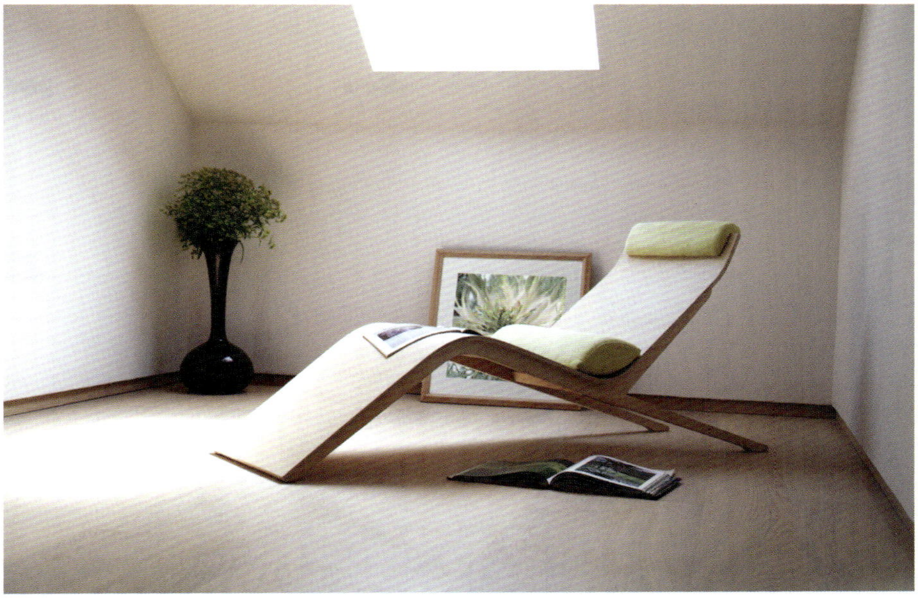

ABOVE LEFT

4.40 Multiple focus points create a sense of action and movement: The different textures in the garments, headdress and floor, and the color contrast in the lips and everything else, create multiple points for our eyes to latch on to, as they flit from one element to another. This produces a dynamic effect of motion and unrest. Model Kristen McMenamy for Alexander McQueen.

Source: Giovanni Giannoni/WWD

ABOVE RIGHT

4.41 A minimalist design such as seen here, with its low-level sensual stimuli, evokes a sense is of emptiness, which can also be felt as a sense of calm or stability.

Source: © Russell Underwood/Corbis

RIGHT

4.42 True dissolution is very difficult to achieve. Underlying structures always rise to the surface. Here, each outfit seems almost chaotic, but taken together a sense of wholeness begins to emerge. Runway shots, Anna Sui, fall/winter 2010–2011, women's wear.

Source: Courtesy of WWD

Choosing to place multiple focus points, as we have seen, also is a way of creating balance. Placing points in a distributed relation to each other and in a saturating relation to the whole makes the eye move over the surface in such a way as to create a sense of structured balance. The counterpoint here would be twofold: either to saturate or overload the surface with focal points or to attempt to do away with focal points altogether. In both cases the same effect is achieved: a negation of focus. One achieves it through overload while the other evokes a sense of emptiness, and the senses of vision and touch are both stimulated. With nothing for the eyes and fingertips to come in contact with, a sense is of emptiness is produced, which may be felt as calm or stability (Fig. 4.41).

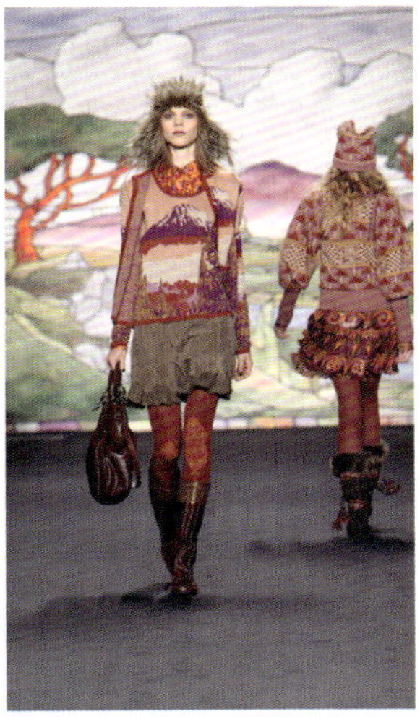

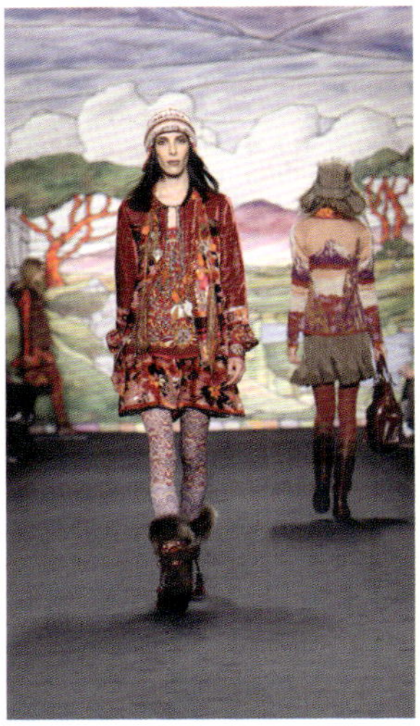

DISSOLUTION

The use of multiple focal points therefore dovetails with the use of none in a sense of balance. One might also see this as a *dissolving* of focus and thereby the dissolving of surfaces. If the eye has nowhere to go, then the surface itself has begun to slip away. However, true dissolution, just like a deliberate lack of pattern in tiling, is very difficult to achieve, with underlying structures always rising to the surface somehow (Fig. 4.42). Even paint splatters start to seem like patterns eventually. But the dissolving of a structure or outfit through multiple or absent focal points can be an interesting way to approach a design. The visual interest becomes intriguing and even a little mysterious.

Total lack of focus is not natural to the human experience. The pattern recognizer is simply too strong. Therefore, a lack of focal points, a lack of pattern, or a lack of structure become uncanny and can give rise to unease. But the fear of chaos is paired with the exhilaration of chaos that is hiding behind the constant order of human experience. The lack of structure also can have a very liberating effect on a viewer. If the visual field becomes a place without forces, then the mind can wander without having to hang on to anything.

USABILITY (EXPERIENCE)

The design elements needed to have time added, to acknowledge the role of lived experience in creating the relationship of the client or end user with the design. In the same vein, experience itself needs to be in the set of principles. **Usability** is a mantra of design that grew out of late-modernist practices, specifically coming to the front of the design discussion as *interactive* became a buzzword around the design of electronic appliances and devices.

The functionality of a design goes beyond the machinelike concepts of mid-20th century modernists, who wrote of houses being "machines for living in" and maintained that functionality was the key to all design. After all, what is the function of many of the consumer goods that are the focus of much of the design profession? That is, what is the function of any designer item? (Fig. 4.43).

We must consider the usability as the practical experience of interacting with the design. But we also must consider the emotional experience, the fulfillment involved that comes from a satisfactory experience of a designed object, which allows us to create a relationship with the design itself over time. The idea that there had to be user friendliness in design was a mantra that arose fully once personal gadgetry and computer software became a widespread and personal side of going through day-to-day life. Design became about ergonomics and user-centered solutions, and the market became heavily researched, as designers and analysts wanted to find out what exactly the end users were up to.

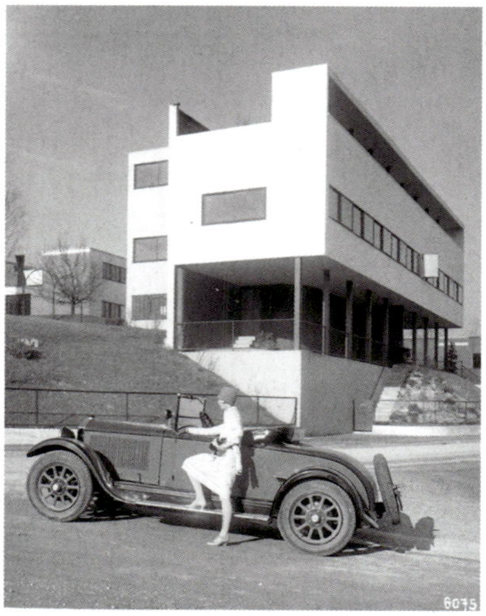
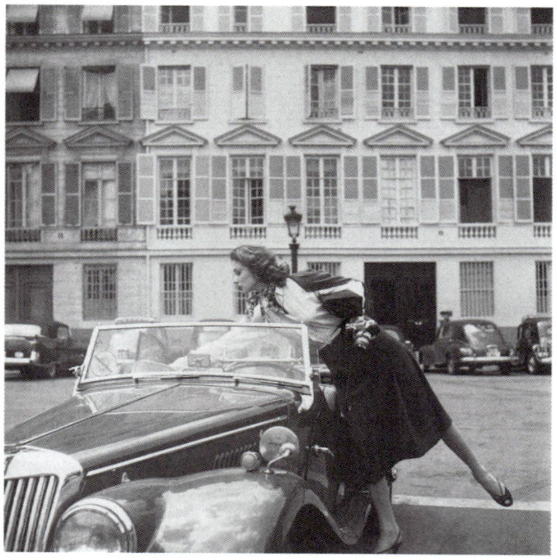
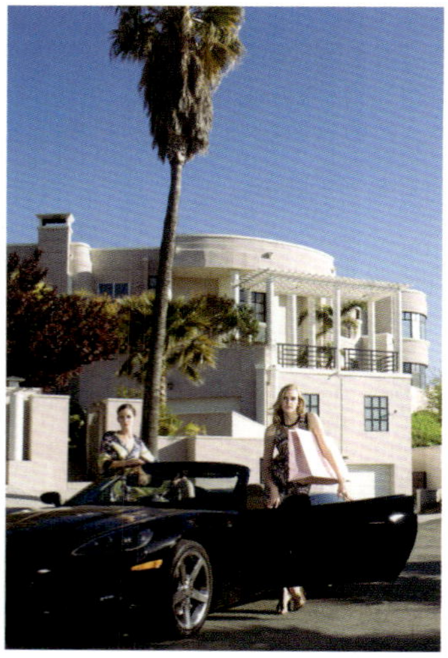

4.43 The 20th-century modernists maintained that functionality was the key to all design. However, we might question what consumer goods, which are the focus of both the modern design profession and modern lifestyles, actually do. The "function" of a designed object may well simply be to look good and to be a designed product. Left to right: 1929, 1954, 2011.

Source: L: Mercedes-Bent Classic Archives. M: © Condé Nast Archive/ Corbis. R: © Velvet/Corbis

NETWORKING: RESOURCES ON PRINCIPLES

The following list contains valuable websites for further exploration:

MATHWORLD: FIBONACCI NUMBER
A website on the Fibonacci series, a mathematical entity related to the golden ratio.
mathworld.wolfram.com/FibonacciNumber.html

GEOMETRY AND ART: SYMMETRY, BALANCE, SCALE (RACHEL BERNSTEIN AND EUNICE LEE, 2011)
A reading from LACMA (Los Angeles County Museum of Art) Evenings for Educators.
www.lacma.org/eduprograms/EvesforEds/GeoEssay.pdf

GESTALT PRINCIPLE OF PERCEPTION (BONNIE SKAALID, 1999)
An excellent website on gestalt perception and design with resources.
www.usask.ca/education/coursework/skaalid/theory/gestalt/gestalt.htm

A COLOR SCHEME GENERATOR
A website that allows you to pick or define a color and suggests a harmonic scheme to go with it.
www.perbang.dk/color+scheme

A POLYRHYTHMIC METRONOME
The best way to understand polyrhythms is to engage with them and you can learn more about doing so on this website.
artsites.ucsc.edu/faculty/Marsh/pages/poly.html

USABILITY.GOV (DIGITAL COMMUNICATIONS DIVISION, U.S. DEPARTMENT OF HEALTH AND HUMAN SERVICES)
A website on best practices and guidelines for user-centered design of digital content. Includes resources, bibliographies, and research plans.
www.usability.gov

This development, a welcome one, has rather different applications depending on what area of design is being investigated and begs the same kind of questions as previously stated: What exactly is the *experience* of a design? What is the experience of a pair of jeans, for example, or a coffee cup or a courthouse? How do we measure satisfaction with something as widely ranging and diverse? The obvious point to make is that the user experience is about the user, not the design. Is the user satisfied in some way or dissatisfied? Why is the end user using this design in the first place? What is the promise of the design, and was it kept? How long does it take to have valid experience with the design and build a comfortable user-relationship with its purpose and functionality?

This gets to the core of the question of what designing actually is. What exactly is it that we are trying to achieve? Paola Antonelli, the curator of the Department of Architecture and Design at the Museum of Modern Art in New York, has written that "designing is the act of making things that are intended to be both sensible and beautiful." On the other hand, Ralph Caplan, who received the 2010 Cooper-Hewitt Design Mind Award, said that design is "a process for making things right, for shaping what people need." In both cases we see the appearance of the thought that design is meant to be a positive force—a sensible solution is to be found to "make it right." The other half of both these quotations, however, become hard to place. In any case the design is meant to be pleasing somehow in its outcome. But what is the meaning of beautiful (or even sensible, for that matter.) The question of what people need becomes equally vague and difficult if looked at closely, with what people *believe* they need probably being the more correct but less elegant phrase.

So, on one hand there is the idea of a design that has to fulfill a need, and on the other a design that fulfils some larger purpose—that is, making something right or is somehow sensible. What is clear is the need for the inclusion of the end user's point of view in these definitions. Otherwise, these theoretical statements simply become more modernist regulation of "true design" and don't get to the dialogue with the day-to-day use of the designed object.

The idea of including the user experience in a design brief allowed the needs of the consumer to be taken into account beyond the actual need that initially prompted the design. So, not only do designers consider whether the design actually "makes it right" but that it does so efficiently—with minimal malfunctions and without enormous amount of training of the user being necessary—and that it does so consistently.

Once that has been included and taken care of, the freedom of the designer to be creative increases immensely. The end user's connection with the design also becomes much better, both in the initial moment of the first impression and over time in creating a relationship and identifying with the designed object as belonging to the framework of his or her life.

CONCLUSION

This kind of connectivity only develops with designs that reach a level of creativity that comes from continually pushing the idea towards better and better solutions of whatever the design problem was initially, whether it is mundane or highly creative (e.g., a better pair of shoes or an interplanetary exploration device). The consideration of the user experience must be considered with the same seriousness as any aesthetic or formal principle. This is the design principle of the 21st century and as such has already become successful.

KEY TERMS

Unity	Proportion	Emphasis
Variety	Scale	Focus
Harmony	Balance	Usability (Experience)
Gestalt	Rhythm	

DISCUSSION AND REVIEW QUESTIONS

1. As with elements in the previous chapter, choose a designed object or environment that you can observe, touch, and move around. Observe how the different principles are experienced by a viewer or user of the design. How do the different principles present themselves from different viewpoints and from different perspectives? How might the designer have approached this?

2. Again, compare two similar designed objects that present design principles in a very different way (e.g., two chairs, two bicycles, two shirts). Consider the relationship of elements that create the totality (gestalt) of the designed object resulting in the presentation of the principle observed. How do the design elements (as detailed in previous chapter) contribute in each case to the principle observed?

3. Consider each of the design principles in turn and consider how their effect contributes to the experience of the design. Is the design more or less usable as a result of the design decisions involved? Is there a relationship between the function of the design and the way the principles appear?

EXERCISES AND ASSIGNMENTS

1. Consider a designed object and describe it in terms of how the principles of design appear (or do not appear).
   a. Unity, variety, and harmony
   b. Proportion and scale
   c. Balance (focus)
   d. Rhythm
   e. Emphasis and focus
   f. Usability (experience)
2. Consider in each case an alternative approach to the principle in question. (Rearrange proportions, move focal points, etc.) For each change:
   a. Why do you suppose this was *not* done originally? (Aesthetics, technical capabilities, nature of the designed object?)
   b. Would the design be altered beyond recognition?
   c. Would the new approach to any of the principles require changing any of the elements?

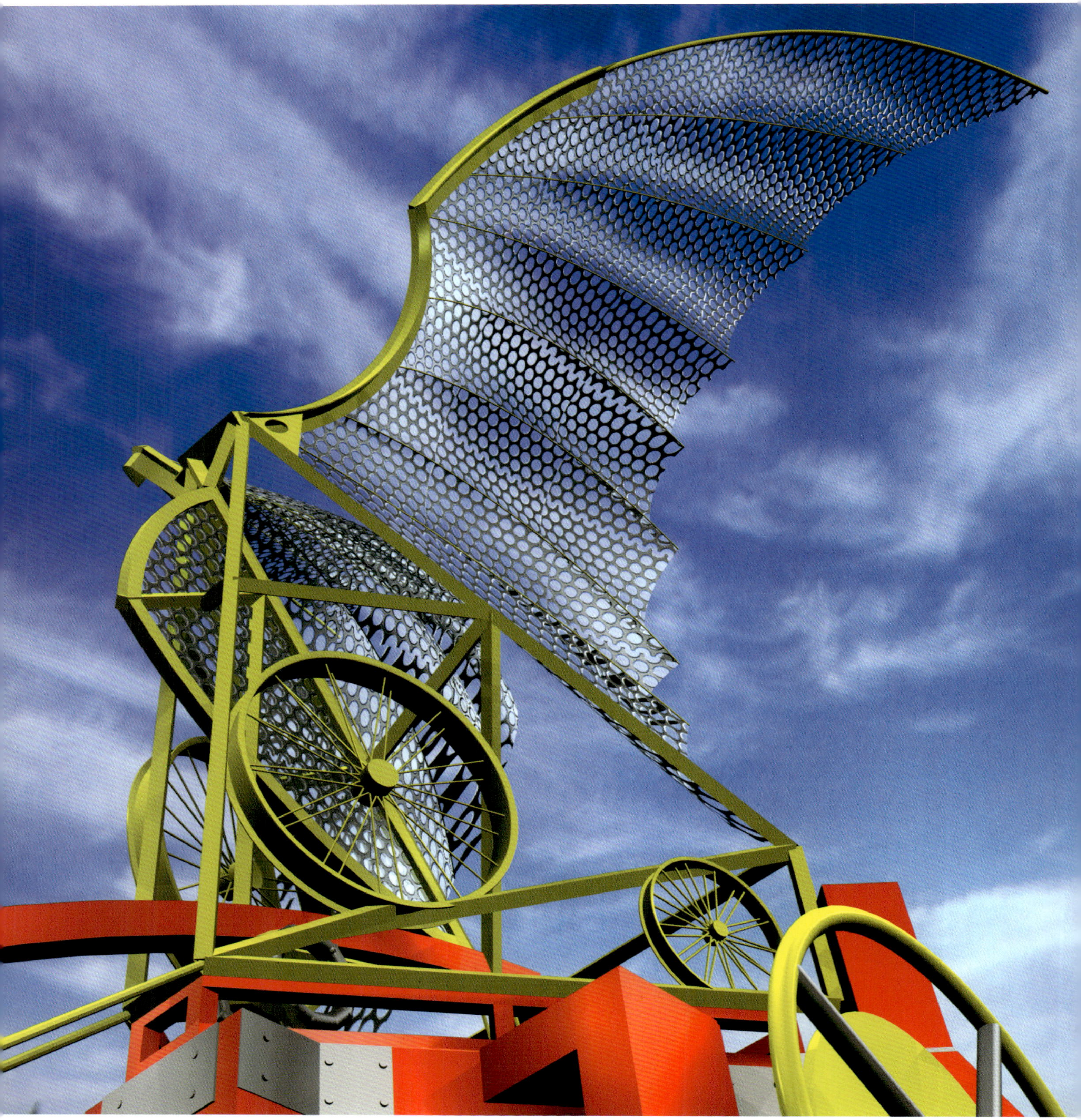

PART II

INFORMING DESIGN

A designer must be an inspired creator and innovator but also an expert communicator. Part Two examines the practical methods for defining and presenting an idea by studying the techniques of conceptualizing, researching, planning, and presenting designs. Chapter 5 looks at the conceptual thinking and brainstorming that may be used, and Chapter 6 follows this with a look at the different ways of presenting designs to different audiences.

OPPOSITE
CAD programs will create precise and elegant technical drawings easily and with much detail and layering of information if necessary, but can also be used to rough out outlines and diagrams, as well as engaging illustrations. (CAD illustrations and diagrams of the artwork "Wing it" by Karl Aspelund and Brent Baggett.)

CHAPTER 5

RESEARCHING AND PLANNING FOR DESIGNS

DESIGNERS SPEAK

"Ideas are like rabbits. You get a couple of them and learn how to handle them, and pretty soon you have a dozen."

—JOHN STEINBECK, *Conversations with John Steinbeck*, Thomas Fensch, ed., University Press of Mississippi, 1988, p. 43

"If you pick up the pencil thinking only of the solution, you will draw without an idea. What's important in architecture is intuition. . . . I have my system of work . . . based on fantasy, but always feeling logical."

—OSCAR NIEMEYER, "Oscar Niemeyer, Brazilian Architect, Dies at 104," AP News, December 5, 2012

This chapter takes a practical slant, considering a designer's concerns from finding and identifying the idea to expanding it, relating it to the world around, and considering the needs and constraints involved. How an idea may become a fleshed-out and clearly defined concept through the use of brainstorming techniques is explored and shown to be a way of examining a concept through looking at it as a totality that is more than the sum of its parts.

OBJECTIVES

Distinguish the importance of inspiration in the design process.

Identify the crosscurrents of artistic and design inspiration.

Recognize techniques for brainstorming and exploring concepts.

Realize methods for planning and researching for design.

Differentiate the components of a design thesis and how to approach them.

THE ART OF INSPIRATION: AVENUES, VECTORS, AND MUSES

A design project, no matter how mundane the end product may seem, is at the outset a creative act. If the project is worth anything, there is a drive to improve, innovate, or enhance an existing situation. Innovation at any level is creative and requires inspiration and energy to combine existing elements and situations into a new configuration in order to solve a problem. There must be a desire to succeed, motivation to continue in the face of obstacles and setbacks, and the energy to fuel the effort. There are a number of ways for a creative person to become inspired and maintain that energy.

Inspiration for a design project can come from any direction, and it is not always obviously connected to the projects end goal. The inspiration may be from the creativity itself, the puzzle-solving element of the job; it can come from a joy of a job well done or from the fulfillment of a desire to be creative. We are all inspired by the act of creation, no matter how small. "Look what I made" is an early declaration of success that arrives almost as soon as we learn to speak. This joy is replicated throughout life for a creative person, even though the expression may be more controlled and subdued as age progresses (Fig. 5.1). Inspiration should be sought in whatever moves you to a desire to work on the projects at hand; it should make you want to do it.

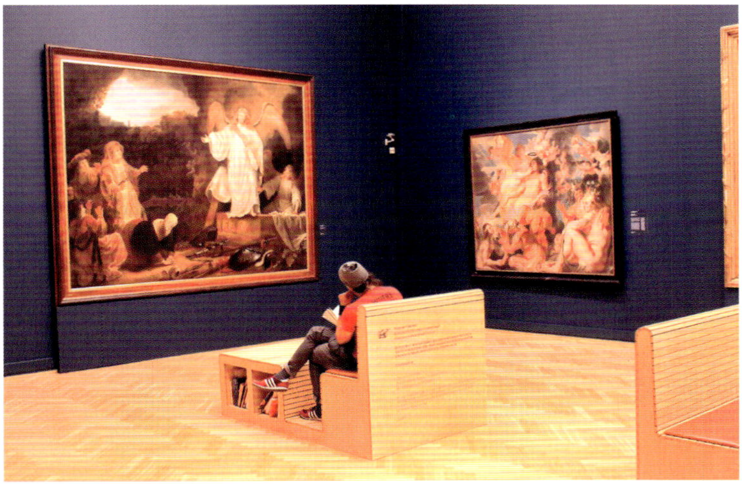

5.1 Inspiration can arrive from any direction. Reading, looking at art, looking at the world, being in a specific place—all can bring the moment of inspiration. For this young man reading in Denmark's National Museum of Art, the moment of inspiration might involve the space, the book, the paintings, the room, and even memories of having been there before.

Source: Photograph by Karl Aspelund

Inspiration arrives from the experiencing of that moment of realization that there is energy to be had from creativity. Reading can inspire, as can looking at a painting, listening to music, watching a movie, listening to a lecture, or admiring a design. The energy transferred excites our imagination and spurs us to action. In order for this to happen, the designer must be open to this influence. We must put ourselves in the place where these influences will move us to creativity. Instead of looking at the rain, we go outside and stand in it and let it wash over us.

FINDING A MUSE

The classical idea of inspiration was a **Muse,** a mythological female figure devoted to one of the arts and sciences, that would visit and endow the fortunate with a gift of artistry of scientific ability (the Muses were equally generous in arts and sciences, and in fact the ancient Greeks seemed to consider the arts and sciences equally in terms of the creativity involved). It is good to have a muse of any kind. Realizing where one's creativity comes from is an individual act of exploration, but it is possible, with some experience and introspection to realize what moves you. What is it that excites you about the act of designing. Why are you moved to investigate it in the first place? (Is there a reason you are you reading this book?) These reasons do not have to be large and earth-shattering, but they do need to be realized and heartfelt so that you can access them when you need them, just in the same way that you realize why you are attracted to certain people and therefore desire their company.

The wonderful thing about being an inspired creator is that this energy is not lost at the end of the project. If you know what music makes you happy, what artists make

TIMELINE: BRAINSTORMING

Although the act of thinking and examining a problem among a group of people is nothing new, the term "brainstorming" only came into being in the mid-20th century, as a result of the ad executive Alex Osbourne, who in 1953 published the book *Applied Imagination: Principles and Procedures of Creative Thinking*. Based on a method he called "thinking up" that he had begun using in 1939 at the BBD&O advertising agency, by the time the book came out, the process was called "brainstorming." The idea that storming the problem, with each individual mind on the team taking his or her own approach without criticism or second-guessing, quickly became a fixture in design and engineering practice, as well as many other creative endeavors.

Many structured methods for problem solving have been developed in the years since. They are of varying degrees of complexity, but most involve frameworks that force the expansion of an idea until as many avenues as possible have been explored. Mapping the ideas components in charts, passing notes back and forth, and using systematic approaches all allow the idea to be separated into its constituent parts or turned around and inside out, until it is understood how far it can go and whether it is feasible. Now software is available where brainstorming can take place among people at a distance. As a designer, find different methods of brainstorming and try them. You are certain to find one that works for you.

you want to create, which designers you wish to emulate, what you want to bring to your clients, and the end users of your designs, then you can revisit and replenish at will. Each design project has an arc—a beginning, middle, and end. At the end a certain distance may be needed to replenish the creative batteries, but if the muse is known, we can come back again and again, without fear of rejection.

DESIGN AND ART/ART AND DESIGN: OVERLAPPING ART FORMS

Designing shares this need for a muse with the sciences and fine art. One might say that the discipline of design bridges the two. Designing requires the methodical rigidity of a scientific approach to problem solving and the incorporation of technical knowledge beyond the actual techniques of the designing itself (building, sewing, molding, chemistry, and so on). But it also requires an artistry that allows freedom from orderly thinking and treading known paths. This combination allows the innovation and aesthetic play to produce a well-designed environment or product. The good news for designers is that the available muses are therefore standing in both camps—science and art. One can take inspiration from the mathematical, physical, artistic, and even poetic aspects of a project, weaving them into a conversation with the other muses.

But designing is not the whole of it. One must also be aware of the wonders involved in other art forms and how these express the joy of creativity. To watch a virtuoso performance of any kind, whether a song, dance, the playing of an instrument, or the molding of a material into a form, is in itself inspiring. But also we must examine the creative approach of practitioners of various disciplines and how they approach their art and their craft. What makes them tick? How does an opera singer or potter approach a challenging piece? What is it that allows a ballet dancer or a guitarist to attack a difficult passage in a performance with joy instead of apprehension? Learning from the desire to perfect a creative mission of any kind, large or small, becomes a way to fuel our own creativity of any kind.

THE ART OF METAPHOR AND SIMILE

The art of writing allows, for example, a quick entry into the mode of creative thinking, even while we engage with the design process at its beginning phases. How to describe a concept that is still only in the earliest planning stages? As we try to define the project at hand and describe to ourselves, our co-designers, and our clients what the solutions require, it is helpful to use metaphors and similes to discuss the nature of things we haven't yet designed into existence.

If the object to be designed is highly innovative, there may be no such objects available to refer to. But by using metaphor, we can discuss it by referring to something familiar but different. We can approach it by using similes: likening it to existing things but then discussing how it will be different and in doing so drawing around it a frame of constraints that create it in the end. A poetic approach to the project can then be brought back to the technical and factual elements of the problem, pulling us back into the world of design.

5.2 In our consumer society, identity is created and maintained by the consumption of designer goods. Designers have in the last century or so acquired the power to shape society well beyond what most people realize. Bargain hunters lining up outside Harrod's department store in London probably don't think of themselves as being part of society's dialogue with itself, but the purchases they will make as well as the commerce involved both direct society's identity and development.

Source: Brian Minkoff/Demotix/Corbis

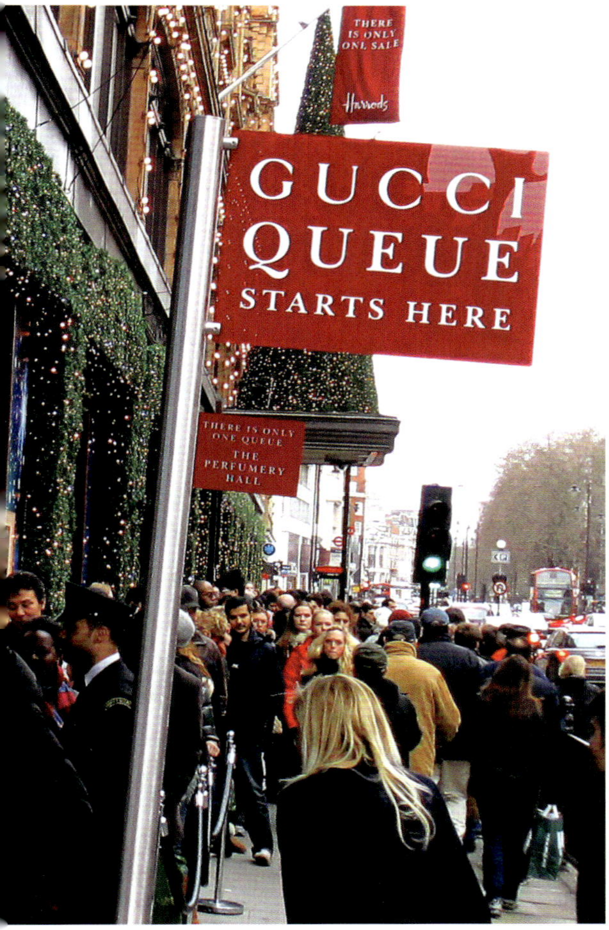

DESIGNER VERSUS ARTIST

Inspiration for design is parallel to inspiration for art, but there are subtle differences in the nature of it from one discipline to the other. These became increasingly blurred during the latter half of the 20th century as art became increasingly commercialized and design entered more and more into the everyday life of the emerging consumer culture. In the classical model, however, the fine artist would find a style and explore this throughout a career, gradually perfecting a vision over a number of years or though a number of commissions or gallery shows. Designers, on the other hand, were expected to provide a fresh vision with each new season, new building, or graphic project for a brand of some kind. The history of 20th century design was therefore one of constant new things. Born as they were of the artisan culture of preindustrial days, designers were less focused on a statement until they began to meld with the art world around the middle of the 20th century. Following on the success of designers such as Paul Poiret and the architects of the early Modernist movement, *vision* would be demanded of fashion designers and high-end architects would present statements and manifestoes outlining their positions.

As designing became a larger and larger part of a consumer culture that now increasingly dominates the globe, designers were looked to by a new class of consumers. The designers became sources of a vision from which to form a lifestyle in a new age of endless choices and opportunities. By consumption of designer goods, identity is created. In being the purveyors of vision, designers have actually moved closer to the fine artists of old, who in their portraits held up a mirror to society and presented a vision of the world to the world (Fig. 5.2). On this vision the world then in turn molded itself. And now the inspiration for designing comes also from the power of design itself—the ability to mold society by a well-considered and well-framed (marketed) product.

THE FREEDOM OF CONSTRAINTS

"The more constraints one imposes," said the composer Igor Stravinsky, "the more freedom one experiences." Creativity must have constraints, especially when the creativity must be channeled toward a specific end, such as a score for a ballet in Stravinsky's case, or a specific product that must fulfill specific needs: This is what must be done, this is the puzzle to solve, our client needs this, production requires this, the world needs that. Now the freedom within the frame is where creativity begins. With all the practical problems outlined, there is now room to maneuver and do something surprising, different, and ultimately creative that brings the solution to a level of proficiency. That will allow the design to wow the client, improve the life of the end user, and be a model for future designers to admire and follow (and perhaps strive to surpass). It is therefore very important for a designer to define the needs and constraints of the project as clearly as possible at the beginning of the project. No matter how mundane or exotic the project, this should always be the first step.

BRAINSTORMING: A HOW-TO GUIDE

Brainstorming is the activity of pulling as many ideas and thoughts about a specific topic as possible out of the multitude of possibilities available. Then, without prejudice, laying them out and considering them as solutions to the problems at hand. Brainstorming, most often undertaken at the beginning of a project, is used in any number of business, scientific, and design situations to get the creativity flowing and allow solutions to emerge from the combined efforts of a group. (It is, however, also possible to brainstorm alone, but then the dialogue has to be forced by assuming multiple roles.) Several different methods can be used, and it is good to be aware of three structured ways of outlining ideas: webbing or concept mapping, SCAMPER, and cubing.

GESTALT

Before the methods are introduced, a more in-depth discussion of a concept introduced in the previous chapter will be helpful. As mentioned, gestalt is a German word that has been incorporated into English to describe a concept for which the English language does not have a good equivalent word. It means "the whole of it" or the *totality* but also carries overtones of this totality being composed of a number of elements that together create something that is larger than simply their grouping. Gestalt is a totality that is larger than the sum of its parts. It includes the sense of an experience or an identity that the elements together do not provide until they are this whole. A piece of music, for example, is a collection of individual notes, but it is also the way it is played and the location and context in which it is heard. A jacket consists of the fabrics, trim, and construction details, but pull it apart and lay them all on a table and you don't have a jacket. One might even say that a jacket's totality is also found in the way it is worn and accessorized: It is not a whole until it is used and experienced, just as the gestalt of the musical piece is an identifiable thing that is not there except in the combination of the elements and in its performance.

A gestalt can be either open or closed. When open, there are gaps in the collection of elements that leave the gestalt open to interpretation; it is not entirely clear what this

THE SUSTAINABILITY CONCEPT MAP

Trying to consider the ecological impact of a designed product can be an extremely complicated exercise, especially if every step in the long process chain of production, lifetime, and disposal or reuse is considered. Building a concept map of the process allows this complex picture to be observed by building it up slowly and piece by piece. The added benefit to constructing a map for the ecological impact is that once a plausible and reliable map has been created, the basic underlying structure will very likely be the same for similar products or for the same product in the near future. Concept maps can therefore be stored and reused to identify weak and wasteful spots in the process of a product in terms of its ecological impact.

Creating such a map would begin simply. The major nodes of materials harvesting, production, shipping, packaging, transportation, marketing, use, reuse, and disposal/recycling form a chain that can then be added to and branched out from until the ecological footprint of the product begins to appear in the form of its myriad components. The next step can then be to question each element now in the map and identify the biggest ecological impact. It is then only a matter of following the chain and interrogating each node until the product has been "greened" as much as possible.

thing is. The more elements that become known, the clearer the concept becomes, and eventually the gestalt is closed: It becomes known. It is recognized as this particular whole. As we approach a design problem, this concept can help us, as it shows how we perceive the world and how we can come to understand ideas and concepts that are foreign to us. We gradually build a gestalt in recognizing the elements and experiences connected with the phenomenon until they are incorporated into our map of the world. We enclose the concept; it becomes a closed gestalt and part of a new world view through which we are able to encounter newer things still.

Brainstorming is essentially a way of approaching the creation of a gestalt in response to a problem or question requiring a solution by design. Webbing, mapping, cubing, and SCAMPER-ing are all tools that allow designers to experiment and explore the possible elements that will be the gestalt of their solution. These methods approach the problem from different directions, trying things out and seeing what sticks, by exploring the unknown elements and going inward as well as the known outward. Attacking a problem from both sides and using more than one method often results in success. You may also find that one is more suited to a particular kind of problem or even to you own way of thinking and working.

The more you experiment, the better. Framing design problems and solutions as a gestalt that needs closing also benefits the role of the designer as communicator. The use of metaphor and simile is an effective approach to discussing, clarifying, and presenting unknown concepts. This is another way of seeing the ideas in terms of the open and closed gestalt. Framing a thought by likening it to some other thing or by comparing it with an existing concept is how the gestalt becomes closed. In trying to explain a design solution to a client or colleague, you may assemble known pieces of information, reference points to known designs, and evoke imagery from familiar places and artworks. From these elements you create for them (and yourself!) the nearly closed gestalt that allows you to converse intelligently and comfortably about the project, even though no objects as yet exist.

WEBBING AND CONCEPT MAPPING

Webbing and concept mapping are two very similar ways of approaching a concept in order to uncover and display its nature. These methods allow the illustration of the elements that make up the concept and how they are connected. **Webbing** is a free association exercise where the main concept is written down and and then related ideas are placed all around and connected by lines. **Concept mapping** is an extended method of webbing where the connecting lines are tagged—preferably with verbs—to give a clearer description of how the elements are related to each other. Webs are therefore less dynamic, but they are also easier to create and clearer in presentation. Webs and maps are excellent tools for clarifying to oneself the nature of an idea, but no less elegant as tools with which to communicate this clearly to an audience.

Using webs and maps allows a designer to show the idea as a whole (a closed gestalt) while retaining the individual elements for inspection. This allows for ease of exploration, as each element can be swapped out, moved around, and reconsidered while maintaining as closed a gestalt as possible. Furthermore, if you are using tagged connectors, the concept map allows the relationships of the various elements to be considered and the cross-connections become all the more clearer by having their function illustrated as well. This can reveal connections in the proposed design solution that would not otherwise have been readily apparent if the elements were not connected. A little time with a stack of index cards and sticky notes, writing up elements, and moving them around on a larger sheet may allow for quick clarity that then facilitates a swift move to the next design phase.

WEBS AND MAPS AS DESIGN TOOLS

A concept of a solution, at the beginning of a design project is a very open gestalt. But we know that even an abstract concept has elements that have characteristics, which in turn are of a nature with a distinct identity. Furthermore, these collective identities are the elements from which the gestalt is derived: They produce the concept's unique identity. We can therefore act *as if* we have them under control, *as if* we know where they belong. The design decision is then in determining how we fill in those gaps to create or confirm the open gestalt so that it closes.

Start by writing the central concept on the center of a sheet of large paper and then creating a series of index cards or sticky notes on which the various elements of the concept (elements of the gestalt) are listed. Then lay them out and consider how they connect, describing these connections with a single verb if possible but with a minimum of words in any case. New concepts are placed in hierarchical relation to it and each other: A bicycle /HAS/wheels/HAVE /spokes /ARE/metal/CAN BE steel, aluminum. . . . Keep going until you run out of new elements or descriptions. (It happens more quickly than you might imagine, and it is not uncommon to come to the end of a thought-train at the fourth of fifth level when you are dealing with maps like this.)

A concept map can be printed out to use in presentation and used as a way of walking the client through the idea (Box 5.1). It can also be broken up into a series of PowerPoint slides, with the elements as headers and connectors in the text. This allows illustration of the ideas as well and can be a very effective way of presenting a design direction as a nearly closed gestalt. Printing a concept map as a large-scale illustration

BOX 5.1

A MIND-MAP: MAPPING A CONCEPT

MIND-MAPS ARE THE BEST WAY to quickly flesh out and outline a concept. They work especially well as they allow for the construction of complex concepts one simple piece at a time while allowing the clear definition of connections between the constituent parts. These maps therefore manage to illustrate very clearly the construction of thoughts in real time. With each added node and connection a new element is added to the totality, and as the brainstorming session continues the concept can be seen to appear before the participants' eyes. Furthermore, once a map has been created, it becomes a record of the creative exploration itself and each step or progression can be isolated and re-explored at will. Whether you are using software or simply sketching out the map in pen or pencil, keeping the elements clear and the connections well-defined is therefore very important, as coming back to the map later may be difficult otherwise. A good rule to begin with is to try to signify all the elements in the nodes with nouns and all the connections with verbs. This may not always be fully possible, but even if the procedure is not perfectly adhered to, it still allows the map to be read or navigated in a way that seems to produce very clear meanings. There is, however, no really wrong way to construct a mind-map as long as the elements placed are produced in a constructive process and the connections between elements are precisely articulated.

can also allow for the addition of further explanation on the presentation wall and makes for a very engaging visual in any presentation setting.

CUBING

Cubing is a simple version of webbing and grew out of techniques used to explore problems in writing. A writing student analyzing a topic by approaching it from six directions: description, comparison, association, analysis, applications, and argument (see Fig. 5.3). We can adapt the method for our purposes by substituting the word *design* for *topic* and adding design principles, as in the following:

1. *Description.* Physically describe your intended design. What would it look like? What color, shape, texture, and size will it be? Identify its parts.
2. *Comparison.* How is your design similar to other designs/things? How is it different?
3. *Association.* What other design/thing does your design make you think of? Can you compare it to anything else in your experience? Don't be afraid to be creative here; include everything that comes to mind.
4. *Analysis.* Look at your design's components. How are these parts related? How is it put together? Where does each component come from? How does each contribute?
5. *Application.* What can you do with your design? What uses does it have?
6. *Argument.* What arguments can you make for or against your design?

5.3 *Cubing*, finding six sides of a design problem, is especially good for thinking on the fly as when making a napkin scribble.

Source: Photograph by Karl Aspelund

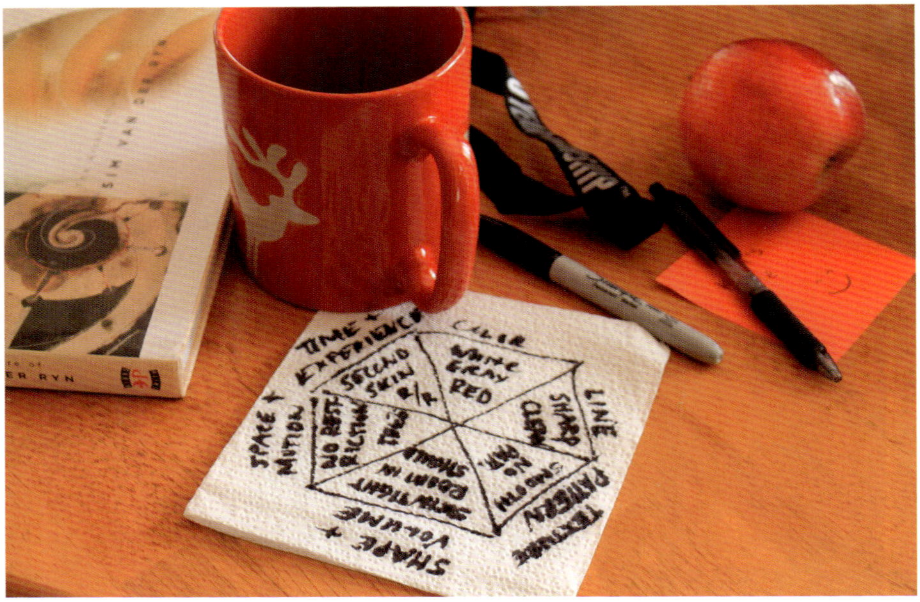

Cubing can also be used very effectively when you are exploring the elements of a design. Here we have six elements that will contribute to the closed gestalt:

1. Color
2. Line
3. Pattern and texture
4. Shape and volume
5. Space and motion
6. Time and experience

Each of these six needs to be addressed in order for the cube to be whole—for the gestalt to close. Cubing can be a very powerful tool when you are working under tight deadlines because it forces the definitions and can be done either in writing or with illustrations as necessary in large or small scale.

SCAMPER

In the early stages of a project, designing is concerned with exploring ideas in order to find out what they contain and what constrains them. The best way to evaluate the constraints in all directions is to isolate the idea's components and, by deliberately changing things around, find the limits of the total concept. Push and prod the intended design to see what it's capable of and whether there may be other directions in which it might go. Once it's gone too far, there's your limit.

Brainstorming usually refers to a group getting together to examine a situation with the express purpose of solving a problem. This is not limited to designing but is found in any structured planning or systematic creativity where a solution must be found by generating new ideas. In a brainstorming session, it is required that

ERGONOMICS: CONNECTING CONSTRAINTS AND NEEDS

The full impact of the power of constraints and needs to frame designing and provide structures for the development of concepts is seen when issues of ergonomics appear. The focus on physical efficiency, safety, and comfort that ergonomics demands is, in fact, as clear an example of the dialogue of constraints and needs in designing as can be found. The constraints of the human body appear in its range and speed of movement, its vulnerabilities, structures, and symmetries. These constraints encounter the needs of the body in the demand for safety and comfort, but design also requires a look at where the constraints relate to the needs of equipment, the environment, or the design capabilities themselves. It is not enough to analyze the relation of the shape of the body and the designed object, but also their interaction and development over time. The human body and the designed object form a system between them. This system can be analyzed if the body and its capabilities are inserted into the design as a component rather than an outside entity that is simply considered at the beginning and end of the process. This gives a whole new meaning to the modernist idea of everything being a machine or system: The body and the design unite as a totality. Design for the body's needs and constraints.

everyone's voice be heard and no ideas are to be dismissed or criticized during the discussion. Critical analysis takes place after a predetermined period of when a certain number of ideas have been generated.

A number of good brainstorming techniques have been developed to assist in a creative process dialogue. The **SCAMPER** technique is an excellent example of how designing can be systematically approached. It is a very good way of exploring the possibilities of idea, as it can easily be applied to any kind of creative venture and is easily done as either a solo activity or as a prompt for group brainstorming. The technique was formally defined by Robert F. Eberle, an educational administrator who wrote on creativity for both children and teachers. SCAMPER is an acronym for:

Substitute

Combine

Adapt

Modify (**m**inimize *or* **m**agnify)

Put to another use(s)

Eliminate *or* **e**laborate

Reverse *or* **r**earrange

Taking an initial idea and running it down the list allows a team or an individual designer to examine the project from various angles, considering various elements and aspects, without getting hung up on any one particular element of the design or even on the nature of the design itself. SCAMPER-ing simply provides a way to rearrange the existing concept and attack it from various levels to get as much out of it as possible. By not binding the discussion to any individual aspect, it allows the idea—as a system—to be taken outside habitual frames of reference and possibly be improved in unexpected ways. Take an idea and do as many of the following as you can. The results may overlap; some may be silly. This is normal and means that you have found a boundary to examine. Consider individual parts of your design, but also think of it as a *system* (you might even be designing an actual system).

SUBSTITUTE

With this step, you take something out and put something else in its place. For example, swap colors or components, or substitute a technique or a method of construction. If there's a process, isolate a step. Then consider doing something else at that point. Where does this lead?

COMBINE

In this step you take two or more components of your idea and combine them (make two pieces into one piece, or several steps into one operation). Combine your entire concept with another idea. Combine styles. What do you find?

ADAPT

This step asks how can your design be adapted to another situation, or for another purpose? For instance, a design for a specific climate is adapted to another, or a system directed at one situation is modified to work for another. Note that adapting involves change, as opposed to the component below of "putting to other uses" where the unchanged idea is directed to another purpose.

MODIFY (MINIMIZE OR MAGNIFY)

This step is probably the most open-ended, as modification can have a very wide meaning. However, begin, without adding new elements, by changing the quality of one or more elements of the design. (Make something bigger or smaller, lengthen or shorten a process, make something curvy that was angular, and so on.) Then consider modifying the functionality of your design; make it do something differently. Finally, consider modifying the overall design by adding a component to the object or a step to the process.

PUT TO OTHER USE(S)

In this step, you consider how your idea could be applied to another problem. How could your design be used elsewhere? What would happen if it were used by someone entirely different than the end user you imagined?

ELIMINATE OR ELABORATE

In this step, you ask, is everything necessary? All the components? Every step in the process? What if you randomly remove an element or function? ("Can't have color," or "mustn't move.") How much can you remove before your idea is no longer what you intended? Conversely, did you leave any thought half finished? What can be increased or made more complex? What can be taken further? At what point is there "too much"? (When is "too much" "just right"?)

REVERSE OR REARRANGE

Here you reverse in whole or in part: Put the back in the front, the end at the beginning, the left on the right. What does inside-out mean in the context of your idea? Is there an order to things that can be rearranged or broken up? Is there an assumption or belief about the order of things that can be challenged out of existence?

PLANNING FOR DESIGNS

Despite the importance of analysis, brainstorming, investigation, and the need for critical thinking about the nature of a project, it is surprising for many students of design to find how much time goes into the nuts-and-bolts planning and organizing of a design project from the start. Setting up the definitions, planning time, looking at organizational issues, and lining up the schedules is extraordinarily important, if for no other reason than to consider the constraints that then reveal themselves. The constraints of time, money, and person-power are usually very rigid, and it is very difficult to deal with changes midstream. Therefore, a lot of energy must go into the planning, even while the joy of creativity must be kept bubbling up. The two-handed approach is often in conflict but must be endured.

SETTING UP A DESIGN THESIS

The design thesis is a simple list of questions that allows the designer to define in very basic terms what the project is about and identify the areas on which the project is to be focused (Fig. 5.4).

The questions are these:

1. What do you need to design? (The product)
2. What is its nature? (A description)
3. Who is it for? (The audience)
4. Why is it needed? (The problem)
5. What are its benefits? (The solution to the problem)
6. Why is it interesting? (A challenge)
7. What will you bring to it? (Your vision)
8. How will you proceed? (Your methods)

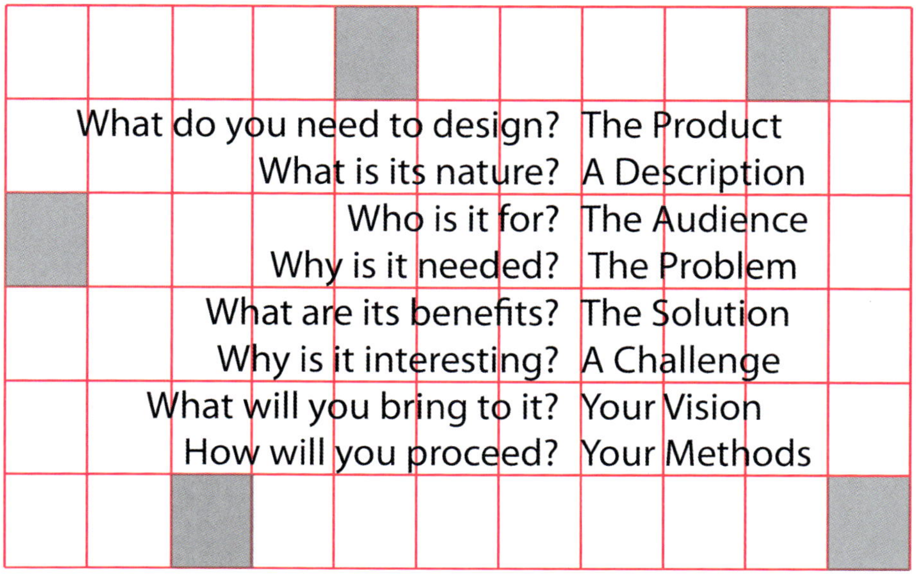

5.4 The design thesis: The questions on the left relate to the concepts on the right. Going down this list, describing the product, its nature, its prospective audience of end users, and so on will create a thesis for your project that serves as a prompt, by identifying where the focus of your thinking needs to be in each stage of the process. By explaining and illustrating the answers, you will force the design to appear.

Source: Illustration by Karl Aspelund

Each of these has a specific area to address and taken together will provide as robust a picture of a design project as is possible in the early stages. They are also in a sequence that is significant, so answering them in order will be helpful. However, depending on the project, some answers may be clearer than others, but all should be readily answerable right at the beginning of a project.

WHAT DO YOU NEED TO DESIGN?

First of all, the precise definition of what the product is must be clear. Note the use of the word *need* in the question. It is implied that there is a specific need involved whether it is considered a trivial need or an urgent one is beside the point. Focus on this need.

WHAT IS ITS NATURE?

Second, consider and describe the nature of the designed product that is to result from the project. What *is* it in terms of what it consists of and what it does? How is it this particular thing and not another (the gestalt of it, yet again). How do we recognize it as the thing that fulfills the above-mentioned need?

WHO IS IT FOR?

The audience for this particular design now comes into play. This may be the actual end user, an observer, or a client that wishes to sell the design. In any case, consider the nature of the client as far as it can be determined and how this might differ between different groups, if there is more than one.

WHY IS IT NEEDED?

Given the nature of the design and the client, the need for this new design should be easily made clear. This may also be phrased as: "What is the design problem?" What needs have prompted the desire for this design, whether it is in your mind or the clients or in the dialogue between you?

WHAT ARE ITS BENEFITS?

The problem that requires the design implies that the design is a solution. Therefore, there must be benefits to the design. Even if they may seem trivial, they are not. If the problem is simple, such as the desire for a new color scheme in a product, the benefits are simply whatever arises from such an exercise. This is the nature of the design job, not trivia.

WHY IS IT INTERESTING?

Regardless of the scale or weight of the problem and the complexity or severity of its solution, you must be able to make a case for why it is interesting to even consider it. Granted, not all design projects are equally interesting. However, it is imperative that you, as a designer, be able to find interest in a project at any level. If you are not interested, the odds of your client being interested in your work rapidly decrease.

WHAT WILL YOU BRING TO IT?

To be interested, the question of inspiration arrives again, and with it the vision that any inspiration will have focused. What do you intend to achieve? How are your talents, abilities, and ideas specifically helpful to the project? Answer this honestly; the design thesis may only be for your eyes anyway. You must be able to articulate this for the same reason as before. If you cannot articulate it to yourself, you will not be in good shape when asked to explain your vision to a client or colleagues.

HOW WILL YOU PROCEED?

This final question is the one that is probably the most difficult to answer in many cases. What do you propose to do next? What will your methods be? If this is not clear, simply consider what you have written in response to the previous questions and ask, "Now what do I need to do? And then what? And then . . . ? How do I intend to do this?" This, and the previous questions, leads you then directly into planning the project in some considerable detail.

PROJECT MANAGEMENT

Having written a thesis for the project, you are in a position to begin planning. The first place to bear down is scheduling (Fig. 5.5). Time is going to be of essence in any design project, and all deadlines, final and interim, are something you'll want to have clear at the beginning. Get as much information from clients and manufacturers and suppliers as you can: when your ideas should be ready and when orders need to be placed for any necessary materials. Know what your options are in terms of presentations and meetings, and if any travel is involved, consider time taken for that. You must work your designing into a time frame; there is generally very little wiggle room for designers in a commercial environment, so do not treat it casually or think that you can wait.

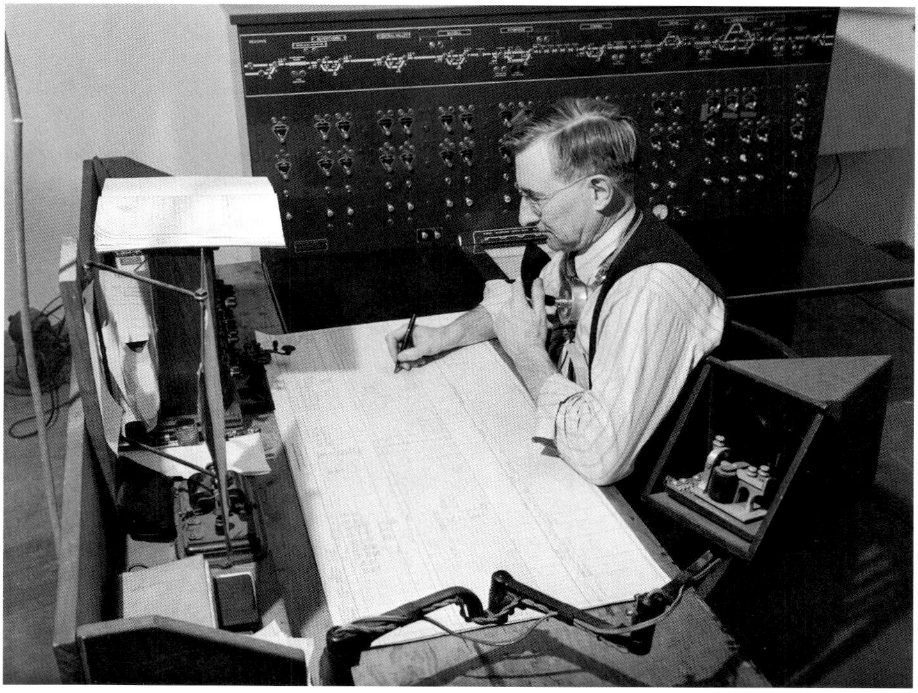

5.5 Like this train dispatcher keeping track of multiple trains on many tracks, heading in various directions at different speeds, a designer must manage multiple thoughts on multiple trajectories for even the simplest project. The only way to make sure everything winds up in the correct place is to start the day by creating a schedule—and then keeping an eye on it.

Source: © Horace Bristol/Corbis

RESOURCES

Next, consider the resources involved. What are the resources you have that can be brought to bear on the project, and what are the resources you'll need? These break down into several categories, the first of which is time, and so begins the scheduling. The next is any technology and materials that you may need in order to get the project started. This comes up quickly, as things may need to be ordered or sought out, and this may take time.

The other resources you will need to consider are whether you need any knowledge that you do not have and whether there are any people or any particular talents that you will need to recruit to assist you in the project (Fig. 5.6). Which brings up the final resource without which not a lot may happen: Do you have the operating funds to allow you to begin the project? If not, where will they arrive from?

KNOWLEDGE

As far as knowledge goes, this can obviously be considered along a very wide spectrum and is a continuing concern in any project that demands or involves innovation. Again, this is an area where you as a designer and project manager must be very honest with yourself: Are you capable of the project? Do you have all the knowledge necessary in order to carry it out, or are you able to access it in a timely fashion? If not, where is that knowledge and how will it be obtained? Consider your co-designers, sample makers, illustrators, and anyone else who may be involved. What knowledge do they need in order for the project to run as well as possible? Is it knowledge you can provide, or will they need to work on that? Is there someone who needs to be brought in to help?

PEOPLE/TALENT

The people involved in a design project are a resource and an asset. If you are your only resource and asset in this department, so be it. If there are more people that need attention, management, and nurturing, then it is very likely your job as the designer to

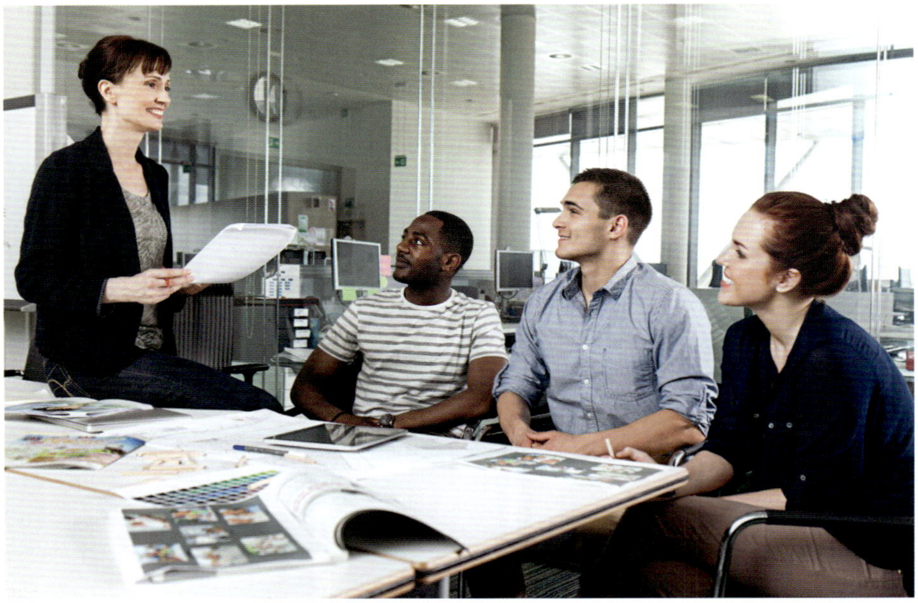

5.6 Different demands come from the client side, the design business side, the marketing team, concerns over production methods, and on and on. The number of different avenues for research and information gathering is very high. Don't skimp on research and make sure every interested party is represented when discussing plans and concepts.

Source: © The Image Source/Alamy

NETWORKING: Six Essential Sites on Brainstorming and Gestalt Perception

FLORIDA INSTITUTE FOR HUMAN AND MACHINE COGNITION

The IHMC provides free downloadable software for creating concept maps (CmapTools). Easy to install and easy to learn and use, it is a very helpful tool when brainstorming.

cmap.ihmc.us

MIND TOOLS

Online since 1996, Mind Tools has a wealth of information, including this very thorough page on brainstorming.

www.mindtools.com/brainstm.html

WRITING CENTER AT THE UNIVERSITY OF NORTH CAROLINA AT CHAPEL HILL

The UNC Chapel Hill Writing Center has an excellent site on brainstorming in the context of writing academic papers, from finding a topic through the revising process. This will serve for any writing project.

writingcenter.unc.edu/handouts/brainstorming

CNET

Free downloadable brainstorming and mind-mapping software.

download.cnet.com/windows/brainstorming-and-mind-mapping-software

INTERACTION DESIGN FOUNDATION

"Gestalt Principles of Form Perception," by Mads Soegaard, focuses on the gestalt perception as it relates to design for the Internet but is applicable to all forms of design.

interaction-design.org/encyclopedia/gestalt_principles_of_form_perception.html

"GESTALT PRINCIPLES" ON SCHOLARPEDIA

A thorough and well-illustrated article by Dejan Todorović of the University of Belgrade.

www.scholarpedia.org/article/Gestalt_principles

provide this. If you do this properly, the talent involved will be put to good use. If you are not able to inspire, educate, and lead the team, the project will suffer. Be positive, straightforward, and interested. Do not assume that all will be well for everyone. Make sure everyone has all the necessary information available, and make sure that everyone's task is clearly defined. In defining a project, it may also be necessary to define team members' areas of expertise, so that each team member is working to the best of his or her abilities and not wasting time.

TIMELINES OF DESIGN AND PRODUCTION

TOTAL—DESIGN—PRODUCTION

We now see that the first thing to do is to create a timeline for the project. Using a spreadsheet or calendar, note any deadlines you can think of and then work backward. What needs to happen to meet this deadline? What needs to happen first to make that happen? What is the order of operations that this requires? (And so on.) Consider who will be required to do what within this order and, again, whether the requisite materials, technology, and knowledge are in place for each step of the way. Even if you are the only person working on the project, it is still important to cover this ground so that there are not uncomfortable surprises on the road. There will come a point where you will need to be ready to hand over to production or the next design phase.

When you are creating a timeline at the beginning of a project, the thing to avoid is wishful thinking. It is very easy to look at a blank calendar and put everything on it in neat and tidy entries and make the plan look good. This happens over and over again in businesses all over the world every day (not to mention government offices). Our desire to make it work must not override our ability to look at the project realistically and see where things may not be exactly as we wish them to be. The whole point of initial planning is to isolate the problems that may arrive down the road, not to paint a picture of open road that then will have to be revised again and again as we go.

Be honest and diligent about considering realistically what can be achieved in a given amount of time. If you don't know, don't guess. Get opinions from whoever else is involved in the process, and be fair to your collaborators and co-designers. It is fair to say that it is nearly guaranteed that you will never have more time than you need, so plan extra time into your project for contingencies and the unexpected. (It is not uncommon to routinely assign as much as 15 percent extra into at time frame to account for emergencies and then tweak as needed when the time comes.)

Finally be aware of what is known as Pareto's Principle that states that 20 percent of any project eats up 80 percent of its resources. In other words, one-fifth of your project will require four out of every five days assigned to the whole project. In planning your time (and other resource management), see if you can identify that crucial 20 percent.

RESEARCH METHODS FOR DESIGN

With all the aforementioned planning and investigating, it is hardly surprising that the number of different avenues for research is also high. Let's look at methods for the research that is necessary to set off on a good journey into a design project. Research must be done on the client side, on the design-business side, on the eventual marketing of the designed product, and on production methods. This research involves the now much-mentioned needs and constraints, functionality, aesthetics, and techniques. Just as with the conceptual investigation, all of this must be carefully placed inside the frame of the project, as with the open gestalt, the possibilities are often limitless and the potential for tangents increases with each step of the process. Constant feedback from the project and collaborators should be taken into account, and the manufacturing side should be kept in the loop at all times.

FINDING AND CHOOSING THE METHODS

Client Side

First there is an investigation into the nature, needs, and constraints of the client. The client may be the end user of your designs but could also be someone intending to sell them to end users, or conversely, you may be designing for an audience to whatever your end user is doing (costume, ceremonial garb, exhibition spaces, theatrical and film sets, etc.). The client will in each case reveal needs and constraints that are defined by demographics, budgets, and previous use and knowledge of the designs you will be providing. When looking at demographics, one may be looking at various different bases, such as location, environment, age, ethnicity, religion, and occupation. It is misleading to consider each of these independently from each other. The concept of *psychodemographics* appears: People are defined by what *kind* of environment they live in more than *where* they live. A person living in a college town may have more in common with another person in a college town a thousand miles away than with someone living in the next town five miles down the road.

Business Side

Second, research into how such projects have been approached in the past is usually beneficial. Seek out articles and books on topics related to the kind of designs you are aiming for. What prompted designers toward new solutions in the past. What problems did they face? How did they overcome these? Which ones didn't they overcome? (These should be noted carefully, as you will run into the same, and they may either be the breakthrough you were looking for or the wall you also hit.) Go look at the products that come closest to the ones you intend to design. How are they successful? What is missing or inadequate? How will you improve on them? Again, the question of clients' needs comes up, as well as the abilities of you and your team. Are you capable of giving clients what they need?

Marketing Side

You may have a wonderful idea. It may make complete sense in all your meetings and brainstorming sessions. But will it sell? Is it actually worth the time and effort to create the new design if it will only become a footnote? Many products have been brilliantly designed and actually better at serving the client than the competitor than won out, but they simply couldn't make it because they were too expensive or not marketed correctly. The late 20th-century tech wars are full of examples of this kind of product. Market research is very tricky and trend analysis even more so, but you simply cannot go out into the world with a new design without having done some investigation into the viability of your idea out there. Look at the markets. Look at the street, or wherever people would be using your design or where there are similar designs in operation. What is going on? Are they selling? Are they "in" or are they "out"? Are trendsetters adopting something completely different?

Production Side

In the end, sending a design to production should be a straightforward proposition. But if the design is truly innovative, if new methods are involved or more complex operations required, then research will be needed into the possibility of production methods. Look into what is possible, what the current production methods are, and how much pressure or strain your new ideas would be on current capabilities. What might need to be emphasized in discussion with production? Perhaps a new process needs to be invented or even a new machine or technique. The main point is this: Do not take for granted that your idea can magically be brought into being, if no similar solutions are available. The reason your idea is not available on the market may well lie in the difficulty of manufacturing it. An early investigation into the viability of your project should help you avoid any shocks.

ORGANIZATION

Organizing your research into the four basic categories of information you need will allow you to better keep track of the myriad streams of information you will be dealing with. Consider keeping folders for (1) needs and constraints, (2) function, (3) aesthetic questions, and (4) production issues. Keeping these four compartmentalized allows you to drop findings into the folders as you go, and not have to ignore one or the other for too long while your eyes are elsewhere.

Function requires a closer look, as it can be broken down into the functioning of individual elements and materials on one hand and then the function of the entire gestalt of the designed object on the other. What does it do on the whole, and how do the individual elements contribute by doing something on their own? This can often veer into rather vague territory. When considering the function of your design, it is almost a trick question brought on by the emphasis on "form follows function" in modernist design philosophy. In all the emphasis on practical functionality, the more nontangible function of a design as it relates to emotional experience tends to be neglected. What is the function of an object that is designed for sensual appeal? How to consider the function of a piece of jewelry, for example? Again, the importance of thinking poetically and metaphorically even when considering practical applications can be a very powerful approach to designing (Fig. 5.7).

Design concerns itself with both aesthetics and functionality, but the two are also interrelated. The function of a design may well be in part to produce an aesthetic effect: to produce an impact of look and feel as in high fashion or interiors. But the functionality of the design may also in itself produce the "look" as in the look of a piece of equipment or a machine. Research on the aesthetic possibilities for your design needs to take into account a number of avenues: Will you be maintaining or breaking with tradition? Are there styles you will reference? What is the relevance of the aesthetics to the nature of the design? Keeping journals and collections of imagery and references is extremely important in order to continually inspire and maintain an aesthetic vision. And in today's globalized multimedia world of information overload you can—and should—be diligent about building up a comfortable knowledge of historical periods and multiple cultural perspectives. This will allow you as a designer to engage with the world, your audience, and the tradition of design in a meaningful and relevant way.

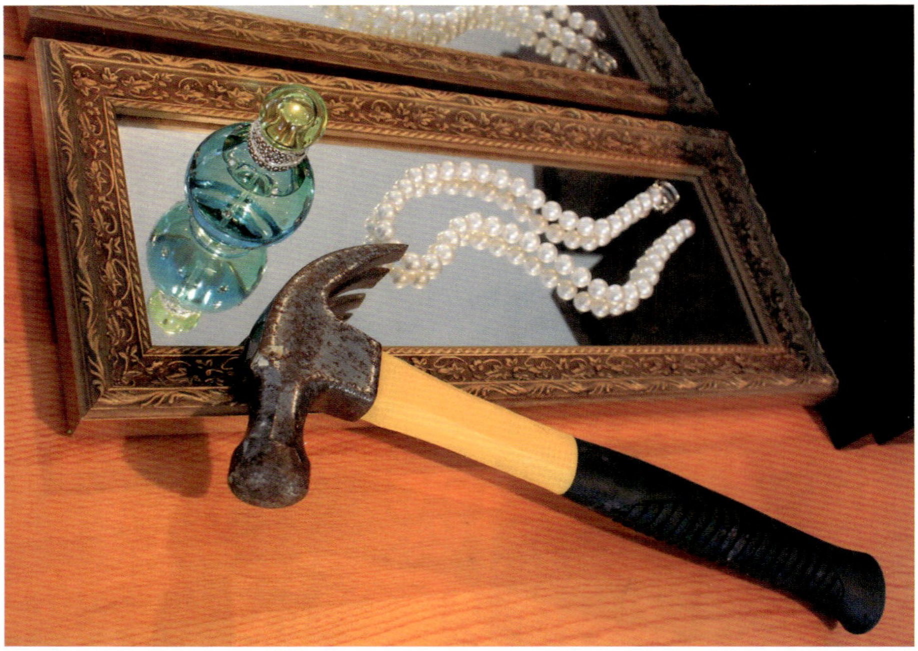

5.7 The emphasis on practical functionality in design theory tends to neglect emotional experience. The function of an object that is designed for sensual appeal, may be open to question and interpretation. If we consider the function of a piece of jewelry, for example, the answer lies in its emotional impact, derived, before any practical or financial functions appear, from its colors, textures, and shapes. The hammer and the necklace above, have very different functions but it is incorrect to say that only one of them is functional.

Photograph by Karl Aspelund

DETERMINING RELEVANCE

But how to determine the relevance of the investigation into history and art? In our fragmented postmodern state, the idea of relevance itself is questioned or regarded as quaint, and meaning, such as it is, is taken to be fluid, malleable, and relative. It is a challenge in designing to consider the relevance of our ideas and aesthetics, when the very idea of a central narrative is increasingly difficult to sustain and rationalize. However, if perspective is all there is to go by, then at least the relevance of our choices can be examined. To look at the research done and the aesthetic choices requires yet again a look at the needs and constraints that are being addressed. Now also one considers the information that can be obtained from modeling and prototyping, by being open to continuous feedback from the project itself, from collaborators, and the input from the manufacturing and production stage.

The task is therefore simply to make sure that you are looking at all the facets involved. Makes sure all the needs are examined and all the constraints have been lined up and their effects accounted for. Go back to the conceptual thinking and consider a concept map of your design idea. Have you covered all the bases? Consider scenarios by putting yourself in the place of your client and imagining yourself interacting with your design (or actually interact with a prototype).

But could you possibly have gone too far? Too many needs being considered? Too many constraints added? In this case, the solution is equally straightforward: If in doubt, consider the opposite as being true. Go down the list of needs and constraints for a project and consider what would happen if they were taken off the list or their effect were the opposite. Be honest about it, and if you find something doesn't actually matter, let it go. That will be one less thing to worry about.

Creating a prototype is one way of assessing the relevance to the design problem of your proposed solution. If your train of thought has gone down the right path and the research and investigations you have carried out have been along the lines necessary, your prototype should affirm your initial thesis. You can use your prototype as a way to point to finer details that need to be examined, now that you have an object that is that much closer to reality. Be careful of one thing, however: Here the desire to be right may override any self-criticism you may muster. Make sure your prototype is looked at and tried out by as impartial an observer as possible. Then go down your list of needs and consider your thesis with the observer and investigate whether you have fulfilled what you intended to do.

Having a prototype is also the opportunity to get assessment from the manufacturer of your design. They can look at your prototype, try it out, test it, and tell you what they would now do differently. They may add constraints, given what has now become clear: This can be done like this, but not that. You can do this with that material, but here you'll need to substitute something else, and so on.

CONCLUSION

All in all, it should now be clear that the researching and planning for designs is nearly a never-ending task and the *nearly* is only there because if your design is going to be produced, there comes a time when you have to let go and trust that the process has been good—that your instincts, knowledge, and research were all that they needed to be.

KEY TERMS

Muse
Webbing
Concept Mapping
Cubing
SCAMPER

DISCUSSION AND REVIEW QUESTIONS

1. For a series of different types of design (apparel, architecture, furnishings, and gadgets), consider what might have inspired their design. Separate functionality from aesthetics, and consider the inspiration in each case.
2. Look at current trendy designs. What may have inspired the look of the design? Is there an overlap with current movements in art?
3. Create a concept map for a design in your immediate environment. Observe how many branches and levels are sufficient to fully describe the design. At what point would you as a designer have to provide tangible samples or measurements?
4. For the same design consider the creation of its design thesis. What would have been clear at the outset? What would have been difficult to define, if anything?

EXERCISES AND ASSIGNMENTS

1. Find three different sources of inspiration that would make you want to be creative in design. Imagine that you are designing the following, and for each, describe how your sources of inspiration would contribute to the design, whether in form, function, emotion, or overall aesthetics.
   a. A bedroom interior
   b. A fashionable outfit
   c. A public square
   d. A magazine ad for an accessory
2. Choose a design you consider—for any reason—to be less than perfect. Imagine you had been asked to improve on it, and attempt to do so by applying the SCAMPER method.
   a. Which of the SCAMPER approaches had the most impact? Why?
   b. Would your solutions be applicable in a production situation?
   c. If not, why not?
   d. If so, why do you suppose this was not done in the first place?
3. Consider an object or environment you consider to be good design. Imagine you were going to design it.
   a. Explain why you think it is good design.
   b. Write a design thesis that would lead to this conclusion.
   c. What are the needs and constraints that define the design and its solutions?
   d. How would you have modeled or created a prototype to test your ideas in order that it would become a good design? What is the most important element to consider? Which is the most important principle to adhere to?

CHAPTER 6 PRESENTING DESIGNS

DESIGNERS SPEAK

"We don't have good language to talk about this kind of thing. In most people's vocabularies, design means veneer. It's interior decorating. It's the fabric of the curtains and the sofa. But to me, nothing could be further from the meaning of design. Design is the fundamental soul of a man-made creation that ends up expressing itself in successive outer layers of the product or service. The iMac is not just the color or translucence or the shape of the shell. The essence of the iMac is to be the finest possible consumer computer in which each element plays together."

—STEVE JOBS, interview, *Fortune Magazine*, January 24, 2000. http://money.cnn.com/magazines/fortune/fortune_archive/2000/01/24/272277/ (accessed 8/12/2013).

"Style for the sake of style alone will have less meaning to the consumer than value. An interruption of the spiral created by boosting sales from year to year with false inducements of style, bulk, and flash gives design a new lease on life. Aesthetic beauty will be the direct result of careful planning and precision manufacturing."

—RAYMOND LOEWY, http://www.raymondloewy.com/about/quotesby.html

A large part of a designer's job is to present ideas, models, and finished designs to a variety of audiences of colleagues, marketers, and clients. Along with a discussion of media that may be useful for creating engaging presentations, this chapter considers techniques, modes, and methods of presenting designs and the problem of presenting to different audiences. The difference between physical and digital presentations is considered as well as different presentation methods and situations. This chapter wraps up by considering the designer's dual role as a performer and salesperson when presenting.

OBJECTIVES

Recognize basic techniques and methods of presenting a design.

Identify the need for different media in various situations.

Distinguish that presenting designs is a performance.

DISPLAY: PROS AND CONS AND SITUATIONS

The mode of display for a design project has a direct bearing on how the audience will receive it, but the choice of method and media is also influenced by the project's needs. Instead of forging ahead with a basic method of presentation and hoping for the best, some thought should be given to the presentation method that is most appropriate for the type of design involved. Some designs may require a more hands-on approach, with samples and functioning models, while others may need a digital animation and technical diagrams. A certain product may need a presentation that references the background of the project itself, perhaps a retro reference or a literary style of some kind (Fig. 6.1).

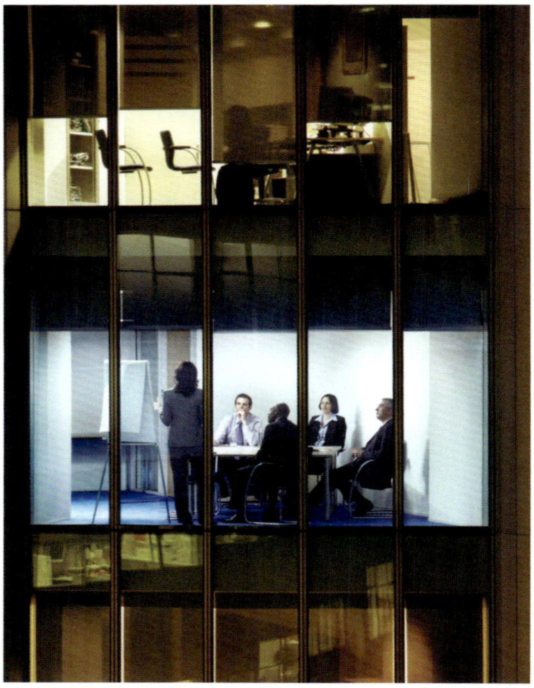

6.1 Some designs may require a hands-on approach, with samples and functioning models, while others may need a digital animation and technical diagrams. Some may be very simple. There is no one rule.

Source: © moodboard/Corbis

However, the **digital presentation** is popular, handy, and, more often than not, expected. Regardless of software, the general format is a slideshow of some kind and possible animations of a varying degree of complexity. Keep it simple. If you have a lot of information to deliver, take the time to go through it, but don't bury your audience. Following are further tips.

Emphasize substance over style. Tailor your presentation to the information, not the other way around. Don't get lost in the bells and whistles. Presentations can be fun, especially in a creative arena. Don't get lost in the entertainment. Don't add effects to your presentation simply for their own sake. An animation is only good if it shows off the design. Slides are only good if they convey the information that is needed. Fancy effects and formatting quickly lose their shine if they are just a pretty surface covering nothing much. Nothing is as devastatingly boring as having someone read a slide to you, so avoid that at all costs.

Be very aware that we are *multisensory* beings. Text is only one away of conveying information. As **multisensory** beings, we also obtain information through images and sound. Creating presentations where the balance of text, spoken word, and visual information requires good insight into how an audience will react to what is being said, shown, felt, and heard. The interplay of the various sensory inputs must be carefully choreographed. Try to put yourself into the experience of your audience: When are you looking; when are you listening, feeling, reading, and thinking? Does one experience collide with another? Do they reinforce each other?

As a rule, it is a lost opportunity if physical samples are not present when you are attempting to engage an audience. As people experience the world through so much more than sight, the feel of an object is better conveyed through the presence of its elements, even if they are present in separate samples. The touch, the weight in the hand, the way the light hits and changes, even the sound or scent of material matters to the overall experience. Modeling software has made great strides in conveying light and visual texture in the past decade, but the full immersion of a physical presence, of weight and texture, still can't be beat.

Presentations of projects that rely on an experience in close proximity, such as clothing or textiles, should include samples of fabrics, trim, and color. The end product is experienced as much by touch as by sight, and a tactile experience in the presentation is crucial, as would be the case for samples of anything novel. A new type of push-button or frame for a handheld device, surfaces that will be touched, anything reflective, and any striking or significant color combinations should be physically present if at all possible, rather than demonstrated only on a picture or screen.

Start with a big-picture overview. Tell your audience about the needs and constraints and how you addressed those. Then go into detail of how the plans and designs came together. Explain any problems or novel situations that need to be clarified, and then sum up with a repetition of the big picture, bringing your presentation full circle back to the way you solved the needs and constraints involved. This can be backed up with slides, boards, or diagrams, and at the end of a presentation, you may want to distribute a handout or "take-home" for your audience outlining main points and perhaps containing more technical or historical information.

Consider the power of face-to-face communication and human interaction. A common misperception, especially among those who have grown up in an always-on digital environment, is that a presentation is essentially a digital or online event where print and speech is supplementary to the digital image on the screen. Speech and body language can have a great effect on winning over an audience. An object provides a physical connection and a memory. Print material, however, in the form of handouts or take-home packages can also provide a sense of connectivity and belonging. Consider creating a handout with facts and figures that the audience can investigate after you've covered the main points. Holding an object in one's hand, especially if it's carefully crafted or purposefully presented, is a powerful way of connecting with an event or person. A well-crafted handout or artifact from a design presentation allows the client again to claim ownership of the project and have a sense of belonging.

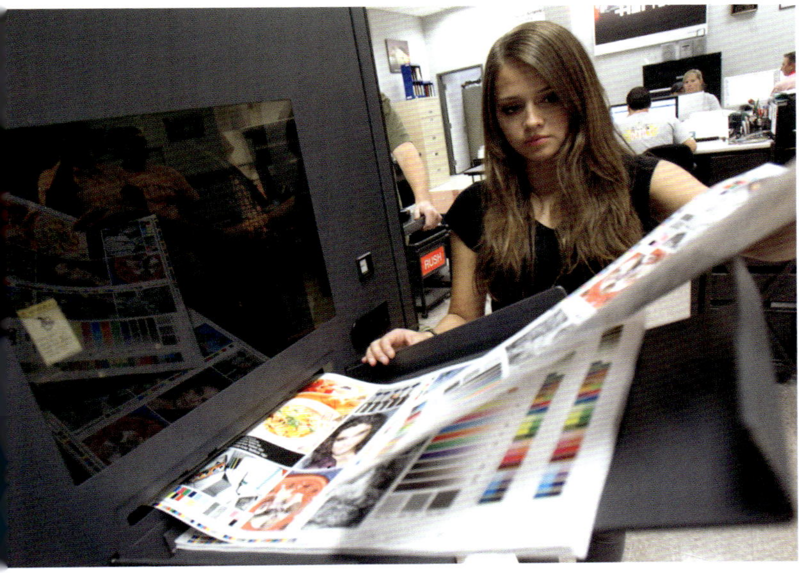

6.2 Color systems also vary widely from screen to page, with the three-color (RGB) system of the screen not translating fully to the four-color (CMYK) of print and the additive process of light on the screen providing a different way of dealing with color than the subtractive of print. High-quality four-color printing, as seen here, is a delicate process requiring careful monitoring, from start to finish.

Source: Courtesy of ASU Print & Imaging Lab.

Consider carefully whether you are creating the best-possible image. Digital presentations can also allow for the creation of artifacts, but these are in danger of losing their power when printed due to the attendant loss of color and size. A screen reads very differently than a page, and if nothing else, the brightness and color saturation of the screen provides a very different experience than that of the printed page. Meanwhile, do not discount the power of holding in your hand a beautifully printed page on high-quality paper.

Printing from digital also requires that you keep a close watch on the resolution of your image and the color process being used. The screen resolution of digital images have until recently been typically 72 dots per inch (dpi), while a printer will print at 300 dpi. Color systems also vary widely from screen to page, with the three-color (RGB) system of the screen not translating fully to the four-color (CMYK) of print and the additive process of light on the screen providing a different way of dealing with color than the subtractive of print (Fig. 6.2).

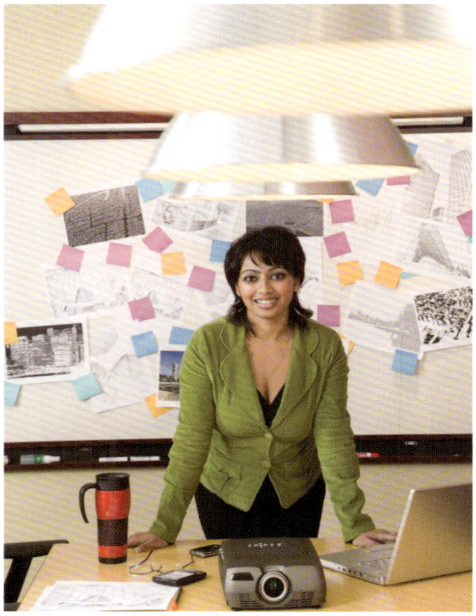

Another twist in the creation and presentation of digital media is that we are now dealing with an increasingly varied world of screens. Not too long ago, one could count on a digital image or presentation being viewed on a certain size of monitor or projection screen. The planning that went into the creation of a standalone digital presentation was—at least in that regard—fairly simple. Now, however, the size of the screen can be almost absurdly different all the way from a couple of inches to a couple of feet, if not even larger. It also is not unreasonable to suppose that a presentation that you email or upload will be viewed in less than favorable circumstances. The recipient may be downloading it anywhere he or she happens to be online. This is not a problem if you simply keep the possibility in mind and do not plan for circumstances over which you have no control.

Whether it is hand-drawn, digital, animated, or printed, keep asking yourself when creating a presentation: Is this representing the work I have done to the best-possible extent? Is the information all correct, and is all the information here? Are there any elements that are being misrepresented and should be thought through in other media?

ABOVE

6.3 When presenting, consider the needs of your presentation, your client, and your colleagues. Balance information with entertainment, visuals with text, and both with spoken word. Balance digital work with physical tangible examples and handouts.

Source: © SuperStock/SuperStock/Corbis

Be aware that no presentation technique and no amount of showmanship can rescue a design. Choose to take time to perfect your ideas and polish your execution of your concept before spending energy, time, and money on a presentation. A good presentation with good illustrations and well-crafted handouts matters, but it is not the product itself.

Don't just dive in. Consider carefully what kind of presentation your project needs, what kind of presentation your client needs, and what kind of presentation your colleagues need. Then balance information with entertainment, visuals with text, both of these with spoken word, and digital work with physical tangible examples and handouts. Then you will have brought the design into the world in a way that it deserves (Fig. 6.3).

TECHNIQUES

Presenting a design usually involves the unveiling of a set of images of varying degrees of artistry and technical prowess and a range of visual and written information. The classic image of a designer sitting at a drawing board, pencil in hand, has given way to a popular image of a designer at a computer screen (Fig. 6.4). Either way, the designer as sketch-artist and image-maker reigns supreme in the public consciousness, and rightfully so. The way to communicate a design concept to an audience is always by way of some visual element or other. Not every technique is necessarily a good idea at all times, nor is every technique strictly necessary for every project. It is therefore fitting to begin the discussion by looking at a few techniques of bringing visual information into a presentation, whether through hand-sketching in the classical mode, modeling, or creating images, diagrams, and presentation slides on computer screens.

BELOW

6.4 The classic image of a designer sitting at a drawing board, pencil in hand, has given way into this: a designer at a computer screen, mouse in hand.

Source: © Peter M. Fisher/Corbis

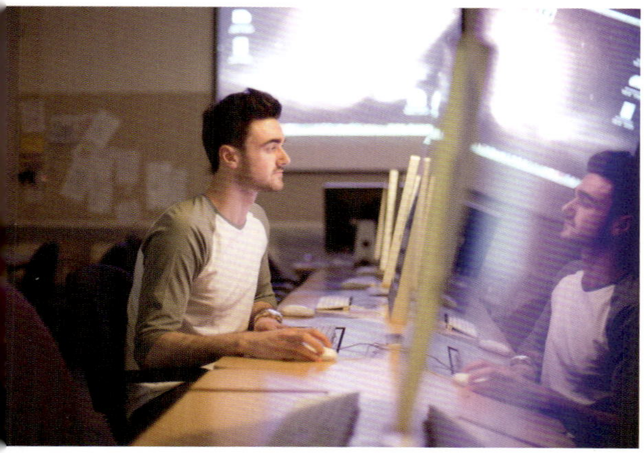

One misconception involving design presentation is that everything needs to be of a highly artistic quality. If the information that is required

TIMELINE: PRESENTATION METHODS AND TECHNOLOGY

For nearly all of human history, oral presentation, based on culturally defined narrative structures, has been the way of conveying information. Manuscript culture and eventually print technology changed how information was stored and altered the role of speeches in the education and presenting of information, but the speech before an audience is still seen as the way for an individual to make a case or teach a subject. Technologically, there was little change until the advent of electricity, and the technology that followed allowed the amplification of voices and the broadcasting of speech by the early years of the 20th century. Image projection technology also arrived and improved quickly, with camera and projectors, and slideshows began to be seen as an essential part of a good presentation. Once computers and digital imagery became common in the late 20th century, the digital slideshow quickly became the industry standard, often to the dismay of overloaded audiences. Videoconferencing and presentations through websites are now commonplace, and the ability to record and store larger and larger files and use greater and greater bandwidth is making presentations at a distance much easier. The ubiquity of handheld devices with high-definition screens and cameras and recording capabilities is also serving to create new options for presentations and discussions. The oral culture of the group gathered around the orator may now be dissolving into individuals, each at their screens, with their devices connecting them to a common experience, separated in space and even in time.

appears and a good level of interest is generated in the viewer, a quick sketch on a bit of scrap paper can be just as impactful as a subtly made, much-labored watercolor or detailed digital image.

Technical drawings aside (they will be discussed a little later), there are basically two ways to think about the designer's handcrafted artwork: either as sketches or as illustrations. The **sketch** is more of an information and exploration tool, quickly done, and not dependent on media or paper choices, whereas an **illustration** has a visual appeal and is carefully created with a consistency of materials, media, and layout. One might say that the sketches are the workhorse tool of designing, on the backs of envelopes or on café napkins, while the illustrations are the image-making elements on good paper, with good pigments and colors, there to establish the design—and charm the client (Fig. 6.5).

In any case, the choice of media will influence how the design is understood. A sketch in pencil or marker, done quickly with a minimum of lines, conveys a message of effortless thought and security. On the other hand, watercolors or highly detailed

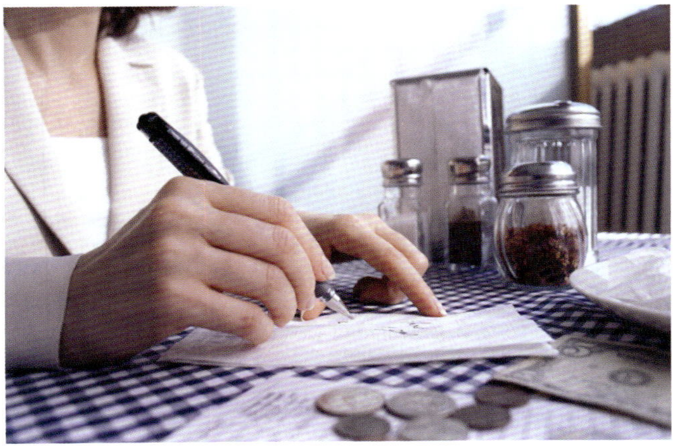

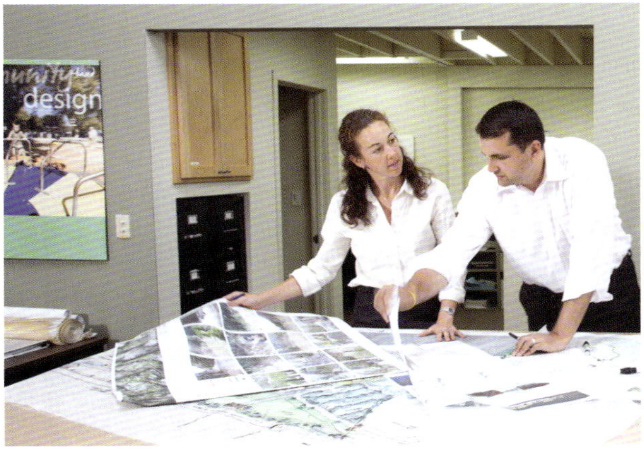

6.5 Sketches are the workhorse tool of designing, while illustrations are the image-making elements that establish the design—and charm the client. Sketching can take place anywhere, in the office, on the run, or as here: in a diner. More detailed presentations of color prints might want to be in a more controlled environment.

Source: L: © Jim Craigmyle/CORBIS; R: © Billy Hustace/Corbis

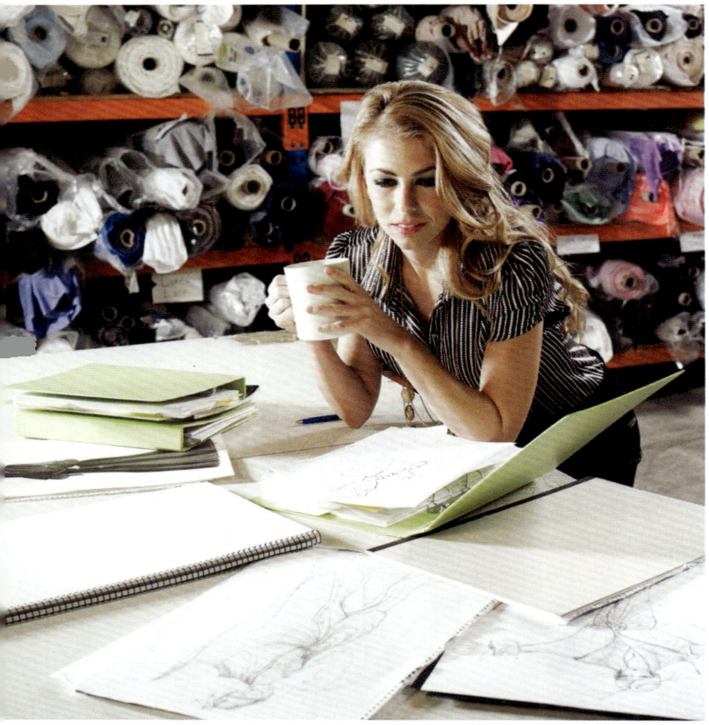

digital illustrations speak of an attention to detail and a focus that goes beyond the surface, even though the information content for the design may be exactly the same in both cases. The audience may be equally wowed by the designer's skill. As designing is by and large a mental activity, the sketches are often a PR issue. Showing the artistry of the design by displaying a handful of rough sketches that led up to it makes the less-than-spectacular technical information come alive. None of the designs may absolutely need the *artistic treatment* to be understood fully, but the visual appeal is very important in how we perceive the world. To capture the audience's attention, a certain amount of fireworks may be necessary.

The *hand sketch* or quick sketch has its pros and cons in a presentation. The first thing to keep in mind when choosing to present rough sketches is that the audience's response to them is also on a visceral level. The *feel* of a hand sketch evokes a sense of creativity and artistry, giving the audience a sense of participation in a creative event (as opposed to being spectators.) The hand sketch is, in the sense of presentation being performance, *live* (Fig. 6.6).

ABOVE
6.6 The *feel* of a hand-sketch evokes a sense of creativity and artistry, giving the audience a sense of participation in a creative event. This designer will bring the feel of her studio to her clients when showing her sketches.

Source: © Serge Kozak/Corbis

BELOW
6.7 Scanning a hand-sketch is a good basis for a CAD illustration.

Source: Courtesy of CGCookie, Inc., www.cgcookie.com.

The downside of the rough sketch comes from the same area, especially now that most people have become accustomed to high-quality computer-generated graphics. The hand sketch can feel low-end or simply not effective in displaying "reality." The audience may simply not be accustomed to perceiving the world through sketches. They will assume that the sketch is meant to be *showing* "reality" not just *pointing toward* it. The mental leap necessary to build the bridge from the sketch to reality requires imagination and a comfort level that is less and less common in a multimedia society.

Producing full-on *illustrations*, in color, with proper layout and formatting, creates a look of professionalism and control, but at the risk of sacrificing spontaneity. Obviously an assessment of the need for one or the other is important, but be very careful not to tilt in the direction of full production when it is simply not needed. Good illustrations take time and money, and it may not be the best use of your resources. On the other hand, if the clients need that level of realism or impact, this is the fastest way toward a good and engaging show.

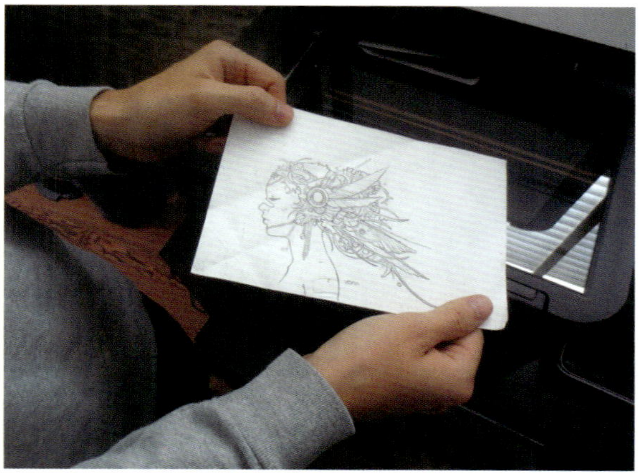

Illustrating can be done with all traditional media, but markers and colored pencils outweigh watercolors and acrylics for speed and control. However, with some training, **computer-aided design (CAD)** programs, such as Photoshop and Illustrator, can allow work habits and methods that very quickly arrive at a consistent level of professionalism. The benefit of these is that digital content is easily transportable, storable, and reusable. However, be careful to not discount the speed with which a good hand sketch can be scanned and cleaned up to use as the basis of a CAD illustration (Fig. 6.7).

SUSTAINABILITY AND PRESENTATIONS

One of the roles a designer plays in presenting a design is to be the educator of the audience, whether they are clients, makers, investors, or end users of the product. This is most important when the design must break with a reigning style or custom or it introduces a new way of operating. The designer must answer the audiences' questions of "why this? why now?" and perhaps get technical, in order to explain the benefits of the (unexpected) change. Industrial manufacturing at this time in history is pressed to move toward more sustainable practices. Enmeshed in a culture of commerce and consumption, we find the reasons for this often to be less than compelling and often confusing. For example, the fact that polyester is currently more eco-friendly than cotton seems counterintuitive. But that's because the client sees and touches the fabric, not seeing what brought them there. The production methods of cotton are more harmful to the environment than those of polyester. That this is even more true if recycling is taken into account leads to what many find to be an uncomfortable conclusion: The future of ecologically conscious design and consumption may not lie in natural fabrics. If the ecological impact is an issue, it would be the designer's job to point this out at a presentation, justifying the fabric choices and making the case for the polyester over the cotton. A debate over comfort and image might ensue, but that would be precisely why the designer would need to present the seemingly contrary view.

Sustainability, green, and eco-friendly are all complex, often counterintuitive, and frequently uncomfortable issues when approached closely. It is therefore all the more important for a designer to have all the facts about the production and supply chain, chemical use, user impact, and recyclability, if these issues are to be included in the design and presentation. In coming years, they will increasingly be there.

COMPUTER-AIDED DESIGN (CAD)

Before looking at CAD, let's consider the nature of **technical drawing** in general. CAD programs have taken over technical drawing from the age of drawing boards and ink, but these are simply new tools for the same purpose. What the novice designer needs to recognize is the fundamental difference in what is conveyed in sketches versus illustrations versus technical drawings. The designer should consider all three and usually include some element of each in a presentation. If the sketches are *emotional* and illustrations *artistic,* then technical drawings are *informational.*

The presentation is where ideas are translated into real-world dimensions, placements, and variations. It is where the maker of the designed object gets the necessary information on construction and where the end user gets to appreciate the functionality and dimensions of things. The maker may be interested but ultimately not really care about the emotional impact of the object except with regard to techniques of building. The end user, on the other hand, may not need to know about every seam or screw or layer of manufacturing. Both traditional and digital types of presentation materials are available to distribute the right level of information to the right people.

CAD covers a lot of territory. Software is available for technical drawing, graphic design, 3D modeling, color manipulation, and the simulation of photographic darkroom techniques, to name a few areas. One area that is often neglected in discussion is the option to use any of these programs as sketching tools. Programs such as Illustrator or Photoshop can be a very elegant solution to the quick sketch, especially if paired with a tablet or touch screen that allows sketching with degrees of pressure and flow. 3D programs such as Trimble's SketchUp can be used to quickly sketch out a 3D object for exploration. CAD programs will create precise and elegant technical drawings easily and with much detail and layering of information if necessary, but they also can be used to rough out outlines and diagrams (Fig. 6.8).

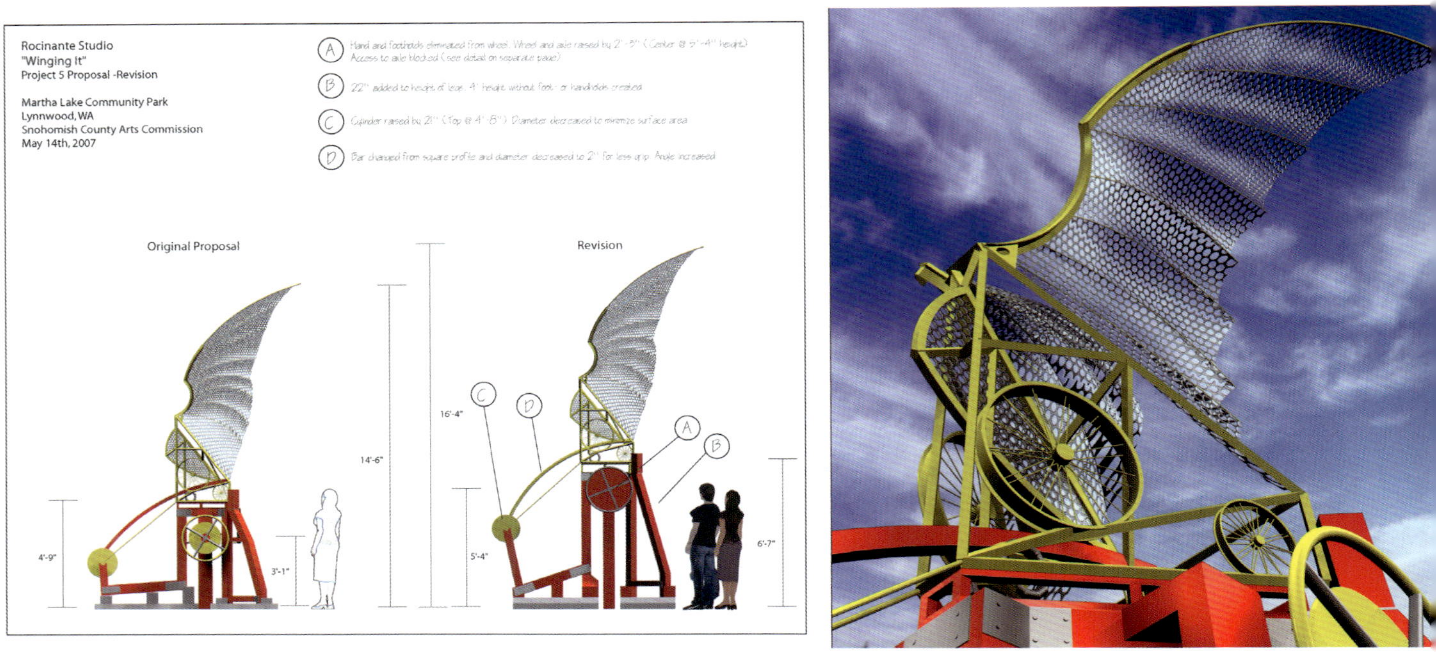

6.8 CAD programs will create precise and elegant technical drawings easily and with much detail and layering of information if necessary, but can also be used to rough out outlines and diagrams as well as engaging illustrations. CAD illustrations and diagrams of the artwork *Wing It,* by Karl Aspelund and Brent Baggett.

Source: Illustration by Karl Aspelund

The danger of CAD it that with all the possibilities available, the novice user (and actually many professionals) tend to get distracted and lost in all the capabilities. It is very important to realize and map out beforehand how intricate or detailed the diagram has to be. Not every CAD drawing needs to be completely perfect and filled with information. Using a program such as Illustrator to block out a quick diagram or create an outline or using Photoshop to cut and paste a series of images together into a concept board can save a lot of time and effort in the sketching phase and produce equally impactful and informative results.

The main goal with a technical drawing is to provide the information that is needed to create the object, but no more. When putting together a diagram for construction, ask yourself every now and then, "Is this necessary information?" and make sure that you are knowledgeable enough about the construction methods and processes involved to recognize whether anything is missing. Do not fall into the trap of being too embarrassed to ask an expert what information you might need to give him or her. The best-case scenario is to have an experienced maker tell you exactly what is needed and if possible have the maker look over your diagrams while you are putting them together. If they are to work on your project later, he or she will appreciate this all the more. By having had input in the process, the maker will approach the project with more confidence and not worry about whether your diagrams are comprehensive. Such a dialogue—if you can enter into it—will potentially save you all a lot of aggravation later.

Programs that allow the creation of illustrations on a computer screen are too numerous to mention, but two of the heavyweights in the field have been the industry standard for a long time. Illustrator focuses on the use of vector-based line creation to create clean and precise illustrations, while Photoshop is a program that grew out

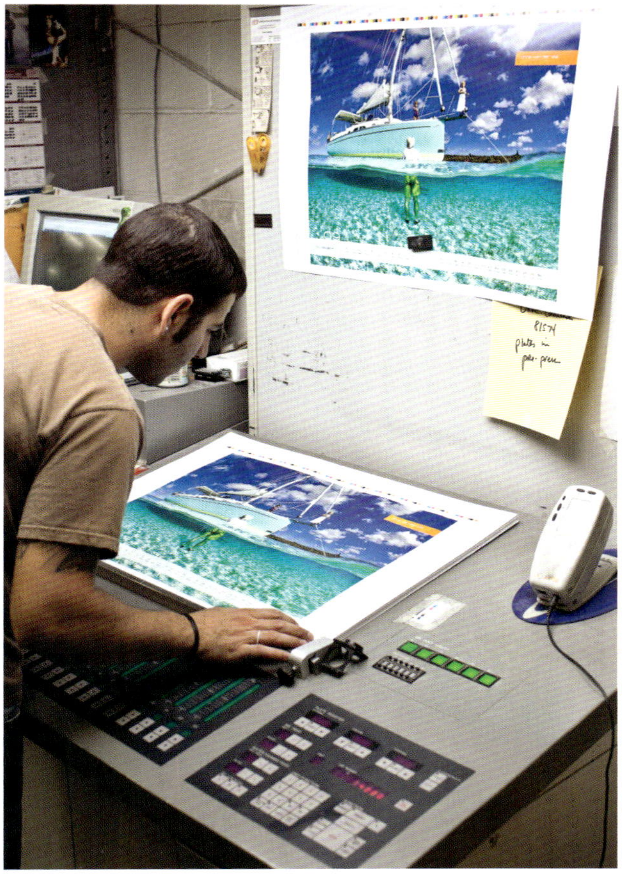

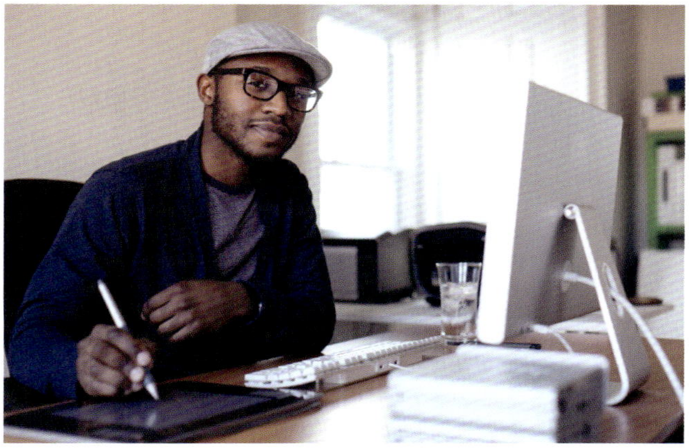

TOP RIGHT

6.9 The use of a tablet or touch screen greatly enhances the experience of designing with CAD programs of any kind by allowing the interaction with software to have the more natural feel and motion of more traditional tools such as pencils and brushes.

Source: © Roberto Westbrook/Blend Images/Corbis

TOP LEFT

6.10 Given the different way in which colors are sensed in inks and on screen, the brilliance and subtlety you see on a screen will not be replicated, especially if the paper you are printing on is not of high quality.

Source: © Onne van der Wal/Corbis

of the methods used in photographic darkrooms of the late 20th century. Although the programs have begun to overlap significantly, together they still provide an incredible range of opportunities for an illustrator. In addition, these programs are invaluable design tools for storing and creating collections of images and elements and components to use. The use of a tablet or touch screen greatly enhances the experience (Fig. 6.9).

It is worth repeating a warning mentioned a little earlier. Keep in mind when working with CAD, especially in illustration, how the final product is to be presented. With the current state of printing technology, make sure that all images and illustrations are created at the correct resolution for printing. Good-quality printers will print at upward of 300 dots per inch (dpi.) Creating images at a lower resolution will result in fuzzy pictures and a sense of low quality overall. Be sure that your printer is able to produce the colors that you require. Most printers have a four-color system (CMYK). The difference from the colors you see on your screen and the color that will be produced on the page can still be very significant, as the colors on the screen are produced via light and are additive whereas the ink on the page is based on pigments and is subtractive. The brilliance and subtlety you see on your screen will simply not be replicated, especially if the paper you are printing on is not of high quality (Fig. 6.10).

The capabilities of CAD programs to allow the quick and accurate creation of models have improved dramatically in the early years of the 21st century. The price of the programs has also come down to where they are easily obtainable by small businesses and individuals. SketchUp, a program available for free online, even allows the creation of good massing models (shapes and spaces) to a degree that makes it nearly impossible to not engage with it in the creation of a 3D design. Creating a CAD model of an object is an invaluable tool for anyone in 3D design, as there is no substitution for the perception of three dimensions on the flat plane of a sketch, and the ability to create multiple views and animations makes the introduction of movement and time irresistible.

A PRESENTATION OUTLINE: Outline It, Tell Them, Summarize, Then Stop

More than 2,000 years ago, the Greek philosopher Aristotle developed a system for the art of persuasion. His lectures were collected by his students and later became a volume known as *The Rhetoric,* which was the main source of instruction in public speaking well into the 20th century. Among other things discussed in *The Rhetoric* is the structure of a public speech and the three-part arrangement, so common today, of:

1. Tell them what you are going to tell them.
2. Tell them.
3. Tell them what you told them.

This is essentially a simplification of Aristotle's breakdown of a speech into *introduction, statement, argument,* and *epilogue.*

The *introduction* is where you tell them what you are going to tell them—a quick overview of the main points that are coming up and a basic outline of what you are going to show, or prove, by your presentation: "I will show that . . . " This is your sales pitch for your concept or design, but not a place to begin any analysis or discussion of detail.

The *statement* and *argument* are in essence one section, which is why our simplification works. "You must state your case, and you must prove it," says Aristotle. Here is where you tell your audience what is important about your design and what is good about it. You iron out any problems, clarify the unclear, discuss opposing possibilities and views and your reasons for going the opposing route, and explain your methods of decision making and the decisions made. In each case you also explain and show *why*; each statement is backed up with proof, where the proof lies in you showing how you have fulfilled the design project's brief, how you have fulfilled the client's needs within the attendant constraints, and how you have even brought the concept to a new height in the hierarchy of design: "Here it is. This is why it works. This is why it is good."

The *epilogue* then serves as a place to reiterate your main points, remind your audience of what you covered, and again connect the dots from the *introduction:* "What I have shown you . . ." This is neither a time to introduce any new information nor to bring in other points of view—that should be done already, in your argument. Wrap it up, thank your audience, and ask for questions. Now you are done.

MODEL MAKING

A digital model might not always do the job. A physical model may need to be built when issues exist that cannot be captured in sketches and illustrations. This is especially important if the design relies on functioning parts or if critical safety issues are involved. Modeling, however, may also apply to *systems*, where the design relies on an order of events, such as in the design of a game, the layout of a screen, or the floor plan of a factory. In such cases the model may simply be a flowchart or a diagram adapted to the structure involved, but time may be a critical factor in the process, and so the events have to take place in real time. Thus, what is actually being modeled in 3D may in fact be the four-dimensional aspect of the design.

Deciding whether to create a digital or physical model may not always be easy. All things being equal, the model exists to show the look and functionality of the upcoming design, so the basic question is this: Which does a better job of showing off the design? Consider your design from the point of view of its look and its function. Which is more important to show; which method does this more effectively? Creating a physical model allows the exploration of gravity and interaction with objects, for example. It can test strength or durability. Creating a digital model allows the exploration of detail and scale (if the object is, for example, of such a size that that modeling will not do the details or situation justice). Digital modeling also allows the exploration of the object in its surroundings and also allows the opportunity for quickly examining different versions of objects and surroundings. Being able to place a design in a virtual environment is invaluable information for both the designer and the client (Fig. 6.11).

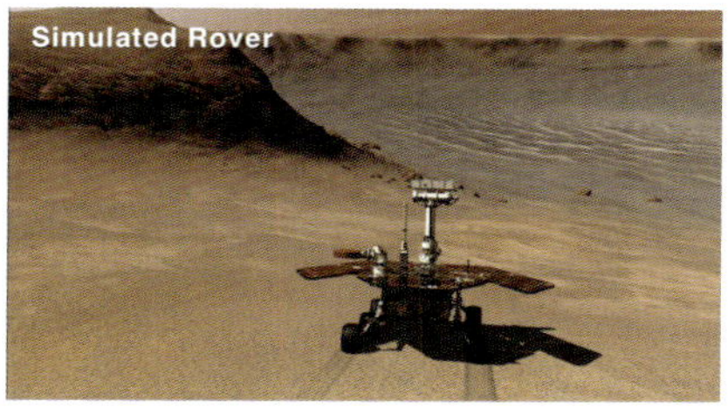

6.11 Digital modeling allows the exploration of the object in its surroundings. This allows the design to be experienced on a level that much closer to reality, and is invaluable for designer and client both by showing multiple views and three-dimensional interaction.

Source: NASA/JPL/Cornell

The quickest way to determine which type of model to create—including the choice between virtual and physical—is to consider whether the model is to be a *look model* or a working prototype. The look model does primarily what its name implies. It exists to display the look of the design as opposed to explore functionality or underlying structure. The look model tends toward surface quality and overall impressions. It may therefore be created out of any materials as long as the finish is the same as would be on the final version.

A *prototype*, on the other hand, is created to allow the testing of a set of attributes or to see how the design will operate under normal and abnormal circumstances. It is, however, of the same—or as close to the same—materials as the final product, in order that the "reality" of the experience be as close to the truth as possible.

Choosing the materials for a prototype model is extremely important, especially if the model is not built at full scale. The materials themselves should be scaled along with the object if the effect of the materials or textures is to be part of the overall effect of the model. Scaling a material may in fact require a substitution of materials, as scaling the model may require a thinner material in order to get the same feel as in the fully scaled object. The relationship between materials may also be distorted if the thicknesses are not altered. The fabric in a scaled-down garment, for example, will not drape the same way, nor will a half-scale sheet bend or a quarter-scale spring deploy in the same way as their full-scale counterparts.

Consider, therefore, not only the look of the material intended for a model but also its motion and feel and its behavior under forces of gravity or impact. Materials that are patterned or textured as part of their visual appeal or identity should also be chosen carefully in a scale model, as the pattern or decoration may scale strangely and not have the same visual or tactile impact as when in full scale. Often, model makers overscale patterns and textures in order to maintain as much of their impact as possible, while placing them in a realistic feel within the model (Fig. 6.12).

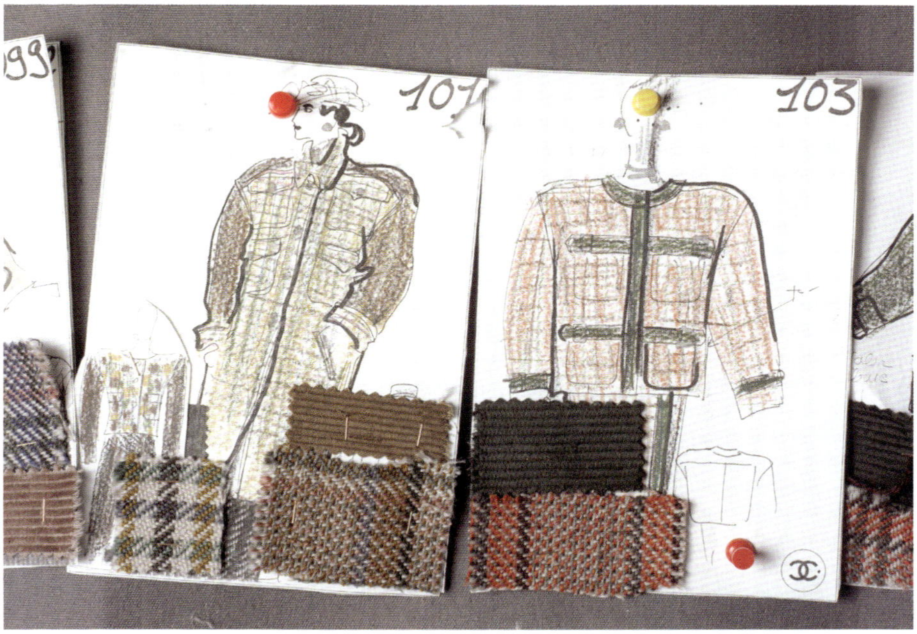

6.12 Often sketches and models have slightly over-scaled patterns and textures to maintain as much of their effect as possible, while giving the artwork a realistic feel. Drawings for Chanel by Karl Lagerfeld.

Source: © Massimo Listri/Corbis

PRESENTATION: A PERFORMANCE

Remarkably, for a profession that is always putting something on display, designers are not always comfortable presenting their work in front of an audience. The presentation of a design or set of designs, just as any presentation to an audience, is ultimately a performance. And just because a designer has the ability to create a design does not mean that he or she will be perfectly capable of presenting it to its makers and users.

A presentation is a combination of speech, active engagement, and emotional connection and can therefore be prepared using the same approach as anyone engaged in theatrical performance or artistic presentation. Here is the moment where the design is explained, shown, and sold emotionally, if not literally. It also therefore has a number of places where it is easy to become entangled and is also very clearly not something to be disregarded or shrugged off. The presentation is a crucial moment in the design process, not something tacked on. A good presentation that allows the audience to take ownership of the design can make or break a project.

The identity of the audience matters a great deal. You may be presenting your work to an informed audience or one that has no knowledge of the background or subtleties of the problems involved. Audiences may be interested in every aspect of the project or—and more likely—they may be only interested in it, as it pertains to them and their involvement. You may be presenting to an audience that will wind up using the design, but they might also invest in it or sell it but never actually use it. Finally, you may be presenting to an audience of makers who will do none of this, but who are interested in how it is to be constructed, with what, and when.

Information needs to be tailored to the audience in each case, in order that the presentation be not wasted time for everyone. Consider very carefully what *this* audience needs to hear, what they will be entertained by, and what information will create in them an interest in hearing more. Remember that the audience may enjoy all kinds of information about creativity and materials, but in the end view it as entertainment. The *important* information for this audience may well be something completely routine. You must create a **narrative**—that is, a story, with a beginning, middle, and end—that hooks your audience, even if your project is simple and requires only a little presentation.

PUBLIC SPEAKING AND STORYTELLING

The art of public speaking is very much about being able to convincingly speak on nearly any topic in a way that makes your audience engaged, interested, and ultimately supportive. Presenting a design is actually a lot easier than public speaking that does not involve props since you have the design there to help you with your narrative and you can reference its look, materials, functionality, and on and on in order to keep the audience engaged and with you. Just remember it all has to have a point sooner or later (preferably sooner). But you are the designer, and therefore by default, you should be able to access a sense of inspiration and accomplishment with which to affect your audience every time.

Now the inspiration that helped you generate and maintain your creativity comes full circle. You not only use it to keep yourself interested and engaged during the presentation, you also convince the audience of the energy within the project itself (and so

NETWORKING: PRESENTATIONS

The following list contains helpful websites for further information:

PUBLIC SPEAKING TIPS—MIT

The following tips are taken from SPEAKING UP, MIT Freshman Advising Seminar 055, that was offered by Norma McGavern (former UROP Director) in Fall 1996.

web.mit.edu/urop/resources/speaking.html

10 TIPS FOR PUBLIC SPEAKING—TOASTMASTERS INTERNATIONAL

www.toastmasters.org/tips.asp

CREATING EFFECTIVE PRESENTATION VISUALS—MINDTOOLS.COM

www.mindtools.com/pages/article/creating-presentation-visuals.htm

DESIGNING EFFECTIVE ORAL PRESENTATIONS—RICE UNIVERSITY ONLINE WRITING LAB

www.rcs.k12.va.us/wbhs/studyskills/oral presentations/Rice OWL Designing Effective Oral Presentations.htm

3 TIPS FOR OVERCOMING THE FEAR OF PUBLIC SPEAKING—HARVARD EXTENSION SCHOOL

www.extension.harvard.edu/hub/blog/extension-blog/3-tips-overcoming-fear-public-speaking

HOW TO ENGAGE YOUR AUDIENCE AND KEEP THEM WITH YOU—HAMILTON COLLEGE, ORAL COMMUNICATION CENTER

www.hamilton.edu/oralcommunication/how-to-engage-your-audience-and-keep-them-with-you

keep your audience interested and engaged). If you are inspired, you will be inspiring; if you are interested, you will be interesting. Share your inspiration along with the presentation of your designs. Everyone enjoys being part of a creative process. Show the audience the inner workings of your creativity and bring them inside. As long as they are also getting the practical information they need, this will allow them to be a part of the process and *own* the design.

A simple and oft-repeated rule for creating a presentation is as follows:

1. Tell them what you will tell them.
2. Tell them.
3. Tell them what you just told them.

Cute and trite as this may seem, it is good advice and worth repeating. Presenting a new concept or design to even the most informed audience requires presenting new knowledge and new applications of what may be very familiar elements in a way that the audience can understand and respond to positively.

Giving an overview first allows the audience to engage with the description and narrative you present, and recapping at the end cements the perceptions and connections you have set up. Your audience will appreciate such thoroughness, and you, in preparing your presentation, will also benefit, as you need to be able to carefully isolate the most important points before you create a thorough narrative of your design.

The narrative of a design in presentation, like any other narrative, must be a coherent story with a beginning, middle, and end. We are accustomed from an early age to receive information about the world this way. We much prefer to have the world presented to us as a tale of things that fit and lead to each other, not as random bits of

6.13 The way you structure your presentation's narrative influences the audience's perception of the presentation as an event and changes how the design is perceived. The location, your wardrobe, and the visuals are all support for the story you are telling. A sales pitch at a restaurant, such as this one, can build to a high point like a theatrical performance (and may result in just as much applause!).

Source: © Bob Barkany/cultura/Corbis

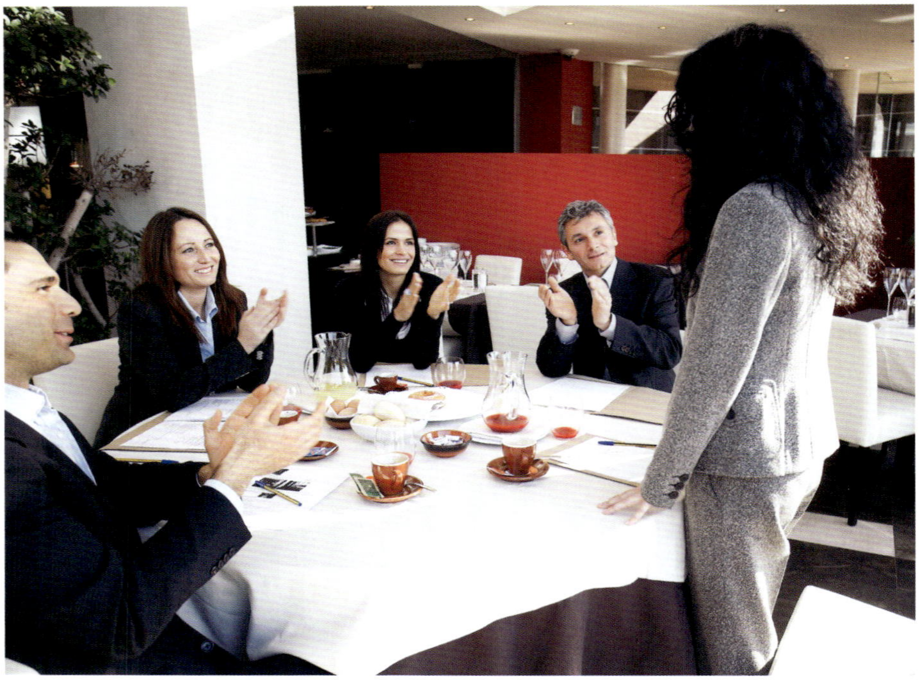

information that we then fit together as best we can. Create a narrative of your design that tells of its *beginning*—your inspiration and the needs and constraints that defined the project—*the middle*—your process of designing up to this point—and *the end*—what it has now become and why this is a good solution to the design problem.

The rhythm of a story helps deliver the message and has an effect on the audience. You can start with a bang and tell them the highlights right at the beginning. Having captured their attention, follow with a detailed explanation building back to the total picture. Conversely, you can start slowly, building your case piece by piece until you arrive at the crescendo: the finished object. Or you can create a narrative that begins slowly with careful preparation, rises to a grand statement, and then cools down by way of discussing what was just presented. Each of these would influence the audience's perception of the presentation as an event and change how the design is perceived (Fig. 6.13).

DESIGNING IS AN ADVENTURE STORY

Designing for a living, once it gets to a career stage, just like anything else that is done without interruption, can cease to be a dream job and one's own fascination may fade. Be careful not to let this happen, at least to the degree where you forget to assume that those coming to it for the first time will be the same. Cynicism about design has no place in a design presentation. Use the magic of design to charm and draw in your audience. No matter what is being designed, the creative act is an adventure, so create a narrative that is exciting and engaging for your audience. The process itself is so full of discovery that even the least informed listener would have to be fascinated by the search for solutions to questions of shape, material, function, color, texture, and pattern.

You may be selling different things to different audiences, so it becomes doubly important to make sure that you and your audience agree that this is what has been delivered. The end users of your designs, as was pointed out earlier, may have heard everything they needed to hear, but the manufacturer, marketer, financier, and management may all leave the presentation without knowing what they need to know. The product you are delivering has many dimensions, and you may be responsible for presenting both the seen and unseen, the tangible and the intangible.

Letting the audience take ownership of your design is very important. They must feel that they can work with it, own it, wear it, drive it, play it, live in it—whatever the interaction is. If you are speaking to an audience involved in the creation or marketing of the design, they may not need to—or even want to—own the design, but the need to become co-owners of your process. In other words, they must feel as if they too have a responsibility to bring your concept to fruition. This again can be achieved in a number of ways, but you have to "own" your design first.

This is not just a labored metaphor. You have to be involved in all the details of your design and know all the functionality, all the elements, and all the particular quirks and characteristics of it before you can be comfortable presenting it to an audience. They may ask any kind of question and pose any kind of problem, and you should be able to address these to a degree that leaves both you and the audience comfortable about what happens next. There should be no question about who has the information that is needed, no question about "what happens if . . . ," and no doubt that any information that is missing will be found. If you own the design, it is yours to sell.

At this point, all **feedback** is beneficial. Positive, negative, or constructive feedback should all be taken into account. First of all, with the project in the presentation stage, it has reached a point where any critique will need to be implemented as soon as possible if it is to have any effect. Positive feedback is always good, but doesn't really require a response except an acknowledgment and a mental check by the box that says "this worked." Negative feedback needs attention: what to fix, what to rationalize, how to deal with the negative perception. Is the critic correct? You must assume so until you can prove the critic wrong. If you can't prove your critic wrong, then you must decide what your response will be.

CONCLUSION

No matter how much you like your designs and no matter how inspired you were, if no one responds, you are in trouble. Information always gives you something to work with. Indifference is never a good thing. Make sure you wrap up by inviting discussion about the project. Ask what your audience feels about it. Find points of commonality between you in why you like the work in question. This will allow everyone a chance at a quick exploration of the finished design as if it now belonged to them. Let them take ownership and speak of it as their own. And do not forget to wrap up your presentation by actually asking your client in any way you choose, "Is this what you wanted?" Get the feedback then and there and welcome it. The dialogue will allow you to be a better designer and will ensure that your client leaves with great confidence in you and your command of the art of designing.

KEY TERMS

Digital presentation
Multisensory
Sketch
Illustration
Computer-aided design (CAD)
Technical drawing
Narrative
Feedback

DISCUSSION AND REVIEW QUESTIONS

Consider your immediate environment at three levels of scale:

- The room you are in
- A piece of furniture
- An object you can hold in your hand

1. If these were new designs, what would be a good way to model each of these for a design presentation?
2. What elements and features would you emphasize for each of the following?
   a. Makers
   b. End users
   c. Marketing
3. In each case, discuss the pros and cons of digital and physical modeling.

EXERCISES AND ASSIGNMENTS

Pick an object that you believe to be a good design (for any reason at all) and consider how you would present it to an audience of end users, makers, or marketers.

1. How would you communicate what is especially important about the design to this audience?
2. How would you describe its design in 100 words to someone who has never seen it before?
3. What if you could only use images to convey it to an audience? How would you do that with six pictures?
4. What would be three to five physical objects or samples that would be especially effective at the presentation for the audience to touch and hold? Explain why in each case.

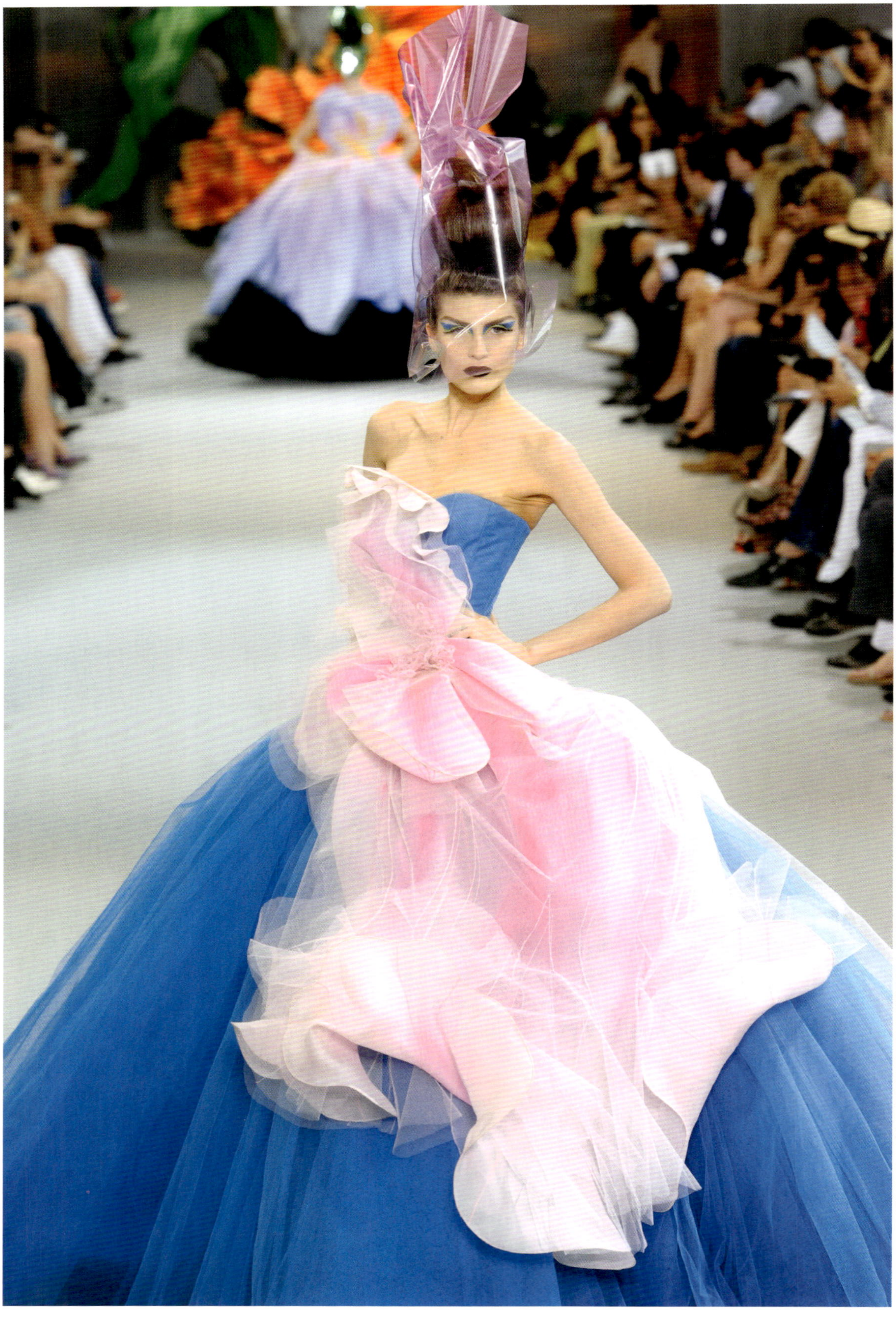

PART III

THINKING DESIGN

A designer has to consider how designs relate to experience in different dimensions. Two, three, or four dimensions may be involved in a project, and different dimensional thinking may be needed at different stages within a project. Each chapter in Part Three involves a different dimension with different needs. Chapter 7 consider two-dimensions and graphic design, Chapter 8 goes into three dimensions and the concerns that follow, while Chapter 9 then dives into four-dimensional thinking, bringing in the time in the context of user experience and emotion. Finally, Chapter 10 considers the shift involved in the transition to an onscreen world.

OPPOSITE
Buildings and architectural structures require support, but designing clothing, for example, needs to take in the drape of fabric and the interaction of the body and supports with the flexible and supple textiles.

CHAPTER 7

THINKING "PRINT": GRAPHIC DESIGN AND ELEMENTS IN TWO DIMENSIONS

DESIGNERS SPEAK

"When a type design is good, it is not because each individual letter of the alphabet is perfect in form, but because there is a feeling of harmony and unbroken rhythm that runs through the whole design, each letter kin to every other and to all."

—FREDERICK GOUDY, type designer, *Typologia: Studies in Type Design and Type Making* (Berkeley: University of California Press, 1940), p. 43.

"If the idea doesn't gel after a certain amount of struggle you have to give it up. I read once about the concepts of the lateral idea and the vertical idea. If you dig a hole and it's in the wrong place, digging it deeper isn't going to help. The lateral idea is when you skip over and dig someplace else."

—SEYMOUR CHWAST, *The Left-Handed Designer*, ed. by Steven Heller (New York: Harry N. Abrams, 1985), p. 8.

OBJECTIVES

Understand the significance of the relationship of graphic design and painterly art.

Identify the areas on which a graphic designer must specifically focus.

Distinguish the challenges of designing two dimensionally for textural and three-dimensional perception.

Recognize the specific challenges of type, space, texture, and balance in graphic design.

Comprehend the importance of understanding the meaning of elements in graphic design.

This chapter discusses the nature of graphic design and its relationship to fine art composition. The mechanics, elements, and inherent meaning of graphic design elements are examined to clarify how this branch of designing is specifically approached and what concerns are immediately evident.

GRAPHIC DESIGN AND PAINTERLY COMPOSITION

In discussions of design practices and principles, topics will tend toward fine art. Even from recent years, examples illustrating design texts are of paintings and sculptures, rather than designed surfaces, spaces, or commercial objects: a Warhol painting rather than a soup can; a sculpture in a plaza rather than the plaza itself, and so on (Fig. 7.1). In part, this has to do with the history of designing, where design, as such, was long considered to be mostly the act of drawing or illustration. There also may be have been a reluctance to discuss commercial design creativity on the same merits as creativity in fine art. Using examples of commercial designs when discussing artistic principles, even in the context of design, may have on some level been seen as a demeaning to fine art, but meanwhile, the discussion of design was simply confusing. On the other hand, by its nature as a two-dimensional application of creative thinking, graphic design is the easiest to discuss in direct connection with fine art. Both deal with the delivery of meaning through symbolic use of forms, objects, and color in two dimensions. Graphic design, however, also deals with text, as information and graphic design is for the most part a commercial endeavor for a commercial entity or client of some kind.

A graphic designer will want to consider the history of painterly arts as well as the history of graphic design itself to be aware of the traditions involved and methods used. The history of graphic arts in many ways even precedes the painters. The visual artists who illustrated manuscripts were working their craft well before the Renaissance, and decorative arts in human habitation have been part of human culture ever since there were walls to paint on.

A look at the history of graphic design in context with the artistic movements of the day shows a clear connection between methods and visions. The obvious parallel is the flat, usually rectangular, plane in which the graphic designer and the painter

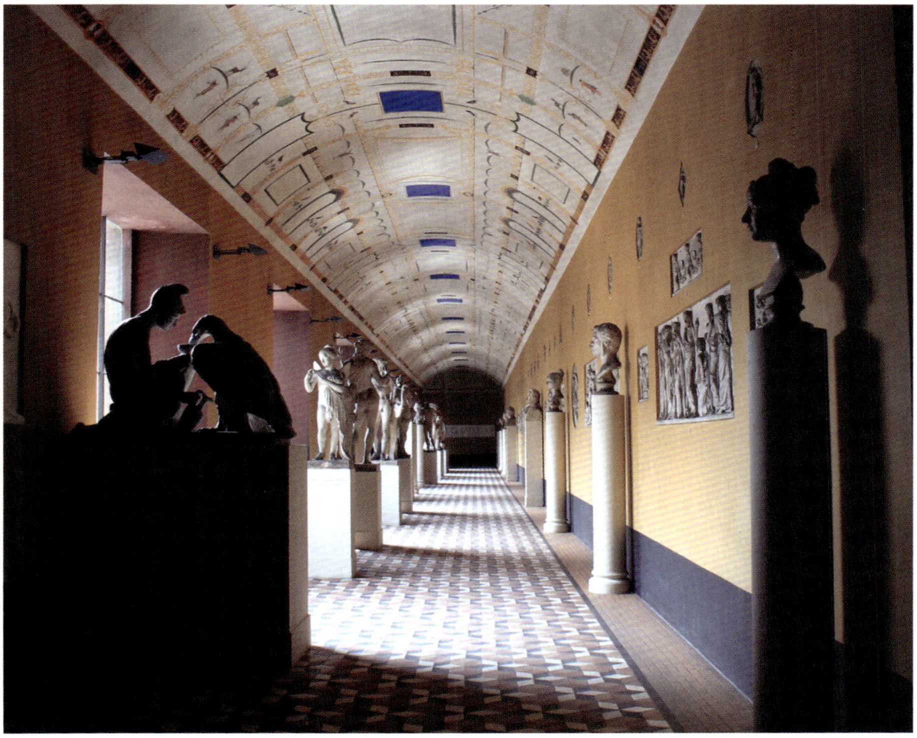

7.1 When design and its practices and principles are discussed, the topics often tend toward fine art. If we are to discuss design here, we might discuss artwork and the hallway separately or we might consider the placement of the artwork in the hallway. Each can be discussed as design, and all together the relationship of the art, architecture, and layout can be by design. The art may be the same, but the purpose is different.

Source: Photograph by Karl Aspelund

PRINTING: A TIMELINE

- **618 to 906:** The first known printing takes place in China using ink on carved wooden blocks.
- **868:** *The Diamond Sutra* is printed in China. It is currently the earliest surviving dated printed book.
- **1241:** Movable type is used by Koreans to print books.
- **1300:** Wooden type is developed in China.
- **1309:** Europeans begin to make paper, as had been done for centuries in Egypt and China.
- **1338:** First paper mill in France.
- **1390:** First paper mill in Germany.
- **1392:** Foundries producing bronze type are operating in Korea.
- **1423:** Block printing is used to print books in Europe.
- **1430s:** Drypoint engravings invented in Germany.
- **1452:** Gutenberg begins printing the Bible. It takes four years. Metal plates are first used in printing.
- **1457:** First color printing by Fust and Schoeffer in Germany.
- **1476:** William Caxton sets up a Gutenberg printing press in England.
- **1495:** First paper mill opens in England.
- **1501:** Italic type first used in a printing press in Venice.
- **1605:** First weekly newspaper published in Antwerp.
- **1640s:** Mezzotint, a print technique allowing half-tomes, is invented in Germany.
- **1702:** Multicolored engraving invented by German Jakob Le Blon.
- **1819:** Rotary printing press is invented by Napier.
- **1829:** Embossed printing is invented by Louis Braille.
- **1841:** Type-composing machine invented.
- **1844:** Electrotyping invented.
- **1846:** Cylinder press invented by Richard Hoe. It can print 8,000 sheets an hour.
- **1863:** Rotary web-fed letterpress, invented by William Bullock.
- **1865:** Web offset press can print on both sides of paper at once.
- **1886:** Linotype composing machine invented.
- **1870:** Paper mass-manufactured from wood pulp.
- **1878:** Photogravure printing invented.
- **1890:** Mimeograph machine introduced.
- **1891:** Diazotype invented (printing photographs on fabric).
- **1892:** Four-color rotary press invented.
- **1904:** Offset lithography becomes common. The first comic books published.
- **1907:** Commercial silk screening developed.
- **1947:** Phototypesetting becomes common.
- **1955:** Xerox produces the first automatic xerographic printer, the Copyflo.
- **1969:** Gary Starkweather invents a laser printer based on a modified xerograph copier.
- **1970s:** The development of ink-jet printers takes place in several companies.
- **1971:** DEC introduces a dot matrix printer.
- **1979:** SATO develops the first thermal transfer barcode printer.
- **1984:** Canon markets the first plain-paper printer.
- **1990s:** Personal computing and the Internet create the possibility of a "paperless" world. This does not develop.
- **2007:** The arrival of iPhones increases the trend in communications toward a more paperless world.
- **2010:** The iPad and subsequent tablet computers imply a further retreat from paper, although the change is still not as marked as many anticipated.

work. The purpose is to create an effect in this limited 2D space that attracts attention and engages the audience in order to deliver a message or emotional impact. But as the modern age of print reproduction and newsprint created a whole new profession in visual design, the cutting edge of urban art began to be found in graphic design. Modern artistic movements made good use of this, with artists such as Toulouse-Lautrec pushing the boundaries of poster art and **Pop Art** later extensively exploring

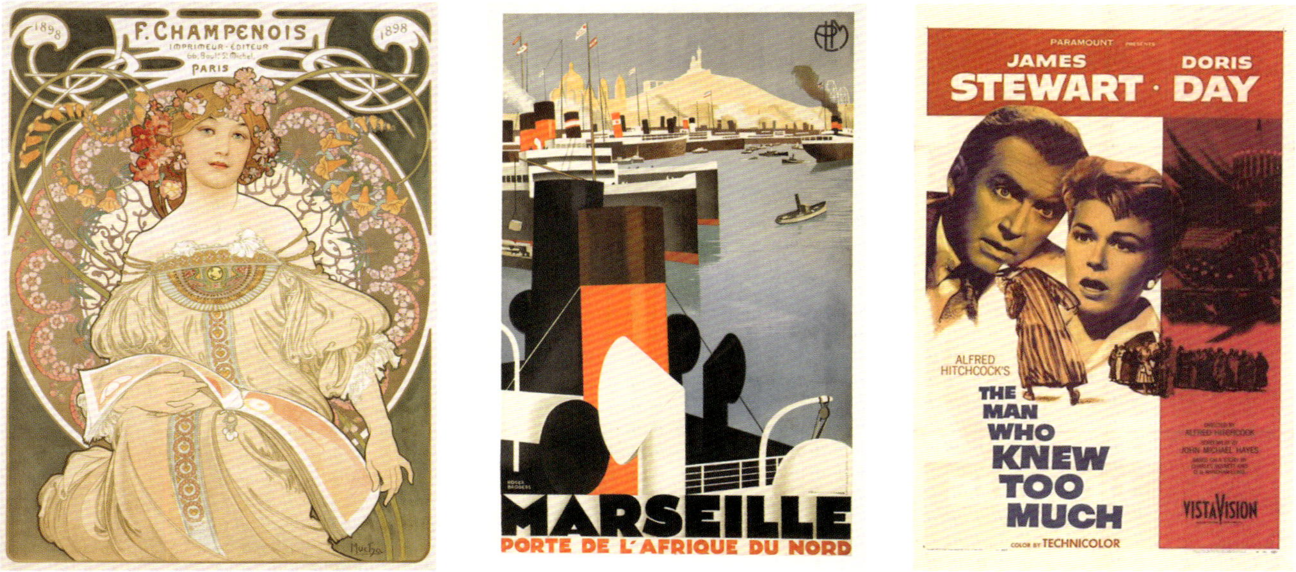

ABOVE

7.2 In Western culture, graphic design has gone so far as to create its own genres and niches with their own devotees of styles and periods. The periods of the modern age are themselves as identifiable by their graphic styling as any other art or creative field, as may be seen in the difference between Art Nouveau (left) and Art Deco (middle) or the iconic styles of the 1950s (right).

Source: L: © Swim Ink 2, LLC/Corbis; M: ©Mucha Trust/ADAGP, Paris

commercial designs. In Western culture graphic design has gone so far as to create its own genres and niches with their own devotees of styles and periods. The periods of the modern age are themselves as identifiable by their graphic styling as any other art or creative fields. This may be seen in the difference between Art Nouveau and Art Deco or the iconic styles of the 1950s (Fig. 7.2.).

The use of color, space, and background/foreground placement to create visual forms and lead the eye relies on the same principles and methods as in a painting. The differences, however, also are marked. The obvious difference is worth looking at first: that of *purpose*. If we compare, for example, a painting of a can of soup with the actual can of soup, the purpose of the creativity is very different (Fig. 7.3). The message involved is entirely different. The label on a soup can is designed for industrial mass production by a designer for a client, with a specific audience in mind: the shopper and

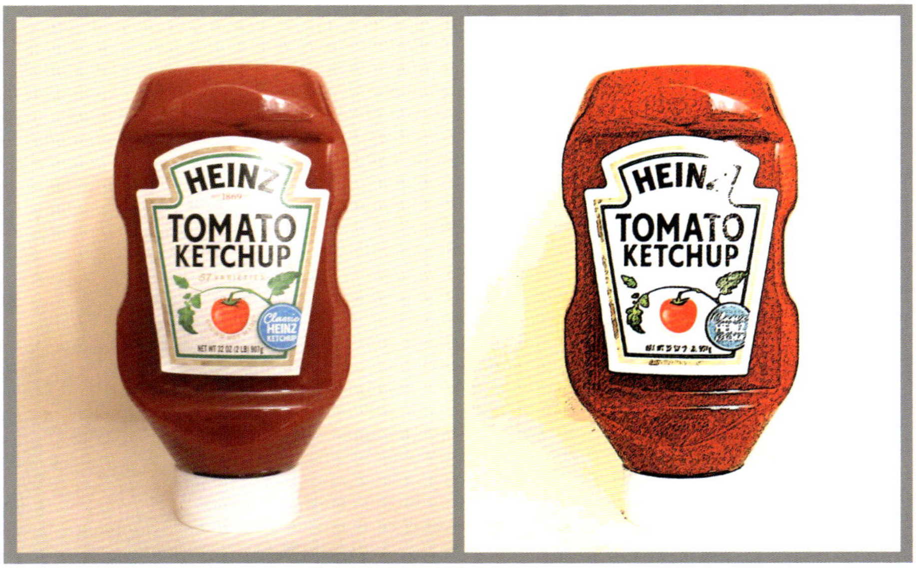

RIGHT

7.3 If we compare a painting of a bottle of ketchup (right), with the actual bottle of ketchup (left), the purpose of the creativity in the design is very different. The painting is intended to make a statement and provoke an emotional or intellectual response. The graphic design of the label is intended to be informational, attention-getting, and easily identifiable.

Source: Illustration by Karl Aspelund

maker of soup. It must attract the shopper's eye as it sits on a store shelf surrounded by dozens of other brands. The text must convey information relevant to the soup: ingredients, instructions, brand name, and content title, for example. The painting however, individually crafted (although very reproducible) conveys a different message. It speaks of the nature of consumer society, or the appreciation of everyday beauty, and the instructions of how to make soup are secondary to the actual social message.

Graphic design, unless deliberately being invoked as an ironic statement, is more often a commercial endeavor than fine art production. However, graphic artists have produced work that in the late 20th century began to be valued equally to fine art, and the power of many 20th-century political poster designs, for example, show an intense vision and command of the media. The difference between painterly art and graphic design blurs especially well in this example, as the message may well be about the artistry of modern design on one hand and the factory-like production of art in the modern age on the other.

It is precisely this blurring that makes the study of fine art essential for the graphic designer (if not all designers). The boundary line between visual effect for attention-getting commercial purposes or for artistic visual pleasure is not really that clear, and often the flow of information and influence is in both directions. Definitely in the stylings of Art Nouveau, the graphic experimentation of the 1920s, and Pop Art of the 1960s, the dialogue of graphic design and fine art shifted irrevocably in each case. Pop Art and graphic design are where the two worlds not only meet but overlap (to the dismay of many high-minded art lovers at the time). The production of graphic design in consumer goods has often been infused with artistry and products such as book covers and album covers often were comparable with works of art. Examining at least these periods of transition is an absolute must for anyone wishing to have a comfortable knowledge of the art and craft of graphic design.

The difference between graphic design and fine art in the end lies in the message. However, the message also may be a result of the same creative spirit that produces the artwork (especially in the early 20th century before the irony exhibited in Pop Art became much the norm). However, for a graphic designer who wishes to tap into the spirit of the times and understand how visual art refers to and makes use of prevailing societal trends, it is an absolute must to study fine artists. The visual language of a period or even an entire culture can contain clues for how to deal with a topic or project. The study of fine art should also be undertaken in order to build a visual language of one's own and to become familiar with the references in works of art as well as the actual works of art in order that they themselves may become references (Fig. 7.4).

COLOR AND INK

Color and all its characteristics come quickly to the fore when one is contemplating the list of things important to a graphic designer. Color language in design works under the exact same principles as in fine art, and color relationships and contrasts generally serve a similar purpose. A full awareness of the various concerns addressed in Chapter 3, such as the difference in print and screen colors, must be absolutely second nature. In addition, thinking about color as a fluid element of varying value and intensity is a must. Designing with color is like playing an acoustic instrument. The basic notes are

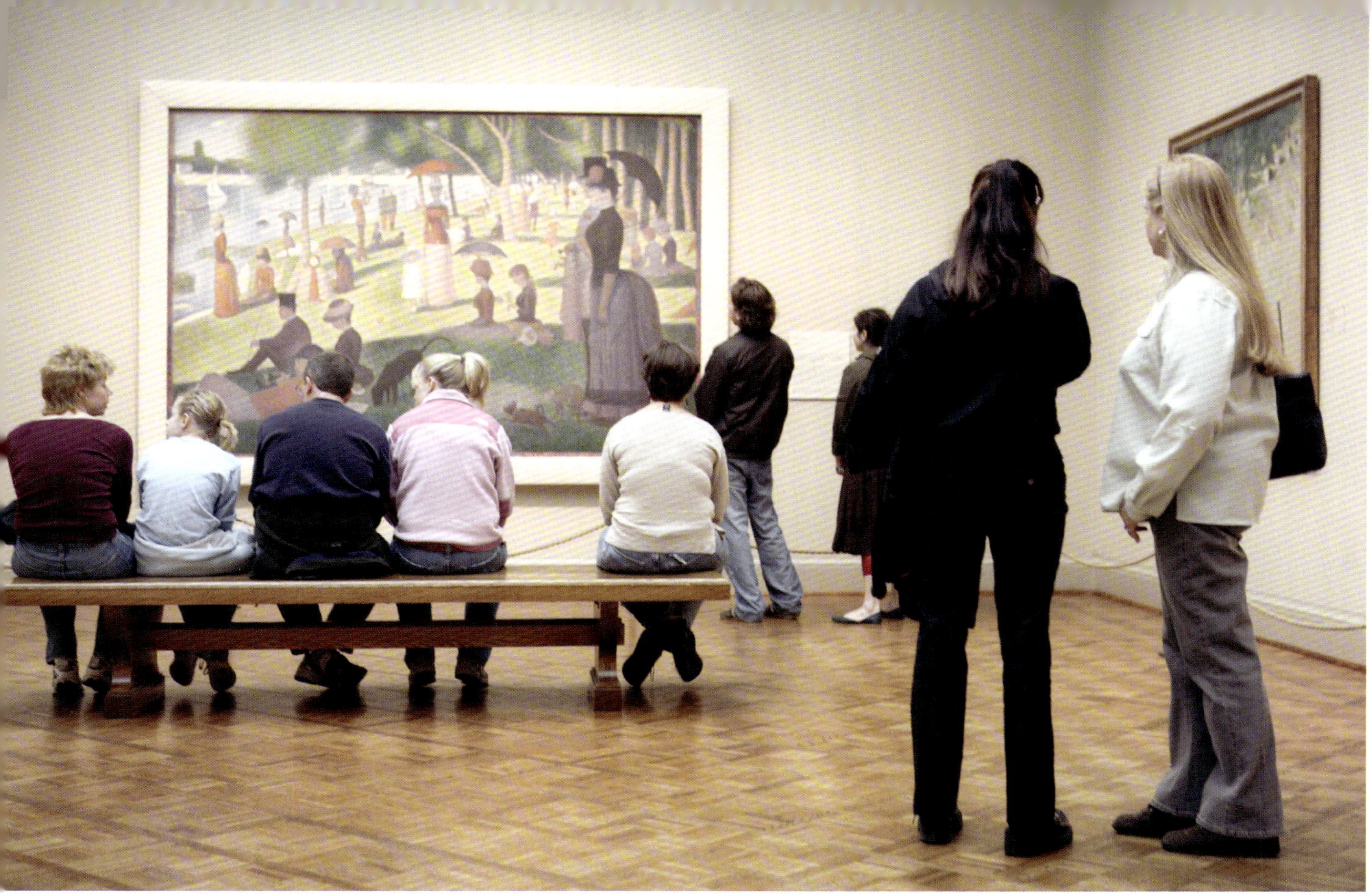

7.4 The study of fine art also should be undertaken to build a visual language of one's own and to become familiar with the references in works of art. Museum visitors looking at Georges Seurat's painting *Sunday Afternoon on the Island of La Grande Jatte* at the Art Institute of Chicago.

Source: © Franz-Marc Frei/Corbis

there in terms of the actual colors, but so much more can be coaxed out of a simple setup by being knowledgeable and instinctive about values and intensities, temperatures, and scales.

The ability to deliver color onto a printed page has improved exponentially in the past few decades, and obtaining the required expertise in different inks and printing processes is far less of a concern for a graphic designer in the present day than a generation ago. However, this does not mean that complacency can set in. Now a working knowledge of the different types of office-grade computer printers and capabilities of larger industrial-scale machines should be part of a graphic designer's arsenal, as should knowledge of paper and coatings and how they interact with printer inks. Ink and paper are surfaces, and surfaces have textures. The beauty of a good piece of print work lies in the combination of these elements—the texture of the paper, the texture of the ink, the quality of the ink, and the coating of the color. Together they produce a page or surface with a feel that should be desired and planned, not just incidental to a process.

In addition, the meaning of color must be considered. Color has cultural connections and emotional weight, but there are also cultural structures that are important and rely on color. Certain colors have become recognizable signals in themselves. But the color coding of cultures is not uniform, and global and local references matter. Right before our eyes the color coding of television election maps gave red and blue a new political significance in the early 21st century in the United States. Both colors are loaded with meaning and perhaps even overloaded as references, but the blue-state/red-state code nonetheless became cultural shorthand. Graphic design for

SUSTAINABILITY

It may seem odd at first glance to approach sustainability from the departure point of graphic design. However, ecological concerns appear when we consider the impact of materials and products have on the environment.

With graphic design so heavily involved in packaging it is, in fact, a perfect vantage point from which to consider the environmental impact of the printing industry, paper manufacturing, chemical content of inks and pigments, and more.

Furthermore the ability of designers to influence the choices of materials toward recyclability is extremely important. The sheer amount of packaging that passes through our hands every day is so great that the habituating of consumers toward the recycling of these is a major goal. Designing packaging in such a way that the needs and constraints of its life cycle from the creation of raw materials to the end-of-life recycling is as environmentally friendly as possible should also be the goal of every graphic designer with every product.

political purposes in the United States has been greatly influenced. Green has become irrevocably connected with ecological concerns to the point where the word itself has new meaning. Graphic design of labeling and signage has become altered as a result (Fig. 7.5).

The presence or absence of color in a design has weighty connections. Text is normally black on white, and when this deviates, we become extra sensitive to the message involved. And as television and film tend toward internationalization of content and programming, the color systems of mass-market designer for these media is rapidly becoming the world's reference. A green-tinged, washed-out color scheme has become the visual cue of horror and desaturated color or graphic black and white has become the color scheme of memory.

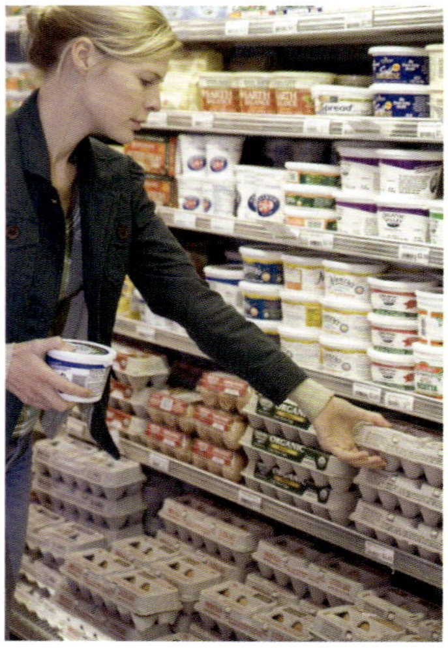

RIGHT

7.5 Green has become connected with ecological concerns to the point where the word has new meaning. Graphic design of labeling has also become altered as a result. Green—both the color and the word—has begun to signal low ecological impact and purity along with any objects of that color. Presumably the green egg cartons contain eggs that are more natural in some way.

Source: © Stella/fstop/Corbis

TYPEFACES

The invention of the printing press in the 15th century allowed the development of **typefaces** for printing, and very quickly in Europe **fonts** based on the Roman lettering and mimicking formal handwriting became the industry standard (Fig. 7.6). (A quick distinction: A typeface is the whole family of fonts available in that family; for instance, Times Roman is the typeface, but Times Roman Bold is a font within that typeface. Many use the terms interchangeably, perhaps incorrectly, but the distinction has blurred over the years.) All manner of variations appeared and in the 20th century the sans serif typefaces were developed for clarity. With the arrival of computer screens that could display varied lettering in the 1980s, typefaces became a matter of choice in people's everyday experiences, yet the basics remain of roman, italic, and the basic san serifs (Fig. 7.7).

Movable typefaces had been invented in China in the 11th century, but due to the complexity of the alphabet, they did not get the same kind of use or distribution. Now

TOP LEFT

7.6 Following the invention of the printing press in the 15th century, roman typefaces quickly became the industry standard. The frontispiece to Miguel de Cervantes' *Don Quixote*, 1655, by the printer Juan de la Cuesta.

Source: [Public domain], via Wikimedia Commons

TOP RIGHT

7.7 Fonts in our surroundings are chosen for a number of reasons and sometimes regulated for official use. The style of commonly use typefaces has, in many cases, become part of the information. For example, sans serif fonts signal information as on road signs and serifed fonts of a Roman type evoke an official and historical feel such as on the WWII memorial in Washington DC.

Source: Illustration by Karl Aspelund

BELOW

7.8 Courier is a font that mimics the typeface of old manual typewriters. Graphic designers make use of this reference to evoke a feel of immediacy of information and old time newsroom urgency.

Source: Illustration by Karl Aspelund

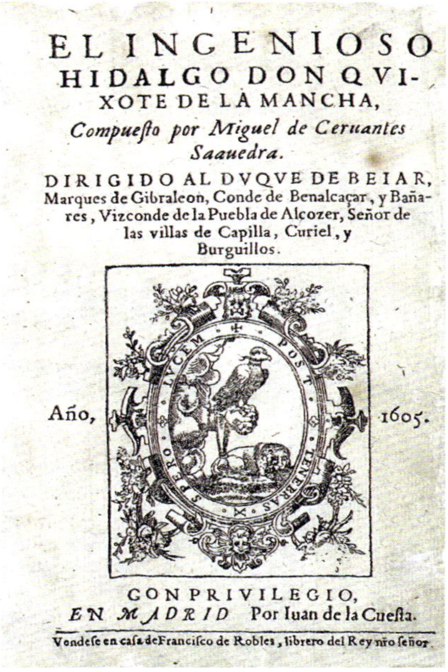
EL INGENIOSO HIDALGO DON QVIXOTE DE LA MANCHA,

Compuesto por Miguel de Ceruantes Saauedra.

DIRIGIDO AL DVQVE DE BEIAR, Marques de Gibraleon, Conde de Benalcaçar, y Bañares, Vizconde de la Puebla de Alcozer, Señor de las villas de Capilla, Curiel, y Burguillos.

Año, 1605.

CON PRIVILEGIO, EN MADRID Por Iuan de la Cuesta.

Vendese en casa de Francisco de Robles, librero del Rey nro señor.

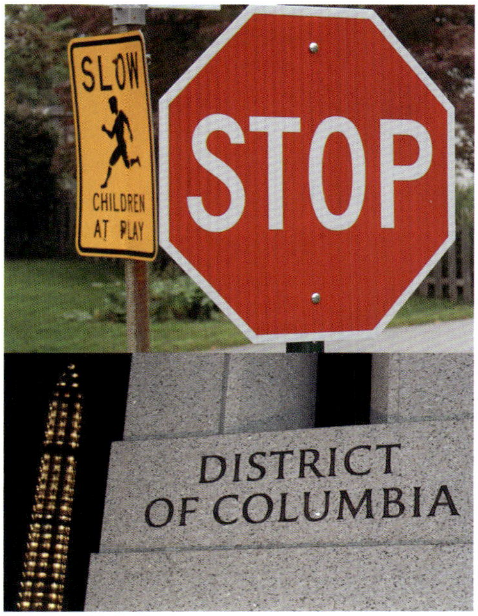

that computers make the manipulation of thousands of characters easier, non-Latin alphabets and the alphabets of Arabic, Chinese, and Japanese, for example, also have developed typefaces. Typefaces went through a flourish of experimentation in the early 20th century along with other modernist design experiments, but the results of this experimentation are typefaces that very strongly bear the mark of their time and are now largely used to reference that era or area (for example, Soviet Russia in the 1920s, or "hip" fonts from the late 1950s and early 1960s).

Choosing a typeface can be a decision involving much difficulty and searching, especially with the number of them available at our fingertips. The main criteria are clarity or legibility and the feel of the designed piece. A particular typeface has a character that it acquires over time as its use becomes associated with a specific kind of information or location. Roman type is associated with printed newspapers and documents and has an official feel. Sans serif typefaces, on the other hand, because of their visual clarity have become informational through their use on signage on roads, in airports, and so on. Meanwhile, handwritten-style typefaces telegraph the emotional content, by way of their association, from comic to romantic. There are even nostalgic typefaces that mimic old typewriters for the feel of old-time correspondence or modernist political headlines (Fig. 7.8).

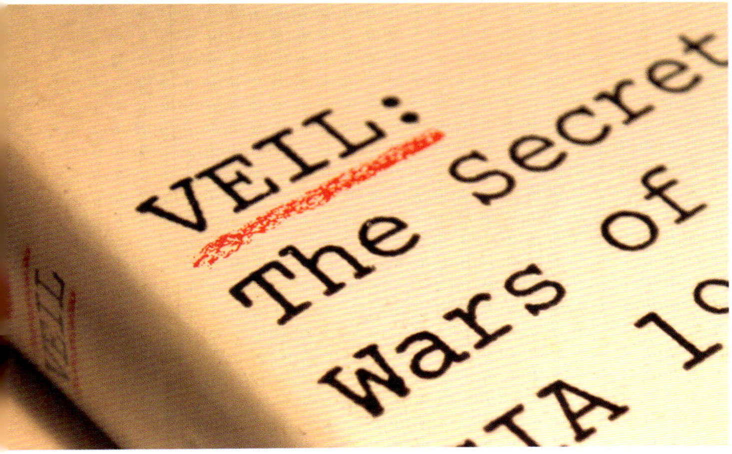

Choosing a font is therefore a way of designing information into the look of the graphic. The viewer can discern emotion or intent, simply by reference to the font itself, even before the meaning of the words or the identity of the logo is decoded. The logo itself may well become associated with the lettering, a development many iconic brands have gone through in the 20th century.

ERGONOMICS AND GRAPHIC DESIGN

Considering ergonomics in relation to graphic design, we find that usability becomes clarity, readability, and accessibility. Your design and the information therein must reach the audience. An ergonomic investigation would, for example, look at the position of the viewer relative to your product (are they children or adults?) eye-level (sitting, standing, where?) lighting, and the covering position of hands on products that will be picked up (readable material on products in supermarkets).

Graphic signage for buildings may consider the motion of people who are walking or driving by: What speed? Can they read it in time? The list and examples could go on and on, but to encapsulate the thought: Don't forget the physicality of the world and people in it. Your design is there to be accessed and interacted with. The interaction takes place on a physical plane. Don't forget the body, its movement, its size, and its limitations.

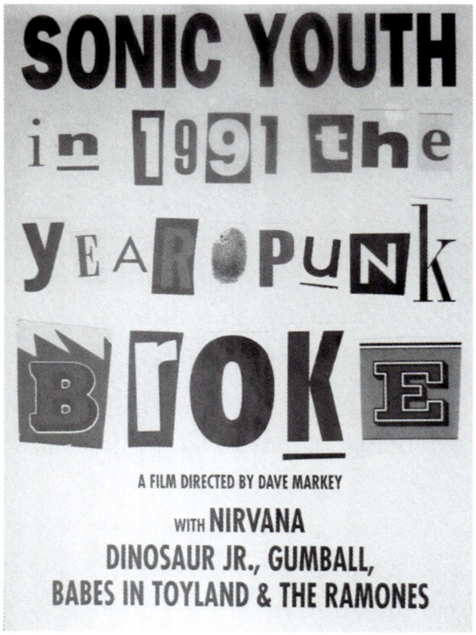

7.9 In this poster, where the rules of type are deliberately broken, the headline and credits are in a coherent typeface, while the title gets a sense of play and motion in the rebellious use of fonts and lettering. Poster for *1991: The Year Punk Broke*, Tara Films, 1993.

Source: Courtesy of David Markey

But lettering can therefore—and is some cases, must—also be thought of as form as graphic visual design elements. The shape, spacing, width of line, and amount of space in and around each letter, word, line, or paragraph all have a say in the visual impact of the designed page or graphic. A good strategy is to block out the text before actually committing to a specific font or style and then proceed to break down the content into text, headlines, and subheadings. Consider what text needs to be highlighted, separated, or even minimized. Then insert various fonts in a graphic design program and note how each impacts the feel of the design. The color of the type can also be coordinated with the total design. The choice of background versus text color can be a simple yet effective way to realize the desired emotional impact of the design.

Finally, the choice of casing—that is, all caps, headline style (where nouns, verb, adjectives are capped and as a general rule articles are lowercase), all lowercase, or sentence style (where just the first letter is capped), or even haphazard—has an impact. The choice of casing can, in its mimicry of classical styles, bring a formality to a designed piece as well as a sense of playfulness, silliness, or even aggressiveness and chaos if rules are deliberately broken (Fig. 7.9).

WHITE SPACE

White space, so called in reference to the white unprinted paper around lettering, is a weighty design element in any graphical layout. Also known as *negative space* (negative as in "nothing there") or *dead space*, the area enveloping and behind the graphic design elements of text, form, and pictures gives balance to the design, provides contrast, and determines the degree of lightness or airiness, depending on how much space the eye has to travel around and rest (Fig. 7.10).

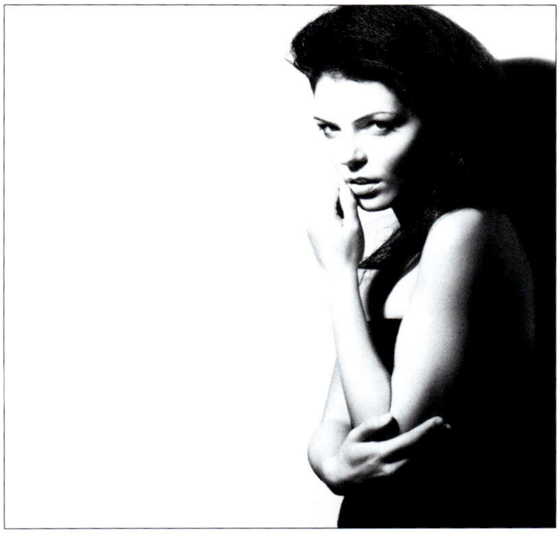

TOP LEFT

7.10 The negative (white) space on this album cover allows the form of the figure to stand strongly in the design, with the contrast of the dark clothes and hair and the subtle shades on the figure "drawing" the picture. The stark contrast in negative/positive in the shading on the face is also remarkable.

Source: © Slawomir Purgal/Alamy

TOP RIGHT

7.11 Negative space can be space. Note how the sky and water provide a negative space against the structure and vague landscape.

Source: © Jefferson Hayman/Jefferson Hayman/Corbis

Approach graphic design using white space as an element, not as *nothing* or *emptiness.* Just as silence in music or pauses in dance create a counterpoint for the tone or movement to be felt more acutely, the white space in a graphic provides the underlying base for the effect of the design elements. The emptiness is full of power and character and must be treated accordingly. Experiment with this balance in the blocking out of a design before going into too much detail, and see what effect the placement of a minor effect into otherwise dead space can have. A hint of shading or texture, for example, can change the entire balance by eliminating the negative space. It is also interesting to play with the notion that the negative space can actually be "space"—as in providing the illusion of three-dimensional space. Using it as such, in terms of background and foreground, by overlapping can be used to strong effect (Fig. 7.11).

We are accustomed to print as information and are acutely aware of the relationship of the placement of text from an early age. As a result, we are very sensitive to minor changes or discrepancies in the design of fonts and layouts, with minute differences in letters or small shifts in placement creating not only a difference of aesthetic feel but also of understanding (Fig. 7.12).

There really aren't any rules, as such, but there are endless rules of thumb about proportions and limits in terms of the space between images and text or the distance of one letter from another (Fig. 7.13). These, however, should be viewed as existing to be broken (or at least verified). The real test comes in simply eyeing the result and determining whether it looks right. There is an element of Zen-like flower arranging or gardening,

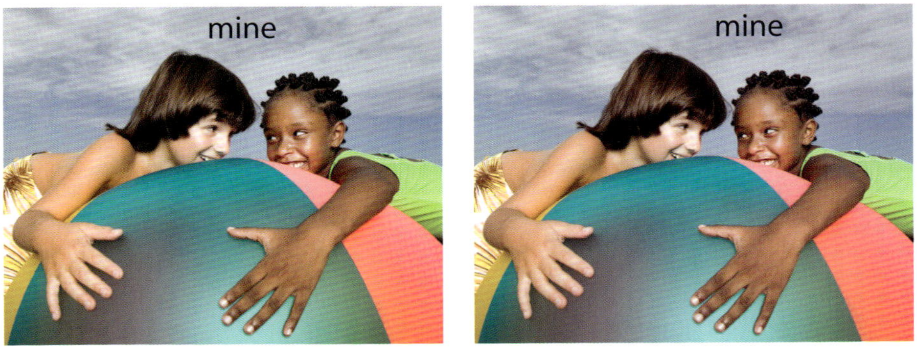

7.12 The very slight and simple shift in the word's placement not only changes the balance of the image but also the meaning. The proximity of the word "mine" to one girl or another signals to whom the "mine" refers and therefore alters the meaning of the image.

Source: © Joson/Corbis

TOP

7.13 The final analysis of a typographic design does not come from rules but from *eyeballing* the result. Here the kerning (the spacing between the characters) has been adjusted to make for a more pleasing result. In the upper configuration, the space between the L and the O was considered problematic, and so the kerning was adjusted to allow the O to nearly overlap the L. The E was also shifted slightly toward the S to reduce the area between them. (Look at the area, not the distance.)

Source: Illustration by Karl Aspelund

MIDDLE RIGHT

7.14 Each element affects all the others and adds to the totality of the design. The simple placement of the headline, with its resulting alteration of the negative space, radically changes the feel of the layout. The headline on the left seems more important, while in the layout on the right the figure has more freedom and its relative impact is increased.

Source: Photograph and illustration by Karl Aspelund

BELOW

7.15 Play around. Do what feels right for the design. The emphasis on "here" in this layout is created by breaking the word out from an imaginary rectilinear grid. The imbalance in placement, alignment, and size pulls the eye toward the key word "here."

Source: Photograph and illustration by Karl Aspelund

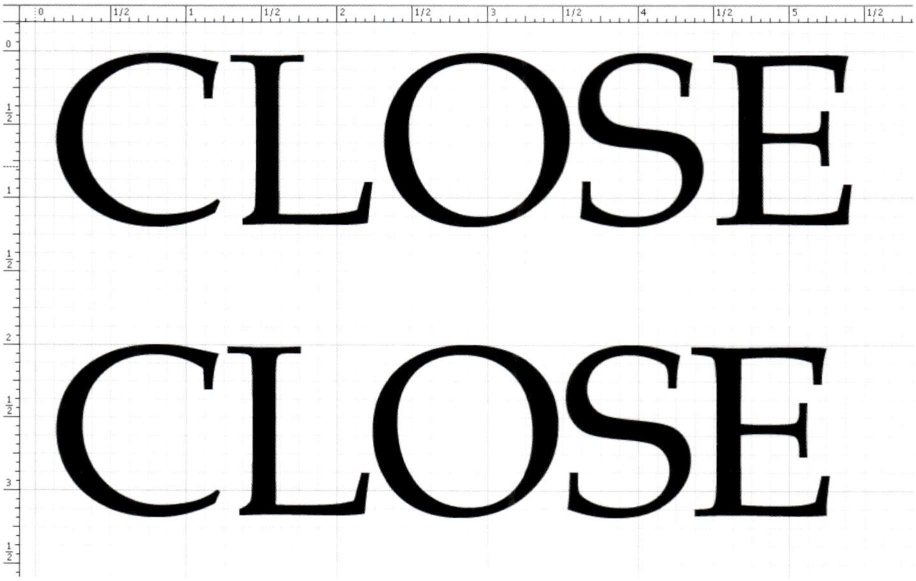

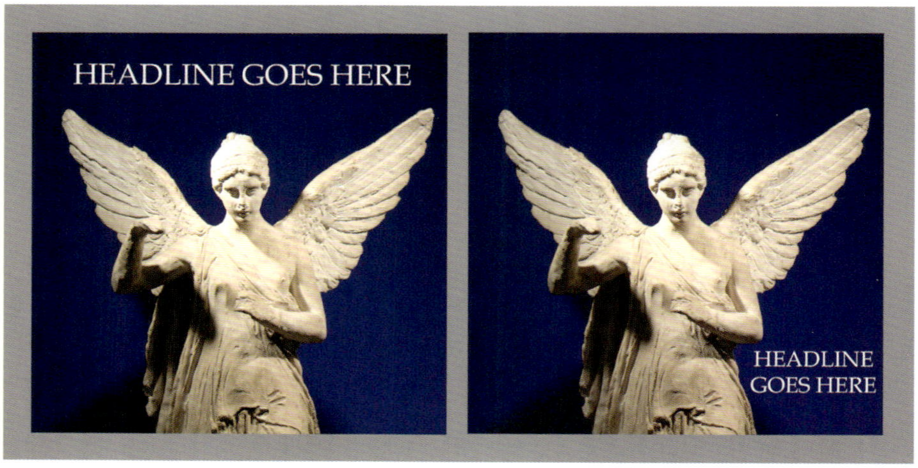

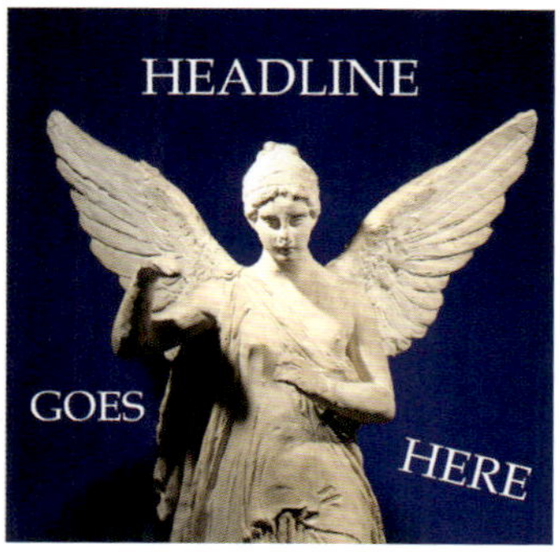

in that the placement of each element should be done with care, as each element affects all the others and adds to the totality of the design. The result must therefore always be viewed as a totality, even as each element is scrutinized in itself (Fig. 7.14).

Do not, for example, always accept default setting on graphic design programs as somehow the right way. This is too easy to do, what with the ease and speed the software allows. The defaults are set by a designer according to some accepted standard, but standards change with the times, and you should not allow this to dictate your moves. Play around, question the assumptions of the program, and do what feels right for the design. It can be very liberating to break all the rules, even if only to then go back to them. In graphic design, especially when it comes to typefaces and white space, the smallest adjustments matter (Fig. 7.15). Give yourself the time to look at your work, and if working in printed material rather than screen-based graphics, don't neglect to print test copies. The experience of the printed work often is radically different from the scale-less and texture-less view on the computer screen with its intense colors and crisp edges.

TEXTURE

In graphic design, the idea of texture may too easily be neglected. How can texture, which is a three-dimensional and tactile phenomenon, be a concern in two-dimensional work? Texture in graphic design is usually executed as a pattern within a color field, or cloudiness or *noise* in an image. The idea of texture in graphic design is more than that. We must remember that texture is experienced through both sight and touch, and that the total look of a graphic design has, in the end, both spatial and textural qualities. We need only to compare graphic designs from the Art Nouveau style with a Constructivist design of only a few years later to sense a difference in texture between the two. Colors, shapes, shading, and references to natural things (with their own textures) creates a feel experienced through sight but can be felt in an evoked sense of touch as well: we see, but the sight also brings a sensation to our fingers and hands.

Humans are, in the end, three-dimensional beings (or four- depending on how you look at it), and our perception is hardwired to this. We are habituated to experiencing the world through all our senses, and sight and touch work together from day one to inform us of the world. We see texture and space in a two-dimensional design by default. Texture is part of the two-dimensional experience and built in the mind from shapes, colors, and space, implied or otherwise. Designers must take this into account and use it as much as they can.

Closely related to texture is pattern. Two-dimensional graphic design tends toward and relies on patterns, as humans have an inherent ability for pattern recognition. We automatically create a totality from the elements in our surroundings (see Gestalt, Chapter 3). Considering the two-dimensional plane on which a graphic design is to be implemented, the idea of a pattern can be thought of in the widest possible sense, as in placing elements on a grid (Fig. 7.16). The subsequent placement of text and images follows a pattern of sorts, even if the underlying map is not obvious.

True patterns, in the sense of repeating elements in a field, also can be used to great effect, either to lead the eye or for decorative purposes or to create a sense of motion. A disrupted pattern can be used for emphasis (Fig. 7.17).

BOTTOM LEFT

7.16 A "pattern" in graphic design can be thought of in the widest possible sense, as in placing elements on a grid. The evenly spaced symmetry of the grid here allows for an underlying pattern to the broken-up text.

Source: Photograph and illustration by Karl Aspelund

BOTTOM RIGHT

7.17 Disrupting a pattern creates a focal point for emphasis. The importance of the switch on the far right is signaled as much by its color as in the fact that it is a different color.

Source: © Paul Burns/Corbis

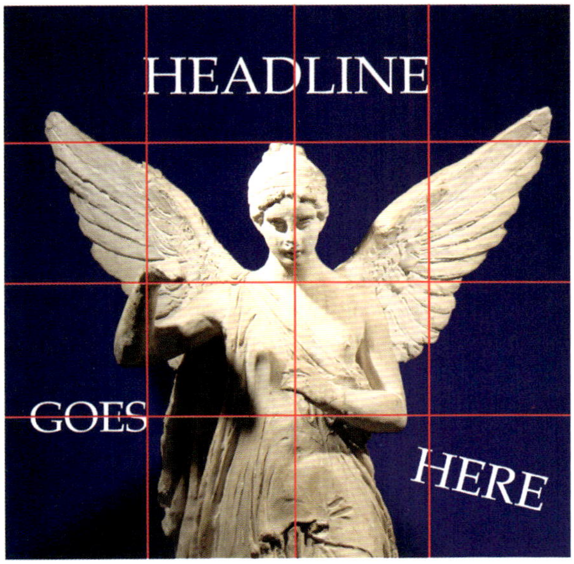

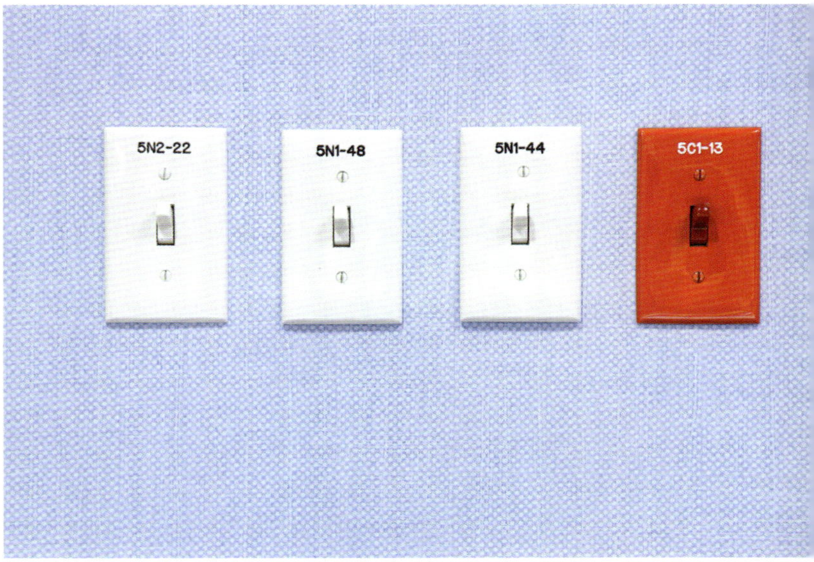

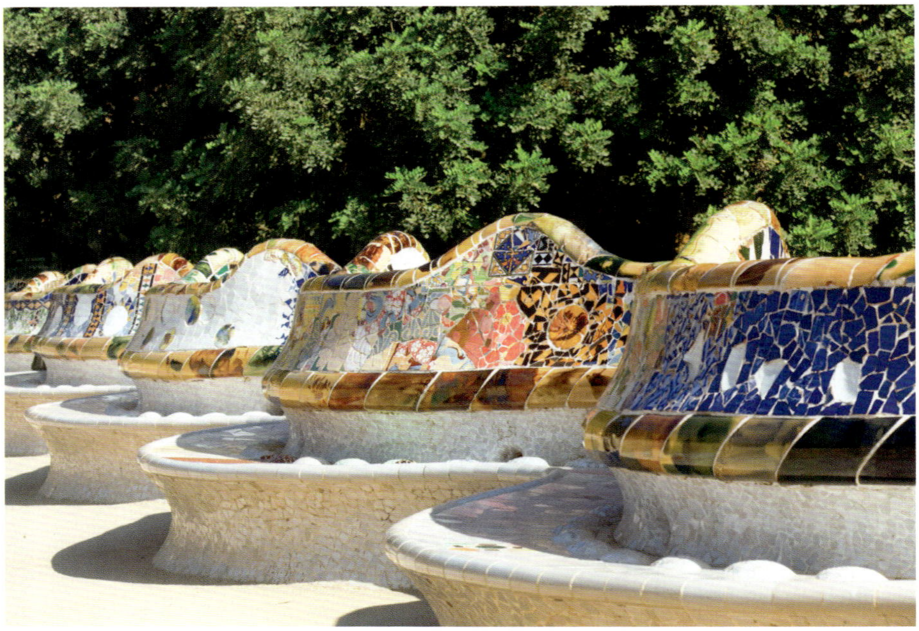

RIGHT

7.18 Colors in patterns can allow a sense of movement and space within the pattern's field. Looking at this bench, the eyes will follow a certain dominant color or pattern to evoke motion, and light-dark contrast is interpreted as space. Bench by Antoni Gaudi, Park Güell, Barcelona.

Source: © Jean-Pierre Lescourret/Corbis

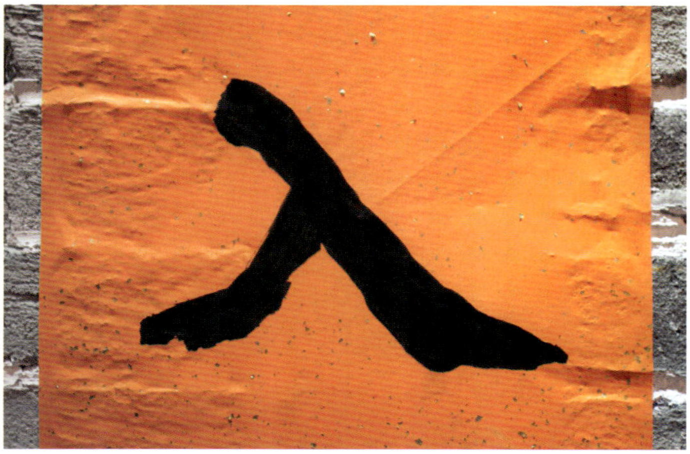

BELOW

7.19 Physical texture will contribute to the visual, just as the visual contributes to the textural. In this photograph of a sign pasted to a brick wall, the sense of texture is enhanced by the contrast of smooth paper and rougher masonry. But the shadows on the paper are what create, in the photo, the visual sense of interesting texture that is far more prominent on the paper than on the stone. "Enter" sign on Hong Kong Museum of History.

Source: © Sean Gallagher/National Geographic Society/Corbis

Patterns in conjunction with color can be more powerful still, as the degree of intensity (or subtlety) can influence the sense of movement and space within the pattern's field (Fig. 7.18). A high-contrast pattern is an eye-catcher, but it may become difficult to look at for an extended period. A low-intensity combination, on the other hand, may not speak as loudly to the audience, but it affords a calmer experience that draws the viewer in. There is much room to play. Between them, the "tricks" that can be played are as many as the different shapes and colors will allow—nearly infinite.

Just as with text on a computer screen that is intended for print, any graphic design that is to be taken off the screen and into the physical world must be tested on the material it is to appear, using the media with which it is to be executed.

If it is to be printed on paper, a print test is needed to see what happens to the feel of it once the paper's texture contributes to the totality. The difference between a glossy print and a nonglossy photograph is all the proof we need of the effectiveness of paper quality to contribute to a design. It is not a given either way. Highly textured or glossy paper might contribute well, or it might not. It must be seen (and felt!).

If the design is to be executed on building materials, perhaps painted on a concrete wall or wood, it may not be possible to do a test of the design itself, but a test of the paint on the type of concrete or wood will be helpful in realizing how the design will work once it is in place. Once again, do not let the default bind your hands. Look at different kinds of surfaces and consider different types of paints, undercoatings, and brushes. See what the actual physical texture will contribute to the visual, just as the visual contributes to the textural (Fig. 7.19).

TEXT/IMAGE BALANCE

The balance between images and text must be evaluated on several levels: the visual effect of the overall layout, the relative weight and balance of text-based information against images, and the individual visual impact of each element (for instance, images, headlines, text blocks, and capital letters). The blocking out of the overall space is a good start, and whether you are working on a screen or physically on a sketchpad, it is a good idea to move the blocks around to find the right layout by eyeballing it and then seeing what logic may be found. If creating within a format, such as when designing pages for a book or magazine or a web page for onscreen viewing, creating a master layout within a grid or framework is a good first move (Fig. 7.20). An evaluation of the relative importance of each element should then lead to an experimental layout where the relative importance of each element is reflected in the relative placement and overall layout.

This is one of the intuitive (Zen) moments mentioned above, as the balance between visual impact and informational importance has to be assessed in place on a gut level. You "don't see it until you see it" and "it isn't there until it's there" are the kind of phrases used at this point. A highly impactful image may require more aggressive use of text to balance it, or large text blocks may require inventive layout or inventive placement of small elements to break up the page. Placing a grid before placing the

7.20 Creating a master layout with a grid or framework is a good first move when you need to create multiple pages or layouts of similar material. This simple layout allows the faculty of a college department to create uniform promotional posters by cutting and pasting in their information.

Source: Illustration by Karl Aspelund

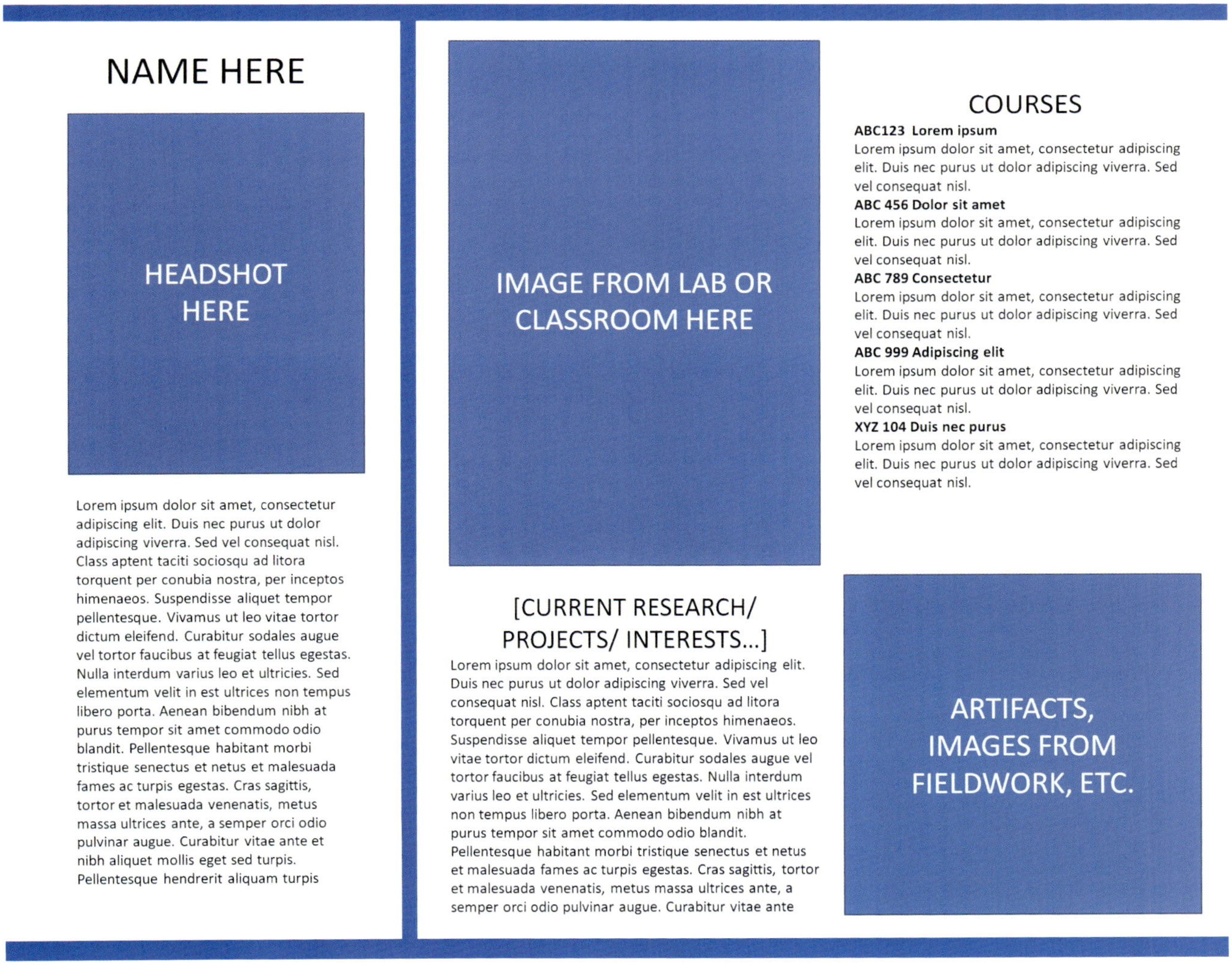

elements will always be helpful, regardless of whether you are designing one layout or more. But you will still need to take a moment to "see it when you see it" and maybe then tweak the results.

The balance between text and image is also cultural, and as many things cultural, it is related to the development of technology. It is interesting, for example, to note the ever-increasing amount of images relative to text in newspapers and magazines over the past 100 years. This is largely due to improved print techniques and cheaper print materials. But it is also due to the cultural dependence on visual information that increased as the 20th century progressed. The culture shifted from being print-oriented in terms of information to being occupied with the distribution and broadcasting of images. From printed sheets to illustrated pages to color-printed magazines, film and television (also shifting to color), and the explosion of visual interaction with the arrival of Internet browsers in the 1990s, the shift has been in every way toward an increasingly visual culture (Fig. 7.21).

The more we learn the instinctive use of images and icons, the more we require them in our daily navigation of information. The idea of the "normal" **text–image balance,** that is, the visual impact of text and graphics together and the weighting of each on the page, changes with demand and is a self-perpetuating evolution. The notion of a full-text cover on a magazine, a newspaper without pictures, or a food-product label that is text-only seem quaint and old-fashioned, and such a design is used to that effect. Websites and screen interfaces also have moved in past decades

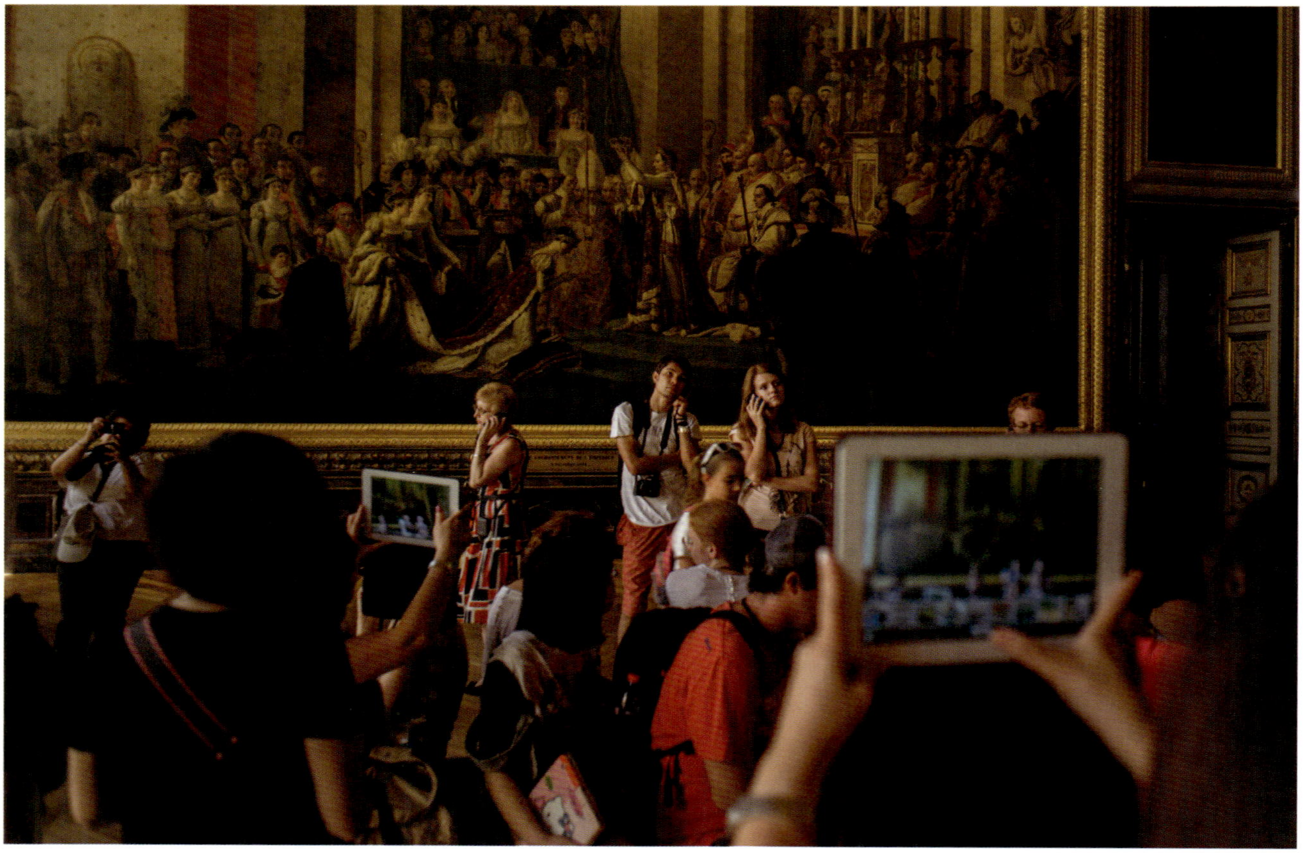

7.21 Since the invention of printing, the move has been toward an increasingly visual culture, to the point where we are viewing the world through imagery and creating images of our immediate experiences far more than we are reading or writing about them. Tablets and phone-cameras are constantly being used to create and disseminate visual information, not words.

Source: © Richard Baker/In Pictures/Corbis

from text-based interfaces to images and visual graphic elements that can be understood and interacted with faster and without reliance on language.

The Web-based environments are, in fact, a different world by now, and should not really be considered as an extension of print media, even though the webpage is delivering text and images. It may look like a page up to a point and be discussed like a page, but websites are, by nature of their interactivity, an experience of a different order than, say, magazines or newspapers. The ability to resize, navigate, scroll, and click changes the approach to the page, and the idea of a layout is different than for that of a fixed and static bit of print. Graphic images and photos are taking over the medium, and as handheld devices have tipped the norm from desk-based screens, text has come to be presented in smaller units.

MEANING

We see that when designing a piece using images and text, we are capable of investing the content with meaning. To state the obvious, the meaning must be the meaning desired. The graphic designer juggles images, text, layout, and format to create and (occasionally) balance the meaning of the elements involved.

But what is the meaning, and how to assess it as one goes along? The words and images may have a clear meaning in themselves. The text says what it says, and the picture is what it is. However, put them together and now their meaning is not necessarily clear (Fig. 7.22). How to construct meaning out of disparate elements, such as corporate colors, text, and various evocative images or product? This is where the art of the graphic designer transcends the artful manipulation of elements and becomes one of interpretation, understanding, and insight. How meaning is constructed in the mind of a viewer, how the gestalt is assembled, is one thing. How the individual elements are culturally understood often with subtle ironies or humor or nostalgic references (or all of the above) relies on knowledge of the elements themselves, their history, the history of their meaning and cultural context, and the understanding of a present-day audience (Fig. 7.23).

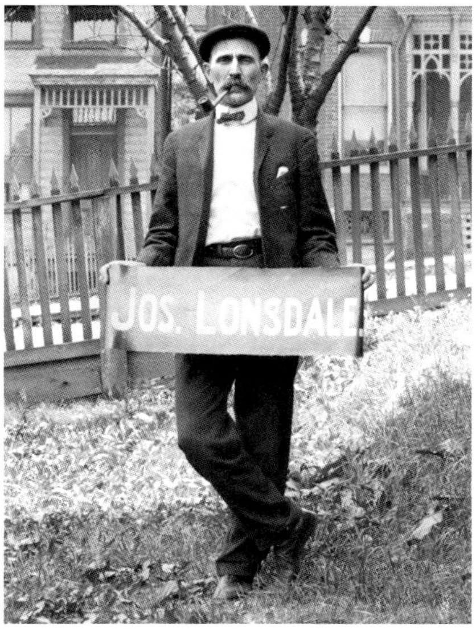

7.22 Text and images combine to create meaning. It is clear in this photograph that this is a man smoking a pipe and holding a sign. We might imagine that the man's name is Joseph Lonsdale, but why he would be holding a sign with his name on it (or anybody else's for that matter) can only be speculated upon and could be debated. If the sign had said "House for Sale," the meaning of the sign would not be open to much except wondering which of the houses behind him are for sale. The text on the sign defines the focus of the image, it can shift the focus from the person to the building, even when we really don't know what is going on.

Source: © Kirn Vintage Stock/Corbis (Illustration: Karl Aspelund)

Cultural references change not only geographically but also over time. The time frame of a cultural signal can be very short or span generations, and it is important to understand that a significant image, artistic reference, or style may have no meaning to an audience that did not grow up in a specific place or live through a certain time. The graphic designer must keep one eye on the meaning of things and understand the cultural context of a font, a color combination, or the juxtaposition of a set of images.

Meaning is created among people in the interaction of daily activities, and the things we use and surround ourselves with begin to acquire meaning personally. The

NETWORKING

The following list contains beneficial Websites for further information:

WHAT IS GRAPHIC DESIGN? AIGA
www.aiga.org/guide-whatisgraphicdesign/

DESIGNINGWITHTYPE.COM
A site devoted to the art and appreciation of typography.
www.designingwithtype.com

MUSEUM OF THE IMAGE, BREDA, NETHERLANDS
www.motimuseum.nl/en/home/4

PRINTS & PHOTOGRAPHS ONLINE CATALOG (LIBRARY OF CONGRESS)
www.loc.gov/pictures/

DESIGNHISTORY.ORG—A PRIMER OF SYMBOL TERMS
www.designhistory.org/Symbols_pages/symbols.html

personal can then aggregate through public interaction into a cultural structure. This is where graphic designers need to be aware of the constant movement of culture, keeping an eye on television, ads, video games, and blockbuster films, as well as the more esoteric and specific subcultures, high-society fashions, and cultural institutions.

The graphic designer can create new meanings out of such structures by using known references and the language of current culture to invest a client's concerns with connections to the world of the viewer. A designer may refer to memory or daily experience, to expressions of the mundane or evocations of exciting pop-culture moments. Figuring out the buttons to push for different generations in terms of nostalgic references or significant events has also become more important even as it has become easier. The constant accessibility to images and history works both ways in society. As the cultural group revisits its references, designers and marketers do so as well. The graphic designer needs only to keep slightly ahead of the curve to revitalize the meaning of things and present a fresh look and energized design.

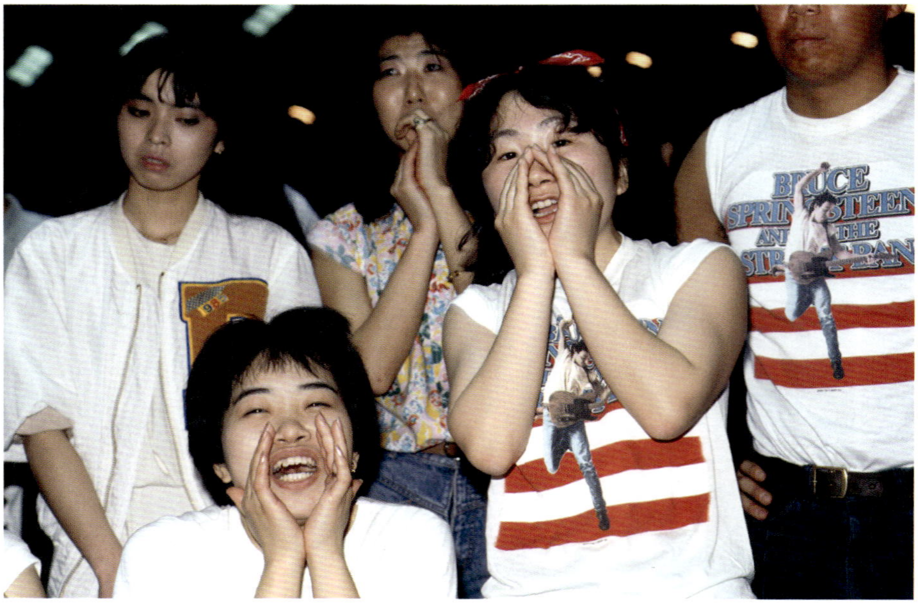

7.23 How the individual elements are culturally understood relies on knowledge of the elements themselves, their history, the history of their meaning and cultural context, and the understanding of a present-day audience. The significance of the flag on the T-shirt–and the shirt itself becomes very different once one understands these are fans at a Bruce Springsteen Concert in Japan.

Source: © Neal Preston/Corbis

CONCLUSION

We see in graphic design a discipline that is on the cusp of craft and art, related to the painter and the printer. The 2D designer is by no means operating in 2D only. The two-dimensional nature of the work does not fully imply the feel for the multidimensional experience of textures, space, balance, and movement that is required. The 2D designer must think in 3D and 4D and be constantly aware of the dialogue between the elements of the design and any text. Creating meaning becomes the task, and doing so requires a wide knowledge of the world.

KEY TERMS

Pop Art	Font	Text–image balance
Typeface		

DISCUSSION AND REVIEW QUESTIONS

1. Pick a classic painting and imagine it was the basis for a poster or book cover. Conversely, take a classic poster or print ad and use it as the basis for a work of art. Observe what needs to change in each case and how the basic approach may have needed to be different in each case, if at all.
2. Translate the concepts, elements, and principles observed in a three-dimensional design into two dimensions and vice versa. What changes? How can you compensate for changes in texture, dimensionality, and space?
3. Find a design that conveys some kind of message. How is this done? How do the elements and principles play in? How is the message interpreted literally, culturally, and experientially? How might the meaning be misunderstood, if at all? Is so, how would a redesign prevent that?

EXERCISES AND ASSIGNMENTS

1. Cut a full-page ad out of a magazine. Cut a 3-inch-×-3-inch square in a sheet of paper. Lay it over the ad until you have framed a section of the ad that you would present as artwork for an exhibition. With the same ad, find three such possibilities and either photograph or photocopy the results so you have all three as framed artworks.
   a. What made this work, in terms of elements and principles?
   b. What did you consistently crop out and leave in, if anything?
   c. What does this tell you about the relationship between art and design?
2. Find three surfaces in your immediate environment where texture makes a significant contribution to the design.
   a. What other materials might be used for these surfaces to the same effect?
   b. What materials would you use for a totally different effect? Would this be as good a design? Why? Why not?
3. Print your name on a sheet of paper using five very different fonts.
   a. Which is the most pleasing to you? Why?
   b. Which would you use (and why) on:
      A business card? Your front door? A T-shirt, if you had a business?

CHAPTER 8

THREE-DIMENSIONAL THINKING

OBJECTIVES

Identify the nature of the design challenges of three dimensions beyond those of two-dimensional design.

Recognize that three dimensions bring the laws of physics into play, notably gravity.

Identify the need to understand 3D as a physical sensory experience.

Distinguish that working with 3D as a physical sensory experience requires attention to space, motion, and time.

Be aware of the human body, with its symmetries, as the ultimate frame of reference of human design.

Understand *proxemics* as a frame for considering the physical interaction and relationship of people in spaces.

Detect the transition to virtual space and the repositioning of spatial thinking involved.

DESIGNERS SPEAK

"Have you looked at a modern airplane? Have you followed from year to year the evolution of its lines? Have you ever thought, not only about the airplane but about whatever man builds, that all of man's industrial efforts, all his computations and calculations, all the nights spent over working draughts and blueprints, invariably culminate in the production of a thing whose sole and guiding principle is the ultimate principle of simplicity?

"It is as if there were a natural law which ordained that to achieve this end, to refine the curve of a piece of furniture, or a ship's keel, or the fuselage of an airplane, until gradually it partakes of the elementary purity of the curve of a human breast or shoulder, there must be the experimentation of several generations of craftsmen. In anything at all, perfection is finally attained not when there is no longer anything to add, but when there is no longer anything to take away, when a body has been stripped down to its nakedness."

—ANTOINE DE SAINT-EXUPÉRY, *Wind, Sand, and Stars,* translated by Lewis Galantière (New York: Harbrace, 1967 [1939]), n.p.

In this chapter the nature of three dimensions (3D) as a design challenge is discussed, followed by a presentation of the application of three dimensions in design and the need to understand 3D as a living experience grounded in the human form.

3D VERSUS 2D

Three-dimensional designing requires a different stance toward the project than two-dimensional in more ways than might be immediately apparent. The demands of three dimensions are at once practical, tangible, and philosophical. Going from the flat-plane thinking of 2D, as discussed in the previous chapter, to the physical world of motion and depth bring to us problems related to the physical world, such as structure, gravity and motion, the need to account for spatial differences in perception, the presence of an inside and outside, and the perhaps disconcerting realization that by requiring attention to motion and experience, three-dimensional design is, in fact, four-dimensional.

These issues become easily framed and discussed when we look at them through the lens of human bodily experience, and our discussion will be brought home by looking at the relevance of the human body itself to human experience and how its shape, structure, and mobility influences our perception and experience of the world. Finally, we will look at motion in three-dimensional space, leading to a brief examination of the relatively new world of virtual environments and the nature of their "space." How the virtual reflects on our bodily perception of the world may well change how we view the notion of three-dimensional design in the near future.

In the transition from 2D to 3D in designing, the first thing to notice is the very different degree of freedom involved. The two-dimensional plane is a remarkably unfettered space, with an enormous amount of freedom from the constraints of the physical realities of the three-dimensional world. There is a complete lack of gravity, and no need for supporting structures. There is a much higher level of control over how the work is viewed and a very limited stance toward the viewer in the sense that the object involved (e.g., the picture, poster, label, page) only turns one face toward the world. Put simply, there is no back to anything.

The three-dimensional world with its spatial distortions does not interfere, as the illusion of space and gravity can be affected in a two-dimensional design rather easily. Two-dimensional designs also allow a degree of freedom from the constraints and demands of the human body itself. Apart from the basic needs of being visible and within range of the audience, a two-dimensional design has no need for any interference that intends to accommodate the body of the viewer, except in being presented in a human scale of some kind. No issues of shape, motion, or bodily impact and weight will matter.

The transition from 2D to 3D is a standard move in nearly all designing. The preparation for a three-dimensional object, such as a shirt, a car, or a railway station, nearly always begins with a two-dimensional representation on a page or computer screen. The danger of this is largely in keeping with the above-mentioned issues: the ease with which something can be put on a page does not necessarily translate into the ease with which the two-dimensional design becomes the three-dimensional object. Materials behave in certain ways and have certain affordances, gravity will pull at things, and use and motion will provide stress and impact that cannot be simulated in 2D.

This is not to say that designers neglect to consider this on a routine basis. Rather, it is simply too easy to fall into a relationship with your design that is based on the environment in which you are working. If your idea is taking shape in two dimensions on a screen or page in front of you, your own thinking and involvement with the

TIMELINE: 3D DESIGN

A timeline of 3D design may not in itself make much sense. Human environments are and have been 3D and to pinpoint any particular moment in the development of this thinking may invite some rather odd statements. However, there are three areas relating to the designing of 3D spaces that are worth considering in a historical context, although the timeline is different from culture to culture and even from country to country. First, the designing of habitats has gone through transformations in different cultures in different times in such a way that the three-dimensionality of the collective space becomes more and more pertinent to how things are done. This is most clearly seen in a culture's transition into urban living, when the designing of cities requires much more rigid planning than the more organic growth of a town or village. On a smaller level, the designing of buildings for larger public business of governmental purposes begins to expand with the rise of cities, and the designing of these calls for a systematic approach to space and utility. The aesthetics follow, and in the history of 3D design as architecture, we see the modernist solutions to these problems essentially become the attempt to answer the question of how to build spaces in these new types of human communities. Even now, with global populations moving between cultural spheres and new materials and methods that allow the redefining of public space, we see this thinking evolve. Moving through our cities, the timeline is right in front of us at all times.

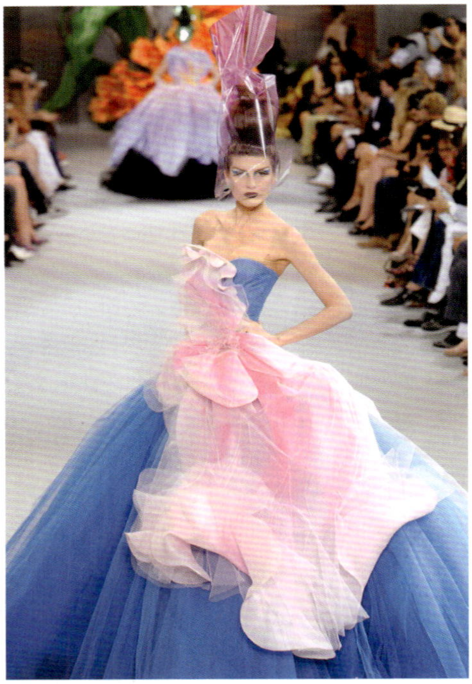

8.1 Buildings and architectural structures require support, but designing clothing, for example, needs to take in the drape of fabric and the interaction of the body and supports with the flexible and supple textiles.

Source: Giovanni Giannoni/WWD

project will tend toward the problems at hand and they will invariably be of a two-dimensional nature, unless you remind yourself continually of the requirements of the three-dimensional world.

Dealing with gravity is actually a good way to visualize the transition. Even though the concerns are tremendously more complex, the basic message is that going from two dimensions to three requires the addition of structure. Buildings and architectural structures require support, of course, but designing clothing, for example, needs to take into account the drape of fabric and the interaction of the body and supports with the flexible and supple textiles (Fig. 8.1). Smaller objects need to stay structurally sound but also need to resist the impact of being dropped or withstand the weight of other objects.

This may seem very obvious, but the opposite is also true. The beauty of working in two dimensions before committing to the structured object allows the freedom from the earthly constraints of gravity and its attendant falling, crushing, and crumbling. However, the simple nod to gravity begins to require an investigation into the engineering of structures, choices of materials of specific tolerances and strength, and the definition of the capabilities that are to be inherent in the final design. As a designer, one can only stretch this freedom so far before the engineers, makers, and materials specialists need to be called in.

A slightly more nuanced way of approaching the transition to three-dimensional thinking is to consider the challenges of spatiality—to now have to consider things in the round. Designing an object for a human (or a living, moving being of any kind, actually) involves considering the spaces around and in between the object and user and how the user's body interacts with or approaches the designed object.

We must consider the view toward the designed object from multiple viewpoints—the front and the back of a garment or building or vehicle—but at the same time realize the limitation of human vision that will not allow the viewing of the object in the round, unless by mirrors or cameras. In considering the effect of movement and space, we must also take into account the changing views with distance or the distortions of perspective and angles. The point of view becomes important in the approach to a building, for example, and the distance from an outfit or decorative elements may reveal or hide detail. Meanwhile, the relationship of a designed object or space to other objects or surrounding spaces may not be clear unless by a certain distance or approach.

The rather obvious fact that a 3D object has an inside and an outside is something that the transition to 3D brings to add to the flat-surface experience of **2d design.** Clothing and furniture is around the body, buildings are inhabited, cars sat in, devices held in the hand, and so on. Devices have interiors for components, and structures are hidden way inside any number of constructed creations. To consider the inside and outside and the relationship of the two is always an interesting exercise and, of course, can split the design problem easily into the exterior *look* and the interior *function*. The layout of electronics or machinery dovetails with the efficient performance of the device or machine, and here is where the designer's role as artist and the role of engineer can blur.

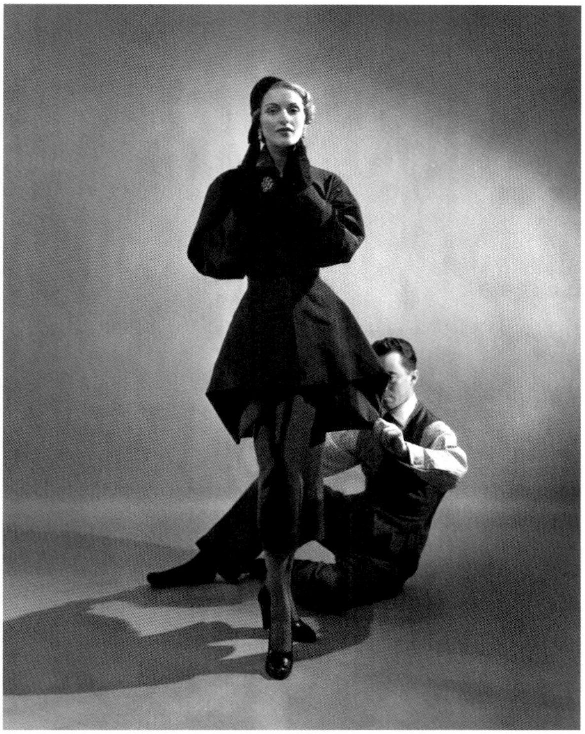

8.2 In clothing the aesthetics are about the exterior, but also the construction design of the structures and elements between layers as well as the interior of a garment in the choice of linings, interior pockets, and the feel of a garment on the skin of the wearer. Designer Charles James pinning a suit on model.

Source: Cecil Beaton/© Condé Nast Archive

In clothing the aesthetics can actually extend or be layered from the exterior inward, with the design of the exterior look providing a surface of sorts, the construction design of the structures and construction elements coming in next in between layers, and then again the aesthetic and tactile choices apparent in the interior of a garment in the choice of linings, interior pockets, and the feel of a garment on the skin of the wearer (Fig. 8.2).

But *inside* and *outside,* like *distance* and *approach,* have no meaning without the possibility of movement, leading to the realization that **3D design** is, in fact, like 3D experience actually presented in four dimensions. Just as our interpretation of two-dimensional design incorporates the ability to inhabit 3D in a 2D format, three-dimensional perception is dependent on the ability to navigate around or with an object in time. The fourth dimension of time allows us the (albeit one-directional) transition from past to future and not just to move but to experience space, life, and the effects of the world. This may seem like an obvious and perhaps needless distinction, but in the designing of interactive spaces, physical or virtual, the question of experience is always that of experience in and over time.

Experience over time may be considered simply as the time an action takes—the crossing of a public space, the response time of a system to input, or the time between one sensory input and another. Taking that further, one might consider the rhythmic design of a hallway, the movement of an airport escalator past an artwork on the wall, or the shifting scenery on a theater stage. Rhythm, change, and anticipation are all experiences in time, and a designer relying on these for impact must take time into account.

SUSTAINABILITY

Considering sustainability within the framework of 3D design is not specifically a problem set one can isolate as such, as 3D design does not change or add to the concerns. However, what changes is right along the lines of other changes in attitude and approach. Going from 2D to 3D is a change in *stance* and *attitude.* Moving off the flat plane of graphic design and 2D illustration brings us into the physical world of weight and wear and tear, potential movement, and physical perception of distance. As we must recognize the interplay of space, time, and motion, we begin to design for forces that do not necessarily act in two dimensions. The environmental impact of a design invariably takes place in three (four) dimensions, and no impact is without consequences. Every design that is going to be a physical object will require materials, resources, and space. As such, every manufactured design is by definition an environmental concern.

The question of light in a designed space is also a question of sustainability. Spaces can be designed to make the best use of natural light and therefore minimizing energy use for illumination. Lighting designed into a building can be specified according to LEED standards, and fixtures and equipment can be chosen according to how they impact the environment. More and more architects, interior designers, and their clients are realizing the power of design to have a positive effect in this way.

THE HUMAN BODY AS THE ULTIMATE FRAME OF REFERENCE

We are beings in time and space. We navigate the world through four-dimensional space–time of which we are able to be conscious by virtue of the spatial and neurological capabilities of our bodies. Our consciousness becomes layered with experiences through these interactions, and the bodily experience is in the end what we know of the world. All knowledge and experience is filtered through the capabilities of our nervous system, transmitted to us through a collection of senses, and classified into experience by a brain of magnificent complexity. Until we are able to run experiences past the senses of our bodies and directly to our brains, this will be the measure of designing for human consumption.

The size and scale of our designs are intimately bound to the size and scale of the human body, and although a few human endeavors in design—such as microchips—do not interact with the body in such a way as making the body the measure of things, most retain a measure of human scale in their design (see Chapter 4 for a discussion of scale). Even structures that are way out of scale, when seen from a distance, such as ancient pyramids or modern cities or space vehicles, contain in their designs human-scale elements that are the fingerprints of our structure as a species. Another being of some other size would, on discovering these thousands of years after we are gone, be able to discern the approximate size of the species that created the structures in Figure 8.3 by the various commonly scaled elements such as steps, handles, hatches, and doorways.

In the end it is the human body and its capabilities that are the ultimate reference points for human design. What we can and cannot do, see, hear, feel, taste, and smell was the limit to our interaction with the world and at the same time the framing of the capabilities that modern-era designing was meant to improve on or at least work with. Subsequent technological developments have led us to a place where all of the senses are in some way or another enhanced by design (in its widest sense, where engineering is on some level design).

The human scale of abilities and the human mode of perception define the technology that then improves on itself and so on. We are, however, largely defined by

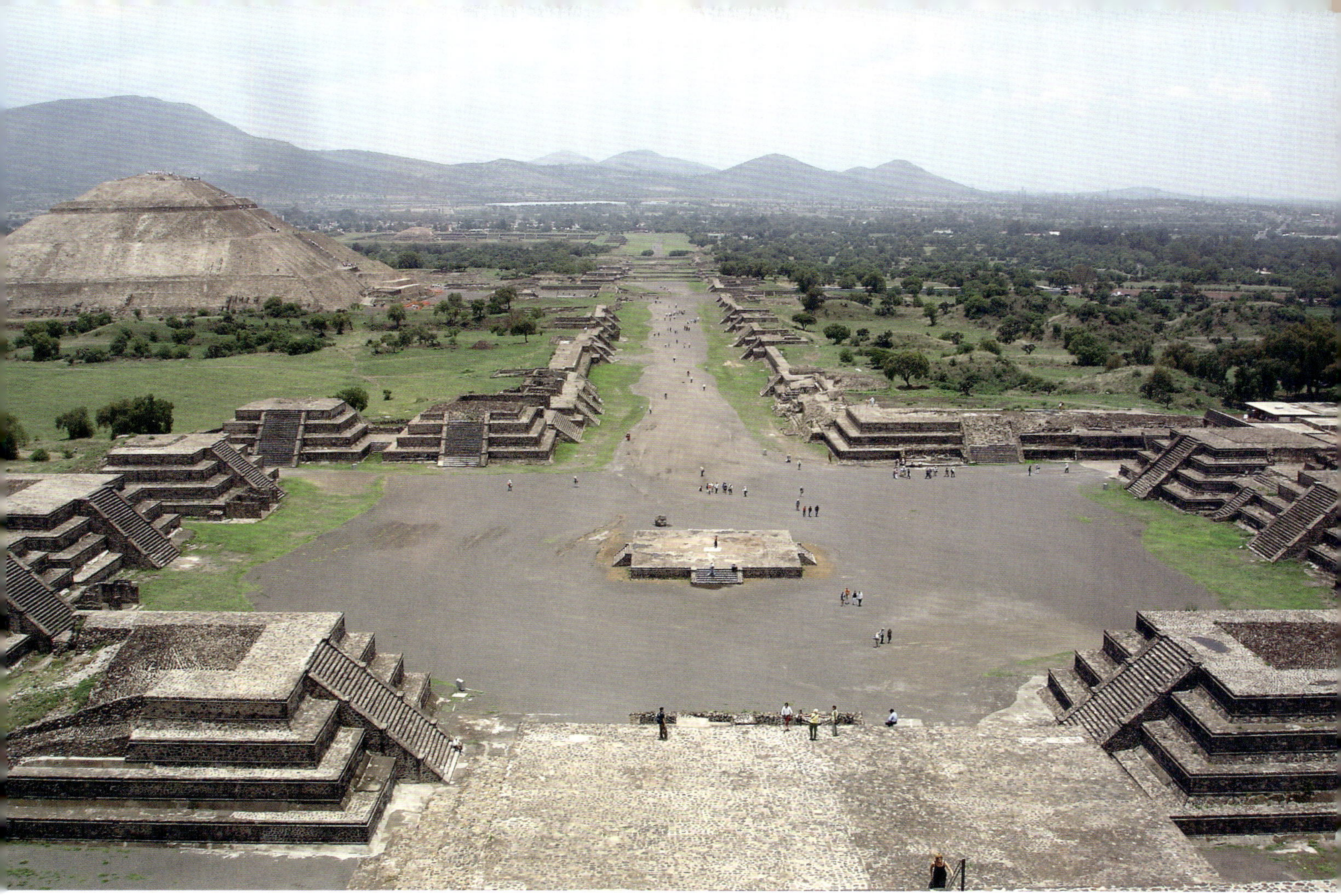

8.3 City planners will often overscale elements for a sense of grandeur or a statement of power. Without the humans for reference, how do we discern the scale of these constructions? The pre-Hispanic City of Teotihuacan, in modern-day Mexico, is an exercise in scale-deception. The steps can be either large or small and the avenue and plaza seem to belong to the larger steps to further the illusion. View from the Pyramid of the Moon of the Avenue of the Dead and the Pyramid of the Sun.

Source: Photo © Jack Hynes

humanness, and we are not accustomed to seeing what is behind us or sharing what other people hear as part of our daily life. We maintain bodily separation as part of our individual identities.

Meanwhile, our bodies, when stripped of technology, are roughly on par with humans of thousands of years ago. We can withstand the same temperatures, need protection from the same elements and chemicals, and function more or less in the same way in relation to food, drink, and sleep. In fact, the most basic needs and constraints of our creature comforts and habits are so similar through at least 40,000 years of human history that the technological developments toward the industrialized human culture brought by the past three centuries of Enlightenment and industrialization may be seen as still being relatively recent. Although the demands and possibilities afforded by consumer culture have changed the way many live their lives and medical science has changed the physical experience of those lives (not to mention their length) considerably, the basic functionality with which the world is experienced and navigated has not changed very much at all.

Our relationship with the world has until very recently in history been bound to the limitations of our physical bodies, most specifically in terms of the scale of human activity. We are operating in what seems to be in a comfortable zone, midway between the atomic and the natural, within a timescale that allows for generational development, but that is anchored by much longer-term processes in natural cycles.

ERGONOMICS

Ergonomics, the *science of work,* frequently translates into an analysis of the relationship of the human body to its environment and any equipment in use. How a body is placed at a desk, sits in a chair, moves with a tool, fits in a shoe—all become a question of space and motion and the range and strength of the human form. Designing in 3D for any human interaction must therefore include ergonomic thinking from the beginning: How will the bodies move, rest, and relate to your design? What will be the effort involved? How desirable is a more or less free range of motion? Finally, in designing human spaces, whether they are large and structured (interiors, buildings) or small and flexible (clothing, interactive, or online spaces), the interactive space, or *space between* people and objects, becomes a significant ergonomic factor, for comfort and navigability. When designing in 3D, whether large or small, virtual or physical, think *motion* and from there you leap to ergonomics.

Another side to ergonomics and space is the issue of light in space. Designing a space whether it be buildings, interiors, stage of film sets, or any other 3D configuration of shapes in which the human body is to operate requires a good sense of light and how illumination, natural light, reflected light, and shadows will play together to create both practical and aesthetic effects. Visibility, definition, comfort, navigability, and legibility all stem from the amount of light present. Where will it come from? How might it change? Is it sunlight or electric light? If electric, what kind? How powerful, how adjustable, and on and on. All we see is a result of reflected light. How can you use it to the best-possible effect for the people in your designed space?

Our view of the world is based on our size and scale. We are large in comparison to much of the animal world, but small compared to natural formations and geological timeframes. Our frame is *anthropocentric*—placing the human at the center—reading the world and its processes as if human scale were the determining factor. We cannot see molecules and atoms, and have limited spectrum of vision and sound within which our world presents itself. Technologically we have managed to extend our perception and capabilities over the past couple of hundred years, but we are still entrenched in a very human frame of perception, and what we see through microscopes, telescopes, and infrared goggles, although incorporated into our common visual references, is still on some level just outside the normal of our day-to-day perception.

HUMAN PLANES AND SYMMETRIES

The **symmetries of the human body** (see also Chapter 3) are very much a determining factor in the construction and development of habitats and equipment. Our adaptation of nature has not, for example, extended to multiple symmetries. We have a left-right symmetry that is weighted to one side or another by the predominance of our own handedness. Our front-back and top-bottom asymmetries, however, define our approach to the constructing of nearly everything we create, own, and do. This is an unavoidable framing of 3D design that will not be taken out of human experience unless the human creature itself is redesigned or engineered beyond its natural limits (Fig. 8.4). Meanwhile, tools, clothing, furniture, vehicles, buildings, and other structures will be conceptualized within a frame that is essentially *of* the human body, *for* the human body. The bodily symmetries and the directionality they imply will direct designs toward structures dictated by our three-dimensional life in the world. For some areas of design, this is more obvious and appropriate than others. Our clothing and furniture, for example, will tend toward left-right symmetry as opposed to

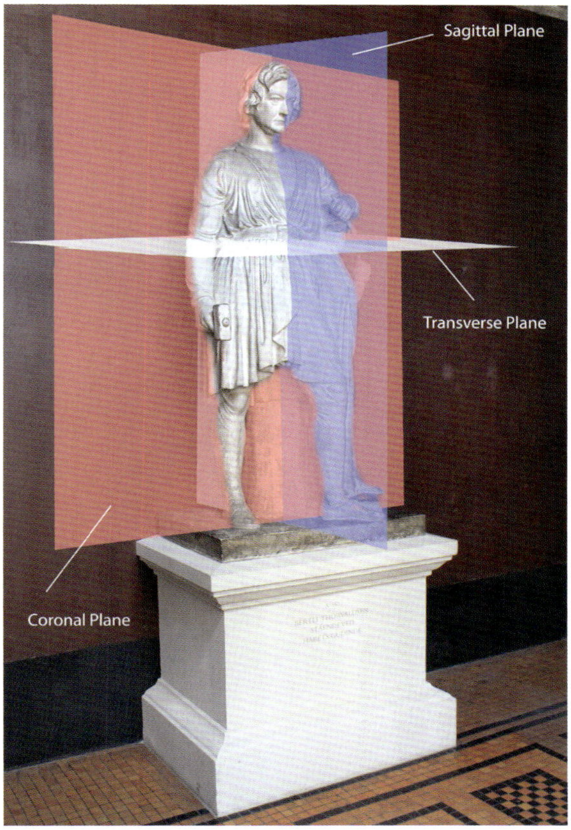

front-back or top-bottom. No matter what the style or decorative element, the strict human-body reference shines through and overrides history and cultural differences.

Another obvious but nonetheless illuminating point to consider is how much our range of motion and our physical sense of balance dictates the designing of our equipment and surroundings. Our positioning being so bound to the strictly vertical or horizontal makes for frameworks and symmetries in these planes and allows a simple diagonal to seem aggressive or invasive in a design, slashing across the planes we exist comfortably within.

Personal space is also measured in the arm's length and goes well beyond a metaphor, and the height of a counter in a reception area, bank, or post office may, for example, be either welcoming or intimidating depending on a variation of only a few inches in height or width. The feel of having to bend down to speak to a person in a kiosk is a very specific stance, as is sitting or standing at a lower or higher level than those around you. The distance between seats in a movie theater, the height of a step, the width of a locker—these are all designs that involve direct sensations of personal space (Fig. 8.5).

The comfortable reach of our bodies and arms forms ideas of comfortable proportions in the design of personal spaces. The distances placed between people and the above or below eye-level positioning of focal points creates a sense of space in itself, and where information is concerned, the placement creates a sense of importance or urgency. The higher the sign, the more important it seems.

ABOVE

8.4 Our front-back and top-bottom asymmetries define our approach to the construction of nearly everything we create, own, and do. This is an unavoidable framing of 3D design that will not be taken out of human experience unless the human creature itself is redesigned or adapted beyond its natural limits.

Source: Illustration by Karl Aspelund

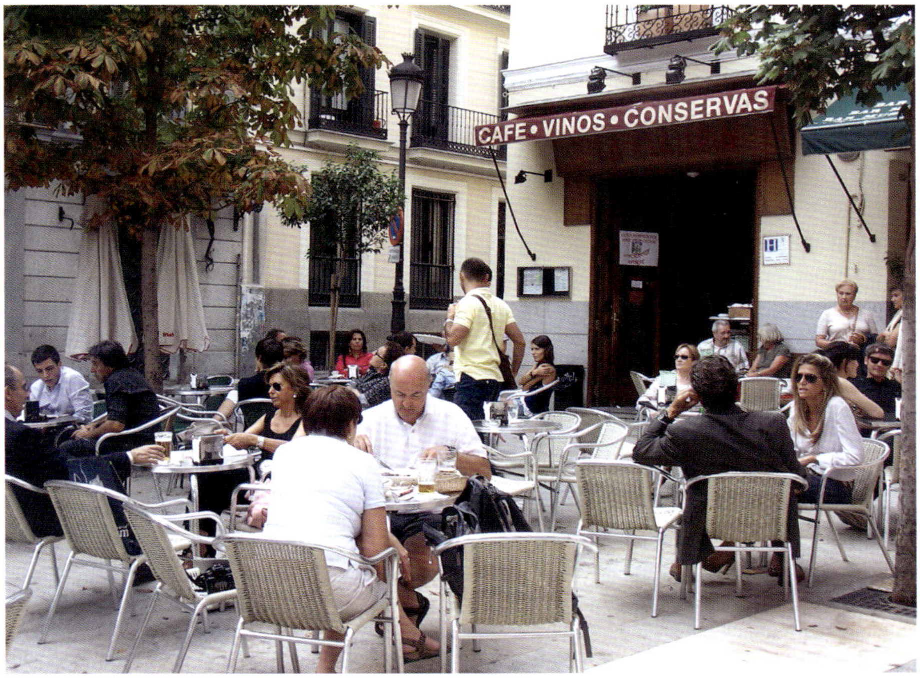

RIGHT

8.5 The design of public spaces involves direct sensations of personal space. In a café, for example, the size of the chairs and tables, the distances between them, and their proximity to the buildings all contribute to both public and private space. Café in Madrid by the Prado Museum.

Source: Image source: Sandie Parrott, Freelance Writer, Blogger, and Photographer

The same is true of situations in which we move our bodies. Our methods of locomotion are in fact extremely limited, and so our spaces, public and private, are directed by very simple constraints and needs. Our general situation is toward the vertical, and the motions we perform in getting from one place to another are usually fairly limited whether walking or in a vehicle. Our spaces are generally narrow, and public venues will usually accommodate a number of people in a very limited space. Sidewalks are narrow, elevators and escalators are small, staircases are not generally very wide unless for aesthetic reasons, and the vehicles we travel in are narrow and tightly placed, and seating does not afford much motion or changing of position.

NEED FOR PROTECTION AND SHELTER

Bodily needs for protection and shelter define much of designing through the centuries. Clothing and habitats have the basic function of protecting our rather fragile structures and skin from the elements and providing shelter from the eyes of fellow humans. The basic interaction of clothing with skin and furniture and furnishings with the shape and strength of our bodies has created various systems of how to shape and create basic garments, chairs, tables, shoes, and any number of utensils and equipment. Materials are defined by their interaction with skin, such as protective coverings on tools to avoid blisters and the choices of materials for clothing, depending on how close to the skin they are to be worn. Jewelry is shaped and rounded to avoid abrasion and pricking, and so on.

As was noted in Chapter 7, texture is experienced in both the eyes and the fingertips. The world as experienced through our sense of touch can therefore be understood to be a three-dimensional experience. The sensations that arrive in our consciousness through our skin are an interaction of surfaces, temperatures, and subtle differences in texture that are also taken in through sight and even sound, such as in the crinkling of paper in our hands or the scratching of a sand-covered floor underfoot. The invasion of the world into our immediate experience can thus be designed in, by considering the impact of touch, when choosing fabrics or surfaces for clothes and habitats. It is a very intimate gesture to place an experience directly on someone's skin (Fig. 8.6).

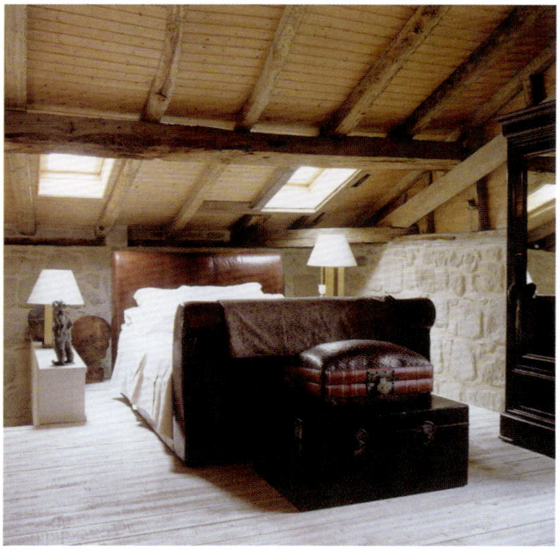

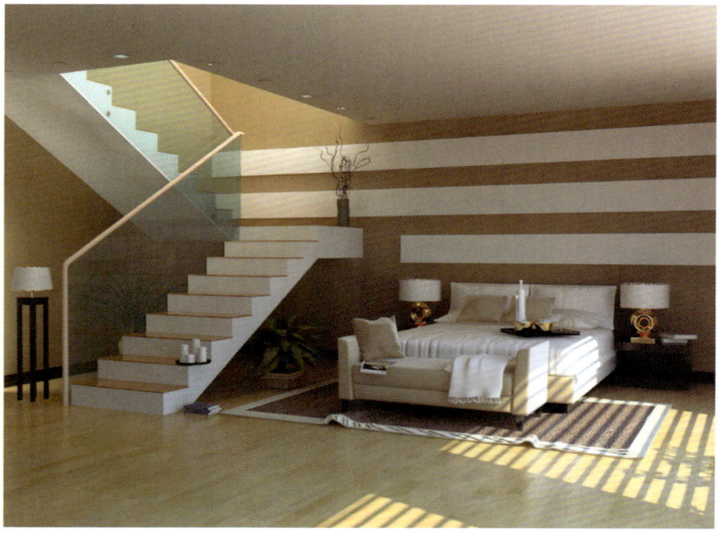

8.6 Choosing fabrics or surfaces for clothes and habitats is a very intimate gesture. The designs are experience directly on someone's skin. Consider the feel of being in these two bedrooms. The surface textures, the space, and even the colors combine in a three-dimensional physical experience that is also emotional. (Which would you rather sleep in? Why?)

Sources: L: © Andreas von Einsiedel/Alamy; R: © YAY Media AS/Alamy

SPACE IN DESIGN

In Chapter 3, we looked at space in design, especially in terms of how 2D and 3D space relate. Here we will consider 3D in its own right, as an experience, and as such as the experience of motion through time. The same applies to space in three dimensions as it does in the illusion of space in two dimensions. There is an experience of positive space and negative space. Again, this is not a statement of value but instead indicates the space where there is something versus that where there is nothing. In design, the simple juxtaposition of positive and negative—something and nothing—can create a number of illusions and allows the creation of an emotional quality in a space. Our bodies themselves may become the positive element within a negative space, such as when placed on a stage or in relation to furniture. The relationship of body and object is an experience that creates a sense of comfort. What also defines space in our experience is the motion we experience either by going through it or even by simply imagining our traversing it.

The illusions of space as outlined in Chapter 3 come into play as a way of experiencing actual space by moving through it: size, vertical location, front/back, and perspective. Objects' apparent sizes change as we move toward or away from them. Apparent vertical location as seen on our visual plane moves up or down. We get a full sense of *in front* and *behind* as we move around or past objects. Perspective shifts with even the smallest movement of our heads and eyes. It is very likely more valid to interpret space from experience of motion to two dimensions as it is the other way around—to understand what we see in three-dimensional motion from that of our experience in viewing a two-dimensional plane. It is simply our learned familiarity with interpreting images and our constant referral to two dimensions that makes it natural to see the world in 2D before we understand it in 3D. But understanding space in design requires both.

The sum of this thinking is that when a designer considers three-dimensional spaces—large or small, personal, social, or public—space and motion are inextricable and experience in time is therefore a factor to be considered in the relationship of the body moving in and through space. Also, the perception of space as the result of an experience implies that the spatial illusions in 2D design should be thought of as the actual 3D forms they imply. Finally, the body is the measure of all human experience, and this applies especially clearly to spatial experience. We are a three-dimensional being operating in time. This brings us to the new space that is increasingly a part of people's lives all over the world: virtual space (Fig. 8.7).

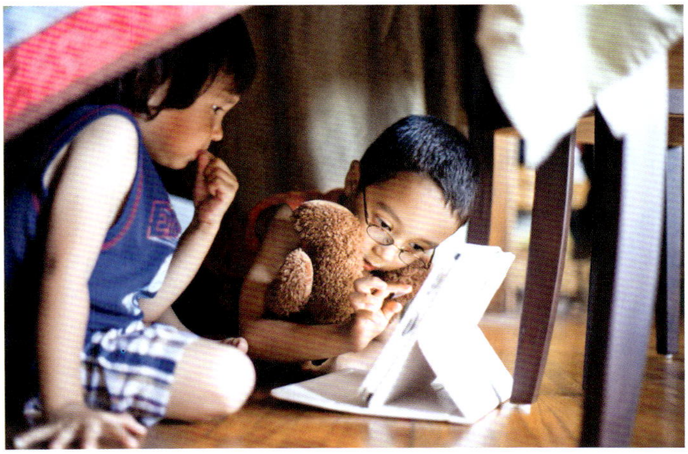

8.7 The late 20th century introduced a new space that is increasingly a part of people's lives all over the world: virtual space. The experience of being in virtual space seems to engage the same centers in our brains as those that get activated by real space. Our experience of the world changes as a result.

Source: © Adam Hester/Corbis

In virtual space the sense of movement comes strictly through the 2D illusions coupled with the sense of time passing. The experience of being in virtual space thus seems to engage the same centers in our brains as those that get activated by real space. Without the full dimensionality of the physical world to work with, the designing of virtual space must use the dimension of time to convey the motion and spatial quality of the environment. Using scale and position, for example, one gets a decent sense of placement, but the time factor of how quickly things move relative to each other also creates a sense of three dimensions. By creating the illusion of proximity to the viewer's body along with the fake perspective involved makes for a real experience in the virtual space, much as in an animated film.

POSITIVE AND NEGATIVE SPACE

In 3D space, the concept of positive and negative space becomes a critical issue compared to that of 2D space, as the negative space is now where the body operates. The negative *emptiness* of a designed 3D space is the place in which we are and where our bodies become the positive space itself. We travel within rooms, seat ourselves into cars, drape clothing around ourselves, and place our feet into shoes and our hands around, on, and within gadgets and equipment. (One might say that the negative of the space is something of a misnomer, as this is the space where actions take place, while the positive space is static.) As has been pointed out above, the body itself must not be forgotten in the equation. It becomes the measure of the negative and positive interaction and defines the effectiveness of the design by the reactions it becomes capable of within the space so defined. The sense of scale, the freedom or enclosure in buildings large or small, or the sense of comfort in an enveloping garment or piece of furniture can easily become its opposite through different experiences. One person's "snug and cozy" may well be another person's claustrophobic (Fig. 8.8).

Actual three-dimensional space is relative for the experience that it affords. Designing a space involves far more than simply geometric constraints, although they are of great consequence. The size of a space can have a very different statement by the inclusion or absence of any number of elements in the overall design. Colors, internal shapes, materials, and proportions can all influence the experience of a space in ways that might contradict expectations raised by the dimensions involved. An enormous space of polished steel obviously feels very different from the same space made of redwood or stone. The interior of a small tent evokes a very different response than the

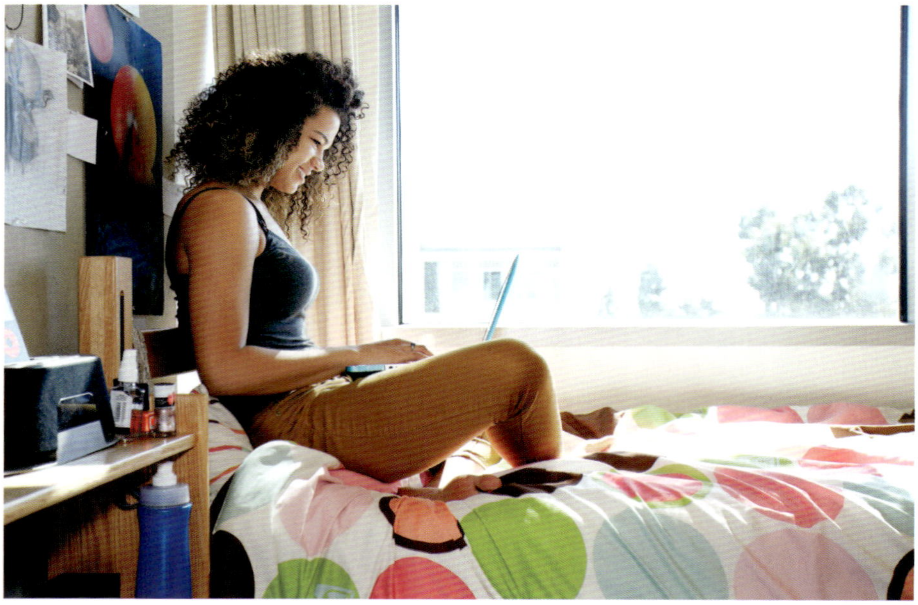

8.8 The sense of scale, and freedom or enclosure in a large or small room, or the sense of comfort in an enveloping garment or piece of furniture can easily become its opposite through different experiences. This young women sitting on her bed in a dorm room seems to be enjoying her moment, but on a bad day having nowhere else to sit may be irritating and uncomfortable.

Source: © Peathegee Inc/Blend Images/Corbis

interior of a paper box of the same size, and so on. The interior of a car might have a completely different appeal depending on the materials used or the color involved. The relative size of a room to its furniture may change the experience of both the room and the furniture, as well as the overall experience of being in the space. Even the number of people in a space can alter the dynamic and change how we behave and react.

PERSONAL SPACE

All space is in this way **personal space.** Navigating through the world, we are continuously aware of our surroundings and the distance between us and the people around us. The experience of this distance is an experience of the space itself as much as it is about the people and surrounding structures. Standing alone in an elevator makes the elevator into one thing, a second person makes it into another, and four more people completely alter the experience of the elevator space, even though the space itself is, in a strictly geometric sense, the same. But this sense is only in the abstract. The actual space is only the experience of the space, and the designing of it must take that into account. There is no getting away from the human element that contributes to the dialogue between body and object and body and other bodies. Personal space is in this way a variable in designing, and the design must accommodate the varying experience of the person and persons involved. The etiquette of personal space varies from culture to culture, and the distance between people may therefore create a very different level of comfort in different places and situations (Fig. 8.9).

8.9 The etiquette of personal space varies from culture to culture and the distance between people may therefore create a very different level of comfort in different places and situations. The proximity of body to body is usually negotiated carefully and without words.

Source: © CKDJ/Corbis

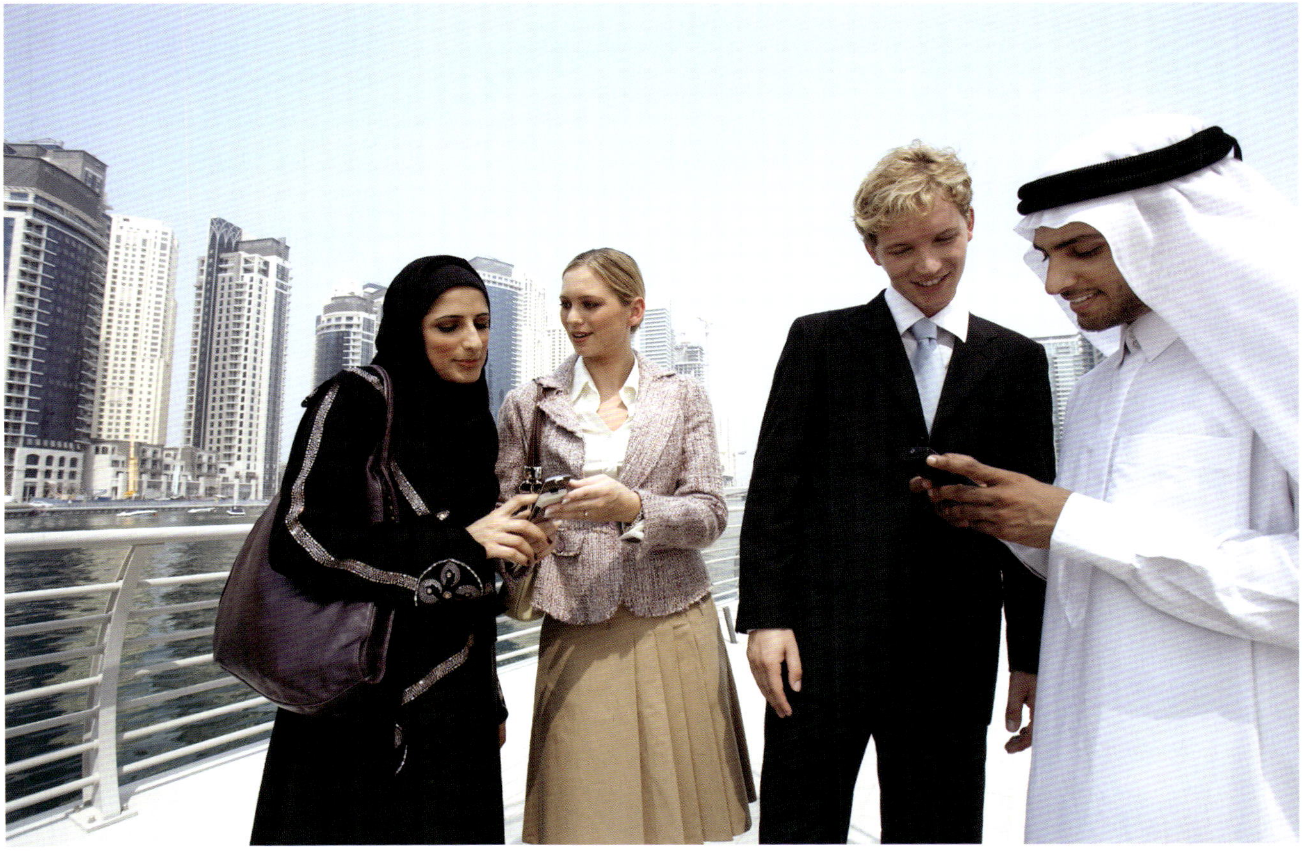

NETWORKING

SKETCHUP

A free downloadable 3D design software package from Trimble.

www.sketchup.com

THE GUARDIAN'S 10 BEST THEATRE DESIGNS

A theater critic chooses ten sets that changed the face of modern theater.

www.theguardian.com/stage/gallery/2011/may/22/set-theatre-design-in-pictures

DESIGNSPIRATION.NET

A design community where users share their inspiration.

www.designspiration.net

THE MUSEUM OF ARTS AND DESIGN

The museum that "explores the intersection of art, craft and design today."

www.madmuseum.org

STANFORD ENCYCLOPEDIA OF PHILOSOPHY

Theories of space and motion. As much as you might want to know and more!

plato.stanford.edu/entries/spacetime-theories

Designers can take advantage of this inherent relationship of humans to space by playing with scale. Over- or undersized objects create a different sense of proximity by altering our sense of self in the environment, and by creating an instinctive reaction of feeling big or tiny makes our relationship to the space and other people in it different. Sitting next to someone in an oversized couch can, for example, create a totally different sense of closeness to the other person than sitting on a small bench. The creation of intimate space is more powerful in the enveloping scale of the couch, while the proximity on the small bench has a more uncomfortable sense of personal intrusion connected to it. Putting the ceiling of an elevator higher makes for a sense of larger personal space by placing an extra bit of "breathing room" above the passengers' heads. However, this is again based on cultural presumptions that may or may not be accurate. The *correct* distance between people varies, and the appropriateness of touching strangers inadvertently is very different in different environments.

PROXEMICS AND MOTION

The anthropologist Edward T. Hall devised the term **proxemics** to discuss the phenomena of how we use space as a manifestation of local culture and practices. He divided personal space into four increasingly close areas, from *public* space to *social, personal,* and *intimate.* Each one of these has a distance that is variable depending on culture and relationships. Intimate, for example, is being within touchable distance of a person, but whether the touch is appropriate or invited is dependent on acceptable norms, the social and relationship context, and so on. The general division is, however, extremely helpful when the designer is considering the designing of spaces, especially where the different ranges meet. For example, defining a space where all four come into play, such as a restaurant, may require the definition of subspaces and areas in order that the patrons may feel private and intimate in a space that is essentially social and public. We can also consider the privacy of a seat in an airplane or movie theater, or the definition of private space in a place of business, by placing panels and glass walls that create personal space even while maintaining the integrity of the public space. Even the scale and

8.10 Personal space can be created and signaled by clothing. The scale and proportion of outfits creates a sense of separation from the local environment and thereby create a sense of intimate space right around the body.

Source: Satirical cartoon by Honoré Daumier, 1856

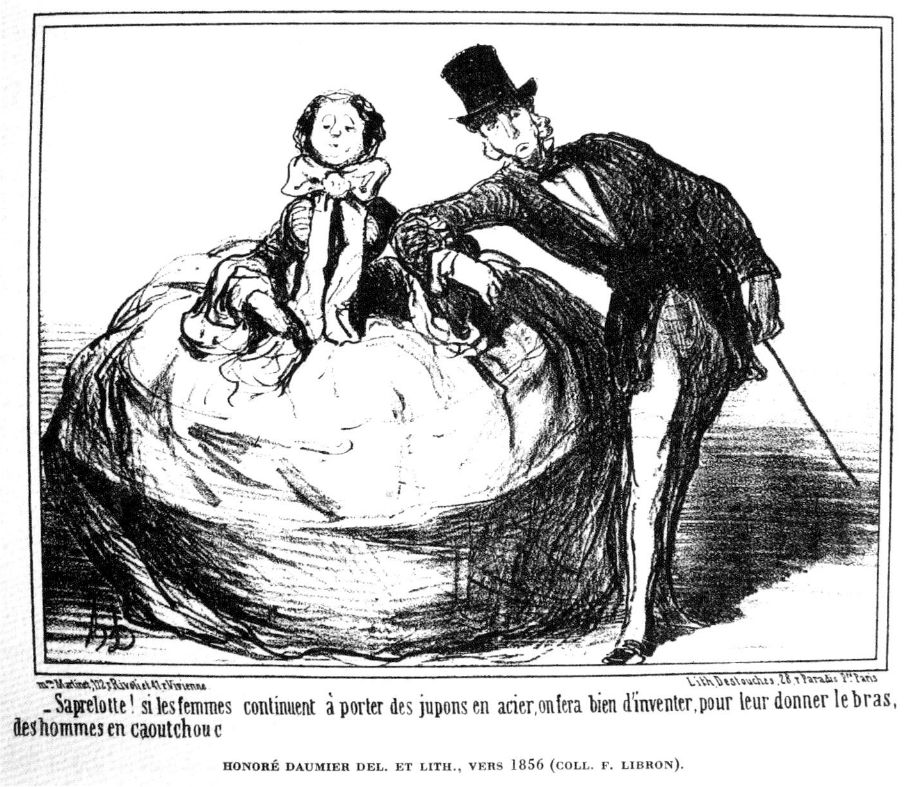

proportion of clothing may create a sense of separation from the local environment and thereby create a sense of intimate space right around the body (Fig. 8.10).

CONCLUSION

Space and motion are intimately connected. It is clear that space needs to be viewed as an experience in time and not an abstract geometric entity. Space *is* the sense of moving through it, regardless of whether the movement is real, implied, or imagined. The space in a 2D design is in this way as valid as the actual 3D space that one may view from a distance or move through. The feeling of being in the space, as created in the mind of the viewer, from the impulses supplied by the designer, is what allows the space to exist as an aesthetic force. The experience of inhabiting the space becomes the reality of the space at that moment. This is the choreography of positive and negative space that a designer must consider when putting together an interior—the choreography of objects within and bodies moving through. This is also the emotional moment of placing oneself into a garment, chair, or vehicle. Being able to project this experience is what makes for a good design.

KEY TERMS

- 2D design
- 3D design
- Symmetry (of the human body)
- Personal space
- Proxemics

DISCUSSION AND REVIEW QUESTIONS

1. In a similar but opposite vein to the previous chapter, translate the concepts, elements, and principles observed in a two-dimensional design (e.g., graphic, poster, logo, etc.) into three dimensions. (If you can create a mock-up, all the better.) What changes? How can you interpret textures or add dimensions and space? How might gravity and construction cause problems if the structure was larger?

2. Pick an item of furniture. What is your experience of it *physically* as opposed to visually interpreted? If touching it, interacting with it, or moving around it, what would be your experience with it? What does it *do*? How is it designed with the human body in mind?

3. Consider a public space. How is it designed to allow a positioning of people in a way that serves a purpose? How does it succeed and/or fail at this? What could be improved through redesign?

EXERCISES AND ASSIGNMENTS

1. Create a logo for an imaginary company by assembling geometric shapes (e.g., circle, square, triangle, rectangle) cut from colored paper. Then create the same concept in three dimensions from whatever materials you choose.

   a. How would you describe the difference as an *experience*?

   b. Does the three-dimensional design work from all angles? Why? Why not?

   c. Identify the most attractive and least attractive angles. What are the spatial qualities that determine your choice?

   d. Now photograph the three-dimensional design from what you consider the best angle. Translate the picture into a two-dimensional design. How has the design developed from the original. What effect did the *three-dimensionalizing* have?

2. Consider a classroom (you may be in one or you can think of one you know; if you don't have one, pick any meeting room or assembly hall you know), and explain what would need to change it were redesigned for:

   a. 10 percent of the people it now holds

   b. Ten times the people it now holds

   c. A virtual space for online interaction

   Describe what conclusions you draw from the above about whether the original room is good design or not.

3. Consider your own personal space.

   a. How close is too close?

   b. How does this change for different people? (Consider at least three.)

   c. How does this change for different situations? (Consider at least three.)

   d. What to you is a comfortable space? Why? How would you design the perfectly comfortable space to share with one other person you don't know?

CHAPTER 9

TIME AND EXPERIENCE: DESIGN *AND* CULTURE/DESIGN *IN* CULTURE

DESIGNERS SPEAK

"You look at where you're going and where you are and it never makes sense, but then you look back at where you've been and a pattern seems to emerge. And if you project forward from that pattern, then sometimes you can come up with something."

—ROBERT M. PIRSIG, *Zen and the Art of Motorcycle Maintenance,* (New York: HarperCollins, 2009), 167–168.

"It's a good feeling to actually know that there's stuff selling and it's not stuck in some showroom for the press to look at. It's got to be wearable. What's the point in doing it otherwise? I mean, you want to see people on the street wearing it."

—ALEXANDER MCQUEEN, interview, *GQ,* October 2007. http://www.gq-magazine.co.uk/men-of-the-year/home/hall-of-fame/alexander-mcqueen-fashion-designer-interview-2007 (accessed 7/27/2013).

OBJECTIVES

Distinguish the different levels of experience that people have in time.

Identify ways in which time is a factor when considering designs.

Grasp the meaning of *usability* in relation to designs.

Understand the concepts behind perceptions of usefulness and beauty in design and how they may be understood as experience.

Recognize the different ways in which we experience a new design over time.

Introducing experience over time as an element of design, this chapter follows with a presentation of practical aspects of time and perception in relation to usability and user satisfaction. Issues of human perception and memory are brought to bear, leading to the idea that in a culture of design, designers influence the culture by designing for a lived experience.

TIME AND EXPERIENCE

User experience and interaction requires a discussion of time. To fully appreciate how a user engages with a design, the designer must consider the very nature of time in human experience. In this way a designer may create more engaging designs by taking advantage of these structures and the different modes of perception. This, however, cannot simply be an abstract discussion of the nature of time, as if in a physics textbook, but rather a look at fundamental structures that lie behind our ability to experience anything at all. A designer must recognize how time is essential in molding and forming experience.

First, we will consider briefly how prevalent and recurring *time* is in design discussions. The word italicized are already an indication of one important point. There is more than one understanding of time involved, making it necessary to take a closer look. The different aspects of time are different forces influencing user experience. We will see how time is involved in the understanding of culture by being the necessary framework within which we understand the identities being formed throughout the creation and use of designs.

Rhythm and patterns also are functions of time, experienced as sequences. This can be a way for a designer to set up a dialogue with the viewer that relies only on wordless communication of sensory detail. Finally, designers must understand that experience of the world comes through the lived body as it moves and encounters things and experiences in space over time. The experience of 3D space is a function of time, as space is understood in relation to the human body as the body moves and anticipates moving through it, encountering things and other bodies.

CLOCK TIME VERSUS LIVED TIME

Experience of design is in **lived time.** What this simple notion brings is the first distinction to make when considering time as a factor in design. There is **clock time,** which is scientific. This is the time of seconds, minutes, and hours, the time of calendars, historical chronologies, and timelines. It is both measured and used for measurement, but not time as we experience it. This is time as we organize it and contain it precisely because we do not normally experience it as discrete measured units any more than we experience three-dimensional space as feet and inches.

Then there is the other time, the time of lived experience, or *sensory time.* This is the time we sense in our being and the time of thought and memory—the kind of time that is adapted to the narrative of whatever is going on in a situation even as it is being experienced. Time drags, speeds up, and even seems frozen in a particular memory or framing of an event. We interpret experiences even as we are going through them, and in doing so, we allow a creation to take place. The interpretation of events as they are happening or in hindsight allows a stretching or shrinking of time to suit the observation needed for our internal narrative. This kind of time may be characterized as the time of storytelling and mythology. Note that sensory time *includes* clock time. Clock time is a subset of the way we as natural beings sense and experience events taking place.

EXPERIENCING TIME

A short tangent is in order at this point, to observe how we actually seem to experience time passing. The image in Figure 9.1 shows a simplified version of the way the philosopher Maurice Merleau-Ponty describes the process. We experience time as a function of our ability to anticipate on one hand and to remember on the other. In the space between anticipation and memory is the moment that we describe as *now* but in fact is continually being shifted into the just-experienced past and from there into memory or the past.

The future is just a bit trickier, as it does not actually exist as such. The diagram is not meant to imply that the future is out there waiting to be funneled into existence. It is simply that the current experience, the *now,* allows us—once we have a sense of cause and effect and a sense of continuity—to anticipate what is next. We turn a page of a book and fully expect (without thinking) to see the text continue and the next word in the sentence to be there. (Without this, reading would be very confusing.) Or a ball gets thrown and we have a sense of its trajectory even before we see it land—a skill essential to all ball playing.

This may seem like a rather wild tangent in the context of an introduction to design, but in fact it is very relevant in terms of understanding the flow of experience that creates the relationship of people, their surroundings, and the items they encounter and use. The constant layering of experience onto itself as we continually move the now into the past becomes a way of understanding how an audience relates to a design: The object is anticipated, encountered, seen, learned, incorporated into experience, and included in an individual's world framework. A designer, especially in the current culture of immediate information and interactive technology, must have an instinctive sense of how the audience reacts to—and forms a relationship with—the designed object, environment, or space.

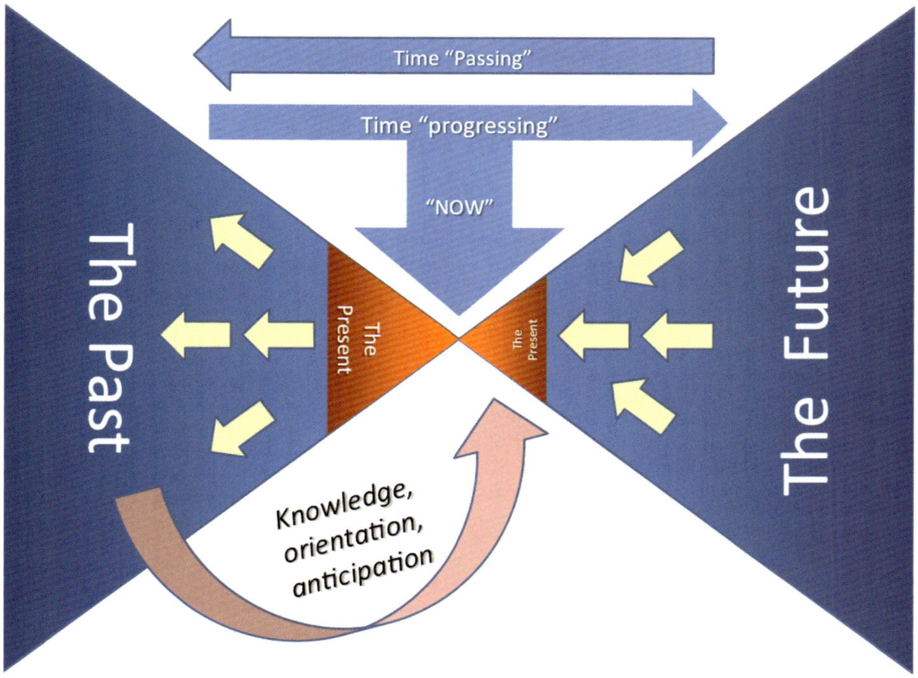

9.1 This graphic represents a basic approach to which philosopher, Maurice Merleau-Ponty describes the process of experiencing time. We experience time as a function of our ability to anticipate on one hand and to remember on the other. In the space between anticipation and memory is the *moment* that we describe as *now* but in fact is continually being shifted into the just-experienced past and from there into *memory* or *the past*. The current experience, *the now,* then allows us—once we have a sense of cause and effect and a sense of continuity—to anticipate what is coming.

Source: Illustration by Karl Aspelund

TIMELINE: ON "USEFULNESS"

- **1750:** Jean-Jaques Rousseau complains about the lack of an appreciation of utility, equating it with truth and virtue: "We no longer ask if a man has integrity, but if he has talent, nor whether a book is useful but if it is well written. The rewards for a witty man are enormous, while virtue remains without honor." (*Discourse on the Arts and Sciences*)
- **1853:** John Ruskin writes that the first architectural virtue is "that [a building] act well, and do the things it was intended to do in the best way." (*The Stones of Venice,* Vol. I Ch. II)
- **1880:** William Morris says: "Believe me, if we want art to begin at home, as it must, we must clear our houses of troublesome superfluities that are forever in our way: conventional comforts that are no real comforts, and do but make work for servants and doctors: If you want a golden rule that will fit everything, this is it: Have nothing in your houses that you do not know to be useful or believe to be beautiful." (*Hopes and Fears for Art,* Ch. 3)
- **1920:** Le Corbusier (Charles-Édouard Jeanneret-Gris): "If we eliminate from our hearts and minds all dead concepts in regard to the house, and look at the question from a critical and objective point of view, we shall arrive at the 'House Machine', the mass-production house, healthy (and morally so too) and beautiful in the same way that the working tools and instruments which accompany our existence are beautiful. Beautiful also with all the animation that the artist's sensibility can add to severe and pure functioning elements." (*Towards a New Architecture: Guiding Principles*)
- **Mid-20th Century:** Charles Eames: "We've always been aware of not . . . attempting to solve the problem of how people should sit, but rather accepting the way people do sit . . . and operating within that framework." (From *100 Quotes by Charles Eames*)
- **1980s:** Dieter Rams: "Good Design Makes a Product Useful: A product is bought to be used. It has to satisfy certain criteria, not only functional, but also psychological and aesthetic. Good design emphasizes the usefulness of a product whilst disregarding anything that could possibly detract from it." (*Ten Principles of Good Design*)

EXPERIENCE *IN TIME*

Within the framework of time and experience as described in this text there are four basic stages of user interaction in forming a relationship with the world of objects and experiences (all of which in modern society are *designed* in one way or another as products, systems, or environments). First, there is the *initial impact*, the first encounter with the design and the time for first impressions. In terms of design, now is when the audience (or end user) forms the desire to engage, to know more, to be in contact, to own, to operate or to experience what has appeared. The initial impact is a moment that is not in clock time, but in sensory time so it may or may not be short or instant. It is simply the time when the experience is completely new. However, the designer's problem is to make sure that the newness in that moment isn't so overwhelming that the experience is off-putting or overwhelming. There must be a level of familiarity that allows engagement, even when presenting something completely new.

Points of reference must be available for the users so they may appreciate the design as something known and encounter it without having to completely reorient their frame of knowledge beyond a certain level of comfort. Designers of high fashion will, for example, often play with the disorienting of audiences in this way (Fig. 9.2). What the disorientation may be depends on the situation. However, a good example of the opposite orientation might be the introduction of touch screens on handheld devices and computers and how they initially emulated *buttons* and other physical hardware to give the users a familiar place to encounter the new technology.

RIGHT

9.2 Designers of high fashion often play with disorienting their audiences. Known elements and recognizable forms are presented out of context or in a new situation, such as the undergarment structures seen here, presented as luxury garments. This allows an appreciation of the design, but not a complete reorienting of frames of knowledge beyond a certain level of comfort. It is new and startling, but not uncanny. Spring RTW 2013 Sarah Burton for Alexander McQueen.

Source: Giovanni Giannoni/WWD

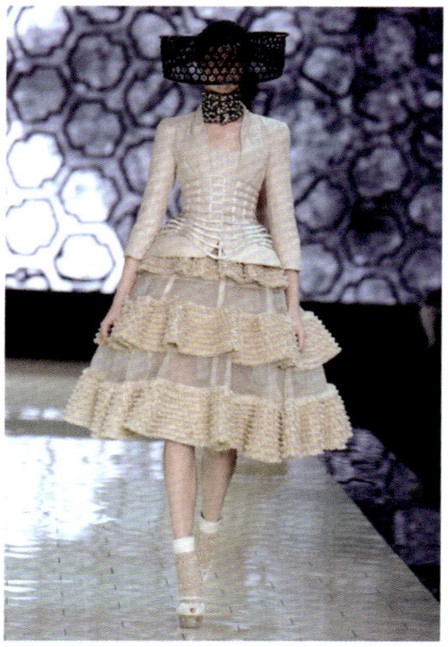

The user then forms a *relationship* with the design over time, and this is the next stage of experience. As the relationship progresses and solidifies, the user becomes comfortable and habituated to the situations offered, and any initial discomfort or hesitation disappears. Familiarity and habit take over, and this is where new versions of the design may be introduced and be accepted, as the design is considered *safe.* Soon the design has an *identity* in the world and is fully incorporated into the worldview of the users. People stop questioning it, challenging it, or wondering over it. It is in the realm of memory and is *known.*

The design can now be a reference for other similar experiences or even a baseline for the introduction of new designs and new encounters. It then gets to the ultimate stage of the relationship of experience in which it becomes *familiar.* Through repetition, commonality, and, ultimately, ubiquity, the design is now fully incorporated into the world frame and requires no introduction or instruction. It is recognized and passed over, and may in fact become so familiar as to almost disappear. The moment of initial encounter has faded from memory. Even forks, cups, and doorknobs required some introduction, learning, and habituation at some stage in everyone's life. Very few of us remember this each time they are encountered again.

DIFFERENT TIME DEMANDS

Different designs present different time demands. One distinction is determined by the amount of time the design demands of us. Another is how the experience of the design enhances its value over time. There are objects that are initially absorbed into our lived experience almost instantly, through a combination of our senses. The totality of the design is experienced in a moment of encounter or recognition, such as when a garment is tried on or a new chair is tested out.

With the exception of designs that are momentary experiences in themselves (rides in amusement parks, fine dining), the initial moment of absorption gives way to a longer moment of familiarity, a continuing experience. The experience of the design is repeated and becomes a part of the framework of daily life (whatever that means in the context of the user). There are other experiences that put this into relief. Consider the difference between (a) the experience of seeing a tool or gadget, (b) holding it, and then (c) using it. The design may appeal to the visual sense immediately; take a longer moment to register in the hand for feel and heft and how comfortably it responds. Then the longer time frame takes over as habitual usage becomes a part of daily operations and certain benefits or concerns are revealed over time. Perhaps it would be better in a different weight or material; maybe the surfaces begin to wear out; perhaps the use goes well only in certain circumstances and not in others that are less common. This interaction and experience over time, through revisiting and reuse allows the identification and conceptualizing of new implementation and perhaps new designs altogether. The designer must be aware of these factors both in creating new designs and in analyzing old ones. "What worked?" is a good question. "What worked when, how, in what time frame?" although not as snappy, is better.

USABILITY

A primary constraint of designing is that of **usability.** The design must be experienced by the end user or audience to be as accessible as possible. What this means is defined by the time frame in which such accessibility is evaluated and measured. A good design may be immediately recognized as such in the moment of initial encounter, or it may need a longer time of repeated and complete interactions over longer time periods. The user experience may be practical (strict usability), or it may be emotional, derived from the satisfaction with its performance. This has been phrased traditionally as a guiding principle of design in that designing is about creating that which is both **useful and beautiful.** (The definitions of which can become slightly problematic, as will be discussed later.)

Usability is the concept that allows a framing of the ease into which the user enters into a proficient interaction with the design. Since the early 20th century, the industrialized world has become largely habituated if not entirely dependent on the ability to interact with all manner of devices, products, and physical and virtual environments. How the interaction takes place and what it is meant to produce can range anywhere from the satisfaction derived from a basic consumer product to the efficient functioning of a complex interactive system of devices and people, such as the designing of a city. But is there a way to encapsulate such diverse experiences in such different circumstances of so varied a nature?

PRACTICAL AND EMOTIONAL EXPERIENCE

First, let us examine the more straightforward notion of practical experience. This is usually what is thought of when usability is discussed, but it is not the whole picture of user experience. Practical experience may come closer to defining usefulness, as what is generally considered useful in our culture is that which is practical. This again may require questioning of how, why, and when it is practical and to what end. But largely the usability of a design is a measure of how well we can approach it, engage with it, and rely on it to do what it is supposed to do. In terms of practical, we find that the design has functioned well. A bicycle, for example, can give a good practical experience by simply getting you where you needed to go in suitable comfort, safely and without breaking down. As a whole, its practical purpose is successful and serves well as such. But perhaps the mechanisms didn't function well, the wheels were not of the right type for a city bike, or the brakes were too weak for the size and speed involved. The usefulness of the bike is relatively unimpaired, but the usability is less than it could be. The experience of riding the bike was not satisfactory due to a number of design decisions that didn't add up to a good totality. *Useful* is a quality, but usability is an experience. There is clearly space between the usability of a design and usefulness of it. User satisfaction is what this concern comes down to in the process of designing.

When considering usability, we must take into account more than the simple binary of success or failure of the practical function of the design. It may work, but

SUSTAINABILITY: TIME AND EXPERIENCE

Time in design has everything to do with sustainability. When we design for sustainability, we attempt to design for the entire life cycle of the product. We must, in other words, consider the movement of its elements thought time. From the gathering or harvesting of materials through manufacture, markets, use, reuse, and recycling, the designed object must be seen as a series of elements on a journey through time rather than a product of only one end-stage. This requires a shift in the designer's thinking; the product, as such, must be perceived as temporary (limited in time), whereas its components and materials must be considered to be more permanent and have a time-wise trajectory that is far larger than the consumer product they lend themselves to for the limited time. If a designer, for example, considers the material for an object not just in terms of the current use but also its past use and its future use, then designing has a whole new dimension and the challenge of sustainability becomes built into the journey of materials though time. A game with polyester, for example: a plastic bottle becomes a jacket that becomes a shirt that becomes a park bench. The park bench will live the longest, but it too could be melted down.

not well. The function may be satisfactory, but a particular component caused trouble and so on. There is also a continuum of emotional responses to the experience of an object, system, or environment that can range from complete satisfaction to complete frustration. These responses derive from whether the design is fulfilling the defined needs within the required constraints of the problem. There are many degrees between completely fulfilled needs and complete failure, depending on the time frame involved or the repetition of the experience. The emotional response of *never works* may simply mean *never works well;* the statement "always works" may mean *never breaks down* but not *always works well.* And to complicate matters, in a field this varied, designing screwdrivers, cocktail gowns, or transit systems, what actually is meant by *works* may be very hard to pin down. When is a design good design?

THE USEFUL AND THE BEAUTIFUL

For over a century a catchphrase of the nature of good design has included the words *useful* and *beautiful.* William Morris, for example, stated in a lecture in 1880 that the key was to have "nothing in your houses that you do not know to be useful, or believe to be beautiful" (Fig. 9.3). Instinctively, we can relate to these statements, but on closer examination, we note that the words are wide open to interpretation. What is useful and what is beautiful is dependent on a number of factors. The relative usefulness of a design immediately makes the statement difficult (as we wondered earlier about the "usefulness" of a cocktail dress.) Usefulness may have to be defined; beauty is an extremely difficult and disputed definition to pin down. It is culturally, situationally, and personally open to interpretation and very specific to context. Consider, for example, the notion of a beautiful hammer. We may not immediately recognize the beauty of it, but a carpenter could instantly describe the beauty of a particular hammer and compare it favorably with another. No one questions the usefulness of the hammer, however. On the same plane one might see the complete usefulness of a design such as a manila envelope, but would one necessarily be attracted to its beauty? Conversely, the beauty of a piece of jewelry may be evident, while its usefulness could be debated. What *is* usefulness? What *is* beauty? These are the questions we must ask. And the

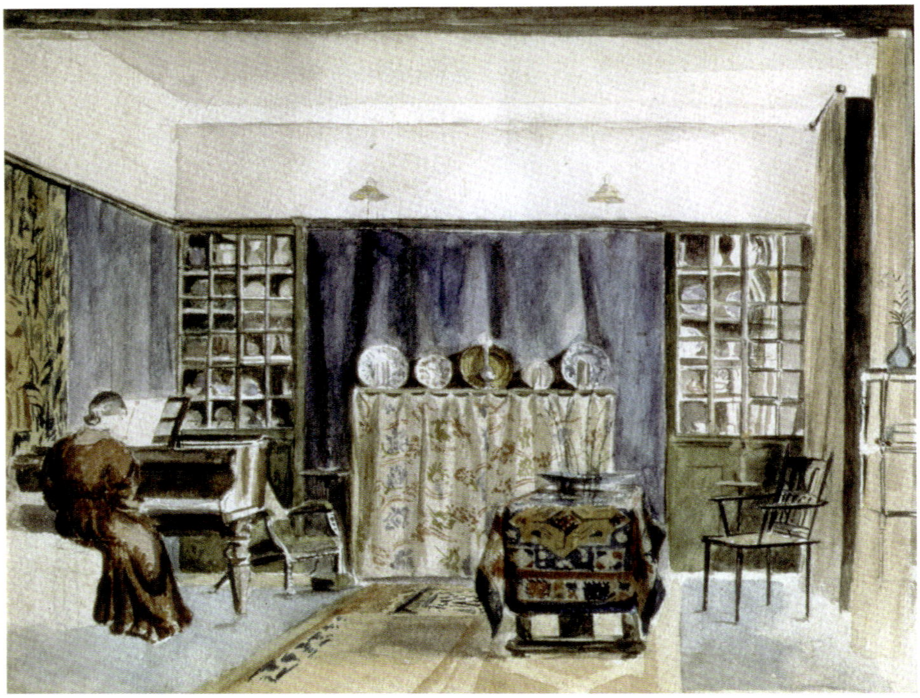

9.3 William Morris (1834–1896), the designer and writer, stated in 1880 that the key was to have "nothing in your houses that you do not know to be useful, or believe to be beautiful." In his watercolor from the parlor of his house Kelmscott Manor, one can see a simplicity of design.

Source: Interior of Kelmscott Manor (watercolor on paper), Morris, William (1834–1896)/Private Collection/The Stapleton Collection/The Bridgeman Art Library

answer may lie in Morris's use of the words *your* and *you.* Perhaps the fact that both are relative accounts for the difficulty in discussing the purpose and meaning of design and that in order to appreciate statements like Morris's, we must look at a larger and slightly more complicated framework.

NEED AND CONSTRAINTS

To begin, it is necessary to look at the framing of design as a creative act that aims to fulfill a certain set of designated needs within a set of defined constraints. The needs come from a problem, a situation, or a desire that is articulated by a client that can be an individual, corporation, social group, or any entity that can express a need for a product or system that fulfils the need. The constraints come from the situation but also from the desired solution itself in that it must be of a certain nature. Some may be very basic, and seem obvious, such as the constraint of designing a chair that requires it to have a surface on which one may sit, or the designing of a jacket that requires it to envelope the upper body. When considering the constraints of a design, one looks for the elements without which the thing is not the thing itself. A cup that cannot contain anything is not a cup but the semblance of a cup, a jacket that cannot be worn is only symbolic of a jacket, and so on (Fig. 9.4).

The *hierarchy of design needs,* as discussed in Chapter 1, shows us the basic level of engagement with a designed object regards its *functionality*, where the design has to actually do what it is supposed to in order to begin to be considered good design. (If this seems extreme to you, consider the number of things you have owned that began their time with you by falling apart, tearing, crashing your computer, etc.) With that out of the way, *reliability* is the next step before getting to *usability*. After that, two steps brought us to *proficiency*, and ultimately *creativity*. Respectively, those two stages of the hierarchy are where designs are improving and even changing our lives. What becomes evident in looking at the hierarchy from the viewpoint of experience is that it represents in effect a heightening of the user experience over time. The *user-friendliness* of the design reaches a middle point in *usability*, after which the interaction with the design begins to become a transformative experience. A gadget allows better communication, a road system allows better transportation, and a garment allows more efficient movement or shelter. Then over time, the expectation of the performance of similarly designed objects or systems becomes embedded in the culture.

The notion of designing for user experience is ultimately about designing for the interaction of the user with the design over time. Whether the design's appeal is about being useful or beautiful or some combination thereof, there are three basic relationships involved: the relationship between the designer and the end user, that of the end user and the designed object or environment, and that of the end user and the internalized experience or memory of the design or environment. The unifying agent in all three is the end user, and it therefore becomes obvious that the designer must have the user's needs and eventual experience firmly in mind even as the analysis of the design project begins.

For example, the design of a garment must allow for the knowledge of the client's needs, the way in which the design will be used, and how the design will be experienced over time. Between the three, the needs and constraints of the design become clear, as do the possibilities for placing the design on the hierarchy of design needs from reliability to creativity.

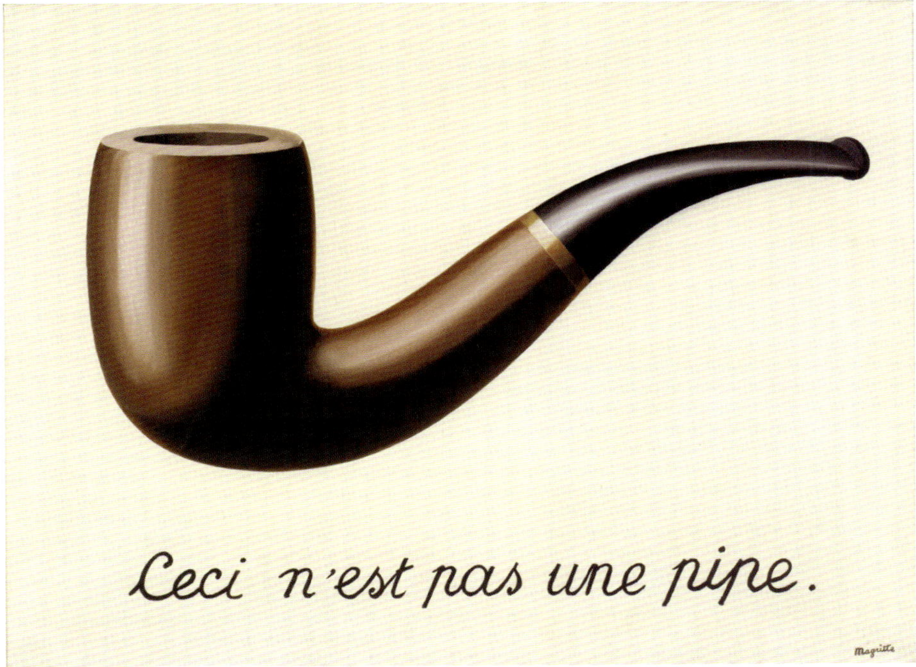

9.4 Is a pipe that cannot be smoked a pipe? Is the image of a pipe a pipe? A cup that cannot contain anything is not a cup, but the semblance of a cup. A jacket that cannot be worn is only symbolic of a jacket. *La Trahison des Images* ("The Treachery of Images," by René Magritte (1928–1929), Belgian artist. (Translation [French]: "This is not a pipe.").

Source: Digital Image ©2013 Museum Associates/LACMA. Licensed by Art Resource, NY © René Magritte Estate/ Artists Rights Society (ARS), New York/ ADAGP, Paris

ERGONOMICS: PERCEIVING TIME

It is an odd thing to think about time. We do not actually know time as we know space through tangible interaction. We only recognize time as a ordering of events and our sense of their separation. To incorporate time into our design thinking, we must consider how the design will be in time: how it will be used over time, how time will change the user's perception of it, and how time will change it. Changes over time can be seen to be both physical and in terms of a design's relevance. It may be a revolutionary concept or avant-garde fashion at first, but over time it becomes mundane and even old-fashioned, without having changed in itself. Physical changes may be for the better or for the worse. Wear and tear can be charming or detrimental to the viewer's experience. Interaction may create comfort, such as when something is worn in or it may be worn out. The designer must be aware not only of the effects of time's passing but also of the user's impression of time passing in relation to the designed object. Sometimes we see the trajectory and we say, "It won't last." Sometimes we desire a designed object for its newness, sometimes for its ability to age well.

BEAUTY AND THE LIVED EXPERIENCE

To aim designing at *the lived experience* is therefore really a reframing of basic functionalist design practices. The useful is fairly easily framed, if defined within the relevant area of needs for that particular end user and situation. The experience of the design is useful for the particular needs it is designed for and the constraints it must operate within. For example, a hammer is not useful for eating spaghetti, but no one would thereby argue that a hammer is useless; a longbow used to be useful in battle, but after the invention of more efficient weapons, that usefulness faded. Examples such as these could be formulated for any designed object. It is always the context that defines the usefulness. The philosopher Socrates is quoted as having said, "In general all things capable of being used by man are regarded as at once beautiful and good relatively to the same standard—the standing being in each case what the thing happens to be useful for."[1]

So, what of beauty? Where will beauty arrive from and how are we to define that? Which is most beautiful: the hammer, the spaghetti bowl, or the longbow? The question is meaningless without context. The usefulness of a design we have seen as being tied to the hierarchy of needs within constraints. It is also about context in a *lived experience.* Just as a relationship is formed with a design over time, bringing with it a sense of appreciation of its usefulness, a sense and appreciation of beauty also arrives with experience. Beauty *is* an experience, but a different *kind* of experience. Our sense of beauty is culturally determined; molded by family, education, and past experiences; and influenced by our surroundings and media.

If design is about the useful and beautiful, then there must be a beautiful conclusion at which we may arrive when designing. How to determine that this is so? When is one thing beautiful and another not? The perception of beauty is not objective, but at the same time, there are socially acceptable concepts at any given time, especially when it comes to art and design. However, ideals of beauty change, as anyone who pays attention to society will quickly notice. For nearly all of its history, Western society placed emphasis on the classical Greek and Roman notions of beauty in design, which implied strong symmetry and mathematical proportions of certain ratios. Recent decades have seen a shift away from these ideals with late-Modernism playing with asymmetries and odd proportions, as well as influences from cultures from all over

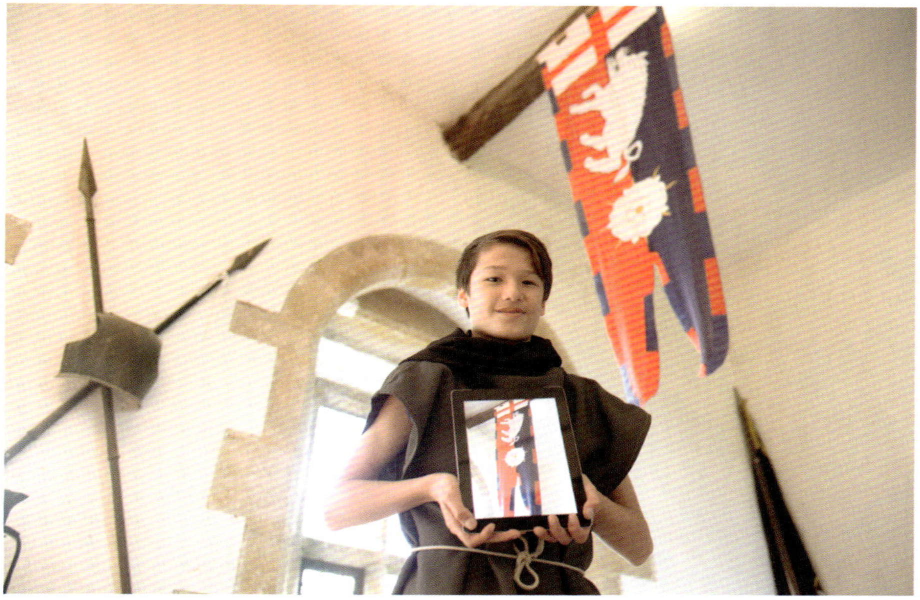

9.5 Time and experience have become compressed in the instant-information, multiconnected world of the Internet and digital imagery. The constant capturing and broadcasting of immediate experience in images changes the way in which the world is navigated and understood. When a moment is lived through a screen, rather than physical experience (such as when this student takes an instantaneous picture on a computer of the flag hanging above), the experience and sense of style and beauty are compressed into a moment on an image rather lived than over time. This changes the lived experience of the flag and the room and its history, with the development of multiple perspectives and contexts that time and memory allow.

Source: © Monty Rakusen/cultura/Corbis

the globe. Within cultures, ideals of beauty can change from one year to the next, especially after the modern media-driven culture took hold around the middle of the 20th century.

In the late 20th century, however, there appeared a tendency to consider all that was old to be of a beauty that could not be denied. Nostalgia and longing for a past became a guiding principle for design and taste-making. At the end of the 20th century, the method of *retro* referencing and the revitalizing of older styles became an established design direction in itself. Instead of looking for the *new new thing,* design critics would wonder what the *new old thing* would be. Our desire for the past appears in designs that appeal to nostalgia for a time before we were born or when we were very young, usually somehow associated with a time that is perceived as *better* on some (emotional) level. Each generation since the 1970s has, for example, had a wave of nostalgic design in clothing. The nostalgia has re-created the past in ever tightening circles. A decade into the 21st century, the nostalgia now overlaps with itself into a retro chic style of many facets. Time and experience have become compressed in the instant-information, multi-connected world of the Internet, and all the past is available at once. The experience of *current beauty* is therefore also compressed into many historical and multicultural notions of "beauty" (Fig. 9.5).

Given the experiential nature of aesthetic perception, this is very significant for design. Another notion of beauty is that it has to be observed from a distance—that there is a need for stepping back and appreciating the quality (whatever it may be) that creates the sense of beauty. In effect, this means that the perception of beauty has to be always remote, abstracted, and self-conscious. Since all styles are now viewable and available with varying degrees of detachment, the perception of beauty in design is no longer restricted, but is multilayered and situation-specific. Just as the media age has given us multiple futures to consider, it also has given us multiple pasts and multiple cultures, and with that, multiple images of beauty to attach to.

ATTACHMENTS AND THE LAYERING OF EXPERIENCE

We have compressed time and history, making all accessible at once. We are therefore able to create attachments to any and all styles and imagery that attracts us. So how does a designer navigate this territory? The designer in an environment where there is access to near-endless references and information must help the audience navigate. Again, time and experience are key. The designer must link concepts to the needs and constraints of the project but also link to the client's previous experience of similar designs. What do the clients know? What have they seen? What would startle them, comfort them, romance them? The designer must find the sense of history and memory that the end user will bring. For example, if one is designing an interior, will there be classical references? The occasional bit of décor from a childhood era for comfort? A complete break from the past to create a sense of now? An appeal to nostalgia does not have to be an appeal to memory; it can be an appeal to a mythological image or a fictional gilded version of a past era. Time and memory create its own version, and the search for the perfect past has become a way of dealing with the uncertain futures of the late modern age.

The interaction with the past of choice and the imagined future takes place on both an emotional and physical level. The designer can consider the experience of the audience and whether the references are relevant to their lives. This would make an enormous difference where direct physical contact matters, such as in interiors and clothing where the sense memory of a texture may convey a range of emotions. Conversely the negation of memory experience (say, a new material, with hitherto unseen properties) can create a sense of wonder and newness in an architectural environment or graphic design. It is important to consider what the audience will consider "the way it should be" and then navigate around that. There is no correct way of doing this; it depends entirely on the three-way relationship of the designer, the user, and the design. What is the game being played? There could be hidden cultural signals, fantastical references, or strict replaying of the past. Each in its own way will trigger a response.

Continuing along this train of thought, the response triggered can be within the frame of one of three kinds of experience. Knowing what elements will trigger which of these allows the designer to fully engage with the audience. The first and most basic of these would be the idea of a *shared experience*, where the designer inserts direct references to known and common cultural signs into the design. Certain patterns, elements, signs, and referents show up and create familiar territory. The dialogue and interaction with the design becomes about recognition and the sense of belonging that arrives from being part of a shared cultural framework: "These are the patterns of my childhood/my homeland/my college days/my ancestors," and so on.

The second level is also of cultural reference, but more personal, not relying on common signals but appealing to the personality of the intended audience or end user. Instead of recognizing common signs, the audience now recognizes a *totality* that is appealing. The totality (gestalt) is such that there is a connection of personality with the design: "This is the kind of thing that should belong to a person like me," or conversely, "this is where I belong, among such things." Finally, the references can be of a more immediate nature. In this case, the design may be of a nature that challenges the audience with innovative, new, or uncommon combinations of elements. The immediate sensory reaction becomes part of the dialogue and creates in the moment a lived

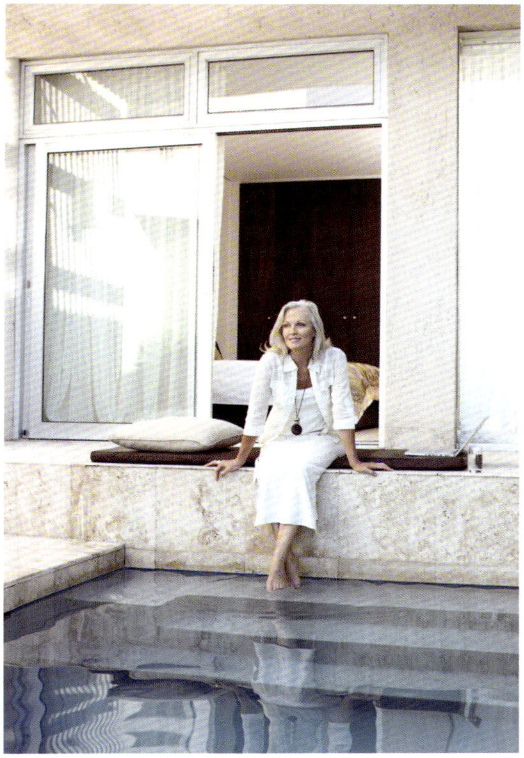

9.6 The color, the texture, the sound and feel of the water, and the marble surface encompassing the pool—any number of sensory cues can be built into a design.

Source: © Johannes Mann/Corbis

experience of the design. The moment, as was discussed above, is not a measured unit, but a period containing an experience, it is the interval experienced now (also known as **the specious present**). This can be understood as the experiencing of an interactive design, the viewing of an event, or indeed any moment of realization and recognition that the first encounter with sensory stimuli can produce. A flash of color, the light on a surface, the feel of fabric on the skin, the sound created by walking across a marble floor—any number of sensory cues can be built into a design (Fig. 9.6).

The layering of experience thus produces a totality that is created out of the design, the reaction to the design and its references, the use of the design, and the eventual familiarity and memory of the design. In addition, the totality over time may acquire a nostalgic feel of its own, or a comfort level that makes it into a classic. To anticipate this, the designer must perceive the creation as it exists through time and anticipate the memories it will create. There are four layers to keep an eye on to anticipate this: impact, knowledge, ownership, and familiarity. First, there is the initial *impact,* the very first encounter that evokes the multisensory experience in the now, that forms the threshold for a future experiences. Any design that will compete or overtake this one will have to produce a stronger first impression. Second, there is the acquisition of *knowledge*, where the relationship is formed and the user/observer takes *ownership* of the design. At this level, the position on the hierarchy of design is evaluated and the usability question comes to the fore. Then, with the design folded into the world of experience, it enters into the realm of *familiarity*, where the comfort of the known is in tension with the excitement of the new, and new designs can overtake the old if the loyalty to the design has not been strengthened already. Finally, *memory* allows new encounters with new situations. With the design "filed away" in unconscious knowledge, new designs can be experienced and referenced based on the knowledge of the previous experiences. Just like people only have one chance to make a first impression, there is only one chance for a new design. After your design becomes *known* and spawns competitors or is simply incorporated into the world, the familiarity cuts both ways. The user does not have to relearn anything for the next round, but the next round also must try harder to engage the user. Having already gotten over the excitement of the new, the user of the latest handheld gadget, fashion, car, or software expects the thrill of the first encounter to be repeated with new features or design tweaks in the next generation.

USER PERCEPTION, HABITS, AND MEMORY

The effect of time and experience on design is deeply engaged with user perception and memory. A designer that wishes to fully engage with an audience works with this by understanding the structures that evolve among and within people as they live their lives in society. A designer must look at the defining structures that are formed around us and within us as we mature as individuals with needs and constraints of our own. This is more than saying that we are creatures of habit. There are what the

NETWORKING

The following list contains practical websites for further information:

DIGITAL COMMUNICATIONS DIVISION, U.S. DEPARTMENT OF HEALTH AND HUMAN SERVICES
A site on best practices and guidelines for user-centered design of digital content. This site includes resources, bibliographies, and research plans.

www.usability.gov

JESSE JAMES GARRETT ON USER EXPERIENCE
JJG was way ahead of the curve on this and wrote one of the better and more accessible books on the topic of user experience. He comes at it from information architecture, but the discussion applies to all design.

www.jjg.net/ia/

THE WORLD USABILITY DAY CHARTER
"Technology should enhance our lives, not add to our stress or cause danger through poor design or poor quality."

worldusabilityday.org/charter

UNIVERSAL DESIGN RESOURCE LIST
Office for AccessAbility at the National Endowment for the Arts

www.nea.gov/resources/accessibility/rlists/UDesResources.html

French sociologist Pierre Bourdieu calls the "habitus," the structures that we operate in through being brought into the world in a specific place where things are done a certain way at certain times.[2] Think of waiting in line at a store counter, for example. This is not something you think about each time, wondering whether you should stand in line this time for this counter. Or think of unspoken dress codes in a school, workplace, or community. You do not wonder each day whether today is the day you might wear pajamas, a Halloween mask, or a swimsuit. Or how do you know how certain foods are appropriately eaten with a fork and others with your fingers? These are the things you simply know on some level. How and where you learn them is not necessarily clear. It's as if you absorb the knowledge as you grow and become who you are, but you do so through observation and instruction of various degrees of subtlety. You can then bring these codes into new situations and quickly adapt yourself (your *self*) to new structures in new places. ("I see. . . . This is how they do that, here.")

POLARITIES OF EXPERIENCE

Our ability to adapt to unseen structures affords a designer much room to play and intervene. One can work inside the structure or attempt to break it open and add to it. By identifying the structures involved, designs can be created to either support or disrupt the unspoken plans. On one hand, one can appeal to the known and comfortable routines. On the other, one can work to support the innate desire for novelty. The balance between the need for the known and the desire for novelty creates a set of experiential polarities that can drive design. Designers can play with this tension by placing their designs anywhere on the spectrum between them.

EMOTIONAL ATTACHMENT—EXCITEMENT OVER NOVELTIES

On one hand, the sense of belonging and self that we find from attachment to known things, things we've had for a while, and things we've grown up with. On the other, we have a sense of wanting new things, new experiences, and new ways of doing things. Designs on the edge are frequently either the familiar with a twist or the unfamiliar with a hint of the known. Being able to manipulate the experience of the design along this spectrum affords a quick and engaged reaction to the initial moment of encounter.

LONGING AND ANTICIPATION—SURPRISE AND SHOCK

We can easily fall into longing for an item or an experience. Luxury designs tend toward such longing, and a design problem is to not disappoint when the longing is fulfilled. There is an anticipation that builds for the use, touch, feel, and sense of the design, and when it happens, it must be of the caliber anticipated. To this end, the designer must be very aware of the history of such designs, the needs of the audience, and the conventions, standards, and myths that go with them. Designers mess with classics at their peril, but the shock of a successful manipulation can be very attractive to an audience.

SAFETY—CHALLENGE

Once people form an identity, they mostly tend to stay within its safe confines, only gradually reforming or slowly being reformed by surrounding structures. The safety afforded by the known is experienced on an individual level as well as in larger-scale interaction in society. We design into cultural norms that then mold us, and we operate within the safe confines of how things are. For the most part, radical changes are seen as disruptive. However, every so often, societies as well as individuals will be ready to respond to a challenge and will take up a new way of being by design. The change may come through technology, politics, unexpected cultural events, or the arrival of charismatic figures on the scene. Being able to spot a trend from *safe* to *switch* is a valuable design tool, and a designer who is aware of the forces operating in society is ahead of the game.

HOME—FOREIGN

Finally, there is in modern culture a strong drift toward the exploration of the *foreign* or exotic that is more than a historical remnant. There seems to be a playful side to our notions of identity that makes us attracted to the "other" even as we retreat into the safety of home. This is visible in storytelling from fairy- and folktales to science fiction and is reflected in the desire of cultures to take up foreign habits and practices and the subsequent reaction of cultural conservatives to reject such developments.

CONCLUSION

A way to encapsulate **culture** is to think of it as the things we do, the things we do them with, and how we do them *over time*. The time involved depends on the current situation and very often politics. In societies, a cultural shift usually has involved a significant time period, at least a generation or two, but often referring back to an uncertain or invented mythological past of forebears. However, the language allows for other more immediate framings such as a corporate culture, sports culture and so on. These are usually manufactured in a significantly shorter time frame. The definition, however, remains the same in practice: "We, here, do this, like this, and have done so since then."

Designing into a culture therefore requires an investigation into the history of it and its practitioners. Time and experience is what makes identities on both an individual and societal level. What are the long-term facts of the history and practice, what is the *current* practice? What are actually facts and what is mythology and storytelling? This may not really matter; just because a culture is *made up* at some point doesn't mean it isn't valid for its practitioners. In fact, the invention may have been triggered by a very meaningful need. Ritual and routine matter to people, and the objects, clothing, and surroundings in which they go through their activities give them meaning. Historical and cultural references in design must be understood as *lived* references, if they are not to be just meaningless décor. The lived experience over time creates identity, and designing creates the things, spaces, and systems in which the identities flourish and are maintained. This is the power of design in society.

KEY TERMS

- User experience
- Lived time
- Clock time
- Usability
- Useful and beautiful
- The specious present
- Culture

DISCUSSION AND REVIEW QUESTIONS

1. Pick a designed object that is familiar to you. How does someone encounter it in stages over time: (a) impact; (b) knowing; (c) familiarity? Describe how your relationship changes.
2. Think of three different designs that you encounter every day: an object, a system, and an environment. How has your experience of them changed over time? How would you characterize your *relationship* with them? How would you turn this into good information for a designer?
3. Look around the room you are in. Imagine (if you don't remember actually doing so) entering it for the first time. What would be the first thing you noticed? What would be the element to first become invisible to you?

EXERCISES AND ASSIGNMENTS

1. Consider your experience of a family or community holiday, religious or otherwise. Consider in terms of design:
   a. The comfort of sameness: What is always the same? Why? How?
   b. Recognition: What object immediately signals this holiday? How?
   c. Culture: Are any of these objects determined by a group or society with which you identify? Does this influence the design of the objects?

2. Then consider:

   a. What is the relevance of designed objects to your experience?

   b. What are these and why are they significant?

   c. What is significantly sensory? Which senses are involved?

   d. What is important by nostalgia or familiarity?

   e. Has anything ever changed radically? If so, how did that affect you?

REFERENCES

1. Xenophon. *Memorabilia [Book III, VIII]*. Translated by H. D. Dakyns. British Columbia, Canada: Blackdog Media, 2003.

2. Pierre Bourdieau, "The Logic of Practice," Stanford University Press, 1990, p. 53.

CHAPTER 10

THINKING "ON-SCREEN"

DESIGNERS SPEAK

"If there's one thing you learn by working on a lot of different websites, it's that almost any design idea—no matter how appallingly bad—can be made usable in the right circumstances, with enough effort. And almost any good design idea can be made unusable by messing up the details of the implementation."

—STEVE KRUG, *Don't Make Me Think: A Common Sense Approach to Web Usability* (Berkeley, CA: Pearson Education, 2009), n.p.

"If a major project is truly innovative, you cannot possibly know its exact cost and its exact schedule at the beginning. And if in fact you do know the exact cost and the exact schedule, chances are that the technology is obsolete."

—JOSEPH G. GAVIN, JR., discussing the design of the lunar module that landed the first astronauts on the moon, "Fly Me to the Moon: An Interview with Joseph G. Gavin, Jr.," *Technology Review* 97, no. 5 (July 1994), p. 62.

OBJECTIVES

Be aware of the place and significance of today's screen culture.

Recognize how design practices apply to designing for on-screen applications.

Identify constraints of designing for a screen.

Identify good practices of on-screen designing.

Be acquainted with the specific applications of elements and principles of design in on-screen environments.

Understand the design process as it applies to on-screen design.

Screens surround us and are carried along with us throughout our days. This chapter looks at designing for on-screen applications, an area where 2D graphic design, three-dimensionality and 4D design come together. Designing for on-screen life is not much different than design in general, except for the fact that the screens themselves are not an environment or a media as such. Rather they are a framing device for incredibly diverse content. The main concern for design, justifying a separate chapter at this time, is the cultural transition that is evident in the shift from print to visual narrative and the fragmentation of the media itself in an age of **electronic culture.** The elements, principles, and design process itself are more or less in line with traditional practices already discussed in previous chapter, but with a larger emphasis on four-dimensional thinking. This difference requires a quick look at pre-screen design practices.

SCREENWORLD

Here is an odd point: It is quite possible that this chapter will become obsolete to some extent, or even entirely, while you are reading it. If current trends continue, it may well be that the devices common now will be transformed within a year or two. However, the paradigm of online activities and video gaming will very likely be around for quite a while, so the discussion can continue on that account. The chapter is put together in such a way as to minimize the effect of a sudden shift in technology, by looking at larger principles and keeping the discussion with one eye on the realm of possible futures.

Another point to consider is that the character of on-screen environments is actually not as distinct, widespread, or overwhelming as was initially thought might be the case at the beginning of the 21st century. The virtual world is *less* three-dimensional than was expected, with much activity taking place on flat screens with two-dimensional interfaces. Games have, of course, reached levels of sophistication in terms of their graphics and motion, but the interface is still a screen and a gadget. The late-20th-century imaginings of holograms and virtual immersions may have gone the way of the flying cars dreamt of in the mid-20th century. Nothing has been added to the paradigm of film and television of the 20th century; things appear on rectangular screens.

A larger issue is the fusing of the online activities of mundane communications and commerce with the normal rhythm of life in the physical world. However, one must be careful not to overemphasize the position of new technologies. It is necessary to remember that every new technology goes through a beginning stage where it is seen as the answer to everything with a myriad of applications. Then things calm down, the excitement wears off, and the technology takes its place in the world. It remains possible that this is the case with all the instant-access technology that we have today. It may well be that a few years from now, the idea of being online constantly and tweeting and texting our every action, thought, and position will be seen as the *excitement stage* of the *handheld and tablet phase* of computing and communication.

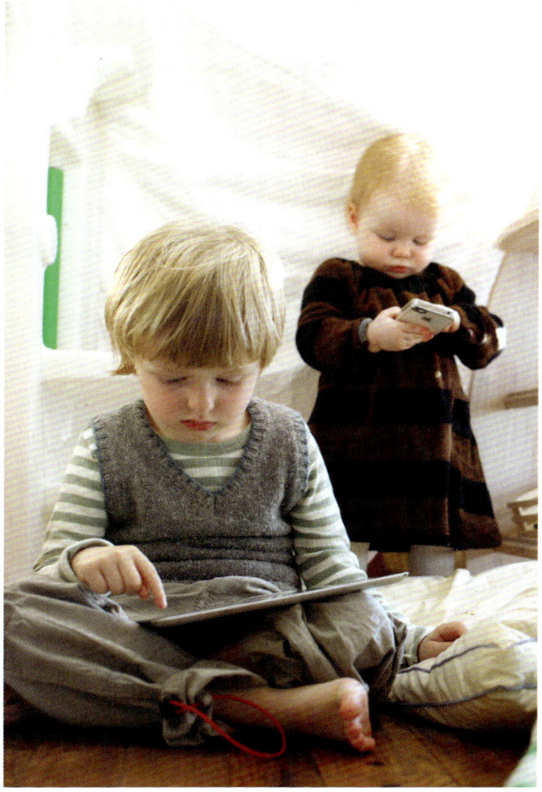

10.1 There has been a generational shift in screen-size preference. Younger users prefer the smaller screens with their mobility and immediate access.

Source: © Mark Makela/Corbis

The first observation that is worth considering is that even though the virtual world is less 3D than was thought, the world of screens is a far different kind of world than was expected only a couple of decades ago. With the swift advent of touch screens and handhelds, the world is returning to a touch sensibility, which may result in some changes in coming years. Not too long ago, vision was meant to be what the next generation of personal computing would involve. Virtual reality was to take over the physical interface to a large degree, and the physical world was to become secondary. Instead, we have a world where communications, entertainment, and daily information are channeled through relatively small handhelds and tablets with touch screens, while the large screens that we were so enamored of in the early part of the century have mainly become passive portals for entertainment and stations for office work. Essentially, we have seen a division of labor among the devices take place, as well as a generational shift in screen-size preference (Fig. 10.1).

TIMELINE: SCREENS (GUIS)

- **1969:** Alan Kay develops the concept of the graphical user interface (GUI) at the University of Utah.
- **1970:** Xerox Co. management is fearful of the "paperless future" and decides to control new computer technology. Palo Alto Research Center (PARC) is formed.
- **1973:** The Alto, the first computer with a modern graphical user interface, is developed at Xerox PARC.
- **1974:** Dan Ingalls at PARC invents BitBlt, a display algorithm that allows the development of overlapping screen windows and pop-up menus.
- **1975:** PARC engineers demonstrate for their colleagues a graphical user interface including icons, windows, and pop-up menus. Done on an Alto computer, this was the first major demonstration of a GUI.
- **1977:** Steve Jobs and Steve Wozniak found Apple computer.
- **1977:** The first LED flat-panel TV screen (monochrome) is developed by James Mitchell and shown in Washington, D.C., in 1978.
- **1984:** The GUI is popularized by Apple computer with the Lisa and the Macintosh. The Macintosh becomes the first successful mass-marketed personal computer with a GUI.
- **1993:** Apple introduces the first tablet computer, the Newton MessagePad 100.
- **1998:** Windows 98 is released, which later becomes Windows Me (Millennium Edition) in 2000.
- **1999:** GUI-based operating systems are developed for web phones, PDA computers, and other devices.
- **2003:** The Blackberry smart phone is released.
- **2007:** First generation of iPhones is released.
- **2007:** Amazon releases the first generation of its Kindle e-reader.
- **2009:** Sony introduces the first LED TV.
- **2010:** Apple iPad goes on sale.

The online world, in which we spend so much of our time, has not become the virtual space that many predicted and, as such, not the three-dimensional design extravaganza of worlds and avatars that many imagined. The immersion into virtual reality (VR) has not been seen to be necessary, and the idea that we would be wearing VR helmets or lying on benches with screen-goggles strapped to our heads has not materialized and is even considered a bit quaint in a retro sci-fi kind of way. There is a sense that games might be still heading in this direction and no reason why they shouldn't, but for other applications, we seem to have found a place where the usage of screens is just as efficient and productive and there simply does not seem to be a need for immersion devices.

The on-screen environment can be of several kinds, with the major (albeit disappearing) distinction being whether one is online or not. The activities taking place are innumerable. There may be basic office-work taking place, social interactions, entertainment pursuits, information gathering and so on. The design problems involved are therefore of a very varied nature. Mostly the environments involved are tailored for one person to be at the controls at each time. Following on from the last chapter we recognize that being online is an *experience*, regardless of which of these activities are taking place, and that this requires the inclusion of time as a concern.

Mainly however, we recognize that the on-screen experience is interactive and that the designing of the experience requires a consideration of the dialogue that is taking place between the user and the system on the screen. There is always information flowing from the screen, and most often the input from the user is coming right back. Here is the greatest difference from what has come before. Environments in which humans have operated until now have not been so deliberately interactive into a focused interface. We, as a species, have not had in our history such a channeling of our activities into a single framework, where a significant portion of our activities takes place via a single device or set of devices. To paint it in almost absurd terms, the physical space in which our bodies operate does not react to our input in the same way, nor does it require our prompting in order to operate, and our activities have tended toward different spaces with different equipment for each activity we undertake. The on-screen environments have their tools and interfaces, but it is the gathering of all onto the single two-dimensional surface that is the radical change.

ON-SCREEN ENVIRONMENTS

So, what are these **on-screen environments**—and are they indeed environments? Clearly there are variations in both form and content, and there are significant differences and similarities to the physical world. We must consider the effect that the actual technology has on our perceptions and behavior. The compression of space and time involved demands a different mind-set in designing. The interaction that is expected has different requirements than when designing physical tools. But the physicality of the screen itself matters, even though not all on-screen life is the same. There is software with very specific abilities, there are apps for handheld devices, tablets running the same environments in different sizes and resolutions, and of course, varying screens of laptop and desktop computers. Finally, there are gaming consoles hooked to television screens of increasingly large and varied scale. Some of the content on these screens is utilitarian; some is for gaming. Degrees of interactivity vary, and some of the on-screen environments are simply portals for content, such as on news media sites or sites for shopping. With the diversity of applications available, our discussion must be general, just as the rest of the discussion in this book does not necessarily address the specific problems of each possible discipline involved.

The fact that there still are screens at all may be the most significant thing to note. When the social theorist Marshall McLuhan wrote in the 1960s that "the medium is the message," he was referring to television, but his observation has received new attention in the Internet age. What McLuhan meant was that the technology delivering information has a larger impact on a culture than the information itself. Telegraph, radio, telephones, movies, and television had all transformed how information was delivered and as such had changed the world. The combination of the Internet and easily portable cell phones and tablets has now created yet a new situation in human history, an **electronic culture** where, to those with the technology, information is available everywhere at all times. And the information is not only current and mainstream but also historical and peripheral, strange, mundane, true, and false. There is no limit to what can be archived and found.

More information that is more easily accessed on ever smaller and more portable devices has not just made the world a smaller place; it has compressed history and cultures into a common space. The resulting disintegrating of boundaries between historical and current, local and global is already apparent in the styles of our time. All space and time are compressed in our current *moment* as we access images and information from nearly any place and time, read texts from all eras in a multitude of languages, and view films and artworks from all over the globe. The relevance and impact on design practices should be clear: The opportunities we have are dramatically transformed from that of the previous generations, and we are able to access information and seek inspiration, as well as find sources, details, and references, at any time. Conversely, whatever we design to be put on the Internet can in equal measure be seen and accessed by any and all in places we hadn't thought of or imagined. The ultimate message is that we now have an *expectation* of being able to access all the world of information and a further expectation that designers will make something of this.

But what happens if (some say "when") the screen itself disappears? What of the shift in the accessibility of information to the point where one is always online. Say the screen disappears because the computer/Internet is no longer bound to devices, but everywhere. Ideas of wearable Internet portals and tabletop computers are nothing new, and marketable solutions might beat this manuscript to market. But the true revolution will arrive in the disappearance of the gadgets altogether into an environment where *online or off-line* and *in range or not* no longer makes sense. A table surface, the wall, your jacket sleeve, and the mirror might all be access points to a permanent stream of information. This would of course be a design problem in itself, but the point is this: How to approach designing for the *virtual* environment, even when it no longer is a screen?

THE NATURE OF THE SCREEN

Humans are visual thinkers. We not only visualize with known imagery but actively create images and icons to symbolize the things we are thinking of. When writing allowed the shift from **oral information** to **manuscripts,** information became visual and words became writing. Regardless of what happens to the technology, it is likely that no matter what interface replaces screens, there will be a visual component and very likely a printed-page analogy will prevail. The transition from manuscript to **print culture** in the 1600s brought plenty of changes to the world, but the basic idea of a *book* and a *page* did not change. The computer screen and the handhelds and tablets all pick up from the paradigm of books but have moved that project forward. We are, however, very attached to the square, two-dimensional format, set up in columns and headlines and text blocks.

It is a very interesting phenomenon to note that the more the touch-screen gadgets and Internet became part of our daily routines in the first decade of the century, the more the design of sites became two-dimensional. The initial faux-3D designs of early websites and browsers of the 1990s began to give way to gridded layouts of flat space and up and down scrolling. By early 2013, for example, Apple's iTunes and Windows had both gone to a largely 2D look.

All the traditional rules of graphic design are completely valid for on-screen design. Consideration of balancing text and images, dealing with white space, placing margins and headlines, choosing fonts and colors—all these apply, but the tools in the toolkit are enhanced. The significant difference is that the screen can deal with dynamic changes and animations, and will show colors with far more variation and brilliance than the printed page. It is tempting to go off the deep end sometimes, but on-screen as in classic graphic design, the "less is more" rule still holds. Having more colors and fonts doesn't mean you *have to* use them.

The major difference in approach to online design as opposed to print graphics is that time is a large factor. The Internet experience is four-dimensional. A physical paper page is a physical experience and has a flexible approach and narrative. It is a multisensory *object* that can be viewed and read and smelled and heard and touched and held in the hand and then put down. But apart from being a page in a sequence of pages, it does not have a dominant dimension of time attached to it. It has an existence that is very much its own and that remains after it has been read. It is very much a *thing*. A web page, however, is an *event* and a *live* one in that it appears on the screen by command and immediately invites engagement. It is linked in and linked out and may contain any number of different media and dynamic content that can only be interacted with by tapping the screen, a key, or a button. Mainly, it has no physical presence apart from the device that displays it. Therefore, while the user's needs define its nature, it is the device that determines the constraints for its design. The capabilities, size, and interactive nature of the screen will decide the experience of the page. How to scroll, swipe, click, touch, zoom, and otherwise navigate is device-dependent. So also are the visibility of images, the legibility of the text, and the speed of its execution.

The constraints of the device are far more likely to determine the experience than any of the content. With the number of different ways a page can be viewed, from a small cell phone screen to a large high-definition wide screen, the options for control are still somewhat limited. Designing multiple pages for different options has become the norm in most cases. Right now, the interactive nature of on-screen experience is determined by the physical constraints of the devices. Two major factors determine the limits: the size of the screen and the possibilities of physical interaction. Regarding interaction, there are still competing technologies, and even the input hardware itself is of different kinds: stylus, mouse, and physical keyboard versus touch screen. Even the physical dimensions of the device itself and its connectivity has an effect on the usability, in that it determines how easily, quickly, or discreetly it can be used.

The rapid adoption of smart phones since 2005 is resulting in a change of style, as younger users are primarily accessing the Internet through the smaller screens. It is therefore likely that the visual style of the smaller screens will come to dominate unless the screen itself becomes redundant and designing for the Internet becomes *truly* the designing of environments. The designing of experiences and environments may then find its way into a narrative mode that is closer to performance, but this depends on the technology involved and what metaphors it uses. Meanwhile, designing for the Internet is basically graphic design (Fig. 10.2).

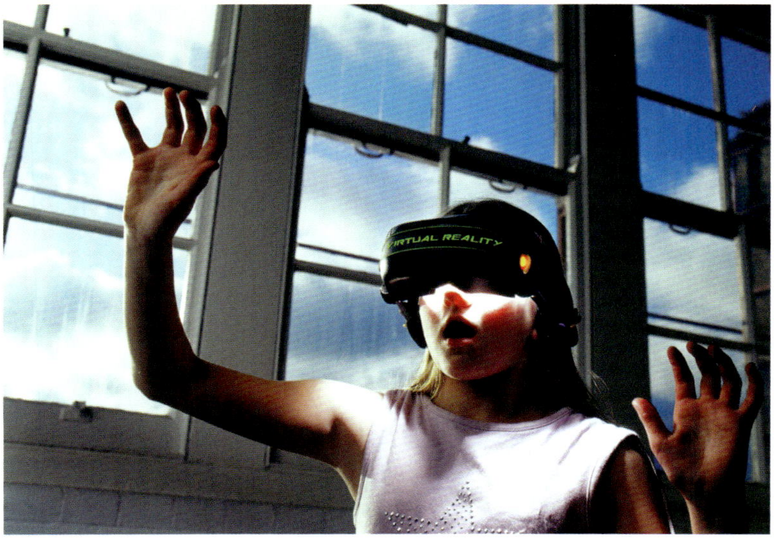

10.2 As virtual environments become less screen-dependent, they will likely move into a narrative mode that is closer to performance, but this depends on the technology involved and what metaphors it employs. This girl, wearing virtual reality goggles, has a far more "immersive" experience. Our interaction with virtual environments become far more physical as the technology itself disappears from view.

Source: © George Logan/Corbis

The prevailing metaphors are still those of the early days of this technology, and some go far back. We speak of "desktops," "wallpaper," and "buttons." Even the "pages" themselves refer to a physical object in a way that was intended to familiarize and comfort early users. However, as things progress, the metaphors have become less and less connected to the real (physical) world and the experience on the screen has begun to develop a language and series of references of its own. For example, a *tweet* is not a sound, *inbox* is a verb, and so is *friend*. As we move away from print culture, on-screen designing is becoming more image-oriented and iconographic, with 2D icons and clear smooth surfaces allowing quick visual recognition in the small spaces of the handheld screens. Decoration is at a minimum, and the content itself is fast becoming the visual element. That is, just as the devices are getting smaller and less intrusive, the on-screen environment itself is becoming less of an issue, with the visual design fading into the background and the functional taking over. (The same happened with early television sets. They were major pieces of furniture in the early years, mimicking large radio cabinets. For half a century, they've gradually been becoming more and more transparent as décor.)

Partly, this allows for easier transferring of the on-screen experience from one device to the other, as we now access our information and entertainment on several different devices during the course of a day, rather than the practice of only a few years ago when television shows and movies were watched on a TV, e-mail was on the desktop of a desktop-bound computer, and phone calls were made on a landline or screenless cell phone. In order to accommodate the rapid shift from one device to another, a certain familiarity is needed and a convergence of styles has thus begun to set in. It is important to have the ability to move from smart phone to large screen to tablet, to someone else's device, and back, without encountering a new situation or different environment each time.

In some ways this is simply the analogy of a standardization of equipment such as happens with any new technology that is developing in many places at once. Eventually the world arrives at a consensus or two (as in metric versus imperial measurements). The virtual tools on our virtual desktops are simply being streamlined. However, this is something for any designer of online environments to keep an eye on, whether it is for office software, information outlets, or gaming. It can be very dangerous to get on the wrong side of such a trend. Even if you think your designs are not part of the larger world of corporate operations, once the users get used to a certain standard look and develop habits of use, then breaking those habits has to be very deliberate and have a clear purpose. Difference for the sake of difference is not always appreciated. On the flip side, being able to improve on a standardizing environment allows for great end user satisfaction.

THE SCREEN: A 4D EXPERIENCE

The designing of an on-screen environment is the designing of an experience at least as much as the designing of a visual. Just as designing in the physical world has a hierarchy, the on-screen world also needs to be approached with the hierarchy of design needs in mind. Without a functioning design that operates reliably and with a satisfying sense of usability, the design is not going to be worth much in the long run.

The interface of any on-screen application, website, game, or application (app) is a 4D experience. We engage and interact, accessing content or applying actions to situations that eventually prove rewarding, either as a functional, informative, or

SUSTAINABILITY

The environmental impact of our computers and gadgets is unfortunately not a pretty sight. The materials, toxic metals, and energy use together create a sinkhole of environmental damage. For a while it was thought that office computers would be environmentally beneficial by saving paper, but this has proved to be untrue, and it seems the opposite may in fact be true. The ease of printing has actually increased the use of paper, as well as that of colored (relatively toxic) inks. Nor has the computer revolution resulted in an increase of telecommuting, which was also predicted to be an environmental benefit of the new technology when it began to arrive in homes and offices in the late 1980s.

As with other matters of environmental concern, the first line of defense is to build awareness. Designers, who now are increasingly reliant on all manner of software, can be responsible about use of paper and energy in the workplace. Designers of software and gadgets, however, should be aware that the hidden costs of the technology we use will come back to be paid by later generations. New materials, more resilient and long-lived gadgets, technologies, and finishes that do not require a heavy use of toxic chemicals and metals would be a start, and the front line of human technology should not be the place to say "can't be done."

entertaining experiences. The three lowest rungs of the hierarchy of design needs are very clearly indicated: *functionality, reliability,* and *usability*. The site or on-screen situation must first and foremost *function*. The speed at which we have become accustomed to operate on-screen does not allow for much room. A game that has hiccups or a Web site that is slow to respond very quickly becomes an irritant. Much like the bicycle that functions, but not *well*, a functioning system that is constantly making us wait will not be considered a good experience and therefore not a good design regardless of whether the visual design is interesting.

All the other guidelines for the physical world apply. Once the functionality is taken care of, *reliability* becomes an issue. A game must respond the same way for the same situation each time, an invited action on a Web page must lead to the desired result each time, and so on. Having fulfilled these, the step to *usability* is open and the user experience can be designed to be pleasurable and effective. Notice that in this quick mention of the hierarchy, functionality is front and center. The on-screen experience is *functional* in time. It therefore requires as much attention as any functional system before getting to the higher stages of the design hierarchy. The look has to be designed in at the beginning stages as with any number of physical products, but only when reliable functioning can be seen to be secure does the look of the site, game, or interface become a critical issue. Moving on to proficiency and creativity then allows the transformation of the user experience into something beyond the norm, and the design of visuals must then support that development.

Designing for the screen is subject to the same principles as off-screen, but the emphasis is different. The *experience* is much more at the fore, and in the case of a game or website, the narrative structure is very important. For gaming, the analogies to film are apparent (Fig. 10.3). A game has a situation, locations, and actions that need to be mapped out. Viewpoints, framings of actions, and sightlines can be an issue. Continuity of the internal world is important, so that the user feels at home in the environment and is not jolted by a change of style appearing at random. Even when

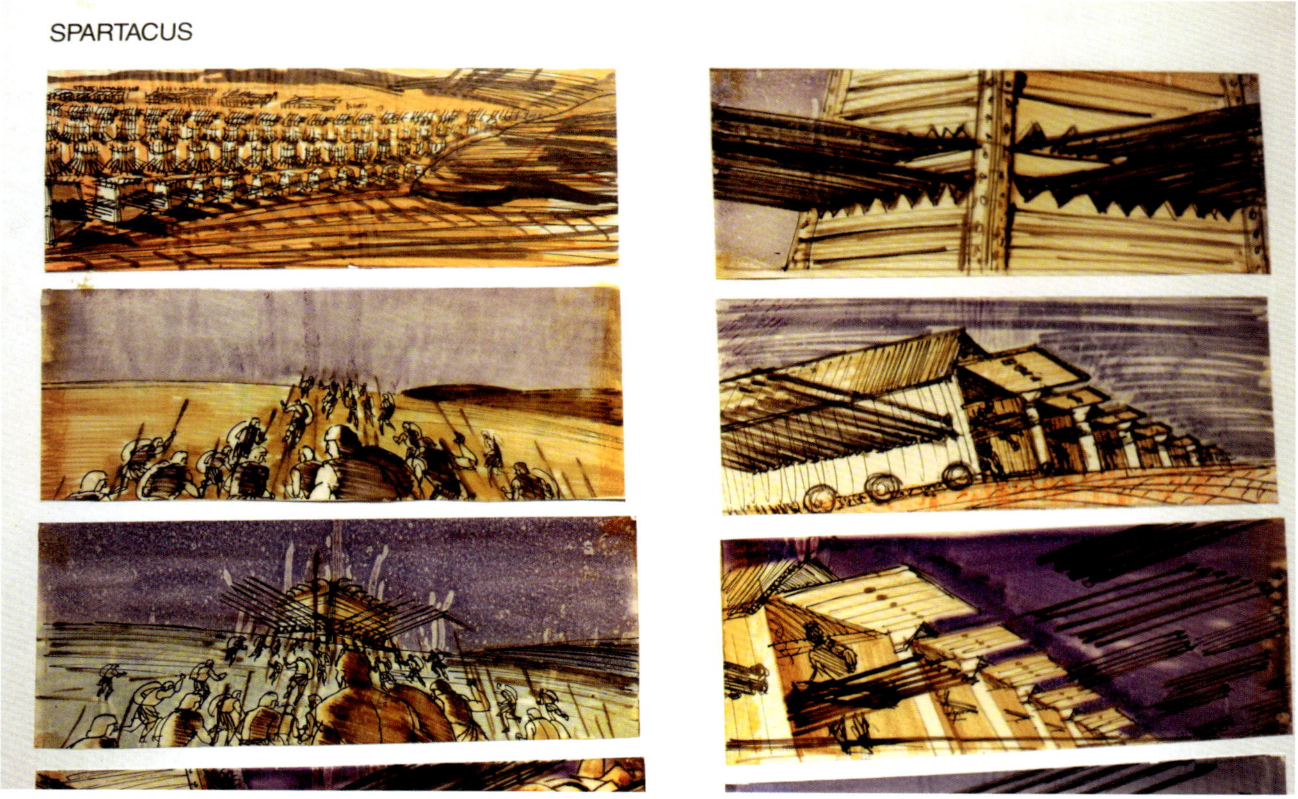

10.3 Designing for the screen is subject to the same principles as off screen, but the emphasis is different. For gaming the analogies to film are apparent. The experience is much more at the fore, and the narrative structure is very important. Game designers storyboard their narratives just like filmmakers.

Source: © Rainer Jensen/dpa/Corbis

different levels may reward the player with a differently styled environment, there is a continuity of the overall feel of the internal world.

The same holds true for any screen environment. The logic of the experience must be consistent. Moving from one page to another must not involve such a large transition that the user becomes lost. Familiar elements, a coherent color scheme, and a consistency of fonts and shapes all help to solidify an inner world of the site. Clicking on a link, for example, must not bring different kinds of responses even though the links transport you to different areas. Any link taking you out of the site should be marked as such, precisely to avoid the jolt. Images must not, for example, be links in one page and not in another, the link back home should always be the same and in the same place, and the help button (if there is one) likewise. If you are designing games, making the user solve a puzzle is OK. If not, the Web site should not be a maze of any kind. There should never be a situation where the user has to ask "Where am I? How did I get here?" Keep it simple. Keep it clear.

ELEMENTS AND PRINCIPLES ON-SCREEN

Designing for on-screen is distinct in how quickly in the process the medium that is being used is the one that will be the final product. That is, the designing of the on-screen environment largely takes place in an on-screen environment and the testing and implementation takes place there as well. It is comparable to a clothing designer dispensing with sketches and working directly into the fabric or a furniture designer working directly into the wood, plastic, or metal involved. Of course, game

ERGONOMICS

In the past 20 years, in the industrialized economies, the methods for interacting with the world at large have been revolutionized. From keyboards, to computer mice, to touch screens, motion detection, and voice recognition, the devices we use have become increasingly attuned to the movements and nuances of our personal physiques. The designing of the gadgets themselves and the interfaces as they appear on the screens have therefore increasingly needed to be thought through from the standpoint of ergonomics. How do we move and what is the range of our hand movements and hand–eye co-ordination? But also, how do we sit, stand, walk, drive, and generally behave with the gadgets, screens, headphones, and on and on who knows what else that we now use to navigate our daily lives? The repetitiveness of motion and sedentary lifestyle creates its own concerns and constraints. The tolerances of the human body and mind for action and motion are one thing, but the effects of a lack of motion and engagement with the physical world is another and increasingly important matter. An awareness of the novelty of all this is very important, but it is also important to be aware of the innate flexibility of human behavior and what its limits may be.

designers frequently sketch characters and storyboards, just as any filmmaker would, and sketches can also be created in any CAD or photo editing software, so the lines are fairly blurry.

It is worth noting that stepping away from the computer and hand sketching even roughly when planning layouts is never a bad thing. The shift in tempo and repositioning involved can often allow new thoughts to develop, just as when a writer moves away from the keyboard to write longhand for a while. It also should be noted that the opposite is true. For anyone used to sketching and building in the physical world, designing on-screen, for on-screen, has a strange feel to it. Being completely free of the physical constraints of materials, gravity, and scale is extremely liberating.

However, the elements and principles of design are equally valid on-screen as off, even though the application may be different. First, it is important to (literally) place the work in the correct frame. The screen form itself is a powerful constraint on any designing. Just like the designing of a film or a theatrical performance, the designer must be aware that the audience sees everything within the basic structure of that rectangular frame. And just like the theatrical proscenium or the movie theater, the frame itself disappears as the audience focuses on the display, but it continues to define the scale and focus of the event. The devices we currently carry around are not large at all, so despite their high-definition displays, which allow the incorporation of more detail and more finesse in textures, the scale of the design is never large. The form of the screens with their wide-angle ratio affords a certain framing of images and pages and implies a direction of text and overall shape of either strongly directed portrait or landscape format. That is to say, a perfectly square format would not be immediately associated with the current style of framing. (See Fig. 10.4.)

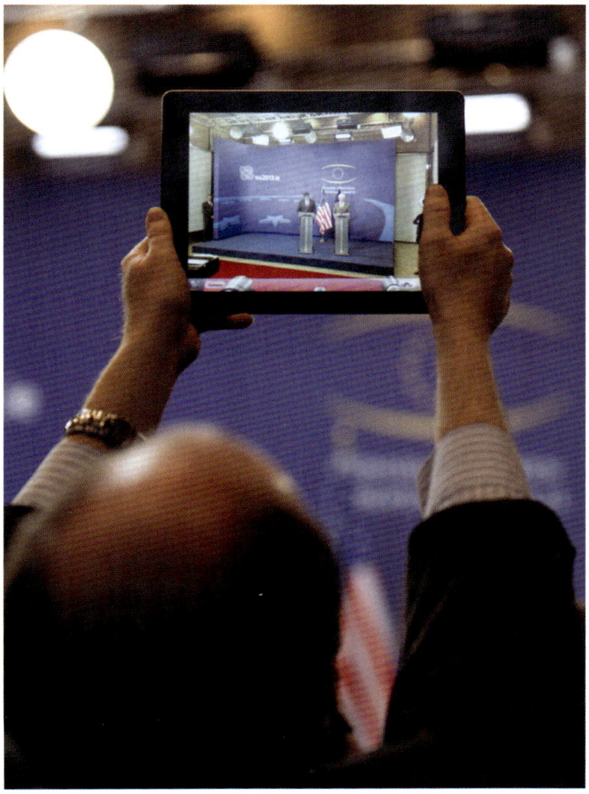

10.4 The form of the screens, whether large or small, is directing text and overall shape into strongly directed portrait or landscape format. This seems to be a form we are settling into over the last decade after several centuries of portrait format print.

Source: © Thierry Tronnel/Corbis

ELEMENTS OF DESIGN

Now let's look at the elements of design and see how each is affected by designing on-screen.

Color. Color is a strong element in on-screen designing. The screen itself is a light source capable of producing innumerable colors in the RGB color model, and care should be taken to make sure the color scheme is valid for the devices and applications intended (see Chapter 3). Also, if there is any possibility that any print material will come out of the designs, then the color scheme needs to be translated into the print scheme of the CMYK model, which may or may not be able to fully deliver the on-screen colors. Be very careful when designing that the screen on which you are designing is correctly calibrated and set so that you are looking at as close-to-correct colors as possible as you work. This is especially important if you are working with subtle differences or with color schemes that are heavily tilted toward one hue or another, in which case a minor adjustment to the screen can alter the entire look (Fig. 10.5). Be also very aware of the effect that sitting in front of a screen has on your own perception and vision. A large, bright screen is a powerful light source and will deaden your sensitivity to colors and subtleties if you stare for too long. Get up, move around, and go into daylight every now and then to recalibrate yourself!

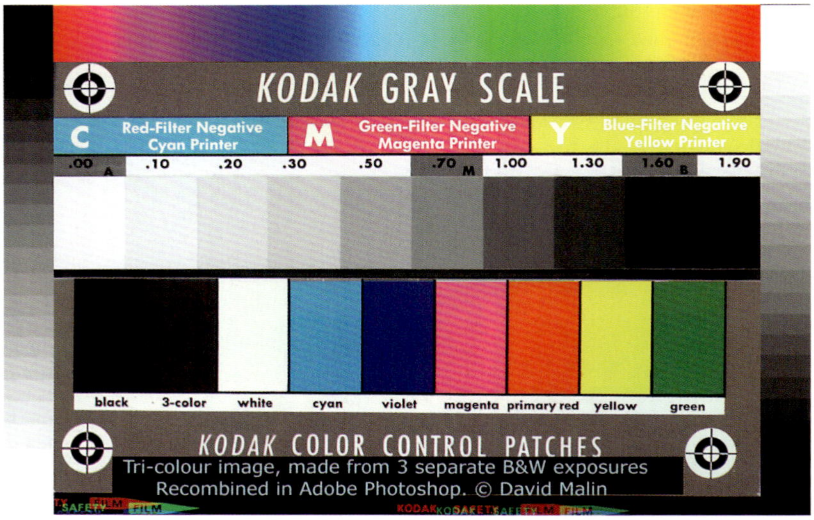

10.5 A color chart, or *control patches,* such as this can be beneficial to have on your desktops—physical and virtual—to make sure by comparison that the colors you see on the screen are the ones that will be produced in printing or production.

Source: © Australian Astronomical Observatory and Photograph by David Malin (image and text)

Line. Line on a screen is a delicate construct, as the smaller the screen, the less well does the line track without the individual pixels making themselves felt. Higher definition has made this a lot better in recent years, but the effect can still be felt, and moving from high definition to standard can cause problems. When using actual illustrative lines in on-screen design, be sure to examine your work on several different screens to check for distortion or even disappearance. The internal construction of a frame on a screen is a graphic design problem. As you begin to break the screen apart with actual or implied lines, it is always a good idea to grid your screen to see what kind of proportions and sections appear (Fig. 10.6).

10.6 When designing a page, grid your screen to see what kind of proportions and sections appear as you begin to break the screen apart with actual or implied lines.

Source: Illustration by Karl Aspelund

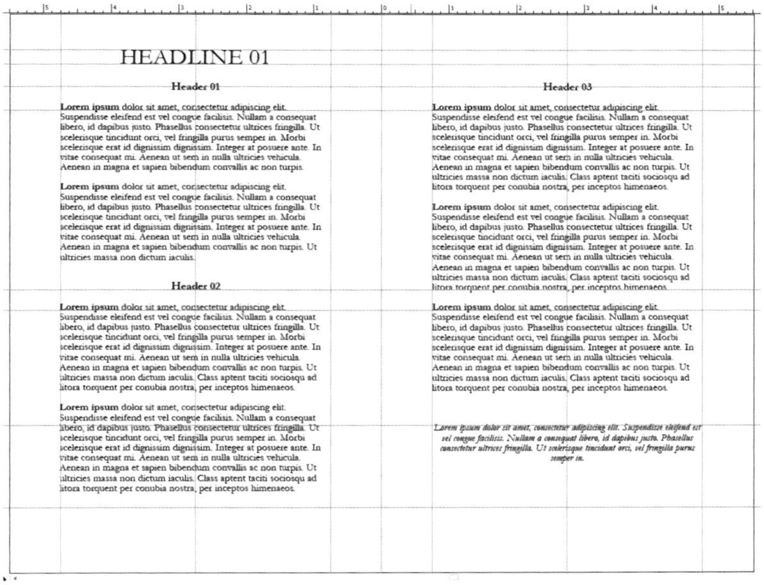

Shape and Volume/Space. Screens, like all traditional illustrative media, are two-dimensional and all the same rules and tricks for creating illusions of *space* apply as in physical media. As discussed in Chapter 3, graphic space *is* volume, and shape and space are practically interchangeable. What on-screen design can add to the overlapping, positioning, and so on is the possibility of *actual motion* being included in the on-screen design when using animation. But remember, it's still a two-dimensional surface.

Time and Experience. Quite obviously, these elements very much come into play, as the on-screen experience is an active experience. Consider your user at every step of the way. What happens first, what happens next, and then what follows? Don't allow yourself to be blinded to the novelty of what you are doing. Things that seem obvious to you, who have sat in front of the design for hours and days, may not seem so to a new user. Another danger of the screen is that because we sit down to it so soon in the design process, we tend to get blinded to the experience of sitting down to the site or game for the very first time. Field-test as much as you can on friends and coworkers. Not on the client! Don't spoil the first impression.

PRINCIPLES OF DESIGN IN DIGITAL DESIGN

The temporal also shows up in the discussion of principles of design for the screen. For example, when addressing the principles of *unity and harmony*, it may seem evident that whatever is on the screen should have a certain totality to it and that colors, fonts, and images should produce a harmony. However, for the dynamic character of a website or game, the unity and harmony also extends to the narrative *over time*. As mentioned above, the different areas, pages and levels of the design should have within and between them a coherent approach.

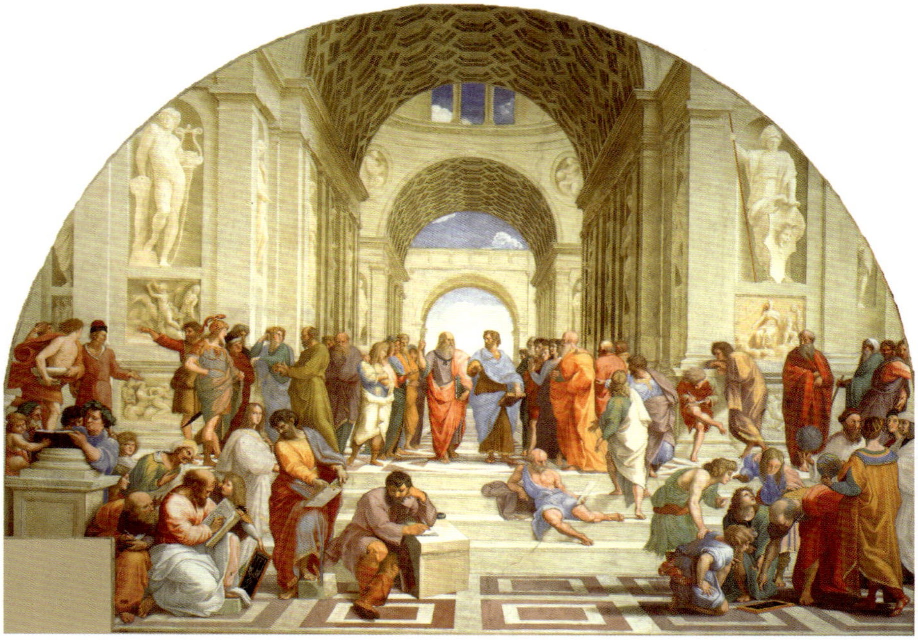

10.7 The two-dimensional framing and classic proportions of our screens allow the same placing of design elements into the frame as practiced by painters and graphic designers through the centuries. *The Scuola di Atene (The School of Athens),* a fresco painted between 1509 and 1511 by the Renaissance artist Raphael in the Apostolic Palace in the Vatican, can be gridded out to reveal underlying structures conforming to the Golden Ratio.

Source: Raphael [public domain], via Wikimedia Commons

Emphasis and focal point on-screen is practically a painterly exercise of the old school. With the strict constraints of the *scale and proportions* of the screen frame guiding the way, placing the design elements into the frame begins to call for the kind of attention traditionally paid by painters and graphic designers through the centuries (Fig. 10.7). Splitting the screen into thirds or fourths, using central axis placement, and placing elements to guide the eye are all games to play with the eye initially being the judge, not the measurements (although they can come in at the end when the placement is fixed). You can also construct the *balance and rhythm* of the screen layout this way, keeping in mind that rhythm is a perception over time, so it also applies to stylistic elements repeated over different areas of the site or game. Go for the feel of it as you design (Fig. 10.8).

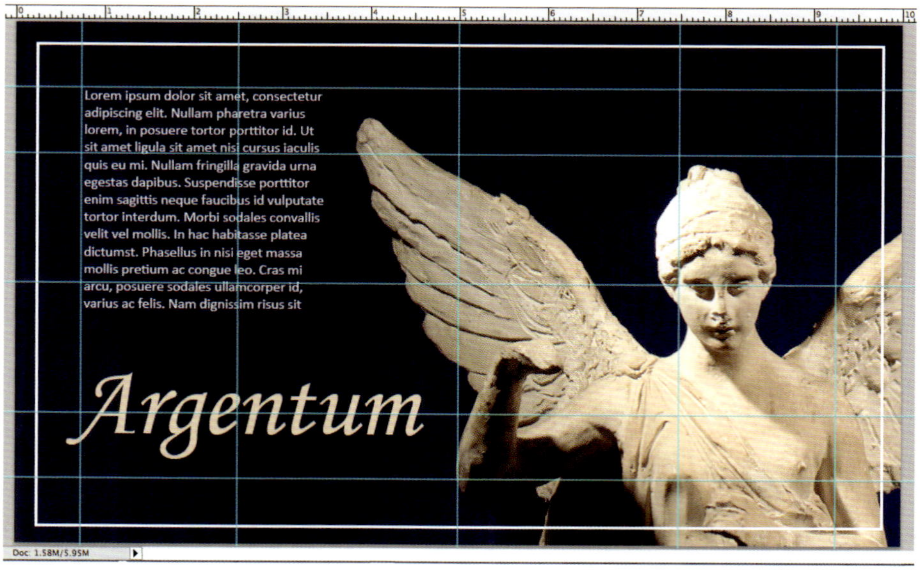

10.8 The balance and rhythm of the screen layout can be constructed with a simple grid. Go for the feel of it as you design—develop a rhythm.

Source: Illustration by Karl Aspelund

A QUICK LOOK AT THE DESIGN PROCESS

The design process is about the same for any design at all. The same holds true as for the elements and principles, in that the major outlines are the same, but the absence of physicality in the product does have a few effects. Beginning with inspiration, looking at the process allows us to see that designing on-screen is a hybrid of 3D design and graphic design, bridging the two by being the arena of both intense 3D gaming and straightforward two-dimensional information-delivery.

On-screen designing is old enough a discipline by now to have numerous sources of *inspiration* and a number of role models to look to and even its own nostalgic tendencies. An important point to consider is to let the media itself be an inspiration rather than just a tool. Consider the needs and constraints of your design project, then consider the screens and the users. Map the actions involved. What do you want them to experience? What happens first, then what next? Draw a layout of the screen and a map of the interaction between the user and your current design. What does this imply? Take the first steps yourself and see if you are on the right track. Remember, this is actually 4D and experience is always the key.

Definition is extremely important. As pointed out above, the complexities of a design for on-screen use can be layered into very functional needs and multiple points of concern before coming to anything that seems like designing artistically. Things need to work; they need to fit together and function reliably. Identify the needs and constraints of your design problem, and map out the possible configurations and actions that can appear in your clients' interactions with your design. Flowcharts are helpful to make sure that all possibilities are taken care of and that your client doesn't get lost or confused. The same care should be taken for any multileveled design of a look to make sure that the identity and style is consistent and that changes are logical, when they appear (Fig. 10.9).

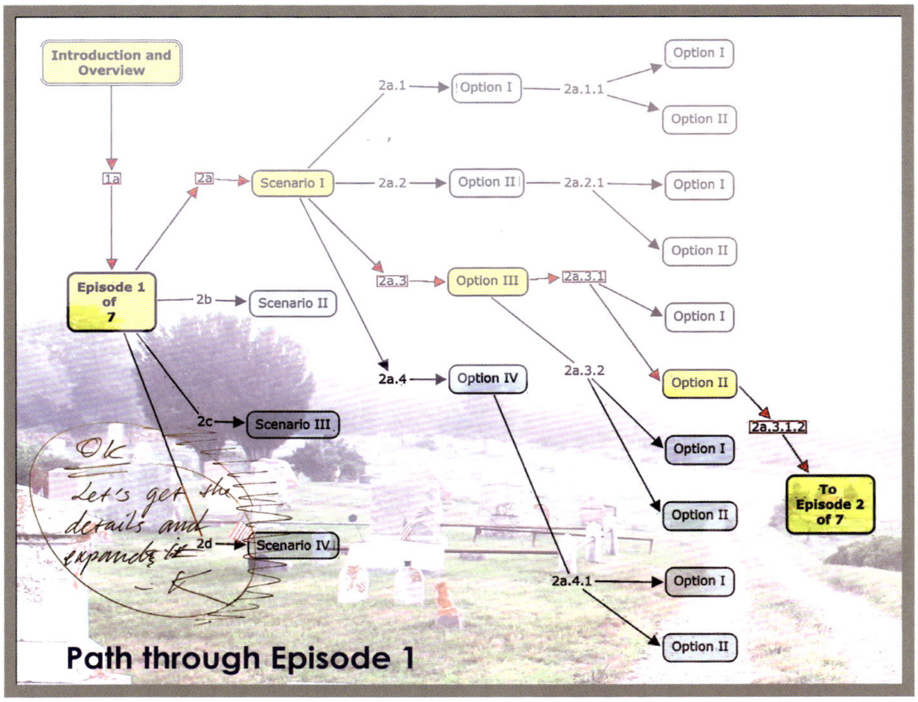

10.9 When a design team is designing a Web site or a videogame, the choices and options facing the user can be many and complex, and the road for the team needs to be laid out in order that the pathways through the site or game are all what they should be. Flowcharts such as the relatively simple one above can be used to make sure all possibilities are taken care of and that no one gets lost or confused. They can also multileveled design of a look to make sure that the identity and style is consistent and changes logically.

Source: Illustration by Karl Aspelund

With all the functionality mapped, the *conceptualizing* of a site grows naturally out of the functionality. A look is settled on and the creation of pages begins. The concept of a design for a game is more complex, but the initial identification of the design problem should lead to an avenue of research into styles and design elements based on situations and characters involved. Here the designing becomes analogous with the art direction for a film or designing for theater. An overall design concept gets applied to individual characters and locations, or *levels,* maintaining a coherent worldview within the confines of the designed world. Again, the emphasis is on the user—what should be the user's *experience*? Keeping track becomes the most difficult aspect of the designing at this point, especially if there are many characters and situations. Who has what and why? Where is this and how did it get there? Where is the user now, if this was the first stop? In both the creation of a simple website and that of a complex gaming world, this problem is found to different degrees. You need to know everything about the internal logic of your design so that any additions and changes that come around later will be logical and not disrupt the relationship the user will have with your work.

Once things begin to develop, you can *explore* and try your design out. Road-test your maps by navigating randomly and finding your way around. Save your work in numerous copies and test different fonts, sizes, and colors. Run the SCAMPER method (see Box 1.1) on the design and see what develops. The danger at this point is that the possibilities are nearly endless, what with the availability of elements, so have a plan for your exploring. Decide to try ten options or three very different fonts. Then simply . . . stop (Fig. 10.10).

Definition will be next, and if all the preceding has been done in an organized way, this should be a fun moment. Because of the practicality of what you are designing and the mapping you've done, what you will have is a row of options to choose from. Then all you have to do is choose. A word of warning: If you are going to let your client in

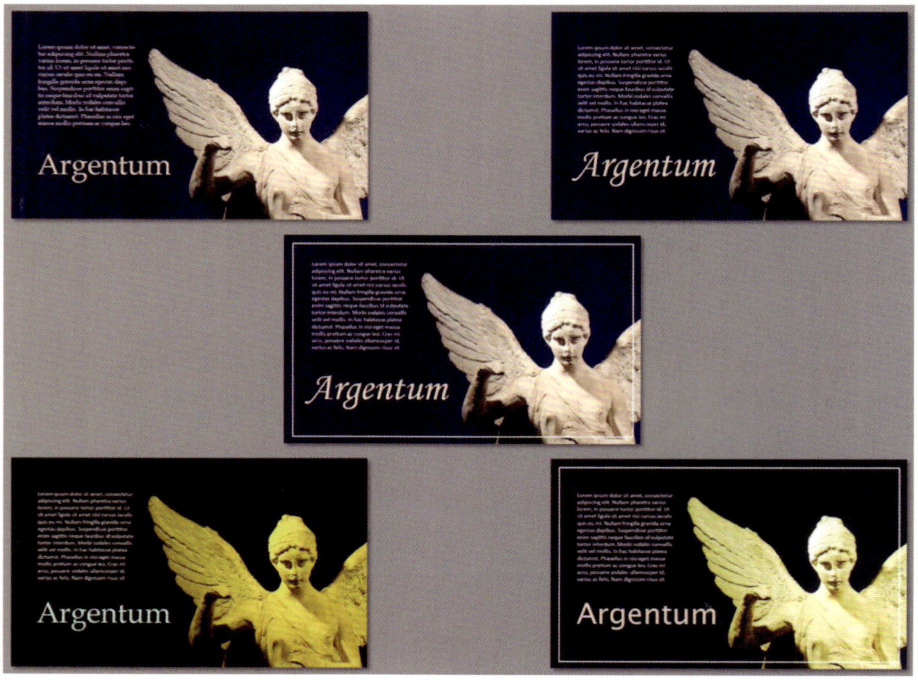

10.10 The possibilities are nearly endless, so have a plan for your exploration. Try a few options and fonts. Then stop, perhaps combine, and choose. Note how the four experiments in the corners contributed to the final design in the middle.

Source: Illustration by Karl Aspelund

NETWORKING

The following list contains helpful websites for further information.

SCREEN CULTURE RESEARCH GROUP—CONCORDIA UNIVERSITY, CANADA

www.screenculture.org

MARSHALL MCLUHAN—THE OFFICIAL SITE FOR THE ESTATE OF MARSHALL MCLUHAN

www.marshallmcluhan.com

HOW TO DESIGN A GOOD WEBSITE—UC, BERKELEY COLLEGE OF LETTERS AND SCIENCE, LETTERS & SCIENCE COMPUTING RESOURCES

lscr.berkeley.edu/advice/web/design

USER INTERFACE DESIGN GROUP—MIT

The User Interface Design group at the Massachusetts Institute of Technology develops and studies new user interface techniques.

groups.csail.mit.edu/uid/index.shtml

WHAT IS USABILITY?—USABILITY PROFESSIONALS' ASSOCIATION

www.usabilityprofessionals.org/usability_resources/about_usability

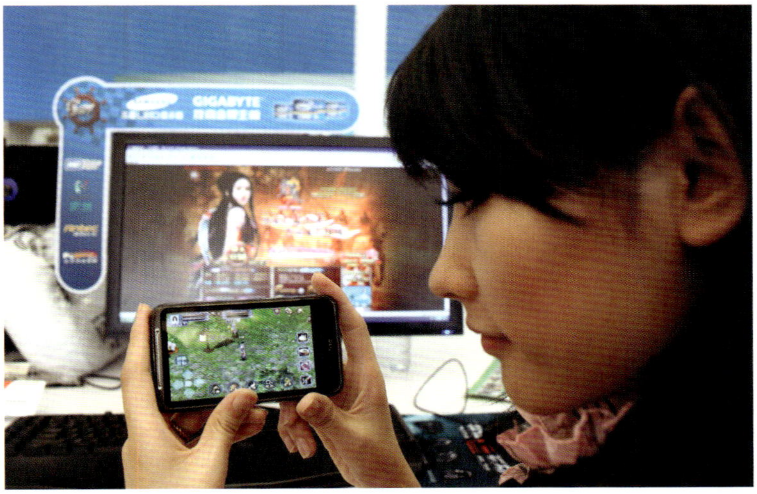

10.11 Test, test, and test again before presentation. If things go wrong, that's all the client will remember, and you may not get a second chance.

Source: © Imaginechina/Corbis

on the definition process, don't give him or her more than three or four options and make *very clear* that this is the moment to make choices, not request changes. It is a natural reaction when hit with options to immediately begin to see the possibility of more options. You, as a designer, should have taken care of that in the exploration stage.

Communication will, as was stated in Chapter 1, be ongoing. However, at the end of a project for on-screen, the communicating of the results is especially easy, as all the material is in digital form. As the project progresses, it is also easy to inform the client of progress in interim deadlines with screenshots and temporary postings online. However, be especially careful to avoid client frustration by labeling anything that is not working, such as a link to an unfinished section or a menu that is not active. Make large and clear error messages that pop up when such things are touched. Best rule: Don't send anything out for approval that requires such actions if you can help it. People always focus on what doesn't work, even when they know they're not supposed to (Fig. 10.11).

Production is again an interesting time in screenworld, as the product is so easily moved and shipped and the production is so easily located. However, the complexity of just a simple website or game is such that the crossing of t's and dotting of i's at this point can seem endless. It is very easy to lose sight of the end product in all the details that need to be polished, especially if things are being done in code rather than graphic interface. Make sure you (and your collaborators) step back every now and then to view the finished product or process from the client-eye view to make sure you're not missing a crucial part of the forest while you focus on the individual trees.

CONCLUSION: FROM WORLD TO SCREEN TO WORLD

Designing for on-screen applications is not that different a process from any other designing, but the technology and rapid changes in the applications of the designs themselves create challenges of their own. Being a proficient designer for virtual spaces, regardless of whether they are straightforward websites or immensely complex online gaming environments, requires a comfort level with the design process for the physical world and knowledge of the elements, principles, needs, and constraints of the same. The translation of this to the screen world is not so difficult as long as the designer remembers that the experience is what matters and that designing for the screen is *limited* by the screen but not *about* the screen.

KEY TERMS

On-screen environment	Manuscripts	Electronic culture
Oral information	Print culture	

DISCUSSION AND REVIEW QUESTIONS

1. Consider the different communication methods that have been used in human history. What could be next? How would you design an interface for it?
2. Which is more challenging, designing physical objects or virtual objects? List three things that are different when designing for online interaction than when designing a physical product. Is "different" better or worse in terms of difficulty in getting it right as a designer?
3. If you were to design for on-screen applications (websites, games, apps) but could only work on products for one screen size, which would you like to do? Why?

EXERCISES AND ASSIGNMENTS

1. Pick a website that you consider to be well designed.
   a. What makes it good design in your opinion? Take both function and aesthetics into account.
   b. How would you communicate what is especially important about the design to someone who had to make it?
   c. How would you describe it to a prospective end user who has never seen it before?
   d. Make a list of the inherent and imposed constraints, and consider how they influenced the outcome.

2. Find a game that can be played on a variety of different screen sizes (phone, tablet, laptop, wide-screen TV) and compare the experience of at least two.

   a. How does the screen size change the experience of the game?

   b. Decide which screen size you like playing on, and consider how you could design a version that would work for another size. Why do you think this works?

   c. If you were to make a recommendation to the game manufacturer to make the game more visually exciting, what would it be?

3. For either the website or the game you chose, do the following.

   a. List the elements and principles of design and how they apply to the design.

   b. What positive changes would you make to any one element and use of a principle?

   c. Why do you suppose the designer made the choices that wound up in the final design?

4. Consider a cell phone. Look at its main screen. How would you describe it in terms of design elements and principles? Try to use as many of the elements and principles as you can.

5. Turn off all your electronic gadgets for a day. Did you miss any of them? Why? Why not? Design a system of behaviors or actions that would make up for their absence, if they didn't exist.

6. Look around the room you are in. How would you represent it as a two-dimensional icon? Sketch out a design that would be understandable as a fingertip-sized image.

APPENDIX 1: NOTABLE ARCHITECTS AND DESIGNERS

ALVAR AALTO, 1898–1976

- *Villa Mairea, Noormarkku, Finland, 1939*
- *Nordic House, Reykjavik, Iceland, 1968*
- *Seinajoki Town Hall, Seinajoki, Finland, 1965*
- *Riola Parish Church, Riola, Italy, 1978*

PETER BEHRENS, 1868–1940

- *Behrens House, Darmstadt, Germany, 1901*
- *A.E.G. High Tension Factory, Berlin, 1910*
- *I.G. Farben Offices, Frankfurt-am-Main, Germany, 1925*
- *Apartments at Weissenhofsiedlung, Stuttgart, Germany, 1927*

MARIANNE BRANDT, 1893–1983

German painter, sculptor, photographer, and designer who studied at the Bauhaus school and became head of the metal workshop in 1928. Brandt created some of the most iconic works of the Bauhaus.

- *Model No. MT49 teapot, 1924*
- *Bauhaus Pendant Lamp,1926*
- *Bauhaus Pendant Lamp With Chains, 1928*

MARCEL BREUER, 1902–1981

- *Wassily Chair, 1925–1927*
- *Campus Center and Garage, University of Massachusetts Amherst, 1965–69*
- *The Whitney Museum of American Art, New York, 1966*

SANTIAGO CALATRAVA, 1951

- *Stadelhofen Railway Station, Zurich, Switzerland, 1984*
- *Alamillo Bridge and La Cartuja Viaduct, Seville, Spain, 1992*
- *Alameda Bridge and Underground Station, Valencia, Spain, 1995*
- *Campo Volantin Footbridge, Bilbao, Spain, 1998*
- *Oriente Station, Lisbon, Portugal, 1998*
- *Sondica Airport, Bilbao, Spain, 1999*
- *City of the Arts and the Sciences Planetarium, Valencia, Spain, 1996–2005*
- *Palace of the Arts, Valencia, Spain, 2001*
- *Milwaukee Art Museum, Milwaukee, Wisconsin, 2001*
- *Sundial Bridge, Turtle Bay, California, 2004*
- *Peace Bridge, Calgary, Canada, 2012*

COCO CHANEL, 1883–1971

"Coco Chanel wasn't just ahead of her time. She was ahead of herself. If you look at the work of contemporary fashion designers as different from one another as Tom Ford, Helmut Lang, Miuccia Prada, Jil Sander, and Donatella Versace, you see that many of their strategies echo Chanel. The way she mixed up the vocabulary of male and female clothes and created fashion that offered the wearer a feeling of hidden luxury rather than ostentation are just two examples of how her taste and sense of style overlap with today's fashion." —*Time*, June 8, 1998

LE CORBUSIER (CHARLES-ÉDOUARD JEANNERET-GRIS), 1887–1965

- *Villa Savoye, Poissy-sur-Seine, France, 1929*
- *United Nations Headquarters, New York, finished 1953*
- *Chapelle Notre-Dame-du-Haut, Ronchamp, France, 1955*
- *Carpenter Center, Cambridge, Massachusetts, 1962*
- *Centre Le Corbusier, Zurich, Switzerland, 1967*

PIERRE DE MEURON, 1950, AND JACQUES HERZOG, 1950

"A building is a building. It cannot be read like a book; it doesn't have any credits, subtitles, or labels like pictures in a gallery. In that sense, we are absolutely antirepresentational. The strength of our buildings is the immediate, visceral impact they have on a visitor." —Jacques Herzog

- *Dominus Winery, Yountville, California, 1998*
- *Gallery of Modern Art for the Tate Museum, London, 2000*
- *Pritzker Architecture Prize Laureates, 2001*
- *Walker Art Center Expansion, Minneapolis, Minnesota, 2005*

CHRISTIAN DIOR, 1905–1957

Dior presented what would be called "The New Look" in women's fashions in 1947, bringing back elegance and femininity after the fashion-starved years of World War II and affirming Paris as the center of haute couture fashion. He began the practice of licensing agreements in the fashion industry.

CHARLES EAMES, 1907–1978 AND RAY KAISER EAMES, 1912–1988

- *Eames Lounge Chair, 1956*
- *Aluminum Group, 1958*
- *Molded Plastic Chair, 1971*
- *"Powers of Ten" installation and film, 1977*

PETER EISENMAN, 1932

- *Wexner Center, Ohio State University, Columbus, Ohio, 1983–1989*
- *Bruges Concert Hall, Bruges, Belgium, 1999*
- *Memorial to the murdered Jews of Europe, Berlin, 1998–2005*

NORMAN FOSTER, 1935

- *Hongkong and Shanghai Bank, Hong Kong, 1986*
- *Millennium Bridge, London, England, 2000*
- *30 St. Mary Axe ("The Gherkin"), London, said to be London's first environmentally sustainable skyscraper, 2004*

FRANK GEHRY, 1929

- *Gehry House, Santa Monica, California, 1979 and 1987*
- *Guggenheim Museum Bilbao, Bilbao, Spain, 1997*
- *Experience Music Project, Seattle, Washington, 2000*
- *Walt Disney Concert Hall, Los Angeles, 2004*
- *New York by Gehry at Eight Spruce Street, New York, 2011*

MILTON GLASER, 1929

Glaser's graphic and architectural commissions include the "I (heart) NY" logo, which has been described as "the most frequently imitated logo design in human history," commissioned by the state of New York in 1976.

EILEEN GRAY, 1878–1976

- *E-1027 (a house planned for her own use) Roquebrune-Cap-Martin, near Monaco, France, 1929*
- *Tempe à Pailla, Castellar, Spain, 1934*

MICHAEL GRAVES, 1934

- *The Humana Building, Louisville, Kentucky, 1982*
- *Team Disney Building, Burbank, California, 1986*
- *Ministry of Health, Welfare and Sport, The Hague, The Netherlands, 1993*
- *Resorts World, Sentosa, Singapore, 2010*
- *Louwman Museum (National Automobile Museum), The Hague, The Netherlands, 2010*

WALTER GROPIUS, 1883–1969

Director of the Bauhaus, Weimar, Dessau, Germany, 1925

- *Gropius House, Lincoln, Massachusetts, 1937*
- *Harvard Graduate Center, Cambridge, Massachusetts, 1950*

ZAHA HADID, 1950

- *Vitra Fire Station, Weil am Rhein, Germany, 1993*
- *Bergisel Ski Jump, Innsbruck, Austria, 2002*
- *Rosenthal Center for Contemporary Art, Cincinnati, Ohio, 2004*

JACQUES HERZOG, 1950 AND PIERRE DE MEURON, 1950

- *Dominus Winery, Yountville, California, 1998*
- *Gallery of Modern Art for the Tate Museum, London, 2000*
- *Pritzker Architecture Prize Laureates, 2001*
- *Walker Art Center Expansion, Minneapolis, Minnesota, 2005*

"A building is a building. It cannot be read like a book; it doesn't have any credits, subtitles, or labels like pictures in a gallery. In that sense, we are absolutely antirepresentational. The strength of our buildings is the immediate, visceral impact they have on a visitor." —Jacques Herzog

VICTOR HORTA, 1861–1947

- *Hôtel Tassel, Brussels, Belgium, 1893*
- *Hôtel van Eetvelde, Brussels, Belgium, 1898*
- *Maison du Peuple, Place Émile van de Velde, Brussels, Belgium, 1898*
- *Horta House (now Musée Horta), Brussels, Belgium, 1898*

ALEC ISSIGONIS, 1906–1988

- *The Morris Mini, 1957–1959*

JONATHAN IVE, 1966

Vice president of Apple Computer's Industrial Design Group from 1992

- *iMac, 1998–2002*
- *G4 Cube, 2000*
- *iPod, 2001*
- *Designer of the Year, London Design Museum, 2003*

ARNE JACOBSEN, 1902–1971

- *Søholm Housing Estate, Klampenborg, Gentofte, Denmark, 1950*
- *Series 7 chair, 1955*
- *Munkegaards School, Copenhagen, Denmark, 1956*
- *Grand Prix Internationale d'Architecture et d'Art, Paris, 1960*

JACOB JENSEN, 1926

- *The Margrethe Bowl, 1955*
- *Kirk E76 Telephone, 1976*
- *Beocenter 9000, 1987*
- *Beosystem 4500, 1989*

PHILIP JOHNSON, 1906–2005

- *Johnson House, aka "The Glass House," New Caanan, Connecticut, 1949*
- *Seagram Building (with Ludwig Mies van der Rohe), New York, 1958*
- *Pennzoil Place, Houston, Texas, 1975*
- *Garden Grove Church, Garden Grove, Los Angeles, 1980*
- *AT&T Building, New York, 1984*

TIBOR KALMAN, 1949–1999

"Kalman was best known for the groundbreaking work he created with his New York design firm, M&Co, and his brief yet influential editorship of [Benetton's] *Colors* magazine. Throughout his 30-year career, Kalman brought his restless intellectual curiosity and subversive wit to everything he worked on—from album covers for Talking Heads to the redevelopment of Times Square. Kalman incorporated visual elements other designers had never associated with successful design and used his work to promote his radical politics. The influence of his experiments in typography and images can be seen everywhere, from music videos to the design of magazines such as *Wired* and *Ray Gun*."

(From the obituary for Tibor Kalman on Salon.com, May 19th, 1999, http://www.salon.com/1999/05/19/kalman/)

REI KAWAKUBO, 1942

Fashion designer Rei Kawakubo, founder of Comme des Garçons (1973, menswear in 1978), was born in Tokyo in 1942. Being untrained as a fashion designer, but having studied fine arts and literature, she conveys her ideas verbally to her patternmakers. The Fashion Institute of Technology honored her in 1987 as one of the leading women in 20th-century design.

ERWIN KOMENDA, 1904–1966

- *VW "Beetle" body, 1936*
- *Porsche 550 "Spyder," 1954*

REM KOOLHAAS, 1944

- *Netherlands Dance Theater, The Hague, The Netherlands, 1988*
- *Kunsthal Rotterdam, Rotterdam, The Netherlands, 1993*
- *Recipient of the Pritzker Architecture Prize, 2000*
- *Seattle Public Library, Seattle, Washington, 2004*
- *Casa da Musica, Oporto, Portugal, 2005*
- *China Central Television (CCTV) headquarters, Beijing, China, 2009*

HELMUT LANG, 1956

Lang is synonymous with the cool minimalism that defined the fashion world in the 1980s.

DANIEL LIEBESKIND, 1946

- *Jewish Museum Berlin, Berlin, 2001*
- *Food Theater Café, London, 2001*
- *World Trade Center Reconstruction Competition, New York, 2003*

MAYA LIN, 1959

- *Vietnam Veterans Memorial, Washington, DC, 1982*
- *Civil Rights Memorial, Montgomery, Alabama, 1989*
- *Groundswell, commissioned by the Wexner Center for the Arts, Ohio State University, Columbus, Ohio, 1993*
- *"The Wave Field," University of Michigan, Ann Arbor, Michigan, 1995*
- *Langston Hughes Library, Clinton, Tennessee, 1999*
- *"Ecliptic" Ice Rink in Grand Rapids, Michigan, 2001*

RAYMOND LOEWY, 1893–1986

- *Lucky Strike packaging, 1939*
- *Greyhound bus, 1954*
- *Shell logo, 1962*
- *In 1975, the Smithsonian Institution opened the Designs of Raymond Loewy, a four-month exhibit dedicated to "the man who changed the face of industrial design."*

CHARLES RENNIE MACKINTOSH, 1868–1928

- *Glasgow School of Art, Glasgow, Scotland, 1897–1899 and 1907–1909*
- *Hill House and the Hill House Chair, Helensburgh, Scotland, 1908*

ALEXANDER MCQUEEN, 1969–2010

Since leaving St. Martins School of Design in London in 1994, McQueen has become one of the most famous and respected international fashion designers in the world. He was named British Designer of the Year four times in 1996, 1997, 2001, and 2003. In October 1996, he was appointed Chief Designer at the French Haute Couture House Givenchy, where he worked until March 2001. He headed his own brand (of which the Gucci group owned 51 percent after 2000) until his death in 2010.

WILLIAM MORRIS, 1834–1896

- *Creation window (design by Morris and Philip Webb) at Church of All Saints, Selsley, Gloucestershire, England, 1863*
- *Sussex Chair, 1865*
- *Marigold Wallpaper, 1875*

JASPER MORRISON, 1959

- *Hanover Tram, Hanover, Germany, 1997*
- *The largest European light rail in production; it was the first vehicle to be awarded the IF Transportation Design Prize and the Ecology Award*
- *Air Chair, 1999*
- *Furniture for the Tate Modern Museum, London, 2000*

I. M. (IEOH MING) PEI, 1917

- *John Hancock Tower, Boston, 1977*
- *Pyramide du Louvre, Paris, 1989*
- *Bank of China Tower, Hong Kong, 1990*
- *Rock and Roll Hall of Fame, Cleveland Ohio, 1995*

RENZO PIANO, 1937

- *Centre Pompidou, Paris, 1976*
- *Kansai Airport Terminal, Osaka, Japan, 1994*

PAUL POIRET, 1879–1944

Poiret broke the mold of 19th century high fashion by introducing loose, corsetless dresses and oriental influences in bright colors. His collaboration with illustrators created iconic images, but his lack of business sense made him the first star designer to be ousted from his own label.

GIO PONTI, 1891–1979

- *La Pavoni coffee machine, 1946*
- *Superleggera Chair, 1955–1957*
- *Villa Planchart, Caracas, Venezuela, 1955*
- *Pirelli Tower, Milan, 1956*
- *Taranto Cathedral, Taranto, Italy, 1970*
- *Denver Museum of Art, Denver, 1972*

KARIM RASHID, 1960

- *Morimoto Restaurant, Philadelphia, 2001*
- *Foscarini Blob lamp, 2002*
- *Semiramis Hotel, Athens, 2004*

GERRIT RIETVELD, 1888–1964

- *Red and Blue Armchair, 1918*
- *Rietveld Schröder House, Utrecht, the Netherlands 1924*

RICHARD ROGERS, 1933

- *Centre Pompidou, Paris, 1976*
- *Lloyds Building, London, 1984*
- *Millennium Dome, London, 1999*

EERO SAARINEN, 1910–1961

- *Kresge Auditorium, Cambridge, Massachusetts, 1950–1955*
- *Yale Hockey Rink, New Haven, Connecticut, 1961*
- *TWA terminal, New York, 1962*
- *Dulles Airport, Chantilly, Virginia, 1962*
- *John Deere and Company, Moline, Illinois, 1963*
- *Gateway Arch, Saint Louis, Missouri, 1966*

YVES SAINT LAURENT, 1936–2008

After "rescuing French fashion" as Christian Dior's successor, Saint Laurent went on to turn haute couture upside down by seeking inspiration from beatniks in Paris and subsequently opening "Rive Gauche," a ready-to-wear line.

ELSA SCHIAPARELLI, 1890–1973

A leading fashion designer in the 1920s and 1930s, she worked with many surrealist artists, including Salvador Dali, Jean Cocteau, and Alberto Giacometti, between 1936 and 1939. Her innovations included her use of color: notably "shocking pink," animal print fabrics, and zippers dyed the same colors as the fabrics.

PAUL SMITH, 1947

Presenting his first Paul Smith menswear collection in 1976, Paul Smith has established himself as the preeminent British designer. His numerous collections of apparel and accessories consistently inspire and anticipate trends.

- *"Mondo" collection of furniture, in collaboration with Italian furniture manufacturer Cappellini, 2002*
- *"Bespoke" upholstery textile, in partnership with textile manufacturer Maharam, 2003*

ETTORE SOTTSASS, 1917–2007

- *Carlton Sideboard (Mobile diviorio), 1980*
- *Wolf House, Ridgway, Colorado, 1989*
- *Cofounder of the Memphis Group, 1980*

PHILIPPE STARCK, 1949

- *Costes chair, 1982*
- *Royalton Hotel, New York, 1988*
- *Juicy Salif juicer, Alessi, 1990*
- *Paramount Hotel, New York, 1990*
- *Kong restaurant, Paris, 2003*

GUNTA STÖLZL, 1897–1983

A textile artist and weaver who became the only female master at the Bauhaus. She ran the Weaving Workshop there from 1927 to 1931. It was the most financially successful workshop of the school. Stölzl moved the art and design of weaving into the realm of modern art and design and worked on incorporating new techniques and materials. Her work can now be seen, among other places, in the Museum of Modern Art in New York and the Vicotria and Albert Museum in London.

YOSHIO TANIGUCHI, 1937

- *Shiseido Museum of Art, Kakegawa, Japan, 1978*
- *The Gallery of Horyuji Treasures, Tokyo National Museum, Tokyo, 1999*
- *Museum of Modern Art addition, New York, 2004*
- *Kyoto National Museum, Kyoto, Japan, designed 1998–2000, completed in 2007*

BERNARD TSCHUMI, 1944

- *Parc de la Villette, Paris, 1983–1998*
- *Alfred Lerner Hall, Columbia University, New York, 1999*
- *Le Fresnoy Art Center, Tourcoing, France, 2004*

EARL S. TUPPER, 1907–1983

- *Tupperware, 1946*

LUDWIG MIES VAN DER ROHE, 1886–1969

- *Apartments at Weissenhofsiedlungen, Stuttgart, 1927*
- *H. Lange House, Krefeld, Germany, 1928*
- *Barcelona Pavilion, Barcelona, 1929*
- *Villa Tugendhat, Brno, Czech Republic, 1930*
- *Farnsworth House, Plano, Illinois, 1950*
- *Lake Shore Drive Apartments, Chicago, 1951*
- *Crown Hall, Chicago, Illinois, 1956*
- *Seagram Building (with Philip Johnson), New York, 1958*
- *New National Gallery, Berlin, 1968*

ROBERT VENTURI, 1925

- *Ohio Center for Performing Arts, Cincinnati, Ohio, 1991*
- *Aronoff Center for the Arts, Cincinnati, Ohio, 1995*
- *Petronas Towers, Kuala Lumpur, Malaysia, 1998*
- *20 River Terrace—The Solaria, New York, 2004*

HANS WEGNER, 1914–2007

- *Peacock Chair, 1947*
- *Wishbone Chair, 1949*
- *Flag Halyard Chair, 1950*

CHARLES FREDERICK WORTH, 1826–1895

Worth was the first to open a couture house in Paris and became the defining designer of France's Second Empire due to his work for the Empress Eugénie. His influence was such that the period is often called "the age of Worth" and defined high-fashion design for over a hundred years.

FRANK LLOYD WRIGHT, 1869–1959

- *Fallingwater, Bear Run, Pennsylvania, 1937*
- *Johnson Wax Building, Racine, Wisconsin, 1939*
- *Boomer Residence, Phoenix, Arizona, 1953*
- *Guggenheim Museum, New York, New York, 1959*

APPENDIX 2: RESOURCES FOR DESIGN

ONLINE PERIODICALS DEVOTED TO DESIGN

Applied Arts: appliedartsmag.com
Architectural Digest: architecturaldigest.com
Architectural Record: archrecord.construction.com
Azure: azuremagazine.com
Communication Arts: commarts.com
Creative Quarterly: cqjoural.com
Curve: curvelive.com
Design Week: designweek.co.uk
Dwell: dwell.com
eVolo Magazine: evolo.us
Foam Magazine: foammagazine.nl
Frame Magazine: frameweb.com
Graphic Design USA: gdusa.com
Graphis: graphis.com
How Magazine: howdesign.com
Icon: icon-magazine.co.uk
ID Magazine: id-mag.com
IdN Magazine: idnworld.com
Interior Design Magazine: interiordesign.net
Metropolis Magazine: metropolismag.com
PRINT: printmag.com
Wallpaper: wallpaper.com

WEBSITES

THE BAUHAUS DESSAU

The site of the iconic and influential German design school

www.bauhaus-dessau.de

BROWN UNIVERSITY'S COMPUTER SCIENCE DEPARTMENT

Apps for Color Theory

cs.brown.edu/exploratories/freeSoftware/catalogs/color_theory.html

CLEMENT GREENBERG: "MODERNIST PAINTING"

An essay on Modernism in Art from 1961 by the influential art critic Clement Greenberg

www.sharecom.ca/greenberg/modernism.html

F. T. MARINETTI (1909) "THE FUTURIST MANIFESTO"

vserver1.cscs.lsa.umich.edu/~crshalizi/T4PM/futurist-manifesto.html

INTERNATIONAL COLOR CONSORTIUM

Promoting the standardization of color-management systems

www.color.org

JESSE JAMES GARRETT ON USER EXPERIENCE

JJG was way ahead of the curve on this and wrote one of the better and more accessible books on the topic of user experience. He comes at it from information architecture, but the discussion applies to all design. This is his Web site.

www.jjg.net/ia/

KENT STATE UNIVERSITY, EDUCATION IN VISUAL LITERACY: LINE

www.educ.kent.edu/community/vlo/design/elements/line/index.html

NAUM GABO AND ANTOINE PEVSNER (1920) "THE REALISTIC MANIFESTO"

davidrifkind.org/fiu/library_files/gabo.the-realistic-manifesto.lib-iss.pdf

SHODOR.COM: INTERESTING PATTERN GENERATOR USING TESSELATIONS

http://www.shodor.org/interactivate/activities/Tessellate/

STANFORD ENCYCLOPEDIA OF PHILOSOPHY: ENTRY ON "POSTMODERNISM"

plato.stanford.edu/entries/postmodernism/

STANFORD ENCYCLOPEDIA OF PHILOSOPHY: ENTRY ON "THE EXPERIENCE AND PERCEPTION OF TIME"

plato.stanford.edu/entries/time-experience/

UNIVERSAL DESIGN RESOURCE LIST (OFFICE FOR ACCESS ABILITY AT THE NATIONAL ENDOWMENT FOR THE ARTS)

www.nea.gov/resources/accessibility/rlists/UDesResources.html

http://arts.gov/publications/design-accessibility-cultural-administrators-handbook

USABILITY.GOV (DIGITAL COMMUNICATIONS DIVISION, U.S. DEPARTMENT OF HEALTH AND HUMAN SERVICES)

A site on best practices and guidelines for user-centered design of digital content. Includes resources, bibliographies, and research plans

www.usability.gov

THE VKHUTEMAS SCHOOL (HIGHER ART AND TECHNICAL STUDIOS, RUSSIA)

Lesser known than the Bauhaus, but equally interesting and influential

monoskop.org/VKhUTEMAS

WALTER BENJAMIN (1936) "THE WORK OF ART IN THE AGE OF MECHANICAL REPRODUCTION"

An essay from 1936 that can be seen to presage the position and relationship of art and design in the years since

marxists.org/reference/subject/philosophy/works/ge/benjamin.htm

WOLFRAM MATHWORLD ON PENROSE TILING

Creating aperiodic tilings and non-repeating patterns

http://mathworld.wolfram.com/PenroseTiles.html

THE WORLD USABILITY DAY CHARTER

"Technology should enhance our lives, not add to our stress or cause danger through poor design or poor quality."

worldusabilityday.org/charter

MUSEUMS WORLDWIDE

DESIGN MUSEUM DANMARK (COPENHAGEN)

designmuseum.dk

VICTORIA AND ALBERT MUSEUM, LONDON

www.vam.ac.uk

DESIGN MUSEUM LONDON

designmuseum.org

THE RISD (RHODE ISLAND SCHOOL OF DESIGN) MUSEUM

risdmuseum.org

DESIGN MUSEUM BOSTON

designmuseumboston.org

SMITHSONIAN COOPER-HEWITT, NATIONAL DESIGN MUSEUM IN NEW YORK

www.cooperhewitt.org

VITRA DESIGN MUSEUM (GERMANY)

www.design-museum.de

MUSEUM OF MODERN ART (NEW YORK)

www.moma.org

DESIGN MUSEUM GENT (BELGIUM)

www.designmuseumgent.be

DESIGN EXCHANGE (CANADA'S DESIGN MUSEUM)

www.dx.org

GLOSSARY OF KEY TERMS BY CHAPTER

CHAPTER 1

"The medium is the message" Marshall McLuhan's catchphrase from the 1960s implying that the power of communication technology came from its ability to change society by how it conveyed information rather than by what it was conveying.

Human culture There are a number of definitions of human culture and they vary depending on the size and nature of the group involved and the discipline under which it is being discussed. For the purpose of this book—considering human society as a whole as a designed environment—a definition can be relatively simple: Culture is the sum of the things we do, the things we do them with, and how we do them, over time.

Mass production The manufacturing of goods under a standard format, usually in large quantities, in a factory setting.

Industrialization The process by which a society moves from an economic system based on agriculture to one based on manufacturing. Usually connected to a shift from rural to urban societies, industrialization also entails a changing attitude toward nature as well as an increasing specialization of work and activities.

Urban living The gathering of people into localized and usually densely structured towns and cities.

Consumerism The idea that the consumption of goods is good for the economy and society.

Capitalism A political system where the means of production and markets are in private hands and are run for the profit of the private owners.

Modernity The historical period, after the medieval period, that is generally marked as beginning with the rise of urban living in the 1500s, with its attendant specialization of labor, centralization of power, and systematic approach to society and culture. It is thought to have begun to transition in the late 20th century to a postmodern condition.

Stages of a design project The (often overlapping) phases through which the development of a design will usually go: inspiration, identification, conceptualization, exploration, definition, communication, and production.

Constraints and needs (of a design project) The idea that designing is the fulfilling of defined needs within a set of identifiable constraints. This allows the definition of the design problem to be phrased as a discrete problem set within which the overall problem can be solved.

Inherent and imposed constraints (of a design project) Inherent constraints are those that can be seen as being crucial to the identity of the object, such as the qualities that make a shirt recognizable as a shirt and not, say, a jacket. The imposed constraints are those qualities that a designer can add to the totality of the design without changing the basic identity of the object. For example, the color of a shirt can be altered without the shirt losing its basic identity (its "being a shirt").

Hierarchy of design needs A hierarchy that outlines the importance of fulfilling various needs in order to create good designs that are original creative and useful. Structured after Maslow's concept of a hierarchy of human needs.

Transparency in experience The idea that we can become so habituated to an object or an action that we do not really see it in our experience until something disrupts our experience. For example, walking up stairs, we generally do not think of the steps and their shape and structure unless there is something unusual about them They are uneven or too high.

CHAPTER 2

Classicism and Neoclassicism In design, it denotes the practices that reference the principles as applied in classical antiquity, mainly ancient Rome.

Modernism The term can refer to a number of artistic and philosophical movements, but in design, modernism can be seen as an approach that arose in the late 19th century in tandem with the increase in industrialized production. Modernism rejected the classical and traditional leanings of the 19th century and aimed to continually overthrow the present by a systematic questioning of practices, materials, and forms.

Futurism An Italian philosophical and artistic movement of the early 20th century that focused on futuristic themes of machines and technology, especially in terms of cars, airplanes, and warfare.

Constructivism An early-20th-century philosophy of art and design that began in Russia. Constructivism focused on art and design as an integral part of society and emphasized design for industrial production.

Postmodern Condition As set forth by Jean-François Lyotard, the social theory of the postmodern condition states that modern society has given way to a decentralized order where the grand narratives of previous eras have disappeared and a worldview has taken their place that emphasizes multiple perspectives and different cultural views.

CHAPTER 3

Elements of design The basic components of a design, traditionally line, shape and volume, color, texture and pattern, and space. In this discussion, time has been included, as the user experience must be considered, and experience, with all its attendant learning, memory, and references, is a function of time.

Line The implied, built, or illustrated connection between two or more points, such as in a *line* of trees, the *lines* of an outfit or a building, or a drawn line in an illustration.

Shape and volume The contours and limits of an area, defining an object in two or three dimensions.

Color The perception of properties resulting from wavelengths of light striking the light receptors in the eyes. Color is defined by its hue, value, intensity, and temperature.

Texture and pattern A perception resulting from either or both visual and tactile stimuli. Rhythmic stimuli produces a pattern, but humans are predisposed to perceiving patterns and will therefore do so in random signals as well.

Space The three-dimensional extent occupied by an object (positive space) or between objects (negative space), or the perception of such an extent in two-dimensional images.

Time The fourth dimension that allows the ordering of events into past and future, with the transition between them identified, along with the (specious) present.

CHAPTER 4

Gestalt A *whole* or *totality* where the combined elements produce an entity that is experienced as more than the sum total of its parts. A jacket, for example, is more than the fabrics and notions it consists of. It is also the feel of it, the look of it, and the weight, warmth, style, and so on of it. It is the total experience of it.

Principles of design Basic concepts framing the application of design elements into perceptual categories. To understand these and how they work is to understand how designs will be perceived.

Unity, variety, and harmony States in which a combination of elements may find themselves, where they produce—to a larger or smaller degree—a sense of belonging together by the number and intensity of the qualities they share.

Proportion and scale Concepts relating to the relative size of objects. A design can be considered in terms of its internal scale—the relative proportions of its components—or external scale—the relative size and proportions of the design compared to its surroundings or location.

Balance The concept of having design elements work in relationship to each other in a way that their relative impact is significant, either toward or away from a sensory equilibrium.

Rhythm A repeated occurrence of sensory stimuli such as shapes, color, or sound, or any of the design elements over space or in time.

Emphasis and Focus The action of placing design elements in such a way as to lead the eye as it scans the designed area.

Usability (experience) Considering the end user's experience of the design and designing in such a way as to making this as good as possible whether from a functional or sensory point of view.

CHAPTER 5

Muse The force behind inspiration. In classical Greece, the Muses were the goddesses of inspiration for the arts and sciences.

Gestalt A *whole* or *totality* where the combined elements produce an entity that is experienced as more than the sum total of its parts. A jacket, for example, is more than the fabrics and notions it consists of. It is also the feel of it, the look of it and the weight, warmth, style, and so on of it. It is the total experience of it.

Webbing, mapping, and cubing Concept mapping techniques.

SCAMPER A method of exploring a design concept that includes the following steps: substitute, combine, adapt, modify (or minimize/magnify), put to another use, eliminate or elaborate, and reverse or rearrange.

CHAPTER 6

Digital presentation Any presentation, slides, website, animation, or otherwise designed for on-screen display.

Multisensory Relating to an experience to which more than one sense contributes sight and sound, flavor and scent, touch, sight, and sound, and so on.

Sketch A representation, in any media, aiming to display a design or design detail quickly and in general.

Technical drawing A diagrammatical representation of a design, formerly executed in ink or pencil with fine-point instruments. Now nearly exclusively created using any of a number of computer programs, these aim to provide information for construction and modeling.

Illustration A representation of a design aimed to be visually appealing as well as informative.

CAD For computer-aided design, any use of computer systems to create designs, either through sketching, illustration, technical drawing, or modeling.

Narrative The telling of a story or a linear description of events.

Feedback A response to information, often including an evaluation or correction of direction.

CHAPTER 7

Pop Art The appropriation of commonly used or popular cultural items into gallery-style art.

Text–image balance The relationship of placement, space used, and subsequent attention paid by the viewer to a designed informational space.

Type Blocks of letters used for printing text.

Font A style of letter for printing or on-screen viewing.

CHAPTER 8

Proxemics The study of the cultural, behavioral, and sociological aspects of spatial distances between individuals. In proxemics two distinct ways of relating to space are observed: *Physical territory,* for example how we arrange our space around us (placement of furniture and architectural elements,) and *personal territory,* the space we maintain, for comfort, between ourselves and other people.

2D design Designing in flat-plane space, on surfaces; space without the possibility of motion *into* the area involved, only *onto.*

3D design Designing in space that has the possibility for motion *into* the area in question, if time is added.

Symmetry (of the human body) The left/right symmetry of the human frame.

Personal space The concept that people have a sense of space around them that has degrees of intimacy and personal contact depending on distance and cultural habitation.

CHAPTER 9

User experience The outcome, satisfactory or otherwise, of an end user's engagement with a designed object, system, or environment.

Usability The ease or lack thereof in engaging with a design.

Useful and beautiful A classic evaluation of good design.

Clock time and lived time Two different ways of experiencing time. Measured by instrument and physically experienced.

Specious present The moment that is experienced as *now.*

Culture The aggregate of the things we do as a group or society, the things we do them with, and how we do them over time.

CHAPTER 10

On-screen environment A website, computer game, or any other interactive application engaged with by a user on a screen.

Oral, manuscript, print, and electronic culture Four stages of human communication culture. Each stage brought about significant changes to how human society operates and sees itself.

BIBLIOGRAPHY

Ando, Tadao. "What Is Wabi-Sabi?" In *The Wabi-Sabi House: The Japanese Art of Imperfect Beauty*. New York: Clarkson Potter, 2004.

Banham, Reyner. *Theory and Design in the First Machine Age.* Cambridge, MA: MIT Press, 1980.

Benjamin, Walter. "The Work of Art in the Age of Mechanical Reproduction." In *Median and Cultural Studies*, edited by Meenakshi G. Durham and Douglas M. Kellner. Malden, MA: Blackwell, 2006, 18–41.

Benyus, Janine M. *Biomimicry: Innovation Inspired by Nature*. New York: William Morrow, 2002.

Berghaus, Günter. "Futurism, Dada, and Surrealism: Some Cross-Fertilization among the Historical Avant-Gardes." In *International Futurism in Arts and Literature.* New York: de Gruyter, 2000.

Boucher, Francois. *20,000 Years of Fashion*, expanded ed., New York: Harry N. Abrams, 1987.

Bristol, Katharine G. "The Pruitt-Igoe Myth." *Journal of Architectural Education*, 1991.

Burkhardt, Lucius. *The Werkbund: History and Ideology.* Hauppauge, NY: Barron's 1980.

Crane, Walter. *Ideals In Art: Papers Theoretical Practical Critical.* London: George Bell & Son, 1905.

Danchev, Alex, ed. *100 Artists' Manifestos: From the Futurists to the Stuckists.* London: Penguin Books, 2011.

Debord, Guy. *The Society of the Spectacle*. New York: Zone Books, 1995.

Eco, Umberto. *The History of Beauty.* New York: Rizzoli, 2004.

Gablik, Suzi. *Has Modernism Failed?* New York: Thames and Hudson, 1987.

Gabo, Naum. "The Realist Manifesto." In *Gabo: Constructions Sculpture Paintings Drawings Engravings*, edited by Naum Gabo, London: Lund Humphries, 1957.

Gale, Monica R. *Myth and Poetry in Lucretius*. Cambridge: Cambridge University Press, 1994, p. 223.

Henshilwood, C. S., and C. W. Marean. "The Origin of Modern Human Behavior: Critique of the Models and Their Test Implications." *Current Anthropology* 44, no. 5 (December 2003): 627–651.

Hughes, Robert. *The Shock of the New.* New York: Knopf, 1996.

Kiaer, Christina. *Imagine No Possessions: The Socialist Objects of Russian Constructivism*. Cambridge, MA: MIT Press, 2005.

Koolhaas, Rem, and Bruce Mau. *S, M, L, XL: OMA, Rem Koolhaas and Bruce Mau*, edited by Jennifer Sigler. New York: Monacelli Press, 1995.

Le Corbusier. "Eyes that Do Not See." In *Toward an Architecture.* Translated by John Goodman. Los Angeles: Getty Research Institute, 2007.

Le Corbusier, *Précisions*. Paris: Cres, 1930.

Lipovetsky, Gilles. *The Empire of Fashion: Dressing Modern Democracy.* Translated by Catherine Porter. Princeton: Princeton University Press, 1994.

Lucretius. *On the Nature of Things*. Translated by William Ellery Leonard. Cambridge, MA: MIT Internet Classics Archive, 2009.

Lukacs, Georg. *Goethe and His Age*. London: Grosset & Dunlap, 1969.

Lupton, Ellen, and J. Abbott Miller, eds. *ABC's of the Bauhaus: The Bauhaus and Design Theory*. New York: The Cooper Union for the Advancement of Science and Art, 1993.

———. *Design, Writing, Research: Writing on Graphic Design*. New York: Kiosk, 1996.

Lyotard, Jean-François. *The Post-Modern Condition: A Report on Knowledge*. Minneapolis: University of Minnesota Press, 1984.

Marinetti, F. T. *The Futurist Manifesto.* Translated by James Joll, 1909.

McDonough, William, and Michael Braungart. *Cradle to Cradle: Remaking the Way We Make Things*. New York: North Point Press, 2002.

McLeod, Mary. "Undressing Architecture: Fashion Gender and Modernity." In *Back from Utopia*. Rotterdam, The Netherlands: nai010 Publishers, 2002.

McLuhan, Marshall. *Understanding Media: The Extensions of Man*. Cambridge, MA: MIT Press, 1994.

Mitter, Partha. *Art and Nationalism in Colonial India, 1850–1922: Occidental Orientations*. New York: Cambridge University Press, 1994.

Moffet, Marian. *A World History of Architecture*. New York: McGraw-Hill, 2003

Morris, William. *Useful Work versus Useless Toil.* William Morris Internet Archive, 1884.

Muller, Ulrike. *Bauhaus Women: Art, Handicraft, Design.* Paris: Flammarion, 2009.

Owen, David. *Green Metropolis: Why Living Smaller, Living Closer, and Driving Less Are the Keys to Sustainability.* New York, NY: Riverhead Books, 2009.

Pevsner, Nikolaus. *Pioneers of Modern Design: From William Morris to Walter Gropius*, rev. ed. New York: Viking Press, 1975.

Pike, et al. "U-Series Dating of Paleolithic Art in 11 Caves in Spain." *Science* 336, no. 6087 (June 15, 2012): 1409–1413.

Pile, John. *A History of Interior Design.* New York: John Wiley & Sons, 2004.

Pirsig, Robert M. *Zen and the Art of Motorcycle Maintenance: An Inquiry into Values*. New York: Morrow, 1974.

Pulos, Arthur J. *American Design Ethic: A History of Industrial Design to 1940,* Cambridge, MA: MIT Press,1983.

Ruskin, John. *The Seven Lamps of Architecture*, Project Gutenberg, 2011.

———. *The Stones of Venice*. Vol. 1. Foundations The Internet Archive, 2008.

———. *The Stones of Venice*. Vol. 2. Project Gutenberg, 2009.

———. *The Stones of Venice*. Vol. 3. Project Gutenberg, 2009.

Said, Edward. "Orientalism." In *Colonial Discourse and Post-Colonial Theory : A Reader.* Edited by Patrick Williams and Laura Chrisman. New York: Columbia University Press, 1994.

Schwartz, Frederic J. *The Werkbund: Design Theory and Mass Culture before the First World War*. New Haven, CT: Yale University Press, 1996.

Sennett, Richard. *The Craftsman*. New Haven, CT: Yale University Press, 2008.

Sullivan, John. *The Tall Office Building Artistically Considered,* 1896, https://archive.org/details/tallofficebuildi00sull.

Venturi, Robert. *Complexity and Contradiction in Architecture.* 2nd ed. New York: Museum of Modern Art, 1977.

Venturi, Robert, Denise Scott Brown, and Steven Izenour. *Learning from Las Vegas: The Forgotten Symbolism of Architectural Form.* Cambridge, MA: MIT Press, 1977.

———. *Learning from Las Vegas: The Forgotten Symbolism of Architectural Form.* Cambridge, MA: MIT Press, 1977.

Vitruvius, Marcus Pollio. *Vitruvius: Ten Books of Architecture.* Translated by Ingrid D. Rowland. New York: Cambridge University Press, 1999.

Volker Albus, Reyer Kras, and Jonathan M. Woodham, eds. *Icons of Design: The 20th Century.* New York: Prestel, 2000.

von Hoffman, Alexander. *Why They Built the Pruitt-Igoe Project.* Joint Center for Housing Studies, Harvard University. http://www.soc.iastate.edu/sapp/PruittIgoe.html

Weston, Richard. *Modernism.* Boston: Phaidon Press, 2001.

Xenophon. *Memorabilia.* Translated by H. D. Dakyns. British Columbia, Canada: Blackdog Media, 2003.

INDEX

Page numbers followed by *f* indicate figures and those followed by *b* indicate boxes.